FINTAN O'TOOL

1900

The Irish Times Book of the Century

1999

GILL & MACMILLAN

KU-592-458

Gill & Macmillan Ltd

Goldenbridge

Dublin 8

with associated companies throughout the world

www.gillmacmillan.ie

© *Fintan O'Toole 1999*

0 7171 2749 4

Research of articles and photographs by Edel Morgan

Time line by Ian McGuinness

Index by Julitta Clancy

(Due to considerations of space, the index was reduced and amended by publishers.)

Print origination, design and layout by Identikit Design Consultants, Dublin

Printed by Butler & Tanner Ltd, Frome, Somerset

All rights reserved. No part of this publication may be copied,

reproduced or transmitted in any form or by any means

without permission of the publishers.

1   3   5   4   2

This book is typeset in Bembo, Frutiger

and Bauer Bodoni

An online version of this book will be published by

The Irish Times on the Web: www.ireland.com

Contents

Note to the Reader

This book is designed so that each two-page spread is read as one page.

A time line runs to the extreme left and right. The two outer columns contain Fintan O'Toole's text and

the inner columns contain original articles published in The Irish Times *throughout the century.*

Queen Victoria

1900

'That Jaundiced Journal of West-Britonism'

1923

1900–1923

'That Jaundiced Journal of West-Britonism'

On *New Year's Day 1900* The Irish Times *headed its front page with the news that 'Her Majesty the Queen sent a Christmas greeting to all the troops in South Africa.' Developments in the Boer War, the appointment of a new commander of her majesty's forces in Ireland, the New Year honours list and the operations of the Irish Regiments' Widows' and Orphans' Fund dominated the front page. In an item on the 'marvellous growth of the National prosperity' it went without saying that the nation so blessed was the United Kingdom of Great Britain and Ireland. And it was a nation at the height of its fortunes. With stirring optimism the article pointed out that 'the progress of the United Kingdom has been of a steady and sterling character and never at any time in the course of all British history, have Imperial interests been founded upon so strong and solid a basis.'*

1900

This was the world of *The Irish Times*. Ireland was part of the greatest empire the world had ever seen, and the paper was happy that this should be so. It seemed likely, after all, that the new century would be dominated by a few great empires, and that all of humanity would eventually belong to one or other of them. The conquest of Africa by Britain, France, Germany and Portugal was virtually complete. In South Africa the Boer War, in which the United Kingdom was engaged, was a struggle not between natives and invaders but between rival groups of European colonists, the British and the Dutch. Even the greatest of republican democracies, the United States of America, had joined the imperial game in the previous few years, replacing Spain as the overlord of Cuba and the Philippine Islands. With the Turkish, Russian and Austro-Hungarian empires dominating much of Europe

New Year's Day

New Year's Day was not very extensively kept in Dublin as a holiday. All the banks, Government buildings, and business establishments were open, and trade was pursued as briskly as on any ordinary day. The fact that practically for the first time since its institution—at all events for the first time within tolerably recent memory—there was no Lord Mayor's show, deprived the festival of one of its most picturesque features, and, of course, left the children without that which for generations has been one of their annual luxuries. The 'Ginger Bread' coach remained within gates; there was no civic procession. This, of course, was in consequence of the operation of the Local Government Act, which fixes the annual municipal elections late in January, and the time-honoured pageant has, accordingly, been deferred until St. Patrick's Day. The crowds, which in former years lined the principal thoroughfares to catch a glance at the outgoing and

Queen Victoria in Dublin in April 1900

incoming Lord Mayors, were absent, and the streets did not, therefore, wear their customary New Year's Day appearance. Nevertheless there was a good deal of animation throughout the city, and such thoroughfares as Grafton Street and Sackville Street were crowded with shoppers. Another custom, that of holding morning performances at the theatres, was also abandoned, so the youngsters were deprived of another favourite mode of celebrating the occasion; indeed it would seem as if New Year's Day runs a close chance of becoming extinct altogether. The matinees will be given tomorrow instead of yesterday. The weather was rather better, but despite many threatenings the rain kept off. The streets, however, were in a very sloppy condition. At the churches services were held, and were attended by large congregations.

The Stock Exchange and Municipal Offices were closed. At Baldoyle the usual race meeting was held, and a morning performance was given at the Royal Italian Circus.

from The Irish Times
2 JUNE 1902

Peace

Boers Sign Surrender Terms

Despatch from Lord Kitchener (Official Telegram): 'From Lord Kitchener to Secretary of State for War: 'Pretoria, 11.15 p.m., 31st May: 'Negotiations with Boer Delegates: 'The document containing the terms of surrender was signed here this evening at 10.30 p.m. by all the Boer representatives, as well as by Lord Milner and myself.'

An earlier despatch telegraphed by Lord Kitchener was as follows: 'Pretoria, May 31, 5.15 p.m.: It is now settled that the Boer representatives will come here immediately, and also the High Commissioner from Johannesburg. It is possible that the document will be signed to-night. I have received from them a statement saying that they accept, and are prepared to sign.' (Reuter's Telegrams)

Pretoria, Friday: The deliberations between the Boer delegates at Vereeniging have resulted practically in the acceptance of the British terms, and the delegates may arrive here at any moment for the purpose of signing the document embodying the terms.

Sunday, 10.25 a.m.: The terms of peace were signed at half-past ten o'clock last night.

and Asia, imperialism was normal. It seemed clear that whatever change the twentieth century might bring to Ireland would take place within the context of the steady and sterling progress of a British Empire that already ruled nearly a quarter of the world's population.

This was, after all, a time of relative calm. The number of convicts (that is, prisoners serving three years or more) in Irish jails had dropped from over 3,400 in 1855 to just 292 in 1901, partly reflecting the decline of rural unrest as land agitation died down. Dublin, Belfast and other cities were far more heavily policed than equivalent cities in Britain, but serious crime was rare. Half of those committed for minor offences were accused of being drunk and disorderly, and even those were, in these more enlightened times, more frequently sent to the newly established Inebriate Reformatories, intended to treat, rather than punish, habitual drunkards. Dublin, admittedly, still had much more crime

Major John McBride pictured in South Africa, where he fought against the British in the Boer War

THE IRISH TIMES, THURSDAY, APRIL 5, 1900.

ARRIVAL OF THE QUEEN.

ROYAL PROGRESS THROUGH DUBLIN.

MAGNIFICENT RECEPTION.

PRESENTATION OF ADDRESSES.

HER MAJESTY'S REPLIES.

THE LANDING AT KINGSTOWN.

PRESENTATION OF ADDRESS.

THE IRISH TIMES, WEDNESDAY, JANUARY 23, 1901.

DEATH OF THE QUEEN.

CLOSING SCENE AT OSBORNE.

PARLIAMENT TO MEET TO-DAY.

The following message was received from the King by the Lord Mayor of London at 6.45 p.m. last evening:—

"OSBORNE, 6.30 P.M.

"MY BELOVED MOTHER HAS JUST PASSED AWAY, SURROUNDED BY HER CHILDREN AND GRANDCHILDREN.

"ALBERT EDWARD."

(OFFICIAL BULLETIN.)

The following bulletin was issued at Osborne last night:—

"OSBORNE, JANUARY 22, 1901, 6.45 P.M.

"Her Majesty the Queen breathed her last at 6.30 p.m., surrounded by her children and grandchildren.

(Signed)

"JAMES REID,
"R. DOUGLAS POWELL,
"THOS. BARLOW."

THE QUEEN'S LAST HOURS.

The following official bulletins were issued at Osborne during yesterday before the Queen died:—

"OSBORNE HOUSE,
JANUARY 22, 1901.

"The Queen this morning shows signs of diminishing strength, and Her Majesty's condition again assumes a more serious aspect.

(Signed)

"JAMES REID, M.D.
"R. DOUGLAS POWELL, M.D.
"THOMAS BARLOW, M.D."

"OSBORNE, TUESDAY, 12 o'clock.

"There is no change for the worse in the Queen's condition since this morning's bulletin. Her Majesty has recognised the several members of the Royal Family who are here. The Queen is now asleep.

(Signed)

"JAMES REID, M.D.
"R. DOUGLAS POWELL, M.D.
"THOMAS BARLOW, M.D."

"OSBORNE, TUESDAY, 4 P.M.

"The Queen is slowly sinking.

(Signed)

"JAMES REID, M.D.
"R. DOUGLAS POWELL, M.D.
"THOMAS BARLOW, M.D."

"... her last at 6.30 p.m., surrounded by her children and grandchildren."

(Signed)

"JAMES REID, M.D.
"R. DOUGLAS POWELL, M.D.
"THOMAS BARLOW, M.D."

The Lord Mayor sent to Osborne the following reply:—

"Your Royal Highness's telegram announcing the nation's great loss I have received with profound distress and grief, and have communicated this most sad intimation to my fellow-citizens. Her Majesty's name and memory will live for ever in the hearts of her people. May I respectfully convey to you ... members of the Royal Family the sincere sympathy and condolence of the City of London.

(Signed)

"FRANK GREEN, Lord Mayor of London."

AT THE MANSION HOUSE.

From an early hour till evening the large crowds which had gathered at the Mansion House at intervals during the day waited in the great anxiety of all classes of Her Majesty's subjects in the welfare of the Queen. To these, no doubt, the news published in the morning papers had been sufficiently disquieting. This, no doubt, led the people to assemble at the official residence of the Lord Mayor and the Royal Exchange. When the noon bulletin was posted outside the Mansion House the people eagerly scanned it, but the worst had not happened. Among those plainly waiting were many young women who were thus spending a portion of their dinner hour. When the good news was passed around that the Sovereign was no worse, and was peacefully asleep, their anxiety was considerably removed. Before the fateful news of the Queen's death ...

In the touching message which His Majesty sent to the LORD MAYOR OF LONDON ...

(Editorial / Leading Article)

To write such a life as the QUEEN'S with anything like fulness will take many volumes. Moreover, it is so closely entwined with the diplomatic history of the past sixty-four years that it can never be attempted until many of the Sovereigns and Statesmen now living have also passed away. For that reason we have dwelt chiefly, in the Memoir which is published elsewhere, on the QUEEN as a Woman rather than as a Monarch. It was in the former aspect that she so deeply touched the hearts of her subjects. The purity of her Court, her early married life, the visits to the Highlands, and her unaffected intercourse with some of her poorest subjects,—all these things appealed to the popular mind, and gave all ranks and classes of her people a living interest in her personality. The deep sympathy with their sorrows and anxieties which Her Majesty so constantly exhibited during the Crimean War and the Indian Mutiny gave her a further hold on their affections. Then followed her own crushing bereavement, and her withdrawal from much of the pageantry of State. It was a strain on her subjects' loyalty to see so little of their much-loved monarch. But the feeling was by this time too deeply-rooted to be upset, and gradually the relation between the QUEEN and her subjects assumed another form. She began to be regarded as the Mother of the people, as well as their QUEEN. Never an incident, whether of joy or sadness, stirred their hearts without a sympathetic message coming from the QUEEN to show that she, too, shared their feelings. This extraordinary gift of sympathy has been exhibited in its highest degree during the sad events of the past fifteen months, and it partially responsible, it cannot be doubted, for the national bereavement that we are all mourning to-day. Messages to those whose dear ones had fallen, personal visits to the wounded, and constant thought for the care and comfort of her soldiers—all this at last overstrained the aged heart and put on a life whose value we can never be over-estimated.

We are reminded of what the QUEEN herself wrote in her diary on the receipt of a letter from Lord DERBY, announcing the death of the Duke of WELLINGTON. "Alas! it contained the confirmation of the fatal news; that England's, or rather Britain's pride, her glory, her hero, the greatest man she ever had ...

...

To-day the people desire to blend my sorrows. It is only fitting to recall the last incidents of that dramatic life. Yet there are offences of the Sovereigns who have had much and stirred, but through all the vicissitudic changes of the time our star shone bright and steady, and remained serene and immovable. Twenty years passed, and Death robbed her of her noble helpmeet, follow their father into the silent land; fifty years passed, and the Nation rose up to do her honour; sixty years passed, and the Nation's plaudits were drowned by those of an Empire. The Nineteenth Century had merged into the Twentieth ere we began to recognise that some day the QUEEN, too, must have an end; at last, the end has come with startling, if merciful, suddenness.

... KING EDWARD VII. of ENGLAND now succeeds the Throne. We may go back to the year 1819, when the family outlook of the British Home was not very bright. Then the old King, GEORGE III., was lingering on in seclusion—a pathetic figure, blind and imbecile. His son, the PRINCE REGENT, afterwards GEORGE IV., had hardly done honour to his position, nor had he brought happiness to anyone connected with him. The children, as it is elsewhere shown, the DUKE of KENT, born in 1767, fourth son of GEORGE III., became the father of our territory. ...

"BELFAST HOUSE."
BY DIRECT and MANUFACTURED RATE-PRICE IMPORT

WALPOLE BROS., LTD.,
Its now on Sale an

Unusually Cheap Lot of

IRISH CAMBRIC
HANDKERCHIEFS

Ladies' and Gentlemen's Sizes, slightly imperfect, Made up in Half Dozens, at

1s, 6d., 2s., 2s. 6d., 3s. 3s. 6d., 4s., 4s. 6d., 6s. 6d. PER HALF DOZ.

SUFFOLK STREET, DUBLIN.

LADIES'
WATERPROOF JACKETS, ULSTERS,
CAPES, CLOAKS.

ELVERY'S SPECIAL WATER-
PROOF ULSTERS.
2s., 3s., 4s., 5s.
NO RUBBER. A SPECIALITY.
WATERPROOF DRIVING APRONS.
Our Special Apron, 1s. 6d., 2s.

J. W. ELVERY & CO.,
ELEPHANT HOUSE,
46 & 47 LR. SACKVILLE ST., DUBLIN.
114 NASSAU STREET.
AND
78 PATRICK STREET, CORK,
AND
31 CONDUIT STREET, LONDON.

HIGH-CLASS TAILORING
READY-MONEY PRICES.
FIT AND FINISH GUARANTEED.

TAAFFE & COLDWELL,
81 GRAFTON STREET, DUBLIN.

BY ROYAL WARRANT.

WEDDING PRESENTS.

PEARL AND TURQUOISE FLEXIBLE BRACELETS, SOLID SILVER BLUE ENAMEL COLOGNE CASES, &c., &c.

All the latest Novelties at the lowest possible prices for Cash.

WEST & SON,
HER MAJESTY'S JEWELLERS AND SILVERSMITHS,
18 AND 19 COLLEGE GREEN,
DUBLIN.

ADVERTISEMENT INDEX.
The following is the order of advertisements in to-day's Irish Times:—

1901

22 January
Queen Victoria dies.

23 January
A vote of condolence for Queen Victoria is rejected by Dublin City Council by 42 votes to 35 but is eventually passed with abstentions.

15 September
William O'Brien of the United Irish League calls for a national strike against ranching and land-grabbing.

6 October
The first annual meeting of the Pioneer Total Abstinence Association of the Sacred Heart takes place.

12 December
Guglielmo Marconi receives the first transatlantic signals in Newfoundland from a station in Cornwall.

1902

20 January
John Dillon of the Irish Party speaks

Oscar Wilde died as the century opened

than comparable British cities such as Sheffield and Birmingham; but Belfast and Cork were remarkably law-abiding.

In Ireland the general expectation of continuity was so great that, as *The Irish Times* reported, 'New Year's Day was not very extensively kept in Dublin as a holiday.' At least in the serene professional suburbs where *The Irish Times* had its deepest roots, the previous evening's celebrations had been notably decorous: business at Kingstown Police Court on 1 January 1900 was 'of an extremely light character and reflects most creditably on the district.' With the banks, government offices, businesses and shops operating 'as briskly as on any ordinary day,' there was nothing to distinguish the start of the new century from the end of the old one. Even the usual Lord Mayor's Parade was not held. The years were passing with such equanimity, indeed, that the paper speculated that 'it would seem as if

from The Irish Times **1903**
7 APRIL

James Joyce hoped to be appointed Paris correspondent of The Irish Times. His only published contribution, however, was this interview with the racing driver Henri Fournier.

The Motor Derby
Interview with the French Champion

In the Rue d'Anjou, not far from the Church of the Madeleine, is M. Henri Fournier's place of business. 'Paris-Automobile'—a company of which M. Fournier is the manager—has its headquarters there. Inside the gateway is a big square court, roofed over, and on the floor of the court and on great shelves extending from the floor to the roof are ranged motor-cars of all sizes, shapes and colours. In the afternoon this court is full of noises—the voices of workmen, the voices of buyers talking in half-a-dozen languages, the ringing of telephone bells, the horns sounded by the 'chauffeurs' as the cars come in and go out—and it is almost impossible to see M. Fournier unless one is prepared to wait two or three hours for one's turn. But the buyers of 'autos' are, in one sense, people of leisure. The morning, however, is more favourable, and yesterday morning, after two failures, I succeeded in seeing M. Fournier.

M. Fournier is a slim, active-looking young man, with dark reddish hair. Early as the hour was our interview was now and again broken in upon by the importunate telephone.

'You are one of the competitors for the Gordon-Bennett Cup, M. Fournier?'

'Yes, I am one of three selected to represent France.'

'And you are also a competitor, are you not, for the Madrid Prize?'

'Yes.'

'Which of the races comes first—the Irish race or the Madrid race?'

'The Madrid race. It takes place early May, while the race for the International Cup does not take place till July.'

'I suppose you are preparing actively for your races?'

'Well, I have just returned from a tour to Monte Carlo and Nice.'

'On your racing machine?'

'No, on a machine of smaller power.'

'Have you determined what machine you will ride in the Irish race?'

'Practically.'

'May I ask the name of it—is it a Mercedes?'

'No, a Mors.'

'And its horse-power?'

'Eighty.'

'And on this machine you can travel at a rate of —?'

'You mean its highest speed?'

'Yes.'

'Its highest speed would be a hundred and forty kilometres an hour.'

'But you will not go at that rate all the time during the race?'

'Oh, no. Of course its average speed for the race would be lower than that.'

'An average speed of how much?'

'Its average speed would be a hundred kilometres an hour, perhaps a little more than that, something between a hundred and a hundred and ten kilometres an hour.'

'A kilometre is about half a mile, is it not?'

'More than that, I should think. There are how many yards in your mile?'

'Seventeen hundred and sixty, if I am right.'

'Then your half-mile has eight hundred and eighty yards. Our kilometre is just equal to eleven hundred yards.'

'Let me see. Then your top speed is nearly eighty-six miles an hour, and your average speed is sixty-one miles an hour?'

'I suppose so, if we calculate properly.'

'It is an appalling pace! It is enough to burn our roads. I suppose you have seen the roads you are to travel?'

'No.'

'No! You don't know the course, then?'

'I know it slightly. I know it, that is, from some sketches that were given of it in the Paris newspapers.'

'But, surely, you will want a better knowledge than that?'

'Oh, certainly. In fact, before the month is over, I intend to go to Ireland to inspect the course. Perhaps I shall go in three weeks' time.'

'Will you remain any time in Ireland?'

'After the race?'

'Yes.'

'I am afraid not. I should like to, but I don't think I can.'

'I suppose you would not like to be asked your opinion of the result?'

'Hardly.'

'Yet, which nation do you fear most?'

New Year's Day runs a close chance of becoming extinct altogether.'

There was, of course, another Irish world, Catholic and, for the most part, nationalist, aspiring towards Irish autonomy within the United Kingdom, the home rule that had been a perennial political question since the eighteen-eighties. Catholics made up three-quarters of the population, and the Catholic Church had become, in the half century since the devastating famine of the eighteen-forties, almost an alternative state. It controlled much of the health care system and the

out in the House of Commons against British concentration camps in South Africa.

25 February
The Boers defeat the British at Klerksdorp.

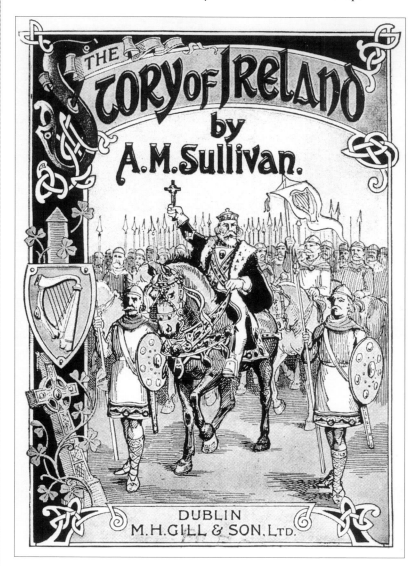

A. M. Sullivan's story of Ireland was originally published in 1867. This was the cover of the turn-of-the-century edition, complete with Celtic Revival triumphalist design.

2 April
Yeats's play
Cathleen Ni
Houlihan *has its
first performance.*

31 May
*The Boers surrender
to the British in
South Africa.*

12 July
*Arthur James
Balfour becomes
British Prime
Minister.*

13 July
*The Intoxicating
Liquors (Licences)
(Ireland) Act
reduces the number
of pub licences.*

9 August
*King Edward VII
is crowned in
Westminster Abbey.*

2 September
*John Shawe-
Taylor writes to
newspapers,
inviting represen-
tatives of landlords
and tenants to a
conference to settle
the land problem.*

8 November
*Sir Antony
McDonnell is
appointed
Under-Secretary
for Ireland.*

The arrival of King Edward VII in 1904

great majority of the nine thousand national schools, a basic but effective education system that by 1911 had reduced illiteracy to just 12 per cent. The growing Catholic professional class was catered for by the secondary schools run by the Jesuits and other orders. The lower middle class was schooled by teaching orders such as the Christian Brothers, which had, by 1903, about thirty thousand pupils. The brothers, moreover, were self-consciously promoting a specifically Irish Catholic identity: Brother M. T. Moylan, elected superior-general in 1900, was a 'thorough Gaelic Leaguer' and a staunch nationalist. By the end of the nineteenth century about 80 per cent of the prizes and exhibitions in the state-run intermediate examinations were being taken by Catholic schools.

There were also some major social organi-sations dominated by Catholics. The Gaelic Athletic Association, founded in 1884, was flourishing. The Gaelic League, founded in 1893, was in its golden years, growing at a steady rate and not yet riven by religious or political differences. (The speaking of Irish had fallen

'I fear them all—Germans, Americans, and English. They are all to be feared.'

'And how about Mr Edge?'

No answer.

'He won the prize the last time, did he not?'

'O, yes.'

'Then he should be your most formidable opponent?'

'O, yes . . . But, you see, Mr Edge won, of course, but ... a man who was last of all, and had no chance of winning might win if the other machines broke.'

Whatever way one looks at this statement it appears difficult to challenge its truth.

from The Irish Times **1904**
15 NOVEMBER

A great deal was expected from the inebriate homes which have been established within the last few years as a result of what may be called reformatory legislation. It seems, however, that too much may have been expected from these institutions, especially so far as the women patients are concerned. It is a very old belief in Ireland that a woman drunkard cannot be cured, and certainly the reports from the various homes in England are calculated to strengthen the conviction in that belief. The last report issued comes from the London County Council Home at Farmfield. There were twenty-two patients licensed during the year. Eleven of them were brought back, eight of the eleven were again brought back, and only four of the twenty-two are known to be doing well. It is a strange thing that the authorities in charge of the home complain that unsatisfactory 'cases' are sent to them, and they ask for 'a better type of woman.' We should be inclined to think that such homes would be reserved, in the first instance, for the worst cases. But, as *The Hospital* remarks, this 'in plain terms would appear to mean that there are a number of women inebriates who are beyond redemption by any known method of reformatory effort and discipline.' But the very important point brought out is that the hopeless cases, which appear to predominate, exercise a most prejudicial influence on the hopeful cases. These homes cost a large amount of money annually. Is the money being actually thrown away? Not only that, but is it actually the medium through which harm is being done? *The Hospital* sums up the position very concisely when it says—'To cope successfully with inebriety, as is the case also with many other diseases, demands preventive rather than curative measures, and in this direction there is much opportunity for both State and municipal effort.'

from The Irish Times
28 DECEMBER **1904**

Irish National Theatre

Opening Performances

The Irish National Theatre Society made its bow to an expectant public at the newly-equipped theatre in Abbey Street last evening. Those who came, either by invitation or by the simple British method of paying at the door, were much impressed and delighted by the change wrought externally and internally on the old theatre premises ... The leaders in the Irish Literary Revival movement were present in strong force, prominent among them being Mr W. B. Yeats, Mr Stephen Gwynn, Mr Edward Martyn, and Mr George Russell. Lady Gregory, who had a play for presentation, was, it was explained, unable to attend, but Miss Horniman, to whose generosity the Society owes the existence of the building, was prominent among the ladies present. Otherwise the audience was fairly representative of literary and artistic culture, and the occasion was, as an

William G. Fay, one of the members of the early Abbey company, in a drawing by John B. Yeats

Lady Augusta Gregory

20 December
A conference of landlords and tenants begins in the Mansion House in Dublin to settle the land issue once and for all.

1903

3 January
The report of the Irish land conference recommends that tenants be allowed to buy out their land with loans from the Treasury.

27 March
St Patrick's Day is made a bank holiday.

11 June
Dissidents form the Independent Orange Order in Belfast.

2 July
A 370-mile road race for the Gordon Bennett trophy between Carlow and Kildare is won by Mikhael Jenatzy, driving a Mercedes.

3 July
Dublin City Council considers an address to King Edward VII on his

visit to Ireland, but the meeting is broken up by nationalists.

21 July
King Edward VII and Queen Alexandra arrive in Ireland on an official visit, which lasts until 2 August.

9 August
Giuseppe Sarto is enthroned in Rome as Pope Pius X.

14 August
The Irish Land Act (1903) becomes law, allowing tenants to buy out their landlords.

17 December
The Wright brothers make the first successful flight in North Carolina.

1904

1 January
The Motor Car Act enforces a £1 registration for cars and a driving licence fee of 5 shillings (25p). Speed is limited to 20 miles per hour, or 14 miles per hour for motorcycles.

A west of Ireland family in the early 1900s

drastically over the previous fifty years, however: in 1851 there were 1½ million Irish-speakers, but in 1901 there were just 641,000, of whom just 21,000 spoke Irish only.)

There was, too, a fringe of militant nationalism beyond the respectable parliamentarism of the Irish Party at Westminster; but in 1900 it too expressed itself most forcefully in an imperial context, with demonstrations of support for the Boers organised by the romantic nationalist Maud Gonne and the journalists Arthur Griffith and D. P. Moran. Neither expressed any interest in the black majority of the South African population, and both Griffith and Moran laced their Anglophobia with attacks on 'the swarming Jews of Johannesburg.' This new nationalism was largely confined to the intelligentsia in Dublin and Cork, but its propaganda was vigorous and innovative. In the early weeks of the Boer War the Irish Transvaal Committee,

experiment, and possibly as an epoch marker, invested with unique interest ... To come now to the dramatic matter of the evening, it constituted, if we may be pardoned the crude Englishism, a triple bill. Three one-act plays, two by Mr W. B. Yeats and the other by Lady Gregory, were performed, and so well was the enterprise steered on its inaugural night that this compound entertainment was over a little after 10 o'clock. The first piece was 'On Baile's Strand,' by Mr Yeats. It was a first production so it calls for a little more than a passing mention. The author has dipped once more into that realm which is paradise to him, the legendary period of Cuchullain of Muiretemne, already dignified in fragmentary episode, in poetry, and in poetic prose. It was a period when kings and princes throve exceedingly in our land, and when the glamour of romance brightly coloured the simplest deeds of a simple peasantry. Mr Yeats has drawn his episode from that mystical past, and has shaped it fairly well within lines of dramatic action ... [The play] is written in blank verse. There is a considerable amount of random talking in the earlier stages of the piece, and the audience experience some difficulty in striking out the central motive. But, when action is proclaimed by the entry of the youthful champion, interest increases at once, and it is well maintained to the close. This antique subject has been appropriately given an antique dressing in diction and imagery. The lines do not always carry us away with the assurance of a masterpiece; but there are many passages of decided literary finish. The catastrophe, too, is well led up to, and the colourisation proves interesting. At one point the audience suspected a not very agreeable *double entendre*, but the author may presumably be acquitted from any such poor intention. The scenery was crude, but good enough to explain the play. It certainly did not by its gorgeousness wean interest from the literary matter. The costumes were according to orthodox ideas of ancient Irish dress, and were worn with grace and dignity. This leads naturally to a consideration of the work of the actors, which was, all things considered, excellent. It must be remembered that the company is one of unsalaried amateurs, whose enthusiasm as art revivalists has been the sole guiding star ... At the fall of the curtain there were loud cries for the author, and Mr Yeats without delay made his way to the stage and bowed his acknowledgments. He also took the occasion to express how pleased the members of the Society

The congested districts, underdeveloped areas in receipt of direct government assistance

for example, had mounted an outdoor screen in College Green, Dublin, onto which they projected text and photographs hailing the Boers' successes against the British.

To *The Irish Times* this nationalist agitation was no more than a foolish distraction, and it could note with satisfaction that the years of the Boer War (1899–1902) marked a historic high point in the recruitment of Irishmen to the British army, with Catholic Dublin supplying far more recruits than 'loyal' Belfast. (Thirty thousand Irishmen served in the British army during the Boer War, while fewer than two hundred fought for the Boers.) In the first week of the new century the paper's leader-writer maintained, 'as all sensible and unprejudiced people here always knew, that the real difficulties of Ireland are economic and agrarian, rather than political. For nearly twenty years much of the energy which could have been profitably applied to the development of the country's material interests has been expended in a vain and unpractical pursuit of the *ignis fatuus* of Home Rule.'

Looking back on the century just passed, the leader-writer drew certain lessons for the future. One was that England had now emerged victorious from a prolonged struggle with 'nearly all the Powers of Europe' and that such a nation would never 'yield to threats what they deny to justice.' Another was that 'England has lost many delusions in dealing with this country and not the least of these was the idea that the vapourings of windy orators had behind them any real body of public opinion.' *The Irish Times* was sure that pro-Boer agitation was no more than vapouring and that the 'flotsam and jetsam' who engaged in such protest 'need not disturb the equanimity of those who desire for us a period of peace and progress.' For *The Irish Times*, peace and progress would be achieved when the Irish settled down within the United Kingdom and devoted themselves to the hard-headed improvement of their social and economic conditions.

The Irish Times had been founded by Major Lawrence Knox in 1859 (it had a brief

Licence-holders must be aged seventeen or over.

25 February
Synge's play Riders to the Sea *receives its first performance in Dublin.*

17 March
All pubs close on St Patrick's Day at the behest of the Gaelic League.

26 April
King Edward VII revisits Ireland and stays until 5 May.

4 July
Coláiste na Mumhan opens in Co. Cork, the first summer school for training teachers of Irish.

26 September
Sir Antony McDonnell, Under-Secretary for Ireland, and Lord Dunraven publish their report, which becomes the programme of the Irish Reform Association. It suggests that a form of power be devolved to the Irish administration by the transfer of control of more than £6

million from the Treasury to an Irish Financial Council.

1 November

Shaw's play John Bull's Other Island *receives its first performance in London.*

2 December

The United Unionist Council is established in the wake of Lord Dunraven's proposed scheme for devolution.

27 December

The Abbey Theatre opens with a performance of Lady Gregory's Spreading the News *and Yeats's* On Baile's Strand.

1905

5 March

George Wyndham resigns as Chief Secretary.

4 December

Henry Campbell-Bannerman forms a Liberal government in Britain.

5 December

Electric trams begin running in Belfast.

The Belfast dock strike of 1907 was led by James Larkin, his first significant impact on Irish life. He is shown here (seated, third from the left) with other labour leaders addressing a meeting in Queen's Square, Belfast.

previous existence from 1823 to 1825) as a thrice-weekly paper selling for a penny. Knox was a member of Isaac Butt's Home Rule movement and was elected as a Member of Parliament for Carlow on a reformist Home Rule platform. He supported Ireland's union under the crown with Britain, but believed that its economic destiny was largely its own and would depend on Irish initiative. Knox saw *The Irish Times* as a way of consolidating progressive Protestant opinion, and he understood his market so well that within less than four months the paper became a daily. The first editor was Dr John Wheeler, who was also a member of the teaching staff at the Faculty of Divinity in nearby Trinity College. Rev. Wheeler later became curate at the parish of Ballysax in County Kildare and continued to minister to his flock on Sundays while 'returning to his labours at the press' during the week, as his obituary reported. He died in an accident when his coach overturned near Newbridge, returning to the capital. He was succeeded by his brother-in-law, Frederick Shaw, a Fellow of Trinity College. Shaw, in turn, was succeeded by Robert Scott

were to see that they were numerously accompanied on their pilgrimage in quest of truth and beauty ... Having now got a liberal instalment of serious drama, the audience were in a mood to appreciate a sprightly bit of comedy. Lady Gregory's little play 'Spreading the News,' supplied that need most soothingly. It is a tripping little piece, founded on a simple idea of modern Irish life, but yielding in its short compass abundance of rich comedy ... This play was very favourably received ... Mr W. G. Fay, who came before the curtain at the close, said that the authoress, Lady Gregory, was not able to be present, but they would convey to her an assurance of the hearty appreciation of the audience. Thus was a most interesting event brought to a close. Its success—which was decided—cannot but prove of the highest value to the Society in the movement which they are so courageously forwarding.

from The Irish Times
16 NOVEMBER **1909**

The Vote and After

What are the Women Doing?

Talk of women's rights has ceased with the franchise which was now to remedy women's wrongs. But women who took such a big part in the movement to obtain the vote have for the most part retired from the scene, and are in blissful ignorance that their work had only begun when they were put on the register. They suffered imprisonment and social ostracism in order to have a voice in the affairs of the country, but now they have a right to be heard they are inarticulate—I mean the majority.

Of the minority, whose main hobby still seems to be the disfigurement of walls with wild threats, I am not speaking. They still live in that dark period when women were denied the vote. Now they have got it they seem still to prefer militant to constitutional means for to remedy their grievances.

And some of these were going to lead women like the Israelites of old into the Promised Land directly they got the vote. If their leadership, or lack of it, persists, then women can look for more than forty years of wandering in the wilderness.

Way to Progress

If only some of the women connected with the suffrage movement of a few years ago would only come forward and tackle the problems that they thought so strongly about in those days, some progress of a real and lasting sort would be possible.

Perhaps it is that fighting women, as well as fighting men, are bad politicians. Few soldiers have shown in the British Parliament any outstanding capacity for dealing with constitutional procedure, and it may be—although I hope events will falsify this conclusion—that the women who won the vote are incapable of carrying through the reforms that they promised us in their fighting speeches.

If they are to function they must have a rallying point; they must have leaders and a programme. And then they can build up an organisation without which no political movement can hope to succeed. If they remain in their retirement the cause for which they risked life and limb and liberty is lost.

Women who were to introduce a new and finer note into politics will have fought in vain if they allow the vital questions of the day to be discussed with less fire and conviction than they would impart into a teatime talk about the latest thing in hats!

Surely those who gained notoriety in those days are not afraid of the hard work and the application of politics to the problems they then propounded and the grievances they then spoke about so eloquently.

The task they are called upon to shoulder is not so spectacular as the militant suffrage movement, but it is far more serviceable.   A.C.B.

and Scott by Algernon Lockyer. When Knox died in 1873 the merchant Sir John Arnott, born in Scotland but domiciled in Cork, bought the paper for £35,000 and developed it as a successful commercial and political enterprise. In the first year of the new century, marking its own belief in the prospects for steady and sterling progress, the paper turned itself into a limited company, chaired and controlled by Sir John Arnott's son and namesake. It was, in effect, an example of the virtues preached in its own leader pages: a solid, practical achievement by Protestants who, instead of standing aloof, threw themselves into the daily life of Ireland.

The Irish Times had a natural market among the Protestant middle and upper classes. There were at least 1.1 million Protestants in Ireland, 327,000 of them in the twenty-six counties of what would eventually become the Republic— the area in which the *Times* had its core readership. In the other six counties Protestants made up a majority of the population, but even outside that bastion their presence was, in some places, very pronounced. In Counties Wicklow, Cavan, Monaghan, Kildare and Donegal about one person in five was Protestant. In the cities of Dublin, Cork and Limerick the figure was in or around 10 per cent. A few suburbs of Dublin were almost as heavily Protestant as any part of Ulster: in the districts of Kingstown (Dún Laoghaire), Pembroke, Rathmines and Rathgar, Blackrock and Dalkey over 60 per cent of the residents were Protestant. And this substantial minority was top-heavy with the well-to-do and well-educated. Even in the twenty-six counties half the lawyers, surveyors and engineers, a third of the doctors and 70 per cent of the bankers were Protestant.

Though most Catholics were outside of this world, there were nevertheless some Catholic unionists. The Irish Unionist Alliance, formed to campaign against home rule, claimed the support of 'all the Irish Roman Catholic gentry (except Sir Thomas Esmonde), three-quarters of the Roman Catholic professional men, all the great

14 December
James Bryce is appointed Chief Secretary for Ireland.

1906

7 February
The results of the general election are a Liberal landslide and a strong Irish Party representation in the House of Commons.

18 April
More than five hundred people die in an earthquake in San Francisco, which has a particular significance in Ireland because of the number of Irish people in the city.

5 May
Arthur Griffith publishes the first edition of Sinn Féin.

31 May
Michael Davitt dies in Dublin.

1 August
Belfast City Hall is opened.

30 August
The Waterford– Rosslare–Fishguard railway line is opened.

As the Home Rule Bill of 1912 made its way through Parliament, nationalist Ireland began to believe that Parnell's dream would be fulfilled

24 October

Eleven women suffragists are jailed in London for their activities.

29 November

A law to make the closing of public houses on Sunday permanent is passed.

1907

28–30 January

Riots occur at the Abbey Theatre as audiences object to the portrayal of Irish people in Synge's Playboy of the Western World.

6 May

James Larkin begins a series of strikes involving the dockers

Roman Catholic merchants and half of the domestic class.'[1] These were partisan claims, but they were not entirely without foundation, and at least some of these Catholic professionals formed a part of the unionist constituency to which *The Irish Times* addressed itself. At least one senior figure at the paper itself was a Catholic. J. J. Simington, appointed general manager and a member of the board in 1907, had been educated by the Christian Brothers in Synge Street. And *The Irish Times* certainly had some Catholic readers in the early years of the century. In 1914, for example, the *Catholic Bulletin* referred disparagingly to the paper being 'patronised by certain indifferent Catholics.'

Yet for all the confidence expressed in the early years of the new century, the political power of the once-dominant Protestant and unionist minority was on the wane. The process of transferring the land from the old Ascendancy to a new Catholic peasantry was proceeding at an astonishingly rapid pace and would culminate in the Irish Land Act of 1903. The Reform Act of 1884 had already given the vote to the majority of ordinary Catholics, ensuring that in the south and west a Protestant could no longer expect to be elected to Parliament unless he happened to be a home ruler. No less significantly, the

from The Irish Times 1912
12 APRIL

In Parliament

Home Rule Bill

Even Home Rule Bills lose their 'drawing' power by repetition. Though all the seats on the floor of the House of Commons were occupied today, there was no necessity to bring in chairs for the accommodation of members, as was done in 1886 and 1893, and there was plenty of room in the side galleries. It was noticed that Mr Bottomley put in an appearance for, I believe, the first time this session. In the Peers' Gallery were Lords Dunraven, MacDonnell, Monteagle, and Oranmore and Browne, while the distinguished strangers included Sir Edward Clarke, who led the Unionist attack nineteen years ago; Sir George Reid, Mr Commissioner Bailey, the Russian and American Ambassadors, and two or three Irish Roman Catholic dignitaries.

Just before three o'clock a great burst of cheering from the Ministerialists heralded the entry of the Prime Minister from behind the Speaker's chair. A minute later Mr Redmond came in from the Lobby entrance, and received a similar greeting from his supporters. Shortly afterwards it was the turn of the Unionists to give a rousing welcome to Sir Edward Carson.

The few questions on the paper were run through with great rapidity, and it was only five minutes past three when Mr Asquith rose. He began with a reference to Mr Gladstone's mammoth speeches of 1886 and 1893, and declared that they contained 'the classic exposition' of the case between Great Britain and Ireland. He would not attempt to 'bend the bow of Ulysses,' but would take up the narrative where Mr Gladstone left it. Mr Asquith is usually very concise, but in this instance he occupied more than half an hour with preliminary arguments. First he dwelt upon the persistence of the Irish demand, as witnessed at eight successive General Elections. The Government did not underrate the importance of North-East Ulster's opposition, but could not admit the right of a minority to veto the verdict of the vast body of their countrymen. But in other respects Ireland had changed. There had been a great improvement in social order, so that Home Rule was no longer a counsel of despair. Irish relations with Great Britain had been largely affected by Imperial legislation, the working of which had blunted some of the arrows in the Unionist quiver. In particular, land purchase and old age pensions had made the idea of separation more unthinkable than ever. Turning to the Imperial aspect of the question, Mr Asquith dwelt on the imperative need for emancipating Parliament from local burdens. Our present system was one of 'centralised impotence.' Home Rule all round could not be accomplished at one blow, but the present bill was introduced with the full and direct purpose of further applications of the principle. Here the Opposition broke in with sarcastic cries of 'Preamble.' After some remarks upon Colonial analogies, Mr Asquith at last entered upon the exposition of the bill, the details of which you will have set forth in your news columns. Towards the end of his closely packed oration he broke into an attack upon Mr Bonar Law's speech at Belfast, sneered at 'the new style,' which was 'all very well for Ulster,' and seemed deliberately to provoke the storm of interruptions and gibes which at once arose from the Unionist benches. It was an unworthy conclusion to a speech which otherwise had been interesting and innocuous.

Sir Edward Carson, who led off for the Opposition, is not the man to refuse a challenge, and he quickly showed that he was in fine fighting form. A more ridiculous and fantastic proposal had never been put before any Parliament. It was absolutely unworkable. A safeguard for the minority was a nominated Senate—a wise proposal, that, from a Radical Government. The supremacy of the Imperial Parliament meant nothing, and was only inserted to satisfy some uneasy consciences. The Government policy had twice been rejected by the voters when it was submitted to them in concrete form. Would they allow this bill to be put before the electorate? 'Answer,' cried the Opposition. But Mr Asquith sat in mumchance. Then Sir Edward pointed out that, so long as the Government had an independent majority, we heard nothing of Home Rule. It was only now, when the Constitution was in suspense, and they were dependent on Nationalist support, that they felt constrained to introduce it. He claimed that the Unionist policy had been thoroughly justified by the events of the last twenty years in Ireland, and quoted from the speeches by Lord MacDonnell and Mr T. W. Russell in support of his assertion.

Mr Redmond rose next, and began by declaring that this was a 'great and historical occasion,' deserving calm and serious discussion, and he regretted that it was apparently the interest of some persons to engender passion. This sounded like a hit at Mr Asquith, but, presumably was intended for Sir Edward Carson. The rest of his speech

Protestant gentry had lost control of local government in 1898, when the Local Government (Ireland) Act created elected county, urban district and rural district councils.

It is hardly surprising, therefore, that by June 1901 *The Irish Times* was beginning its editorials with questions such as 'What is to become of Irish Conservatism?' The answer, it suggested, was that 'Irish Conservatives must find work for themselves if they are to retain their position in the country.' The paper realised that,

of the Belfast Steamship Company.

7 May
The Irish Councils Bill is introduced in the House of Commons, the aim being to give

John Redmond, the leader of the reunited Irish Party

Marconi, the inventor of wireless telegraphy. His transatlantic service between Clifden, Co. Galway, and Cape Breton in Canada opened in 1907.

Ireland more autonomy; on 3 June it is abandoned.

6 July

The theft from Dublin Castle of the regalia of the Order of St Patrick (sometimes called the 'Irish crown jewels') is discovered.

10 July

King Edward VII and Queen Alexandra visit Ireland.

with just twenty-one Irish Unionist MPs in the House of Commons in London, the political influence of their cause was decidedly weak. But it believed that, at a local level, the natural abilities of the Protestant gentry might still allow them to take the lead: 'We would appeal to the Conservative gentry of Ireland no longer to stand aloof from local affairs, but by coming forward as candidates for the county councils to give the electors a chance of availing themselves of their services.' *The Irish Times* also urged 'young men of the landlord class' to throw themselves whole-heartedly into the 'grand and essentially Irish work' of the co-operative movement.

The Irish Times was edited by Algernon Lockyer and, from 1907, by John Healy, described by Lionel Fleming, who worked under him in his later years, as 'a man of remarkable inflexibility of mind.'[2] Healy, who had studied to be a Church of Ireland clergyman before entering journalism, epitomised the ideal of Protestant

consisted largely of an endorsement of the Prime Minister's assertions. No word of criticism broke the even tenor of his praise. Even as regards finance, he considered this a better bill than either of its predecessors. It was 'a great measure' and an 'adequate' measure, and he would recommend the coming Convention to accept it.

The Labour Leader (Mr Ramsay Macdonald) added nothing new to the situation. He extended a warm welcome to the bill. Lord Castlereagh, who said he was proud to be a descendant of one who was responsible for the Act of Union, naturally had no good word for the bill. Mr William O'Brien, who followed was, of course, listened to with much attention. He made more of the fact that he had not been privileged to see a draft of the measure, a lack which rendered it impossible for him to give a considered or final judgment upon its terms, but in a general way he remarked that it was a complex bill and one of transcendent importance to Ireland. While he wished the government had been more courageous, and given to the Irish Legislature complete power over the purse, he congratulated the Cabinet upon its determination to complete land purchase under Imperial auspices, this being a more vital necessity.

For very nearly an hour, Captain Craig held forth against the bill, and other speakers followed on both sides, including Mr Eugene Wason, Sir Thomas Esmonde, and Mr Harry Lawson. Mr Ronald MacNeill, as an Ulsterman proud of his race, congratulated the House on having got away from vague and bombastic rhetoric to definite proposals. He utterly denied Mr Redmond's statement that Parnell had accepted the bill of 1886 as a final settlement, and quoted Parnell's contrary statement of St Patrick's Day, 1891. He suggested that the Nationalist leader's acceptance of today's bill was liable to similar modifications. Mr MacNeill's speech made a considerable impression.

The debate was adjourned on the motion of Mr Balfour.

from The Irish Times 1912
15 APRIL

Irish Public Opinion

Lack of Interest in the Bill

A remarkable lack of general interest in the Home Rule Bill is manifesting itself amongst all classes. So far as Dublin is concerned, the bill, which was heralded with so many words, has fallen like a stick from a spent

The might of empire: British hussars in Grafton Street, Dublin

rocket. Honest Nationalists, if not hostile in their criticism, are lukewarm in their general approval, while Unionist business men openly condemn it as political trickery, in which they can see no good. The bill is looked upon with serious apprehension by the Civil servants, who are proposed to be transferred to the Irish Executive. Legal servants, when asked for their views, preferred to wait for the text of the bill before expressing any opinion. The Post Office officials were equally

respectability. R. B. McDowell describes him as 'dignified, austere and rather reclusive.' Lionel Fleming remembered him 'going in and out of the office—always alone, always with the neatly-rolled umbrella, the neat bowler-hat, and the neat iron-grey moustache.' His grammar was extra-ordinarily conservative and his aversion to certain constructions was so great that he would change

30 July
The RIC, angry at conditions and pay, go on strike in Belfast and are replaced by soldiers on the streets and by members of the RIC from the

south. Riots result, in which two people die.

2 August
The decree Ne Temere is issued by Pope Pius X, affecting marriages between Catholics and Protestants.

12 August
Riots on the Falls Road in Belfast are suppressed by the British army, which kills four civilians.

a phrase such as 'it is hardly credible' to 'it hardly is credible.' His inflexibility was such that he insisted that the first editorial always consist of three paragraphs of twenty-two lines each and the second of a single paragraph of thirty-five lines.

Yet the unionism of both Arnott and Healy was not that of the Protestant landlords, nostalgic for the good old days of Ascendancy rule. It was modernising, industrial, and urban, anxious to see the rest of Ireland follow the lead of industrial Belfast into the twentieth century. Healy, in particular, was also sympathetic to the notion of a federalist unionism that would keep Ireland within the United Kingdom but give it more control over local affairs. And although the Ireland of *The Irish Times* was Protestant, unionist, and imperial, it was nonetheless Irish.

reticent. A retired official stated that undoubtedly the postal service at present laboured under many grievances, but he was inclined to think that a transfer to a Nationalist Executive would only mean to the postal service that it has, to use a homely phrase, got 'out of the frying pan and into the fire.' This phrase, so far as our inquiries have gone, practically sums up public opinion in Dublin on the measure.

from The Irish Times **1912**
16 APRIL

Almost as we go to press the awful news reaches us of the loss of the Titanic, with nearly seventeen hundred out of the two thousand three hundred and fifty-eight passengers and crew who formed her immense burden of human life. The telegrams are brief. They upset all the reports which reached us between midday and midnight, but it is to be feared that they are true. We cannot be surprised that the public received with something like complete incredulity the first reports yesterday morning that the giant liner was sinking off the Newfoundland banks, as the result of a collision with an iceberg. To sudden tidings of another tragedy of the sea we are only too well accustomed. But the imagination halts at the suggestion that the latest and most marvellous mechanisms of ocean traffic are exposed to dangers every whit as awful as those which lie before any tramp steamer of a few tons burden. 'Floating palaces' is a common phrase of description for such vessels as the Titanic, or her sister-ship, the Olympic, and even vessels of much smaller size. The Titanic was appointed throughout in a way which no hotel on solid earth could hope to rival. She had suites of luxurious apartments, carried a large staff of first-class cooks, and was fitted with spacious lounges containing all kinds of costly furniture and decorations. The sight of a swimming bath helped to convey to the mind of the traveller who wandered through her corridors the suggestion that he was in a magnificent hotel. There was nothing to remind him that he was on board ship except the far-off throbbing of the screw. We do not suppose that those who parted from the Titanic's passengers at Southampton or Queenstown felt any more emotion than if their friends were stepping into the security of a train. We can imagine that this happy and comfortable hotel-party of hundreds of passengers were inclined to regret that their voyage across the Atlantic was nearly ended. Then, with all

The marriage of Count Casimir Markievicz and Constance Gore-Booth, 29 September 1900

Saving the harvest in Co. Antrim at the turn of the century

the horror of the totally unexpected, just before midnight, they suffered a sea-change. A sudden shock of collision, and the largest vessel in the world lay helpless, fighting a losing battle against time, while her wireless apparatus sent out urgent messages that she was sinking and called for help. The substantial reports which reached an anxious public throughout yesterday of the saving of the passengers and crew by means of the boats of other liners, hastily summoned by wireless telegraphy, appear to have had no foundation; their origin has yet to be explained. If it be, indeed, true that only 675 women and children have been saved out of the ship's immense passenger list, this is one of the supreme tragedies of the sea. The loss of the Titanic finally disproves the confident assertion that her system of watertight compartments made her absolutely unsinkable. It is hardly profitable to speculate at present upon the causes of the collision. But this accident, following upon the collision between the Olympic and HMS Hawke, seems to lend colour

Few unionists in the early years of the century would have disagreed with the words of one of their MPs, Colonel Edward Saunderson, a former Deputy Grand Master of the Orange Order, when he insisted on behalf of Protestant landlords that 'we are Irishmen as much as the tenants are … we love our nation as much as they do.'

That nation, like the world in general in 1900, was emphatically a rural one. Just one-tenth of the world's population lived in cities. There were, nevertheless, sixteen cities with a population of a million or more. And the concentration of these cities was radically different from what it had been a century earlier. In 1800 just three of the world's ten largest cities—London, Paris, and Naples—were in the West. In 1900 cities like Beijing, Guangzhou, Istanbul and Hangzhou had lost their place in the

16 October

Marconi's wireless telegraph opens for transatlantic press telegrams at Clifden, Co. Galway.

1908

17 January

Sinn Féin wins fifteen seats in the Dublin municipal elections in its first substantial electoral victory.

Queen Alexandra at Maynooth in July 1903. Dr Daniel Mannix, the president of the college and later Archbishop of Melbourne, is on her left. Dr William Walsh, Archbishop of Dublin, is on her right.

29 January

The Municipal Gallery of Modern Art opens in Harcourt Street, Dublin.

21 February

Sinn Féin stands in a by-election for the first time but loses to the Irish Party in North Leitrim.

ranks of urban expansion, and Tokyo was the only city outside Europe and North America to figure in the top ten.[3] Ireland, however rural it remained, was part of this increasingly urbanised civilisation. There were large Irish communities in five of the world's ten largest cities: London, Manchester, Chicago, New York, and Philadelphia. By the early twenties, 43 per cent of Irish-born men and women were living abroad, with over a million in the United States, over half a million in Britain, roughly 100,000 each in Australia and Canada, and substantial numbers in New Zealand, South Africa, and India.

to the theory then put forward that the suction of such enormous vessels exposes them to a danger hitherto unknown. These two accidents to the largest vessels in the world must give pause to naval architects who scout the suggestion that the very size of modern vessels may be a source of weakness to them. It is, at least, certain that misfortune has dogged the steps by which the tonnage of liners has increased to that of the two largest examples that the world has yet known. The Olympic had to be returned shortly after completion to the hands of her builders. Her sister-ship, whose building cost more than that of a Dreadnought, has ended her maiden voyage at the bottom of the Atlantic.

from The Irish Times
16 SEPTEMBER 1912

Riot in Belfast

Wild Scenes at a Football Match

A fierce riot occurred at a football match at Celtic Park, Belfast, this afternoon. The match was in the Irish League competition, and was between the Belfast Celtic and the Linfield teams, who are keen rivals, and whose supporters are of a different religious and political persuasion. So great was the interest taken in the match, which promised to be one of the best of the season, that there was an attendance of about 20,000 people.

How the Fight Began

A few minutes before half-time Linfield was leading by one goal to *nil*, and at the interval a scene unprecedented in the annals of Irish football occurred. A party of Celtic supporters in the unreserved area, carrying the club colours—a green and white striped flag—marched through the crowd in the direction of the Linfield supporters, who carried aloft a Union Jack. Their approach was resented, and a fight ensued. The disturbance rapidly developed into a riot, and the crowds overran the playing pitch. Stones were thrown, and the air soon became filled with flying missiles. In the *melée* a number of revolver shots were fired, and this so terrified the other spectators that they scattered in all directions, and many were knocked down and trampled under foot. The riot raged for about half an hour, and the ground resembled a battlefield owing to the number of men lying about in all directions. The ambulances were summoned, and about sixty men were conveyed to the two city hospitals, five of whom, it is stated, were suffering from revolver shot wounds. Dozens of others who received injuries were able to proceed home without receiving any attention at the hospitals. The police force on the ground and the officials were unable to cope with a riot of such magnitude, and reinforcements of constabulary were hurriedly sent. When they arrived the riot had terminated, and the majority of people had gone home. No arrests were made. The military were confined to barracks as a precautionary measure in case of renewal of disturbances during the evening ...

The Party Element

No such regrettable blot has ever besmirched the history of football in Belfast. Although the riot took place at a football

Edwardian Eccles Street, Dublin, with the Mater Hospital in the foreground and St George's Church, Hardwicke Street, in the background. Further down on the left, Number 7 was the most famous address in Irish literature, the fictional home of Leopold Bloom in James Joyce's Ulysses.

These emigrants had left behind in rural Ireland a society that was more stable and more conservative than it had been for decades, perhaps for centuries. The Famine of the eighteen-forties and the exodus that followed had disproportionately affected the propertyless labourers, cottiers, and very small tenant-farmers. As the remaining farmers were enabled to buy their holdings from their landlords, rural society was transformed, by the early years of the twentieth century, from a teeming mass of poor families into a solid, mostly frugal peasantry. Farms were small—only 58 per cent were over fifteen acres in 1901—but housing was far better than it had been: 70 per cent of the population lived in houses categorised as 'good farmhouses' or better.

Within these houses a new domestic sphere was emerging, one in which women were increasingly confined. Respectability was taking hold. The paradox of Irish Catholics in the early twentieth century was that, as the historian D. G. Boyce has put it, they had 'taken enormous strides towards enjoying the fruits of majority status; but, more than any other of the peoples of the Celtic lands of Britain, they had advanced at the expense of their traditional ways of life.'[4] Irish had been largely abandoned in favour of English. A fierce

31 March

The University Bill proposes two new universities, one in Belfast, the other in Dublin, with constituent colleges in Dublin, Cork and Galway.

5 April

The leader of the Liberal Party, Herbert Henry Asquith, becomes British Prime Minister.

7 May

Introduction of the old age pension at the rate of 5 shillings (25p) per week.

9–12 November

Dockers and carters in Cork go on

strike, an action
partly organised by
James Larkin.

11 November

The Irish Women's
Franchise League
is formed.

21 December

The Housing of
the Working
Classes (Ireland)
Act grants to local
authorities the
power to build
houses and to
establish funds to
support home
construction.

1909

1 January

The first old age
pension is paid to
people over the age
of seventy.

9–10 February

A meeting of the
United Irish
League in Dublin
illustrates the
divisions that exist
among nationalists
over land and
language issues.

24 March

The writer John
Millington Synge
dies, aged
thirty-seven.

*This illuminated address was presented to Douglas Hyde
during his American trip in 1905*

sense of propriety had replaced the older, more
convivial attitudes. Even the popular nationalist
ballads were infused with the rhythms and
sentiments of British nineteenth-century verse.

All of this was proof that Ireland was by no
means untouched by modernity. In the
countryside, even in the remote and infertile areas
of the west, there was by 1900 ample evidence of
commercial agriculture and a money economy.
After the Famine, pasture had taken over from
tillage, and the export of cattle to Britain had
become a huge and very lucrative trade. Whereas
in the eighteen-fifties less than 300,000 cattle a
year had been exported to Britain, by the early
years of the twentieth century the number had
risen to well over 800,000. These cattle fetched,
in the first two decades of the century, steadily
rising prices, so that between 1916 and 1920 store
cattle were worth twice what they had been
worth between 1901 and 1905.

By the beginning of the new century,
however, the cutting edge of modernity was in

match, it, however, possessed all the elements of a party
disturbance on a large scale. The Linfield and Celtic colours—
blue and green respectively—are in Belfast regarded as party
emblems, and the expressions, 'Go on the blues' and 'Go on
the stripes,' if used in an 'opposition' locality, are regarded by
the magistrates as party expressions. Therefore, while the riot
today must be regarded as a football *fracas*, similar to that
which occurred at Hampton Park, Glasgow, several years ago,
it also had a party element which cannot be overlooked in any
consideration of the affair. Party feeling has been running very
high in Belfast since the Castledawson outrage and the
subsequent shipyard disturbances in July, but there was some
reason to hope that these feelings had to a considerable extent
died down, now that the majority of the Nationalist and
Roman Catholic workmen have returned to their employment
at the shipyards. However, having regard to what took place at
the Celtic Park ground today, one is forced to the conclusion
that, in some quarters at any rate, and among a certain section
of irresponsibles, party feeling is more bitter than ever. One can
only express the hope that the trouble has spent its force, and
that there will be no recurrence of the evidence of the passion
and party feeling which today had such startling results.

from The Irish Times 1912
30 SEPTEMBER

The Ulster
Covenant Signed

Unparalleled Scenes in Belfast

Being convinced in our consciences that Home Rule
would be disastrous to the material well-being of
Ulster as well as of the whole of Ireland, subversive
of our civil and religious freedom, destructive of our
citizenship, and perilous to the unity of the Empire,

We, whose names are underwritten, men of Ulster, loyal
subjects of His Gracious Majesty King George V, humbly
relying on the God whom our fathers in days of stress and
trial confidently trusted, do hereby pledge ourselves in
Solemn Covenant throughout this our time of threatened
calamity to stand to one another in defending for ourselves
and our children our cherished position of equal citizenship
in the United Kingdom, and in using all means which may be
found necessary to defeat the present conspiracy to set up a
Home Rule Parliament in Ireland.

And in the event of such a Parliament being forced upon us, we further solemnly and mutually pledge ourselves to refuse to recognise its authority,

In sure confidence that God will defend the right, we hereto subscribe our names, and further, we individually declare that we have not already signed this Covenant.

The Women's Pledge

We, whose names are underwritten, women of Ulster, and loyal subjects of our Gracious King, being firmly persuaded that Home Rule would be disastrous to our country, desire to associate ourselves with the men of Ulster in their uncompromising opposition to the Home Rule Bill now before Parliament, whereby it is proposed to drive Ulster out of her cherished place in the Constitution of the United Kingdom and to place her under the domination and control of a Parliament in Ireland.

Praying that from this calamity God will save Ireland, we hereto subscribe our names.

(From our Reporters) Belfast, Saturday

Today the Solemn League and Covenant, in resistance to Home Rule, has been signed by many thousands of Ulstermen all over the United Kingdom. Here, in headquarters of Ulster Unionism, many impressive incidents have marked the day which will be remembered for years, perhaps for generations, as 'Ulster Day'. The sun shone this morning on innumerable Union Jacks, flags large and small flying from houses, business establishments and institutions all over the city. Everywhere it was the prevailing element in the decorations which abounded all over Belfast. Union Jacks fluttered, sometimes four or five in number, at the 'bows' of motor cars; people carried small editions of the flag, and horses were decorated with Union Jack rosettes. Where other flags occurred, they were always British standards of some sort—in preference, red or blue ensigns embodying the Union Jack. The appearance of the city was suggestive of high festival.

Such were the externals. What was the 'internal' feeling of Belfast today? Outsiders can judge but by actions. The principal thing that most Belfast people did this morning was to take part in a religious service. The principal thing they did this afternoon was to sign a document of solemn and pious import, committing all of them to a course of action, which may involve them in consequences which none can foresee accurately, but from which, whatever they may be, none—as

Edward Carson, with James Craig standing to his right, signs the Ulster Solemn League and Covenant on 28 September 1912

A Unionist anti-home rule postcard

the north. Belfast had overtaken Dublin as the country's largest city. It represented, literally, a new Ireland: its population had quadrupled since 1850. With the biggest shipyard in the world and thriving engineering plants, linen mills, rope works, and distilleries, Belfast was a flamboyant participant in the industrial revolution, fully integrated into the imperial economy of the United Kingdom. Well over a third of the men and 70 per cent of the women employed in the city had industrial jobs. Its huge, confident and opulent City Hall, built in 1906, declared its prosperity to the world.

29 April

Lloyd George introduces the 'People's budget', involving extra taxes on spirits and tobacco.

16 August

The Fianna Éireann scout movement is founded by Constance Markievicz.

The Volta cinema in Abbey Street, Dublin, opened in 1909 under the brief management of James Joyce

4 November
The 'People's budget' is passed on its third reading in the House of Commons.

30 November
The House of Lords rejects the Liberal budget.

10 December
At a speech in London, Asquith states that Ireland

Dublin, in spite of its relative decline, was also showing signs of entering the industrial age. By 1901 its electric tramway system was complete, and fifty miles of tramway radiated across the city from the Nelson Pillar in O'Connell Street. Electric street lighting was being installed. Cars were becoming a common sight. The Irish Automobile Club was founded in 1902; the Gordon Bennett Trophy race was held in Ireland in 1903; by 1905 there were 138 private cars and nine commercial vehicles licensed in Dublin.

Ireland belonged too to that part of the world (by 1914 it comprised Australia, Austria, Belgium, Denmark, Finland, France, Germany, Italy, Norway, Sweden, Switzerland, the United

everyone who knows the people acknowledge—will shrink. Another feature of the day's proceedings, worthy to be set beside the religious observance and the solemn pledge, was the display in various ways of a spirit of entire confidence in, even of strong devotion to, the chosen leader of militant Ulster—Sir Edward Carson. These are the three special features to be remarked in the conduct of Belfast today; the rest was, by comparison, merely the expression of mannerisms. The processions, the closing of shops, the turn-out of people in the streets, the display of flags and decorations (though more general today than ever before) are Belfast's usual accompaniments of a great occasion. The spirit expressed today was to be identified by the solemn offices in the churches, by the resolute attitude of every man who went to affix his name to the pledge of resistance, and the profession of loyalty to the leader who understands his people.

SEPTEMBER 1913

William Butler Yeats

What need you, being come to sense,
But fumble in a greasy till
And add the halfpence to the pence
And prayer to shivering prayer, until
You have dried the marrow from the bone?
For men were born to pray and save:
Romantic Ireland's dead and gone,
It's with O'Leary in the grave.

Yet they were of a different kind,
The names that stilled your childish play,
They have gone about the world like wind,
But little time had they to pray
For whom the hangman's rope was spun,
And what, God help us, could they save?
Romantic Ireland's dead and gone,
It's with O'Leary in the grave.

Was it for this the wild geese spread
The grey wing upon every tide;
For this that all that blood was shed,
For this Edward Fitzgerald died,
And Robert Emmet and Wolfe Tone,
All that delirium of the brave?
Romantic Ireland's dead and gone,
It's with O'Leary in the grave.

Yet could we turn the years again,
And call those exiles as they were
In all their loneliness and pain,
You'd cry, 'Some woman's yellow hair
Has maddened every mother's son':
They weighed so lightly what they gave,
But let them be, they're dead and gone,
They're with O'Leary in the grave.

Douglas Hyde by Seán O'Sullivan. He was one of the key figures of the Irish Revival and was later to be first president of Ireland.

Kingdom, and the United States) in which some form of extensive, though by no means universal, manhood suffrage was in operation. Public opinion was becoming more important, and the 'public' increasingly included the lower middle class. The first purpose-built public library was opened in Dublin's North Strand in 1900. At least seven daily newspapers were published in the city. *The Irish Times,* with a circulation of about 45,000, vied with the pro-home-rule *Freeman's Journal* and *Evening Telegraph,* with circulations of about 40,000 and 26,000, respectively. Conservative papers such as the *Daily Express* and *Evening Herald* had small but respectable circulations, as had the broadly non-partisan *Daily Independent* and *Evening Mail.*[5]

Commercial mass entertainment was well established. The first cinema in Dublin, the Volta, was established under the management of

must be given a measure of home rule.

20 December
The Volta, the first cinema in Ireland, opens in Abbey Street, Dublin.

31 December
The first aeroplane flight on Irish soil takes place near Hillsborough, Co. Down.

1910

15–31 January
A hung Parliament is the result of the general election, with the Irish Party holding the balance of power.

21 February
Edward Carson replaces Walter Long as leader of the Ulster Unionist Party.

27 April
The House of Commons passes the reintroduced budget.

6 May
King Edward VII dies and is succeeded by George V.

The lock-out of 1913 was the most climactic moment in Irish labour history. Here the Dublin Metropolitan Police baton-charge the crowd in Sackville Street (now O'Connell Street). Two people died and several hundred were injured.

7 May

The Abbey Theatre refuses to close in mourning for the British king.

25 May

Halley's comet is visible in Dublin for half an hour.

23 June

Irish is made a compulsory subject for matriculation at the National University, to be enforced from 1913.

James Joyce in 1909, and by 1914 the city had twenty-seven commercial picture-houses. English comics were widely read in the cities; C. S. Andrews, a shopkeeper's son born in Dublin in 1901, grew up with them. 'From the comics we read,' he recalled, '*Chips, Comic Cuts,* and later the *Magnet* and the *Gem* and the *Union Jack,* we absorbed the correct British imperial attitudes to the "Fuzzy Wuzzies", the "Niggers" and the Indian Nabobs ... soccer football was the game talked of and played everywhere on the vacant lots in the city ... In cricket we followed the fortunes of Surrey and Kent, Hobbs and Hayward ... Our nursery rhymes were English and we knew all about Dick Whittington, Robin Hood and Alice in Wonderland, but we never heard of Fionn or Cuchulain.'[6]

Even nationalists believed that Ireland was becoming, culturally, more like England. Douglas

from The Irish Times 1913
7 OCTOBER

Letter to 'the Masters of Dublin'

Sirs—I address this warning to you, the aristocracy of industry in this city, because, like all aristocracies, you tend to go blind in long authority, and to be unaware that you and your class and its every action are being considered and judged day by day by those who have power to shake or overturn the whole Social Order, and whose relentlessness in poverty today is making our industrial civilisation stir like a quaking bog. You do not seem to realise that your assumption that you are answerable to yourselves alone for your actions in the industries you control is one that becomes less and less tolerable in a world so crowded with necessitous life.

Some of you have helped Irish farmers to upset a landed aristocracy in this island, an aristocracy richer and more powerful in its sphere than you are in yours, with its roots deep in history. They, too, as a class, though not all of them, were scornful or neglectful of the workers in the industry by which they profited; and to many who knew them in their pride of place and thought them all-powerful, they are already becoming a memory, the good disappearing together with the bad. If they had done their duty by those from whose labour came their wealth they might have continued unquestioned in power and prestige for centuries to come.

The relation of landlord and tenant is not an ideal one, but any relations in a social order will endure if there is infused into them some of that spirit of human sympathy which qualifies life for immortality. Despotisms endure while they are benevolent and aristocracies while *noblesse oblige* is not a phrase to be referred to with a cynical smile. Even an oligarchy might be permanent if the spirit of human kindness, which harmonises all things otherwise incomparable, is present.

You do not seem to read history so as to learn its lessons. That you are an uncultivated class was obvious from recent utterances of some of you upon art. That you are incompetent men in the sphere in which you arrogate imperial powers is certain, because for many years, long before the present uprising of labour, your enterprises have been dwindling in the regard of investors, and this while you carried them on in the cheapest labour market in these islands, with a labour reserve always hungry and ready to accept any pittance. You are bad citizens, for we rarely, if ever, hear of the wealthy among you endowing your city with the munificent gifts which it is the pride of merchant princes in other cities to offer, and Irishmen not of your city who offer to supply the wants left by your lack of generosity are met with derision and abuse. Those who have economic powers have civil powers also, yet you have not used the power that was yours to right what was wrong in the evil administration of this city.

You have allowed the poor to be herded together so that one thinks of certain places in Dublin as of a pestilence. There are twenty thousand rooms, in each of which live entire families, and sometimes more, where no functions of the body can be concealed and delicacy and modesty are creatures that are stifled ere they are born. The obvious duty of you in regard to these things you might have left undone, and it be imputed to ignorance or forgetfulness; but your collective and conscious action as a class in the present labour dispute has revealed you to the world in so malign an aspect

The Daily Mirror

THE MORNING JOURNAL WITH THE SECOND LARGEST NET SALE.

No. 3,076.   Registered at the G.P.O. as a Newspaper.   TUESDAY, SEPTEMBER 2, 1913.   One Halfpenny.

MR. JAMES LARKIN, DISGUISED IN FALSE BEARD AND FROCK COAT, ARRESTED BY POLICE IN CONNECTION WITH DUBLIN STRIKE RIOTS.

In a brilliant coup, Larkin defied a ban on a public meeting he had planned for Sunday 31 August 1913. Not only did he appear in disguise but he did so from the balcony of the Imperial Hotel, which was owned by the employers' leader William Martin Murphy. He was afterwards arrested by the DMP.

Hyde, president of the Gaelic League, had inspired the new cultural movements with a famous lecture in 1892 'On the Necessity of De-Anglicising the Irish People'. But the very title contained the concession that the Irish people were already Anglicised. Similarly, in 1900, when Maud Gonne founded Inghinidhe na hÉireann as a feminist vehicle for cultural and political separatism, the organisation's concern with 'the reading and circulation of low English literature, the singing of English songs, the attending of

1 October

Jim Larkin is released after serving three months in prison for his labour activities.

30 November

The House of Lords again rejects the Liberal

Grafton Street, Dublin, hung with decorations for the visit of King George V in 1911

*budget, forcing a
general election.*

3–19 December

*A second general
election takes place
in an to attempt to
give the Liberals an
overall majority to
face down the
House of Lords.*

10 December

*It is announced
that reform of the
House of Lords
and home rule for*

vulgar English entertainments at the theatre and music hall and [the] … English influence which is doing so much injury to the artistic taste and refinement of the Irish people' implied that these pastimes and influences were already well established. Likewise, the fact that the Gaelic Athletic Association instituted a formal ban on its members playing such English games as soccer, rugby, cricket and hockey was an indication of how strong the pull of these sports really was. Especially in Dublin, soccer was indeed far more popular than Gaelic games. In 1913 there were 2,272 applications to play soccer on the pitches in the Phoenix Park but just 90 applications to play hurling or Gaelic football.[7]

Yet the appeal to a separate Irish identity was very strong. The search for an apparently

that the mirror must be held up to you, so that you may see yourself as every humane person sees you.

The conception of yourselves as altogether virtuous and wronged is, I assure you, not at all the one which onlookers hold of you. No doubt, some of you suffered without just cause. But nothing which has been done to you cries aloud to Heaven for condemnation as your own actions. Let me show you how it seems to those who have followed critically the dispute, trying to weigh in a balance the rights and wrongs. You were within the rights society allows when you locked out your men and insisted on the fixing of some principle to adjust your future relations with labour, when the policy of labour made it impossible for some of you to carry on your enterprises. Labour desired the fixing of some such principle as much as you did. But, having once decided on such a step, knowing how many thousands, men, women and children, nearly one-third of the population of this city, would be affected, you should not have let one day to have passed without unremitting endeavours to find a solution of the problem.

What did you do? The representatives of labour unions in Great Britain met you, and you made of them a preposterous, an impossible demand, and because they would not accede to it you closed the conference; you refused to meet them further; you assumed that no other guarantees than those you asked were possible, and you determined deliberately in cold anger, to starve out one-third of the population of this city, to break the manhood of the men by the sight of the suffering of their wives and the hunger of their children. We read in the Dark Ages of the rack and thumb screw. But these iniquities were hidden and concealed from the knowledge of man in dungeons and torture chambers. Even in the Dark Ages humanity could not endure the sight of such suffering, and it learnt of such misuses of power by slow degrees, through rumour, and when it was certain it razed its Bastilles to their foundations.

It remained for the twentieth century and the capital city of Ireland to see an oligarchy of four hundred masters deciding openly upon starving one hundred thousand people, and refusing to consider any solution except that fixed by their pride. You, masters, asked men to do that which masters of labour in any other city in these islands had not dared to do. You insolently demanded of those men who were members of a trade union that they should resign from that union; and from those who were not members you insisted on a vow that they would never join it.

Your insolence and ignorance of the rights conceded to workers universally in the modern world were incredible, and as great as your inhumanity. If you had between you collectively a portion of human soul as large as a threepenny bit, you would have sat night and day with the representatives of labour, trying this or that solution of the trouble, mindful of the women and children, who at least were innocent of wrong against you. But no! You reminded labour you could always have your three square meals a day while it went hungry. You went into conference again with representatives of the State, because dull as you are, you know public opinion would not stand your holding out. You chose as your spokesman the bitterest tongue that ever wagged in this island, and then, when an award was made by men who have an experience in industrial matters a thousand times transcending yours, who have settled disputes in industries so

Main Street, Swords, Co. Dublin, at the turn of the century

older and more authentic culture was one way of coping with the startling confusion of modern life. This was, after all, a time when almost all common-sense assumptions seemed to be disintegrating before the merciless onslaught of science and technology. H. G. Wells was publishing novels in which he imagined time machines, invaders from outer space with weapons that 'generate an intense heat in a chamber of practically absolute non-conductivity,' and men landing on the moon (*The First Men in the Moon* came out in 1901). Einstein's theory of relativity, published in 1905, challenged the most basic ideas of time and space. Solid flesh had become transparent: Wilhelm Conrad Röntgen's X-rays, discovered in 1895, were coming into general use. The common notion of what was real was being dramatically expanded by the arrival of the cinema. New kinds of noise and speed, unprecedented visions and ideas that brazenly defied the common sense of countless generations, were everywhere.

Throughout the modern world, governments and political movements were responding to all this change, and to the development of mass democracy, by discovering or inventing a national past that seemed to offer security and community in an uncertain and increasingly open world. This was the great era of monuments, flags, anthems, and commemorative stamps. Even the socialist movement, bent on

Ireland are now on the Liberal Party's agenda.

1911

2 April
The census is taken throughout Ireland, which shows the population to be 4.39 million.

11 April
The Home Rule Bill is introduced in the House of Commons.

21 April
The Parliament Bill, first introduced in the House of Commons in April 1910, is reintroduced. It radically curtails the powers of the House of Lords to veto legislation.

overthrowing the old order, was inventing its own rituals, such as the annual celebration of May Day.

Throughout Europe, young intellectuals were asking the same questions that Irish writers, artists and journalists were putting to the country. From the perspective of Great Britain, Irish nationalism may have looked like something of an anomaly; but in a wider context it was very much in tune with the mood of the times. In Russia, Jews were declaring themselves a nation and demanding autonomy. In Finland the nationalist movement was campaigning for equal status for Finnish and for greater autonomy within the Russian empire. The Latvians, Estonians and Lithuanians were turning the dialects that had survived only among the remote peasantry into standardised literary languages. Poland, Ukraine, Hungary, Georgia, Slovakia and practically every other European nation within the Austro-Hungarian, Russian and Ottoman empires were in the throes of a 'revival' that was really a re-invention or a synthesising of a distinctive language, culture, and historical narrative.

In Ireland, moreover, the reaction against cultural absorption and confusion was not confined to Catholics; and the establishment of the Abbey Theatre in 1904 as a forum for distinctively Irish theatre was largely the work of two Protestants, William Butler Yeats and Lady

Goods being delivered by motor vans to the docks under police protection during the Belfast dock strike of 1907

great that the sum of your petty enterprises would not equal them, you withdraw again, and will not agree to accept their solution, and fall back again upon your devilish policy of starvation. Cry aloud to Heaven for new souls! The souls you have got cast upon the screen of publicity appear like the horrid and writhing creatures enlarged from the insect world, and revealed to us by the cinematograph.

You may succeed in your policy and ensure your own damnation by your victory. The men whose manhood you have broken will loathe you, and will always be brooding and scheming to strike a fresh blow. The children will be taught to curse you. The infant being moulded in the womb will have breathed into its starved body the vitality of hate. It is not they—it is you who are blind Samsons pulling down the pillars of the social order. You are sounding the death knell of autocracy in industry. There was autocracy in political life, and it was superseded by democracy. So surely will democratic power wrest from you the control of industry. The fate of you, the aristocracy of industry, will be as the fate of the aristocracy of land if you do not show that you have some humanity still among you. Humanity abhors, above all things, a vacuum in itself, and your class will be cut off from humanity as the surgeon cuts the cancer and alien growth from the body. Be warned, ere it is too late.

—Yours, etc. Æ

from The Irish Times 1914
23 MARCH

The Army and Ulster

Grave Crisis at the Curragh

The story I now relate is one of supreme importance in the history of Ireland, and especially in its relation to the present political crisis. I will state what has actually happened as clearly and concisely as possible, and readers may form their own conclusions from the narrative. The facts can be relied on as being substantially correct.

On Thursday night instructions were conveyed to the Commander-in-Chief in Ireland to carry out certain movements of troops to Ulster, and other precautionary measures, details of which had previously been agreed upon by a conference at the War Office, to which Sir Arthur Paget was specially invited. It was then known that a certain number of officers would decline service in Ulster, but the exact numbers and positions were not accurately known. To meet this difficulty it was tentatively agreed that any officer whose domicile was in Ulster should not be asked to accompany his regiment there, and that he would be given the option of resigning his commission or of requesting prolonged leave, which it was agreed upon would be granted in exceptional circumstances, and for just cause shown. To give effect to this decision what has been generally described as an *ultimatum* was sent out by the War Office to all the officers in Ireland on Thursday night, asking them to state definitely if, under certain contingencies, they would be willing to serve in Ulster, and, should they be unwilling to do so, to send in their papers within twelve hours. The sending in of papers, of course, involved dismissal from the Army, and the forfeiture of all right to pension. In a word, the officer sending in his papers ruins his career, and places himself entirely at the mercy of the War Office.

Circulars Received at the Curragh

These circulars were received at the Curragh on Friday morning, and after roll-call and morning parade, the officers of the 3rd Cavalry Brigade, which comprises the 4th Hussars and 16th Lancers, were addressed by the officer in command, Brigadier-General H. De la Poer Gough, C.B., who, in a short address to his colleagues, explained the position of affairs, and asked them to consider carefully how they should act. The officers, with practical unanimity, promptly stated that they would decline service in Ulster. This involved the sending in of papers, and the decision was at once conveyed to the Commander-in-Chief at headquarters in Dublin. Sir Arthur Paget immediately got into communication with the authorities at Whitehall, which explains the unusual bustle which occurred there on Friday night, and kept the heads of Departments, together with Colonel Seely and Mr Winston Churchill, in conference to the early hours of Saturday morning. Though the War Office were fully cognisant of the serious turn of events at the Curragh on Friday night, it was not expected that the officers' papers would reach Whitehall before this (Monday) morning ...

War Office Changes Its Attitude

A different attitude was adopted by the War Office on Saturday morning. Early in the day there was a prolonged conference between Sir Arthur Paget and the officers of the 3rd Cavalry Brigade stationed at the Curragh, as well as representatives of the officers of the 5th (Royal Irish) Lancers,

The corner of New Row and Blackpitts in the Dublin Liberties in Edwardian times

Augusta Gregory. *The Irish Times* gave extensive and often sympathetic coverage to their work. Yeats was not, of course, a natural admirer of the paper's unionism. In 1900 the worst accusation he could think of making against Trinity College, which he hated with a vengeance, was that it had 'turned our once intelligent gentry into readers of *The Irish Times*.'[8] In his collection of folklore, *The Celtic Twilight*, Yeats also reported the alleged experiences of a County Mayo woman who encountered the Devil: 'Something came flapping and rolling along the road up to her feet. It had the likeness of a newspaper, and presently it flapped up into her face, and she knew by the size of it that it was *The Irish Times*.'[9] Yeats complained in 1905 that *The Irish Times* critic tended to review Abbey plays without actually seeing them, because, as he allegedly put it, 'plays depress my spirits.'[10]

Yet *The Irish Times* was in fact quite well disposed towards the new theatrical movement. In August 1904, when the Irish National Theatre Society was about to be granted its patent, the paper welcomed it as 'an earnest effort by talented writers and readers to do something better for the play-going public than is being done by the stock dramatists of the day.' The southern unionist readership of *The Irish Times*

25 September

Carson declares that the Ulster Unionist Council intends establishing a Provisional Government in Northern Ireland.

1 October

A monument to Parnell is unveiled in Upper Sackville Street (O'Connell Street).

13 November

Andrew Bonar Law becomes leader of the Unionist Party in the House of Commons in succession to Balfour.

16 December

The Local Authority (Ireland) (Qualification of

Steerage passengers on the **Titanic**

Women) Act allows women to become members of county and borough councils.

1912

5 January
Colonel Wallace of the Grand Orange Lodge of Ireland applies for permission to legally begin drilling men in

was, on the whole, able to identify with both the Irish literary revival and its British cultural connections. It could, as R. B. McDowell has put it, 'take a possessory pride in and enjoy Yeats and Synge, Hardy and Kipling, Lady Gregory's plays and Gilbert and Sullivan.'[11]

The Irish Times therefore had a rather ambivalent relationship not just with the Abbey but with Yeats. On the one hand, the paper's reports of Yeats's addresses on spiritualism and magic were loaded with scepticism. A lecture by Yeats on 'A New Theory of Apparitions' in January 1912 was summed up with subtle but unmistakable irony. The reporter noted that Yeats had explained that spiritualist mediums were invaded by 'strange promptings to

a portion of the same Brigade, stationed at the Marlborough Barracks, Dublin (almost all of whom have also formally handed in their papers). The conference was held in the Fire Brigade Station of the Curragh Camp, the entrances to which were specially guarded with double sentries. The greatest secrecy prevails as to what actually took place, and the officers present at the conference stated at the close that they were in honour bound not to disclose the nature of the proceedings, but did not deny that matters had taken a nasty and unexpected turn. From information subsequently elicited from quarters which can be regarded as perfectly reliable, it seems that the Commander-in-Chief intimated that the War Office would not accept the resignation of the officers as a body, but were prepared to accede to the applications of two individual officers, the position in regard of the other officers being that their requests to be relieved of their commission not being

March past and review of troops bound for France. This photograph was taken in Belfast in the early days of the Great War.

granted, it would be a personal matter with each officer whether he would obey the command to go to Ulster or not.

The Officers' Decision

These terms were considered at length by the officers. It was intimated that the movement of troops to the North was largely a precautionary measure, and that the outbreak of actual hostilities was extremely unlikely. The new conditions having been considered by the officers, it was agreed that they would lead their men to Ulster for the purpose of making a demonstration, performing what may be called police duty, or protecting Government property, but that under no conditions would they order their men to fire on the Ulster loyalists. This decision was at once conveyed to Whitehall. . . .

from The Irish Times 1914
5 AUGUST

Ireland and the War

We believe that the people of these kingdoms are today more cheerful than they have been at any time since the war cloud began to gather over Europe. The period of suspense and uncertainty is ended. In

wickedness' and added that 'Mr. Yeats' theory, it would seem, explains the notorious fact that much of the history of modern spiritualism is a record of trickery, deception and even uglier things.' Later in the same year, when the poet protested to the editor about a similarly sceptical report of a similarly airy lecture by Yeats 'and his friends the spirits,' the editor responded: 'We agree with Mr. Yeats that life is too short for explanations of his psychical adventures.'

Nor was the paper especially supportive of the Abbey's greatest and most controversial playwright, John Millington Synge. Reviewing the premiere of *Riders to the Sea*, the paper's critic remarked that 'there are some things which are lifelike, and yet are quite unfit for presentation on the stage, and *Riders to the Sea* is one of them.' In January 1907, when *The Playboy of the Western World* was first staged, the paper was not as virulent in its condemnation as much of the rest of the press, but it was hardly helpful either, praising the realism and the dialogue but complaining that the offensiveness of some of the

defence of the realm, in fact to oppose home rule.

8 February
Winston Churchill addresses a crowd of seven thousand at Celtic Park in Belfast with the leader of the Irish Party, John Redmond.

11 April
Asquith introduces the Home Rule Bill in the House of Commons.

14–15 April
The White Star liner Titanic, *built*

THE IRISH TIMES, MONDAY, JUNE 2, 1902. 5

PEACE.

BOERS SIGN SURRENDER TERMS.

DESPATCH FROM LORD KITCHENER.

(OFFICIAL TELEGRAM.)

"From Lord Kitchener to Secretary of State for War.

"PRETORIA, 11.15 P.M., 31ST MAY.

"Negotiations with Boer Delegates,

"The document containing the terms of surrender was signed here this evening at 10.30 p.m. by all the Boer representatives, as well as by Lord Milner and myself."

An earlier despatch telegraphed by Lord Kitchener was as follows :—

"PRETORIA, MAY 31, 5.15 P.M.

It is now settled that the Boer representatives will come here immediately, and also the High Commissioner from Johannesburg. It is possible that the document will be signed to-night. I have received from them a statement saying that they accept, and are prepared to sign."

(REUTER'S TELEGRAMS.)

PRETORIA, FRIDAY.

The deliberations between the Boer delegates at Vereeniging have resulted practically in the acceptance of the British terms, and the delegates may arrive here at any moment for the purpose of signing the document embodying the terms.

SUNDAY, 10.25 A.M.

The terms of peace were signed at half-past ten o'clock last night.

RECEPTION OF THE NEWS.

REJOICINGS IN LONDON.

LONDON, SUNDAY EVENING.

The announcement giving official and definite news that peace had been concluded was first posted outside the War Office shortly after five o'clock this evening. Unlike the early days of the war, when every item of intelligence was eagerly scanned as it was published, this passed comparatively unheeded for a considerable time. Meanwhile the news had been officially communicated to the Press, which simultaneously gave the first public intimation by the display of flags across the street. The good news was also conveyed to the Lord Mayor of London and the Church dignitaries, so that the glad tidings might be as widely distributed as possible.

As soon as the news became known people began to make their way to the Mansion House, the Lord Mayor expressed satisfaction at the news, but intimated that he would await communication from the War Office before making the public announcement from the balcony. Meanwhile word was passed to the police and those on duty in the vicinity assembled in front of the historic building.

About six o'clock Sir Joseph Dimsdale received the following telegram :—

"War Office, Sunday.

"I have received the following telegram from Lord Kitchener :—'Pretoria, 11.15 p.m., May 31st,—Negotiations with Boer delegates. The document containing terms of surrender was signed here this evening at 10.30 p.m. by all the Boer representatives as well as by Lord Milner and myself.'

"SECRETARY OF STATE FOR WAR."

A copy of this message was immediately posted on the outside of the Mansion House by one of the attendants, and was eagerly read by an excited group of citizens. Loud cheers were immediately raised, and the spectators rushed to the front of the Mansion House, where the Lord Mayor, who was attired in his official robes, accompanied by Lady Dimsdale and a group of ladies, made his appearance. The Lady Mayoress and her young daughter attached the ends of a large streamer bearing in red lettering the significant message "Peace is Proclaimed" to the pillars of the historic facade. This brief message acted like a talisman. People rushed to the spot from the side streets, Tube subways, and passing vehicles, cheering wildly. The passengers on the outside of the 'buses rose and waved their

of the acceptance of the peace terms offered to the Boers, and it is significant that Mr. Brodrick waited upon the King as late as midnight. But it was not until the early hours of this morning that definite news came to hand of the signature of the peace agreement. The War Office was the first department to be informed. Lord Kitchener and Lord Milner have been associated in the communication with the Boer leaders, but it was left to the soldier to make the bold announcement of the result, while the diplomatist undertook the task of giving to the Colonial Secretary a detailed account of the steps which led to it. Ministers had in some instances left town in the expectation that they might be recalled to meet in council, but it was fully recognised that this was probable only in the event of a hitch at the last moment.

Fairly early this morning the War Office was in possession of its definite tidings, and of course the first step taken was to advise His Majesty the King and other members of the Royal Family, all of whom, it is understood, received the news with deep thankfulness, although it had been discounted to some extent by confident anticipation.

The next step was to telegraph those Ministers who were out of town, including Lord Salisbury and Mr. Balfour. The Colonial Office got the despatch from its sister department, and was evidently looking for it, seeing that the staff of the South African Department was in attendance. These gentlemen went out to Mr. Chamberlain at Prince's Gardens, and communicated the tidings to him, and the right hon. gentleman did not go at all to Downing street. Lord Onslow, the Under Secretary of State, called at the Colonial Office in the course of the afternoon, just about the time at which the cablegram to Mr. Chamberlain had been received from the Governor of Natal. About the same time, too, a long despatch in cipher came to hand from Lord Milner, giving his full account of the proceedings and their result. For some time the authorities were minded to keep the good news quiet until to-morrow, and a Press representative was informed, some hours after he had learned definitely of the receipt of a despatch of some kind from Lord Kitchener, that "No statement could be made to-day."

Later on the decision was modified, and it is believed that the Government decided to publish the news late this afternoon as being the least likely time to provoke any demonstration unfitted for the Sabbath, and the publication took the form of posting on the railings in front of the War Office, Lord Kitchener's brief message.

The King and Queen, the Prince and Princess of Wales, and other members of the Royal Family attended Divine Service this morning at the Chapel Royal. Nothing had then been allowed to transpire as to the conclusion of peace, and it cannot even be definitely stated —although it is probably a fact—that their Majesties were then in possession of the formal news, but it was noticed by members of the congregation that the demeanour of the Royal worshippers, always devout, was especially and obviously so to-day, and the deep thankfulness in their hearts at the termination of a long and dire struggle can well be imagined, assuming that they then knew of the exact position of affairs. The Bishop of Kensington preached the sermon. Dr. Edgar Sheppard took the evening service, and just before the assembling of the congregation heard of the official declaration, and although he made no pulpit allusions he arranged for a special hymn at the close of service, "Now Thank we all our God." The choir and the congregation then united in singing with great fervour "God Save the King."

Stepney. The assembly of worshippers was not so large as usual, owing, doubtless, to the inclemency of the weather. The preacher was Rev. E. J. Kennedy, Vicar of St. John's, Boscombe, who during his sermon, incidentally referring to the blessings of peace, said, "Of which we hear to-night." This was the only intimation made in the sermon. The Bishop of Stepney then ascended the pulpit and said "I desire to announce to the congregation that God has been pleased to answer our prayer, and to give us the blessings of peace." He added "I will read to you the telegram which has been sent by the Commander-in-Chief to the Secretary of State for War—"The document containing the terms of surrender was signed at Pretoria this (Saturday) evening at 10.30 p.m. by all the Boer representatives, as well as Lord Milner and myself." Comment is needless, but I ask you to offer your heartfelt thanks to Almighty God by singing, instead of the hymn on the paper, a hymn suitable to the occasion, and to follow by singing two verses of the National Anthem. The hymn referred to was "Now thank we all Our God." The organ pealed forth the tune, and the congregation sang the hymn with much feeling and impressiveness. Following this the people sang two verses of the National Anthem, and the solemnity of the National hymn appeared all the more marked by the historic occasion which called it forth. The worshippers again knelt for the Benediction, the General Thanksgiving Prayer being read by the Bishop of Stepney, who interpolated the words, "for Thy late mercies vouchsafed to us in restoring peace." The congregation quietly left the cathedral, and on reaching the street the fact that the news had become widespread was made manifest by thousands of people shouting patriotic songs and flags being waved in hundreds.

No arrangements have yet been made for thanksgiving services at the cathedrals, though it may be taken for granted that such service will be held to-morrow. The bells of the cathedral will be pealed, and at the conclusion of the afternoon service the *Te Deum* will be sung. to the majority of the congregation, which, despite the inclemency of the weather, practically filled St. Margaret's, Westminster. Canon Hensley Henson's announcement of the official news when he entered the pulpit was the first intelligence. The subdued murmur of pleasurable excitement having died away, the Canon made the following remarks :—"It is, perhaps, a happy circumstance that the glad news of peace which we have waited for so long and desired so earnestly, should happen to be first publicly announced in church, for the aspect of the war now at last ended which is best worth remembering is that which can most fitly be dwelt on here. This war, let our enemies say what they will, has been a high-toned war, worthily fought out on both sides, and a high-toned war properly leads to a generous and equitable settlement. It has left behind a legacy of mutual respect, and there could be no better guarantee of genuine and lasting harmony. But we cannot forget that this peace has been dearly purchased. The very greatness of the price we have had to pay in suffering and sorrow indicates the special responsibilities attached to it. Be it our task as Christian citizens to heal the sufferings of this long conflict, and to join hands with our gallant opponents, now become our fellow-subjects, in order to build a Christian civilisation on the land which has been for so many months ravaged by war. South Africa was a land without traditions, without history, one of the blanks in the moral geography of mankind. It is now a land rich in memorials of sacrifice and heroism, able to provide a worthy environment for a manly and high-minded society. South Africa has had its baptism of blood. We have, indeed, much to thank God for."

The *Te Deum* was then sung with great heartiness, and after the Benediction the congregation with great fervour gave a verse of the National Anthem. As they slowly filed out of the great edifice the bells of St. Margaret's rang out a joyous peal.

OPPOSITION LEADER AND THE INTELLIGENCE.

A Press representative this evening communicated to Sir Henry Campbell-Bannerman the fact that the peace conditions had been signed. Sir Henry remarked —"Undoubtedly the whole country will rejoice that peace is assured. I know nothing of the terms or conditions, but I hope they are such as will be full of promise for the future."

SCENES IN THE STREETS.

The news arriving on a Sunday militated greatly against anything in the nature of a big demonstration in London. Nevertheless as the evening advanced there were many outbursts of enthusiasm in the principal thoroughfares of the City and West End. A few newspapers published editions containing

THE NEWS IN DUBLIN.

TELEGRAM TO THE LORD MAYOR.

The Lord Mayor of Dublin received the following telegram from the Secretary of State for War at 5.4 last evening :—

"From the Secretary of State for War

"To the Lord Mayor of Dublin.

"I have received the following telegram from Lord Kitchener :—'Pretoria, 11.15 p.m., 31st May. Negotiations with Boer delegates. The document containing terms of surrender was signed here this evening at 10.30 p.m. by all Boer representatives as well as by Lord Milner and myself.'"

Shortly afterwards the intelligence reached the newspaper offices, and "stop press" editions of evening issues were on the streets, and were quickly bought up. The principal city thoroughfares were rather deserted owing to the heavy rain which descended continually all the evening, but the great body of pedestrians seemed much elated by the welcome news. About ten o'clock a large bonfire was lit by a number of students in that famous portion of Trinity College known as Botany Bay, and was watched by many persons in the vicinity of College green. On receipt of the welcome news that peace had been signed the bell-ringers of St. George's Church assembled, and by permission of the Rector, Rev. Canon Scott, rang a peal on the bells from 9.55 to 10.30 p.m. The following members of the St. George's Society Amateur Change Ringers took part:—Messrs. J. G. Wilson, C. Purdie, A. E. Deane, A. Corrigan, G. Moore, J. R. Ennis, C. M'Cullagh, A. E. Greene, and S. C. Gregg.

LONDONDERRY.

A message announcing the signing of the terms of peace was handed to the preacher in Derry Cathedral last night, and he read it to the congregation, who sang the Te Deum and the National Anthem, and a team of bellringers went into the tower, and pulled the joy-bells for half an hour, thus spreading the news throughout the city.

MR. JOHN REDMOND AND THE BOERS.

Mr. John Redmond was the chief speaker at a meeting in Kensington last evening in aid of the Irish Parliamentary Fund. He denied that Ireland had been in sympathy with the Boers out of any feeling of hostility to England. After peace had been settled, Cape Colony would return a Parliament hostile to England and friendly to the Dutch. England would lose the whole of South Africa. Mr. Redmond ridiculed the idea that any Liberal party could ever gain office without Irish support. As to our Colonies, their value sank into insignificance compared with that of Ireland. Ireland would be absent from the Coronation celebrations.

PASSING EVENTS.

MONDAY MORNING.

We have received from the hon. secs. of the Irish Unionist Alliance a copy of that very useful publication, "Notes from Ireland," for June. The scope of the journal is enlarged, and an editorial article is one of the new features. Political incidents are more fully treated than formerly. The Blessington street meeting is dealt with in detail, and its connection with certain affairs in the West proved to demonstration. The journal has always been a valuable aid to Unionist speakers and organisations, and its success is sufficiently proved by the fact that it has been forced to extend the scope of its subjects and comments.

As there still exists considerable misconception regarding the nature of the Coronation Oath, we should like to draw attention to a small leaflet on the subject by "an Irish Churchman," published by Messrs. Hodges, Figgis, and Company, Limited. The text of the oath is given, and it is pointed out that the declaration against Transubstantiation forms no part thereof.

To-day, in the London Divorce Court, sixty-seven applications to make absolute as many decrees *nisi* will be almost automatically granted. It will be interesting to note the number disposed of by Sir Francis Jeune in the space of an hour—should the list take so long to get through.

So far 139 entries have been received for the Paris-Vienna motor race. These include nine Mors cars, twelve Panhards, eight Daimler Mercedes, four Serpollets, six Darracqs, and twelve vehicles made by the new firm of Charron, Girardot, and Voight. Among the drivers who have put their names down for these and other cars are the Hon. Charles Rolls, Baron de Caters, and Henry Fournier, who will all pilot Mors cars ; the Chevalier Rene de Knyff ; the Duc de Valencay, second son of the present Duc de Sagan ; and Messrs Henry and Maurice Far-

THIRD EDITION.

PEACE.

KING'S MESSAGE TO HI[S] PEOPLE.

The following gracious message was issu[ed] from the King late last night :—

The King has received the welcome news [of] the cessation of hostilities in South Africa wi[th] infinite satisfaction, and trusts that peace may [be] speedily followed by a restoration of propert[y] in his new dominions, and that the feelings n[e]cessarily engendered by the war will give pla[ce] to the earnest co-operation of all His Majesty['s] South African subjects in promoting the welfa[re] of their common country."

MEN AND THE WORLD.

(FROM OUR CORRESPONDENT.)

LONDON, SUNDAY.

Lady Airlie and Mr. Andrew Carnegie are [to] receive the Freedom of the City of Dundee.

Lord Churchill is to act as Master of the Asc[ot] Racecourse under the King, and he and Maj[or] Clements are responsible for the arrangement[s]; when the whole thing is over they will bo[th] have earned a holiday. It is understood tha[t] Lord Churchill will head the Royal procession [to] the course.

Mr. William M. Barclay sailed for We[st] Africa yesterday as a special com[]missioner from Liverpool and Ma[n]chester traders with that part of the Afr[i]can Continent who desire to co-operate with th[e] chiefs and native traders, Oil Rivers Colony, [in] opposing the monopoly which now practicall[y] controls the trade in the West African river[s]. Under the present system the native trader[s] have to take any price they can get for the[ir] produce.

There will be a numerous attendance of mil[i]tary officers at the Levee on Monday. Th[is] function is known as the Derby Levee, the ex[]planation being that officers who get leave to a[t]tend the Levee can generally make that leav[e] spread over the Derby and Oaks. The result [is] that the Derby Levee is very popular in th[e] Army, and is very generally selected as a mo[st] favourable opportunity for paying respect to th[e] Sovereign.

It is said that the Earl of Hopetoun's incom[e] is between £60,000 and £70,000 a year. If thi[s] is so no trifle has induced him to resign th[e] Governor-Generalship of Australia on the scor[e] of insufficient salary. Some idea of what he ha[s] spent out of his private purse ma[y] be gathered from the fact that when he repre[]sented the Sovereign in Victoria he [is] believed to have disbursed £10,000 a year i[n] addition to his official income. The estimat[e] was made by Australians in a position to judge. As he showed no objection to that tax on hi[s] private resources, it is not unreasonable to sup[]pose that the one he has lately borne was muc[h] greater.

Sir George Faudel Phillips, who, it is re[]ported in Anglo-Jewish circles, will b[e] one of the Coronation Peers, was Lor[d] Mayor of London at the Diamond Jubilee and carried out his functions of that year wit[h] great success. He has a long family connectio[n] with the "one square mile" of the City o[f] London, his father, the late Sir Benjami[n] Phillips, having filled the Lord Mayoralty man[y] years ago. Sir George in charitable matters ha[s] been prominently identified with the Jew[s'] Hospital and Orphan Asylum at Norwood.

Many happy returns of the day to Viscoun[t] Villiers, who will be 29 to-morrow. Lor[d] Villiers is the eldest son of the Earl of Jersey and heir to Osterley Park, Middleton Park, an[d] the share in Childs' Bank, which is the backbo[ne] of the wealth of the family. Lord Villiers is [a] thorough sportsman, and a member of that centr[e] of sport, the exclusive Turf Club in Piccadilly, but he is also preparing himself for the mo[re] serious work of legislation in the future by ac[t]ing as a County Councillor in Oxfordshire.

To-day is the 54th birthday of Lord Langfor[d], an Irish Peer, who is well-known to a[ll] who have attended the State function[s] at the Viceregal Castle, Dublin. He was [for] some time State Steward, and now he [is] Comptroller of Lord Cadogan's household, a p[ost] which gives him a good deal of work. He ow[es] his appointments mainly to his activity [in] politics, which has also made him a repre[]sentative Peer, but his K.C.V.O. is a memen[to] of the late Queen's visit to Dublin, and his sha[re] in the work of reception.

Considerable interest attached to the ascen[t] from the grounds of the Ranelagh Club yesterda[y] by members of the Aero Club. The balloons (thre[e] in number) were inflated on the polo practic[e] ground, and at 3.30 p.m., the time appointed, everything was in readiness, and the balloon[s] sailed away gracefully at intervals of about five minutes each. Sir Vincent Kenneth-Barring[]ton's Shropshire, with a capacity of 35,000 fe[et], in addition to its owner, carri[ed] the well-known motorist, Mr. S. F. Edge, an[d] the aeronaut, Mr. Percival Spence[r]. Mr. Frank H. Butler's Graphic, 45,000 feet, carried the owner, his sister, Miss Vera Butler, and Messrs. John Holder and C. F. Pollock, whilst Mr. Leslie Bucknall's new balloo[n] Vivienne, of similar capacity to the Shrop[]

THE IRISH TIMES, TUESDAY, APRIL 16, 1912.

THE LOST TITANIC.

Photo by]   [Tuttle, Belfast.

PICTURE OF THE LEVIATHAN IN BELFAST DOCK.

HOME RULE BILL IN PARLIAMENT.

FIRST READING DEBATE.

MR. BALFOUR'S BRILLIANT CRITICISM.

DEFECTS OF THE MEASURE EXPOSED.

MR. SAMUEL ON THE FINANCIAL PROVISIONS.

IRELAND'S POWER OF TAXATION.

LAND PURCHASE SECURITY.

MR. JOHN DILLON'S ATTITUDE.

MR. WILLIAM MOORE STATES THE CASE OF ULSTER.

HOUSE OF COMMONS—Monday.

Mr. BALFOUR, who was received with prolonged Opposition cheers, on rising to continue the debate on the motion that leave be given to bring in the Home Rule Bill, said:—

IN PARLIAMENT.

HOME RULE BILL.

CRITICISED BY MR. BALFOUR.

MR. SAMUEL AND THE BILL'S FINANCE.

IRISH POWERS OF TAXATION.

(FROM OUR CORRESPONDENT.)
LONDON, Monday.

Though there were more vacant places in the House of Commons than on Thursday last, it was well filled to hear Mr. Balfour resume the debate on the Home Rule Bill.

TITANIC'S FIRST WAGES PAID.

The first half-pay notes given to the wives and dependents of the members of the Titanic's crew became payable yesterday, and after receiving their money the women gathered in small groups at the Southampton Dock gates, many of them with babies in their arms, and anxiously discussed the latest news respecting the liner. The White Star offices were besieged for the latest informa-

---

NEWS CREATES SENSATION AT QUEENSTOWN.

(FROM OUR CORRESPONDENT.)
QUEENSTOWN, Monday.

143 IRISH PASSENGERS ON BOARD.

The intelligence received here to-day of the serious accident to the Titanic, which left this port on last Thursday afternoon for New York, with 1,463 passengers on board, created quite a sensation, and the regret was, indeed, widespread that this magnificent vessel which graced the waters of the harbour on last Thursday for the first time should have met with such an accident on her maiden voyage.

MESSAGE FROM THE WIRELESS OPERATOR.

The wireless operator on the Titanic is Mr. Jack Phillips, son of Mr. and Mrs. G. A. Phillips, of Farncombe, Godalming, Surrey. He is 25 years of age, and served as telegraphist in Godalming Post Office, afterwards joining the Marconi School at Liverpool. His first wireless appointment was on the Teutonic, after which he was appointed to the Mauretania, Lusitania, and Oceanic, from which last he was transferred to the Titanic for her maiden trip. His parents received a message from him last night as follows:—"Making slowly for Halifax. Practically un-

---

UNK.

LINER ON VAGE.

CEBERG.

DISASTER.

FEARED APPALLING DISASTER.

ONLY 675 SURVIVORS.

OVER 1,600 LIVES LOST.

MEAGRE DETAILS.

The following telegram, received at 2.50 a.m. this morning, points to appalling loss of life by the Titanic disaster. It is now admitted that the 675 survivors on board the Carpathia are nearly all women and children, and that probably over 1,600 of the passengers and crew went down with the ill-fated steamer:—

(REUTER'S TELEGRAMS.)
NEW YORK, Monday, 8.45 p.m.—

A despatch from Cape Race says:—
All Titanic's boats accounted for.
About 675 souls saved of crew and passengers.

Latter nearly all women and children.
Carpathia returning to New York with survivors.
9.10 p.m.

The Titanic's survivors on board Carpathia are stated at White Star offices to include all first-class passengers. She is expected to reach New York on Friday morning.
9.50 p.m.

White Star officials now admit that probably only 675 out of the 2,200 passengers and crew on board the Titanic have been saved.
NEW YORK, 8.45 p.m.

The following despatch has been received here from Cape Race:—
"The steamer Olympic reports that the steamer Carpathia reached the Titanic's position at daybreak, but found boats and wreckage only.
"She reports that the Titanic foundered about 2.20 a.m. in latitude 41.16, longitude 50.14.
"All the Titanic's boats are accounted for.
"About 675 souls saved of the crew and passengers—the latter nearly all women and children.
"The Leyland liner California is searching in report of the disaster.
"The Carpathia is returning to New York with survivors."

in the Harland and Wolff shipyard in Belfast, sinks in the Atlantic Ocean with the loss of 1,490 lives.

7 May
The Capuchins report to Rome that their temperance crusade has resulted in more than a million pledges since 1905.

18 June
Attempts by the Liberals to introduce an amendment to

language 'brought what, in other respects, was brilliant success, to an inglorious conclusion.'

The play generated riotous opposition from nationalists, led by Arthur Griffith's small but vocal movement, Sinn Féin, founded two years previously on a programme of self-reliance in economics, culture and politics but stopping short of endorsing violent separatism. An *Irish Times* reporter recorded the shouted dialogue he heard during the third performance:

'That's worthy of the slums of London.'
'Shut up your mug.'
'Go to Hell.'
'That's your country.'
'Go home and kill your father.'
'This travesty should be beaten off the stage.'
'There's a picture of the west!'
'They're more modest there than the girls of Dublin.'
'Where's Cardinal Logue now?'

Arthur Griffith, the founder of Sinn Féin

Ireland today the national feeling is not merely one of courage and confidence. Faced with terrible and urgent danger though we be, our hearts find room for thankfulness—even for exultation. In this hour of trial the Irish nation has 'found itself' at last. Unionist and Nationalist have ranged themselves together against the invader of their common liberties. A few weeks ago it used to be said by despairing English politicians that Ireland was two armed camps. Today she is one armed camp, and its menace is directed against a foreign foe. Mr Redmond's speech is receiving from Irish Unionists the whole-hearted welcome which we claimed and predicted for it yesterday. It gives to Southern Unionists, in particular, the boon which was hitherto denied to them—the opportunity of asserting their nationality, of rendering personal service to the motherland. Today Mr Bryan Cooper, former Unionist member, and present Unionist candidate, for South County Dublin, announces that he has joined the National Volunteers. The Earl of Bessborough and Lord Monteagle, both Irish Unionist Peers, invite support and sympathy for the same movement. We believe that hundreds of young Unionists will be glad to follow Mr Cooper's example, and to stand shoulder to shoulder with their Nationalist fellow-countrymen in the danger that threatens us all. We are sure that co-operation between the Ulster and Nationalist Volunteer forces will now prove to be a simple and easy thing. The Nationalist army has hastened to endorse Mr Redmond's speech. It is not only ready, but eager, to unite with Ulster's army for purposes of home defence. We do not pretend that the political question of Home Rule is affected by this splendid act of union, but Sir Edward Carson and Mr Redmond have done a noble work for Ireland. They have achieved the beginning of national reconciliation: they have opened a great door.

from The Irish Times
25 APRIL **1916**

The Outbreak

This newspaper has never been published in stranger circumstances than those which obtain today. An attempt has been made to overthrow the constitutional government of Ireland. It began yesterday morning in Dublin—at present we can speak for no other part of Ireland, for there has been an abrupt stoppage of all means of external communication. At this critical moment our language must be moderate, unsensational, and free from any tendency to alarm. As soon as peace and order have been restored the responsibility for this intended revolution will be fixed in the right quarter. The question whether it could have been averted will be discussed, and will be answered on the ample evidence which the events of the last few months afford. Today we can deal only with today's and yesterday's facts. During the last twenty-four hours an effort has been made to set up an independent Irish Republic in Dublin. It was well organised; a large number of armed men are taking part in it; and to the general public, at any rate, the outbreak came as a complete surprise. An attempt was made to seize Dublin Castle, but this failed. The rebels then took possession of the City Hall and of the *Dublin Daily Express* Office. During these operations a soldier and a policeman were shot dead. The General Post Office was seized, and a green flag was hoisted on its roof. Several shops in this quarter of Sackville Street were smashed and looted. It appears that the invaders of the Post Office have cut the telegraph and trunk telephone wires. Harcourt Street Station and Westland Row Station were seized; the South Dublin Union was seized. In the very centre of the city a party of the rebel volunteers took possession of St Stephen's Green, where, as we write, they are still entrenched. The military authorities were in motion soon after the beginning of the outbreak. Fierce fighting has taken place between the soldiers and the rebels in various parts of the city, and there is reason to fear that many lives have been lost. The Fire Brigade ambulance was busy during yesterday, and brought wounded soldiers and some wounded civilians to the various hospitals. The soldiers have retaken the City Hall and some other positions which were seized by the rebels; but, as we write, many places are still in rebel hands. Of course, this desperate episode in Irish history can have only one end, and the loyal public will await it as calmly and confidently as may be. Nothing in all yesterday's remarkable scenes was more remarkable than the quietness and courage with which the people of Dublin accepted the sudden and widespread danger. In the very neighbourhood of the fiercest fighting the streets were full of cheerful or indifferent spectators. Such courage is excellent, but it may degenerate into recklessness. Perhaps, the most useful thing that we can do now is to remember that in quietness and confidence shall be our strength, and to trust firmly in the speedy triumph of the forces of law and order. Those loyal citizens of Dublin who cannot actively help their country's cause at this moment may

The town hall at Kingstown was a world away from Poole Street. Here was the smug suburban assurance of the Edwardian middle classes.

The paper stood up for Synge's right to be heard. It first published 'a friendly warning to Mr. Synge' from Francis Sheehy-Skeffington, who disliked the play but pointed out that it was no more vulgar than most pantomime and urged readers to see it and judge for themselves. This was followed by an editorial in which Synge's language was described as indelicate but Sinn Féin's insistence on the moral impeccability of the peasantry was ridiculed and attempts to disrupt the performances were condemned. The paper then published a subtle and sophisticated analysis of the play by Pat Kenny, who suggested that Synge had shown the effect of emigration on the west of Ireland by exposing a society in which it was better for a woman to marry a parricide than an idiot. 'The difference between a hero and a murderer is sometimes, in the comparative numbers they have killed, morally in favour of the murderer … Can the Western peasantry have a truer friend than the one who exhibits to criticism and to condemnation the forces afflicting their lives?'

The Irish Times was also the medium for the first publication of some important Yeats poems. And in 1914 it published an enthusiastic review of Lady Gregory's *The Irish Theatre*, in which it

the Home Rule Bill that would exclude the four north-eastern counties from home rule is defeated.

28 June

At its annual conference in Clonmel, the Irish Trades Union Congress becomes the Irish Trades Union Congress and Labour Party.

29 June

A sectarian attack occurs on a Protestant Sunday school party in Castledawson, Co. Derry, during a march by the Ancient Order of Hibernians.

A very bourgeois family. The Pearses, showing Patrick (standing centre) *and Willie* (left). *Both were to be shot after the 1916 Rising.*

2 July

Protestant shipyard workers in Belfast expel Catholics in response to the attack in Castledawson.

18–20 July

The British Prime Minister, Asquith, visits Ireland.

14 September

Riots occur between Celtic and Linfield supporters during a soccer match in Celtic Park, Belfast.

remarked of the work that she, Synge and Yeats had done in establishing the Abbey Theatre that 'the founders of the theatre have done a big thing even if it were not so big as some of their fulsome admirers would have us believe.'

This mixture of praise and scepticism was typical of the paper's attitude to the new cultural movement. The editor, John Healy, was a former student of the influential professor of English in Trinity College, Edward Dowden. Dowden's line was one that sought to balance local pride in the distinctive contribution of Irish literature in English with an insistence that it was precisely that: a contribution to a larger British culture. The repeal of the Union would lead, he warned, to cultural isolationism. *The Irish Times* echoed Dowden's concerns. In 1913 it noted that Ireland was 'pulsating with intellectual activity,' but at

help it indirectly by refusing to give way to panic, and by maintaining in their households a healthy spirit of hope. The ordeal is severe, but it will be short.

from The Irish Times
25 APRIL 1916

A First Impression

The Opening Shots

A few minutes after twelve o'clock I was coming into the city by tram from the North side. The streets, to all appearance, were in their usual Bank holiday guise. People attired in holiday garb were to be seen on every side, some making their way from the city, others—country cousins—who had come to Dublin to enjoy themselves. The trams proceeding towards the Phoenix Park had upon their side the legend, 'Zoological Gardens half price today,' and, judging by their crowded state, many, old and young, were bent on availing themselves of the treat thus advertised. Around the Nelson Pillar was the usual group of holiday idlers, and just as I was idly wondering what attraction the Pillar had for the public my attention was attracted by a slight commotion in front of the General Post Office. The crowd there was not of large dimensions, but the people seemed to be agitated by some unusual happening. A small group was gathered round a young man in the uniform of a Volunteer—either a Sinn Féiner or one of the Larkinite Citizen Army—who was standing between two pillars under the portico. This young man had a rifle with a fixed bayonet in his left hand, whilst in his right he held a bright-edged axe. These Volunteers have been so familiar a sight in our thoroughfare that I was not a little puzzled to know the cause of the commotion.

Something Very Unusual

A closer scrutiny, however, revealed that something very unusual, indeed, was afoot. Into the new porch of the GPO were crowding other men in Volunteer uniforms, all of them armed after the fashion of the young man who stood between the pillars under the portico. Above the slight commotion in the street and the noise of the traffic could be heard the crash of breaking glass. The pavement was strewn with fragments from the broken windows. Along by the Prince's Street side of the GPO other men in similar attire and similarly armed were breaking in the windows. The door leading on to Prince's Street, through which the mail vans pass, was opened, and a considerable body of men in Volunteer uniforms passed through. In front of the GPO was a travel-stained motor car in which the men in Volunteer uniform were taking a proprietary interest. The majority of the onlookers seemed to regard the entire proceedings at this stage more or less in the light of a joke. In Abbey Street other men in Volunteer uniform had taken possession of two licensed premises—those of Messrs Mooney and Mr John Davin—and were piling up furniture as though to form barricades inside the building and out upon the street. At the corner of Bachelor's Walk there was also the crashing of glass, some Volunteers, who had a hand barrow outside, having broken into the premises of a retailer of gun-powder. In Westmoreland Street nothing unusual was happening at this time, but from the directions of Dame Street, Parliament Street and Capel Street could be heard the ominous crackling of rifle shots.

Members of Fianna Éireann on a training routine in the years before the Easter Rising. The Fianna were founded in Dublin in 1909 by Constance Markievicz and Bulmer Hobson with the object of 're-establishing the independence of Ireland' and, by 'training the youth of Ireland, mentally and physically, to achieve this object by teaching scouting and military exercises, Irish history and the Irish language.'

the same time it warned that 'we take ourselves and our new movements too seriously' and that 'our gloomy enthusiasts' shut themselves up within the four walls of Ireland.

That warning reflected a growing feeling that the cultural revival could not be insulated from political separatism. As early as 1907 *The Irish Times* was noting 'the bitter hostility of a growing section of Nationalists to any sort of connection with England, and … their open ambition for complete separation from the British Empire.' The number of Irish soldiers in the British army was declining rapidly, from 30,000 in 1904 to 20,000 in 1913, largely because of better economic conditions in the countryside and to the introduction of unemployment benefit in 1910. But the decline was also influenced to some degree by the success of anti-recruitment propaganda and the rise of 'national' sentiment.

In Ireland, however, there was more than one 'national' culture and more than one narrative of history. Nationalists paid little attention to the Protestant militancy of the north, seeing it either as a bluff that could be called by Home Rule or as a delusion conjured up by the

28 September
Nearly half a million unionists sign the Ulster Solemn League and Covenant against home rule.

1913

16 January
The Home Rule Bill is passed on its third reading in the House of Commons. The House of Lords rejects it.

31 January
The Ulster Volunteer Force is formed.

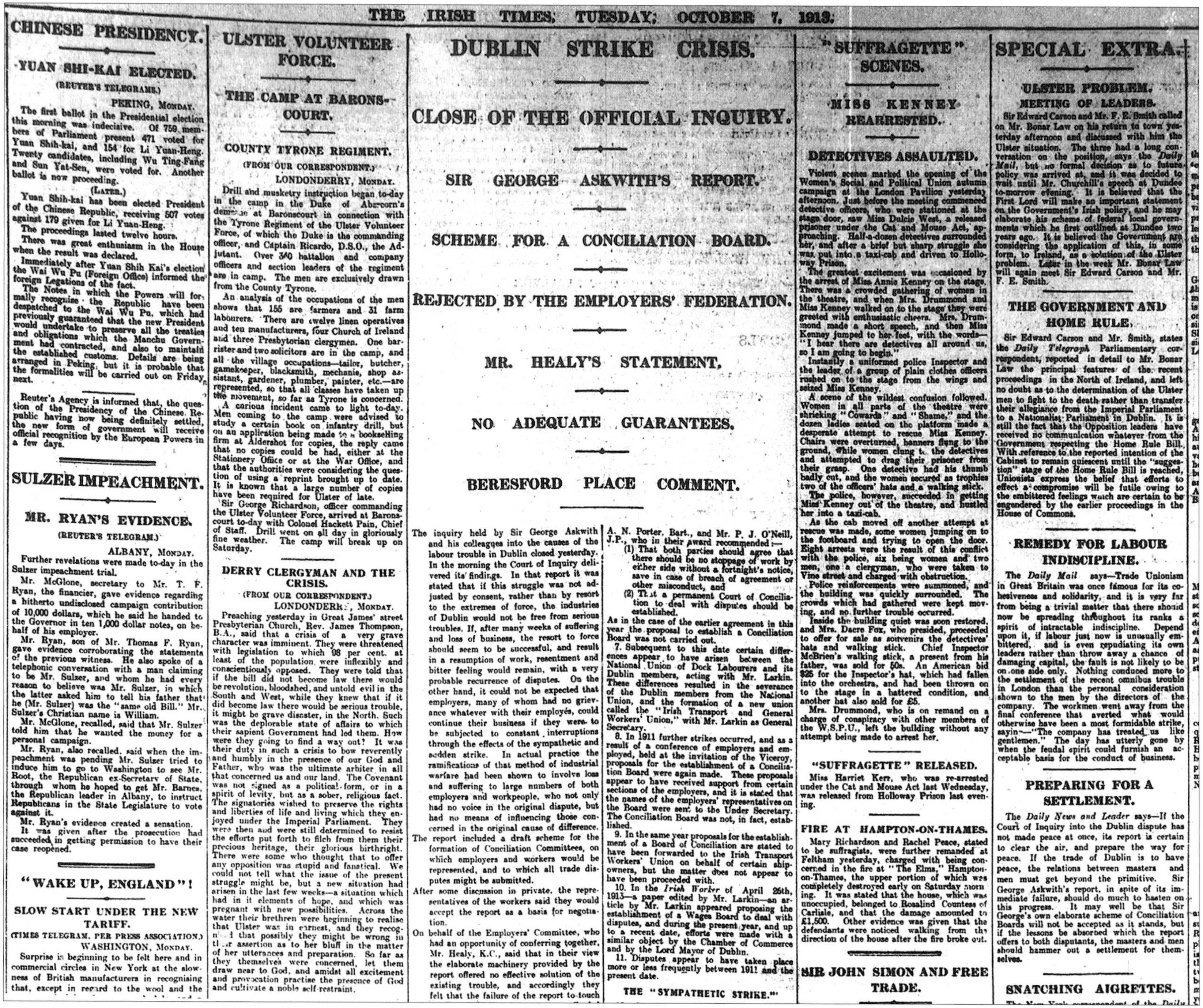

THE IRISH TIMES, TUESDAY, OCTOBER 7, 1913.

CHINESE PRESIDENCY.

YUAN SHI-KAI ELECTED.

(REUTER'S TELEGRAMS.)

PEKING, MONDAY.

The first ballot in the Presidential election this morning was indecisive. Of 759 members of Parliament present 471 voted for Yuan Shih-kai, and 154 for Li Yuan-Heng. Twenty candidates, including Wu Ting-Fang and Sun Yat-Sen, were voted for. Another ballot is now proceeding.

(LATER.)

Yuan Shih-kai has been elected President of the Chinese Republic, receiving 507 votes against 179 given for Li Yuan-Heng.

The proceedings lasted twelve hours.

There was great enthusiasm in the House when the result was declared.

Immediately after Yuan Shih Kai's election the Wai Wu Pu (Foreign Office) informed the foreign Legations of the fact.

The Notes in which the Powers will formally recognise the Republic have been despatched to the Wai Wu Pu, which had previously guaranteed that the new President would undertake to preserve all the treaties and obligations which the Manchu Government had contracted, and also to maintain the established customs. Details are being arranged in Peking, but it is probable that the formalities will be carried out on Friday next.

Reuter's Agency is informed that, the question of the Presidency of the Chinese Republic having now being definitely settled, the new form of government will receive official recognition by the European Powers in a few days.

SULZER IMPEACHMENT.

MR. RYAN'S EVIDENCE.

(REUTER'S TELEGRAM.)

ALBANY, MONDAY.

Further revelations were made to-day in the Sulzer impeachment trial.

Mr. McGlone, secretary to Mr. T. F. Ryan, the financier, gave evidence regarding a hitherto undisclosed campaign contribution of 10,000 dollars, which he said he handed to the Governor in ten 1,000 dollar notes, on behalf of his employer.

Mr. Ryan, son of Mr. Thomas F. Ryan, gave evidence corroborating the statements of the previous witness. He also spoke of a telephonic conversation with a man claiming to be Mr. Sulzer, and whom he had every reason to believe was Mr. Sulzer, in which the latter asked him to tell his father that he (Mr. Sulzer) was the "same old Bill." Mr. Sulzer's Christian name is William.

Mr. McGlone, recalled, said that Mr. Sulzer told him that he wanted the money for a personal campaign.

Mr. Ryan, also recalled, said when the impeachment was pending Mr. Sulzer tried to induce him to go to Washington to see Mr. Root, the Republican ex-Secretary of State, through whom he hoped to get Mr. Barnes, the Republican leader in Albany, to instruct Republicans in the State Legislature to vote against it.

Mr. Ryan's evidence created a sensation.

It was given after the prosecution had succeeded in getting permission to have their case reopened.

"WAKE UP, ENGLAND"!

SLOW START UNDER THE NEW TARIFF.

(TIMES TELEGRAM, PER PRESS ASSOCIATION.)

WASHINGTON, MONDAY.

Surprise is beginning to be felt here and in commercial circles in New York at the slowness of British manufacturers in recognising that, except in regard to the wool and the

ULSTER VOLUNTEER FORCE.

THE CAMP AT BARONSCOURT.

COUNTY TYRONE REGIMENT.

(FROM OUR CORRESPONDENT.)

LONDONDERRY, MONDAY.

Drill and musketry instruction began to-day in the camp in the Duke of Abercorn's demesne at Baronscourt in connection with the Tyrone Regiment of the Ulster Volunteer Force, of which the Duke is the commanding officer, and Captain Ricardo, D.S.O., the Adjutant. Over 340 battalion and company officers and section leaders of the regiment are in camp. The men are exclusively drawn from the County Tyrone.

An analysis of the occupations of the men shows that 155 are farmers and 31 farm labourers. There are twelve linen operatives and ten manufacturers, four Church of Ireland and three Presbyterian clergymen. One barrister and two solicitors are in the camp, and all the village occupations—tailor, butcher, gamekeeper, blacksmith, mechanic, shop assistant, gardener, plumber, painter, etc.—are represented, so that all classes have taken up the movement, so far as Tyrone is concerned.

A curious incident came to light to-day. Men coming to the camp were advised to study a certain book on infantry drill, but on an application being made to a bookselling firm at Aldershot for copies, the reply came that no copies could be had, either at the Stationery Office or at the War Office, and that the authorities were considering the question of using a reprint brought up to date. It is known that a large number of copies have been required for Ulster of late.

Sir George Richardson, officer commanding the Ulster Volunteer Force, arrived at Baronscourt to-day with Colonel Hackett Pain, Chief of Staff. Drill went on all day in gloriously fine weather. The camp will break up on Saturday.

DERRY CLERGYMAN AND THE CRISIS.

(FROM OUR CORRESPONDENT.)

LONDONDERRY, MONDAY.

Preaching yesterday in Great James' street Presbyterian Church, Rev. James Thompson, B.A., said that a crisis of a very grave character was imminent. They were threatened with legislation to which 98 per cent. at least of the population were inflexibly and conscientiously opposed. They were told that if the bill did not become law there would be revolution, bloodshed, and untold evil in the South and West, while they knew that if it did become law there would be serious trouble, it might be grave disaster, in the North. Such was the deplorable state of affairs to which their sapient Government had led them. How were they going to find a way out? It was their duty in such a crisis to bow reverently and humbly in the presence of our God and Father, who was the ultimate arbiter in all that concerned us and our land. The Covenant was not signed as a political form, or in a spirit of levity, but as a sober, religious fact. The signatories wished to preserve the rights and liberties of life and living which they enjoyed under the Imperial Parliament. They were then and were still determined to resist the efforts put forth to filch from them their precious heritage, their glorious birthright. There were some who thought that to offer any opposition was stupid and fanatical. We could not tell what the issue of the present struggle might be, but a new situation had arisen in the last few weeks—a situation which had in it elements of hope, and which was pregnant with new possibilities. Across the water their brethren were beginning to realise that Ulster was in earnest, and they recognised that possibly they might be wrong in their assertion as to her bluff in the matter of her utterances and preparation. So far as they themselves were concerned, let them draw near to God, and amidst all excitement and provocation practise the presence of God and cultivate a noble self-restraint.

DUBLIN STRIKE CRISIS.

CLOSE OF THE OFFICIAL INQUIRY.

SIR GEORGE ASKWITH'S REPORT.

SCHEME FOR A CONCILIATION BOARD.

REJECTED BY THE EMPLOYERS' FEDERATION.

MR. HEALY'S STATEMENT.

NO ADEQUATE GUARANTEES.

BERESFORD PLACE COMMENT.

The inquiry held by Sir George Askwith and his colleagues into the causes of the labour trouble in Dublin closed yesterday. In the morning the Court of Inquiry delivered its findings. In that report it was stated that if this struggle was not adjusted by consent, rather than by resort to the extremes of force, the industries of Dublin would not be free from serious troubles. If, after many weeks of suffering and loss of business, the resort to force should seem to be successful, and result in a resumption of work, resentment and bitter feeling would remain, with a very probable recurrence of disputes. On the other hand, it could not be expected that employers, many of whom had no grievance whatever with their employés, could continue their business if they were to be subjected to constant interruptions through the effects of the sympathetic and sudden strike. In actual practice the ramifications of that method of industrial warfare had been shown to involve loss and suffering to large numbers of both employers and workpeople, who not only had no voice in the original dispute, but had no means of influencing those concerned in the original cause of difference.

The report included a draft scheme for the formation of Conciliation Committees, on which employers and workers would be represented, and to which all trade disputes might be submitted.

After some discussion in private, the representatives of the workers said they would accept the report as a basis for negotiation.

On behalf of the Employers' Committee, who had an opportunity of conferring together, Mr. Healy, K.C., said that in their view the elaborate machinery provided by the report offered no effective solution of the existing trouble, and accordingly they felt that the failure of the report to touch

A. N. Porter, Bart., and Mr. P. J. O'Neill, J.P., who in their award recommended:—

(1) That both parties should agree that there should be no stoppage of work by either side without a fortnight's notice, save in case of breach of agreement or other misconduct, and

(2) That a permanent Court of Conciliation to deal with disputes should be established.

As in the case of the earlier agreement in this year the proposal to establish a Conciliation Board was not carried out.

7. Subsequent to this date certain differences appear to have arisen between the National Union of Dock Labourers and its Dublin members, acting with Mr. Larkin. These differences resulted in the severance of the Dublin members from the National Union, and the formation of a new union called the "Irish Transport and General Workers' Union," with Mr. Larkin as General Secretary.

8. In 1911 further strikes occurred, and as a result of a conference of employers and employed, held at the invitation of the Viceroy, proposals for the establishment of a Conciliation Board were again made. These proposals appear to have received support from certain sections of the employers, and it is stated that the names of the employers' representatives on the Board were sent to the Under Secretary. The Conciliation Board was not, in fact, established.

9. In the same year proposals for the establishment of a Board of Conciliation are stated to have been forwarded to the Irish Transport Workers' Union on behalf of certain shipowners, but the matter does not appear to have been proceeded with.

10. In the *Irish Worker* of April 26th, 1913—a paper edited by Mr. Larkin—an article by Mr. Larkin appeared proposing the establishment of a Wages Board to deal with disputes, and during the present year, and up to a recent date, efforts were made with a similar object by the Chamber of Commerce and by the Lord Mayor of Dublin.

11. Disputes appear to have taken place more or less frequently between 1911 and the present date.

THE "SYMPATHETIC STRIKE."

"SUFFRAGETTE" SCENES.

MISS KENNEY REARRESTED.

DETECTIVES ASSAULTED.

Violent scenes marked the opening of the Women's Social and Political Union autumn campaign at the London Pavilion yesterday afternoon. Just before the meeting commenced detective officers, who were stationed at the stage door, saw Miss Dulcie West, a released prisoner under the Cat and Mouse Act, approaching. Half-a-dozen detectives surrounded her, and after a brief but sharp struggle she was put into a taxi-cab and driven to Holloway Prison.

The greatest excitement was occasioned by the arrest of Miss Annie Kenney on the stage. There was a crowded gathering of women in the theatre, and when Mrs. Drummond and Miss Kenney walked on to the stage they were greeted with enthusiastic cheers. Mrs. Drummond made a short speech, and then Miss Kenney jumped to her feet, with the words—"I hear there are detectives all around us, so I am going to begin."

Instantly a uniformed police Inspector and the leader of a group of plain clothes officers rushed on to the stage from the wings and seized Miss Kenney.

A scene of the wildest confusion followed. Women in all parts of the theatre were shrieking "Cowards" and "Shame," and the dozen ladies seated on the platform made a desperate attempt to rescue Miss Kenney. Chairs were overturned, banners flung to the ground, while women clung to the detectives and attempted to drag their prisoner from their grasp. One detective had his thumb badly cut, and the women secured as trophies two of the officers' hats and a walking stick.

The police, however, succeeded in getting Miss Kenney out of the theatre, and hustled her into a taxi-cab.

As the cab moved off another attempt at rescue was made, some women jumping on to the footboard and trying to open the door. Eight arrests were the result of this conflict with the police, six being women and two men, one a clergyman, who were taken to Vine street and charged with obstruction.

Police reinforcements were summoned, and the building was quickly surrounded. The crowds which had gathered were kept moving, and no further trouble occurred.

Inside the building quiet was soon restored, and Mrs. Dacre Fox, who presided, proceeded to offer for sale as souvenirs the detectives' hats and walking stick. Chief Inspector McBrien's walking stick, a present from his father, was sold for 50s. An American bid $25 for the Inspector's hat, which had fallen into the orchestra, and had been thrown on to the stage in a battered condition, and another hat also sold for £5.

Mrs. Drummond, who is on remand on a charge of conspiracy with other members of the W.S.P.U., left the building without any attempt being made to arrest her.

"SUFFRAGETTE" RELEASED.

Miss Harriet Kerr, who was re-arrested under the Cat and Mouse Act last Wednesday, was released from Holloway Prison last evening.

FIRE AT HAMPTON-ON-THAMES.

Mary Richardson and Rachel Peace, stated to be suffragists, were further remanded at Feltham yesterday, charged with being concerned in the fire at "The Elms," Hampton-on-Thames, the upper portion of which was completely destroyed early on Saturday morning. It was stated that the house, which was unoccupied, belonged to Rosalind Countess of Carlisle, and that the damage amounted to £1,500. Other evidence was given that the defendants were noticed walking from the direction of the house after the fire broke out.

SIR JOHN SIMON AND FREE TRADE.

SPECIAL EXTRA.

ULSTER PROBLEM.

MEETING OF LEADERS.

Sir Edward Carson and Mr. F. E. Smith called on Mr. Bonar Law on his return to town yesterday afternoon and discussed with him the Ulster situation. The three had a long conversation on the position, says the *Daily Mail*, but no formal decision as to future policy was arrived at, and it was decided to wait until Mr. Churchill's speech at Dundee to-morrow evening. It is believed that the First Lord will make an important statement on the Government's Irish policy, and he may elaborate his scheme of federal local governments which he first outlined at Dundee two years ago. It is believed the Government are considering the application of this, in some form, to Ireland, as a solution of the Ulster problem. Later in the week Mr. Bonar Law will again meet Sir Edward Carson and Mr. F. E. Smith.

THE GOVERNMENT AND HOME RULE.

Sir Edward Carson and Mr. Smith, states the *Daily Telegraph* Parliamentary correspondent, reported in detail to Mr. Bonar Law the principal features of the recent proceedings in the North of Ireland, and left no doubt as to the determination of the Ulster men to fight to the death rather than transfer their allegiance from the Imperial Parliament to a Nationalist Parliament in Dublin. It is still the fact that the Opposition leaders have received no communication whatever from the Government respecting the Home Rule Bill. With reference to the reported intention of the Cabinet to remain quiescent until the "suggestion" stage of the Home Rule Bill is reached, Unionists express the belief that efforts to effect a compromise will be futile owing to the embittered feelings which are certain to be engendered by the earlier proceedings in the House of Commons.

REMEDY FOR LABOUR INDISCIPLINE.

The *Daily Mail* says—Trade Unionism in Great Britain was once famous for its cohesiveness and solidarity, and it is very far from being a trivial matter that there should now be spreading throughout its ranks a spirit of intractable indiscipline. Depend upon it, if labour just now is unusually embittered, and is even repudiating its own leaders rather than throw away a chance of damaging capital, the fault is not likely to be on one side only. Nothing conduced more to the settlement of the recent omnibus trouble in London than the personal consideration shown to the men by the directors of the company. The workmen went away from the final conference that averted what would otherwise have been a most formidable strike, saying—"The company has treated us like gentlemen." The day has utterly gone by when the feudal spirit could furnish an acceptable basis for the conduct of business.

PREPARING FOR A SETTLEMENT.

The *Daily News and Leader* says—If the Court of Inquiry into the Dublin dispute has not made peace at once, its report is certain to clear the air, and prepare the way for peace. If the trade of Dublin is to have peace, the relations between masters and men must get beyond the primitive. Sir George Askwith's report, in spite of its immediate failure, should do much to hasten on this progress. It may well be that Sir George's own elaborate scheme of Conciliation Boards will not be accepted as it stands, but if the lessons be absorbed which the report offers to both disputants, the masters and men should hammer out a settlement for themselves.

SNATCHING AIGRETTES.

THE IRISH TIMES. TUESDAY, APRIL 25, 1916.

IN DUBLIN.

wanton destruction of property. But they were quickly given to understand that serious business was afoot, for a volley of rifle shots fired through the vacant windows sent the hitherto listless pedestrians scampering at full speed in all directions. "O Lord save us," cried a few old women as they hurried away from the scene, "it's the Citizen Army," and they have taken the Post Office." And so the first act in this latest of Irish rebellions was performed.

Meanwhile other parties of the revolutionists were not idle, for the noise of fusillading was heard from other parts of the city, notably from Dublin Castle. Excitement grew intense, and women and children who were out for the holiday found themselves cut off from the means of getting to their homes. The tramcar service was suspended at one o'clock, and all the cars were sent to their depots. One large car was perforce kept at the entrance to North Earl street, it might be supposed as a sort of street barricade. All the publichouses within a certain distance of the Post Office were closed, and trembling spectators gathered on O'Connell Bridge and at the corners of Westmoreland street and D'Olier street, expecting every moment to see the military coming from one direction or another.

LANCERS ATTACKED.

Shortly after the trouble began a troop of lancers came along from the direction of the North Wall, escorting four or five waggons of munitions which were being conveyed to the magazine in the Phoenix Park. They crossed from the Eden quay side of Sackville street, and passed up Bachelor's Walk, knowing nothing of what was happening in the neighbourhood. They proceeded up the quays, and presumably having deposited their charge, returned to the city, and came into Dublin by the north end. As soon as they got in front of the Post Office they were met with a volley from the occupants of that building. The shots came for the most part from men who had got on the roof, from which position they had a great advantage over the lancers. Four of the latter were shot, and the horse of one of them fell dead on the street. The dead bodies of these men were taken to Jervis street hospital. The Lancers withdrew to the Parnell Monument, where they remained for a short while before returning to barracks. The ambulances were busy for a couple of hours in the middle of the day, conveying the wounded to hospital. Early in the proceedings a party of the Volunteers turned into Abbey street, and, having smashed several large shop windows, entered the Ship Hotel, and "took" that, too. Armed men posted themselves in the upper windows, but they relinquished that position in the course of the afternoon. The police meantime had withdrawn to their several stations.

SHOPS LOOTED.

Shop windows in North Earl street were smashed, and the shops were looted. Noblett's sweet shop at the corner, and that of Lewers and Co., next to it in Sackville street, were sacked, and youngsters, male and female, might be seen carrying bundles of sweets, or caps and hats, or shirts, of which those shops were despoiled. There was no one to prevent them from helping themselves as they listed. A publichouse in North Earl street was looted, and when the looters had partaken of the ardent spirits some of them beat each other with the bottles so violently that they were under the necessity of having their wounds dressed in hospital. Another of the shops that suffered was that of Messrs. M. Kelly and Son, gunsmiths and gunpowder merchants, at the corner of Bachelor's Walk and Sackville street. The looters took away with them such ammunition as they could lay their hands on. A couple of motor cars were stopped as they were passing the Post Office, and the occupants had to leave them in possession of the "boys." One of the victims of this high-handed procedure was Judge Law Smith, County Court Judge of Limerick, who was accompanied by a couple of ladies.

As the afternoon wore on the fusillading became less frequent, and the rebels in possession of the Post Office might be seen behind the "barricades" by anyone who ventured near enough to the building. They sat or lounged on mail sacks with their rifles at the "ready." They commandeered all the food that the larder of the adjacent Metropole Hotel afforded.

FIRES IN SACKVILLE STREET.

Looting was resumed after six o'clock, when a publichouse near Nelson Pillar was attacked and raided. Its contents were seized, and the mob struggled for whiskey and stout bottles, and, instantly drank their contents. Shops of clothiers and boot and shoe-factors were visited in turn, and plate glass windows were smashed. The Fire Brigade was twice summoned to quell fires that occurred at boot shops. Their efforts were not obstructed, and they were quickly successful.

ST. STEPHEN'S GREEN.

One of the boldest acts of the rebels was their seizure of St. Stephen's Green Park, and the systematic way in which they set about digging themselves in. There was no parade about the earlier proceedings. The men came up shortly after mid-day in two

THREE LADIES SHOT IN ST. STEPHEN'S GREEN.

A grave incident occurred in St. Stephen's Green as the people were returning in motors from the Fairyhouse Races. Two ladies—Mrs. Smithwick, of Kilkenny, and Mrs. Fleming, wife of a District Inspector in the Royal Irish Constabulary—were caught in the midst of a fusillade of bullets and were wounded. They were conveyed in their own motor car to Mercer's Hospital, and thence they were taken in the Fire Brigade ambulance to a private hospital, where they are receiving every attention. A third lady—Miss Mabel McGlynn, aged 26, of 30 Home villas, Donnybrook—sustained a bullet wound in the left leg at about the same time. She was removed in the Fire Brigade ambulance to a house in Upper Rathmines.

"G.R." VETERAN KILLED.

Several members of the "G.R." Veterans Corps were wounded, as a company, 35 strong, under Captain Browning, was returning to its headquarters at Beggar's Bush Barrack's, after a field day at Ticknock. The first man wounded was hit by a shot fired from the railway bridge at the end of Haddington road, and the Veterans were then the objects of a volley fired by the rebels from a house in Northumberland road. Though the Veterans had rifles they were entirely without ammunition. They made no demonstration against the rebels, being probably unaware of the state of affairs, and were shot down without any warning. Three of them were severely wounded, including Mr. William Horne, of the Great Northern Railway, and five other Veterans were also wounded. They were taken in motor cars to the Royal City of Dublin Hospital, where one of them died during the evening from a wound in the head.

SOUTH DUBLIN UNION SEIZED.

SEVERE FIGHTING.

Fighting of a serious character took place between James's street and Mount Brown. The Volunteers shortly after midday took possession of the South Dublin Union, and occupied it in military fashion. Their action caused indescribable commotion. Another detachment entered Messrs. Roe's distillery, and proceeded at once to place it in a state of defence. The presence later of men of the Royal Irish Regiment created much excitement, and occupants of houses in the vicinity became greatly agitated. At the approach of the military the rebels opened fire. Soon a fierce fight was raging, the soldiers firing numerous volleys when the rebels showed themselves at the windows or on the roofs of the premises. At the Union they were fortified with a machine gun, and the insurgents freely utilised it. The north and south gates were strongly held, but an entrance was effected through the grounds on the west side of the building, and the soldiers were thereby enabled to get closer. An attack on the detachment holding the southern gate resulted in the capture of the machine gun, but unfortunately it also resulted in a private of the Royal Irish Regiment being fatally injured. A lieutenant and two men received severe wounds, and some of the insurgents were also wounded, two, it is believed fatally. The fighting continued during the day, and about twenty prisoners were secured and taken to Kilmainham Police Station. Sniping was maintained at intervals until dusk, when the rebels still preserved their attitude of defiance. Under cover of darkness many of them endeavoured to evacuate the building. Some of them succeeded, but several could not elude the vigilance of the soldiers, and they were lodged with their fellow-insurgents in the police cells. The military succeeded in driving those who remained, not more than fifty, into a corner of portion of the Union grounds, and held them there during the night. The approaches to the Union were carefully guarded by soldiers, and traffic was stopped, communication with the city being maintained by side streets.

MILITARY CONVOY ATTACKED.

THREE LANCERS KILLED.

The first ambulance was seen in the streets of Dublin at about one o'clock in the afternoon, and from that hour onwards the nine men of the Dublin Fire Brigade on ambulance duty had as much as they could do to cope with the calls upon them. The initial call came from Charles street, near the Four Courts. A few minutes before a body of cavalry had come up the north quays, escorting several waggons of what were apparently military stores and munitions discharged from a vessel, which arrived at the North Wall in the morning. The convoy passed unmolested across Sackville street, which was crowded with the ordinary holiday throng at the time. When they had arrived within a short distance of the Four Courts, however, they were fired upon by a body of the rebel Volunteers gathered in the vicinity, and several men and horses were struck with bullets. The ambulance arrived on the scene in a few moments, and promptly removed three dead soldiers of

WESTLAND ROW STATION SEIZED.

ALL TRAINS STOPPED.

BARRICADES ERECTED.

Up to noon ordinary crowds of holiday makers who wend their way to the various popular resorts between the city and Bray were to be seen going through Great Brunswick street in the direction of Westland row Station. Traffic from the station had proceeded as usual during the forenoon hours, and there was every evidence that a big holiday throng would have to be provided for. All arrangements to meet the rush had been made by the Dublin and South-Eastern Railway Company.

Almost precisely at mid-day, however, a sensational incident occurred. A body of armed men in the uniform of the Irish Volunteers marched up to the station and took possession of the entrances, of the platforms, and of the entire station premises. The first body of armed men who entered the station would not be more than thirty in number, but they took the staff of the railway company completely by surprise. They pushed back the crowd, closed the main doors, and bolted them. By 12.10 p.m. the entire station premises were completely in possession of the Volunteers, the staff having been driven out at the point of the bayonet. So far as can be ascertained, no member of the railway company's staff sustained any injuries of a serious character. Intending passengers, many of them women and children, pushed forward with their little bundles of sandwiches and so forth, and showed their tickets, but all alike were promptly ejected, and the doors of the station barred against them.

The last train to leave Westland row Station was the twelve o'clock "local" to Kingstown. From that hour onwards there was no train in or out during the day. So far as the street was concerned nothing was to be seen save a throng of bewildered citizens, who found their holiday interrupted. Inside the station, however, there was considerable bustle and activity. The telephones in the stationmaster's offices were disconnected and telegraphic communication cut off. The officials in charge of the traffic department sought the assistance of the police in Brunswick street and the Castle, but up to seven o'clock in the evening none was forthcoming. Meantime, the Volunteers had erected barricades at both the goods and passenger entrances, and the carriage way leading to the station was also barricaded. All the barrows in the station, all the seats, all the sweetmeat machines, milk churns, and, in fact, all the movable articles were utilised for the erection of the barricades.

The Volunteers also took possession of the signal cabins as far as Lansdowne road and of the railway workshops in Grand Canal street. This condition of affairs continued throughout the entire afternoon and evening, and disappointed passengers were to be seen wandering aimlessly about the streets until such time as the tragic incidents which they witnessed only too frequently forced upon them the necessity of seeking such shelter as they could find. Some of the residents in the coast districts set out to walk home, whilst others found refuge with their friends.

HARCOURT STREET STATION.

At Harcourt street Station similar scenes to those described at Westland row were enacted. Possession was taken of this station at 12.5 p.m. and the premises barricaded, but at about 3 p.m. the Volunteers evacuated the premises, and the railway officials then resumed peaceful possession. The first train down the line after it had been evacuated left Harcourt street at 5.30 p.m., and another followed about 6.15. The railway line outside the station was blocked with sleepers and other obstructions, and these had to be removed before traffic could be resumed.

ATTACK ON GREAT NORTHERN RAILWAY.

ATTEMPT TO BLOW UP A BRIDGE.

Shortly after three o'clock in the afternoon an attempt was made to blow up the culvert bridge at the inlet of the sea, about half-way between Donabate and Rush, on the Great Northern Railway. The bridge is in target before the 2 p.m. train from Dublin was due in Donabate the stationmaster there heard a loud explosion. At first he thought the sound came from blasting in the quarries, which are close by, but the smoke was immediately apparent over the culvert bridge. The stationmaster and some of the men on duty ran there as fast as they could, and found that an attempt, which was fortunately unsuccessful, had been made to blow up the middle section of this bridge. No one was about at the time, nor was there any trace of anyone in the vicinity. A short time before this the stationmaster at Lusk, when walking over the line near this bridge, was stopped by an Irish Volunteer in uniform with a loaded rifle and fixed bayonet. He told the stationmaster he would not be allowed to proceed further, and it was shortly after this that the explosion took place. The telephone

A FIRST IMPRESSION.

THE OPENING SHOTS.

(FROM A CORRESPONDENT.)

A few minutes after twelve o'clock I was coming into the city by train from the North side. The streets, to all appearance, were in their usual Bank holiday guise. People attired in holiday garb were to be seen on every side, some making their way from the city, others—country cousins—who had come to Dublin to enjoy themselves. The trams proceeding towards the Phoenix Park had upon their side the legend, "Zoological Gardens half price to-day," and, judging by their crowded state, many, old and young, were bent on availing themselves of the treat thus advertised. Around the Nelson Pillar was the usual group of holiday idlers, and just as I was idly wondering what attraction the Pillar had for the public my attention was attracted by a slight commotion in front of the General Post Office. The crowd there was not of large dimensions, but the people seemed to be agitated by some unusual happening. A small group was gathered round a young man in the uniform of a Volunteer—either a Sinn Feiner or one of the Larkinite Citizen Army—who was standing between two pillars under the portico. This young man had a rifle with a fixed bayonet in his left hand, whilst in his right he held a bright-edged axe. These Volunteers have been so familiar a sight in our thoroughfares that I was not a little puzzled to know the cause of the commotion.

SOMETHING VERY UNUSUAL.

A closer scrutiny, however, revealed that something very unusual, indeed, was afoot. Into the new porch of the G.P.O. were crowding other men in Volunteer uniform, all of them armed after the fashion of the young man who stood between the pillars under the portico. Above the slight commotion in the street and the noise of the traffic could be heard the crash of breaking glass. The pavement was strewn with fragments from the broken windows. Along by the Prince's street side of the G.P.O. other men in similar attire and similarly armed were breaking in the windows. The door leading on to Prince's street, through which the mail van pass, was opened, and a considerable body of men in Volunteer uniform passed through. In front of the G.P.O. was a travel-stained motor car in which the men in Volunteer uniform were taking a proprietary interest. The majority of the onlookers seemed to regard the entire proceedings at this stage more or less in the light of a joke. In Abbey street other men in Volunteer uniform had taken possession of two licensed premises—those of Messrs. Mooney and Mr. John Davin—and were piling up furniture as though to form barricades inside the building and out upon the street At the corner of Bachelor's Walk there was also the crashing of glass, some Volunteers, who had a hand barrow outside, having broken into the premises of a retailer of gunpowder. In Westmoreland street nothing unusual was happening at this time, but from the direction of Dame street, Parliament street, and Capel street could be heard the ominous crackling of rifle shots.

ATTITUDE OF THE PEOPLE.

The people in the streets were becoming somewhat excited and alarmed, and saying one to the other, in a half-incredulous way, that a Sinn Fein revolution had broken out. Across the wide expanse of Sackville street, from Eden quay to Bachelor's Walk, there slowly passed a body of cavalry in khaki. The impression in the crowd seemed to be that the cavalry would charge, but they did nothing of the kind. They passed on up Bachelor's Walk and out of sight. Anon, a ripple of rifle shots could be heard in the distance, but people in the vicinity of O'Connell Bridge could see nothing of their purpose or effect. A few moments later the Fire Brigade ambulance dashed off in the same direction as the cavalry had gone, and the word was soon passing about that the Volunteers and the cavalry were in collision on the quays.

AT COLLEGE GREEN.

Crowds of holiday makers were by this time growing thinner and thinner. Up along Dame street, in the direction of the Castle, could be heard the loud noise of rifle firing almost incessantly. There were soldiers in khaki and sailors in navy blue in the thoroughfares, and they seemed to be inclined to regard the whole affair very lightly. Citizens with pale faces were to be seen now making hurriedly towards their homes. Some little children were crying, either through disappointment because of an abandoned holiday or through vague apprehension of what was afoot. Occasionally there were rushes along the street. As one approached the corner of South Great George's street the noise of the rifle shots grew louder and louder. An attack was being made on Dublin Castle—policemen had been shot down—such was the talk that passed from lip to lip. A crowd gathered round a woman who was describing something tragic she had witnessed. Civilians and some soldiers out for the holiday were passing along with an air of indifference that somehow seemed a trifle forced. The offices of the *Daily Express* and *Evening Mail*, we were told, were in the hands of the *Sinn Feiners*, who were firing on Dublin Castle. Despite the fusillade and the occasional patter of bullets upon the walls, people passed up and down Cork Hill with assumed indifference.

A SOLDIER SHOT.

A soldier passing along with a cane in his hand was shot as he walked on the flagway

THE CASUALTIES.

JERVIS STREET HOSPITAL.

Three soldiers died in Jervis street hospital, and one was dead when admitted as the result of gunshot wounds. They belong to the 5th Lancers. One was Sergeant[?]nan, and the names of the others are not be ascertained. A young married woman, Mrs. Shiels, of Jervis street, was severely injured in Sackville street, and taken to the hospital last night. Her husband was wounded from France, and he was at her bedside when his wife died. Two Sinn Feiners were treated for slight wounds, and are, in addition, seven patients in the hospital suffering from wounds received during the fighting.

CITY OF DUBLIN.

Three deaths occurred:—
Mr. J. E. Gibbs, 58 Belgrave square, and Mr. Cleary, both members of the Veterans' Corps.
Private James Nolan, R.I. Rifles, reached the city yesterday morning from France.
Seriously wounded:—
Mr. F. H. Browning, Commandant, and Mr. Ford, another member of the Corps.
Mr. Browning was shot through the arm and spine.
Five other cases are under treatment.

THE MEATH.

Four deaths occurred in the hospital:—
Lieutenant Calvert, R.I. Rifles.
Ella Warbrook, aged 17, 7 Fumbally.
A police constable, shot through the body.
A man named Kelly, who resided in Brazil street.
Seriously wounded:—
Lance-Corporal Thomas Cox.
Private Michael Burns, 10th Battalion Dublin Fusiliers.
Richard Walsh, 77 Maddison terrace.

ST. VINCENT'S.

Two patients have died. Both are named Kearney and Armstrong.
The former is supposed to be a native of Rathdrum and the latter of Dublin.
Amongst the cases of serious injury:—
David Roberts, tram driver.
G. Knox.
Michael Kavanagh.
Francis O'Brien.

MERCER'S.

A private in a cavalry regiment died an hour after admission.
Captain M'Cullagh, R.A.M.C., is injured, being shot through one of his legs. Amongst other serious cases are two men, and a civilian, who received a bullet in the forehead.

STEEVENS'.

Died—Two soldiers, one of whom was Private Treacy, Royal Irish Regiment. One Sinn Fein Volunteer.
Eleven cases are being treated, some very critical.

KING GEORGE V. HOSPITAL

On inquiry at the King George V. Hospital at 2 o'clock this morning we were told that the total casualties treated there up to that time were:—
One officer killed.
Eleven soldiers wounded.

RICHMOND HOSPITAL.

The authorities at the Richmond this morning report four deaths from wounds.

MIDNIGHT RIFLE FIRE

THE STREETS DESERTED.

There was a renewed outbreak of rifle firing in the vicinity of Annesley Bridge and North Wharf road after midnight, as a result of which the Fire Brigade ambulance was summoned to the scene. Three persons suffering from bullet wounds were removed to hospital.

At 1.30 o'clock this morning there was a vigorous renewal of rifle-firing in the street, as a result of which the ambulance was again summoned to remove casualties to hospital. As it was very dark, intense rifle-firing broke out in the very central area of the city, and continued without remission for fully half an hour. As there were then very few ordinary pedestrians about the streets. Up to midnight, however, large numbers of persons of both sexes, some of them young, were parading the principal thoroughfares such as Westmoreland street, Sackville street, D'Olier street, College Green, and streets, singing and shouting, apparently excited by the events happening around. At one o'clock these perambulations of irresponsibles had almost entirely dispersed, and, save for the noise of shots in the dark, scarcely a sound was heard.

A RUSSIAN RAILWAY

The Russians, it is well known, have for a long time past busy with the construction of a railway communicating with the coast of Lapland, which, unlike Archangel, is not blocked by ice during the year. A Swiss engineer, M. C[?], who has recently visited this line, the *Journal de Genève* publishes, on his authority, some interesting details. The progress which has been made. The line, says M. Cruvellier, is divided into four manipulation of the mass of Protestants by a reactionary minority. It was not in fact entirely unreasonable to suppose that threats of violent resistance to home rule were merely rhetorical. Unionist opposition to the Home Rule Bills of 1886 and 1893 had been vocal but non-violent, and its leaders had been most concerned to impress mainstream British public opinion. But unionist politics had been changing. For one thing, the Parliament Act of 1911 deprived the House of Lords of its power to block legislation, depriving unionists of their most formidable parliamentary means of preventing a Home Rule Bill from becoming law. For another, the formation of the Ulster Unionist Council in 1905 had created, for the first time, a broadly based political structure capable of mobilising the Protestant masses. Unionists had both an incentive for militant resistance and the means of organising it.

from The Irish Times
27 APRIL **1916**

Martial Law

Every wise citizen of Dublin is a loyal man, but loyalty alone does not confer wisdom in all the details of life. Plain as are the terms of the Regulations to be observed under Martial Law, which we print today, we think it well to impress the necessity of a rigid observance of them on the civil population of Dublin. The censorship will permit us, perhaps, to say that we live in times which demand that we walk with more than customary wariness. By keeping these regulations with religious strictness we shall help the State, and we shall be doing a very valuable service to ourselves. The first of them commands that all persons in the City and County of Dublin, with specified exceptions, shall stay in their houses, until further notice, between the hours of 7.30 p.m. and 5.30 a.m. In present circumstances this restriction will not irk even the well-known citizen of Dublin

The scene in Sackville Street (O'Connell Street) following the Easter Rising

who said—'I dined in a strange place last night,' and when asked, 'Where?' replied, 'In my own house.' . . .

As a rule, the citizens of Dublin are not home-birds. They have the Continental love of the open air. The season is just beginning when the lengthening daylight invites to evening walks. Yesterday—if anybody happened to notice it—was a beautiful day. The new confinement to the house between those hours—say 7.30 p.m. to 11 p.m.—when people usually take their walks abroad, play a quiet game of bridge at a neighbour's, or visit the theatres, will confront the heads of many respectable families with a novel problem. It is not often that a workable bridge party is found under one roof—even if people had a head for bridge at this time. Current light literature has ceased to be accessible. There is little or no news (we admit frankly) in the only newspaper; that, however, is not the newspaper's fault, and it may claim, perhaps, as a merit that it comes out at all. What is the fire-side citizen to do with those three hours? We make two or three suggestions. He can cultivate a habit of easy conversation with his family: the years may have made his efforts in this direction spasmodic or laconic. He can put his little garden into a state of decency that will hold promise of beauty. He can do some useful mending and painting about the house. Best of all, perhaps, he can acquire, or re-acquire, the art of reading—that is to say, the study, with an active and receptive mind, of what the great writers of the past have said nobly and for all time. How many citizens of Dublin have any real knowledge of the works of Shakespeare? Could any better occasion for reading them be afforded than the coincidence of enforced domesticity with the poet's tercentenary?

from The Irish Times
28 APRIL 1916

The Insurrection

The 'Sinn Fein' Insurrection, which began on Easter Monday in Dublin, is virtually at an end. Desultory fighting continues in suburban districts. The severity of martial law is maintained; indeed, it is increased in the new Proclamation which we print today. Many streets and roads are still dangerous for the careless wayfarer. But the back of the insurrection is broken. Strong military forces, skilfully directed by a strong hand, have decided the issue sooner than most of us had dared to hope. The cordon of troops which was flung round the city narrowed its relentless circle until further

Patrick Pearse surrenders to General Lowe at 2:30 p.m. on Saturday 29 April 1916. The Easter Rising is over.

The result was that, in the words of Alvin Jackson, between 1905 and 1911 Ulster unionism had developed 'from an essentially parliamentary movement into an army of resistance, retaining a residual and peripheral parliamentary presence.'[12] After the Liberal government in Britain introduced the third Home Rule Bill in April 1912, the great majority of Protestant men in Ulster signed the Solemn League and Covenant, pledging themselves to repudiate the authority of any parliament forced on them. Protestant women signed their own version of the Covenant. This overwhelming display of mass resistance to home rule, backed by the explicit threat of force, suggested to many that Ireland was beginning to slide towards civil war.

As Ireland became more unsettled it had also become more significant to all sorts of people with an interest in the undermining of empires. In the summer of 1907 a young Indian, Jawaharlal Nehru, took a holiday in Dublin while

after Murphy says he will not recognise unions. It is typical of the conflict between Dublin trade unions and employers, who refuse to recognise the unions.

30 August

Two workers die and six hundred are injured as members of the Dublin Metropolitan Police run riot among a proscribed rally in O'Connell Street, Dublin, at which

Poole Street, Dublin

*Jim Larkin speaks.
The police also
attack workers'
houses. The Irish
Citizen Army is
later formed as
a result.*

2 September

*Houses collapse in
Church Street,
Dublin, killing
seven people.*

3 September

*Most delegates at
the Dublin
Employers'
Federation agree
to impose a
statement on their
employees forcing
them to state that
they will not join
the Irish
Transport and
General Workers'
Union.*

waiting to begin his studies in Cambridge. He wrote to his father: 'Have you heard of the Sinn Fein in Ireland? ... Their policy is not to beg for favours but to wrest them. They do not want to fight England by arms, but "to ignore her, boycott her, and quietly assume the adminis-tration of Irish affairs."'[13] Six years later Ireland attracted the attention of an obscure Russian agitator, Vladimir Ilyich Ulyanov, living in Geneva under the pseudonym Lenin. Having witnessed the bloody defeat of an attempt at revolution in his own country in 1905, Lenin was watching for signs of incipient revolt elsewhere, and in 1913 he thought he could see them in Dublin. Ireland, he wrote, was 'something of a British Poland,' increasingly dominated by the rising Catholic middle class. 'At the present moment, the Irish nationalists (i.e. the Irish bourgeoisie) are the victors. They are buying up the land from the British landlords; they are getting national Home Rule ... they will freely govern "their" land in conjunction with "their" Irish priests.' But, Lenin imagined, Ireland was about to 'turn into a land with an organised army of the proletariat.'[14]

Side by side with the stirrings of prosperity and modernity in Dublin there was poverty of the most primitive kind. Even at a time when the lot

resistance became impossible. On Saturday, P. H. Pearse, one of the seven ring-leaders, surrendered unconditionally with the main body of the rebels. Yesterday other bodies came in dejectedly under the white flag. Of the buildings which were seized a week ago not one remains in rebel hands. The General Post Office, save for its noble portico, is a ruin. The premises of the Royal College of Surgeons and Messrs Jacobs' factory were evacuated yesterday. St Stephen's Green was cleared on Thursday. Liberty Hall is no more than a sinister and hateful memory. It is believed that most of the ring-leaders are dead or captured. The outlaws who still 'snipe' from roofs may give a little more trouble, but their fate is certain. So ends the criminal adventure of the men who declared that they were 'striking in full confidence of victory,' and told their dupes that they would be 'supported by gallant allies in Europe.' The gallant ally's only gift to them was an Irish renegade whom it wanted to lose. Ireland has been saved from shame and ruin, and the whole Empire from a serious danger. Where our politicians failed—and worse than failed—the British Army has filled the breach and won the day. The Dublin Insurrection of 1916 will pass into history with the equally unsuccessful insurrections of the past. It will have only this distinction—that it was more daringly and systematically planned, and more recklessly invoked, than any of its predecessors. . . .

from The Irish Times 1916
6 MAY

The Proclamation of the Irish Republic

Few people have heard the beginning of the official declaration of an Irish Republic. Fewer stayed to the end. Though Sackville Street was fairly crowded at the time, the majority of the people paid little attention to the doings of the rebels, and preferred the more practical process of looting.

At 1.30 there came from the Post Office a small man in plain clothes with a bundle of papers under his arm. Escorted by a guard of revolutionists, he made his way to Nelson's Pillar, and began to speak, surrounded by not more than 30 men.

'Citizens of Dublin', he said, 'the last of the public buildings of the city is now in our hands. We have captured the General Post Office, and in this memorable day Ireland, as a Republic, has freed herself from the Republic of England.'

The ruins of the Metropole Hotel beside the GPO, O'Connell Street, after the Rising

The speaker then launched into the well-worn theme of Ireland's wrongs and England's oppression. The subject was evidently equally familiar to the orator and his hearers. As he gained fervour and thundered out the phrases he had used so often before his audience became progressively bored. A sweet shop was broken into, and nearly all rushed across the street to join in the spoil. A few old men and women who had lost their desire for sweets remained. Even these soon became discontented. 'Isn't Clery's broken into yet?' said one. 'Hivins, it's a great shame Clery's isn't broken.' On a rumour that this great event was going to happen they moved over to the shop windows and left the speaker finishing his peroration with no one to listen to him but his guard.

Like the revolution itself, the proclamation was a great fiasco.

of the urban poor throughout the world was generally brutal, Dublin stood out for the savagery of its social conditions. In the period 1910–14 the infant mortality rate in London was 106 per thousand live births; in Dublin it was 147—higher, at this time, than the prevailing rate in Moscow or Calcutta. In 1901 the death rate in Dublin for those aged between one and sixty was 75 per cent higher than the English level.[15] Of the 9,000 people who died in the city every year, 1,600 died in workhouses. Official attitudes to public health can be judged by the fact that in 1907, of the 167 national schools in Dublin, 104 had no toilets.[16]

Though there was still desperate poverty in the countryside, most people in rural Ireland had

23 September

The Provisional Government of Ulster is established by Unionists.

23 October

Priests lead crowds in an attempt to stop locked-out workers sending their hungry children to England to be cared for during the dispute.

27 October

James Larkin is sent to jail for seven months for using 'seditious language'.

1 November

The Gaelic League newspaper An Claidheamh Soluis publishes an article entitled 'The North Began' by Professor Eoin MacNeill calling for nationalists to follow the example of the Ulster Volunteer Force and organise and arm themselves.

25 November

A mass meeting at the Rotunda in Dublin launches the Irish Volunteers.

27 November

The newly formed Irish Citizen Army holds its first drill.

4 December

King George V proclaims all of Ireland and forbids the importing of arms.

an adequate, if hardly exciting, diet, consisting of potatoes, milk, brown bread, and increasingly meat, particularly bacon. In the cities, however, many lived in a state of constant undernourishment. Labourers in Dublin were judged to require a minimum of 3,500 calories a day; but a representative working-class diet drawn up in 1913–14 by Dr Mabel Crawford of the Women's National Health Association, consisting, in the course of a week, of white bread, sugar, potatoes, a pig's head, some fish, and a little beef, yielded only 2,600 calories.[17] This poor diet was a direct reflection of the poverty wages on which unskilled workers and their families had to subsist: earnings per family averaged just over £1 2s (£1.10) a week. Such people were, inevitably, in constant debt. Every year about four-and-a-half million items were pawned in Dublin alone.

While in Belfast most of the housing stock was reasonably new, and tenements were rare, in Dublin housing for the unskilled working class consisted of what one historian describes as 'some

Tom Kettle was a rising star of the Irish Party when he volunteered for the western front. He died at Ginchy in September 1916. His body was never recovered.

from The Irish Times
6 MAY **1916**

Obituary of a soldier
Lieutenant Trimble

Second Lieutenant Noel Desmond Trimble, 12th Inniskillings (Ulster Division) attached to the 8th Inniskillings (16th Irish Division), has been killed in action. He is the son of Mr W. Copeland Trimble, JP, Enniskillen, editor and proprietor of the *Impartial Reporter*. He is an old Portora boy, had a distinguished scholastic career, and was a scholar of Trinity College, Dublin. He has two other brothers on active service, Lieut R.S. Trimble, 6th Royal Irish Fusiliers (10th Division), wounded at the Dardanelles, and A.E.C. Trimble, 7th Inniskillings (16th Irish Division). He left for service only 4 weeks ago.

from The Irish Times
6 JULY **1916**

Irish Soldiers and Settlement

When the full story of the British advance from Albert is known it will add a new and glorious chapter to Irish history. At this moment Ulster is torn between anxiety and pride. Her 36th Division has fought splendidly, and, it is to be feared, with heavy loss. The Division was in action north of Montauban. The exact locality has not been revealed. It may have been Thiepval, where the fighting was desperately fierce. It may have been Gommecourt, where the British troops advanced as on parade through a double barrage of shells and against machine-gun and rifle fire. Wherever it was, the Ulstermen won immortal fame for Ulster and for Ireland. 'Their heroism and self-sacrifice,' says *The Times*, 'continue to be the theme of mournful praise among their comrades in arms.' The price will be grievous, but Ulster will pay it with a steadfast heart. Her young soldiers have now earned their place beside the veteran Dublins and Munsters and Inniskillings who went through the hottest furnace of war at Helles. We have reason to believe that some of those great battalions are now north of the Somme, giving a taste of their quality to the Germans as they gave it to the Turk. It is no secret that the 16th (Irish) Division is also within sound of the British guns between the Ancre and the Somme. Here, surely, is an inspiring thought for Ireland. At home we are once more torn by political contentions. The blood of Irishmen shed by Irishmen is hardly dry upon the streets of Dublin. Out there, in the forefront of Ireland's and the Empire's battle, the men of all our parties, all our creeds, all our social classes, are fighting side by side. The only conflict between them is a conflict of honour in Ireland's name. They are living and dying for one another, and they are fighting for Ireland even more grandly than they know. No political hates or passions can survive that brotherhood of action. These Irish soldiers from all the provinces are not merely crushing the might of Germany; they are laying the foundations of a new Ireland on the plains of France.

We are confronted, however, with a tragic paradox. Who have the best right to order Ireland's destinies—the men who are making war profits and talking angry politics at home, or the men who are dying that Ireland's destinies may be great and free? There are a thousand arguments against Mr Lloyd George's scheme. The strongest of all is the fact that it is being contrived behind the backs of the very Irishmen for whose sake the rest of the world honours Ireland. When these young men from North and South went to the war the political leaders whom the 16th Division follows were solemnly pledged against the dismemberment of Ireland. The political leaders whom the 36th Division follows were solemnly pledged against the dismemberment of Ulster. The men who thought that they were fighting for the glory of all Ireland will be told when they come back that they were only fighting for the glory of twenty-six counties. The men to whom the nine counties of Ulster are what Rome was to the Roman legions will come back to learn that a third part of their heritage has disappeared. Mr Lloyd George's scheme is not merely a crime against good government; it is a crime against patriotism. Moreover, it is an unnecessary crime—if any crime can be accounted necessary. In the first place, the absurd plea of Imperial urgency is now tacitly abandoned. In the next place, it is our firm belief that there need be no partition if our Irish fighting men are given that voice in Irish affairs to which, more than any other body of Irishmen, they are entitled. We know that the Ulster soldiers would have agreed to the exclusion of the whole of Ulster before they went to the war; but nobody has any right to assume that, having discovered the essential unity of Ireland in the trenches, they would agree today to the exclusion of all Ulster—much less to the partition of Ulster. We refuse to

of the worst slums the world has ever seen.'[18] Even Belfast's disadvantaged Catholics, confined to the older parts of the city by sectarian housing policies, were far better housed than the Dublin poor. Over a quarter of Dublin's population— some 20,000 families—lived in one-room flats in tenement buildings. 1,500 of the 5,000 tenements had been formally condemned as unfit for human habitation. And even these miserable dwellings were not occupied with any security. The Lord Mayor of Dublin claimed in 1914 that 30,000 notices to quit were served each year on tenement dwellers, a figure that, as the historian Mary Daly points out, 'makes evictions in rural Ireland, even at the peak of the land war, pale into insignificance.'

Though it was in general conservative, *The Irish Times* had led the way in calling for state intervention in these social problems. In January 1900 the paper suggested that 'the time has come to direct very serious attention to the phenomenally high death rate of the city of Dublin.' In 1903 a leading article claimed that 'it is daily becoming more evident that the question of the poor, their housing and the manner their children are employed, will require to be taken in hand by the government.' Ironically, because *The Irish Times* supported the state it was much more inclined to such appeals than nationalists, suspicious

Kingstown harbour in the early years of the century

1914

19 January
The Inchicore works of the Dublin United Tramway Company opens after five months, as carters and labourers return to work.

14 February
A report published by an inquiry into Dublin housing states that 28,000 Dubliners live in houses 'unfit for human habitation.'

20 March
Newspapers report that the majority of the officers of the 3rd Cavalry Brigade would refuse to serve in Ulster, in what

Hugh Moore and his staff stand in the ruins of their business premises after the Easter Rising

becomes known as the 'Curragh Mutiny'.

2 April

Cumann na mBan is founded as the women's wing of the Irish Volunteers.

24 April

The Ulster Volunteer Force smuggles 35,000 guns and three million rounds of ammunition into Bangor, Larne, and Donaghadee.

29 April

Carson welcomes Churchill's proposal for the exclusion of north-eastern Ulster from home rule.

of almost all government actions. In 1911 the paper demanded an inquiry into the failures of Dublin City Council and remarked that without changes in local policy 'the slums of Dublin will still be there whether we get Home Rule or not.'

Sir Roger Casement

believe that our Nationalist soldiers would agree today to be divided permanently from their fellow-soldiers of the North. The rifles of the 36th and 16th Divisions, firing together towards Berlin, call for unity in Ireland. Their sound has been overpowered by the crack of the rebel rifles in Dublin, and Mr Redmond calls for dismemberment ...

from The Irish Times
4 AUGUST **1916**

Roger Casement

Roger Casement's death is a miserable end to a life which for the greater part of its course was honourable and distinguished. The story of his guilt and fate points its own moral; he has paid the full penalty of his crime. Very willingly we should have allowed the rest to be silence if we had been able to ignore the attempt which already is being made to represent him as a victim of British brutality. The Cork Board of Guardians adjourned yesterday 'to mark our sense of horror and detestation at the murder of Sir Roger Casement.' It is false and foolish to say that Casement was 'murdered,' or to suggest in any way that he had not forfeited his life to the State. This wicked resolution compels us to recall the facts. Casement had served the British State with distinction, had received many honours from it, and was its pensioner. Deliberately he decided to do his best to subdue it to its worst enemy. In the middle of our greatest war he went to Germany and put his brains and influence at the service of the German Headquarters Staff. He tried to seduce Irish soldiers from the allegiance. He came secretly to Ireland on the eve of the rebellion, in company with a shipload of German arms. He was captured in circumstances which forbade the slightest doubt about his guilty acts and intentions. In like circumstances any other European Government would have executed him promptly, without forms of law. The British government, however, gave Casement a conspicuously careful trial before eminent and impartial judges. His counsel was allowed to make every possible point in his favour. He was convicted on overwhelming evidence, and appealed. The appeal was heard with equal patience and charity, and the conviction was upheld. No prisoner ever received a fairer trial from a court of justice; the guilt of no prisoner was ever more clearly established. To say that Casement was 'murdered' is to say either that his judges were prejudiced and vengeful, or that the crime of which he was properly found guilty did not deserve death. It is permissible to argue that a reprieve might have been granted on grounds of clemency or policy; it is sheer treason to say that Casement's punishment was not just and lawful. The resolution of the Cork Board of Guardians is a disgrace to themselves and a libel on the county of the Munster Fusiliers.

from The Irish Times 1917
26 OCTOBER

The Sinn Fein Convention

The first day's proceedings at the Convention of the Sinn Fein Party in Dublin have not illuminated the party's policy, but they throw some new light on its quality and strength. They show that Sinn Fein is a powerful and popular movement; that all classes of Nationalists, including large numbers of the Roman Catholic clergy, have joined its ranks; that it is well organised; and that it is still free, and hopes to remain free, from those meaner political vices which have helped to wreck the Nationalist Parliamentary Party. There were signs yesterday of the existence of the personal jealousies and suspicions which have always infected Irish politics; but we do not advise the enemies of the movement to set much store on them. Sinn Fein's ruling passion is hatred of England, and it is likely to abstain, for the present at least, from the minor luxury of 'witch-hunting' at home. It is perfectly open in its aims: yesterday's proceedings were a public challenge to British authority. The Convention represents, we are told, 250,000 affiliated members throughout the country, and it would be foolish to deny that these 250,000 men and women share among them a large measure of the brains, education, and character of Nationalist Ireland. Yesterday the Convention adopted a constitution—which is, of course, a very different thing from a policy. The main article of this constitution is the establishment in Ireland of 'an independent Irish Republic,' with international recognition. Sinn Fein proposes to 'make use of any and every means available to render impotent the power of England to hold Ireland in subjection by military force or otherwise.' Yesterday a couple of clergy-men were frightened by this large commitment, but Mr de Valera, with a dramatic gesture, swept their scruples out of court. Mr

Sir John Lavery's painting of Casement's trial in London in 1916

These slums went to war in the Dublin lock-out of 1913. The lock-out began on 21 August 1913 when the employers' leader William Martin Murphy dismissed employees in two of his companies, the Dublin United Tramway Company and the *Irish Independent*, because they had joined James Larkin's Irish Transport and General Workers' Union. He then ordered his remaining employees to leave the ITGWU if they were members and to pledge not to join if they were not. The lock-out intensified five days later when tram-drivers and conductors came out in support of their sacked colleagues, leaving their passengers stranded during Horse Show week. It became an all-out class conflict on Sunday 31 August when the police baton-charged Larkinite marchers in O'Connell Street, creating the first of many Bloody Sundays in twentieth-century Ireland. By early September the majority of Dublin's employers had joined Murphy in locking out their employees until they signed the anti-ITGWU document. Over 20,000 workers had been dismissed and over 100,000 people in the city had been reduced to a state of destitution.

As a conservative paper, *The Irish Times* was naturally inclined to identify with the employers and to abuse Larkin and the ITGWU. Its

6 May
The House of Lords rejects a bill that would give some women the vote.

25 May
The Home Rule Bill gets its third reading in the House of Commons.

28 June
Archduke Franz Ferdinand and his wife are assassinated in Sarajevo.

10 July
The Ulster Provisional Government meets in Belfast.

21 July
A conference of nationalists and

A tenement bedroom in Waterford Street in Dublin. The conditions in which the Dublin poor lived before the Great War were among the worst in northern Europe.

unionists begins at Buckingham Palace to find a solution to the home rule question. It breaks down on 24 July.

26 July
The Dublin Battalion of the Irish Volunteers smuggles 1,400 guns into Ireland at Howth. British soldiers shoot dead four civilians and injure thirty-seven in Batchelor's Walk after crowds jeer them because they failed to recover any weapons.

1–2 August
The Irish Volunteers run guns into Kilcoole, Co. Wicklow.

editorials, especially in the early days of the lock-out, rang with apocalyptic warnings that the bosses were fighting 'for the very life of the city' and that whatever short-term losses the city might sustain from the lock-out, it would be nothing to the 'ruin' that would follow a labour victory. The paper acknowledged nonetheless the appalling social conditions that created Larkin's following among the slum-dwellers. In early September it reported the collapse of two tenement houses in Church Street, with the death of seven people. An editorial remarked that members of the ITGWU lived 'for the most part in slums like Church Street' and that 'the condition of the Dublin slums is responsible not only for disease and crime but for much of our industrial unrest … The workers, whose only escape from these wretched homes lies in the public house, would not be human beings if they did not turn a ready ear to anybody who promises to improve their lot.' The writer concluded that 'if every unskilled labourer in Dublin were the tenant of a decent cottage of three or even two rooms, the city would not be divided into two hostile camps.'

On 8 September 1913 the paper published for the first time a Yeats poem, rather awkwardly

Arthur Griffith has resigned the presidency of the organisation in favour of this young man who believes in the efficacy of 'ten-foot pikes' against British machine guns. The constitution, and the speeches which supported it, confirm absolutely the Prime Minister's and Mr Duke's descriptions of the intentions of Sinn Fein. It proposes to arm and drill its members in defiance of the law. It proposes to kill the Irish Convention. Its dream is the erection of some sort of new Ireland on the smoking ruins of the Ireland of today.

Madness does not cease to be madness when it exists on a large scale and disguises itself in the vesture of careful and competent organisation. The Sinn Fein Party is advancing with the utmost deliberation towards the destruction of its own hopes and the infliction of untold calamity on Ireland. It recognises—this gleam of sanity survives—that it cannot dethrone England in Ireland without the help of the great nations, yet in the last few months it has been wonderfully successful in estranging the sympathy of every one of them except the nation which is now the pariah of humanity. Sinn Fein has boasted that its sheet-anchor at the Peace Conference will be the United States. The recent arrests in that country prove that, if America had her way, she would show far less mercy to Sinn Fein than it is receiving today from the British Government. Whatever harm Sinn Fein may continue to do, however frightful the bill which Ireland may have to pay for its folly, its programme is doomed to failure. Posterity will regard it as one of the most incomprehensible aberrations in history …

from The Irish Times
11 MARCH 1920

From The Times *of today (By special arrangement with the proprietors of* The Times*)*

The Decision of Ulster

The Times, in a leading article dealing with yesterday's decision of the Ulster Unionist Council upon the Home Rule proposals of the Government, says:—It is obvious that the Government have left no stone unturned to secure yesterday's result, and have been prepared to jeopardise every chance of conciliating Nationalist opinion by the prodigality of their provision for Ulster Unionism. We need not here restate the limits set by abstract justice in this course of action—limits which, we

National Executive of Irish Trade Union Congress (ITUC) and Labour Party. This is one of the few photographs that show James Connolly **(back left)** *and James Larkin* **(sitting second from right)** *together.*

hold, have been exceeded by the bill. Nevertheless we do not underestimate the importance of the concession which has been made by Ulster, or its far-reaching effects upon the nature of Irish policies. After remarking that it is now almost possible to view, as a whole, Sir Edward Carson's conduct of the Ulster case, *The Times* adds—If Unionism were merely the desire to keep North-East Ulster beyond the control of an Irish Parliament, Sir Edward Carson might have claimed a victory. But Unionism is more. It is a tradition of government, a social and economic conception. It involves the maintenance of a common civilisation in Ireland and Great Britain. Judged by such a standard, he has suffered a terrible and humiliating defeat, of which the full magnitude has yet to be seen. We do not disguise our profound disappointment, proceeds *The Times*, at a decision which threatens to confine Unionist influence for all practical purposes to an area of six Irish counties. We had hoped that

titled 'Romance in Ireland (On reading much of the correspondence against the Art Gallery)'. It was one of the greatest of literary polemics, and under its revised title, 'September 1913', it would become one of Yeats's best-known poems. It is essentially about the failure of the Dublin merchant class to support the establishment of a modern art gallery in the city; but since the leader of the opposition to the gallery, William Martin Murphy, was also the leader of the employers who had locked out their workers, it had, especially in the newspaper, broader overtones. *The Irish Times* also published George Russell's stinging open letter 'To the Masters of Dublin', described by the first historian of Irish labour, W. P. Ryan, as 'the most enduring document of the 1913 struggle, the one thing through which those

2 August
Germany invades Luxembourg.

3 August
The leader of the Irish Party, John Redmond, says in the House of Commons that the Irish Volunteers will protect Ireland so that regular soldiers can leave the country.

4 August

War breaks out in Europe, and Britain declares war on Germany.

8 August

The British expeditionary force lands in France.

10 August

The Education (Provision of Meals) (Ireland) Act permits local authorities to provide meals for schoolchildren.

18 August

The Home Rule Act becomes law but is suspended indefinitely.

masters of Dublin, so proud and cruel in their little day, will live in history.' (The paper did not, however, publish a second open letter by Russell, which he submitted in November.)

The workers were eventually defeated by starvation. By February 1914 *The Irish Times* was reporting that no strike pay was being doled out at the ITGWU's head office in Liberty Hall and that two loaves of bread for each applicant was all that the union could muster. By then the workers were drifting back to their jobs, though after twenty-two weeks, five deaths and losses of over £1 million there was no real victory for anyone. In a final comment on 3 February 1914 *The Irish Times* reminded its readers of the underlying causes of the conflict: 'The brooding discontents which exploded in the mad attempt to "hold up" Dublin gathered force and volume in the pestilential atmosphere of the Dublin slums ... It is a cynical commentary on our social sense that we needed the stimulus of the strike to realise the squalor and misery which, in the last analysis, produced it.'

Yet there were other, equally bitter conflicts in the air. The Irish Women's Franchise League, led by Hannah Sheehy-Skeffington, was

Tom Kettle's sister-in-law, Hannah Sheehy-Skeffington. Her husband, Francis Sheehy-Skeffington, was murdered by the deranged Colonel Bowen-Colthurst during the 1916 Rising.

Ulster Unionists might have looked further than the immediate situation, and have sought to build upon broader foundations than those which their now shrunken province can supply. Belfast Unionism seems to care nought for the morrow. It seems determined to hold what it has got as long as it can. There is no sign of the vision and energy that might have inspired more daring minds to create a new tradition of good government, which should establish a harmony in the whole of the nine counties, with influence far beyond them. It is not, however, *The Times* further adds, on the phrases of a carefully drawn document that we base a fleeting hope than they encourage, but rather on the expectation that many North-Eastern Unionists will yet realise that the only effective safeguard which they can confer upon their former comrades lies in seeking the fulfilment of every possibility of extra-provincial action on the part of North-East Ulster, for which the bill provides.

This portrait shows the kilted William Gibson, the second Lord Ashbourne, president of the Gaelic League, in the foreground. The central figure is that of Stephen McKenna, journalist and translator. Both men were prominent in Dublin intellectual life in the early years of the century.

from The Irish Times
22 JULY **1920**

Disturbances in Belfast

Our Belfast Correspondent, telegraphing last night, says:— Serious disturbances broke out in the Belfast shipyards this afternoon, as the result of which a number of men were injured. Ten of these were treated in hospital. Most of them are alleged to be Sinn Féiners. The origin of the disturbances is difficult to trace, but for some time there has been a considerable amount of ill-feeling developing in the shipyards amongst Unionist workers against Sinn Féiners being employed in the yards, on account of the atrocities that are being perpetrated in other parts of Ireland. This ill-feeling has on more than one occasion before the 12th of July holidays almost led to disturbances.

outraged by the absence of a provision for votes for women in the Home Rule Bill that was eventually proposed by the Liberal government in London. In his Lenten pastoral for 1912 the Bishop of Limerick, Edward O'Dwyer, noted that hitherto the question of votes for women 'has been merely academic, and provoked a smile of amusement, rather than serious consideration. Now it has come within the range of practical politics.' He felt sure, however, that most of his women listeners would regard the idea that they should have the vote as 'an absurdity' and be glad that Catholic reverence for women had 'restricted the activities of woman's life to the peace and quiet of her home. She was made by God too frail, too delicate, too good, to mix in the rough ways of men in the world.'

21 August
Six new divisions of the British army are created, including the 10th, which is made up of Irishmen.

20 September
Redmond, speaking at Woodenbridge, Co. Wicklow, calls on the Irish Volunteers to go 'wherever the firing-line extends.'

The great gantry at the Harland and Wolff yard in Belfast, symbol of Belfast's industrial might

An Claidheamh Soluis *was the official organ of the Gaelic League. It first appeared on 17 March 1899 and was an important voice in the Irish Revival.*

2–4 December

Three newspapers are suppressed by the British military and the police: Sinn Féin, Irish Freedom, *and* Irish Worker.

1915

5 January

William T. Cosgrave is elected unopposed for Sinn Féin to Dublin City Council.

25 April

Irish regiments are among those that land on the Gallipoli front.

On the streets, however, the women of the Franchise League were perfectly capable of mixing in the rough male world of political agitation. Shortly before the bishop's pastoral they had showered a huge nationalist demonstration in Dublin to hail the Home Rule Bill with VOTES FOR WOMEN leaflets dropped from their office in O'Connell Street after being roughly handled by stewards when they tried to distribute them on the street.

Throughout 1912, 1913 and 1914 there were signs that women too were prepared to turn to violence. A suffragist threw a hatchet at the Prime Minister, H. H. Asquith, as he rode through the streets of Dublin on his way to a Nationalist meeting at the Theatre Royal, which feminists tried to set on fire the same day. Windows of government buildings and political offices were smashed, and the home of the Nationalist MP John Dillon was attacked. In the north, women activists burned mansions such as Orlands House in the countryside and in Belfast set fire to the Bellevue Tea House, Annadale Hall, and the pavilion of the Cave Hill Bowling and Tennis Club.

The Irish Times was broadly supportive of the demand for women's suffrage though against

Unionist Workers' Resolution

During the shipyard dinner-hour today an informal meeting of Unionist workers in the yards of both Messrs Harland and Wolff, and Messr Workman, Clarke, and Co. was held, and was attended by over five thousand workers. Resolutions were adopted calling upon the workers to boycott all Sinn Féiners and refuse to work with them.

Later a large body of workers went to the new East Yard of Messrs Harland and Wolff, and advised a number of men there to leave at once. Instead of doing so, it is stated, these men became aggressive, and indulged in Sinn Féin cries. Blows were exchanged, and a number of men were injured. Seven or eight men ran away, and either jumped or were pushed into the Musgrave channel, and had to swim to the other side. Here they were met by a large crowd and compelled to turn back. They were badly mauled during the disturbance.

Subsequently the same crowd went to Messrs Harland and Wolff's joiners' shop, where a similar warning was given. One man produced a revolver and shouted: 'Up the rebels!' He was immediately knocked down and the weapon taken from him. He was beaten, and had to be taken to hospital. Other men also received minor injuries. Some of them were taken away in the ambulance, while others escaped on tramcars. During the afternoon, small parties of men searched the works endeavouring to find Sinn Féiners. A number of the parties were headed by Union Jacks.

The ss. Cedric, which is lying at the Thompson Wharf, was also searched, and a number of men were advised to leave.

Owing to the excitement prevailing, work ceased at both yards, but was subsequently resumed ...

Sinn Féin Provocation

The principal trouble took place in the new East Yard of Messrs Harland and Wolff Ltd., where a number of men, stated to be Sinn Féiners, were engaged in navvying and general labouring work. Some of these men, it is alleged, have been displaying partisan feelings recently, and indulging in provocative talk in regard to events in other parts of Ireland. One worker stated that these men have been more than once advised about their conduct and the possible consequences, but, he added, they paid no attention. Before 5 o'clock this afternoon all was reported quiet in the East Yard, admission to which was strictly refused except to all on business, for which they could produce the recognised authority. A gate into a joiner's shop at the new extension was smashed with heavy sledge hammers ...

Military Fire Over Crowd

Telegraphing at an early hour this morning, our Belfast Correspondent says:— The neighbourhood of the Falls Road was, at a late hour last night, the scene of very serious rioting. The trouble arose through an attempt by Sinn Féiners to attack a number of Unionist workers who were engaged late at a mill. Incensed by the attack on the Sinn Féiners at the shipyards, they repeatedly expressed their determination to 'get their own back,' and when the workers attempted to leave the mill they were beaten. Police were rushed to the place, and the crowd immediately turned their attention on them. The police were assaulted with stones, bolts, rivets, and other missiles. It became necessary to call on the military, and they arrived, fully armed and equipped with machine guns. Revolver shots were fired at them by the mob. So menacing did the crowd become that an order was given to the soldiers to fire over their heads. A volley was discharged. This and a baton charge by the police had the effect of compelling the crowds to withdraw.

Meanwhile, the people in the district leading from the Shankill to the Falls Road had attacked a number of spirit groceries supposed to be tenanted by Nationalists. The contents of the shops were looted, quantities of the drink being consumed. Everything that would burn was thrown into the street, where barrels, beds, shop fittings, and furniture were set on fire. The Fire Brigade were called on to quell several outbreaks of fire ...

from The Irish Times 1920
22 NOVEMBER

Dreadful Series of Murders in Dublin

Concerted Attacks on Officers of His Majesty's Forces

Yesterday morning there was enacted in Dublin a series of crimes unparalleled in the history of the city. As a result, fourteen members of His Majesty's Forces were murdered in their houses, and a number of other seriously wounded.

The attacks, which were apparently preconcerted, in every case occurred at the same hour. At nine o'clock in the morning the houses and hotels where these officers resided were entered by civilian bands. Most of the officers were in their bedrooms; some were dressed and ready to go to breakfast.

Sir Hugh Lane, connoisseur and collector, who went down with the Lusitania *in 1915. His priceless collection of modern masters is now housed in the Dublin gallery that bears his name.*

the more militant tactics of the Irish Women's Franchise League. In 1909, in one of many editorials excoriating the failure of Dublin City Council to tackle poverty, bad housing, and poor sanitation, the leader-writer suggested that one of the strongest arguments for women's suffrage was that women would be more concerned with such social issues. 'We need woman's wit and sympathy in dealing with social and domestic evils at home as much as we need man's strength and judgement in maintaining our supremacy abroad.' Women's involvement in politics would 'secure in the State that completeness of thought

7 May

The Lusitania is torpedoed off Kinsale, with the deaths of 1,502 people, including Hugh Lane.

25 May

A war coalition Cabinet is formed in London that includes Edward Carson.

Crowds gather in Merrion Square, Dublin, to watch the funeral cortège of Jeremiah O'Donovan Rossa on 1 August 1915. Pearse delivered the funeral oration at Glasnevin, one of the most famous Irish speeches of the century.

29 July

Douglas Hyde steps down as President of the Gaelic League at its ardfheis in Dundalk.

1 August

The body of Jeremiah O'Donovan Rossa, the veteran Fenian, is returned to Ireland. An immense crowd turns out as he is laid to rest in Glasnevin Cemetery in Dublin.

and judgement which in the home can be only obtained by a combination of the ruling attributes of the sexes.' About the same time as Bishop O'Dwyer's pastoral letter in 1912, the paper gave prominence to a letter from a suffragist, Isabella Richardson, decrying the fact that 'violence has become the vogue and many women who would not themselves indulge in wanton destruction of property nevertheless applaud those who do. I try to remonstrate, and am met with the reply "Oh, it's a very good thing. We have drawn the attention of the whole world!" Unfortunately, so does a man who murders his wife ...'

As well as the divide between workers and employers, and the struggle for women's rights, there was also increasing tension between Protestants and Catholics. By 1913 *The Irish Times* was becoming increasingly aware of itself as the

At least twelve were shot dead in this way, while two auxiliary police officers who were on their way to procure assistance were set upon and taken into a private house, where in a back garden they were shot dead. The official report indicates that most of these men were in some way connected with the administration of the law.

Later in the day, while a Gaelic football match was being played at Croke Park, Jones's Road, where many thousands of people were assembled, Forces of the Crown arrived, with the object of searching for perpetrators of the crimes of the morning. According to the official report, these forces were instantly fired on by pickets of civilians guarding the grounds, and the Crown Forces immediately replied.

The result of this action was a violent stampede amongst the spectators and more firing, in the course of which it is estimated that ten persons were killed and upwards of fifty wounded. In addition to those wounded by gunfire, many suffered from injuries received in the stampede ...

The Murder of Captain Fitzgerald

About nine o'clock yesterday morning (Sunday) a man knocked at the door of 28 Earlsfort Terrace, which was opened by the servant. He asked her if Mr Fitzgerald lived there. She answered in the negative, and he said that he knew Captain Fitzgerald lived there. He asked her to point out his room, and pointed his revolver at her. There were seven men at the door, of whom two entered, and took up a position in the hall. The first man who entered went to Mr Fitzgerald's room, and a moment later the servant heard Captain Fitzgerald utter a loud shout. She heard one of the men who had entered the room say 'Come on.' Four shots rang out immediately, and the man left the room at once and ran away, the others following.

When the police arrived shortly afterwards they found Captain Fitzgerald dead in his bed, with three bullet marks— one in the forehead, one in the heart, and one in the right wrist.

voice of a religious minority that might yet find itself under a specifically Catholic autonomous government. Sectarianism was, at least in the south, rather muted. But the fears and resentments sparked by the approach of home rule crystallised around the case of a Protestant clerk, G. H. Walton, in which *The Irish Times* itself became the object of fierce Catholic resentment. In October 1913 the Catholic booksellers and publishers M. H. Gill dismissed Walton from his job on the grounds that he was a Protestant proselytiser. Walton regularly served tea on Sunday mornings for the Dublin Free Breakfasts for the Poor, a Protestant missionary charity. When the firm discovered this, it sacked him.

The Irish Times published a letter from Thomas Hammond, a Protestant rector, and

1916

5 January
The Compulsory Service Bill, allowing conscription for men between the ages of eighteen and forty-two, excludes Ireland. A depot for four thousand wounded Irish soldiers is established in Co. Tipperary.

Members of the Irish Women Workers' Union photographed at Liberty Hall in 1913

10 February

The leader of the Irish Party, John Redmond, attends a recruitment meeting in the Mansion House with the Lord Lieutenant.

20 April

The Aud *arrives at Banna Strand, Co. Kerry, with twenty thousand rifles for the Irish Volunteers. It is intercepted by the British and eventually scuttled by its German captain.*

21 April

Casement lands at Banna Strand from the Aud *and is arrested immediately.*

24 April

Easter Rising: insurgents seize Dublin city centre and declare the Irish Republic.

25 April

The Lord Lieutenant proclaims martial law in Ireland as 350 people die at the start of the rising.

William Rothenstein's portrait of George Moore, the novelist. After many years in London and Paris, Moore returned to Dublin in 1901 and lived there for the next ten years. His mordant, sardonic wit was reflected in the three volumes of autobiography, **Hail and Farewell,** *which have left an unforgettable account of bohemian life in the city in the first decade of the new century.*

Henry O'Connor, general secretary of the City of Dublin Young Men's Christian Association, outlining Walton's plight and asking for 'the co-operation of every fair-minded Roman Catholic in the effort to repair as far as possible the unmerited injury which has been done to Mr. Walton.' Gill's company secretary replied that the organisations that Walton assisted 'bear to all Catholic minds one, and only one, aspect, namely proselytism—and that in one of its most insidious forms. Under these circumstances, my board did not conceive it consistent with their obligations as recognised Catholic publishers that a gentleman engaged in such practices should continue in their service.' He accused Walton of 'endeavouring to wean little children from the faith of their fathers.'

Captain Fitzgerald had been lodging in the house for a month, and the people in the house believed him to be attached to the Auxiliary RIC Forces. He was, as a matter of fact, an ex-military officer, and had served as a barrack defence officer in the RIC somewhere in the County of Clare. While on that duty he was kidnapped. He was placed against a wall and shot at, but he was not much injured. He dropped to the ground pretending that he was dead, and seized an opportunity to climb over the wall, and so escaped from his torturers. He was an Irishman, and was attending a hospital in Dublin.

Fight in Lower Mount Street

At 22 Lower Mount Street, at about nine o'clock, a man knocked at the door. He asked the servant if he could see Mr Mahon. She replied that she did not know, and at the same time twenty men rushed into the hall, one of whom, she noticed, had a revolver. The man asked her to show him Mr Mahon's room, and she led him to it, and a number of men entered the hall. She immediately heard five shots. The men asked her for another officer's room, and she showed them the door of the apartment. The door was locked, and shots were fired through it, but the officer managed to make his escape.

Thomas J. Clarke, Fenian and first signatory of the proclamation of the Republic in 1916

The British army patrols the grounds of Jervis Street Hospital, Dublin, in 1920

The occupant of a neighbouring house having heard the shots, shouted and attracted the attention of some Auxiliary Police officers who were passing. They fired into the house, and the raiders ran out by the back door. They were pursued by the officers, who wounded one and took him prisoner. They also arrested three others.

The Auxiliaries rescued the officer, and sent two of their number to the nearest barrack for reinforcements. Those men, whose names were Garrin and Morris, never reached the barracks, and their dead bodies were subsequently found in a garden some distance away.

Three Killed in Morehampton Road

A party of about twenty armed men called at 117 Morehampton Road a few minutes before 9 o'clock. The house is called 'Brianna,' and was occupied by Thomas Herbert Smith, aged 45 years, with his wife and three children. He had in the house as lodger Captain Donald Louis Maclean, aged 31, with his wife and child. There was also in the house Mr Smith's brother-in-law, a gentleman named

The Irish Times then published a calm and sober editorial on the Walton case. It condemned proselytism from any church but added that, even if Walton's actions in serving tea to the poor were interpreted in such a light, he should not be sacked for practising his religion as he saw fit in his own spare time. The demand that he be responsible to his employers for his religious activities 'sets up a claim which, if many employers were to assert it, would justify the hardest things that Mr. Larkin has said about employers as a class.' And the paper put Walton's sacking forward as a 'test case' for whether or not home rule would indeed be Rome rule. 'We hope that, for the sake of public enlightenment on a really vital question, representative Irish Nationalists will tell their Protestant fellow Irishmen what they think about Mr. Walton's case.'

The invitation was not taken up by any prominent home-ruler, however, and it was the

29 April

Patrick Pearse, one of the seven signatories of the proclamation of the Irish Republic, unconditionally surrenders to the British. Three thousand people have been injured in the week-long rising and 450 killed.

1 May

About four hundred insurgents arrive in Britain for internment there.

Main Street, Wexford

3 May

The British army begins executing leaders of the Rising. Patrick Pearse, Tom Clarke and Thomas MacDonagh are shot by firing-squad.

4 May

Joseph Plunkett, Edward Daly, William Pearse and Michael O'Hanrahan are executed.

Catholic Bulletin, coincidentally published by Gill, that put itself forward as the voice of Catholic opinion. It defended the sacking of Walton without qualification and turned its anger on *The Irish Times*, whose staff it accused of being 'calculating and unscrupulous bigots,' whose stock in trade was 'distortion, interpolation and the other traditional devices of West-British journalism.' The paper's editorial was 'strung together by the shabby misrepresentations, the cunning innuendos, and the bare-faced half-truths which one mostly expects from that jaundiced journal of West-Britonism.'

The *Bulletin* returned to the attack in January 1914, searching for new insults and

Cadlow, a native of Prestwick. Mr Maclean belonged to the Rifle Brigade, and had been lodging there for some months. While all the inmates were still in bed a knock and a ring brought Mr Smith's son, aged ten years, to the door.

About twenty men rushed into the house and upstairs. They ordered Captain Maclean and Mr Cadlow, who occupied separate rooms, out of their beds. The raiders brought them to a spare bedroom on the upper landing. They brought Mr Smith there also, and there Captain Maclean and Mr Smith were shot dead; Mr Cadlow was very seriously wounded.

The raiders then ran out of the house, and went along into Herbert Park Road. Two constables, passing the house about five minutes later, were informed of the murders by Captain Maclean's widow …

from The Irish Times
22 NOVEMBER **1920**

Shooting at Croke Park

Wild Scenes at Football Match

The murders which occurred in the morning were followed by an unexpected fusillade at Croke Park in the afternoon, when nine people were shot dead and a great many wounded.

It had been arranged that the challenge Gaelic football match between County Tipperary and County Dublin should take place in the grounds of Croke Park, Jones's Road, Dublin, and it is estimated that about 15,000 spectators had assembled to witness the contest.

finding, among others, 'pampered bigotry', 'cowardly and contemptible paper', and 'journalistic blackguardism'. Such a furious response to a mild editorial on a simple issue of religious freedom can hardly have encouraged Protestants to accept assurances that their rights would be protected under home rule. And there were many Protestants, especially but by no means exclusively in the north, who were only too happy to seize on such incidents as further evidence that their faith and their power would be crushed by an autonomous Irish government. That rhetorically inflated fear of obliteration in turn encouraged the idea of armed revolt against home rule.

5 May

John MacBride is shot.

8 May

Éamonn Ceannt, Michael Mallin, Con Colbert and Seán Heuston are shot.

9 May

Thomas Kent is shot in Cork.

*Erskine Childers' yacht **Asgard** landed 1,500 guns for the Irish Volunteers at Howth in July 1914. The photograph shows Childers' American wife, Mary Ellen Osgood, and Mary Spring-Rice, the nationalist daughter of Lord Monteagle, on board the **Asgard** bound for Howth.*

12 May

*James Connolly and
Seán Mac Diarmada
are shot by firing-
squad. The British
Prime Minister,
Asquith, visits
Ireland.*

26–29 June

*The trial of Roger
Casement takes
place in England.
He is found guilty of
treason and
sentenced to death.*

1 July

*A massive offensive
begins on the
Somme on the
western front, and
thousands of Irish
soldiers are killed or
injured. The 36th
(Ulster) Division
(comprising the
Ulster Volunteer
Force) suffers five
thousand casualties.*

22 July

*Writing in the
Manchester
Guardian, George
Bernard Shaw asks
that Roger
Casement be
treated as a
prisoner of war.*

3 August

*Roger Casement is
hanged in
Pentonville prison.*

The interior of the Abbey Theatre

As early as November 1910 the Ulster Unionist Council had formed a secret committee to procure arms and form an army of resistance. English politicians such as Winston Churchill predicted that when the worst came to the worst, civil war would evaporate in uncivil words. But the Ulster unionists were serious, and when the Home Rule Bill was passed by the House of Commons in 1913 a Protestant militia, the Ulster Volunteer Force, began to take shape. Protestant support for the UVF was by no means universal, and there were protests from radical Presbyterian farmers and Liberals. But in April 1914 the UVF succeeded in landing 216 tons of rifles and ammunition at Larne and, in the first recorded military use of motor cars, dispersed them to prepared dumps around the province. After an absence of almost half a century, the gun had returned to Irish politics.

According to what can be gathered from inquiries, the match had been in progress for about fifteen minutes when a force of armed men arrived in lorries and armoured cars. It is difficult to discover what actually happened, but it appears from statements of spectators that during the progress of the match armed men in uniform arrived simultaneously at the four corners of the field. Almost immediately afterwards there was firing. There was great activity in the district by forces of the Crown, armoured cars and military lorries moving about, and a general stampede followed after the first volley.

A great many shots were fired, and numbers of people were injured by being knocked down in the rush and trampled upon in the scrimmage. After the shooting it was stated that the death toll was heavy.

The shooting was heard in the suburbs, and people were generally alarmed.

Going toward Clonliffe Road one could see excited persons hastening from the direction of Jones's Road, and at all the exits the same anxiety to get away was evident. Some people ran so quickly that they lost their hats and did not stop to search for them. The common object seemed to be a tramcar, and these vehicles were quickly crowded.

An *Irish Times* representative conversed with a number of men who said that they had just escaped from Jones's Road. One of these men, with some others, had lost his hat in rushing away, and he gave a vivid account of what he saw. He said that lorries and armoured cars arrived at the football ground and divided into four groups. The four corners of the field were occupied by the armed forces, and shots were fired from machine guns in armoured cars, and from rifles carried by the occupants of the lorries. A man who was standing beside him was shot and fell at his feet, and he then rushed away ...

In response to the rise of the UVF, nationalists had formed the Irish Volunteers in November 1913. By June 1914 the Volunteers, numbering 129,000, had been taken under the control of the Irish Party. *The Irish Times* understood the choice facing the country as one between 'settlement and civil war'; but for a conservative paper it was extraordinarily indulgent of the division of the country into two armed camps, neither of them under the control of the government. In May 1914 two editorials lauded both the Ulster Volunteers and the Irish Volunteers, on the grounds that, if civil war was to come to Ireland, it was better that it be fought by drilled and trained men than by violent mobs.

23 August
Greenwich mean time is introduced in Ireland in place of Dublin mean time (25 minutes behind Greenwich).

13 November
The Somme offensive ends with more than a million casualties suffered by the British, French, and Germans.

One of the many Guinness warehouses in Dublin. The great brewery was the biggest employer in the city in the early years of the century.

Éamon de Valera arrives home on 18 June 1917 in the aftermath of the Rising

7 December

David Lloyd George is appointed Prime Minister in a coalition government.

22–23 December

Interned insurgents are released from Frongoch and Reading jail, but those convicted remain behind bars.

It praised the 'proud spirit of the young men' in the Volunteers and reflected that 'the best elements of the young Nationalism of Ireland were fired at the example of Ulster's self-sacrifice and discipline.' Even in late July 1914, when the Irish Volunteers landed thousands of rifles at Howth and brought them into Dublin, a leading article acknowledged that a paper that had supported gun-running by loyalists in Ulster could not very well condemn similar actions by nationalists in Dublin. 'It is not for us to criticise the conduct of the Nationalist Volunteers in landing a cargo of rifles at Howth yesterday. We cannot fairly blame their almost exact imitation of deeds which we have not condemned in Ulster. The coup was cleverly and boldly made …'

The Irish Times opposed the Home Rule Bill on national rather than imperial grounds.

from The Irish Times 1921
17 AUGUST

Some Impressions of Dáil Éireann

Sinn Féin in the Flesh

First the opening of the Northern Parliament by His Majesty the King, then the hollow farce of the 'Southern Parliament' in the Department's building in Merrion Street, and now the Dáil. One approached the Mansion House yesterday morning in a certain spirit of adventure. One was about to meet Sinn Féin in the flesh and to see for oneself the men whose names have become household words throughout the country, and around whose figures popular legend has woven a web of almost mediæval romance. There was nothing romantic about the young men with green badges who were keeping order in Dawson

Street. This was downright efficiency, possibly a little over-accentuated through eagerness, but working with admirable ease. A late comer had his yellow ticket carefully inspected by a self-possessed youngster, and was ushered into the Mansion House by a courteous guide, for whom the young men on the steps evidently had great respect. Inside the Round Room the atmosphere was stifling, and every available seat was occupied. There must have been at least fifteen hundred people in that room, and, so far as could be seen, there was no ventilation, with the exception of the doors. The large space roped off for the members of the Dáil was empty, and one envied their prospective occupants the luxurious arm chairs inside the bar of the House. All sorts and conditions of men and women were among the spectators. The gallery was thronged, and the body of the house was a dense mass of intensely interested relatives and friends of the members.

Shortly after the scheduled hour the crowd sprang to its feet, and the tall figure of Mr de Valera could be seen striding through an avenue of clapping hands and agitated bodies. He was followed by his colleagues of the Sinn Féin ministry in

Ironically, the paper essentially agreed with the militant nationalists of Sinn Féin that there was no habitable half-way house between independence and union. 'There are only two conceivable forms of government for Ireland: government under the Act of Union and full self-government. The latter, however much Unionists might fear and hate it, would, at any rate, give the country incentives to generous action, fine enterprise, and courageous economies. This Bill robs us of the Union, and gives us none of the heroic possibilities of self-government. It is a mean, suspicious, nation-killing measure. For our present great position in the Empire it substitutes a status of fiercely invigilated subordination.' Instead of self-government Ireland would get 'perpetual and harried subservience to Imperial authority.'

The bill was passed by the House of Commons early in 1913, only to be duly and

29 December
James Joyce's A Portrait of the Artist as a Young Man *is published.*

1917

5 February
Count Plunkett, father of the executed Joseph Plunkett, wins the North Roscommon by-election but he declines to take his seat in the House of Commons.

Leinster Lawn in the dying days of British rule

8 March

A revolution in Russia leads to the establishment of a Provisional Government and the overthrow of the Tsar.

6 April

The British government proclaims meetings or processions between 8 and 15 April. The United States enters the war.

overwhelmingly rejected by the House of Lords. (It was not passed again by the House of Commons until May 1914, at which time it required only the royal signature to become law.) And while the bill was stalled the prospects of civil war rose. The Curragh Mutiny of March 1914, in which sixty officers under the command of General Gough offered to resign rather than lead their men against Ulster loyalists, placed *The Irish Times* in a difficult situation. It shared the mutineers' political views and their insistence that Ulster Protestant resistance could not and should not be crushed by force; but it was also horrified by 'the extraordinary gravity of the military crisis that has suddenly been superimposed upon the political crisis.' It tried to steer a middle course.

Indian file, and the remaining members of the Dáil in long procession. Mr O'Kelly, the Speaker of the old Dáil, took his seat in the leather-upholstered chair which, on a high dais, dominated the assembly. He was flanked on the right by the Lord Mayor of Dublin, and, on the left by Mr Frank Walsh, of the United States. Beneath him, to the right, Mr de Valera and the other Ministers—among whom, by the way, was Countess Markievicz without a hat—took their seats, and, as soon as the rank and file had distributed themselves on the cross benches—Mr Duggan being wise enough to secure one of the aforesaid arm chairs—the Speaker called upon the Reverend Father O'Flanagan to open the session with prayer. Thenceforth up to Mr de Valera's speech the proceedings were conducted in the Irish tongue. The new Speaker, Mr Eoin MacNeill, was elected and led to the chair by his predecessor, who was elegantly attired in morning dress.

Crowds welcome home republican prisoners at Westland Row station in 1917 following their release from Frongoch prison camp in Wales

The Irish Convention, which lasted from July 1917 to April 1918, was yet another attempt by Lloyd George to settle the home rule question. Here the suffragist Mrs Connery interposes herself between Andrew Bonar Law and Edward Carson, while a zealous member of the DMP springs into action on the right.

Taking the Oath

The administration of the oath of allegiance to the Irish Republic was very interesting. It was taken by all the members standing with upraised right hands, and, of course, was repeated after the Clerk of the House in Irish. As the members came up individually to sign the register one had a good opportunity of taking stock of the better-known men. The calling of Mr Michael Collins's name was the signal for an outburst of applause, which, however, was silenced quickly by the Volunteer stewards. Mr Collins's appearance upset all the preconceived ideas of one who had known him only through the newspapers. He is tall, with a slight leaning towards *embonpoint*, and, with a great mass of jet black hair, gave one the impression of an almost Falstaffian geniality. Unless his looks belie him, Mr Collins has an abundant sense of humour. Mr Barton was *debonnair* and very well groomed,

'That the Government should contemplate the use of armed force against the Covenanters of Ulster is tragic and terrible. That the forces of the Crown should refuse to obey the orders of the Executive is a matter even more important and more sinister.'

Yet the paper could not resist the temptation to rejoice at the mutineers' victory (the War Office refused to accept their resignations and told them that the government had no intention of taking offensive action against the Ulster Volunteers) and at the massive blow they had struck at the government's plans for home rule. 'We congratulate the officers on their vindication. Especially do we congratulate General Gough, whose fearless and honourable

10 May

Joseph McGuinness wins the South Longford by-election for Sinn Féin while still in prison.

16 June

Republican prisoners are released from jail, including Constance Markievicz, Éamon de Valera, Joseph McGuinness, and Eoin MacNeill.

British troops search a car in Dublin during the War of Independence

10 July
Éamon de Valera is elected for Sinn Féin in the East Clare by-election.

23 July
Constance Markievicz, recently released from prison, is granted the freedom of the borough of Sligo.

25 July
The Irish Convention opens in an attempt to resolve the Irish question.

conduct has added lustre to the laurels of a great Irish family. We do not recant what we said yesterday about the gravity of these unfortunate events in the Army, or the vital necessity of maintaining the highest possible standard of military discipline and obedience. But all the blame rests on the government.'

The threat of civil war was not just a domestic affair. It was also one of the factors encouraging Germany to believe that it could win a war on Britain and its allies. Europe was increasingly locked into a complex set of alliances between the rival imperial powers— Germany and Austria-Hungary on the one side, France, Russia, Turkey and, perhaps, Britain on the other. Uncertainty about Britain's likely role in a Continental war was an important restraint on Germany's military ambitions. But the crisis in Ireland, and its divisive impact on British

while his cousin, Mr Erskine Childers, looked rather worn and pale. Mr J.J. McKeon, whose approach to the table was greeted with uproarious enthusiasm, is the athlete *pur sang*. He, too, was different from what one had expected him to be. One of the most interesting figures of all was Mr Richard Mulcahy. Quiet, rather delicate-looking, and with features cast in an austere mould, he seems to be a man who is rather shy, but full of nervous energy.

A pathetic impression was made by Mrs O'Callaghan in her widow's weeds. Mr Brugha was unobtrusive, and confined his activities to occasional remarks to Count Plunkett. The others were mostly young men, very serious, and evidently impressed by the solemnity and magnitude of the task that awaits them. With a few exceptions they seemed to be well under forty years of age, and only one of them, Mr Pierce Beasley, who looked rather shaken, showed any outward signs of the ill-effects of his recent experiences.

When Mr de Valera got up to speak every body held his breath. What was he going to say? His first few sentences

Constance Markievicz

were terse and to the point, and one was impressed by the excellence of his delivery. 'We are not Republican *doctrinaires,*' he exclaimed, and a flash of hope lit up the atmosphere. But it soon disappeared. Speaking with great emphasis and obvious sincerity, Mr de Valera soared into the realms of pure theory and lofty idealism. One felt that like Yeats's poet he was hiding his head amid a crowd of stars; and reality began to dissolve in the quickening flow of his eloquence. One's thoughts were carried back to the frosty January morning in the Clock Room of the French Foreign Office when President Wilson was making his famous speech at the opening of the Paris Peace Conference. One had the same impression of moral fervour and passionate sincerity and the same unwelcome conviction that disillusionment lay in store. As a shrewd observer of human affairs remarked on that occasion when the American President resumed his seat. '*C'est magnifique*; but it is not hard tacks.'

politics, suggested that Britain could be neutralised. The American ambassador to Germany reported that it was 'believed by the Germans that Ireland would rise in rebellion the moment war was declared.' In Berlin, General von Bernhardt was sure that the Irish situation would paralyse Britain 'if it ever comes to war with England,' and Field Marshal Conrad von Hotzendorff felt that the Ulster crisis would give him a free hand. As the historian George Fielding Eliot puts it, 'there is little doubt that both German statesmen and leading German soldiers believed that Britain was hopelessly divided and not to be reckoned with in the European situation.'[19]

That situation was one in which almost any crisis could spark war on a massive scale. The

10 August
The Kilkenny borough by-election is won by William T. Cosgrave for Sinn Féin.

25 September
The republican prisoner Thomas Ashe dies in Mountjoy prison in Dublin after he is forcibly fed during his hunger strike.

crisis came in the Balkans, where trouble had been simmering since 1908, when Austria-Hungary annexed the provinces of Bosnia and Herzegovina, formally under Turkish control. Serbia, dreaming of the establishment of a Greater Serbia, had designs on the same territory and mobilised its army. Germany and Austria, however, forced Serbia, and its Russian allies, to accept the annexation. A deep sense of humiliation fed nationalist sentiment in Serbia. On 28 June 1914 the Archduke Franz Ferdinand, heir-apparent to the Austrian throne (ironically, the member of the ruling elite most sympathetic to nationalist demands), and his wife were assassinated in Sarajevo by a young Serbian nationalist, Gavrilo Princip.

What followed was a chain reaction in which individual causes had a cumulatively explosive effect. Austria threatened Serbia; Russia supported the Serbs; Germany supported Austria; France supported Russia. Germany declared war on Russia on 1 August and on France on 3 August. The following morning the Germans crossed into Belgium on their way to attack France. When a British ultimatum to withdraw from Belgium was ignored, Britain declared war on Germany. Ireland, as part of the United Kingdom, was at war.

In its edition of 5 August 1914 *The Irish Times* rejoiced that 'the call to arms has come. At eleven o'clock last night Great Britain declared war on Germany. We are glad that the formal declaration has come from our own Government, and not from the enemies who forced the quarrel upon us. This is the fitting answer to a direct and insolent challenge. The whole nation will welcome the ending of suspense.' In this exultation the paper was in tune with the general mood throughout Europe. On every side the rhetoric of violence was dominant. Marxists who confidently predicted that the workers of the world would never slaughter each other in the name of their ruling classes were stunned by the almost immediate collapse of the international socialist movement into rival

John Redmond staked his political future on his support for the British war effort. It was to prove a fatal blunder.

from The Irish Times
7 DECEMBER **1921**

The Treaty

The Irish situation has undergone a swift and almost bewildering change. Men rubbed their eyes yesterday like people who step suddenly from darkness into sunshine. Forty-eight hours ago a renewal of civil warfare seemed imminent. Today we are offered, in Lord Birkenhead's words, 'the sure and certain hope' of peace—not only of peace in Ireland, but of a *pax Hibernica* throughout the English-speaking world. 'A Treaty between Great Britain and Ireland' was signed in the small hours of yesterday morning by the leaders of the British Government and the plenipotentiaries of *Sinn Féin*. If the Treaty is ratified by the British Parliament and by the Southern Irish Parliament, the Free State of Ireland will come into existence before the end of 1922. It will have the same *status* as Canada in the community of nations known as the British Empire. In other words, it will have complete control of its own finance, customs and excise, and internal affairs. The British Government retains certain naval rights which satisfy the Admiralty; but Ireland may establish a military defence force on a proportional basis. The members of her Legislatures will take an oath of allegiance to the Free State and will swear fidelity to the King as Head of the Empire. She will pay her share of the war debt, subject to legitimate counter-claims which will be decided by arbitration. No law of the new State shall impose disabilities on account of religious belief or in the field of education. An important article of the treaty safeguards the rights of judges, police, and other public servants under the Government of Ireland Act. Such are the main terms of the charter which, if it is ratified and executed, will constitute the greatest transaction in Anglo-Irish history. If the plans of Downing Street and Washington prove to be

imperial armies. Intellectuals everywhere welcomed the war as a test of manly virtue, an opportunity for a great cleansing, a rite of passage into a more uplifting world, the cauldron of spiritual awakening.

As well as this general enthusiasm there was for *The Irish Times* a more particular reason for welcoming the war. It seemed, at a stroke, to cut through all the hopelessly knotted complications of loyalty and rebellion, empire and nationality. Home rule was, for the moment, out of the question. Ulster Volunteers and Irish Volunteers, at one moment heading for a civil war, were at the next moment gallant allies in the anti-German cause. The Irish Party leader John

Ireland is introduced in the House of Commons.

16 April
The Irish Conscription Act becomes law, but it is never implemented.

18 April
A conference is held in the Mansion House against conscription and is

John Redmond and Joe Devlin MP inspecting a detachment of National Volunteers in the Phoenix Park in 1915

attended by
nationalist and
republican
representatives.

21 April

*An anti-conscription
pledge is taken by
people throughout
Ireland. Two days
later there is a
national one-day
strike.*

23 April

*Much of Ireland
comes to a standstill
in a one-day strike
in protest at the
possible introduction
of conscription.*

Redmond, long a *bête noire* for *The Irish Times*,
earned its approval by pledging Irish support for
the war effort and in September urging the
Volunteers to join up and fight in France and
Flanders. This led to a split in the Volunteers,
with the vast majority (possibly 150,000 men)
supporting Redmond in splitting off to form the
National Volunteers and only a minority of
between 3,000 and 10,000 remaining as the more
radical Irish Volunteers. Underlying the paper's
euphoria in August and September was the belief
that the war would shock Ireland out of its
squabbles and transform its politics for the future.

In 1914 it was a full century since there had
been a large-scale war involving a majority of the
world powers. Those wars that had been fought
on a large scale, the Crimean War of the
eighteen-fifties and the Franco-Prussian War of
1870–71, had been relatively brief; nothing like
the thirty-one years of almost incessant conflict
that would develop between 1914 and 1945

equally successful, 1921 will stand as an *annus mirabilis* in
the records of the world. The King has been 'overjoyed to
hear the splendid news.'

One question remains. Will the Treaty hasten the event
towards which everything that was best in the heart and soul
and brain of the Irish people has yearned for a hundred
years? Will it give us now, or in the near future, a united
Ireland? Everything will depend on the spirit in which the Free
State applies itself to its greatest task. Here will be the
supreme test of its fitness for the tremendous responsibilities
which the Imperial Parliament will be asked to confer upon it.
The machinery which the Conference has contrived for
bringing Ulster into the national fold is exceedingly
ingenious. We may agree with Lord Birkenhead that the
Government has kept its promise to Ulster. She remains free
from coercion and she will be protected against any menace
of coercion. Nevertheless, strong inducements towards unity
will begin to accumulate from the moment when the Free
State is formed. The State will include North-East Ulster; but
within a month from the passing of the Act she may
withdraw herself by means of an address to the King. In that

National Volunteers at rifle practice

Thomas Traynor of the Irish Volunteers was hanged in Mountjoy jail on 25 April 1921, while members of Cumann na mBan recited the Rosary outside the prison gates

event Ulster will retain all her existing powers and privileges under the Government of Ireland Act; but her decision will involve a new delimitation of the Northern boundaries. She will continue to pay her taxes to the Imperial Exchequer and, if Southern Ireland is so well and economically governed that Southern taxation is lower than Imperial taxation, a mighty lever in favour of unity will begin to operate in the commercial North. If and when Belfast turns its face towards Dublin, the Treaty offers it a variety of safeguards for its fiscal and industrial interests and for the protection of minorities. At this stage we can say only—but we say it with sincere satisfaction—that at last the foundations of Irish unity have been laid. Will Ireland build upon them?

We shall not indulge in premature felicitations. Though the whole outlook has been transformed, the future is still uncertain. It is possible that the Imperial Parliament may hold that the promise of Irish peace has been bought too dearly. It is possible that *Dáil Éireann* may raise objections on the question of allegiance. The decisions of both assemblies may be affected by Ulster's attitude to the new agreement. One

seemed conceivable. But wars had previously been waged for limited and specific ends. The First World War was, as the historian Eric Hobsbawm put it, 'waged for unlimited ends.'[20] Each of the major powers believed that its future economic growth would depend on political and military dominance. And economic growth itself seemed limitless. The spoils of victory would not be measured in territory or captives but in the indefinable but infinitely alluring possibility of being able to set the terms for the progress of the twentieth century itself. With such a huge, abstract end in mind, the powers of Europe embraced a conflict that would, they thought, give a shape to the coming decades.

Yet at the start of the war, few suspected that it would in fact be a defining moment, not just for the twentieth century but for civilisation. A few visionaries, such as the Polish-Russian industrialist Ivan Blokh in his *Technical, Economic*

17 May

Arthur Griffith, Constance Markievicz, Éamon de Valera, William T. Cosgrave and eighty other prominent republicans are arrested in a fictitious 'German Plot'.

20 June

Arthur Griffith wins the East Cavan by-election for Sinn Féin.

Standing in the ruins of the Custom House following its destruction by the Irish Volunteers, 26 May 1921

3 July

The Irish Volunteers, Sinn Féin and the Gaelic League are proscribed.

16 July

Tsar Nicholas of Russia and his family are murdered by the Bolsheviks.

10 October

The mail steamer Leinster is sunk

and Political Aspects of the Coming War, published in 1898, and the Austrian peace campaigner Bertha von Suttner, had predicted a catastrophic war of attrition, with trench warfare, mass slaughter, and huge social and political convulsions. But the scale of what was to happen, with 20 million soldiers under arms in August 1914 and 65 million by 1918, was so far beyond anything in history that it was almost unfathomable.

In the entire nineteenth century the total number of deaths caused by all the wars waged throughout the world was about 19.4 million. In the Great War, 26 million would die, half of them civilians killed by the malnutrition, disease, lack of medical care and the breakdown of social services that resulted from the conflict. A further

thing, however, is certain. If this Treaty is ratified, if Irishmen of all creeds and parties combine to administer it in a spirit of broad-minded patriotism, if it bridges the gap between North and South, if it reconciles Ireland to the Empire—if it gives us all these blessings, it will be one of the most fruitful and most glorious achievements of modern statesmanship. It will close a hideous era of strife and bloodshed and will open a new era of material and intellectual progress. It will give to the rising generation in Ireland a scope for effort and prospects of happiness that their fathers never knew. Nobody will welcome it more gladly than the loyalists of Southern Ireland. For them Ireland does not exist, and never will exist, apart from the Empire which the blood of their sires and sons has cemented. If Ireland accepts the Empire with her heart, and not merely in the cautious wording of an oath, and if she accepts themselves as Imperial Irishmen, they will come joyfully to her aid. The

The Great Square in Royal (Collins) Barracks following the truce. There would not be many more displays like this by the British military in Dublin.

Southern loyalists' gifts of education, character, and experience are essential to the building up of a new nationhood. They will rejoice to put those gifts into the common stock. During the darkest hours, they never lost their faith in Ireland's high destiny. Will that faith be rewarded now?

from The Irish Times 1921
20 DECEMBER

The Two Voices

Yesterday Mr Arthur Griffith and Mr Michael Collins invited Dáil Éireann to ratify the Articles of Agreement between Great Britain and Ireland. Mr de Valera, Mr Austin Stack, and Mr Erskine Childers were the chief opponents of the Treaty; and we use the language of moderation when we say that the mass of the Irish people will

20 million would be maimed, permanently shell-shocked, or otherwise disabled. So immense was the war that some of its individual battles inflicted more casualties than entire wars of previous eras. In the Battle of the Somme alone, half a million French, German and British soldiers were killed, more than in the two big wars of the late nineteenth century—the Franco-Prussian and the US-Spanish wars—put together. Who could imagine such slaughter or expect that three times as many people would die in wars between 1914 and 1999 than in all the wars in all previous recorded history?[21]

And the war was unprecedented in another sense as well: it was truly global. Every state in Europe was involved, with the exceptions of

by a German torpedo while en route to Holyhead from Dún Laoghaire. More than five hundred people are killed.

1 November
The Irish Labour Party announces that it will not stand in the coming general election.

Michael Collins addresses a mass meeting in Cork

11 November

An armistice is declared on the western front in the Great War.

12 December

John Dillon becomes leader of the Irish Party.

28 December

The results of the post-war general election give Sinn

Spain, the Netherlands, the three Scandinavian countries, and Switzerland. Almost one-and-a-half million Indians served with the British army. Canadians joined up in large numbers, while Australia and New Zealand forged their national consciousness on the Aegean peninsula of Gallipoli. Africans fought for the French, and Chinese labour battalions were employed by the combatants in western Europe. Japan joined the war soon after it started, planning to take over Germany's possessions in the Far East and the Western Pacific. Even before the United States joined in the fighting in 1917 the war was shaping American society in the most profound ways. The economic boom it created drew thousands of

read their speeches with mingled feelings of anger and despair. If they are to have their way, the hunt for the chimera of absolute independence is about to be renewed. It was always hopeless, but—if there are degrees of hopelessness—its renewal will be the most hopeless adventure for which a people ever sacrificed their peace and the blood of their young men. Until Great Britain made her astonishingly generous offer to Ireland the Sinn Féin movement enjoyed a large measure of foreign sympathy—not as a Republican movement, but as a struggle for the just and reasonable rights of nationhood. All those rights are now Ireland's, to take or reject. None of the hostile arguments yesterday was able to discredit the Treaty as a real concession to this country of all, and more than all, for which her sons have striven through seven hundred years. Ireland is now a nation without any grievance that could induce any other nation to lift a finger or contribute a sixpence in her defence. The world applauds the British Empire's greatest act of Imperial magnanimity. It judges Britain to be wholly in the right, and will judge Ireland, if she rejects the Treaty, to be wholly in the wrong. Yet for the sake of an impossible idea—indeed, as it seems, for the sake of a mere quibble—Mr de Valera and his supporters are ready to drag Ireland down from the topmost pinnacle of hope fulfilled into the old slough of misery and despond ...

The goal of every member of Dáil Éireann is a united Ireland; but yesterday's discussions have not served the cause of a united Ireland. Some of the speeches will disappoint and alarm the loyalist minority in the South and West. They have accepted the Agreement as a final declaration of peace between Great Britain and Ireland. They were encouraged to put their fears and prejudices behind them by the hope that

black workers from the rural south to the industrial cities of the north, setting off the Great Migration, which would transform urban life, politics and race relations in the coming decades.

In the first year of the war eighty thousand Irishmen enlisted in the British army, including thirty thousand UVF men, who formed the 36th (Ulster) Division. The war seemed to have created the national unity that had eluded the politicians. With both Carson and Redmond urging their followers to join up, and only a small minority of the Irish Volunteers rejecting Redmond's policy, it seemed possible that the small conflicts of Ireland would be submerged in the greater confrontation. In all, some 206,000 men from Ireland, along with tens of thousands of Irish emigrants in England

Féin 73 of the 103 Irish seats. Constance Markievicz is the first woman to win a seat in the British House of Commons.

1919

21 January
Sinn Féin establishes Dáil Éireann, the first

Members of the Dublin Labour Conference at Liberty Hall in 1921

parliament in Dublin since 1800. On the same day an IRA party, including Dan Breen, kills two RIC men at Solloghod, Co. Tipperary. The Anglo-Irish War begins.

31 January
An tÓglach, the paper of the Irish

and Scotland, would serve during the war, and about 30,000 would die.

Partly because of censorship and partly because all the main newspapers supported the war, there was no critical coverage of the military's tactics and no real reflection of the horror of life in the trenches. The Catholic Bishop of Limerick, Edward O'Dwyer, summed up the coverage in his Lenten pastoral letter of 1917: 'All the newspapers are on the same note. Unionist and Nationalist, they are all on the side of the war ... The people read nothing but war, war: hatred of Germany, the certainty of victory, but never a word of human responsibilities and the torrents of innocent blood that are crying to God from the earth.'

the Irish Free State would settle down to the task of making this country a peaceful and progressive partner in the community of the Empire. Are they to learn now that, even if the Agreement is ratified by a small majority, a section of Irishmen will refuse to be bound by it? They expect a constitutional Opposition in the Irish Free State, as in all free States; but are the first workings of our own infant State to be harried by the hostility of an unconstitutional Opposition? Is the dreary maxim, *Plus ça change, plus c'est la même chose,* to be true of the new Ireland with her Canadian *status*? Again, Ireland will not be Ireland without Ulster. Will Ulster's misgivings be abated by the menace of an unappeased sentiment of hostility to the Imperial allegiance in an Ireland from which the last remnant of the Imperial forces will have been withdrawn? The Dáil must ratify the Agreement, but

The last Lord Lieutenant of Ireland, Lord FitzAlan of Derwent, takes the salute in Dublin in 1921

mere ratification will not suffice. The manner of its ratification must prove that Mr Griffith, not Mr de Valera, is the authentic spokesman of the Irish people.

from The Irish Times 1922
4 APRIL

More Light on Castlebar
No Regard for Free Speech

Experience of previous pro-Treaty meetings prepared one for the tactics that were adopted to prevent the assembly at Castlebar. Displacing railway tracks, blocking roads, cutting wires, 'holding up' motor cars—these were already common features at political meetings—but the uniformed interrupters were hitherto absent. They were to be seen at frequent intervals in the large crowd which assembled on the square, and they kept shouting and gesticulating while Mr Collins was addressing the meeting. There were many civilians also who indulged persistently in interruptions, and it was obvious that there was a good leavening of anti-Treaty civilians in the crowd. Mr Collins, however, had a big following, mainly drawn from the town, as his outside supporters were unable to reach the venue.

There was nothing unusual in the interruptions until Mr Campbell, solicitor, of Swinford, attempted to harangue the crowd from a motor car drawn up beside the motor lorry from which Mr Collins was speaking. As this second 'Richmond,' an elderly gentleman of impassive demeanour, appeared there was a storm of boohing, and the proceedings became distinctly lively. Mr Collins invited him to bring along the typewritten list of questions which he was calmly waving in his hand. Mr Campbell, quite unperturbed by a hurricane of groans, made his way on to the lorry, and endeavoured to make himself heard, but the din was deafening.

Mr Collins spoke to Mr Campbell, and the last-named was seen to shake his head. Mr Collins was heard to shout, 'He won't give them to me.' He then endeavoured to continue his speech, but he was interrupted by Mr Campbell's declaring that he was afraid to answer his questions.

An attempt was made to get at Mr Campbell, but it was frustrated by some clergymen, and Mr Campbell said that he did not want physical force.

The Rev. Father Joyce appealed for order, but Mr Campbell declared that he did not want this clergyman to

Revolutionaries: Seán Mac Eoin and Seán Moylan in 1922

The Irish Times was certainly no exception. Long after the early hopes for a noble and uplifting war had been ground down by the brutal realities, it clung to the belief that the suffering was somehow ennobling. During the Battle of the Somme, while the Ulster Division was being torn asunder, with 5,500 of its men dead or wounded on the first two days alone, an editorial suggested that Ireland was better off than peaceful and prosperous America, then still holding aloof. 'It will seem to many of us that we are living today on a higher plane of thought and feeling than those fortunate neutrals on the other side of the Atlantic. To-day the United Kingdom is living more intensely, more nobly, more seriously, than

Volunteers, declares that every volunteer is entitled to use 'all legitimate methods of warfare against the soldiers and policemen of the English usurper, and to slay them if it is necessary to do so to overcome their resistance.'

General Eoin O'Duffy (centre left with holster) and other officers of the fledgling Free State army

3 February

Éamon de Valera escapes from Lincoln jail in England.

9 February

The Irish Labour Party and Trades Union Congress demands a 44-hour working week and a minimum weekly wage of 50 shillings (£2.50) for adults.

it has ever lived before. It is being purified by suffering and sacrifice. Discipline has brought out its best, and submerged its weakest, qualities. There is hardly a household which is not sanctified by great sorrow, or does not glow with the pride of gallant deeds done by those who, before the war, were careless schoolboys or quiet men of affairs. In spite of all our bereavement, our anxiety, and our financial losses, we feel the exultation of a people that is living up to the greatest tradition of its past, and is fighting in the noblest cause that ever inspired a soldier.'

In the month ending 15 April 1916, 1,827 Irishmen joined the British army, 448 of them in Dublin. For the authorities, the overwhelming priority was to keep this flow of recruits going

interfere. Amid the ensuing din there were shouts of 'Who stoned Michael Davitt?' but Mr Campbell remained unmoved, and declared that Mr Collins was a faithful subject of King George. This retort stung Mr Collins to the quick, and he replied, angrily: 'Your conduct is worthy of your record: you took good care to be in jail when there was danger.'

Rushing the Lorry, A Revolver Drawn

There was another rush towards Mr Campbell, who again declared that he did not want physical force used. Mr McCabe, MP, and others endeavoured to calm the crowd near the lorry, but excitement reached fever pitch, and there was much commotion. The lorry began to move slightly, as if an attempt were made to take it away. Several of those who had been interrupting Mr Collins made a rush towards it, and Mr McCabe, who was standing near the driver's seat, drew a revolver. Those who were approaching halted for a moment, and produced revolvers also.

There were a few moments of painful tension, and it looked as if a terrible tragedy was about to be enacted. Revolvers flashed, seemingly by the score, as by this time Mr McCabe's supporters had gathered round him, and also flourished weapons. Portion of the crowd took to flight, fearing the worst. Mr McCabe's uniformed opponents declared that they would arrest him. An angry scene ensued, and a priest rushed up and declared that they would not do so.

The dramatic scene was interrupted in a startling manner. A tall, young man was seen dashing through the highly-strung crowd, and being pursued by officers in uniform. He rushed down a side street, and several shots were heard. Many women screamed, and others fainted, but the crowd generally remained around the lorry, where Mr Collins maintained his post. There was a lull in the excitement, and he proceeded with his speech. He was now the sole 'Richmond' on the lorry, as his antagonist had vanished.

After a few minutes had elapsed an officer in uniform came on the platform, and addressing Mr Collins, said:— 'Aren't you ashamed of the man who shot the woman?' Amid cheers, Mr Collins replied:—'Everyone here knows I am not responsible for that.'

General Richard Mulcahy

and to avoid any action that might stir up nationalist resentment. This involved turning a blind eye to the increasingly flagrant drilling of the Irish Volunteers. As Sir Matthew Nathan told a royal commission, as reported by *The Irish Times* in May 1916, the difficulty for the authorities was that they could not suppress the 'disloyal' Irish Volunteers without also disarming the 'loyal' Ulster Volunteers and Redmond's National Volunteers. 'In the circumstances, especially if the Volunteers to resist Home Rule had been allowed to continue, the Nationalist union would have been completely alienated, and with it that large body of Irish feeling which had been favourable to Great Britain and the war, and had sent some 55,000 Irish Catholics to fight for the Empire.'

The authorities found it particularly difficult to read the feelings of ordinary people, especially in Dublin. As the Chief Secretary, Augustine Birrell, put it before the same inquiry, 'I always felt I was very ignorant of what was actually going on in the minds and cellars, if you like, of the Dublin population.' He and his advisers were taken aback, then, when, on the morning of 24 April 1916, a faction of the Irish Volunteers and the small Irish Citizen Army seized buildings around Dublin and declared an Irish Republic.

Like all the Dublin newspapers, *The Irish Times* was directly affected by the rising. The paper's reserve printing office in Abbey Street was raided by the rebels in the early morning of Tuesday 25 April, and the huge bales of newsprint stored there were used to make a formidable barricade. The office was set ablaze, probably by British army shelling, on Thursday 27 April, and the conflagration spread across the barricade, eventually destroying much of Lower Abbey Street and O'Connell Street. There were even some *Irish Times* employees among the rebels. A clerk, Edward Keegan, wounded at the South Dublin Union, was subsequently sacked for 'disloyalty'.

But the main *Irish Times* office was saved from insurgent occupation or British army shelling by raking fire from loyalists in Trinity

19 December

Republicans attempt to assassinate Viscount French in the Phoenix Park.

22 December

Lloyd George's Better Government of Ireland Bill proposes two home rule governments, one for the six north-eastern counties of Ulster and another for the rest of the country, to come into effect in May 1920.

College, which kept the rebels out of Westmoreland Street. For much of the rising, therefore, *The Irish Times* was the only newspaper on the streets. On the second day of the rising the *Irish Independent* managed to get an edition out, but on 26 and 27 April and again on 1 and 2 May *The Irish Times* was the only source of news. On two days, 28 and 29 April, however, gunfire in Westmoreland Street was so heavy and continuous that it was impossible to move about safely, and the paper did not make it to the streets.

On the days it did appear the paper carried the government's martial law proclamations, but because of censorship and the practical difficulty of getting access to the areas where the fighting was heaviest it was not otherwise able to report in any detail on the conflict. It filled its pages

'Proclaimed', 'In the Interests of Peace'

A second officer suddenly appeared and announced that the meeting was 'proclaimed in the interests of peace.' Then somebody started the engine, and the lorry, containing some priests and ladies and Colonel Moore, was hurriedly driven away, but Mr Collins, profiting probably by his Dungarvan experience, jumped off before it got going.

The meeting then came to an abrupt close, and Mr Collins and his colleagues returned to their hotel ...

from The Irish Times
17 APRIL 1922

Critical Days

Irishmen are living on the edge of a volcano, and have come to be thankful for every hour which spares them the horrors of an eruption. In spite of sinister portents the peace has been kept during the last two days. Easter

National Army recruiting office

Members of the National Army sailing for Cork Harbour to take republican positions in the rear during the Civil War

Sunday was a calm and quiet festival in Dublin. Mr Arthur Griffith exercised without mishap his right to plead the cause of the Treaty with the citizens of Sligo. We may hope now that the anniversary of the Rebellion of 1916 will be allowed to pass without disturbance. Mr Rory O'Connor has declared that the seizure of the Four Courts is not the beginning of a *coup d'état* and that his forces do not contemplate a revolution. We are quite ready to accept the assurance; for all Mr O'Connor's statements have been frank and candid. On the other hand, the Provisional Government presents to every form of provocation an attitude of careful restraint. It is keeping the troops of *Dáil Éireann* under strict control, and intends, we may infer, to rely less upon arms than on the support of a public opinion which becomes daily more conscious of the significance of recent events. The fighting men on both sides are reluctant to commit themselves to the tragedy of civil war, and the people pray earnestly that it may be averted. Nevertheless, the situation is full of peril. The country is divided into two armed camps, and the normal activities of the Irish capital are paralysed by an all-pervading uncertainty. The task of the peace-makers has become terribly urgent.

with 'special articles of literary interest and some items of local events.' On the Thursday, for example, an editorial declared that 'there is little or no news (we frankly admit)' in the paper. A leader had been written calling on all true patriots to stand firm, but the censor struck it out and it was replaced with a bizarrely frivolous piece enquiring 'how many citizens of Dublin have any real knowledge of the works of Shakespeare? Could any better occasion … be afforded than the co-incidence of enforced domesticity with the poet's tercentenary?'

Nevertheless copies of the paper were sold by news vendors for as much as a shilling each. The city was infested with rumours. The novelist James Stephens met 'a wild individual who spat rumour as though his mouth were a machine gun or a linotype machine … He said the Germans had landed in three places. One of these landings alone consisted of fifteen thousand men. The other landings probably beat that figure. The whole city of Cork was in the hands of the Volunteers, and,

2 January

The RIC enrols demobilised British recruits, who soon become known as the Black and Tans.

15 January

Elections take place for boroughs and urban districts. Sinn Féin, with other nationalists and the Labour Party, wins control of 172 out of 206 councils, including 72 out of the 127 municipal councils.

20 March

Thomas MacCurtain, Lord Mayor of Cork, is shot dead by the RIC. On 17 April the inquest returns a verdict of wilful murder against the RIC and indicts Lloyd George and the British government.

16–19 May

A 'soviet' is established at the central creamery in Knocklong, Co. Limerick.

to that extent, might be said to be peaceful. German warships had defeated the English, and their transports were speeding from every side. The whole country was up, and the garrison was out-numbered by one hundred to one.'[22]

Even the official news published in *The Irish Times* was read with suspicion. On Wednesday, Stephens got a copy of the paper. 'It contained a new military proclamation and a statement that the country was peaceful, and told that in Sackville Street [O'Connell Street] some houses were burned to the ground ... Into the newspaper statement that peace reigned in the country one was inclined to read more of disquietude than of truth, and one said: Is the country so extraordinarily peaceful that it can be dismissed in three lines? There is too much peace or too much reticence, but it will be some time before we hear from outside of Dublin.'

The paper made up for the absence of immediate coverage by publishing a triple issue of the *Weekly Irish Times* on 13 May, with full details of the fighting, lists of casualties, the names of prisoners sentenced and deported, and photographs of the protagonists. It proved, as the paper reported, 'immensely popular and had a colossal circulation, which far exceeded anything ever previously claimed by any Dublin newspaper—morning, evening, or weekly.' Updated and expanded, it was republished in 1917 and became a standard reference work on the history of the rising.

The paper obviously had better sources on the government side than among the rebels. It thought, for example, that the Edinburgh-born James Connolly was 'a Monaghan man' and that Patrick Pearse may have 'intended to occupy the post of Provost of Trinity College in the event of the rebellion being a success.' But its reporters did capture the human tragedies, ironies and ambiguities of the conflict. They described the fate of Thomas Moran Jozé, a well-known Dublin chemist, shot dead by the rebels because, being deaf, he failed to respond to a challenge from a sentry; of the former editor of the *Northern*

Terence MacSwiney, Lord Mayor of Cork, who died in Brixton jail, London, after a hunger strike of seventy-four days.

If the conference of political leaders can arrange a *modus vivendi* on Wednesday, the cause of peace will receive a very important reinforcement. The united voice of the conference would be the united voice of both parties in the existing Parliament of Southern and Western Ireland. Messrs de Valera and Brugha are not asked to repudiate the Republican policy. They are asked only to recognise the people's right to vote freely upon the Treaty—not necessarily for the Treaty—at the coming elections, and to co-operate in the task of maintaining a *régime* of law. We never have been able to fathom Mr de Valera's objections to this natural course, and our perplexity is increased by his speech yesterday at Tullamore. He said that the Treaty did not exist for the people until they had given it the sanction of their votes; but why is he unwilling to put the Treaty to the test of a general election? The more free the elections are, the more free will the people be to reject the Treaty, if they so desire. Does Mr de Valera profess to know the people's mind better than the people themselves know it? He said, too, that the elections of 1918 gave the Republic 'a democratic basis which could not be questioned anywhere.' If the register was so satisfactory in 1918, why is it not good enough for 1922? Mr de Valera suggested also that the people had not studied the text of the Treaty—that they had allowed the newspapers to mislead them. The proposed Constitution of the Free State will be submitted to the electors in June. Would any English autocrat venture to hint that Irish democracy could not be trusted to form its own judgment on its own affairs?

The only true, the only sound, the only democratic principle is that which Messrs Griffith and Collins defended yesterday at Sligo and Naas. The people know what they want, and it is the people, not Mr Collins, Mr de Valera, or Mr O'Connor, who must decide. The Provisional Government offers peace with Great Britain, prosperity and virtual independence for the Free State, and a substantial prospect of union between North and South. Mr de Valera offers a Republic to which, as Mr Churchill has told us, Great Britain would be hostile from the outset. In his Easter message to the country, Mr de Valera says: 'Ireland is yours for the taking! Take it!' How does he propose to take North-East Ulster? On this point, and on many others in the Republican programme, the people await enlightenment. Mr de Valera

Standard in Monaghan, Lieutenant T. J. Kennedy, who was mentioned in dispatches for his attempts to protect the Catholic Pro-Cathedral while commanding British forces in the area and who was killed a few months later fighting with the Ulster Division at the Battle of the Somme; of Second Lieutenant A. L. Lucas, shot dead by his own soldiers in Guinness's brewery when they mistakenly came to the conclusion that he was a rebel sympathiser; of Robert Mackenzie, who survived the sinking by the Germans of the liner *Lusitania* only to be killed by a stray bullet that hit him as he was sitting in his shop in Rutland Square (Parnell Square); of Count Casimir Markievicz, who was fighting with the Russian army in alliance with Britain while his wife, Constance, was taking a leading role with the rebels in alliance with Germany.[23]

While clearly on the side of the government, *The Irish Times* nevertheless gave

12 August
The Lord Mayor of Cork, Alderman Terence MacSwiney, is arrested by the British army.

23–31 August
Riots, arson and intimidation in Belfast claim thirty lives.

20 September
The Black and Tans sack Balbriggan, Co. Dublin.

National Army troops line up for inspection in Munster during the Civil War

De Valera addresses an anti-conscription meeting

28 September

Mallow, Co. Cork, is sacked by the British.

14 October

The IRA leader Seán Treacy is shot dead in a gun battle with British forces in Talbot Street, Dublin.

detailed and extensive coverage to atrocities by the army. When Captain J. C. Bowen-Colthurst of the Royal Irish Rifles was court-martialled in June for the murders of Francis Sheehy-Skeffington, Patrick McIntyre and Thomas Dickson in Portobello Barracks, the paper published a full account of the evidence. Likewise, it gave a long account of the inquest in May on the bodies of Patrick Bealen and James Healy, two working men shot dead by the army in North King Street.

In one sense the rising was a protest against the imperial system that had plunged the world into carnage. But in another, it was itself a part of will have every opportunity to give it to them in the next few weeks. He can address meetings, without fear of disturbance, in every one of the twenty-six counties. The columns of every Irish newspaper, including this newspaper, will be open to him. If his cause is the people's cause, it will prevail. If he is a real democrat, he will accept the people's verdict, whatever that verdict may be. We are very unwilling to suppose that any section of the Irish Army would set itself above the people's choice after that choice had been declared freely according to the custom of all civilised lands. The first safeguard of free elections must be an agreement of the political leaders in their favour, and the country expects and requires such agreement as the outcome of the Mansion House Conference.

from The Irish Times 1922
1 MAY

Repertory Theatres

A Dublin Experiment

One might imagine that the people of Dublin obtained enough drama in their ordinary lives without frequenting the theatre. Why pay for a seat in the pit when you can stand outside the Dáil and see comedians and tragedians for nothing? Who can expect to be thrilled by the pistol shot in 'Bulldog Drummond' if he is fortunate enough to live near Beggars' Bush? And yet the play seems to be flourishing in our midst. The Dublin Drama League has closed its activities for the year with a credit balance, the Rathmines and Rathgar Amateur Operatic Society is producing a Gilbert and Sullivan opera which has never been seen in the city, and no sooner is the Abbey Theatre vacated by its usual tenants than a season of repertory is to be installed therein ...

from The Irish Times 1922
10 MAY

Modern Magic

Science invents or discovers marvels, and society puts them to very common-place uses. Take, for instance, the contrast between the possibilities of a wireless telephone in every home and the actual use to which it is being put. The 'broad-casting' system is well established in the United States and is now being introduced on a large scale in England. For a few guineas you buy a box which is capable of transmitting to you, along with thousands of other box-holders, at fixed times of the day, the noblest thoughts and sweetest sounds that the world's wisdom and imagination can create. It is a miracle compared with which the fisherman's bottled genie pales into insignificance. If Plato could have foreseen this invention, he would have proposed a connection of all the home telephones with a centre from which a little band of the supremely good and wise would raise the intellectual stature of mankind. In fact, the typical American programme for a wireless telephone recital consists of a weather forecast, a 'bed-time story' for children, 'late news flashes,' police reports, and a popular concert. It appears that the typical English programme will be of a similar kind. Science has tamed Pegasus and commerce has harnessed him to a dray.

that carnage. The home front was getting a taste of life on the battlefield. The war itself had invaded the city. James Stephens, listening to the gunfire, noted that 'during daylight, at least, the sound is not sinister nor depressing, and the thought that perhaps a life has exploded with that crack is not depressing either. In the last two years of world war, our ideas on death have undergone a change. It is not now the furtive thing that crawled into your bed and which you fought with pill-boxes and medicine bottles. It has become again a rider of the wind whom you may go coursing with through the fields and open places. All the morbidity is gone, and the sickness, and what remains to death is now health and excitement. So Dublin laughed at the noise of its own bombardment, and made no moan about its dead—in the sunlight. Afterwards—in the rooms, when the night fell, and instead of silence that mechanical barking of the maxims and the whistle and screams of the rifles, the solemn roar of the heavier guns, and the red glare covering the sky. It is possible that in the night Dublin did not laugh, and that she was gay in the sunlight for no other reason than that the night was past.'[24]

The rising was intended as a 'blood sacrifice', but, as usual in wars, most of those doing the sacrificing did not choose to do so. Of the 450 killed in the fighting, 132 were soldiers or policemen, about 60 were rebels, and 250 were civilian non-combatants, many of them from the slums of Dublin. Likewise, about 2,000 of the 2,614 wounded were ordinary citizens. But it was the fourteen rebel leaders executed between 3 and 12 May who were destined to be remembered.

In retrospect, nationalists were inclined to blame *The Irish Times* for the executions and the policy of repression after it. P. S. O'Hegarty, a member of the Supreme Council of the IRB, subsequently wrote of the executions that 'the army and *The Irish Times* demanded blood, and blood they got.' The Sinn Féin leader Arthur Griffith, he wrote, was interned 'under instructions from *The Irish Times*.' The subsequent British resort to terror tactics in 1920 and 1921

25 October
Terence MacSwiney, Lord Mayor of Cork, dies on hunger strike in prison.

1 November
Enrolment begins for three new categories of special constables in Northern Ireland: A, B and C Specials. An eighteen-year-old IRA volunteer, Kevin Barry, is hanged in Dublin.

21 November
Eleven British intelligence agents are shot dead in Dublin by the IRA, on the orders of Michael Collins. That afternoon the Black and Tans murder twelve civilians in Croke Park; three republican prisoners are shot in the back by the British army in another reprisal.

27 November
The IRA carries out a wave of arson attacks in Liverpool.

THE IRISH TIMES, MONDAY, NOVEMBER 22, 1920.

DREADFUL SERIES OF MURDERS IN DUBLIN.

CONCERTED ATTACKS ON OFFICERS OF HIS MAJESTY'S FORCES.

FOURTEEN SHOT DEAD AND MANY OTHERS WOUNDED.

WILD SCENES AT GAELIC FOOTBALL MATCH.

Yesterday morning there was enacted in Dublin a series of crimes unparalleled in the history of the city. As a result, fourteen members of His Majesty's Forces were murdered in their houses, and a number of others seriously wounded.

The attacks, which were apparently preconcerted, in every case occurred at the same hour. At nine o'clock in the morning the houses and hotels where these officers resided were entered by civilian bands. Most of the officers were in their bedrooms; some were dressed and ready to go to breakfast.

At least twelve were shot dead in this way, while two auxiliary police officers who were on their way to procure assistance were set upon and taken into a private house, where in a back garden they were shot dead. The official report indicates that most of these men were in some way connected with the administration of the law.

Later in the day, while a Gaelic football match was being played at Croke Park, Jones's road, where many thousands of people were assembled, Forces of the Crown arrived, with the object of searching for perpetrators of the crimes of the morning. According to the official report, these forces were instantly fired on by pickets of civilians guarding the grounds, and the Crown Forces immediately replied.

The result of this action was a violent stampede amongst the spectators and more firing, in the course of which it is estimated that ten persons were killed and upwards of fifty wounded. In addition to those wounded by gunfire, many suffered from injuries received in the stampede.

OFFICIAL REPORT OF ATTACKS ON OFFICERS.

SHOOTING AT CROKE PARK.

WILD SCENES AT FOOTBALL MATCH.

CONFLICT WITH ARMED FORCES.

TEN PERSONS KILLED AND OVER FIFTY INJURED.

STATEMENTS BY ONLOOKERS.

MER MOUNT STREET FIGHT.

BATTLE BETWEEN OFFICERS AND RAIDERS.

POLICE AUXILIARIES KILLED.

OFFICER SHOT DEAD.

SCENES IN PEMBROKE STREET.

OFFICERS KILLED IN THEIR BEDROOMS.

FOUR OTHERS WOUNDED.

ATTACKERS ESCAPE.

THE IRISH TIMES, WEDNESDAY, AUGUST 23, 1922.

GENERAL COLLINS DEAD.

KILLED IN AMBUSH.

CHIEF OF STAFF'S MESSAGE TO ARMY.

CALM DISCIPLINE AND NO REPRISAL.

A message reached Dublin this morning to the effect that General Michael Collins was killed yesterday in an ambush near Bandon, County Cork.

On inquiry at Army Headquarters this sad intelligence was confirmed.

The following message from the Chief of Staff to the men of the Army was issued this morning:—

TO THE MEN OF THE ARMY.

Stand calmly by your posts.

Let no cruel act of reprisal blemish your bright honour.

Every dark hour that Michael Collins met since 1916 seemed but to steel that bright strength of his and temper his gay bravery. You are left each inheritors of that strength and of that bravery.

To each of you falls his unfinished work. No darkness in the hour; no loss of comrades will daunt you at it.

Ireland! the Army serves—strengthened by its sorrow.

(Signed), R. UA MAOLCATHA,
Chief of General Staff.

DAMPED ARDOUR.

OPERATIONS CHECKED BY RAIN.

FIGHTERS GOING HOME.

(FROM OUR SPECIAL CORRESPONDENT.)
LIMERICK, Tuesday.

IRISH FUNDS IN AMERICA

NOT TO BE PAID TO MR. DE VALERA.

NEW YORK SUPREME COURT ORDER.

GERMANY'S GOOD INTENTIONS

THWARTED BY MARK'S COLLAPSE.

POINCARÉ'S SPEECH EXPLAINED.

"SABRE RATTLING."

FROM TO-DAY'S LONDON PAPERS

M. POINCARÉ'S SPEECH

ALLIED DIFFICULTIES ACCENTUATED

SITUATION IN GERMANY

PREVAILING UNCERTAINTY

ANXIOUS TO PAY.

BUT CANNOT GIVE PLEDGES.

"A THUNDERING MENACE."

POINCARÉ SPEECH DIRECTED AT GERMANY.

STOCK EXCHANGE

M. POINCARÉ'S ATTITUDE

CLONMEL'S ISOLATION.

BUSINESS SERIOUSLY THREATENED

(FROM OUR SPECIAL CORRESPONDENT.)
CLONMEL, Monday.

CORK TOWNS OCCUPIED.

GENERAL COLLINS'S TOUR.

(FROM OUR SPECIAL CORRESPONDENT.)
CORK, Tuesday Night.

THE LATE COMMANDER-IN-CHIEF.

28 November

The IRA kills eighteen British soldiers in Kilmichael, Co. Cork.

11–12 December

The Black and Tans and Auxiliaries sack Cork.

23 December

The Government of Ireland Act, dividing the country into two home rule statelets, comes into effect.

1921

4 January

Martial law is declared in Munster.

13 January

Cork is placed under curfew.

4 February

Carson stands down as leader of the Ulster Unionist Party.

28 February

Six IRA men are executed in Cork.

was 'the policy recommended to England by *The Irish Times* in 1916.'[25]

In fact, however, the paper, unlike much of the nationalist press, did not directly demand the execution of the leaders. A leading article on 1 May rejoiced at the end of a 'criminal adventure' whose defeat meant that 'Ireland has been saved from shame and ruin, and the whole Empire from a serious danger.' It paid, however, a grudging tribute to the rebels. 'We do not deny a certain desperate courage to many of the wretched men who today are in their graves or awaiting the sentence of their country's laws.' But it certainly implied the need for stern measures. 'In the verdict of history weakness today would be even more criminal than the indifference of the last few months. Sedition must be rooted out of Ireland once and for all …'

By 10 May, indeed, the paper seemed to be almost welcoming the rising because it had led to the imposition of military government on Ireland. 'The fact is that martial law has come as a blessing to us all. For the first time in many months Dublin and large areas in the provinces are enjoying real security of life and property.' In the House of Commons, John Dillon MP read extracts from this 'very significant and very terrible' editorial from 'undoubtedly the leading journal of the Unionist party in Ireland.'

Perhaps no more than a thousand people took part in the 1916 rising—about seven hundred in Dublin—while hundreds of thousands of Irishmen were fighting with the British army. But militant nationalism had seized the political initiative. It had created a force to which resentment of the war, now grinding on at an increasingly fearful cost in lives for an increasingly meaningless purpose, could attach itself. Particularly in 1917, when there was an imminent threat that the British government would extend conscription to Ireland, the 'men of 1916' seemed to offer both an alternative to an intolerable present and a degree of certainty with which to face an unpredictable future. Partly because *The Irish Times* had mistakenly

from The Irish Times 1922
19 MAY

Attempt to Seize Police Headquarters
Men in Police Uniforms

A daring raid took place here early this morning, when an attempt was made to seize the Central Police Barracks, Musgrave Street, the headquarters of the City Force.

At four o'clock the guard at the day-room of the barracks—Constable John Collins and Special Constable McKeown—heard a knock at the front gate. Collins, before opening the gate, inquired, 'Who is there?' and received the reply, 'Police on duty.' He opened the door about a couple of inches to satisfy himself that they were police who demanded admission, and saw seven or eight men dressed in police waterproof coats and caps. They were tall, well-built men, and Collins, believing that they were Royal Irish Constabulary, opened the door.

On entering the men carefully closed the gate, and pushed their way into the day-room, with Collins in front of them.

McKeown paid little heed to the men, as it is quite customary for police to be passing in and out of the barracks at all hours of the day and night.

As soon as they entered the day-room, however, the raiders all produced revolvers and gave the order, 'Hands up!' Still the two men of the guard were not surprised. They thought the affair was a joke. They were in the difficulty of not knowing any of the men personally; but that was only natural, owing to the large numbers of strange men who are being drafted into the city stations every day. The raiders repeated the command, and then the guard realised that the strangers were not police at all.

The two Royal Irish Constabulary men were at once relieved of their revolvers, and, finding all means of resistance from firearms gone, the raiders released their hold on the police to some extent.

McKeown, who was nearest to the door of the day-room, then made a dash for the yard for the purpose of giving the alarm, but one of the raiders, who were stated to be Sinn Féiners, struck him a severe blow on the back of the head with the butt of a revolver.

A dining hall in High Street, Dublin

Although somewhat dazed by the blow, McKeown staggered out to the yard, but before he could give a call for assistance several shots were fired after him, and he collapsed in the yard, wounded in the leg. At the same time several other shots were discharged in the day-room, and Constable Collins also fell.

The raiders then made a rush upstairs towards the arms room, but they met with a hot reception.

The sound of the shooting below put Sergeant Toomley, who was in charge of the arms and ammunition, on the alert, and, opening the door, he saw several men rushing up stairs. As soon as the door was opened the Sinn Féiners fired several shots at the sergeant, who briskly returned the fire, and in the meantime a special constable who was on guard in another part of the barracks hurried to the scene and fired several shots.

christened the rising 'the Sinn Féin Rebellion', Sinn Féin became the label for a deep reservoir of resentments and aspirations among the Catholic majority.

When Éamon de Valera, the senior surviving commandant of the rising, won a parliamentary by-election in Clare in July 1917 under its banner, it was obvious that the war had not, after all, dissolved the differences between nationalists and unionists. It had in fact exacerbated them, polarising the country still further between an even more militant nationalism and a unionism made still more implacable by outrage at the perceived treachery of the 'stab in the back' delivered by the rising. When, in the general election of December

7 March

The Mayor of Limerick is shot dead by the British army.

14 March

Six republicans are executed in Mountjoy prison, resulting in tens of thousands protesting outside and a general work stoppage.

British troops in Limerick following the truce

2 May

Viscount
FitzAlan becomes
the first Catholic
Lord Lieutenant
since the reign of
King James II.

25 May

The Custom
House in Dublin
is burnt to the
ground by the
IRA, which loses
eleven men in
the attack.

1918, Sinn Féin won seventy-three seats to the Irish Party's six, with the Unionists dominating the north and taking twenty-six seats, a crude divide into a southern Catholic and separatist Ireland on the one hand and a northern Protestant and unionist Ireland on the other had been set in stone. The Sinn Féin representatives refused to take their seats in London and established their own Dáil in Dublin. When militant nationalism took the form of the Irish Republican Army and began to attack the policemen of the Royal Irish Constabulary, it seemed that the Great War had put down a small but deeply rooted offshoot in Ireland.

In this, again, Ireland was not untypical of the wider world. The war proved to be the

Finding that the opposition was getting greater as time went on, the gang saw there was no hope of carrying out their plan. They escaped over the high walls and disappeared, some in the direction of the markets and other towards the Queen's Bridge.

Subsequently the two injured policemen were taken in the ambulance to the Royal Victoria Hospital. Collins, who had received bullet wounds in the head and body, died shortly before five o'clock. McKeown, in addition to the injuries inflicted by the butt of the revolver to his head, got a bullet through his right leg near the ankle. His condition is not regarded as serious.

McKeown has been about seventeen months in the special Constabulary, and came to Musgrave Street four months ago. He came on the same draft to the city as that which contained Special Constables Chermside and

Cunningham, who were murdered in May Street about two months ago. Constable Collins, who was 50 years of age, had almost 27 years' service in the force, and was to have resigned in a few weeks' time ...

from The Irish Times
8 JUNE 1922

Refugees in Dublin

Fresh Arrivals

Yesterday afternoon a party of 79 refugees arrived at Amiens Street Station, Dublin, from Belfast. The arrangements for their reception were in the hands of Commandant Henderson, from the Four Courts, who was acting on behalf of the North East Ulster Boycott Committee. A fleet of motor vehicles carried the refugees, many of whom were little children, to Marlborough Hall, Glasnevin, where five hundred Belfast men, women, and children are now housed.

An *Irish Times* representative, who visited Marlborough Hall soon after the arrival of the party, was afforded every facility of speaking with them, and of seeing the arrangements that have been made for their comfort. As a rule they do not care to discuss their recent experiences in the Northern city, and try to forget them in the new surroundings. Some of the women looked pale and ill. More than one had lost her husband or some other member of her family, and had not yet recovered from the blow. One woman, whose husband was killed, is accompanied by her six children. Many of them have lost their homes and almost everything that they possessed in the way of property.

At Marlborough Hall the refugees look after the cleaning of their rooms and make themselves generally useful. The cooking, however, is done by cooks of the Republican Army. Strict attention is paid to the health of the women and children, and a doctor and a trained nurse are in constant attendance. Medicine is also provided. Some of the women need careful attention.

Every able-bodied man is expected to look for work, and, with this object in view, they leave early every morning to find suitable positions in the city. So far none of them has been successful, and until there has been a general improvement in trade and business there can be little expectation of finding openings for the majority of them.

Last evening an impromptu concert was held in the grounds of Marlborough Hall, and it appeared to give much

ultimate test of how fully and efficiently the imperial regimes had modernised themselves. The least modern, the Tsarist government of the Russian empire, collapsed first, creating the conditions for two revolutions in Russia in 1917, in the second of which Lenin's Bolsheviks—a strange hybrid of libertarian socialism and vengeful authoritarianism—took power. Turkey collapsed next. Then Germany and Austria-Hungary, which had partly modernised but had retained powerful monarchies, ultimately lost the war, leading to a grand sweep of European imperial dynasties. In the aftermath of the war, revolutionary regimes ruled, sometimes very briefly, in Berlin, Munich, Hungary, Portugal, and Romania. There was martial law in Spain, food rioting in Japan, and civil war in Mexico. In Glasgow a general strike led to violence in January 1919. In India in April 1919 the British army massacred 379 people in Amritsar, wounding a further 1,200, all within the space of ten minutes.

Nor was Ireland unusual even in the complicated nature of its internal national and political divisions. After 1919 about 25 million Europeans found themselves part of a minority within a state dominated by another group. In Poland, only two-thirds of the population spoke Polish. Czechoslovakia was not only divided, in a close parallel with Ireland, between rural Slovak Catholics and urbanised Czech Protestants but there were also 4.6 million Germans, Poles, Ruthenes and Magyars out of a total population of 14.3 million. In Yugoslavia the Croats, like the Ulster Protestants, saw themselves as a civilised and prosperous people surrounded by what they regarded as a less developed people, the Orthodox Serbs. Ireland's unsettled state was part of a larger pattern of problems that attended the breaking up of empires and the foundation of nation-states.

The Irish Times itself was now a symptom of these anomalies—a unionist paper in an increasingly nationalist city. And nationalists identified the paper more and more explicitly as

5 June
The Northern Ireland Parliament sits for the first time. James Craig is appointed Prime Minister on 7 June.

22 June
King George V formally opens the new Belfast Parliament.

9–15 July
Riots in Belfast kill more than twenty people. Many are Catholics who are killed at the hands of loyalists and the Special Constabulary. 161 homes are destroyed.

11 July
A truce is agreed in the Anglo-Irish War.

27 July
Dáil Éireann meets openly for the first time in the Mansion House in Dublin.

16 August
The second Dáil is convened.

Two young boys outside the sandbagged Four Courts before the bombardment in June 1922

11 October

Negotiations begin between British and Irish plenipotentiaries.

6 December

Articles of agreement for a treaty between Britain and Ireland are completed at the end of two months of negotiations in London.

14 December

Dáil Éireann meets to discuss the Treaty.

part of the old regime. In the general strike against conscription in April 1918 a meeting of six thousand trade unionists in Navan resolved to burn copies of *The Irish Times*.[26] The paper, however, clung more and more desperately to the belief that Britain, which had after all weathered the Great War, would ultimately prevail and that a negotiated peace would keep Ireland within the empire. In 1919 *The Irish Times* mocked the first sitting of Dáil Éireann, calling it a 'stage play at the Mansion House' and claiming that the deputies were living in 'cloud-cuckoo land'. 'The press gallery,' said the paper, 'witnessed a solemn act of defiance of the British Empire by a body of young men who have not the slightest notion of the Empire's power and resources. The quicker Ireland becomes convinced of the folly which elected them, the sooner sanity will return.'

Sinn Féin had, as Jonathan Bardon puts it, 'no policy on Ulster, no plan for conciliating or

pleasure, especially to the women and children. Some of the young girls, who were dressed in bright costumes, sang songs of a patriotic character and danced lively Irish dances.

It is expected that arrangements will be completed shortly for continuing the education of the children. Teachers will soon be available to conduct the classes.

from The Irish Times 1922
13 JUNE

The King's Farewell
Disbandment of Six Irish Regiments

There was an impressive ceremony at Windsor Castle yesterday, when the King received the Colours of the six Irish regiments that are to be disbanded.

In accepting the Colours, His Majesty said:—'I pledge my word that within these ancient and historic walls your Colours will be treasured, honoured, and protected as hallowed memorials of the glorious deeds of brave and loyal regiments.'

You'll hang in the Castle at Windsor,
And dust will enshrine every fold
On which are emblazoned the honours
We gained in the battles of old.
But none will write on you the legend
How we strove to be worthy your fame.
You will fade, and our deeds, all forgotten,
Fade quicker—not even a name.

Will the plains of the Tigris remember?
At Anzac, burned bitter with pain,
There are crosses that speak of the Rangers,
There are more by the Marne and the Aisne.
From Guillemont flashes our glory,
And the Serbian mountains reply.
You may rot: in our hearts we still cherish
The Colours that never will die.

Bryan Cooper

from The Irish Times 1922
1 JULY

The Four Courts

I f there is an Elysian Field for beautiful buildings, Dublin's General Post Office, her Custom House and her Four Courts will keep sad company there. The destruction of the Four Courts is at once the heaviest and the most tragic of the three losses. Last week the Courts were a monument to the taste and ambition of eighteenth century Irishmen. Today their blackened ruins are a monument to the selfish folly of a small minority of a later generation. The explosion which destroyed our great treasury of legal and public documents has torn whole chapters out of Irish history and has involved some of the country's most important business in costly confusion. The full responsibility lies, of course, with the men who offered a reckless defiance to the authority of the Irish Government and the will of the Irish people. It is not the Government's fault that the seat of Ireland's law has been laid in ruins. The law is more precious than its house. Only in the last resort, only after a hundred appeals to reason and patriotism, did the Provisional Government take action to save the country from imminent anarchy. It was a hateful, but an inevitable, task. We pray God that, after peace has been restored, no such duty will ever fall again upon the national Army. If need be, Mr Collins and his colleagues must continue

compromising with the Protestant majority in the north-east.'[27] The depth of nationalist understanding of Protestant Ulster was illustrated by the despatch of a summons in Irish to Edward Carson, leader of the Ulster Unionists, requiring him to attend the first sitting of Dáil Éireann on 21 January 1919. There was laughter in the Dáil when Carson's name was called in the roll-call: even committed nationalists knew that the formality of expecting Carson's presence was an absurd joke. Sinn Féin's instinct was to identify Ireland with the agricultural society of the south rather than the shipyards, engineering works and red-brick terraces of the industrial north. In *What Sinn Féin Stands For*, published in 1921, the party made this explicit. 'Every Irish social thinker envisages the Gaelic polity as a rural polity. The great crowded industrial cities of Britain or America are regarded in Ireland generally as horrible perversions of the natural order … The average Irishman is not much attracted to the town. He loves rural sports and manners. Given the choice between ownership of a city business and a farm of equal capital value, he would, generally, decide for the farm.'[28] The impression this would have made on a Belfast shipyard worker—or for that matter on an Irish emigrant in New York—can only be imagined.

Yet militant nationalism was not a monolith. As the country became more and more unsettled, elements of class war crept into the conflict, with strikes, cattle drives, agitation by landless labourers and even soviets being woven into the general unrest. *The Irish Times* could point, not without evident satisfaction, to the problems that social agitation caused for Sinn Féin. From its peculiar vantage point outside the nationalist consensus it could see the clear lines of class and economic divisions that tended to be obscured by Sinn Féin's appeal to national unity. In April 1920, while workers throughout the country were striking in support of demands for controls on food prices, an editorial stated that 'we are on the eve of a critical struggle between Socialism and anti-Socialism in this country, and it is probable that forces which profess an equal hostility to British rule will be found in opposite camps. Sinn Fein as a body is anti-socialist. The Sinn Fein farmers are as little in love with Labour's claim to control food prices as are the unionist farmers of North-East Ulster. The agrarian agitation in the West—wholly a Labour movement—is viewed with intense alarm by the shopkeeper proprietor of grazing land. We imagine that a good deal of unpleasant thinking is being done in Ireland today by people who were content hitherto to shout with the loudest crowd. They are beginning to appreciate—now that it has disappeared—Pax Britannica.'

A mark of the complexity of the underlying situation is the fact that the paper most passionately opposed to what now seemed the inevitable partition of the country was *The Irish Times*. It was the staunchest upholder of a united Ireland, a unity that it believed could be preserved only within the framework of the United Kingdom. The reasons were obvious: partition would isolate southern unionists as a small minority within an overwhelmingly Catholic and nationalist state. At first the paper believed that the ferocity of Ulster Protestant opposition could be used as a means of defeating home rule; but it began to suspect from early on that Ulster was primarily concerned with its own position and that the rhetoric of its defiance was, from the point of view of southern Protestants, decidedly double-edged.

Even in its enthusiastic coverage of the signing of the Solemn Covenant on 'Ulster Day' in September 1912 there were undertones of unease. What the paper called the 'intense and absolute fusion of religion and politics' that was so evident in the event was uncomfortable for southern unionists, whose position depended on a belief that the Union was good for the Catholic majority as well as the Protestant minority. An editorial noted that 'the outstanding feature of Ulster Day was the part which religion played in it. We have never concealed our own dislike for the introduction of religion into politics. The

to use that stern weapon until Dublin is once more safe and free. They cannot allow the sniper's bullet to fill the city's hospitals and to kill its trade. The people will endorse every measure that may be required for the suppression of the desperate attack upon their lives, their property and their prospects. Surely, however, we may expect now some recognition of their awful responsibility by the Republican leaders. Mr de Valera has associated himself openly with the men who are firing on Irish troops and are filling thousands of Irish homes with misery and sorrow. What does he expect to gain? His political cause is hopeless.

from The Irish Times 1922
3 JULY

Dublin's Days of Trial
Impressions of the Fighting

All the time while revolvered youths were seizing buildings in the city, the bombardment of the stately Four Courts continued. The light 18-pound shells did not seem to be making much impression on the façade, but the eastern wing was showing signs of wear, and the tower supporting the great dome bore a distinctly pock-marked appearance. Somebody—I think it was a demure-looking lass of about eighteen years of age, who reminded me vaguely of Lily Elsie in 'The Quaker Girl,' thrust a copy of Rory O'Connor's communiqué into my hand. Other people were paying a shilling for it. I paid nothing. But I was sorry that she gave it to me, for it reminded me that they were Irishmen over yonder, and I wanted badly to forget it.

Along the quays the crowd was as dense as ever. From Grattan Bridge to the corner of Westmoreland Street there must have been well over a thousand spectators, and that enterprising street entertainer who makes a crazy little doll step-dance to the lively tune of a mouth organ, was doing a roaring trade. The vicious spit of a sniper's rifle did not worry him in the least. Hi-tiddely-hi-ti—ti-ti; the staccato rhythm of the foolish little puppet's feet seemed to synchronise with the beat of the gun-play. Where else but in Dublin could one find such a contrast? 'I never thought it would come to this,' remarked a tough old customer who was leaning on the parapet of the river. And he spat deliberately into the Liffey.

All night on Wednesday the bombardment was kept up, and all day on Thursday. Wednesday's series of ambushes had had a sobering effect on the people, and now one began to notice shops being shut, and a steady shrinkage in the number of persons on the streets. Several further buildings, including Carlisle Building, beside O'Connell Bridge, had been seized by the Irregulars, and snipers were beginning to make things lively from the roof tops. Now and then an armoured car would dash through the streets, but one saw very few signs of military activity, although one heard plenty of them.

It was becoming clear that the Four Courts could not hold out much longer, as a large breach had been made by the field guns, and the moment for an attack by storm was rapidly maturing. But as the chances of a successful resistance in the Four Courts lessened, more and more daring began to be shown by the Irregulars in other parts of the city. They were swooping down into most unexpected places, 'commandeering' foodstuffs, pots and pans, bedding, medical appliances, and what not. Apparently they were going to dig themselves into the heart of the city. One

Ireland of our own day bears many sad testimonies to the bad results of this practice. We have always assumed that Churches historically connected with Ireland are resolved to continue their work there under any circumstances, and, therefore, ought not to identify themselves with any particular form of government. We feel that no Church is entitled to bind all its members to a political creed—much less to a political collect. In his sermon at the Ulster Hall, on Saturday, Dr. M'Kean [the former Presbyterian moderator] claimed for the Church "a right to lay the Divine measuring line on every attempted form of legislation bearing on the character, the freedom, and the well-being of the people." We think that this is a very dangerous claim for Churches which denounce the doctrine of infallibility.'

17 February
The first postage stamps are issued by the Provisional Government of the Irish Free State.

21 February
Recruitment begins for the new police force in the Free State. Sinn Féin's ardfheis adjourns, and elections are postponed for a month.

Volunteers during the War of Independence

The Chief Secretary for Ireland, Ian Macpherson, introduces the second reading of the Government of Ireland Bill in the House of Commons in March 1920. Lloyd George sits crouched beside him on the Treasury bench.

29–30 March

The Provisional Government, the British government and the Northern Ireland government formally reaffirm the Craig-Collins pact and call for an end of IRA activity north of the border and fair policing of Catholic communities.

14 April

Anti-Treaty IRA members seize the Four Courts in Dublin.

In March 1920 the paper was dismayed by the decision of the Ulster Unionist Council to formally accept the exclusion of six Ulster counties from the remit of a Dublin parliament (declaring rather unconvincingly as they did so that they regarded their acquiescence in the establishment of a Belfast parliament as a 'supreme sacrifice'). An editorial complained that the Ulster Unionists had thus 'resolved to slam, bar and bolt the door of six counties against the other twenty-six … The Unionists of Cavan, Monaghan and Donegal are thrown into outer darkness, unwilling victims to the permanent segregation of the six-county area … Thus the Unionists of two-thirds of Ulster have crossed the Rubicon. They have accepted a form of self-government which will give them complete control of their own fortunes. They have re-established the Tudor Pale—save that on this occasion some half million of the King's loyal

noticed that people were getting appreciably more nervous as the day advanced, and the news that, as a friend of mine put it, the postal services had 'gone west' sent a number of excellent citizens scurrying to the Kingstown mail boat. Sniping was in progress all over the city. Here, there, and everywhere one heard of civilian casualties. A woman killed on the bridge, another in Cavendish Row, and so forth.

Steadily the hospitals were beginning to fill. By the middle of the afternoon virtually every shop in the city had closed its doors. Dapper youths and pale-faced girls hurried homewards from their places of business. A few of the more curious lingered to watch what they were pleased to call 'the fun.' A drunken woman staggered across O'Connell Bridge, singing a snatch of maudlin song in quavering tones. Suddenly a burst of machine-gun fire tore the air. The streets seemed to duck with a fearful shudder. Then they were empty.

That night everything was strangely quiet. The guns seemed to have grown weary of their roaring, and but for the odd whip-like snap of a sniper's bullet one could hear no evidence of the drama that was rushing swiftly to dénouement on the quays. Then came the startling news. The troops had stormed the Four Courts. Newspaper men dashed frantically about, linotypes rattled with excitement. Out in the darkened streets all was quiet; a Red Cross car flew across the bridge and was lost in the night.

Three-quarters of the building were now in the hands of General Ennis's men. The Irregular leader, with a remnant of his youthful force, was fighting desperately to hold the last fort. Morning came. The whole city seemed to be astir at an early hour, as the news had flown wildly from house to house. Sniping was still keeping pedestrians on the alert; but the trams were running, and a few shopkeepers daringly opened their shops. The Four Courts taken! Was it all over? 'Not yet,' came the reply from the young Irregulars as they seized half Sackville Street and extended their activities to Poyntz's and Yeates's corner.

About mid-day an ear-splitting explosion shattered Dublin. Compared with this, the booming of the 18-pounder gun had been the merest murmur. Windows were smashed, houses shook from roof to cellar, the sky was darkened with a cloud of flying debris as the Four Courts disappeared into

subjects are outside it.' In accepting the exclusion of the six counties, the paper said, the government 'will pass a measure for the permanent division of Ireland, for the maintenance of sectarian strife, for the perpetuation of all the grotesque machinery of trisected railways and double judiciaries. It will doom the Irish people to secular unsettlement, and will convert thousands of law-abiding men to the cause of revolution.'

If *The Irish Times* spoke for one minority on the 'wrong' side of the emerging divide, there was another whose situation was even more perilous: the Catholic population of the six northern counties that, under the Government of Ireland Bill introduced in February 1920, were granted their own devolved parliament. That parliament was opened by King George V in June 1921 with a plea for 'forbearance and conciliation,' but the dawn of self-government in Northern Ireland arrived in the midst of the most

22 April
The Civil Authorities (Special Powers) Act (Northern Ireland) comes into effect.

20 May
De Valera and Collins agree a pact, which is ratified by the Dáil and the Provisional Government, for the forthcoming elections.
A national coalition panel of candidates is to

A contemporary Belfast cartoon predicting the ruin of prosperous Belfast under a home rule parliament. The Albert clock tower is being demolished to make room for a statue of John Redmond.

Michael Collins carries the coffin of Arthur Griffith on 12 August 1922. A little more than a week later, he would be dead himself.

smoke. A brown-robed monk with a large red cross on a white background across his breast led a grimy, red-eyed crowd of shaken boys on to Ormond Quay. Rory O'Connor was taken injured in a car. Liam Mellowes, grim and determined as ever, walked defiantly to Jameson's Distillery en route for Mountjoy ...

from The Irish Times 1922
6 JULY

MacArthur & Co

79 Talbot St., Dublin, Auctioneers, House, Land, and Estate Agents. Established 1880. Burned Out July, 1922.

Announcement

We regret to inform our numerous Clients that during the Disturbance OUR PREMISES WERE BURNED OUT. Although considerable damage has been done to the Building, we are hopeful of RESUMING BUSINESS AS USUAL AT OUR OLD ADDRESS IN THE COURSE OF A FEW DAYS. Meanwhile, Correspondence can be forwarded to PERCY E. MacARTHUR, 55 WELLINGTON ROAD.

from The Irish Times 1922
14 JULY

Seen From a Motor Car

A Favourable Opening

The real trial of strength is not yet. To use a metaphor from chess, the opening has not yet become merged in the middle game. But from what I have seen there can be little doubt that the opening has gone in favour of the National forces. There may still be serious attempts by the Irregulars to attack the lines of communication. In a mountainous district such as that which extends to the south of Dublin, it is almost impossible to prevent a concentration of malcontents who might create an awkward diversion. The further a force is advanced from its base, the more vulnerable are its supplies; but, at the same time, the more precarious is the position of troops operating in its rear. Even with the initial advantage of fighting without uniforms, and so being able, chameleon-like, to turn their appearance from that of a solider to a harmless and necessary civilian, such a force could only prove a nuisance, and not a danger.

sustained and vicious sectarian violence in Ireland since 1798. With the IRA still on the offensive, the Unionist leadership resurrected the UVF. Riots in the Bogside area of Derry turned into gun battles, and the British soldiers sent in to restore order sided with the UVF. Catholics and socialists were driven from their jobs in the shipyards of Belfast, accompanied by kicks, blows, and showers of rivets. Catholic homes, shops and pubs were burnt down. Thousands of Catholics were forcibly expelled from the big engineering firms. In the last week of August 1920 alone there were 180 major fires in Belfast, causing almost £1 million worth of damage.

The violence was at its worst in the spring of 1922, after the IRA had renewed its campaign to destabilise Northern Ireland by kidnapping forty prominent loyalists in Counties Fermanagh and Tyrone. Loyalist attacks on Catholic areas were met with fierce resistance from the IRA. Sectarian atrocities on both sides reached new levels of barbarity. In the last week of March, uniformed men, believed to policemen, broke into the home of Owen MacMahon, a Catholic publican, and murdered five members of the family; only the youngest child, who hid under a table, survived. A week later a bomb was thrown into the home of Francis Donnelly, a Protestant, maiming him and his two daughters and killing his two small sons, aged twelve and two. In all, between 1920 and 1922 about two hundred Catholics and a hundred Protestants were killed in the conflict. The new Northern Ireland, moreover, had become something like a police state. By April 1922, with the UVF militias transformed into a special constabulary and with the establishment of the Royal Ulster Constabulary, there was one policeman in Northern Ireland for every two Catholic families.

The Irish Times reported these events in vivid and disturbing detail but was also awash with news of violence in the south. By 1920 the IRA's armed campaign had become a serious one, with 192 policemen and 150 soldiers killed in that year. The British responded with the

be put forward to represent the pro-Treaty and anti-Treaty sides of Sinn Féin throughout the thirty-two counties.

23 May
The Northern Ireland Parliament outlaws the IRA, Cumann na mBan, and Fianna Éireann.

31 May
The RUC is officially established.

16 June
The general election takes place in the Free State as newspapers publish the draft consti-tution.

22 June
The IRA assassinates Field-Marshal Sir Henry Wilson, adviser to Craig on law and order in Northern Ireland, in London.

recruitment and deployment of seven thousand ex-soldiers, known as the Black and Tans, and six thousand officers, known as the Auxiliaries—too few for an effective reign of terror but more than enough to commit a constant stream of atrocities that alienated liberal opinion in America and in Britain itself, while undermining the attempts of *The Irish Times* to present the conflict as a struggle between anarchy and order. Pax Britannica, as interpreted by the Black and Tans, did not look very peaceful.

Particularly after the opening of the Belfast parliament had closed off the paper's preferred option of a united Ireland within the United Kingdom, *The Irish Times* became increasingly conciliatory, demanding above all a truce leading to negotiations and a peace settlement. By the

Travelling about Ireland in a motor car is at present a very enjoyable and sometimes exciting occupation. Watching the shadows chequering the Dublin hills, diving down a slope into a green tunnel of trees which edge and overhang the road, watching the village children playing the great new game of war, you forget that the miles which are rolling under your wheels are bringing you further and further into districts which have not yet been completely tidied up.

How softly green is the tunnel which stretches before you, as if the wood had grown into the road itself. Hullo! brakes quickly! there is a tree down! The foot brake checks our swift rush, the hand brake grinds into action, and the heavy car—over twenty-eight hundredweight—comes finally to a stop three or four yards from the huge beech which has been felled artfully at a corner of the road, so that from a slight distance its leaves blend indistinguishably with the curving line of trees behind it. Then starts the hunt for an

De Valera speaking on the steps of Ennis courthouse before his arrest in 1923

alternative route. Sometimes by going back a mile or two you can find a by-road which leads round by a detour to the main route on the other side of the obstacle. Sometimes you have to dig your way through a hedge and ditch and bump along through woodlands and over fields ...

from The Irish Times 1922
23 AUGUST

Michael Collins

As we go to press we learn that General Michael Collins, Commander-in-Chief of the Irish Army, and Chairman of the Provisional Government, has been wounded fatally in an ambush in County Cork. The Irish nation will be shocked beyond measure at this awful news. General Collins stood for stable government and the restoration of civilised conditions to our distracted country. He applied all his abundant energy to the performance of the task to which he set his hand last December, when he signed the Treaty with the British Government in London, and his courage and sincerity rallied round him all the best and sanest elements in Irish life. His death is a disaster for Ireland. Irishmen the world over will mourn him, and will sink their heads in shame at the deep damnation of his taking-off. That he should have met his tragic end at Irish hands is the darkest feature of this national calamity. He dared much and suffered much for the ideal to which he devoted his life and in the achievement of which he played such a decisive part. Like his friend and teacher, Arthur Griffith, General Collins was a firm believer in the destiny of the Irish people and in its fulfilment through the medium of the London Treaty. He has fallen now within sight of the goal towards which he strove with such tenacity of purpose, but his death will serve only to strengthen the resolve of the Irish people that his work shall be carried to complete success.

from The Irish Times 1922
23 AUGUST

General Collins Dead

The Late Commander-in-Chief

We much regret to announce the death of General Michael Collins, Commander-in-Chief of the National Army, which occurred yesterday under the circumstances related above. . . .

summer of 1920 the paper was urging southern unionists to recognise that 'the innate sanity as well as the unrestrained idealism' of their compatriots (including, at least by implication, Sinn Féin) demanded a generous settlement. By September the paper had formally adopted a policy of supporting full self-government within the Commonwealth, including the establishment of a parliament with full control over its own taxation. It urged 'the great force of Southern unionism' to be 'a vital factor in any settlement.' In the summer of 1921 it supported the four southern Unionist representatives who took up an invitation to meet de Valera at the Mansion House in Dublin, a meeting that resulted in de Valera agreeing to go to London for talks with the Prime Minister, David Lloyd George.

These talks in turn led to a truce in July and the opening of formal treaty negotiations in October. On 6 December 1921 the Irish delegates in London signed an agreement giving Ireland dominion status, equivalent to that enjoyed by Canada. Members of the parliament of the new Irish Free State would have to swear an oath of allegiance firstly to their own constitution and then to the British crown, by virtue of common citizenship and of Ireland's membership of the Commonwealth. This was a significant advance on home rule but went slightly further than de Valera's draft terms—the so-called Document No. 2—for the inevitable compromise. The main difference was over the form of recognition to be given to the British monarchy. Instead of the oath, de Valera contemplated recognition of the king 'as head of the Association' of Ireland and the states of the Commonwealth. The difference may have been negligible, but it was enough to give an opening to those within Sinn Féin who were psychologically unprepared for any compromise. The Treaty was bitterly opposed by a large minority within the Dáil—where it was ratified in January 1922 by 64 votes to 57—and something close to a majority within the IRA.

It was a mark of the utter transformation of Irish politics that *The Irish Times*, for so long an

Waterford, crushing the 'Munster Republic'.

9 August
A new style of shop, a department store called Clery's, opens in Dublin.

12 August
Arthur Griffith dies. Cork is seized by Free State forces.

17 August
The RIC is disbanded and replaced by the Civic Guard.

22 August
Michael Collins, Commander-in-Chief of the Free State army, is shot dead in an IRA ambush near Macroom in his native Co. Cork.

9 September
Dáil Éireann reconvenes; republicans abstain. William T. Cosgrave is elected President of the Executive Council (head of government).

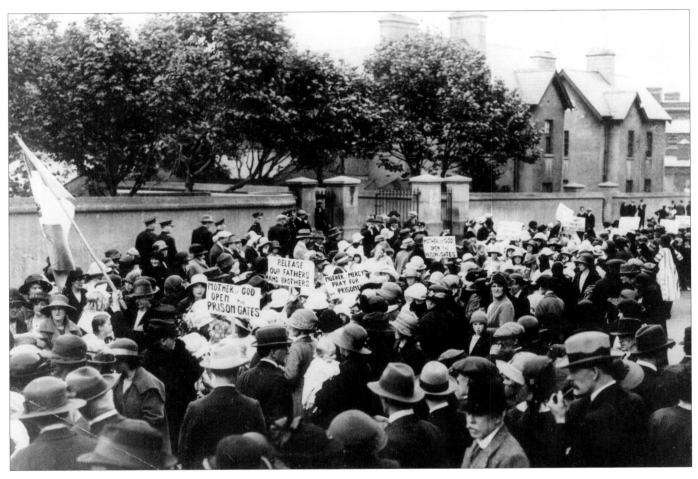

Protesters outside Mountjoy prison during the Civil War

28 September
Dáil Éireann approves a motion to establish military courts.

15 November
The British general election returns a Conservative government and a Unionist majority in Northern Ireland.

implacable opponent of home rule, now endorsed the more radical settlement of the Treaty. Admitting that the Treaty settlement went 'far beyond anything that the boldest reformer' among the southern unionists 'had dared to contemplate,' the paper expressed, in the midst of the Dáil's fierce debates on the Treaty, the anxious hope that the Dáil might 'make the pax Hibernica a real substitute for the pax Brittanica.' When it became clear that the pax Hibernica endorsed by the Dáil would be challenged in arms by the hard-line minority, the paper threw its weight behind the pro-Treaty Provisional Government, led by Michael Collins and Arthur Griffith. It suggested that southern unionists should form local committees to support and influence the choice of pro-Treaty

We print below a character sketch of General Collins by 'Nichevo,' which appeared under the heading 'Irishmen of Today,' in *The Irish Times* of 1 April.

One day, about eighteen months ago, I was sitting with a friend in a Dublin restaurant. He was one of those people who seem to know everything and to be hail-fellow-well-met with everybody from Davy Stephens to the Lord Chancellor of England. We were talking politics, of course, when suddenly I noticed that my companion had turned very pale. 'Don't look round yet,' he said beneath his breath, 'Michael Collins has just come in.' I must confess that my heart promptly took refuge in my boots; but curiosity is generally stronger even than fear, and I could not resist the temptation to have a look at the elusive 'Mike'. The man to whom my friend referred was small, thin, with mouse-coloured hair, and looked rather like a jockey. What he lacked in physique, however, he made up in facial ferocity, for a more villainous looking individual I never saw. 'Are you sure that he is Collins?' I asked in doubt. 'Of course,' he replied jauntily, 'don't I know him well?'

For nearly a year, therefore, I guarded the guilty secret of having been within touching distance of the most badly 'wanted' man in Ireland; but I might have known my friend the *quidnunc* better. The man was no more Michael Collins than I was.

I discovered the fraud last August, when Dáil Éireann met in the Mansion House to discuss Mr Lloyd George's invitation to a conference. I scanned the assembly in vain for the gentleman of the restaurant. None of the members resembled him in the very least, and I was just beginning to be afraid that Mr Collins was a myth after all, when the Clerk of the House began to call the roll. 'Míceál Ó Coilean' was the first name on the list, and I knew enough Irish—but just enough—for that. There was the famous 'Mick,' *sed quantum mutatus ab illo!* Here was no emaciated little jockey-man, furtive of eye, and hang-dog of look. A big, burly, broad-shouldered individual with a shock of pitch-black hair and a broad smile, walked across the floor and signed the register. All my preconceived ideas were shattered. I could not have been more completely taken aback if the Moderator of the General Assembly had answered to that name ...

from The Irish Times
4 SEPTEMBER 1922

Dancing in Dublin

The new Metropole Ballroom opens its doors on Monday next. The management have arranged with Mr and Mrs Leggett Byrne to personally superintend the inaugural dances. For the past 30 years Mr and Mrs Leggett Byrne have been engaged at most of the principal functions in the City of Dublin. They were the pioneers of children's dances and ballrooms at the Ballsbridge Fêtes, almost all of which they organised since the great 'Kosmos' Fête of 1893. An excellent band has been engaged for these dances.

Mr and Mrs Leggett Byrne have also arranged to re-open their classes on Thursday next for children and adults. Morning and afternoon sessions will be held during the season. Children will be taught on Thursdays and Saturdays, and adults on Tuesdays and Thursdays.

candidates at the next general election, a suggestion that was endorsed by a meeting of unionists under the chairmanship of Lord Mayo.

In the event, the election of June 1922 was a confusing one, fought on the basis of a pact between de Valera and Collins intended to return pro-Treaty and anti-Treaty Sinn Féiners in numbers proportionate to their strength in the previous Dáil. The pact broke down on the eve of the election, however, and the result was a strong endorsement of the Treaty, with de Valera's rejectionists winning just 36 of the 128 seats and taking fewer votes than the Labour Party.

The fact that *The Irish Times* supported them was, in the eyes of de Valera's followers, sufficient proof that Collins and Griffith were traitors. A handbill distributed by the Republicans during the election campaign of 1922, with the heading 'Unionists and the Treaty,' reminded voters that 'in its issue of March 21st, the "Irish Times", organ of the Irish Unionists, asks its readers to support the Treaty Party and to subscribe to its funds. Do you think the Unionists regard the Treaty is [*sic*] freedom? Do you think they would help to make the "mere Irish" independent? They support the Treaty because they know it will make Ireland British through and through.' Yet, for the first time in its history, the paper had the experience of being on the same side as the mainstream of Catholic and nationalist opinion in an election. For it was clear that the Treaty did have the support of the emergent Irish democracy.

Before the new Dáil could convene, in any case, hostilities had broken out with an attack by Collins's new Free State army on Republicans ensconced in the Four Courts in Dublin. In early July 1922 an *Irish Times* reporter gave an eye-witness account of the public mood after the attack on the Four Courts. 'For the first time in our history a Government using force to put down an insurrection had had the overwhelming support of the common people. As one moved about in the back streets, it was possible to gather the general feeling. Certainly there was some support for the Irregular cause, and what support they had was of

17 November
The first executions of IRA men occur in the Free State.

24 November
Erskine Childers, anti-Treaty republican and 1914 Irish Volunteers gun-runner, is shot by Free State army firing-squad for possession of a revolver, a gift from Michael Collins.

8 December
Four prominent republicans—Rory O'Connor, Liam Mellows, Dick Barrett, and Joe McKelvey—are shot by the Free State army in what is a typical action. Their deaths are a retaliation for the shooting dead of Seán Hales TD the previous day.

1923

28 March
Legislation in the South abolishes the workhouse system.

a vociferous quality. It was apparent, however, that its mainspring was Sentiment and personal ties of kinship … For every vehement harangue there were twenty solid and silent opponents, who only vented an occasional growl of disapproval to show their real opinion. When it came to deeds, not words, the kindly attention paid to the [Free State] troops wherever they were quartered showed their own personal popularity and the popularity of their cause.'

The Irish Times reported too on the enthusiastic reception given to the Free State forces in many of the main towns as Collins's forces gradually wrested control of the south and west from the Republicans. It described night-long celebrations in Claremorris, County Mayo, when the IRA was driven out. In Tipperary at the end of July the entry of the Free State forces was greeted by huge crowds, alienated from the IRA by the burning down of the town's main factories. One of the IRA's weaknesses, reflected in the paper's reporting, was that its soldiers were not paid and therefore resorted to taking money and food from local people. One dead IRA man in County Mayo was found to have what was then the huge sum of £800 in his pocket. In Clonmel, which had been a garrison town and was therefore especially likely to oppose the IRA, *The Irish Times* reported that 'the soldiers were shaken by the hands, and doors were thrown open for their welcome. Captain Mackey, a native of the town, had a remarkable reception. He was raised shoulder-high by the people, and borne triumphantly through the streets.'

The paper's support for the Free State government was strengthened by reports it published of the intimidation of Protestants by anti-Treaty forces. It reported on 1 May on an atrocity in Clonakilty, County Cork, in which a Protestant man and his son were forced to dig their own graves and then shot. The man's nephew, a former soldier who fired on the raiders, was overwhelmed and hanged. As a result, according to *The Irish Times*, there was an 'exodus' of Protestants from the Dunmanway and

from The Irish Times 1922
16 SEPTEMBER

The New Ireland

Type, Culture, and the Hark-back to Race

A new tilth of nationality is manifest now; a new culture in Ireland. It is not the product of the hectic side of the last few years, but that helps to emphasise it. Rather it has been quietly silting upwards in the growth of generations, though in direct issue it comes from the broader education and outlook in this country.

It is puzzling, it is extraordinary; but, even more, it is exhilarating. For a human type has arisen and is now prominent from our mixed blood, harking back to the features of the most purely-kept of the Irish races, the farthest from the Pale; and today this manifestation of the ancient race is the most imbued with modern ideals—a being developed by culture and education, a national tradition, and the automatic evolution of race.

Walking our streets, it can be recognised by physical characteristics, akin to those who have been accustomed to attribute to the Connemara peasant those Spanish features giving rise to the stupid tradition that ship-wrecked sailors of the Spanish Armada are responsible for dark eyes and narrow faces among the 'men of the West' of Ireland. But important is this: these physical characteristics denote certain set traits, un-Irish to strangers, but to those of the mixed races who have been used to pondering upon what may, indeed, be the true Irish racial type, nearest to the essential Irish. These traits are silence, a keen, rather morose intelligence, brooding and watchful; the extremes of either a rock-firm placidity or temperamental spasmodic vivacity; a fidelity to rooted affections and opinions, and utter coldness to all outside them. But none of the accustomed ebullient simplicity that is found where English blood runs strongly.

Our new Irishman is less of a fighting man than a scholar, and when not wrought up to scholar's pitch, is a type of normality with intelligence, irony and a touch of intellectualism holding him out of the drift of life. He will not drift: there lies his value. He is a separate entity, and conscious; and out of a past and present national bewilderment he is a promise for the future. See—there are examples of it around—a man and a woman of this type marry; and look at their children. The children will, to guess at it, be more generous of self-expression that the parents, since removed

National Army troops with a Lewis gun

somewhat from the necessity of hardening defence against chaotic influence, while maintaining their evenness, purpose, and intelligence.

Essentially and by vocation are these men and women of the spiritual breed that makes builders of the city in the desert, unchangeable of direction for all the stormy seas of circumstance. They may be in any occupation, belong to any class-stratum; but they remain themselves.

Clerks in offices, a man in an engineering shop, a saleswoman, doctors and nurses, teachers and university professors—wherever they are, they make their own atmosphere, and it is a steadying one. In it minds and bodies can expand and grow, men and women can work and rest. As though, in fact, from out of the toils of time had begun to

Bandon areas, some fleeing for the boat to England without a bag or a coat. On 13 June the paper described an incident in County Westmeath when a Protestant grocer fled to Belfast after being taken out into the countryside by armed men who threatened to shoot him. Three days later it reported that Protestants in Ballinasloe, including the local agent for Guinness's brewery, the manager of a boot shop, and the stationmaster, were ordered to leave the town.

Adding to southern unionist unease, the leaders to whom they had reconciled themselves, Griffith and Collins, both died in August 1922, the former of natural causes, the latter in an

1 July

The number of republicans interned in the Free State reaches its highest level at 11,480.

16 July

The censorship of films becomes possible under Free State law.

8 August
The Garda
Síochána is
established
by law.

15 August
De Valera is
arrested by the
forces of the
Irish Free
State. Sinn
Féin wins
forty-four seats
in the general
election, but
Cumann na
nGaedheal
remains the
largest party in
the Dáil.

10 September
The Free State is
admitted to the
League of
Nations.

14 October
Hundreds of
republicans in
the Free State
go on hunger
strike, which
lasts for a
month and
a half.

14 November
W. B. Yeats
is awarded
the Nobel
Prize for
Literature.

ambush. The loss of such seasoned leaders may have contributed to the increasing ferocity with which the Free State side pursued the war. Official violence reached its height after December 1922 when the Republicans shot dead a Free State deputy, Seán Hales. The government, now led by William T. Cosgrave, responded by executing four Republican leaders, a policy of reprisal that continued until seventy-seven in all had been killed in cold blood. Unofficial violence reached a peak in March 1923 when Free State troops tied nine Republican prisoners to a land mine in Ballyseedy, County Kerry, and exploded it, killing eight of them.

One of these deaths, that of Erskine Childers, was particularly poignant for *The Irish Times,* because it summed up the tormented passage from empire to independence that the country as whole, and indeed the paper itself, had followed since the beginning of the century. Executed as a Republican diehard in November 1922, Childers had begun the century as an English imperialist and had supported many of the same causes as *The Irish Times.* In an editorial on his death the paper noted that he had 'fought against the tyranny of the Boers' and that 'many years ago, in a brilliant book [*The Riddle of the Sands*], he foretold the German attack on the liberties of Europe, and when his vision was fulfilled, he defended those liberties on sea and in the air.' Even now, while supporting his execution as a grim necessity, the paper could not deny Childers the praise due to 'an idealist, a thinker of high thoughts, and a brave man.' Faced with the cruel blighting of so many of the hopes with which the century had begun, the paper could only ask, 'What is the mysterious difference which sometimes, in ardent minds, perverts the ideal of freedom from a blessing into a curse?' It was a question to which the previous decade of almost universal violence had supplied no answer and which would be asked again and again in the coming times.

breathe in this land the old race that once made scholarly achievement throughout the world, and made Ireland the source of an out-spreading civilisation—until the confusion and Babel of mixed races brought desolation like Nemesis.

CYNTHIA

from The Irish Times **1922**
10 NOVEMBER

Bridge

Cure for Nervous Breakdown

Bridge parties are very popular in Dublin today, and at nearly all the stakes are so small that the old argument used by people who dislike cards, that the game causes financial loss that many of the players cannot afford, has disappeared.

The only argument that I have heard against bridge that has carried any weight with me is that it produces a 'card face.' The card face as seen at tables, however, is not seen so frequently nowadays, but I confess that it is not pretty, and it is a natural supposition that only a hardened gambler would sacrifice good looks to cards.

Bridge is one of the few recreations that does not affect the nerves, in spite of what many people say.

'Bridge has saved me from a nervous breakdown,' declared more than one woman beset by many cares. 'I can never be thankful enough that I am fond of cards. By becoming keenly interested in bridge for a few hours every evening I forget all my worries and enjoy complete mental rest.'

Bridge does incalculable good by drawing out of seclusion women who would fall into a rut and become old before their time.

It has brought enjoyment into the lives of hundreds of women who, before they cultivated an interest in cards, were eating their hearts out with melancholy.

Of course, one could argue that women who lead dull lives could go in for intellectual effort, for charitable work, or some pursuit, but how few do it, or are fitted for it?

Cards seem to provide for these women their only escape from deadly depression, and anything that does that cannot be evil. Though, perhaps, the 'die-hard' opponents of bridge would maintain that the cure is worse than the disease.

Bridge-Player

After ten years in the United States, James Larkin returned to Dublin in 1923. This photograph, one of the most graphic images of twentieth-century Ireland, was taken as he spoke in O'Connell Street on his return.

Éamon de Valera shortly after his election victory in 1932 and before the formation of his first government.

He was just fifty years of age and was set to dominate Irish politics for a generation.

1924

The Plain People of Ireland

1957

1924–1957

The Plain People of Ireland

ooking back in anger at the end of the Civil War, the veteran nationalist P. S. O'Hegarty, now Secretary of the new Department of Posts and Telegraphs, felt that the internecine violence had shattered the illusion that the Irish were somehow better than everyone else. 'The "Island of Saints and Scholars" is burst, like Humpty Dumpty, and we do not quite know yet what to put in its place.'[1] The bloody and bitter feud over the Treaty—often more bloody and more bitter than the conflict with the British—dispelled the notion that Ireland's sorrows would cease with independence. The need to adopt a defensive posture as the Free State fought for its life meant that there was no honeymoon of utopian experiment. And with the death of Michael Collins the new regime had also lost its most formidable and potentially mercurial figure, leaving the state in the hands of less colourful leaders such as William T. Cosgrave, President of the Executive Council (head of government) and his deputy, Kevin O'Higgins, who remarked of himself and his colleagues that 'we were probably the most conservative minded revolutionaries that ever put through a successful revolution.'

1924

The sobering effect of the Civil War on nationalists was, from the point of view of the Protestant middle class, for whom *The Irish Times* spoke, rather welcome. It dampened messianic expectations of radical change. It was clear in the early twenties that the best hopes of radical nationalists and the worst fears of conservative unionists were not going to be realised. The Free State would settle down into a rather dull orthodoxy. Whatever mild tinge of social revolution there had ever been to the nationalist revolt was washed out by the bitterness and exhaustion that followed the Civil War. Any remaining likelihood that the new government might adopt an expansive attitude disappeared with a series of dock strikes in 1923 and poor weather that year and in 1924, both of which helped to depress the economy and to hamper the cattle trade with Britain, on which, in spite of all the political turmoil, the new state remained dependent. With the exchequer already

from The Irish Times
11 MARCH 1924

'The Pictures'

Yesterday was the twenty-fifth anniversary of the birth of the moving picture. Although the first film story was made and shown in America, it was the work of two Englishmen, Mr J. Stuart Blackton and Mr Albert E. Smith. Their first picture, 'The Haunted House,' was one hundred feet long and was shown in one-and-a-half minutes. From this modest source have sprung the 'super-productions' of the present day. That we owe to Messrs. Blackton and Smith one of the most powerful influences in modern life cannot be doubted, although opinions may vary on the point whether they were benefactors of the race or the reverse. Today the *clientèle* of the picture-house is larger than that of any other form of entertainment, dramatic, musical or sporting; and the influence of the 'pictures,' for good or ill, on the human mind is immeasurable. A few years ago they were held by many people to be the origin of numerous crimes. 'I saw it on the pictures,' was an explanation of all sorts of offences against person and property. Recently another aspect of the film

The first Executive Council of the Irish Free State. The president, W. T. Cosgrave, sits at the head of the table. Desmond Fitzgerald is third from the left. Ernest Blythe and Kevin O'Higgins are on the right.

The Abbey Theatre in the twenties

industry has caught the public eye, and startling episodes in the lives of 'stars' have been used as a peg for disparaging criticism. As surely, however, as nothing in human affairs is wholly good, nothing is wholly bad, and the 'pictures' may claim to have brought real solace to a weary world. At any rate, they are an established institution which the wise moralist will seek to improve, knowing that he cannot abolish it. No Voltaire could hope now to flout, or no new 'Histriomastix' to scourge, the film out of the affections of young and old.

from The Irish Times 1924
13 MARCH

Army Manoeuvres

At the end of last week two officers of the Free State Army, acting 'on behalf of the IRA organisation,' presented an ultimatum to the Government. It was in part a political manifesto and in part a veto upon the policy of the Ministry of Defence. The Executive Council, regarding the conduct of these officers as mutiny, issued orders for their arrest; and President Cosgrave, in Dáil Éireann on Tuesday,

burdened with the cost of the Civil War (about £17 million for the Free State army's campaign and material damage of about £30 million), there were powerful incentives to fiscal, and therefore social, conservatism.

The peace that followed the Republican surrender was, moreover, an uneasy one. The last of the executions were carried out in June 1923, a month after the IRA Chief of Staff, Frank Aiken, had given the order to 'dump arms.' The political leader of the anti-Treaty forces, Éamon de Valera, was arrested by Free State troops in Ennis in August 1923 and imprisoned for almost a year, but he retained a substantial following in the country. In the general election that followed his arrest his supporters took 28 per cent of the vote, against 39 per cent for Cosgrave's pro-Treaty party, now called Cumann na nGaedheal. (Labour took 12½ per cent, and other broadly pro-Treaty parties took 21 per cent.) Since the Republicans refused to take their seats in the

6 November
The Boundary Commission, which the Free State hopes will reduce the size of Northern Ireland, meets for the first time.

1925

29 January
Reports state that the Free State sells £40 million worth of food to Britain and almost none elsewhere.

11 February
Cosgrave carries a Dáil motion urging the Senate to agree to standing orders that would prohibit the introduction of bills allowing divorce.

5 March
Cosgrave's proposal reaches the Senate; the Chairman rules that no such motion can be adopted, as the termination of an existing legal right could only be attained by statute and not by a resolution. As no divorce bill can be inaugurated without the approval of a motion of both

THE IRISH TIMES, MONDAY, MAY 17, 1926.

EMIGRATION FROM IRELAND.

1,000 PERSONS LEAVE BY QUEENSTOWN.

LETTERS TO THE EDITOR.

THE NATIONAL WAR MEMORIAL.

THE POUND AT PAR.

FIRST TIME IN ELEVEN YEARS.

FRENCH DEBT.

FINANCE MINISTER IN LONDON.

FALL OF THE FRANC.

"AN ATTACK ON FRENCH CURRENCY."

From "The Times" PARIS, Sunday.

AFTER THE STRIKE.

CHURCHES AND THE STRIKE.

A RECONCILIATION SERVICE.

THE PRESS.

FORGIVE AND FORGET.

FORGET AND FORGIVE.

NEXT GENERAL ELECTION.

MR. O'HIGGINS SOUNDS ADVANCE NOTE.

THE GOVERNMENT'S RECORD.

VIGOROUS ATTACK ON THE PRESS.

END OF A CHAPTER.

GOVERNMENT'S WORK REVIEWED.

From Our Reporter.

CLONMEL, Sunday.

THE IRISH TIMES, MONDAY, SEPTEMBER 4, 1939.

7

[BRITAI]N AND FRANCE AT WAR WITH GERMANY

[MES]SAGE TO [EM]PIRE

[Wh]at We Should [C]hallenge"

ANNOUNCEMENT MADE BY WIRELESS

Dominions Rally to Support Great Britain

KING'S CALL TO STAND "CALM AND FIRM AND UNITED"

Mr. Churchill and Mr. Eden become Ministers

GERMANY REFUSES TO ACCEPT ULTIMATUM

Blames Britain for Giving Poland Blank Cheque

BRITAIN and France are at war with Germany. The first announcement of the momentous decision was conveyed in a broadcast made by Mr. Chamberlain soon after 11 o'clock. The House of Commons heard the decision at noon. Later it was announced that the French Government had given the German Chancellor until 5 o'clock to give an answer to the Note sent on Friday last, and that, failing a reply, or in the event of a negative reply, France would consider herself at war with Germany from that hour.

Hitler's reply to the British ultimatum was handed to the British Ambassador twenty minutes after the time had expired. Hitler blames Britain for the outbreak of war, and refuses any demands made in the form of an ultimatum.

VOICE OF THE KING

The King, broadcasting at 6 o'clock, called on his people to stand calm and firm and united. "The task will be hard," he said, referring to the "conflict we have been forced into," and added: "But we can only do the right as we see the right, and reverently commit our cause to God. With God's help we shall prevail."

Australia, Canada and New Zealand have already intimated their intention to join Britain and France in the fight. The Viceroy of India has called on India to play her part. Eire's decision to remain neutral already has been announced.

M. Daladier, in a broadcast to the French nation last night, said:—"By standing up against the most horrible of all tyrannies, and by making good our word, we are fighting to defend our land, our homes and our liberty. The cause of France is that of all peaceful and free nations. It will be victorious."

WAR CABINET FORMED

THE German reply to the British Note calling for the withdrawal of German troops from Poland, and the subsequent ultimatum expiring at 11 a.m., was handed to the British Ambassador in the form of a memorandum.

"The Reich's Government and the German nation refuse to accept, or even to satisfy, demands in the form of an ultimatum from the British Government.

"For many months there has been a virtual state of war on our Eastern frontier. After the German Government had torn up the Treaty of Versailles all friendly settlements were refused to the German Government.

"The National Socialist Government has endeavoured repeatedly since the year 1933 to remove the worst forms of coercion and violations of its rights contained in this treaty.

"It was always in the first instance the British Government that, by its unbending attitude, prevented any practical revision.

"But for the intervention of the British Government a settlement, reasonable and satisfactory to both sides, would have been found to the dispute between Germany and Poland, and this is well-known not only to the German Government, but also to the German people.

"Germany has neither the intention, nor has she put forward the demand, to annihilate Poland.

"The Reich only demanded the revision of those articles of the Treaty of Versailles which far-seeing statesmen of all nations regarded at the time the diktat was being drafted as intolerable, and, therefore, impossible in the long run, not only for the whole of a great nation, but also for the whole political and economic interest of Eastern Europe.

"British statesmen also described the solution in the East at that time as the germ of wars to come.

"It was the intention of all German Governments, and of the new National Socialist Government in particular, to remove this danger.

BRITAIN IS BLAMED

"The British Government is to be blamed for having prevented this peaceful revision. By an action which is unique in history the British Government gave for the Polish State a blank cheque for any action against Germany which that State might intend to carry out.

"The British Government promised military help to the Polish Government unreservedly in the event of Germany's defending herself against any provocation or attack. Thereupon the Polish terror assumed intolerable dimensions against the German living in territories torn

this. On the contrary, while constantly stressing its pledge to assist Poland under all circumstances, it encouraged the Polish Government to continue its criminal attitude, which endangered European peace. In accordance with this spirit, the British Government rebuffed Signor Mussolini's proposal, which could still have saved the peace of Europe, though the German Government had declared itself willing to accept it.

THE RESPONSIBILITIES

"The British Government, therefore, bears the responsibility for all the misfortune and suffering which has now come upon many nations and will come in the future.

"After all attempts to find and conclude a peaceful settlement had been rendered impossible by the uncompromising attitude of the Polish Government backed by Great Britain, after conditions similar to the civil war which had existed for months on the eastern frontier of the Reich, without the British Government making any objection, gradually developed into open attacks on Reich territory. The German Government decided to put an end to this continuous threat, intolerable to a great Power for the external and ultimately the domestic peace of the German people, with the only means that remain at its disposal, to defend the peace, security and honour of the German Reich, after the Governments of the democracies had virtually wrecked all other possibilities of revision.

"The German Government has answered the latest attacks by the Poles which threaten the Reich territory with the same measures.

REFERENCE TO PALESTINE

"Whatever British intentions or obligations may be, the German Government is not willing to tolerate on its eastern frontier conditions similar those existing in Palestine under the British protectorate.

"The German population also is not willing to tolerate further ill-treatment from Poland.

"The German Government, therefore, refuses all efforts to force Germany by means of ultimatums to recall the troops which have been sent out for the protection of the security of the Reich and thus put up with the old disorder and the old

---

[left column, partially cut]

thinkable that we should refuse to meet the challenge.

... to this high purpose that I now call my people at home and my peoples across the seas, who will make our cause their own. I ask them to stand calm and firm and united in this time of trial.

... task will be hard. There may be dark days ahead, and war can no longer be confined to the battlefield, but we can only do the right as we see the right, and reverently commit our cause to God. If, one and all, we keep resolutely faithful to it, ready for whatever service or sacrifice it may demand, then, with God's help, we shall prevail.

[...] He bless and keep us all"

[...] the King spoke to his people from his [...] at Buckingham Palace. He wore the [...] blue undress uniform of an Admiral [...] the Fleet—his first appearance in [...] form since the war began. He was [...] in the room as he broadcast.

[...] the Queen listened to the speech from [...] her room in the palace.

The King spoke in serious, measured [...], suppressing the stress under which [...] addressed his peoples with firmness.

[...] voice rose a little and his pace increased when he spoke of meeting the [...] of a principle which, if it prevailed, would be fatal to civilised order [...] the world, and he again laid emphasis [...] the passage declaring, that this [...], if established, would place the [...] British Commonwealth of Nations anger.

[...] firmness of his voice increased when [...] said: "We can only do the right as we see the right."

[...] before the broadcast the B.B.C. [...] played the National Anthem, and [...] then Britain entered the war at 11 [...] the King and Queen were together [...] their private rooms at Buckingham [...].

11.15 Their Majesties listened to the [...] Minister's broadcast.

They had spent the morning [...]

[BROADC]AST

[DECISION] [ANNO]UNCED

chambers, divorce proposals are stopped in their tracks.

3 April
Unionists take nearly two-thirds of the seats in the Northern Ireland Ireland Parliament.

28 April
Some Nationalist MPs take their seats in the Northern Ireland Parliament for the first time and swear the oath.

4 July
Legislation authorises a hydro-electric scheme on the Shannon.

3 December
The British and Free State governments agree to nullify the proposals of the Boundary Commission, leaving the North-South border as it is.

1926

19 January
The Minister for Finance, Ernest Blythe, puts forward a bill to establish an Irish coinage.

Ernest Blythe, Minister for Finance in the twenties, notorious for reducing the old-age pension. In later years he was Managing Director of the Abbey Theatre.

Dáil, this left well over a quarter of the voters unrepresented.

And even on the pro-Treaty side there was dangerous dissent. The government managed with remarkable success to establish an unarmed, non-political police force, the Garda Síochána; but the creation of a democratically controlled army was more difficult. By 1924 the Free State army was almost fifty thousand strong and was taking 30 per cent of the national budget. Attempts by the Minister for Defence, Richard Mulcahy, to effect a drastic reduction in its size led to tensions within the army, especially among a faction associated with the old IRA that had close connections with some members of the government, notably the Minister for Industry and Commerce, Joseph McGrath. On 7 March 1924 two senior officers, Major-General Liam Tobin and Colonel Charles Dalton, issued an ultimatum to the government from the old IRA

described the ultimatum as 'a challenge to the democratic foundations of the State, to the very basis of Parliamentary representation and of responsible government.' Immediately afterwards the Minister for Industry and Commerce announced his resignation as a protest against the alleged mishandling of affairs by a public department. It was arranged that Mr McGrath should explain his position to the Dáil yesterday, but between Tuesday evening and Wednesday morning several things happened. Mr McGrath made no explanation yesterday, but the President read a letter and made a brief statement. The letter was from the two officers, who declared that they now recognised the supremacy of Parliament and would consider their object achieved if the 'Army situation' were 'righted.' In his statement the President announced the Government's intention to hold an inquiry into the administration of the Army. Mr McGrath will be consulted on the matter. The whole Executive Council—including the Minister whose policy Mr McGrath denounced—will constitute the court and the proceedings will be private. The debate which followed did not disclose whether Mr McGrath persists in his resignation or has cancelled it.

The President is satisfied that a crisis has been survived or side-tracked; but the country will ask the question: 'Another such crisis and another such solution, or evasion, and what will have become of the Free State?' We are fully conscious of the Government's difficulties and, for that reason, are willing to be gentle with its arguments. It is true that the relations between the National Army and civil authority are less clearly defined than in older and more stable communities, and that the ex-politician is apt to be a restive soldier. Probably it is true also that some modification of the Government's plans for the reduction of the Army is required. The decision to reduce the *personnel* from fifty thousand to eighteen thousand in a few months was very drastic, especially when the Government had taken no adequate measures for the relief of unemployment. The country will not criticise the inquiry; but it will be perplexed and alarmed by the manner in which the whole business has been arranged. Mutiny is mutiny, and, with all respect for Mr Kevin O'Higgins, who must have been acutely uncomfortable yesterday, twenty-four hours cannot change it into a merely frank expression of military discontent—not even twenty-four hours of treatment in the secret alembic of Cumann na nGaedheal. The unhappy truth is that in a situation which demanded courage, decision and faith in Irish democracy the Government has failed to justify the people's hopes ...

The newly formed Garda Síochána or Civic Guard replaced the RIC from 1922. The most obvious difference between the new force and the old was that the Gardaí were unarmed from the beginning.

from The Irish Times 1924
28 APRIL

An Alternative

President Cosgrave has announced that, as the result of the failure of the London Conference, 'there is no alternative to the Boundary Commission.' At this critical time it is all-important that the two Irish States shall appreciate each others' difficulties, and we wish to impress an essential fact on the Government and people of Northern Ireland. The Free State Government's insistence on the Boundary Commission is not an act of spite or defiance, intended merely to exasperate the North. It is an act of self-preservation and, therefore, virtually inevitable. There is in the twenty-six counties, and in Dáil Éireann itself, a very large number of persons who have accepted the Anglo-Irish settlement *faute de mieux*; and a considerable minority in the country is bitterly hostile to it. The settlement exists today because, by a most scrupulous observance of its terms, the British Government has given no sort of handle to its enemies. A refusal by President Cosgrave to demand the

demanding a suspension of the plans for demobil-isation and the removal of the Army Council. A nervous government eventually agreed a compromise with the mutineers. Mulcahy and the senior officers who had arrested the leaders of the mutiny were forced to resign.

For *The Irish Times* these were disturbing developments, shaking the paper's faith in the Cosgrave government. An editorial on 20 March described what had happened as 'astonishing events … which the public will read with bewilderment and alarm.' Showing its willingness to temper its general support for the government with stinging criticism, the paper stood up for Mulcahy. 'Mutiny has been condoned, and resignation has been the fate of those responsible persons who refused to condone it. Soldiers are simple men and they can put "two and two together." The "two and two" in this case are represented by the facts that the mutinous ultimatum demanded the removal of the Army

The Free State members of the Boundary Commission. Eoin MacNeill is second from the right.

11 November

George Bernard Shaw is awarded the Nobel Prize for Literature.

1927

22 May

Charles Lindbergh's plane The Spirit of St Louis *is spotted over Dingle Bay en route to Paris after a solo crossing of the Atlantic.*

Council and that the Army Council has been removed.' The following day the paper's alarm was increased by a strange incident in which men dressed as Free State soldiers opened fire on a party of British soldiers and civilians who were landing at Cóbh from the British base on Spike Island, killing one soldier and wounding dozens. The recently resigned Mulcahy told the paper, however, that this was 'an isolated act of blackguardism.'

Yet the Free State gradually established itself as a functioning democracy. By 1926 de Valera himself was convinced that the institutions established under the Treaty had become facts of life and began to adjust to them. He proposed a motion to the Sinn Féin ardfheis to the effect that if the oaths of allegiance were removed, a

Boundary Commission would be the end of his Government, and a refusal by Great Britain to constitute the Commission might be the end of the Free State. Unhappily, the establishment of the Commission will create a most dangerous conflict of wills—perhaps, even of material forces—between the two Irish States, whereby, in all probability, the peace and progress of both States will be set back for many years.

It is in the equal interest of both States to find a way out of this difficulty. The destruction of the Free State would be a calamity for Northern Ireland. Any attempt at this time to enforce a new frontier on the North would kill for ever the Free State's hopes of a united country. We regard the demand for the Boundary Commission less as a claim upon Northern territory than as an assertion of that principle of unity which hitherto Northern Ireland has refused to recognise. We believe that the border issue would lose most

W. T. Cosgrave

of its urgency in the minds of Southern Irishmen if Northern Ireland would make an immediate profession of faith in the principle of ultimate unity, and would agree immediately to initiate measures by which such unity would be made possible in the course of few or many years. If the Northern Government will offer to take the first step, in return for a postponement of the boundary question, we believe that every succeeding step will be easier and longer. In the first place, some simple basis of co-operation must be found. We have suggested that it might be found in an agreement for joint settlement—a really national settlement—of the Irish railways. Then there are services, at present duplicated services, which in both States pursue identical policies towards identical ends—for instance, the two Departments of Agriculture. Co-operation in agricultural policy not only would mean reduced expenditure and increased efficiency, but would involve such a coming together of the two Governments and peoples as, in twelve months, would rob the border question of half its terrors. Thereafter the same principle of co-operation and co-ordination might be applied, with ever-growing confidence and goodwill, to other public services in the two States ...

decision to take seats in the Dáil and the Northern Ireland Parliament would be 'a question not of principle but of policy.' When this motion was narrowly defeated he led his followers out of Sinn Féin and formed a new party, Fianna Fáil. When it contested the June 1927 election the party was attacked by *The Irish Times* and most of the rest of the press but took 26 per cent of the vote, to Cumann na nGaedheal's 27 per cent. Its deputies tried to gain admission to the Dáil but were turned away when they refused to take the oath.

On 10 July, however, the Vice-President of the Executive Council, Kevin O'Higgins, was shot dead by Republicans on his way to Sunday Mass in the Dublin suburb of Booterstown. The government responded with a bill requiring all future Dáil candidates to sign an affidavit to the effect that they would, if elected, take the required oath. On 11 August, a week after the passing of the act, Fianna Fáil TDs took the oath, and their seats in the Dáil, without incident.

9 June
The general election results in a hung Dáil.

10 July
The Vice-President of the Executive Council and Minister for External Affairs, Kevin O'Higgins, is assassinated.

11 August
The Public Safety Act establishes special courts with military members. De Valera and Fianna Fáil enter Dáil Éireann, stating that they are taking no oath in doing so.

16 August
Cumann na nGaedheal defeats a vote of no confidence with the casting vote of the Ceann Comhairle.

20 August
An act is passed allowing for the establishment of a separate currency in the Free State.

15 September
Another general election results again in a hung Dáil,

though Cumann na nGaedheal is still the largest party.

1928

12–13 April

The first east-west transatlantic flight takes place, from Baldonnel to Labrador. The monoplane Bremen *is crewed by Col. James Fitzmaurice and two Germans.*

7 May

The voting age for women is lowered from thirty to twenty-one.

14 October

The Gate Theatre opens in Dublin.

1929

5 February

De Valera is arrested in Armagh and imprisoned for a month.

16 April

Proportional representation is abolished for elections to the Northern Ireland Parliament.

Unlike those of the Free State, the Northern Ireland police and police reserve were an armed militia. Here two members of the B Specials search a suspect. It was invariably the case that the B Specials were Protestant and the suspects Catholic.

There were plans for an immediate change of government, with Fianna Fáil supporting a minority Labour administration. On 13 August the Labour Party leader, Tom Johnson, met his colleagues William O'Brien and R. J. P. Mortished in the Powerscourt Arms Hotel, Enniskerry, County Dublin, to decide the composition of a government. The names were listed on a piece of paper that was then torn up and thrown into a waste-paper basket. By chance, John Healy, the editor of *The Irish Times*, saw the three men waiting at a bus stop to return to the city. He traced their movements back to the hotel, found the bin, pieced the sheet together, and, in a scoop that proved that his journalistic instincts were intact after twenty years as editor, published the names of the prospective ministers the following day. Three days later the government was saved when a Sligo deputy, John Jinks, missed the crucial vote of confidence. The rumour that he had been plied with drink by

from The Irish Times **1924**
10 MAY

Two Army Officers 'Wanted' for Mutiny

Searches in Dublin

'Two Army officers have attempted to involve the Army in a challenge to the authority of the Government.'

In these words General Mulcahy, Minister for Defence, described on Saturday the action of Major-General Liam Tobin and Colonel Charles Dalton, who were said to be evading arrest on a charge of mutiny.

The issue of orders for the arrest of these officers of the National forces on a charge of mutiny was announced officially on Saturday evening. In view of the official statement certain small incidents reported from the provinces seemed to gain significance.

The incidents occurred at the same time as the publication of particulars of the reorganisation of the Army.

The official statement issued from Government Buildings, Dublin, on Saturday evening was as follows:—

'Orders have been issued for the arrest of two officers of the National forces—Major-General Liam Tobin and Colonel Charles Dalton, who are charged with mutiny. For the purpose of effecting their arrests, several houses in Dublin were visited by a party of military last night, but without result. The two officers are at present evading arrest.'

Later it was announced that the following statement had been issued to the Army by General Mulcahy:—

'Two Army officers have attempted to involve the Army in a challenge to the authority of the Government. This is an outrageous departure from the spirit of the Army. It will not be tolerated. Particularly will it not be tolerated by the officers and men of the Army who cherish its honour. They will stand over their posts and do their duty today in this new threat of danger in the same watchful, determined spirit that has always been the spirit of the Army' ...

Healy's right-hand man, Robert Smyllie, a Sligo man who knew Jinks well, and then put on a train home added to the impression that *The Irish Times* had been part of a conspiracy to keep Cosgrave in office.[2]

The political drama, however, distracted attention from the underlying continuity of Irish society. The change of flags had done little to alter the underlying realities of life. The census of 1926 showed that there were still over 800,000 people living in overcrowded conditions. The infant mortality rate in the north of Dublin city was 25.6 per 1,000, compared with 7.7 per 1,000 in the middle-class suburb of Drumcondra, just a few minutes away. As *The Irish Times* reported in November 1925, tuberculosis was causing 4,500 deaths a year. In 1924, influenza had killed 2,073 people in the Free State.

The hydro-electric scheme at Ardnacrusha under construction

22 May

Unionists win more than two-thirds of the seats in elections to the Northern Ireland Parliament.

16 July

Legislation in the Free State provides for a censorship board to censor or ban publications.

21 October

The Shannon hydro-electric scheme begins commercial operation.

29 October

Stock markets around the world crash, throwing economies into disarray.

17 December

The University College, Galway, Act requires preference to be given to Irish-speakers when appointments are being made.

1930

17 September

The Free State is elected to the Council of the League of Nations.

1 October

The Irish
delegates to the
Imperial
Conference in
London demand
independence.

31 December

The Minister
for Local
Government
dissolves Mayo
County Council
for refusing to
appoint a
Protestant as
county librarian.

1931

5 September

The Irish Press is
launched.

23 October

The IRA and
Saor Éire are
declared illegal.

1932

10 February

The Army
Comrades'
Association is
formed. Later it
transforms
itself into the
National
Guard,
commonly called
the Blueshirts.

Armagh Cathedral on the occasion of the funeral of Cardinal Logue in 1924

But the problems of the city were not a high priority for the new state. Cut off as it was from the industrial heartland of the North, it was overwhelmingly rural. 61 per cent of the population lived outside towns or villages, and 53 per cent of the work force was engaged in agriculture. Most of them worked their own small or medium-sized farms. This rural society was overwhelmingly Catholic, making the South a Catholic state to match the Protestant polity of

Cause of Government Action

As regards the latter, it is understood that a few days ago certain officers addressed a document to the Government. The nature of the document has not transpired, but it is apparent from the statements issued on Saturday evening that the Government regarded the contents as indicating mutiny; and they at once issued instructions for the arrest of the two officers mentioned.

Particulars of the scheme of Army reorganisation were issued to the Press by the military authorities on Friday night, and were published in the newspapers on Saturday. It was then stated that the demobilisation of officers surplus to the establishment was completed on Friday, when 900 left the service. It was also announced that in addition to three months' pay, demobilised officers with pre-truce service received supplementary grants for their reinstatement in civil life, and it is understood that in some cases the amount of assistance might reach £250.

The Demobilisation

In 1922 the Army totalled 55,000, with 3,300 officers. The new organisation provides for a force of 18,000, with 1,300 officers.

Demobilisation of the rank and file has been going on for many months past, but the reduction in the commissioned ranks had not been equivalent, and the result was that when the re-organisation came into effect the number of officers who found themselves simultaneously bidding farewell to their jobs was large, and in every military centre there was a group of individuals faced with a blank future in place of the life in positions in which men were at their bidding. Other officers were placed on a new footing involving reduction of rank.

While it cannot be assumed that in places where incidents have occurred they have been inspired by officers due for demobilisation, or reduction in rank, it is likely that expectation of the drastic change brought into force last week was at the bottom of a certain recent restlessness and disturbance of the usual discipline. In this atmosphere certain ideas might have an easy currency ...

from The Irish Times 1925
9 NOVEMBER

The Free State

This newspaper will not be accused of an uncritical attitude to the conduct of public affairs in the Free State. It speaks its mind freely about the Government's sins of commission and omission, and more than once, on that account, has been put in the pillory by angry or peevish Ministers. Perhaps, therefore, a plea from us for fair play for the Free State may have some weight in the quarters to which it is directed. Outside this country there seems to be still a number of persons who have convinced themselves that the Saorstát will come to a speedy and bad end. What capital was not made, for instance, out of the

Kevin O'Higgins, Minister for Home Affairs and strong man of the early Free State governments

Northern Ireland. The Prime Minister of Northern Ireland, Lord Craigavon, made this explicit in 1932 when he remarked: 'They still boast of Southern Ireland being a Catholic State. All I boast is that we are a Protestant Parliament and a Protestant State.'

But for all its veneer of rural, Catholic contentment, the South was not, by any standards, a normal place. The most basic social activity—marriage—was extraordinarily rare. The combined effects of the Famine, mass emigration

16 February

The general election results in a minority Fianna Fáil government.

9 March

De Valera enters government for the first time.

10 March

IRA prisoners are released from jail.

16 March

De Valera announces his plan for government, including withholding the land annuities paid to Britain, the abolition of the oath of allegiance, the introduction of protective tariffs, and the merging of the office of President of the Executive Council with that of Governor-General.

18 March

The government allows the order outlawing the IRA to lapse.

20 April

The Constitution (Removal of Oath) Bill, which eliminates the oath to the British monarchy, is published.

22–26 June

The International Eucharistic Congress is held in Dublin.

26 September

De Valera makes his inaugural speech as

Early Dublin fire engines

and a puritanical brand of Catholicism were revealed in the census of 1926, which showed that the Free State had the highest proportion of unmarried people of any country that kept records. In the 25–30 age group 80 per cent of men and 62 per cent of women were unmarried. Even in the 35–40 age group, 50 per cent of men and 32 per cent of women were unmarried.

absurd story that the Earl of Birkenhead's life would have been in danger if he had visited Dublin! Again, we have before us a copy of the November issue of 'Notes from Ireland,' which is printed in London. This publication consists of eight pages of news items and comment from which everything hopeful, progressive and of good report in the Saorstát's current history is excluded carefully, and the net effect, of course, is horrific in the extreme. The English reader

A fallen dray-horse at O'Connell Bridge, Dublin

of the 'Notes' is told about 'Sinn Féin anglophobia,' about 'disappearing trade,' about the alarming plight of the railways, about the degradation of the learned professions and about the electors' 'apathy of despair.' It is admitted that the harvest has been good, but this fact, the editor adds gloomily, 'merely postpones the prospect of famine.' Three columns of the 'Notes' are packed with reports of crimes, compiled from Free State newspapers.

It is true that Irish trade is depressed, that the Free State railways are in a bad way, and that the Government has done some very foolish things, including its wanton attack on the prestige and efficiency of the medical profession. It is not true, however, that the Free State is the victim of an orgy of misgovernment and is hurrying hopelessly to perdition. Surely the members of the Irish minority who still live in the Free

Freedom was, for many, still an abstract term. Some farm labourers, especially those who lived in their employers' houses (over 36,000 in 1926), continued to experience conditions close to slavery. Hiring-fairs, where labourers had to put themselves on display for prospective employers, continued in Munster, Leinster and Ulster until the thirties. Dan Bradley has evoked their atmosphere: 'Big farmers came to the Limerick fairs from North Cork, East Kerry and all parts of County Limerick. Those for hire gathered in the market places from early morning on the fair day, usually at the beginning of spring. Farmers tested the muscles of those for hire, and scrutinized them closely for signs of illness or

chairman of the Assembly of the League of Nations in Geneva.

1933

24 January
Fianna Fáil wins the general election.

30 January
Adolf Hitler becomes Chancellor of the

Weimar Republic in Germany.

22 February
Eoin O'Duffy is dismissed as Commissioner of the Garda Síochána.

3 May
The oath of allegiance is removed from the Constitution of the Irish Free State.

weakness. The examination struck some observers as similar to that performed on animals.'[3] In Munster the indoor labourer was referred to as the 'servant boy', even if he was in his sixties. Paddy Roche, an indoor labourer in Mountcollins, County Limerick, in the thirties, recalled his typical diet. 'Watery potatoes, green cabbage and a mug of water often constituted dinner. Supper was bread and milk without butter. Around two o'clock there was tea and a few slices of bread.'[4] Even in 1934, when farm labourers' hours of work were fixed by law, they were at the extraordinarily high level of fifty-four hours a week.

Officially, and to a large extent in reality, strict Catholic morality prevailed among this

State can claim to know something of its present conditions. We have the public testimony of many of these residents, including leaders of the Churches of the minority, that they do not despair for the future of the Free State. President Cosgrave's young Executive has established—apart from the folly and injustice of 'compulsory Irish'—admirable traditions of religious and political tolerance. It cannot control the fluctuations of trade, but it has passed laws which, we believe, will give an important stimulus to the country's main industry. It has so comported itself politically that—again with the exception of 'compulsory Irish'—it has done much to disarm the fears and suspicions of the North. Perhaps the Government's most notable achievement has been the restoration of order throughout the land, the establishment of a first-rate police force and the successful reorganisation of

William Redmond, son of the former leader of the Irish Party, founded the short-lived National League Party in 1926. Here he addresses a public meeting in 1929.

Sir John Lavery's painting of the Twelfth of July parade in Portadown, Co. Armagh, in 1928

the whole machinery of the law. Three columns of assorted crimes for the months of August, September and October prove nothing to the contrary: in a single week three such columns could be compiled for the city where the 'Notes from Ireland' are printed. There is, then, as Mr Blythe said yesterday at Clonmel, little excuse for domestic pessimism; and for long-distance pessimism there is no excuse at all …

from The Irish Times 1925
11 NOVEMBER

1914–1925

And some there be which have no memorial; who are perished as though they had never been … Their bodies are buried in peace; but their name liveth for evermore.

S even years ago today the last shot was fired in the greatest conflict that the world has known. After four and a half years of death and ruin mankind was freed from the thraldom of war, and the news that the

unmarried population. But after the Civil War it seemed to some observers that the political turmoil of the previous years had unsettled morals. Writing in 1924, the senior civil servant P. S. O'Hegarty claimed that 'the last years of the wars were years of moral unsettlement, of which waves of loot and materialism were the result. There has been a grave increase in sexual immorality, and a general abandonment to looseness and dissipation.'[5] The following year *The Irish Times* took up this theme. An editorial in November 1925 remarked that 'democracy is more prudish in Ireland than, perhaps, anywhere else in the world.' Sex was seldom discussed in public, and 'for the most part, Press and pulpit are content to respect this conspiracy of silence.' Yet the writer was sure that the 'national morals' were considerably looser than they had been twenty years before, particularly because of 'the effects of our recent years of social and political

11 June
The Communist Party of Ireland is formed.

20 July
Eoin O'Duffy is elected leader of the Army Comrades' Association (Blueshirts).

22 August
The Blueshirts are banned.

8 September
Cumann na nGaedheal, the National Centre Party and the National Guard (Blueshirts) merge to form Fine Gael.

1934

24 April
Lord Craigavon, leader of the Ulster Unionist Party, refers to Stormont and Northern Ireland as 'a Protestant Parliament and a Protestant state.'

21 September
Eoin O'Duffy resigns from his position in Fine Gael.

W. T. Cosgrave with some of his political supporters

1935

28 February
The sale and importing of contraceptives becomes illegal, and the age of consent is raised from sixteen to seventeen.

10 April
The Irish Nationality and

disorder.' Dublin's notorious brothels had been subjected to increasing pressure from the Gardaí but had merely been driven 'under the surface.' Girls were taking to drink and all-night dances. Looser attitudes were not confined to the cities: 'Now the Churches have cause to be as much concerned for country as for city morals, and it becomes daily more difficult to defend our old traditions of rural innocence.' And, the paper hinted darkly, 'an honest statement of the present ravages of venereal disease in Ireland would startle the public conscience.'

This was more than a fit of moral panic. There was strong evidence that all was not quite

Armistice had been signed on the Western front sent a wave of new hope surging through the breast of humanity. The years have passed, and in their passing have begun to dim the memories of those awful days when civilisation seemed to be toppling to its fall; but on this day we who remain devote our thoughts to that great multitude of gallant men whose lives were given gladly for freedom. We think, with sad pride, of the thousands of young Irish soldiers whose blood drenched the soil of France and Flanders ... They, with their millions of comrades of other nations, did not hesitate to throw their lives into the dread hazard of war for their country's sake; and they have laid on us, into whose hands their torch of endeavour has fallen, a responsibility of which we have yet to prove ourselves worthy.

World peace is still a dream ... It is a sobering fact that there are many more armed men on the Continent of Europe today than there were in 1914. Germany has been forced to reduce her army to a skeleton in accordance with the ruling of the Versailles Treaty; but this reduction has been countered by the creation of new armies in Poland and Czecho-Slovakia, the former of which is a stronger military Power than Great Britain. In the background lurks Soviet Russia, with her 'Red' army of more than a million fighting men. Outside the pale of civilisation, she knows no law. The League of Nations may issue its peace compelling edicts, but so long as Russia remains in isolation they will have no real force in the world ... France is engaged in two minor wars; Italy is still living on the brink of the unknown; the German Monarchists are becoming active again with plans of a Wittelsbach

as it seemed. The official figures for 'illegitimate' births were rising steadily, from 1,520 in 1922 to 1,853 in 1929, the latter figure representing over 3 per cent of all births registered that year. And an official report concluded that these figures were 'only a part of the actual situation.' Such was the strain on the inadequate facilities available that the authorities were faced in county homes with 'the objectionable fact that unmarried mothers of first-born children cannot be maintained apart from the other inmates (the decent poor and sick).' Such attitudes underlay the often cruel treatment of unmarried mothers, their children and other children who ended up in institutions. And even the official figures

Citizenship Act allows people born in Northern Ireland after 6 December 1922 to be citizens of the Free State.

1936

19 May
The Free State Senate meets for the last time.

27 May
The first Aer Lingus flight between Dublin and Britain takes place.

17 July
Civil war breaks out in Spain.

20 November
Eoin O'Duffy and other Blueshirts go to the Spanish Civil War to fight on the side of the fascists.

11 December
The Constitutional Amendment Bill removes all reference to the crown in the Free State Constitution.

16 December
Frank Ryan and other left-wing activists arrive in

James MacNeill, the second Governor-General

*Spain to fight on
the side of the
republicans.*

1937

28 May

*Arthur Neville
Chamberlain is
appointed Prime
Minister of the
United Kingdom.*

8 June

*The functions and
powers of the
crown's represen-
tative in Ireland
are transferred to
the Executive
Council.*

22 June

*Eoin O'Duffy and
other fascists return
from Spain.*

1 July

*A referendum on
the Constitution of
Ireland, promoted
by de Valera, is
held at the same
time as the general
election. De Valera
is victorious,
though Fianna
Fáil does not get
an overall majority.*

29 December

*The Constitution
of Ireland comes
into force.*

**Colonel James Fitzmaurice was one of the three-man
crew who made the first east-west flight across the
Atlantic in April 1928.**

acknowledged the incidence of child abuse. The
Gardaí recorded 268 sexual offences against girls
and 174 against boys between 1927 and 1929. In
Dublin alone they estimated that there were
about a hundred women under twenty-one
engaged in prostitution.

Aside from the private defiance of sexual
orthodoxy there was the much more common
outlet of emigration. Between 1926 and 1936,
166,751 people emigrated from the Free State.
Much of the impulse to get away was purely
economic, but much of it too was a desire for a
broader, richer life. It was notable that the rural
Irish settled well in the big cities of America,
where, by the twenties, they were already rising
from the bottom of the heap. Irish emigration
was unusual in that women left in larger numbers
than men. Many of them worked as domestic
servants before they married but were able to get
their children into the middle classes. As early as
1910 a quarter of the public-school teachers in

restoration in Bavaria, and in the Balkan States the old
jealousies and hatreds are breaking out again.

The hope of the future lies with Britain and the United
States. Almost alone among the nations of the world they
have preserved their social and economic stability throughout
the upheavals of the war and its aftermath. Britain, it is true,
has her problems of unemployment; but her body politic is
sound in wind and limb, and her influence throughout the
globe is stronger than ever it was. America was born anew in
the war. Her heterogeneous population was welded together
in its fires, and the work of nation-building, which may be
said to have been begun by Lincoln, was brought to a
triumphant conclusion at the salient of St Mihiel. The great
need of our times is Anglo-Saxon unity; for, if the British
Commonwealth and the United States work together, there is
nothing that they cannot accomplish. By sheer force of moral
influence they can impose peace on the nations of the earth.
What Power, or group of Powers, would dare to go to war
against the will of that mighty combination? Britain and
America control most of the raw materials of the world; the
seas are under their joint sway, and their trade penetrates into
the uttermost corners of the earth. For the moment American
opinion holds aloof from the affairs of Europe; but the time
is coming when its attitude of isolation will be changed.
Pending that change Britain must continue her work of
peace-making alone; and today, when heads are bowed in
reverent memory of their dead, the British people throughout
the Empire will dedicate their lives afresh to that noble task.

from The Irish Times **1925**
20 NOVEMBER

The Boundary Crisis

I t is believed that the Irish Boundary Commission is nearing
the end of its task and that its report, or reports, will be
published within the next few weeks. Many people will be
surprised that the President of the Free State Executive not only
should have discussed this extraordinarily delicate subject in
Parliament yesterday, but should have devoted a part of his
speech to an English newspaper's unofficial and entirely
unauthorised forecast of the Commission's report. While we
may wish, however, that Mr Cosgrave could have remained
silent, we must acknowledge that such silence had become
virtually impossible. The newspaper forecast indicates that the
Free State will lose more than it will gain, and has provoked the

liveliest indignation among Northern Nationalists—especially in Donegal, which, according to this forecast, will be required to surrender territory to Northern Ireland. Furthermore, the Republicans, whose political stock is at a heavy discount, have eager hopes that they may be able to mend their fortunes if the Free State Government loses credit and influence as a result of the Commission's report; and, in the meanwhile, the Government's representative on the Commission is honouring his strict obligation to say nothing at all. Mr Cosgrave's position, therefore, was exceedingly difficult. The country looked to him for reassurance, but his material was scanty and the limitations which his responsibilities imposed on him were severe. The natural outcome is a negative rather than a positive statement. He has given us a fairly clear notion of the sort of boundary settlement which his Government will not accept.

Last week President Cosgrave told the *Dáil* that his Government had informed the Boundary Commission of its contention that no territory now within the *Saorstát*'s jurisdiction could be transferred to Northern Ireland under Article 12 of the Treaty. He renewed this contention in the clearest terms yesterday, and the *Dáil* endorsed it by formal resolution. It appears, therefore, that, if the Commission's report, or a majority report, transfers the smallest portion of Free State territory to Northern Ireland, the Free State Government may claim the right to reject that verdict and to lay an appeal before some higher tribunal. The implications of this contention are enormously important. Certainly it is manifest that any such 'settlement' as the *Morning Post*'s forecast suggests must revive the whole border controversy in its fiercest form. Mr Cosgrave will not tolerate the notion that any part of Donegal shall be given to Northern Ireland, and assumes that any equitable verdict must give Newry to the Free State. His words were impassioned, and we do not doubt that they were sincere. We must admit, quite frankly, that the Free State Government would court political disaster if it should accept any such barren readjustment as the *Morning Post* suggests. On the other hand, there is no prospect that the Government of Northern Ireland will accept any settlement that would embrace what we now conceive to be Mr Cosgrave's *minimum* of concession. Thus a very grave situation becomes imminent. Only one of two miracles, it seems, can save this land from an invasion of new discords at the very season of peace and good-will—a miracle of compromise at Clement's Inn or a miracle of commonsense in Ireland ...

Boston and Rhode Island were the daughters of Irishwomen; in Chicago they made up a staggering 70 per cent. Those prospects were considerably better than those of women who stayed on the farm at home.

Yet the official culture of the Free State remained pious and conservative, and *The Irish Times* was inclined to accept the reality that the Catholic Church would have a dominant role. As early as March 1923, reporting a secret Vatican initiative to mediate between the opposing sides in the Civil War, the paper had remarked that 'we are like those victims of the witch's spell who stumbled for ever in an enchanted wood. If the Pope can help us to break that spell, he will be blessed even in Portadown.'

The editor of *The Irish Times*, John Healy, was determined that the paper should play a constructive role in the new state. He urged former unionists, with 'their special contribution of character, education and experience,' to make

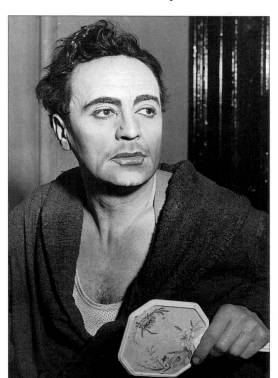

Mícheál Mac Liammóir, who, with Hilton Edwards, founded the Gate Theatre in 1928 and was its artistic inspiration for a generation

1938

11–13 March
German soldiers march into Austria.

26 April
The economic war between Britain and the Free State comes to an end as articles of agreement signed the previous day are published. The British lose control of their military installations in Lough Swilly, Cóbh, and Bearhaven; in return the Irish pay £10 million in a final financial settlement. Tariffs between the two countries on certain products come to an end.

27 April
Seanad Éireann meets for the first time.

17 June
The general election results in an overall majority for Fianna Fáil.

25 June
Douglas Hyde is inaugurated as President of Ireland.

The hydro-electric scheme on the Shannon at Ardnacrusha, just north of Limerick, was the first major industrial and engineering achievement of the Irish Free State

a willing and whole-hearted commitment to the new state. As early as January 1922 the paper had expressed the perhaps naïve hope that a member of the unionist minority might be included in the Provisional Government. Yet there were also worries about the future. The announcement that Irish was to be made a compulsory subject in schools provoked a number of editorials in 1922 and 1923. The paper expressed its good will towards the language but also warned that the minority would resent any attempt to force it down their throats or to make it a condition of their right to full citizenship.

The paper still saw its sincere commitment to the Free State within a British and an imperial context; even in 1926 it was still declaring the British Empire 'the most powerful progressive force in the world.' What for the new men in power were necessary but unwelcome concessions to the British connection were to

The Blackbird of Derrycairn

Stop, stop and listen for the bough top
Is whistling and the sun is brighter
Than God's own shadow in the cup now!
Forget the hour-bell. Mournful matins
Will sound as well, Patric, at nightfall.

Faintly through mist of broken water
Fionn heard my melody in Norway,
He found the forest track, he brought back
This beak to gild the branch and tell, there,
Why men must welcome in the daylight.

He loved the breeze that warns the black grouse,
The shout of gillies in the morning
When packs are counted and the swans cloud
Loch Erne, but more than all those voices,
My throat rejoicing from the hawthorn.

In little cells behind a cashel,

Patric, no handbell has a glad sound.

But knowledge is found among the branches.

Listen! The song that shakes my feathers

Will thong the leather of your satchels.

Stop, stop and listen for the bough top

Is whistling . . .

Austin Clarke

from The Irish Times 1935
CIRCA

Emigration Again

There are definite signs that emigration has begun again, though its present volume must remain a matter for guesswork. Irish emigrants no longer seek the United States, where a careful record was kept of their numbers, but are crossing to Great Britain in search of work. Speaking on Tuesday at the annual meeting of the Cork County Vocational Education Committee, the Rev. F. McCarthy described conditions in his own parish, and said that the tendency for young men and women to emigrate to Great Britain had become 'an epidemic' ... Owing to the 'economic war,' farming is in a deplorable condition. The farmers themselves are in a bad plight, and the farm labourers share their misfortunes—at the best they get low wages, and at the worst they get neither wages nor work. It is no wonder that they should try to 'better themselves' abroad; and, as America now is closed to them, the only remaining hope is Great Britain. *Fianna Fáil*'s policy must take the blame for a great deal of this situation; but it would be unjust to blame it for everything. Emigration, a natural and even a good tendency in most countries, is a chronic evil so far as Ireland has been concerned, and perhaps it was too much to hope that so deeply-rooted a habit could be stopped easily. Nevertheless, when the United States at last closed her doors there was a chance that the drain on our population would be brought to an end. During the last few years, indeed, the numbers have begun to increase for the first time in almost a century; and the new factories of Mr Lemass could have played a useful part in absorbing the young men and women who now were staying at home. As events have turned out, of course, the new factories have not even been able to make good the decay in agriculture, and the

W. B. Yeats, winner of the Nobel Prize for Literature of 1923 and arguably the greatest English-language poet of the twentieth century

The Irish Times, and the southern Protestant minority for which it spoke, vital expressions of identity. When, in a debate on the role of the British courts of appeal, Cosgrave referred to Britain as 'an alien government', an editorial rejected the description. It pointed out that Ireland, with a seat at the Imperial Conference, was a partner in the Commonwealth and that the British legal system was 'the most perfect of their common possessions.' Likewise it deplored the disbanding of six Irish regiments of the British army. Even in 1923 the paper could publish a

19 February

De Valera announces that the Free State will be neutral in any imminent war.

4 May

James Joyce's Finnegans Wake *is published.*

The Governor-General, Tim Healy, in conversation

14 June
De Valera introduces the Offences Against the State Act, allowing for internment and military tribunals against those trying to undermine the state.

25 August
An IRA bomb in Coventry kills five people and wounds seventy.

review of a history of the 2nd Battalion of the Royal Dublin Fusiliers that expressed the hope that the book would soon be in the hands of every Irish schoolboy. Equally, in 1926, when the paper exhorted all sections of the country to join in the 'noble and holy task' of building the nation, it inadvertently revealed the gap between its own cultural background and that of the majority by ending the appeal with a call 'to play up, play up and play the game.'

The paper was out of line too with the prevailing southern attitude to Northern Ireland. It remained fervently opposed to partition and continued to express the hope that the Prime Minister of Northern Ireland, Sir James Craig, would eventually take his place in a united Irish

unemployment figures would be much larger if emigration had not begun again. We do not pretend to say whether the present exodus to Great Britain is serious or not, because any judgment is impossible in the absence of details. Reports from various parts of the country, however, show that many young people of both sexes are leaving the Free State for Great Britain, and some official attempt should be made to find out the actual position. At the present time it is even more important than before to stop emigration by providing work at home. In former days the Irish emigrants to America were reasonably sure to find employment when they arrived there; but many recent emigrants are discovering, too late, that there is no such guarantee now either in America or in Great Britain.

from The Irish Times 1933
27 MARCH

Germany and the Jews

Chancellor Hitler has allowed the anti-Semitic proclivities of his followers to reach wicked lengths. Within the past week international opinion, which had been generally not unfavourable to Nazi aspirations, has swung definitely against their abuse of power. Doubtless, the reports from Germany, which suggest that whole Jewish communities are being extinguished by the bomb and the bayonet, are hysterical exaggerations; but there is enough evidence to show that a ruthless campaign is being waged against the Jews. The professed object of the Nazis, both before and after Herr Hitler's return to power, has been to purge public life in Germany of its 'non-Teutonic' elements. Jews are being turned out of their positions by the thousand; any action taken by them in self-defence is construed as an act of treason, and men of the highest distinction are being driven into exile. Naturally, the Jewish communities throughout the world are in revolt against this treatment of their co-religionists. Yesterday the Jews of the British Empire, through their board of Deputies, condemned the Nazis' behaviour in the strongest terms, and a 'boycott German goods' movement is gaining ground in parts of England. Polish Jews have instituted a similar boycott, and the American Jewish Association, one of the wealthiest and most powerful bodies in the world, is summoning a 'world demonstration' of protest against the German excesses. The vigour of this opposition seems to have frightened Chancellor

Hitler and his Cabinet, but as yet they have done nothing to check the exuberance of their followers.

Many German Jews, of course, are Communists, and some of them are the brains of the Communist movement in Germany—just as Russian Jews were the brains of the 1917 revolution in Russia. As a community, however, the Jews of Germany are not formidable; they number only one per cent of the population, and certainly do not merit the atrocious treatment which is being allotted to them. If they deserve anything, they deserve well of Germany; for during this century they have made huge contributions to her intellectual and scientific advancement. Among the people who have incurred the displeasure of the Nazis are Professor Einstein, Herr Leon Feuchtwangler, and Herr Bruno Walter, one of the most famous conductors in the world. The proscription of these men is a lamentable commentary on Nazi enlightenment and a gloomy portent for Germany's future. It

parliament as 'a rallying point for all the elements of sanity and conservatism.' Once the Union had gone, the ideal of the editor, John Healy, was 'a united, liberal-minded prosperous Ireland, an enthusiastic member of the Commonwealth, cherishing its links with Great Britain and the empire.'[6] But he also warned in his editorials that the only way to achieve unity was through peaceful co-operation and cautioned that a policy compounded of 'half overture and half obloquy' would succeed merely in evoking the 'old war cry, "No surrender."' Particularly after the Boundary Commission established under the Treaty to consider the borders of Northern Ireland and the Free State ended in ignominious failure, southern attitudes and northern responses were precisely those that Healy warned against.

3 September
Beginning of the Second World War.

13 September
Petrol rationing begins in the Free State. Northern Ireland follows suit ten days later.

23 December
The IRA raids the Magazine Fort in the Phoenix Park.

W. T. Cosgrave (right) with Archbishop Byrne of Dublin (centre)

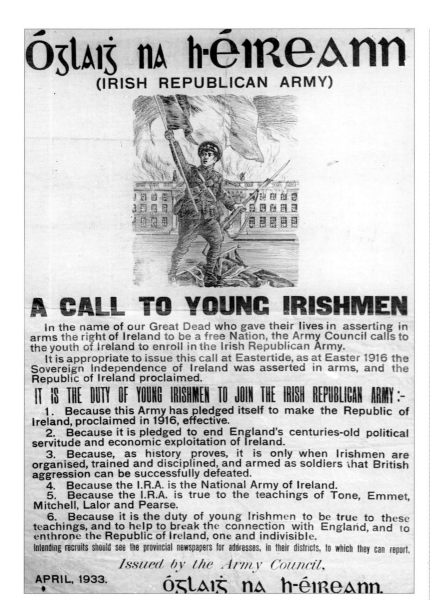

A recruiting poster for the IRA from the early thirties

suggests either that Chancellor Hitler's alleged genius for statesmanship is a much poorer thing than was supposed, or that he and his Ministers are unable to control the ignorant passions of the Nazi rank and file. In either case, while Germany is being deprived by the campaign of some of her worst citizens, she is losing also a great many of the most valuable and the most illustrious.

More sinister, however, and by this time patent to all Germany, is the retribution which almost inevitably will follow her treatment of the Jews. The unofficial boycotts in Great Britain, the United States and other countries are but a first instalment of what Germany may expect from the outraged sentiment of international Jewry.... If she chooses to alienate the Jews within her own borders, their co-religionists elsewhere will be powerful enough to make things exceedingly unpleasant for her. The boycott movements have given Herr Hitler occasion to stop and think; what will happen when the money markets of London and New York offer him a token of their displeasure? He has been given a fair chance by the electors of Germany to reinstate their country as a noble and puissant nation. Will he permit an unjust and tyrannical campaign to ruin that opportunity?

from The Irish Times **1936**
20 JUNE

IRA Declared Unlawful
Order Made by Free State Government

The Free State Government has made an Order banning the organisation known as the Irish Republican Army, and a proclamation has been issued prohibiting the parade announced by that body to be held at Bodenstown tomorrow.

The step declaring the Irish Republican Army an unlawful association has been taken under Article 2A of the Constitution.

Under the proclamation the holding of the parade on Sunday is prohibited on that day, 'or at any other place within one day before or three days after such time.'

The following statement was issued by the Government Information Bureau last evening:—

'The methods and activities of the organisation styling itself the Irish Republican Army, and the commission of crimes of violence obviously organised, make it necessary that

1940

4 January
An emergency session of Dáil Éireann allows the establishment of an internment camp in the Curragh Camp.

In many ways *The Irish Times* under Healy remained an ambivalent presence. On the one hand it was still rooted in a declining imperial world; on the other hand it was so anxious to be respectful of the new state and constructive in its criticisms that its defence of minority rights was rather muted. One of the tests of whether the new state would be a confessional or a pluralist one was the issue of divorce. Under the old regime there were limited and difficult procedures—by way of private parliamentary

A creamery in rural Ireland. Sights like this were commonplace throughout the first half of the twentieth century

it should be made clear that the continuance of this unlawful organisation will not be permitted.

'THE GOVERNMENT HAS THEREFORE DECIDED TO MAKE AN ORDER FORMALLY DECLARING THIS ORGANISATION TO BE AN UNLAWFUL ASSOCIATION UNDER SECTION 19 OF ARTICLE 2A OF THE CONSTITUTION.

'A mobilisation of this organisation has been arranged to be held at Sallins and Bodenstown on Sunday, the 21st instant, and is intended to be used as an occasion for a parade in military order of units of the organisation from different parts of the country. The Government has decided to prohibit the holding of any such mobilisation or meeting, and has issued a proclamation to that effect.

'The Government warns all citizens to avoid visiting the neighbourhood of Sallins and Bodenstown on Sunday next.' ...

bills—for the dissolution of marriage. The Free State Constitution did not explicitly prohibit divorce, but Cosgrave proposed in effect to do so. In June 1925 Protestants in the Senate argued that this amounted to making church law into state law. W. B. Yeats, then a member of the Senate, chose the occasion to make a passionate plea for the rights of the Protestant minority: 'If you show that this country, Southern Ireland, is going to be governed by Catholic ideas, and by Catholic ideas alone, you will never get the North ... I think it tragic that within three years of this country gaining its independence we should be discussing a measure which a minority of this nation considers to be grossly oppressive

5 January

A member of the Garda Síochána is shot dead in Cork.

23 January

Appeals by two IRA men, Peter Barnes and James McCormack, against the death sentence imposed for the bombing of Coventry the previous year are launched.

Two Cumann na nGaedheal posters for the 1932 election designed to ridicule Fianna Fáil and to scare the electorate

5 February

Barnes and McCormack are hanged in Birmingham. Dublin firms shut down for the day, and flags in the Free State fly at half mast.

9 April

Germany invades Denmark and Norway.

10 May

Germany invades the Netherlands, Belgium, and Luxembourg.

… We against whom you have done this are no petty people. We are one of the great stocks of Europe … If we have not lost our stamina then your victory will be brief, and your defeat final, and when it comes this nation may be transformed.'

Yeats's fighting words were at odds with the low-key approach of *The Irish Times*. The paper agreed that 'subjects in the Irish Free State are being deprived of a right which is guaranteed by the constitution and is inherent in citizenship of the British Empire.' But it deplored the manner of Yeats's intervention, which it condemned as hurtful and aggressive. An editorial observed that the 'problem of reconciling the minority's constitutional freedom with the dictates of the majority's conscience is by far the most delicate problem with which this state has been or is ever to be faced.' It remarked ruefully that 'breadth of vision and the appreciation of an unfamiliar moral outlook are plants of slow and fragile growth on this side of the Irish Sea.' The

from The Irish Times
21 NOVEMBER 1936

Irishmen for Spain

General O'Duffy Leaves with Party

General O'Duffy left Dublin last night with about forty members of his Irish Brigade on their way to Spain. They were seen off by a large crowd of people, who collected on the quayside as the B and I steamer left the dock.

General O'Duffy, interviewed on board the ship, stated that, including those leaving from Belfast and Dublin, there were about one hundred of his followers travelling to Spain. Those leaving Dublin included former soldiers of the Free State Army, and was representative of various parts of the country, including a Catholic scoutmaster of 22 years of age.

It is understood that applications for passports to Spain and Portugal have been received in between forty and fifty cases at the Dublin Passport Office recently. It was also learned last night that an ambulance unit would shortly leave in the wake of the latest detachment, and would include a number of doctors.

When General O'Duffy and his followers reach Liverpool today they will be joined by a party of ten Irishmen resident in England, who will accompany them to Spain.

The first contingent of ten men left Dublin last Friday for Spain.

from The Irish Times
19 DECEMBER 1936

The Reign of Error

To the Editor of *The Irish Times*

Sir,—In all his reign of error Mr de Valera has never been so supine and self-contradictory as when last week he hastened to be the first in all this rough island's story to set the name of an English Monarch on its Statute Book. Do not take it that I object to an English Monarch. I have come to realise that ourselves alone would never evolve as sound an idea of either freedom or justice as that to be met with now under the Commonwealth and the Throne.

What I do, as an Irishman, object to is the precipitancy with which this Act was put through at a time that was far from being the darkest in our history and when there was no threat of immediate and terrible war, no reign of terror, to alarm Mr de Valera; a precipitancy which enabled him to slur over the Coronation Oath, which is repugnant to English as well as Irish Catholics. Judging by the way Mr de Valera tolerates the continuance of an oath which puts Catholics in the position of untouchables as regards the Throne, I begin to wonder if it came to maintain his position he would have objected to the Penal Laws. This flaccidity is all the more astonishing when we remember his objection to the oath of allegiance, which he brought himself to take only because the Bible was a few feet away from him at the time of swearing.

Meanwhile, with this exception, I welcome heartily and hopefully each and every repudiation by Mr de Valera of his old self and his drawing closer to the Throne. In this lies the only hope for our country. It is Mr de Valera's only chance of becoming less an 'unique' dictator but efficient like the others.

Yours, etc.,
Oliver St J. Gogarty
Ely Place, Dublin,
19 December 1936

fear, evidently, was that too strong a defence of minority rights would provoke a reaction that would nip pluralism in the bud.

The attitude of its old West British readership to *The Irish Times* was itself somewhat ambivalent. On the one hand the paper was still regarded as at least a relic of the old decencies. Brian Inglis, who grew up in a well-to-do Protestant household, recalled that '*The Irish Times*, though we thought it devoted too much space to the Dáil and to Gaelic games, had at least remained faithful to the Crown.'[7] On the other hand, while it may have been a relatively respectable newspaper, it was, after all, a newspaper, and the trade was a vulgar one. Lionel ('Bill') Fleming, the son of a Church of Ireland clergyman who became a reporter with the paper (and later the BBC's colonial correspondent), recalled that in the early thirties there was still in his social circles a stigma attached to journalism,

27 May
The evacuation of British soldiers from Dunkerque begins.

10 June
Italy declares war on Britain and France.

14 June
German soldiers enter Paris.

2 July
Germany launches its first daylight bombing raid on London.

The Blueshirts

De Valera's first government

12 August

The Battle of Britain begins.

26 August

German bombs kill three women working in a creamery in Campile, Co. Wexford. A ship arrives in Strangford Lough to hold interned IRA prisoners.

27 December

John Charles McQuaid is

an assumption that 'reporters are all seedy and rather unscrupulous men, with a taste for drink, an ignorance of grammar, and a capacity for never getting the facts quite right.'[8]

As it happened, both of these attitudes rather accurately reflected the ambience of *The Irish Times* in the twenties and thirties. It was still suffused with nostalgia for the lost world of British Ireland, partly because, with no pension scheme to allow for retirement, staff from the old imperial days were still employed. As late as the eve of the Second World War there was still a reporter in the news room, John Collins, who claimed that his first assignment had been to cover the Franco-Prussian War of 1870. The general manager, J. J. Simington, had been with the paper since 1878 and was still running the business in 1941. The doorman was still Bill Coyne, who had been batman in the Great War

from The Irish Times
4 SEPTEMBER 1939

Dies Irae

The British Empire is at war. This tremendous and appalling fact overshadows everything else in the world today. Yesterday morning His Majesty's Ambassador in Berlin presented the German Government with an ultimatum, giving it a space of two hours in which to reply to Great Britain's former demand regarding the evacuation of Poland. When the fateful hour struck, no reply was forthcoming; and at eleven o'clock yesterday morning a state of war was declared between Germany and the British Empire. The general public was informed of what had happened in a moving broadcast by Mr Neville Chamberlain, who spoke from his home in Downing Street ...

In this tragic hour the thoughts of all Irishmen, whatever may be their political views, will turn with deep feeling to the agonies that are being suffered by the people

Frank Ryan (third from left at back) with Republican comrades during the Spanish Civil War

of Poland. There has been much in common between the histories of our two nations, and no Irishman can think without sympathy of the days when

Hope, for a season, bade the world farewell,
And freedom shrieked—as Kosciusko fell!

It also would be impossible to expect the people of this country not to feel conscious at this moment of the many bonds that tie them to their neighbours in Great Britain and their kinsfolk in Northern Ireland. Apart from all ideological or political considerations, blood is thicker than water; and, despite their many quarrels, the peoples of Ireland and Great Britain have been living side by side, inter-marrying and intermingling, for the better part of a thousand years. Finally, nobody who has known the German people—the people of Goethe and of Beethoven, of mighty Wagner and the gentle Mozart—will fail to sympathise also with them. We are convinced that they—or, at any rate, the vast majority of them—had no desire either to endure again, or to inflict upon others, the anguish and misery that they experienced in the last war; but in totalitarian States the people have no

Frank Ryan

consecrated Catholic Archbishop of Dublin.

1941

2 January
Three women die in German bombing of Carlow. Two houses are damaged in bombings in Dublin on the same day. The British government places restrictions on Irish ships coming to Britain.

28 January
The Emergency Powers Act provides for the censorship of press messages to places outside the Free State.

19 March
The Germans resume bombing raids on London.

15/16 April
Seven hundred people die in Belfast as German bombers return to the city. Fire brigades from the Free State are sent to Belfast to help fight the fires.

James Craig, Lord Craigavon, Prime Minister of Northern Ireland from 1921 to 1940

4 May

Another bombing of Belfast kills 150 people. Fire brigades are again sent from the Free State to give assistance.

31 May

The North Strand area of Dublin is bombed again.

22 June

Germany invades Russia.

7 December

Japan bombs the American naval base at Pearl Harbor, Hawaii.

to Sir Lauriston Arnott (who succeeded his brother, Sir John Arnott, as chairman of *The Irish Times* in 1940). He was still liable to inflict his memories of the Boer War on passing employees, culminating, as Brian Inglis recalled, in 'an account of the aftermath of one of the battles when "Bobs", Lord Roberts of Kandahar, had told him, "Put down your gun, Bill Coyne, you've killed enough."'

Particularly in the first decade after independence, when John Healy was still the editor, *The Irish Times* remained very much the voice of a defeated and somewhat bewildered minority. Its editorials tended to dwell on the political and economic value to Ireland of the Commonwealth connection and on what a leader shortly before the Imperial Conference of 1923 called 'the interdependency of the Anglo-Saxon peoples.' Healy decried anything that seemed to weaken the link between Ireland and its British past. The paper condemned the suggestion of Kevin O'Higgins that the Free State in 1926 should end the right to appeal decisions

say. The *Fuhrerprinzip* brooks no opinion save that of the individual who has the power. Ireland faces the uncertain future with heavy heart. She is a tiny nation, whose sole interest is in peace; but her geographical position, her economic system and, to a large extent, her history, place her at the mercy of a warring world. Mr de Valera has proclaimed a policy of strict neutrality. In the circumstances, it is the only policy that the Irish Government could pursue. Amid the din and fury of European strife the voice of Ireland is unlikely to be heard by the battling nations; yet such influence as she has will be used in the cause of peace, and it is some comfort to know that already she has provided for thousands of innocent little children a sanctuary from the madness of men.

from The Irish Times
SEPTEMBER 1939

What War Means to You

Some Repercussions

With the coming of war, and, therefore, the contingency that all horse racing will be suspended in England, the Irish Sweepstakes authorities are faced with the probability that the races on which the periodical sweepstakes are run—the Cesarewitch, the Grand National and the Derby—will not take place until the cessation of hostilities ...

The sweepstake organisation—one of the most efficient and highly technical organisations or machines in these islands—may be placed at the disposal of the Éire government for the issue of food and ration tickets and gas masks, or placed on other war-time work, thereby avoiding sudden unemployment for several thousand workers.

Mail boats and other passenger steamers leaving British ports for Ireland yesterday were escorted by destroyers for the greater part of the journey. All pursued a zigzag course, and, as a consequence, were late on arrival. Similarly, boats arriving from Ireland were met by destroyers not far from their port of leaving ...

Works at Dundalk, Co. Louth, have, among others, received orders from the Department of Defence for the manufacture of a large number of steel air-raid shelters, in which sand and steel are incorporated as components.

Advices from principal Irish sea ports show that during the last few days an estimated total of almost 8,000 men

Two views of O'Connell Bridge, Dublin, during the Eucharistic Congress of 1932

8 December

The United States and Britain declare war on Japan.

11 December

The United States declares war on Germany and Italy.

1942

5 March

George Plant, from Co. Tipperary, is executed in Port Laoise jail for his role in the murder

of the Irish courts to the Privy Council, which, it claimed, was to many citizens 'a very precious guarantee of their personal liberties.' It regretted in 1930 the 'cold and disparaging' attitude to the Commonwealth of the Cosgrave government.

Try as it might, the paper could not submerge itself in the orthodox culture of Catholic Ireland. Reporting on the Eucharistic Congress of 1932, when Dublin became the setting for a huge international display of Catholic devotion, and especially on the enormous open-air Mass in the Phoenix Park, it hinted, beneath a surface of awed enthusiasm, at typically Protestant unease in the presence of a devout Catholic throng. 'The beautiful voice of John McCormack … came clear and bell-like, borne without a tremor over the whole silent space, midway through the Service. It was at that moment of the elevation of the Host, the supreme point in

(reservists or soldiers on leave) left Dun Laoghaire, North Wall, Dublin; Cobh, Cork, and Rosslare for Britain.

Trains arriving at Harcourt Street and Westland Row, on the contrary, carried large numbers of women and children from Holyhead and Fishguard, respectively.

All leave in the Irish Civil Service, in the Department of Defence, and in associated departments, has been cancelled. So has leave in the principal departments of the Dublin Corporation—Fire Brigade, Housing, Public Health, etc.

Ireland, being a sparsely populated and mainly agricultural country, food supplies are not as short as in other lands. Milk, butter, eggs, bacon, poultry, fresh meat are in abundance. In addition, owing to the Government's recent industrial policy, there are considerable supplies of tinned food, almost all of which is now produced in this country. Normally a housewife with a full week's store in hand should not need to purchase goods in advance.

A rumoured shortage of sugar is denied by a spokesman of the Irish Sugar Company. Hoarding and advance buying is

Troops of the Irish army in the early days of the Second World War

Scenes at the site of the North Strand bombings in 1941

Scenes at the site of the North Strand bombings in 1941

of the alleged Garda spy Michael Devereaux, who was killed in September 1940.

6 May

Ration books are issued in the Free State; details of the rationing are announced two days later.

Catholic ritual, that one fully realised the common mind that swallowed up all individuality in the immense throng. Flung together in their hundreds of thousands, these people were merely part of a great organism which was performing a tremendous act of faith, with no more ego in them than the sands themselves.'

Early in 1937, on the day before Éamon de Valera (who had finally come to power with a resounding 44 per cent of the vote in 1932) introduced his draft for a new Constitution to the Dáil, *The Irish Times* issued a magazine to commemorate the coronation of King George VI in London. The main editorial that day was

said to be responsible for temporary difficulties which merchants may feel. Large supplies of cane sugar recently have been brought to Ireland.

Citizens who possess gardens or land which might be made available for cultivation are advised to grow root or vegetable crops for their own consumption or for sale or distribution to their neighbours. Every square yard of cultivation, it is emphasised, adds to the resources of the nation.

Raising of pigs (a rapid-paying stock), together with that of sheep and cattle, is advised.

Dublin had its first 'Black-out' last night. Citizens were required to mask all windows, skylights, etc., in which, normally, lights might be seen. Motorists had to drive slowly with only side-lights showing.

Weaving at the Tintawn carpet factory in Newbridge, Co. Kildare. Enterprises such as this were encouraged under the policy of economic protection introduced by Fianna Fáil in the thirties

from The Irish Times 1939–45

Myles na Gopaleen

The Brother

I've a quare bit of news for you. The brother's nose is out of order.

What?

A fact. Some class of a leak somewhere.

I do not understand.

Well do you see it's like this. Listen till I tell you. Here's the way he's fixed. He starts suckin the wind in be the mouth. That's OK, there's no damper there. But now he comes along and shuts the mouth. That leaves him the nose to work with or he's a dead man. Fair enough. He starts suckin in through the nose. AND THEN DO YOU KNOW WHAT?

headed 'Gentlemen, the King', and it asserted that the Commonwealth stood for 'freedom of thought and action, individual liberty, stability, toleration and peace' and against 'exaggerated nationalism, parochial jealousies [and] petty feuds.' And it concluded: 'God Save the King.'

Rather more to the point, in December 1937, when the new Constitution came into effect, *The Irish Times* asked, 'What of the North? Does Mr. de Valera really think that Ireland will be any closer to national unity this evening than she was twenty-four hours ago? When the treaty was signed on December 6th 1921, there was some small chance of a united Ireland. December 29th 1937 will mark the forfeiture even of that small chance.'

23 October

The Battle of al-Alamein begins.

1943

2 February

The Battle of Stalingrad ends in a massive German defeat.

22 June

Fianna Fáil wins the general election.

Emergency transport

26 July

*Mussolini is
arrested after
he resigns as ruler
of Italy.*

8 September

*Italy surrenders
unconditionally.*

1944

7 January

*The ITGWU
serves notice of
disaffiliation from
the Labour Party.*

Lionel Fleming recalled the wistful air of the paper when he joined it in the early thirties. 'It could not, of course, ignore what was going on all around it. It reflected, gently but sadly, upon such things as an old "loyalist" country clergyman might reflect on them. It agreed that, on the whole, the Southern Protestants had been treated very decently. It hoped very much that Mr Cosgrave and his young men would go on being decent, that they would not push things so far as to forget the essential links which bound Ireland to the Empire.'[9]

Yet whatever about the grammar or the facts, the seediness and the taste for drink that Fleming's circles associated with newspapers were greatly in evidence at *The Irish Times*. Brian Inglis describes the place as he encountered it on his first morning as a cub reporter in 1939. 'The

What?

THE—WIND GOES ASTRAY SOMEWHERE. Wherever it goes it doesn't go down below. Do you understand me? There's some class of a leak above in the head somewhere. There's what they call a valve there. The brother's valve is banjaxed.

I see.

The air does leak up into the head, all up around the brother's brains. How would you like that? Of course, his only man is to not use the nose at all and keep workin' on the mouth. O be gob it's no joke to have the valve misfirin'. And I'll tell you a good one.

Yes?

The brother is a very strict man for not treatin himself. He does have crowds of people up inside in the digs every night looking for all classes of cures off him, maternity cases and all the rest of it. But he wouldn't treat himself. Isn't that funny? HE WOULDN'T TREAT HIMSELF.

He is at one there with orthodox medical practice.

So he puts his hat on his head and takes a walk down to Charley's. Charley is a man like himself—not a doctor, of course, but a layman that understands first principles. Charley and the brother do have consultations when one or other has a tough case do you understand me. Well anyway the brother goes in and is stuck inside in Charley's place for two hours. And listen till I tell you.

Yes?

When the brother leaves he has your man Charley in bed with strict orders not to make any attempt to leave it. Ordered to bed and told to stop there. The brother said he wouldn't be responsible if Charley stayed on his feet. What do you think of that?

It is very odd to say the least of it.

Of course Charley was always very delicate and a man that never minded himself. The brother takes a very poor view of Charley's kidneys. Between yourself, meself and Jack Mum, Charley is a little bit given to the glawsheen. Charley's little finger is oftener in the air than annywhere else, shure wasn't he in the hands of doctors for years man. They had him nearly destroyed when somebody put him on to the brother. And the brother'll make a job of him yet, do you know that?

No doubt.

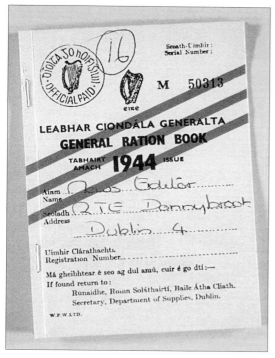

A wartime ration book

office consisted of three houses facing on to three streets which formed a triangle: Westmoreland, Fleet and D'Olier. Between them a network of passages had been constructed, the more confusing in that there were no signs showing which way to go. The editorial staff in those days went in through the main Westmoreland Street door by the counter where people were putting in advertisements, or collecting replies; up the main staircase; past the Manager's office, on the left, and the editor's, on the right, before switching direction to reach the D'Olier Street house, where two rooms had been knocked together for the reporters. Nobody was in any of the upstairs offices when I arrived at nine. They were all dark, dingy, and depressing.' The reporters' room had one telephone and one toilet.

Even for some of the young Protestants coming into the paper at this time there was a certain distance between themselves and the most immediate aspects of the world outside this gloomy room. One of Inglis's first assignments was to check on reports of a Garda baton charge on pro-IRA demonstrators. The news was happening literally on the paper's doorstep in Westmoreland Street. Inglis had no idea where this place might be. Told to go to 'West Moreland Street', he was puzzled; only when he reached the front door and saw the Gardaí dragging some men into a van did it dawn on him that 'the scuffle had been in what I had always pronounced, as our set had always done, as "Westm'land Street."'[10]

Clearly, a newspaper whose young reporters are so unsure of their immediate environment could not hope to survive for long. *The Irish Times* might well have died in the forties had it not been able to break out of its genteel ghetto and find a larger place for itself in the new Ireland. The man who guided the paper from 'Westm'land Street' to 'Westmoreland Street' was the memorable Robert Smyllie. Even if he had not been a crucial figure in the paper's history he would not have been easily forgotten. Patrick Campbell, one of

A week later five Labour Party deputies leave the party to form the National Labour Party.

26 January
Richard Mulcahy is elected leader of Fine Gael in succession to W. T. Cosgrave.

27 January
The siege of Leningrad is broken by the Red Army after two years.

23 February
The Children's Allowances Act provides for an allowance of 2s 6d (12½p) a week for a third and any further child under the age of sixteen.

25 February– 8 April
Workers in the Harland and Wolff shipyard in Belfast go on strike.

30 May
Fianna Fáil wins a snap general election.

6 June
D-day: Allied forces land in Normandy.

GRAMOPHONE RECORDS
Why not renew your Library of your favourite Music, Classical or Popular?
Can we help you to compile it gradually?
Make your RADIOGRAM give full value
Your Programme when You Want it!
PIGOTT
AND CO. LTD.
CORK   DUBLIN   SLIGO

The Irish Times.

CITY EDITION

BIRTHS, MARRIAGES AND DEATHS, PAGE 2.

PRICE 2D. (SATURDAYS 3D.)   DUBLIN, MONDAY, JUNE 2, 1941.   VOL. LXXXIII. NO. 26,172.

Pims FOR WEDDING GIFTS
Visit our unequalled display of Crystal, Cut Glass and China.
(Take Lift to 2nd Floor)
PIM BROTHERS LIMITED, GEORGE'S STREET, DUBLIN

HILTONIA SPRING INTERIOR MATTRESS

GERMAN BOMBS WERE DROPPED ON DUBLIN

GOVERNMENT PROTEST TO BE MADE IN BERLIN

DEAD NUMBER 30; INJURED OVER 80

THE bombs which were dropped in Dublin early on Saturday morning were of German origin.

An official statement last night says:—

"The Government regrets to announce that, as a result of the bombs dropped in Dublin during the early hours of Saturday morning, at least 27 persons lost their lives and about 80 received injuries. Considerable damage to property was caused.

"A further bomb was dropped near Arklow on ... (Sunday) morning. No lives were lost, but there was some damage to property.

"Investigations having shown that the bombs dropped were of German origin, the Chargé d'Affaires in Berlin is being directed to protest, in the strongest terms, to the German Government against the violation of Irish territory, and to claim compensation and reparation for the loss of life, the injuries suffered, and the damage to property. He is being further directed to ask for definite assurances that the strictest instructions will be given to prevent the flight of aircraft over Irish territory and territorial waters."

In a second message the Government, on behalf of the whole nation, expresses its sympathy with all who have been bereaved or have suffered injury or loss in the bombing.

The Government wishes also to express its appreciation of the splendid services rendered by the Garda, A.R.P. organisations, L.S.F., the first-aid and medical services, and, in particular, the Red Cross and St. John Ambulance Brigade, and the staffs of the city hospitals, who gave such devoted care to the injured.

MANY PEOPLE STILL MISSING

With the death yesterday of Mrs. T. Clarke, Lord Mayor; Alderman Cormac Breathnach, T.D.; and Superintendent Henley, retired officer of the Civic Guard, the several with his section of the L.D.F.; Senator of the L.D.F. in the North Strand area.

The public representatives heartily commended the pluck and coolheadedness of people who had been bombed out of their homes but had stayed to help rescue neighbours. Among these was Miss M. Dempsey, who was asleep in her bedroom with her aged mother when one of the first bombs tore a crater in the roadway outside the front door. The front of her house was reduced to rubble, and all that was left was portion of the bedroom walls.

The Dublin City Manager and his staff, including the Housing and Engineering Departments, were in session all day yesterday, dealing with the problems of accommodating the homeless in the bombed areas, and also those affected by the collapse of houses in Bride street earlier in the day, according to an announcement by Alderman A. Byrne, T.D.

It was decided to place at the disposal of the homeless about 100 houses in the Cabra section and all night last night workers were rushing to completion the lighting, sanitary and other arrangements in these houses, which were not scheduled to have been completed for at least three weeks hence. It is expected that by working all day to-day they will have the houses ready for the refugees.

During yesterday the devastated area was visited by Alderman P. S. Doyle, Dr. Hannigan, T.D.; Alderman T. Kelly, T.D.; Councillor P. Medlar, and Senator Michael Staines.

Every effort will be made by the City Manager and the Dublin Corporation to take care of the homeless.

IN OTHER PAGES

TWO FAMILIES

Rescue parties were throughout yesterday very active at North Strand road, where the greatest death-toll occurred, this being the locality of the most violent explosion. Here, at No. 26, seven bodies of the Browne family, who came from Edenderry five years ago, were identified by Mr. John Corrigan, father of Mrs. Browne. Another grievously-stricken family was that of the Fitzpatrick's at No. 28. The bodies of father and mother, their son Noel, and their daughter Madge were recovered on Saturday night. Another daughter, Gretta, aged 10, and a son, Gerard (20), were taken from the remains of the two smashed houses, No. 155 and No. 158, the body of a woman was extricated. Members of the rescue parties said there were more bodies beneath.

WORK OF RED CROSS

...Red Cross worked magnificently.
... Commissioner J. A. O'Connor, official of the St. John Ambulance Medical Department, worked yesterday. Assisted by the Red Cross they handled large numbers of casualties, fatal and injured. ...

During the day the "refugees" were visited by the Most Rev. Dr. ...

DUBLIN HOUSES COLLAPSE

THREE PERSONS KILLED

THREE persons were killed and fifteen others had to receive hospital treatment when two houses collapsed in Old Bride street, Dublin, shortly after 10 o'clock yesterday morning. A third house partly collapsed.

The dead are: Mrs. Bridget Lynskey (30) and her five-months-old baby, Noel, and Samuel O'Brien (72), a pensioner of Messrs. Guinness. They all lived in the tenement house, No. 46 Old Bride street.

Several of the families—there were five families in all—living in No. 46 were preparing to move to new homes in the immediate future. Mrs. Lynskey, the dead woman, had the key to a new Dublin Corporation house at Kimmage in her possession; she and her family were to have moved there to-morrow.

Patrick Harvey, a 15-year-old member of the A.R.P. Emergency Communications Service, who lived in No. 47 Old Bride street—the second of the wrecked houses—told an *Irish Times* representative that he had just got out of bed at 10 o'clock when "I saw bits falling off the wall. Then someone shouted, 'Come on quick—the house is falling.' Part of the wall of No. 46 collapsed, and then our own house fell as I reached the door. Something hit me and I fell. After a minute or two I managed to crawl out."

In escaping from the wreckage young Harvey had saved the light blue helmet which he wears in the Emergency Communications Service. All the other members of the Harvey family, who ran a small cycle shop at No. 47, escaped uninjured. They were Mrs. Harvey, her mother and six children.

TRAPPED IN WRECKAGE

Most of the casualties occurred in No. 46. The Dublin Fire Brigade reached the street within a few minutes of the houses falling, and found that nine of the thirty people who lived in the three houses were trapped in the wreckage. Three persons crawled out while the crew of the Fire Brigade's rescue van worked to save the others. One fireman, George Leigh, forced his way through a narrow aperture to a point where a woman could be seen under the *débris*. She was Mrs. Georgina O'Brien, and he succeeded in bringing her to safety, although badly disturbed himself by gas-poisoning, caused by a fractured gas pipe. Leigh was revived by the apparatus of the rescue van and then taken to the Adelaide Hospital; he was discharged later. Mrs. O'Brien also was taken to hospital suffering from gas-poisoning. One of her children, Elizabeth, also was treated in hospital, but only for shock. Her husband and the other members of the family escaped unhurt.

The firemen brought four persons out of the wreckage, including the body of Samuel O'Brien. O'Brien's wife was uninjured.

An A.R.P. rescue party was called from its work on the bombed houses at the North Strand and took over the rescue duties from the Fire Brigade. They were assisted for some time by a party of military Red Cross men. St. John Ambulance Brigade workers were assisting the injured and those suffering from shock to hospital. L.S.F. men were assisting the guards in holding the crowds back, and, standing by the wreckage were doctors from the Adelaide Hospital, together with the Rev. Father T. A. Walsh, from the nearby Carmelite Church in Whitefriar street, while the search for Mrs. Lynskey and her baby continued. One of the onlookers was Mr. O'Connor, Mrs. Lynskey's father, who could do nothing but watch the pile of debris in which his daughter and grandson were buried.

... were not found until some hours later. Mrs. Lynskey ... her three other young ... are safe, although the husband ... Mr. Lynskey, and two of the children, Esther and Fray, were treated in hospital.

PEOPLE EVACUATED

Orders were given for the evacuation of several neighbouring houses, and 20 persons from No. 44, which were taken to the Red Cross headquarters, in Merrion road. Others found accommodation with relatives and friends in the district.

While the precise cause of the collapse of the buildings is unknown, it is believed to be due to a combination of factors—the old age of the houses, the fact that the houses were shaken when the bombs fell in Dublin on Saturday morning, and a heavy lorry passed the buildings a short time before they collapsed.

Those who received hospital treatment, mostly for shock, were:—
Adelaide Hospital—Joseph Atkinson, Elizabeth O'Brien, Mary Doyle, Georgina O'Brien (children), Miss Margaret Lawlor (midwife), James Doyle, May Doyle, Thomas Lynskey, Esther Lynskey, all of Old Bride street; Florence George Leigh, 15 Purcell road; Patrick Hodges, 15 Cross Kevin street.
Meath Hospital—Fray Lynskey, Patrick O'Brien, Mary Lawlor (detained), all of 46 Old Bride street; Ann James Packman, 48 Old Bride street.

Among those who visited the scene ...

A view of the houses in Old Bride street, Dublin, which collapsed yesterday, killing three people and injuring others.

THE STATE AND THE INDIVIDUAL

POPE DEFINES LIMITS OF INTERFERENCE

POPE PIUS XII. broadcast an address from Vatican Radio yesterday, to commemorate the fiftieth anniversary of the encyclical, Rerum Novarum, issued in 1891 by Pope Leo XIII.

The Pope, having sent Whitsuntide greetings to the members of the Church throughout the world, described his message as being one of love and comfort in the present difficult times.

Wireless transmission, which for many to-day presented almost to a weapon of war, was for the Vatican an instrument of Providence in the Apostolic task of pacification, he said.

RENEWED MIRACLE

Thus it would appear that the miracle of Pentecost was renewed. Just as the many different peoples assembled in Jerusalem were able to hear the voice of St. Peter and the other Apostles, so the Vatican across the ether called to the Catholic community.

"Within the general framework of labour and the responsible development of all physical and spiritual energies of individuals and their free organisations, the Pope said, "a vast field of multiform activities is opened in which the public authority collaborates, finally, by means of local co-operative or professional organisations, and thus by reason of the State itself whose superior and moderating social authority provides for a general economic equilibrium.

"It is, on the other hand, within the competence of the Church in that aspect of the social order into which moral considerations enter, to decide whether such social order is in conformity with the unchangeable order of the Creator manifested by means of natural laws and the Revelation. This is the two-fold manifestation to which Leo XIII appealed, and with reason, in his encyclical."

HEART OF LABOUR

The Encyclical, *Rerum Novarum*, "went deep into the hearts of the working classes." "This call evoked a powerful response, and it is the clear duty of justice to recognise the progress which has been achieved in the lot of the workers through the plans taken by the civil authorities in many lands. Here it can be well understood that the *Rerum Novarum* became the *Magna Carta* of a Christian social endeavour." Meanwhile, the Pope went on, had a century passed, leaving deep furrows and grievous disturbances, both in nations and society, until the years finally poured their dark and turbulent waters into the sea of war, "whose unforeseen currents may affect our economy and society."

The Pope then dealt with the problems likely to arise after the war, beginning with social evolution. Goods were created by God for all men, and "the natural right to the use of material goods provides man with a secure basis of the highest import on which to rise with regard to matters which by their nature are destined to his personal welfare, and thus to facilitate the fulfilment of his duties." The Pope went on, "should be the essential object of every public authority. It follows on this care for such a common good does not imply a power so extensive over the members of the community that in virtue of it the public authority can interfere with the evolution of the individual activity which we have just described, or decide on the natural right to the use of material goods, or take away ... or essentially limit it, ... or, in fine, take away, in whole or in part, the human personality ... inferring at will the manner of its ... physical, spiritual, religious and moral ..."

HUMAN RIGHTS

"To safeguard the rights of the human person and to facilitate the fulfilment of his duties." The Pope went on, "should be the essential object of every public authority. It follows on this care for such a common good ..."

ARMISTICE TERMS
PRESS ASSOCIATION.

CAIRO, Sunday.

The armistice terms in Iraq were officially announced here to-night.
They are:—All hostilities to cease. Return of Iraqi troops to their peace-time stations, including the Rashid Ali group. British prisoners to be released. Axis prisoners to be interned in Iraq, and Iraqi prisoners to be ...

GERMAN CAPTURE OF CRETE

15,000 British Taken To Egypt

SEVERE LOSSES ADMITTED

AFTER twelve days of the fiercest fighting of the war, British troops have been withdrawn from Crete. A communiqué issued in London yesterday states that some 15,000 of the British troops have been removed to Egypt.

It is assumed in London that General Freyberg came out with the troops which were withdrawn, as the latest statement about him had explained that he was alive and with his troops.

The number of troops withdrawn is believed to relate only to British troops and does not include Greek troops. It is not known yet what proportion of Dominion troops are British are among the men saved.

The Germans claim to have captured 10,000 British and Greek prisoners.

AIRCRAFT SUPERIORITY

Against overwhelming odds of air superiority, the British Forces put up a terrific struggle, says the Press Association. The German troops landing from troop-carriers, gliders and by parachute were mown down by the fire ..., but still they came, their planes maintaining a minute-by-minute time-table, and each new arrival being preceded by devastating attack ...

It was the first large-scale airborne invasion attempted in military history, and this led the Germans to put into practice all the tricks by which the Germans have managed to invade Britain.

The deciding factor was the lack of fighter aircraft with the devastation of the German air armada. British fighters had to be withdrawn from the weakly-defended aerodrome, and from that point onwards Germany flung in large numbers of bombers to blast a way for her paratroops.

Aerodromes and beaches were littered with the blazing wreckage of Junkers troop-carriers and the dead bodies of Germans, many of whom were shot before they landed.

NON-STOP METHODS

Still Germany maintained her non-stop offensive British fighters, operating from bases in Egypt, took heavy toll of the troop-carrying 'planes and bombers, but the disparity in distance between the British and German bases from Crete proved too great a handicap.

Attempts by Germans to transport troops and material by sea and convoys were smashed or turned back, and many ships sunk.

It is not yet known how many troops Britain had in Crete, or whether the evacuation is completed or is still being continued, adds the Press Association. One factor that has been proved beyond doubt, adds the Agency is that the magnificent resistance of the British and Greek troops in Crete has not only struck heavy blows at German forces, material and equipment, but it has also given Britain a victory in Iraq. Finding the opposition much more stubborn than was expected, the Germans were unable to fulfil the promise to supply large numbers of aircraft and other forms of aid to Rashid Ali.

Meanwhile, General Wavell has had an invaluable breathing space in which to strengthen his positions on other fronts.

"SEVERE LOSSES"

The British communiqué yesterday evening described the evacuation of Crete in these words:—
"After twelve days of what has ...

HUNDREDS OF 'PLANES USED BY GERMANS

A senior R.A.F. officer, reviewing the Cairo, last night estimated that the Germans used 1,000 ... over Crete.
Hundreds of these machines were destroyed, he said, when they ... off the monasteries were low ...
The parachutists division, in particular, he was considerably 'chewed up,' the officer added. He described the practice of 'firing that it was not the parachutists, but the bombers and fighters who captured Maleme. This enabled air-borne troops to land. It was the air-borne troops, not the parachutists, who were dangerous.

DANGEROUS FIGHTERS

The consensus of opinion from Greece and from Crete was that low-flying fighters were far more deadly than dive-bombers.

While the German successes in Crete had complicated Britain's problem, the Germans, he said, would never find anywhere else such geographical conditions as existed in Crete. As they went further and further resistance would grow, and their commitments would grow, too.

Explaining the difficulties of the R.A.F. in Greece and Crete, the officer said that in winter it was impossible to use aerodromes without properly prepared runways, but after two days' fine weather it was possible to create a number of improvised aerodromes.

"We are hampered by the fact that the weather did not improve until two days after the German advance," he went on. "The Germans had the advantage of fine weather and were also ruthless in comparison with us. The main trouble, however, was that we were being forced into the shape of a triangle, with the Germans having a wider and wider ring of bases round us.

"One of the problems then arising (Continued in Page 8, Col. 2.)"

WAR IN IRAQ ENDED

REGENT RETURNS TO CAPITAL
PRESS ASSOCIATION TELEGRAM.

LONDON, Sunday.

BRITAIN will abstain from any infringement of Iraqi independence and will afford the Regent every help in re-establishing the legal government of the country.

These are the chief provisions of the armistice, signed in Iraq yesterday afternoon. Fighting ceased at 8 o'clock this morning.
PRESS ASSOCIATION.

CAIRO, Sunday.

Six years old King Feisal of Iraq, whom Rashid Ali was reported to have kidnapped when he fled to Iran (Persia), is understood to be safe in Baghdad. The Governor of the Mosul area, Northern Iraq, where the oilfields lie, is now stated to have been opposed to the Rashid Ali movement from the start of the revolt. Thus it is considered in usually well-informed circles here that the trouble in Iraq is virtually at an end.

The anti-British Grand Mufti of Jerusalem, who has left Iraq following the collapse of the Rashid Ali régime, is expected to try to transfer his activities to some other quarter. A correspondent, who states that the terms of the armistice include life exile for Rashid Ali.

The Emir Abdul Illah, Regent of Iraq, entered Baghdad this morning, according to Iraqi sources here.

SYRIA NEXT?
PRESS ASSOCIATION.

ANKARA, Sunday.

Turkish unanimity that Britain's next move should be to take over Syria has become stronger. Cyprus, most Turks say, will be the next German objective, and then Syria, where, according to some reports, the Germans have more materials, and their plans are more advanced than is generally supposed.

Ankara reports that certain barracks have been evacuated by French troops and many boats are being assembled north of Tripoli and are being overhauled under German supervision. It appears that Germany's Near Eastern expert, von Hentig, is now operating along the strip of Syria territory traversed by the Turkey-Iraq railway line, and attempting to organise bands of volunteers.

Influential Arabs are receiving special excess food rations from the Germans, while others, it is reported, have been given large sums of money. It appears that the Germans now control one newspaper in Damascus and one in Beirut.

COAL RATIONING

WALLACE BROS., LTD.

wish to inform their customers that their **Registration Dept.** will be open as from Tuesday morning.

Do not delay. Send us a postcard or fill in coupon attached and you will be registered for your monthly ration.

DEPOTS AND BRANCHES:—
DUN LAOGHAIRE   Dunleary Ho.
BLACKROCK   2 Rock Road

AN APPEAL FOR FUNDS

PROMPT RESPONSE ASSURED

HUNDREDS of people, whose homes have been wrecked or damaged by the bombs that fell on Dublin on Saturday morning, many of whom are mourning the loss of a father or mother or other members of their families, have been and are being looked after by the Irish Red Cross Society and the St. John Ambulance Brigade.

Both these organisations treated hundreds of injured people during Saturday, and their members still are working assiduously in the interests of the unfortunate sufferers.

They have appealed for funds to enable them to help them carry on their humane work, and their joint appeal is meeting with a prompt response. Already subscriptions, large and small are being forwarded through various channels (including the *Irish Times*) to the headquarters of these organisations.

The joint appeal of the Irish Red Cross Society and the St. John Ambulance Brigade reads as follows:—

TO THE EDITOR OF THE IRISH TIMES

Sir,—On Saturday morning, in Dublin, the Irish Red Cross Society and the St. John Ambulance Brigade rendered first-aid to hundreds of casualties, and the Irish Red Cross Society is providing shelter, food and clothing for hundreds of others. Both these organisations are definitely short of funds, and they cannot carry on their work with empty hands. We appeal to the generosity and humanity of your readers.—Yours, etc.,

CONOR MAGUIRE,
Chairman,
Irish Red Cross Society,
20 Merrion square.

JOHN LUMSDEN,
Commissioner,
St. John Ambulance Brigade,
14 Merrion square.
May 31st, 1941.

OVER £4,000

The Hon. Mr. Justice Conor Maguire, Chairman of the Irish Red Cross Society, last night acknowledged receipt of a cheque for £1,000 from Mr. Joseph McGrath in response to the appeal. Mr. McGrath also has forwarded a cheque for £3,000 on behalf of Hospitals' Trust (1940), Ltd. by way of payment on account of what the Trust hopes to raise on the forthcoming sweep.

"While not being on behalf of the Irish Red Cross Society, our very sincere thanks," says the letter, "may I again appeal for an immediate response to our appeal.

Mr. Maxwell Arnott, The Cottage, Clonsilla, wrote to the Editor of the *Irish Times*:—

I enclose cheque for £100 towards the relief of those who suffered by the dropping of bombs in Dublin on Saturday.

"This contribution, and all others received at this office, will be sent to the Red Cross and St. John Ambulance Brigade Joint Appeal."

OVER 500 HOMELESS

Up to late last night the Red Cross Society had 544 people registered on its books as a result of the bombing, and eight of those have been taken away by friends leaving 506 people in the Society's care.

Mobilising on Saturday morning with remarkable speed, the members of the St. John Ambulance Brigade worked uninterruptedly during the day. One of their ambulances alone carried no fewer than 40 victims to hospital. The mobile canteen of the Brigade provided meals for 1,000 people in the bombed area, and distributed a large quantity of food in the afternoon.

During the week-end the Dublin Blood Transfusion Service had a good many calls for blood donors.

WEEK-END AIR RAIDS

FIVE BOMBERS SHOT DOWN

QUALITY Is the best policy!

When a man buys clothes to-day he probably expects them to last him at least 50% longer than they would have done pre-war. That means that they must be really good—long wearing, shape-keeping, well finished. That must be the best available. Let us show you them.

KENNEDY & McSHARRY
WESTMORELAND STREET & D'OLIER STREET

The Irish Times

"Telescopic" Swim Suits

PRICE 3d.   DUBLIN, WEDNESDAY, JUNE 7, 1944.   **No. 27,107**

ALLIES ADVANCE 10 MILES INTO FRANCE

Bridgeheads Established In Normandy

An armoured vehicle being towed ashore from a landing craft.

THE ALLIED INVASION OF NORTHERN FRANCE, BEGUN YESTERDAY AT DAWN, WAS PROGRESSING "SATISFACTORILY" LAST NIGHT, AND, ACCORDING TO MR. WINSTON CHURCHILL, THE LANDING TROOPS HAD SUCCEEDED IN PENETRATING INLAND TO A DEPTH OF SEVERAL MILES IN PLACES. AN ALLIED COMMUNIQUE LAST NIGHT STATED:—

"Shortly before midnight on June 5th, 1944, Allied night bombers opened the assault. Their attacks, in very great strength, continued until dawn. Between 06.30 and 07.30 hours this morning r..o naval task forces, commanded by Rear-Admiral Sir Philip Vian, flying his flag in H.M.S. Scylla (Captain T. M. Brownrigg, C.B.E., R.N.), and Rear-Admiral Alan Kirk, U.S.N., in U.S.S. Augusta, launched their assault forces at enemy beaches.

"The naval forces, which had previously assembled under the overall command of Admiral Sir Bertram Ramsay, made their departure in fresh weather, and were joined during the night by bombarding forces which had previously left northern waters. Channels had to be swept through the large enemy minefields.

"This operation was completed shortly before dawn, and, while mine-sweeping flotillas continued to sweep towards the enemy coast, the entire naval force followed down swept channels behind them towards their objectives.

"Shortly before the assault three enemy torpedo-boats, with armed trawlers in company, attempted to interfere with the operation, and were promptly driven off. One enemy trawler was sunk and another severely damaged. The assault forces moved towards the beaches under cover of heavy bombardment from destroyers and other support craft, while heavier ships

engaged enemy batteries which had already been subjected to bombardment from the air. Some of these were silenced.

"Allied forces continued to engage other batteries. Landings were effected under cover of the air and naval bombardments, and air-borne landings, involving troop-carrying aircraft and gliders carrying large forces of troops, were also made successfully at a number of points.

"Report of operations so far show that our forces succeeded in their initial landings. Fighting continues. Allied heavy, medium, and light and fighter-bombers continued the air bombardment in very great strength throughout the day with attacks on gun emplacements, defensive works, and communications.

"Continuous fighter cover was maintained over the beaches and for some distance inland, and over naval operations in the Channel. Our night fighters played an equally important part in protecting shipping and troop carrier forces and intruder operations.

"Allied reconnaissance aircraft maintained continuous watch by day and night over shipping and ground forces. Our aircraft met with little enemy fighter opposition or anti-aircraft gunfire. Naval casualties were regarded as being very light, especially when the magnitude of the operation is taken into account."

KING GEORGE ASKS VIGIL OF PRAYER

KING GEORGE, broadcasting last night from London, made a solemn call to prayer and dedication "that we may be worthily matched with this new summons of destiny."

"Four years ago," said His Majesty," our nation and Empire stood alone against an overwhelming enemy, with our backs to the wall. Tested as never before in our history, in God's providence we survived that test. The spirit of the people, resolute, dedicated, burned like a bright flame, lit surely from those unseen fires, which nothing can quench.

"Now once more a supreme test has to be faced. This time the challenge is not to fight to survive, but to fight to win the final victory for the good cause. Once again what is demanded from us all is something more than courage and endurance. We need a revival of spirit, a new, unconquerable resolve.

"After nearly five years of toil and suffering we must renew that crusading impulse on which we entered the war and met its darkest hour.

"We and our allies are sure that our fight is against evil and for a world in which goodness and honour may be the foundation of the life of men in every land.

"That we may be worthily matched with this new summons of destiny, I desire solemnly to call my people to prayer and dedication.

"I hope that throughout the present crisis of the liberation of Europe there may be offered up earnest and continuous and widespread prayer. We who remain in this land can most effectively enter into the sufferings of subjugated Europe by prayer, whereby we can fortify the determination of our sailors, soldiers and airmen, who go forth to set the captives free.

"The Queen joins with me in

FOUR YEARS AGO

Four years ago, on June 4th, 1940, the British troops left in France after the evacuation from Dunkirk were fighting their way down the coast as they retreated towards Rouen and Le Havre. The second phase of the Battle of France had started the previous day, with the Germans attacking on a 120 miles front. The evacuation from Dunkirk had been completed on the night of June 3rd-4th, and on June 22nd the armistice between France and Germany was to be signed at Compiègne.

sending you this message. She well understands the anxieties and cares of our womenfolk at this time, and she knows that many of them will find, as she does herself, help, strength and comfort in such vigil upon God. She feels that many women will be glad in this way to keep vigil with their menfolk as they man the ships, storm the beaches and fill the skies.

"At this historic moment surely the Allied invasion forces. They swept their way through the minal areas, established clear water and marked the channels for mile after mile.

"The Allies used upwards of 4,000 ships, with several thousand smaller craft, backed by 11,000 front line aircraft. Mr. Winston Churchill told the House of Commons:—'Everything is proceeding according to plan, and there are already hopes that actual tactical surprise has been attained.' He said that massed airborne landings were successfully affected behind the German lines; that landings on the beaches was proceeding at various points, and that the fire of shore batteries had been largely quelled.

"The invasion troops penetrated, in some cases, several miles inland. Fighting is taking place in the town of Caen, ten miles inland between the Cherbourg peninsula and Le Havre.

"The airborne troops, in the

Operations Proceeding Satisfactorily.

MR. WINSTON CHURCHILL, in a statement to the House of Commons yesterday afternoon, said:—

"I have been at the centre where the latest information is received, and I can state to the House that this operation is proceeding in a thoroughly satisfactory manner.

"Many dangers and difficulties, which this time last night appeared extremely formidable, are behind us. The passage of the sea has been made with far less losses than we apprehended. The resistance of the batteries has been greatly weakened by the bombing of the air force, and the superior bombardment of our ships quickly reduced their fire to dim visions which did not affect the problem.

"The landing of the troops on a broad front, both British and American and Allied troops—I will not give the lists of what different nationalities they represented—the landings along the whole front have been effective and our troops have penetrated in some cases several miles inland.

"Lodgments exist on a broad front.

"The outstanding feature has been the landings of the airborne troops, which were, of course, on a scale far larger than anything that has been seen so far in the world. These landings took place with extremely little loss and with great accuracy. Particular anxiety attached to them because of the conditions of light prevailing in the very limited period just before the dawn. The conditions of visibility made all the difference.

"It might easily have been that something might have happened at the last minute which would not enable the airborne troops to play their part. A very great degree of risk had to be taken in respect of weather, but General Eisenhower's courage is equal to the necessary decisions that had to be taken in all these extremely difficult and uncontrollable matters.

"The airborne troops are well established, and the landings and follow-ups are all proceeding with much less loss than we expected—very much less loss. Fighting is proceeding at various points. We have captured various bridges which are important and which have not

"But all this, although a very valuable first step, gives us no indication whatever of what may be the course of battle in the next days and weeks, because the enemy will now, probably, endeavour to concentrate on this area, and, in that event, heavy fighting will soon begin, and will continue, without any end, so fast as we can push troops in and the enemy can bring other troops up.

"It is, therefore, a most serious time we are entering upon, and we enter upon it with our great Allies, in good heart and in good friendship."

Mr. Churchill, in an earlier statement to the House of Commons yesterday, announcing the invasion, said:—

"During the night and the early hours of this morning the first of the series of landings in force upon the European Continent has taken place. An immense armada of upwards of 4,000 ships, together with several thousand smaller craft, crossed the Channel. Mass airborne landings have been successfully effected behind the enemy's lines.

"Landings on the beaches are proceeding at various points. The fire of the shore batteries has been largely quelled. The obstacles which were constructed in the sea have not proved so difficult as was apprehended.

"The Anglo-American allies are sustained by about 11,000 first-line aircraft, which can be drawn upon as may be needed for the purpose of the battle.

"A somewhat smaller Allied group, consisting of light tanks and armoured scout cars, now stands a few kilometres further to the east in the dunes north-west of Bayeux, and,

Very Secret Weapons

MANY secret weapons were used for the first time by the invasion troops, according to a British Ministry of Supply statement.

They were made in the Ministry factories under conditions of the greatest secrecy, and often the workers themselves did not know what they were making.

biggest parachute descent in history, suffered extremely little loss, landed with accuracy, and are now well established. Naval losses were small, and the tremendous onslaught from air and sea on the coast batteries greatly weakened the resistance. Opposition was less than expected.

"Landings on the beaches are proceeding at various points. The coloured lights were to help pilots keep in formation.

"(I) in the region on both bridgeheads—

"These two areas comprise bridgeheads established by the Allied invasion troops late in the afternoon of the first invasion day.

Turkey Reports New Landing in Greece

The landings took place in Normandy, between 6 a.m. and 8.15 a.m.

"Communiqué Number One," issued from Supreme Headquarters, Allied Expeditionary Force, at 9.33 a.m. yesterday, said:—

"Under the command of General Eisenhower, Allied naval forces, supported by strong air forces, began landing Allied armies this morning on the northern coast of France.

"The Germans had reported earlier on their radio that airborne troops had been landed at the mouth of the Seine.

Hundreds of mine-sweepers led the Allied invasion forces. They swept their way through the minal areas, established clear water and marked the channels for mile after mile.

is trying to establish contact with the main bridgehead.

"Local German forces are warded off thrusts by this group."

The official German News Agency stated last night that the Allied invasion forces had secured a coastal bridgehead between Villers-sur-Mer and Trouville about 20 kilometres (16½ miles) in length and a few kilometres in depth.

"Although they brought up reinforcements from the waters around Le Havre," the agency added, "the Allies could not prevent the Germans from sealing off the bridgehead on all sides and even from narrowing it down locally.

General Eisenhower, Allied Supreme Commander-in-Chief, and General Montgomery (right), who is in command of the Allied invasion forces.

"All other landing in this region between the estuaries of the Orne and Vire Rivers were eliminated by powerful counter-attacks by German coastal guards.

"The greatest German success of the day which ended with a complete defensive success for the German Command, was the smashing of the large Allied landing fleet at St. Vaast de la Hougue. The Allied had operated here in the assumption that they succeeded in St. Vaast, would succeed in neutralising the defences and thus in clearing the way for a huge landing operation.

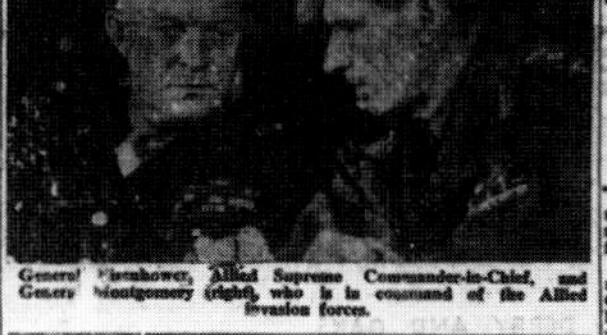

Greatest-ever Air Umbrella Protected Troops

EVERY aircraft in the vast fleet of Ninth Air Force Douglas carriers that flew the first troops and equipment on to the Continent was loaded anti-flak, with broad white and white stripes, and carried coloured lights—yet no flak or fighters opposed them, states an A.F.A.F.

Only small arms fire—mostly from 50-calibre machine-guns—was thrown up against the huge, brightly lighted armada, which stretched more than 200 miles, travelled only a few hundred feet above ground, and took more than an hour to pass.

"The war-paint, added to the aircraft's fuselage only a few hours before take-off, was designed to make them recognisable to friendly forces in the zone of operations. The coloured lights were to help pilots keep in formation.

"The greatest air-borne invasion in history was planned in a riverside cottage in a country village. By night and day over many weeks, with midnight pouring through the windows, or under powerful arc lights, the British Commander and his officers worked out in the minutest details the battle of being fought by the Allied airborne troops.

"Of the airborne troops dropped between Le Havre and Cherbourg some particularly strong formation gained a hold on both sides of the Carentan-Valognes road. During the morning and noon this formation received reinforcements from the air, including, apparently, the main body of the airborne units who were landed from gliders during the early morning. Bitter fighting is in progress along the Carentan-Valognes road."

A German report, quoted by Algiers Radio, said that Allied landings had taken place at Calais and Boulogne.

A few minutes before the invasion got under way via Flying Fortresses swept over northwestern France to warn the people that the blow was about to be struck, and rained down pamphlets

telling the French to seek safety in the open fields and to remain away from highways.

German Overseas Radio earlier reported Allied landings at Cherbourg and Jersey, and last landings at Arromanches, a fishing village 15 miles north-west of Caen. It added that more than 200 craft approached this part of the coast, two hours after the first landing.

The enemy are trying to scale the steep coast with the aid of special ladders," it was stated.

"Continuous landings" in the vicinity of Ouistreham, on the mouth of the Orne, about half-way between Cherbourg and Le Havre, were reported by the official German News Agency.

Berlin correspondents of the Swedish Press quoted a German High Command spokesman as saying that the invasion has now stretches for 240 miles, from Calais through Boulogne, Le Havre, Caen, and the Cherbourg Peninsula to the islands of Guernsey and Jersey.

A Berlin report early to-day said the Anglo-American paratroopers landed between Carentan and Bayeux, as well as the airborne troops and seaborne troops, have been driven back in very heavy fighting. In the area of the Orne mouth other heavy naval artillery the enemy landed 51,000 Allied airmen were in the air over France.

Allied aircraft flew 7,500 sorties, and dropped over 10,000 tons of explosives on invasion coast targets between midnight on Monday and 8 o'clock yesterday morning.

Air activity over the East coast of England reached a crescendo early yesterday evening. For fully an hour there was an incessant deafening roar as swarms of heavy bombers and fighters crossed and re-crossed the coast.

THE ASSAULT SEEN FROM A WARSHIP

ONE of the first eye-witness descriptions of the landing operations is given below by Desmond Tighe, Reuter's special correspondent for the Combined Press. His message was sent from a British destroyer off Bernière-sur-Mer, eleven miles north-west of Caen, at dawn.

The correspondent's account stated:—

Guns are belching flame from more than 600 Allied warships. Thousands of bombers are roaring overhead. Fighters are weaving in and out of the clouds as the invasion of Western Europe begins.

Rolling clouds of dense black and grey smoke cover the beaches south-east of Le Havre as the full power of the Allied invasion force unleashed on the German defences. It is the most incredible sight I have ever seen.

We are standing some 8,000 yards off the beaches of Bernière-sur-Mer and from the bridge of this little destroyer I can see vast numbers of naval craft of all types. The air is filled with the continuous thunder of broadsides and the crash of bombs. Great spurts of flame come up from the beaches in long, snake-like ripples, as shells ranging from 16 inches to 4 inches find their mark in the last ten minutes some more than 2,000 tons of high explosive shells have gone down on the beaches.

FIRST WAVE

It is now exactly 7.25 a.m., and through my glasses I can see the first wave of assault troops touch down on the water's edge and up to the beach.

FOUR PHASES

The plan for the invasion of the coastline allowed for four separate phases:—1. Landings by airborne troops and paratroops in the rear areas. 2. Preliminary bombing by the R.A.F. on the beach and big beaches themselves. 3. An bombardment by sea. 4. The assault proper.

The coastal area between the estuaries of the Somme and the Seine is anything could be expected candidate for invasion.

The spokesman said that the first sea-borne attack came against the mouth of the river Seine, and beginning in the east at Deauville and reaching to the Bay of Seine in the west.

"At Villars massed landings supported by considerable naval forces, are reported. In the bay of Caen across Allied tanks penetrated several miles south, with Paris as their objective.

Rome's Fall "Glorious And Memorable Event"

MR. CHURCHILL in the British House of Commons yesterday, described the fall of Rome as "a memorable and glorious event," which rewards the intense fighting of the last few months in Italy.

Reviewing events in Italy, Mr. Churchill said that the original landing at Anzio on January 22nd last, Mr. Churchill said that the operation held in the first place," he said, "Hitler was induced to send to southern Italy as many as eight or nine divisions which he might well have need of elsewhere. Secondly, those divisions were engaged in severe fighting and their teeth broken by the success-

Landings Going on Constantly

THE German commander yesterday announced the Allied invasion as follows:—

"The long-prepared and expected attack on Western Europe by the enemy began last night. As initiated by heavy air attacks on our coastal fortifications.

"The enemy dropped airborne troops at several points on the coast of Northern France, between Le Havre and Cherbourg, at the same time carried out sea-borne landings, supported by strong naval forces.

"Fierce fighting is going on in the coastal stretches which have been attacked."

The German News Agency gave this account:—

"The Allied landings continue without stop under constant German fire. The Allies continue to fling the main body of their forces into the sector between Cherbourg and Ouistreham. German counter-attacks at Annelise, near the centre of the Seine Bay, led by midday to the destruction of 35 Allied tanks landed by the enemy with great difficulty under fire."

Assault Directed From Trailer

GENERAL EISENHOWER directing the first phase of the invasion of Fortress Europe in English stood near the boats from which the great assault fleets launched their offensive. His headquarters, a trailer, was so placed that no point was visible from the air from a few hundred feet.

It was just after 4 o'clock when we reached a position some 12 miles off the coast of France. This bombarding was in full swing, and 4,520 innumerable assault ships appeared amidships on our starboard bow.

Seven minutes later the night bombing has ceased and the great naval bombardment begins. We move in slowly. Cruisers open fire on our starboard bow. They are firing tracers, and we see the shells curving in high trajectory towards the shore.

The big assault ships start lower their small boats, crowded with troops. There are at least 1,000 ships of all sizes in our sector. The air bombardment intensifies, and the battleships join in. The battleships and cruiser are firing away with all they have got. The destroyers are darting round us. It appears we have taken the enemy by surprise.

6 a.m.—German batteries now opening fire spasmodically, but by now big fires are burning ashore.

6.50 a.m.—The whole invasion fleet is now moving, just seven miles off Courseul.... After half an hour the destroyers close in on the shore, bombarding any target they can see. Then the first wave of Flying Fortresses come in, and the crashing of shells is terrific.

UNMOLESTED

Fighters keep up constant patrol, protecting the invasion fleet. It is early yet, but so far there has been no enemy air opposition.

The invasion fleet came over to the shores of North-Western France unmolested. Away on our port beam a Hun class destroyer is having a ding-dong duel with the coastal batteries, one of which appears to go round her as the German gunners try to find their mark.

Destroyers are steaming up and down close inshore, protecting the landing troops and plugging shore batteries with shells. Gunfire is so terrific that our cars are deafened.

"TOUCH DOWN"

7.25 a.m.—The first wave of landing craft have reached the shore less than touch down. Red tracers from close-range German weapons are sparking across the beach. Mass leap out of the craft and move forward. Tanks follow them. The Flying Fortresses have reached the landing beaches, and a tremendous bombing behind the beaches is their mark.

7.35 a.m.—We move out on patrol. It is too early to know what damage has been done, but they were made to a split second according to time-table. The battle goes on ...

Rome's Fall "Glorious And Memorable Event"

Mr. Churchill has received the following message from Marshal Stalin:—

"I congratulate you on the great victory of the Allied Anglo-American forces in the taking of Rome. This news is being greeted in the Soviet Union with great satisfaction."

Reviewing events in Italy, Mr. Churchill said that the original landing at Anzio on January 22nd last, Mr. Churchill said that the operation had two purposes ... (Reuter.)

Germans Falling Back

The Germans are falling back in disorder with heavy loss, especially in material, in the mountainous country. The Allied forces were grouped with special emphasis to their left flank, and soon deployed against Rome after cutting an important

153

Stormont on the occasion of the state opening of the Northern Ireland parliament. The building became a symbol of Unionist domination.

23 August
Paris is liberated by Allied forces.

1945

20 April
The Red Army reaches Berlin.

25 April
The ITGWU and fourteen other unions form the Congress of Irish Unions.

28 April
Mussolini is killed by Italian partisans.

Smyllie's most brilliant recruits, recalled in the *Spectator* in 1959: 'When, in these trying times, it's possible to work on the lower slopes of a national newspaper for several weeks without discovering which of the scurrying executives is the editor, I count myself fortunate to have served under one who wore a green sombrero, weighed twenty-two stone, sang parts of his leading articles in operatic recitative, and grew the nail on his little finger into the shape of a pen nib, like Keats.'

Smyllie took over as editor on the death of Healy in 1934, having been editorial assistant to Healy since 1920. The contrast between him and his distant and reserved predecessor could not have been greater. Smyllie's traditional late afternoon arrival at the office has been described by Niall Sheridan. 'In anticipation of his coming, the front office was frequently occupied by a straggle of supplicants—impoverished old acquaintances to whom he gave small sums of

Ah yes. Everybody knows that it's the brother that's keepin Charley alive. But begob the brother'll have to look out for himself now with the nose valve out of gear and your man Charley on his hands into the bargain.

Is there any other person to whom your relative could have recourse?

Ah, well, of course, at the latter end he'll have to do a job on himself. HAVE TO, man, sure what else can he do? The landlady was telling me that he's thinkin of openin himself some night.

What?

You'll find he'll take the razor to the nose before you're much older. He's a man that would understand valves, you know. He wouldn't be long puttin it right if he could get his hands at it. Begob there'll be blood in the bathroom anny night now.

He will probably kill himself.

The brother? O trust him to look after Number One. You'll find he'll live longer than you or me. Shure he opened Charley in 1934.

He did?

He gave Charley's kidneys a thorough overhaul, and that's a game none of your doctors would try their hand at. He had Charley in the bathroom for five hours. Nobody was let in, of course, but the water was goin all the time and all classes of cutthroats been sharpened, you could hear your man workin at the strap. O a great night's work. Begob here's me 'bus!

Bye bye.

1944

No more sea

Dove-melting mountains, ridges gashed with water,
Itinerant clouds whose rubrics never alter,
Give, without oath, their testimony of silence
To islanders whose hearts themselves are islands;

money, crackpots seeking publicity for their crazy schemes, a well-known briefless barrister needing money for a cocaine "fix", an elderly lady from some respectable suburb, banging her umbrella on the counter and demanding an interview with the Editor.'[11]

The chaos may have been either a cause or a symptom of the tendency of both Smyllie and his staff to repair to the Palace Bar across Westmoreland Street (or later to the Pearl in Fleet Street) at every opportunity. When Smyllie was still Healy's deputy, Lionel Fleming arrived for a meeting on the important subject of Fleming's prospective employment as a reporter. He found the office full of young men who seemed merely to be standing around. Smyllie suggested that they have their meeting in the Palace instead. 'To my surprise, Smyllie ignored the vacant "snug" just inside the door, and made straight for a large

30 April

Hitler commits suicide in Berlin.

2 May

De Valera calls on the German ambassador to offer his condolences on the death of Hitler.

7 May

Germany surrenders unconditionally.

8 May

Victory in Europe is celebrated.

Jesuits from Clongowes Wood

A road accident

11 May

Press censorship ends in the Free State.

13 May

In his victory speech, Churchill attacks de Valera and the position of Ireland during the war.

16 June

Seán T. O'Kelly is elected President of Ireland. Seán

group which was, I think, discussing the evidence for or against the resurrection. Alec Newman was there with the other leader-writer Michael Eddis, and the only other I can definitely recall was an odd-looking old man with a pepper-and-salt suit, pork-pie hat, and sad, monkey-like eyes—he was Tom Casement, the brother of the Roger Casement executed by the British ... It seemed a bad place to discuss business except on the assumption that everyone else was on the point of going home; and after a few rounds, it became clear that such was by no means their intention. In fact, the group was soon increased by the arrival of several of the characters we had left behind in Smyllie's office. Smyllie himself, now

For whom, if the ocean bed should silt up later
And living thoughts coagulate in matter,
An age of mainlanders, that dare not fancy
Life out of uniform, will feel no envy—

No envy unless some atavistic scholar
Plodding that dry and tight-packed world discover
Some dusty relic that once could swim, a fossil
Mind in its day both its own king and castle,

And thence conceive a vague inaccurate notion
Of what it meant to live embroiled with ocean
And between moving dunes and beyond reproving
Sentry-boxes to have been self-moving.

Louis MacNeice

Éamon de Valera in his capacity as President of the League of Nations

from The Irish Times 1945
2 MAY

Curtain

Adolf Hitler is dead. This tremendous news was broadcast from Germany last night, and transcends everything else in importance. The announcement was made by Admiral Doenitz, formerly Commander-in-Chief of the German Navy and leader of the U-boat campaign during the first years of the war. It seems that on Monday Herr Hitler nominated Admiral Doenitz as his successor, and he now has affirmed his intention to carry on what he describes as 'the fight against Bolshevism.' As we write, no details are available concerning Herr Hitler's death. In these circumstances the whole situation regarding the war in Europe must be reviewed afresh. During the last week Count Bernadotte, a high Swedish official, has been in touch with Herr Himmler, Commander-in-Chief of Germany's Home Army, and, since the retirement of Marshal Goering, generally accepted as Herr Hitler's immediate successor. Apparently, it

wedged tightly into the middle of everything, seemed to have forgotten me altogether. If at that time I had got on to reading Kafka, I would certainly have thought of him then.'

Eventually, at one o'clock in the morning, Smyllie asked Fleming to return to the office to discuss business. Fleming made his way into the building 'to the sound of distant singing—the last movement of Beethoven's Choral Symphony. As I mounted the stairs, the words, as well as the superb melody, rang out clearly:

> Down the hall the butler wandered
> Bent on sodomistic crime,
> For the parlourmaid was pregnant
> For the forty-second time …

'Oh God, what now? … Smyllie at his desk was correcting proofs with one hand and with the other was playing dominoes against Alec Newman, Eddis and someone else. "Ah, Mr Fleming, sir, a pleasure to see you again! Herr

Lemass succeeds O'Kelly as Tánaiste.

5 July
The British general election leads to a Labour majority. Clement Attlee replaces Churchill as Prime Minister.

6 August
The United States drops a nuclear bomb on Hiroshima, Japan.

Neumann, you will search in vain for a five to
put on that—my spies tell me that I have you
finally banjaxed and scuppered."[12]

Yet for all his eccentricity, Smyllie managed
to transform the paper from a vestige of the old
regime into an integral part of Irish culture. The
ardent republican Todd Andrews, Fianna Fáil's
leading technocrat, paid him an unlikely tribute
in his autobiography, *Man of No Property*,
crediting him with having 'integrated *The Irish
Times* and what it stood for into the Irish nation.'
Smyllie became editor, Andrews claimed, 'in
succession to a west British pedant, who for years
had edited the paper and who could not accept
the fact that the establishment of the Free State
represented a major change in Irish relations with
Britain. *The Irish Times* was, until the days of
Smyllie's editorship, a stodgy and poor imitation
of the London *Times* and was read, almost
exclusively, by Church of Ireland clerics, Trinity
dons and the remaining occupants of the "big
houses" and their minions. Under Smyllie's
editorial direction, its readership extended to
businessmen and bank clerks, members of rugby
football clubs, academics of the National
University and, even more significantly, civil
servants and members of government.'

Operating as he did at the highest levels of
the public service, Andrews was able to assess the
paper's growing influence with officialdom. 'The
civil servants were in origin mainly of the lower
middle classes and having attained the first aim of
job security, they wanted social acceptance and
respectability as well. *The Irish Times* was for them
and, indeed, for all the rising lower middle classes
the symbol of "ould dacency" and respectability
and they read it. When anyone in the civil service
offices told you that he had seen such and such an
item "in the paper," you knew that he was
referring to *The Irish Times*. Favourable comment
from *The Irish Times* made a minister's day.
Favourable comment from the other two Dublin
dailies was of no importance to them.'[13]

One important reason for this new
influence was that the paper was becoming less

*Jimmy O'Dea, probably the most popular Irish
entertainer of his generation*

seems that Herr Himmler offered to surrender unconditionally
to the British and Americans, but refused to have any truck
with the Russians; and at this point negotiations—if there
were any negotiations—broke down. During the week-end it
was reported that, in view of the British and American refusal
to dissociate the Anglo-Saxon Powers from Soviet Russia,
Herr Himmler had decided to make a new offer which, this
time, would include the Soviets. Yesterday, however, Count
Bernadotte denied that he had seen Herr Himmler during his
last visit to Germany and Denmark, or that he had
transmitted any message from authoritative Germans to the
Allies. Herr Hitler's death has changed everything. If Admiral
Doenitz has been appointed as his successor, manifestly Herr
Himmler has no authority to speak on behalf of the German
Government. If one may judge by the Admiral's broadcast
last night, he is prepared to carry on the struggle against
Russia indefinitely, and to continue the fight against the
British and Americans so long as they remain associated with
the Soviets ...

For the last ten years, and particularly since the
outbreak of the war, Adolf Hitler had an almost uncanny

Éamon de Valera inspecting a guard of honour at the commissioning of army cadets

instinct for that mysticism which plays such a vital part in the German character, and it was this mystic quality that raised the Führer to such a pinnacle of national hero-worship. Now that he is dead, he can have no heir; for none of the remaining German leaders has been able to exert his peculiar appeal. His death must make a terrific difference to the future conduct of the war by Germany. It must be remembered that every German fighting man took a personal oath to the Führer. Without him, National Socialist Germany finds itself bereft of spiritual leadership. Henceforward the Germans may fight, as men always will fight, in sheer defence of their hearths and homes; but the death of their leader, coming, as it has come, at a moment when their military fortunes have reached their nadir, cannot but tear the heart out of their resistance.

closely associated with Cumann na nGaedheal and its successor party, Fine Gael. The rise of fascism, in fact, was a crucial factor in establishing the independence of *The Irish Times*. With the formation of the quasi-fascist Blueshirts and their subsequent incorporation in Fine Gael, Smyllie in effect withdrew the paper's previous support from the Cumann na nGaedheal wing of Irish nationalism. And this more independent stance was in turn reflected in the paper's coverage of fascist Italy's invasion of Ethiopia in 1935 and the outbreak of the Spanish Civil War the following year, when right-wing soldiers under General Franco launched a rebellion against the democratically elected republican government.

fasting laws because people are undernourished.

24 June
De Valera says that Ireland is 'associated with' the Commonwealth but is not a member.

1 October
Dubliners get their first coal ration since 1941.

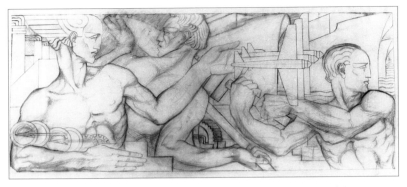

A drawing by Gabriel Hayes for one of the large panels on the balcony of the ministerial suite in the Department of Enterprise, Trade and Employment, Kildare Street, Dublin. The building itself was a rare and notable example of Irish art deco.

30 October
Clann na Poblachta wins two out of three by-elections.

1948

15 January
Gas rationing ends. The rationing of other commodities, such as bread and flour, ends in later months.

7 February
Election results produce a hung Dáil.

18 February
J. A. Costello is elected Taoiseach by the new Dáil. A coalition Government is formed for the first time since the state was established in 1922.

In Ireland there was a good deal of sympathy for Franco's 'Nationalists', who were seen as champions of Catholicism against godless communism, especially in the ranks of Fine Gael. The Catholic hierarchy made a national appeal for prayers and aid for the Nationalists. General Eoin O'Duffy, the former Blueshirt leader, visited Franco in Spain, and eventually sent a 700-strong Irish Brigade to fight (very ineffectively) for the Nationalists. De Valera, on the other hand, supported the League of Nations policy of non-intervention and refused to recognise Franco's government until the war was over. For the first time on a major ideological issue, *The Irish Times* found itself aligned with Fianna Fáil and even with the left wing of the IRA, some of whose members joined the International Brigade to fight for the Republic.

According to Lionel (Bill) Fleming, 'when the Spanish Civil War broke out, the *Irish Independent,* ever the faithful mouthpiece of the Church, sent a man down on to Franco's side to describe the fearful threat to Christianity which Franco was now countering. Smyllie said "Look, Bill, you say you've no money for a holiday. Give you fifty shuddering pounds to go down on the Republican side. I don't give a bugger what your conclusions are, so long as they're honest."[14]

The publication of Fleming's first articles from Spain was followed by a visit to *The Irish Times* office of a 'very polite' priest. He told

from The Irish Times 1945
3 MAY

Herr Hitler's Death
Callers at German Legation

The Taoiseach and Minister for External Affairs, Mr de Valera, accompanied by the Secretary to the Department of External Affairs, Mr J. P. Walshe, called on Dr Eduard Hempel, the German Minister, last evening to express his condolence.

The Swastika at the German Legation was flown at half-mast at 58 Northumberland Road.

An official of the German Legation in Dublin last night told an *Irish Times* reporter that they had heard of the death of Herr Hitler on the German Radio on the previous night, but had received no official intimation from Berlin.

He would not make any statement about the present crisis, but said that the Legation had received many messages of sympathy and there had been a large number of callers.

President Truman stated yesterday that he had it on the best authority that Herr Hitler is dead, states a Washington (Reuter) cable.

The President did not say what his authority was, but he declared that he was convinced that the late Fuehrer had been killed.

from The Irish Times 1945
18 MAY

Turning Away Wrath

The Taoiseach's broadcast reply to Mr Churchill was as temperate as it was dignified. Mr de Valera has his faults as a statesman and a politician; but he has one outstanding quality. He is a gentleman. Never in the course of a long public career has he been either rude or discourteous; and his broadcast on Wednesday night was a model of good manners. We were particularly glad that he took the opportunity to pay a tribute to the late Mr Neville Chamberlain, whose reputation has been sullied in his own country as a result of the Munich episode, but whose dealings with Ireland proved him to be a man of vision and understanding. On the other hand, Mr de Valera is cursed, or blessed, with a metaphysical mind; and the recent war blew metaphysics, as it blew so many other things, sky-high. In the world of today, realism is the only thing that matters. Mr de

Valera's logic, doubtless, may have been unimpeachable; but for all that it was wrong. Let us take two examples. In the first place, Ireland's neutrality was unique. It could not be compared in any way to the neutrality of countries such as Switzerland or Sweden, which are wholly independent States. Ireland's international position—largely, if not entirely, as a result of the Taoiseach's metaphysical outlook—is, to say the least of it, ambiguous. Éire is neither a Republic nor a Dominion of the British Commonwealth. From the point of view of international law, if one can speak in present circumstances of such a thing as international law, the instrument governing this country's position in the world is the Anglo-Irish Treaty of 1921. This instrument, however, in actual fact, has ceased to exist, so far as the Twenty-Six Counties are concerned. Many of its most important provisions have been denounced unilaterally by Mr de Valera's Government, with the result that the relations between Ireland, on the one hand, and Great Britain and the Commonwealth, on the other, are almost impossible to define. Although throughout the war Ireland was neutral, all her diplomatic representatives abroad were accredited under the Executive Authority (External Relations) Act, 1936, by the King of England. A Gilbertian situation arose during the war, when, for obvious reasons, a new Minister could not be sent to Germany, and Ireland was represented only by a *Chargé d'Affaires*. Ireland's neutrality, therefore was *sui generis*. In the second place, Mr de Valera's hypothetical question to Mr Churchill had little relation to fact. There is an obvious difference between the forcible seizure of six English counties by a foreign Power and the unhappy situation that exists in this country. Here, unfortunately, the majority of the inhabitants of the six sundered counties are staunch supporters of partition. 'Tis true, 'tis pity and pity 'tis 'tis true. Mr de Valera's hypothetical analogy may be logical; but again it is false. The relations between Éire and the Six Counties, like those between Éire and the Commonwealth, are unique.

Having said so much, we would venture to suggest once more that Mr Churchill did less than justice to the people of this country. Unfortunately, for some time past there has been a wave of anti-Irish feeling both in Great Britain and in the United States; and in some respects every intelligent Irishman can understand it. We regret, however, that the British Premier should have thought fit to increase its intensity and to exacerbate passions, the continuance of which can do no possible good to anybody. Ireland, admittedly, was neutral

Smyllie that 'by pure chance, he had been talking to several of our advertisers and that, unless *The Irish Times* discontinued this series of articles, they would feel compelled to withdraw their custom.' He spoke, he said, as a 'well-wisher of the paper' who 'would not like to see *The Irish Times* lose money.' He was, nevertheless, shown the door.

The Irish Times was also markedly sympathetic to the plight of Germany's Jews. When the anti-Jewish Nürnberg laws came into effect in 1935, an editorial on 12 September declared: 'The resolve of the Hitlerites to bring about the complete elimination of Jewry from German life makes it essential that some refuge

16 April
The Organisation for European Economic Co-operation is established, and Ireland becomes a member.

5 September
The Sunday Independent *reports that the External Relations Act is to be repealed.*

Edel Quinn, lay missionary and member of the Legion of Mary

Éamon de Valera at Baldonnell Aerodrome in 1936, flanked by Frank Aiken and Charles Lindbergh

Éamon de Valera addressing the nation at the end of the Second World War

during the war. In some ways, largely, as we think, through the operation of the Press Censorship, her neutrality was interpreted *au pied de la lettre*. In its anxiety to avoid any suspicion of sympathy with one side or the other, the Censorship often went to fantastic extremes. In actual fact, however, Ireland's neutrality from the very start operated in favour of the United Nations and particularly of Great Britain. This country had no Foreign Enlistment Act, with the result that at least 100,000—and probably more—of her sons joined the British forces. Their fighting record can bear proud comparison with that of the fighting men of any of the officially belligerent countries. Furthermore, this country sent many scores of thousands of workers to Great Britain, where they not only made valuable contributions to her war effort, but also shared the trials and tribulations of her people

shall be provided for the victims of Nazi fury; and civilised people in every country would welcome an arrangement that would provide a means of escape for them.'

The Irish Times also raised the awkward subject of Irish sympathy for the Nazis. In April 1937 it published a translation of an interview given by the Irish minister in Berlin, Charles Bewley, to the evening newspaper *Uhrblatt*. In it Bewley said, among other things, that 'my government will always do everything to promote the old friendship between Ireland and Germany' and that Hitler and his colleagues had 'many admirers among our youth.' In an accompanying leader the paper asked how 'a

7 September

The Taoiseach, John A. Costello, speaking in Ottawa, announces that Ireland is to leave the Commonwealth.

21 December

The Oireachtas passes the Republic of Ireland Act.

Patrick Street, Cork

1949

30 January

Church-gate collections are taken up throughout the Republic to assist nationalist candidates in the Northern Ireland elections.

10 February

Unionists again win a majority in

democratic state administered by a democratic government, which has made no secret of its abhorrence of dictatorship … could approve the German system.'

Shortly afterwards *The Irish Times* used the occasion of the appointment of the Chief Rabbi of Ireland, Isaac Herzog, as Chief Rabbi of Palestine to remind its readers of the Jewish contribution to Ireland. 'We claim no special credit for Ireland because she never has persecuted the Jews—for therein she has behaved merely as any civilised country ought to behave … Here in Ireland the Jews are not a separate people; they are part of the nation to whose welfare they have contributed in large measure. They have done fine services to our industry, our commerce, and

during their darkest, albeit their most glorious hours. Ireland sent food in vast quantities to the other side, thus helping to relieve the economic strain, and in some measure, to alleviate the rigours of rationing. For most practical purposes, the mere existence of this little country on Britain's western flank constituted a military safeguard, although it must be admitted that at one stage of the war the loss of the Irish ports caused grave embarrassment to the Admiralty. The airport at Foynes was of incalculable value both to the British and to the Americans. Some day, no doubt, the public will be allowed to know the number and the importance of the many trans-Atlantic passengers who took advantage of the facilities at Foynes. In the meantime, one only can guess; but there is small doubt that had the use of this airport been denied to the Allies, serious inconvenience would have been caused. The war is over. Mistakes have been made everywhere, and Ireland has been no more infallible than any other country. Surely the time has come when we all must look not over our shoulders, but towards the hard road that lies ahead. For better or for worse, the destinies of these islands are inseparable. Each has something to gain from the other. Both have much to lose through dissension. The future demands an act of oblivion concerning the past. We rejoice that Mr de Valera, at least, has given the soft answer.

from The Irish Times 1945
9 JUNE

Dieppe

again the last ebb
the dead shingle
the turning then the steps
towards the lights of old

Samuel Beckett

our art, and if we have tolerated them—to use an objectionable phrase—we have been more than repaid by their presence in our midst.'

As it became more horrifyingly clear that the Nazis were intent not merely on impoverishing or humiliating the Jews but on annihilating them, increasing numbers of refugees sought safety in democratic states. The trickle of Jewish refugees entering Ireland was the excuse for anti-Semitic protest. In November 1938 the 1916 Veterans' Association adopted a motion 'that we hereby register our emphatic protest against the growing menace of alien immigration, and urge on the Government the necessity of more drastic restrictions in this connection.' In February 1939 *The Irish Times* carried the text of a manifesto issued by the Irish-Ireland Research Society, declaring its refusal to 'stand by and allow the Jewish hold on our economic life to develop.' The paper accompanied the text with an editorial

the Northern
Ireland general
election.

23 February
*Seán MacBride,
Minister for
External Affairs,
states that Ireland
will not sign the
proposed Atlantic
Pact, because Britain
still occupies the six
north-eastern
counties of Ireland.*

3 April
*The anti-partitionist
Belfast Labour Party
is established.*

Limerick Docks

The **Iolar**, *Aer Lingus's first aircraft, which made the airline's maiden flight in 1936*

9 April
The Northern Ireland Labour Party commits itself to the United Kingdom and co-operation with the British Labour Party.

18 April
The Republic of Ireland Act comes into effect, and Ireland is no longer a member of the Commonwealth.

5 May
Ireland signs the convention to establish the Council of Europe.

pointing out that 'we would treat this effusion with the contempt which it deserves but for the fact that attempts have been made of late to stir up anti-Jewish feeling in this country, which is justly famed for its tolerance.' It concluded that 'anti-Semitism in any country is foolish; in Ireland it is almost criminal.'

Even if it were not for the paper's strong emotional connection to Britain, disgust at Hitler's policies would have ensured that, when the Second World War broke out, the sympathy of *The Irish Times* was entirely with the Allies. The paper had been expecting war at least since October 1938, when it commented on air-raid precautions in Belfast and contrasted them unfavourably with the state of readiness in the South. 'We have heard that there are gas masks in the city of Dublin. Where are they? If war should break out tomorrow … what would the citizens of Dublin be expected to do about it? Nobody knows.' When the war did break out, on 1 September 1939, with first Germany and then the Soviet Union (on 17 September) attacking Poland, *The Irish Times* illustrated the fusion of its own Protestant perspective with a broader anti-Nazi stance by describing the Catholic Poles as fighting 'with a courage reminiscent of the defenders of Derry.' Short-wave radio listeners in

from The Irish Times 1946
24 JUNE

Saint-Lô

Vire will wind in other shadows
unborn through the bright ways tremble
and the old mind ghost-forsaken

sink into its havoc

Samuel Beckett

Alfie Byrne, *the genial populist who was Lord Mayor of* **Dublin throughout the thirties**

A children's tea party in Dublin

Foxford Woollen Mills

The consecration of John Charles McQuaid as Archbishop of Dublin in the Pro-Cathedral in 1941

2 June

*The Ireland Act,
which guarantees
the status of
Northern Ireland
within the United
Kingdom, is passed
by the House of
Commons.*

8 August

*The Minister for
External Affairs,*

Dublin were able to hear the sound of bombs and machine guns in Warsaw, mixed with patriotic appeals from the Polish resistance. *The Irish Times* carried long transcripts of these emotional broadcasts until, in the first of a long series of tussles with the Controller of Censorship, Joseph Connolly, it was prevented from doing so.

The Irish Times broadly supported, on pragmatic grounds, de Valera's policy of keeping Ireland neutral. But this did not, in Smyllie's view, preclude an obvious desire that Germany should be defeated. An editorial on 28 September 1939 summed up the paper's

from The Irish Times
16 JULY 1946

by Patrick Campbell

Greeted by the literary men with a hoarse cheering, and showers of manuscript flung in the air like confetti, the Censorship of Publications Appeal Board came into existence in the spring-time of this present happy year.

The idea was that the Appeal Board would hear the appeals of authors whose work had been banned by the Censorship Board.

The first appeal has now been made. The book involved is *The Midnight Court*, newly translated by Frank O'Connor from the Irish of Bryan Merryman. It is published in Dublin by Maurice Fridberg.

I shall now, with extreme accuracy, trace the course of this appeal from its hopeful beginning to its singularly abrupt conclusion.

It began with a letter addressed to 'The Secretary, Censorship of Publications Appeal Board, 5 Ely Place, Dublin.' The letter was dated 25 June, 1946. This is how it read:—

'Dear Sir,

'We have been consulted by Mr Maurice Fridberg, of 27/28 Clare St, Dublin, in connection with the publication by him of a book entitled "The Midnight Court" described as a Rhythmical Bacchanalia from the Irish of Bryan Merryman, and translated by Frank O'Connor.

position: 'We have said from the beginning that we thoroughly approve of Mr. de Valera's policy of neutrality in the present war. In all the circumstances of internal and external affairs, it is the only feasible policy for Eire. Yet it would be absurd to pretend that the people of this country can remain as indifferent to the fortunes of Great Britain as, say, the inhabitants of Nicaragua. For one thing, there can be very few families in Eire that have not some relatives or friends in one or other of the British services …' In fact about fifty thousand people from the 26 counties joined the British forces or went to work in British war industries.

Seán MacBride, and other Irish delegates attend the first meeting of the Council of Europe in Strasbourg.

1950

23 February
The British general election results in a

Douglas Hyde, first President of Ireland, with his successor, Seán T. O'Kelly, immediately to his right. They are flanked by Éamon de Valera and Frank Aiken.

Climbing
Croagh
Patrick

Crowds at the
summit of
Croagh Patrick

Diaspora power: a St Patrick's Day parade in Fifth Avenue, New York, passes St Patrick's Cathedral

reduced majority for Labour. Unionists again take a majority of seats in Northern Ireland.

6 June
The National Labour Party and the Labour Party agree to reunite.

10 September
The Sunday Independent *reveals the articles of the 'Mother and Child Scheme'*

Nevertheless the war marked a further separation of North and South. In the South the war years were a period of almost stultifying isolation; the North, however, suffered all the consequences of being, as part of the United Kingdom, one of the belligerents. In spite of the impression of *The Irish Times* to the contrary in 1938, Northern Ireland was in fact poorly prepared for war. The Unionist government had done almost nothing to unite the divided population against Hitler. The cities were ill-prepared for German bombing; even in 1940, when the Luftwaffe turned its attention to Belfast, the city council had neglected to fit water pipes for firefighting appliances or to collect building materials for shelters. The city did not possess a single searchlight. When, in April 1941, the Luftwaffe launched a full-scale raid on Belfast, it was able to drop two hundred tons of bombs without meeting any defensive fire. At least nine hundred people were killed. Volunteer

Aer Lingus introduced hostesses for the first time in 1945

Dolphin's Barn in Dublin in the cold winter of 1946

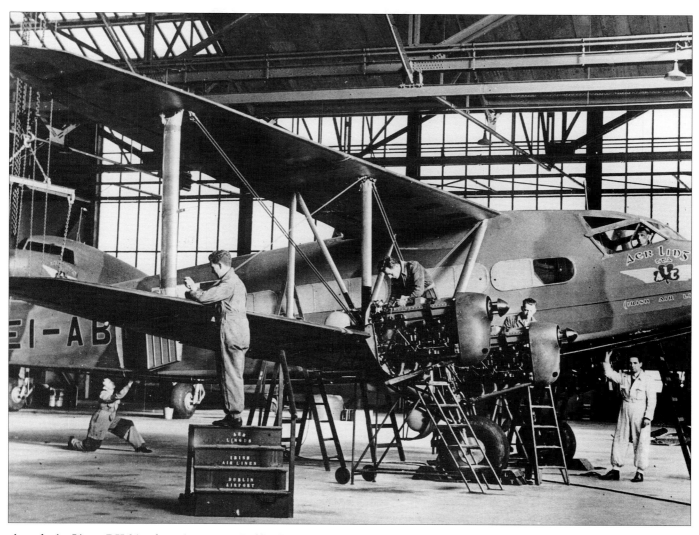

An early Aer Lingus DH 86 under maintenance at Dublin Airport

'We understand from our client that this book has now been placed on the list of banned books, and our client now desires to appeal against the decision of the Censorship of Publications Board in prohibiting the sale and distribution of this said publication.

'We enclose herewith cheque for £5, being the necessary deposit, "together with six copies of the publication," in compliance with the provisions of the Censorship of Publications Act, 1946. We shall be glad if you will acknowledge receipt of this letter and enclosures, and state that this letter will be treated as formal notice of appeal.'

The letter was signed by Mr Herman Good, solicitor.

It was despatched to Ely Place, and the appealing parties sat down to wait for an answer.

firefighters from Dublin, Drogheda and Dundalk sped northwards to help; but it was clear that the two parts of the country were living through different histories.

In the early days of the war *The Irish Times*, as Robert Fisk has remarked, 'sometimes exhibited more confidence in British victory than the British did themselves,' predicting, for instance, that the German tactic of using submarines to attack military and merchant shipping would surely fail. Increasingly, however, the paper's ability to comment on, or even to report, the progress of the war was hampered by the imposition of heavy-handed censorship. The Government's

suggested by the Minister for Health, Noel Browne.

1951

6 March
Dr Noel Browne announces details of his 'Mother and Child' health scheme,

The funeral of the great James Larkin approaches Glasnevin Cemetery, January 1947

offering free maternal care and postnatal treatment to all mothers and their babies.

4 April
The Catholic bishops condemn the 'Mother and Child' scheme, as they say it infringes on the rights of the family.

8 April
Noel Browne resigns as Minister for

determination to prevent any 'expressions likely to cause offence to the peoples of friendly states whether applied to individuals or to the method or system of Governments, or to the culture of the people of such States,' was so extreme that Charles Chaplin's anti-fascist burlesque, *The Great Dictator*, was banned in Ireland.

And *The Irish Times* was the censor's prime concern. A few days after his appointment in September 1939, Connolly sent a memorandum to de Valera noting that 'it seems likely that we will have definite difficulty in the case of certain papers such as *The Irish Times* in restraining them from tincturing all or most of their material with a definitely pro-British tinge, and, particularly in their leading articles, getting them to follow a strictly neutral line of argument.' Strict censorship, he noted, would probably provoke 'an open breach with papers like *The Irish Times* where they might either refuse to obey our

There was no delay. An answer came back by return of post, a swift, but somewhat peculiar-looking document.

It was written in longhand, in sky-blue ink. At the top of the page a number of erasures had been made—the printed words, 'Censorship of Publications Board,' in Irish and English, being crossed out heavily, and the words substituted, in longhand: 'Censorship of Publications Appeal Board.' The Appeal Board seemed to be short of official notepaper.

This is how the letter read: 'I am to acknowledge receipt of your appeal (HW/PH, of 25th instant) on behalf of the publisher, Mr Maurice Fridberg, of 27/28 Clare Street, Dublin, against the prohibition order at present in force against the translation by Frank O'Connor of the book, "The Midnight Court," by Bryan Merryman, together with 6 (six) copies of the aforesaid publication, and the statutory appeal deposit of £5 (five pounds) per your cheque, and to inform you that the matter will have the early attention of the Appeal Board.

'Pending the publication for sale of the official appeal form, the Board has decided to accept informal applications of the type of your communication.'

This letter was signed, in black ink and a different handwriting, 'B. MacMahon, Runaidhe.'

In view of the sky-blue ink, and the black ink, and the longhand, and the erasures, it would seem that the Board's own communications were of a fairly informal nature, too. One was also left with the hope that the man who wrote the letter had the strength left, again in longhand, to make a copy of it.

After this the appealing parties heard no more of the matter for nearly a fortnight. They filled in the time with the preparation of their case, in consultation with senior counsel.

Then a letter arrived dated 10 July 1946. It was on the same notepaper as before, but this time only the English version, 'Censorship of Publications Board' had been crossed out and 'Censorship of Publications Appeal Board' substituted in ink in its place. The Irish version remained undisturbed.

rulings or force us to take action up to the stage of fine or suppression or both.' But he felt that these risks would have to be taken; and the Minister for the Co-ordination of Defensive Measures, Frank Aiken, supported this option even to the extent of preventing the reporting of a speech in favour of the Allies by the Fine Gael TD James Dillon or the most basic factual accounts of Nazi atrocities.[15]

As the censorship took hold, it was gradually extended to reporting that could not possibly offend any of the belligerent powers or undermine Irish neutrality but that merely criticised members of the Government. In May 1941, for example, *The Irish Times* wanted to

Health after the Catholic Church opposes his proposals for the state to provide maternity aid.

30 May

The general election results in Fianna Fáil becoming the largest party in the Dáil. De Valera becomes Taoiseach on 13 June.

Rural electrification was one of the substantial achievements of independent Ireland. This photograph dates from 1949.

15 November

*It is announced
that E. T. S.
Walton, professor
of natural and
experimental
philosophy in
Trinity College,
Dublin, is to
share the Nobel
Prize for Physics
with an English
colleague.*

1952

10 January

*The Aer Lingus
plane St Kevin
crashes in Wales,*

publish a report of a speech by Richard Mulcahy critical of a visit by Aiken to the United States. The page proof was sent to the censor's office in Dublin Castle and came back with the critical words deleted. Smyllie summed up his frustration in a letter to Mulcahy. 'It is damnably difficult for a newspaperman to deal with our friends in the Castle … I have bitter experience of the whole hierarchy of Censors. I have found [Michael] Knightly [chief press censor] reasonable and even sympathetic, [Thomas] Coyne [his assistant] casuistically helpful, Joe Connolly a bitter Anglophobe, and Aiken unintelligently impossible!' De Valera, whenever he appealed to him, Smyllie found 'more than anxious to be fair.'

Aiken later admitted that he took pleasure in thwarting the paper's attempts to report the war. 'I had a lot of fun with Smyllie. When he was censored, he would always write a letter about it. So I would sentence him to one of two pages of Coyne. We used to "hop off" each other.'

This letter, however, was typewritten—the Appeal Board apparently having been able to borrow a machine in the interval. This is what it said:—

'I am directed by the Minister for Justice'—then, 'Minister for Justice' was crossed out, and the word 'Board' written in above it—'to inform you that, at a meeting held on the 9th instant, your appeal, lodged on behalf of your client, Mr Maurice Fridberg, of 27/28 Clare Street, Dublin, publisher of the book, 'The Midnight Court,' as translated from the Irish of Bryan Merriman by Frank O'Connor, from the Prohibition Order in force against the said publication, was dismissed.

'The Board, however, directed the refund of the deposit lodged by you on behalf of your client, and, accordingly, I enclose herewith a pay order, made out in your favour, to the amount of £5 (five pounds), as provided by Section 12(e) of the Censorship of Publications Act, 1946.'

This letter was signed, as before, 'B. MacMahon.' A pay order for £5 (five pounds) was enclosed.

It would be no exaggeration to say that the appealing parties were taken aback by this communication.

A street crossing in Belfast in 1949

An Aer Lingus DC3. This was the all-purpose short-haul workhorse of most airlines in the turbo-prop era.

It surprised them to learn that their appeal had been heard already. They wondered who spoke on their behalf and what he said and if he was defending the right book.

They felt they would like to know how many members of the Appeal Board were present while the matter was under discussion and if they all paid attention to the argument.

They felt, too, that it would be nice to know whether a vote was taken at the end and who voted for what and why. And, when they came later to examine this aspect of the situation, they wondered what they were doing with a solicitor, Senior Counsel and a case of their own when they never even got as far as the halldoor of No. 5 Ely Place.

I cannot see what they are complaining about. The processes of the law are known to be exceptionally expensive and tedious for those involved in them. This new system, however, as inaugurated by the Censorship of Publications Appeal Board, effects an enormous saving in time, money and nervous strain.

You merely wait in the cells while your case is going on and then the warder comes in and tells you what happened. 'Sorry, pal,' he says, 'you weren't too good in the box—ten years.'

Always provided, of course, that the warder remembers you're there and still interested.

Smyllie had to be content with small victories. When a former *Irish Times* journalist, Johnny Robinson, was rescued from a Royal Navy ship sunk off Singapore, the paper sneaked in a report that 'the many friends of Mr. John A. Robinson, who was involved in a recent boating accident, will be pleased to hear that he is alive and well.' Similarly, when Smyllie wanted to draw attention to the fact that many of the top British commanders were from Ireland, North and South, he ran a list of 'Japanese' military heroes:

General Wilson—Japanese (North Island)
General O'Connor—Japanese
General O'Moore Creagh—Japanese
General Dill—Japanese (North Island)
General Brooke—Japanese (North island)
Admiral Cunningham—Japanese
Admiral Somerville—Japanese

On VE Day, 8 May 1945, the paper expressed its delight and got around the censorship at the same time by carrying on the front page a series of photographs of Allied leaders arranged in the shape of a V.

killing all twenty-three passengers and crew.

16 May
President Seán T O'Kelly is re-elected unopposed.

14 June
A co-ordinated system of social welfare is established by the Social Welfare Act.

30 July
The Government publishes a white paper on extended health benefits for lower income groups.

June Weddings—

AT SWITZERS you will discover many delightful ways of conveying your good wishes... through the happy couple on their journey through life, with a fitting memento of their Wedding Day, a present that will give *lasting* *pleasure* and serve as a tribute to your own good taste.

A visit to the Lower Ground Floor is especially rewarding. It offers countless suggestions for Gift Seekers.

Switzer
Grafton St.,
DUBLIN

The Irish Times

CITY — FIRST-RATE EYESIGHT — AT EIGHTY — AXPEL — DIXON & HEMPENSTALL

HAYES, CONYNGHAM & ROBINSON, LTD.
The Chemists,
12 GRAFTON STREET, DUBLIN
AND BRANCHES

PRICE 3d.   DUBLIN, TUESDAY, MAY 8, 1945   No. 27,391

PEACE TO-DAY IN EUROPE

Total Surrender By Reich

VICTORY FOR THE ALLIES, AND THE END OF THE WAR IN EUROPE, WERE ANNOUNCED YESTERDAY. THE NEW FUEHRER, ADMIRAL DOENITZ, ACCEPTED THE ALLIED DEMANDS, AND, ON HIS INSTRUCTIONS, COLONEL-GENERAL GUSTAV JODL, CHIEF OF STAFF, SIGNED THE DOCUMENT OF UNCONDITIONAL SURRENDER TO THE ALLIES OF ALL GERMAN FORCES.

To-day will be V-E day in Allied countries. In Britain, King George, Mr. Winston Churchill and military leaders will broadcast at various times during the day.

The surrender document was signed on the Allies' behalf by Lieut.-General W. Bedell-Smith, General Eisenhower's Chief of Staff; General Ivan Sustoparoff, for Russia; and General Sevez, for France.

The signing took place at Rheims at 2.41 a.m. (French time), in the schoolhouse used by Eisenhower as his headquarters.

Describing the scene at the schoolhouse, A.P. Correspondent Edward Kennedy said:—

General Eisenhower was not present at the formalities, but immediately after Jodl and his fellow-delegate, General Friedebug, had signed for Germany they were conducted to the Supreme Commander.

2,094 Days of War

THE war lasted 2,094 days —526 days longer than World War I.

Germany invaded Poland on September 1st, 1939.

Britain and France declared war on Germany two days later.

Italy declared war on Britain and France on June 10th, 1940.

Germany attacked Russia on June 22nd, 1941.

America entered war on December 7th, 1941.

Italy capitulated on September 8th, 1943.

(War Survey in Pages 2 & 5.)

SOS FROM PRAGUE

AN SOS from Prague, after the Doenitz surrender statement had been published, reached Czechoslovak circles in London yesterday afternoon, says Reuter. It said that heavy fighting in the streets continues.

"The Germans are throwing hand grenades at houses showing Czechoslovak flags. German aircraft have been dropping bombs on Broadcasting House and on other public buildings in the centre of the city."

The Czech National Council calls urgently upon the Allies for speedy help, and particularly for aircraft, the S O S said.

Another Reuter cable states that the Commander of the German troops in Czechoslovakia, refusing to recognise the Flensburg announcement, has issued a "fight on" order. It said: "The Reich Government has only ceased the fight against the Western Powers. In our area the struggle will be continued until the Germans on the East are saved, and until our way back into the homeland is secured."

The situation in the immediate neighbourhood of Prague is not clear, says Reuter.

Germany's New Policy

VON KROSIGK, GERMAN FOREIGN MINISTER, YESTERDAY READ OVER FLENSBURG RADIO AN ORDER OF THE DAY FROM ADMIRAL DOENITZ ANNOUNCING THE UNCONDITIONAL SURRENDER OF ALL GERMANY'S FIGHTING FORCES. "GERMANY HAS SUCCUMBED TO THE OVERWHELMING POWER OF HER ENEMIES. TO CONTINUE WOULD ONLY MEAN SENSELESS BLOODSHED AND A FUTILE DISINTEGRATION," VON KROSIGK DECLARED.

"No one must be under illusions about the severity of the terms to be imposed on the German people by our enemies," the Foreign Minister stated. "We must now face our fate squarely and unquestionably and accept this burden, and stand loyally by the obligations we have undertaken.

"We must recognise law as the basis of all relations between the nations, and we must recognise it and respect it. Respect for treaties will be as sacred as the aim of our nation to belong to the European family of nations, as a member of which we want to mobilise all human, moral and material forces in order to heal the dreadful wounds which the war has caused.

"Then we may hope that the atmosphere of hatred which to-day surrounds Germany" all over the world "will give place to a spirit of reconciliation among the nations, without which the world cannot recover."

Before the German Foreign Minister made his broadcast, Danish radio, now under Allied control, announced the capitulation of German forces in Norway, estimated at 300,000.

The announcer gave no details, but after the statement the Norwegian national anthem was played.

The Germans marched into Norway on April 9th, 1940. Six days later an Allied expeditionary force landed in Northern Norway. On June 10th of the same year they withdrew.

Broadcast To-day by Churchill

THE British Ministry of Information last night announced:—

"It is understood that, in accordance with arrangements between the three Great Powers, an official announcement will be broadcast by the Prime Minister at 3 o'clock tomorrow (Tuesday) afternoon. In view of this fact, Tuesday will be treated as Victory in Europe Day and will be regarded as a holiday.

"The day following, Wednesday, May 9th, will also be a holiday. H.M. the King will broadcast to the peoples of the British Empire and Commonwealth to-morrow (Tuesday) at 9 p.m. (D.B.S.T.). Parliament will meet at its usual time to-morrow."

[Note.—The British Premier's broadcast will be made at 2 p.m., Eire time, and King George's broadcast at 8 p.m. Eire time.]

On behalf of the Government, Mr. Churchill will simply announce to the nation to-day that the war in the West is over, says the P.A. It is constitutionally important that the responsibility for this actual declaration should be taken by the King's Ministers and not by the King.

SCENES IN BRITAIN

THERE were celebrations in London, New York, Paris, and many other cities, when the end of the war in Europe was announced. In the West End of London, especially in Piccadilly Circus, in Whitehall and in the Westminster area, thousands gathered and waited for hours in the expectancy of hearing the news officially.

Buckingham Palace became the focal point of the nation's rejoicing. The area outside the massive railings and the Royal parks around were thronged with waiting crowds.

In Times Square, New York, the city's traditional centre, thousands, yelling ceaselessly, packed the streets, stopping all traffic. As far as the eye could see and hearing could blocked all thoroughfares.

King Sends Message to Eisenhower

KING GEORGE last night sent to General Eisenhower, Supreme Commander, on the Allied victory:—

"Having entrusted to you the Allied Expeditionary Force across the English Channel, carrying with you the hopes and prayers of millions of men and women of many nations.

Baton Charges in Dublin

DUBLIN'S reaction to the stoppage of hostilities found expression in the parading of the principal streets by thousands of people, who had felt relief from the few years' strain too much to keep them to their normal occupations and recreations. At night the main thoroughfares were thronged and the area around College Green was the rendezvous of sight-seers.

Ex-Polish Premier To Make Statement

Virtually complete agreement was reached yesterday between the "Big Four" Foreign Ministers over the revisions of the Dumbarton Oaks proposals, states Reuter.

Mrs. Truman May Visit Ireland

It was learned in Roscrea yesterday that President Truman's wife may visit her relatives in that part of the country when her husband visits London.

Russians Take Breslau

Marshal Stalin last night announced that Soviet forces have captured the town and fortress of Breslau, and taken 40,000 prisoners.

World A Valley Of Sorrow

Vatican Radio last night, in its French bulletin, stated: "In celebrating peace, we must not forget the ruins created by war."

No Early Prospect of Better Supplies

NO early improvement in the supply position is expected to follow the end of the war in Europe.

Plea for Playing Fields At St. Anne's

DUBLIN CORPORATION, at its meeting last night, postponed consideration of a motion by Alderman A. Byrne, T.D., suggesting the provision of playing fields at St. Anne's, Clontarf.

BELL'S SCOTCH WHISKY *"Afore ye go"* An Independent Firm

NOTICE TO GOLFERS The new American-type heeled putters ("Stewart One-Putt") are now available from Elverys. Price: 52/6 Elverys O'CONNELL ST., NASSAU ST., DUBLIN.

THE IRISH TIMES

Price 3d. No. 29,460 DUBLIN, FRIDAY, JANUARY 11, 1952 CITY EDITION

J. H. MOORE LTD. AUTOMOBILE ENGINEERS

Delicious Ready-to-serve dishes D.B.C. delicatessen 37-38 ST. STEPHENS GREEN

AER LINGUS PLANE CRASHES: ALL 23 ON BOARD KILLED

...ome of ...he ...ictims

...HE three members of the crew ... belonged to Dublin, and it is ...ieved that most of the twenty ...ssengers are also Irish.

Following are the names of those ...ieved to be among the victims ... the crash:—

...HE CREW

Captain J. R. Keohane (pilot).
First Officer W. A. Newman ...cond pilot).
Miss Deirdre Sutton (air hostess).

...SSENGERS

Mr. Nick Laker (an Aer Lingus ...ain), his wife and child.
Mr. John Stackpool, Gresham ...el, Dublin.
Mr. Henry C. Richardson, The ...se, Mount Merrion, Dublin.
Mr. Thomas J. Carol, Lexington ...nue, New York, U.S.A.
Mr. W. A. Lynch, New York, ...S.A.
Mr. Maurice Fitzgerald, Cork.
Mr. and Mrs. Aston, Dublin.

...AS IN R.A.F.

...aptain J. R. Keohane, the pilot ...the plane which crashed last ...ht, was 30 years of age, and ...d with his wife and three ...ldren at 174 Iveragh road, White...l, Dublin.

...le joined the R.A.F. at the ...inning of the Second World War ...l did most of his training as ...g in Southern Rhodesia under ... Empire Air Training Scheme. ...served in the Near East and in ...er overseas theatres.

...le joined Aer Lingus as co-pilot ...1946 and took his first command ...hort time afterwards. He was ...ribed last night as a highly ...erienced pilot.

...irst-Officer W. A. Newman (co-...) was 32. He lived with his ... and one child at Dundrum. ...wife was a former Aer Lingus ...ess. Joining the R.A.F. early ...e Second World War, he served ...e Pacific and was shot down, ...nd stated last night. He was ...red by the Japanese. He had ... with Aer Lingus since the ...f 1946 and had been flying ...ly on the company's routes ...ance.

...TY HOSTESS

...s Sutton was aged 22, and ...at 16 Sandford road, Ranelagh, ... her father keeps a grocery ...minion merchant's shop. She ...a small, fair-haired girl, and ...nown as one of the prettiest ...r Aer Lingus hostesses.

...ucated at the Dominican ...ent, Muckross Park, Miss ...n was a keen hockey player, ...at one time played for her ...l. Before going to the staff of ...Lingus, with whom she had ...for three years, she worked in ...hlin department store. It is ...stood that she had been ...ed to be married.

...tain Laker, who is believed ...ve been on the aircraft with ...fe, a Canadian, and their four-...ld child, Melody, was aged ...d is a native of Midhurst ... He served in the R.A.F. ...g the second World War in ...mber aircraft. He had been ...d in Canada and took up his ...ntment as a pilot with Aer ...s about six years ago. He had ...n leave in England and was ... return to duty to-day.

...ng the passengers was, it is ...d, Mrs. Hague, of London, ...party of English people who ...d to visit a Dublin factory. ...ad booked on the flight.

ARNOTTS SALE

Machine nose-dives on Welsh mountain

A Dakota plane similar to the one which crashed.

FLYING FROM LONDON TO DUBLIN

TWENTY-THREE PEOPLE—20 PASSENGERS AND THE CREW OF THREE—WERE KILLED, WHEN AN AER LINGUS DAKOTA AIRCRAFT, EI–AFL ST. KEVIN, EN ROUTE FROM NORTHOLT (MIDDLESEX) TO DUBLIN AIRPORT, NOSE-DIVED INTO A BOG ON THE SLOPES OF 2,860-FOOT MOEL SIABOD MOUNTAIN, IN SNOWDONIA (NORTH WALES), LAST NIGHT AND BURNT OUT.

When the first rescue party had struggled 1,000 feet up the steep Cribau slope of the mountain, its members found the smouldering débris partly embedded in the earth. Most of the passengers were buried in the bog, and early to-day the 23 bodies had been found.

The plane left Northolt at 5.25 p.m., and was due in Dublin at 7.25 o'clock. She reported herself flying normally to Nevin Radio Station, south of Anglesey, at 7 p.m. The crash is believed to have occurred within the next half-hour, during a gale of wind and rain.

Moel Siabod is 6¼ miles east of Snowdon.

The wreckage, with mail scattered around, was found one mile east of Lake Gant Gwynant at the hamlet of Cwm Edno.

The weather was reported "shocking" in the area. There was a terrific storm of hail and rain.

When the news was given, police at once set out from Caernarvon, Bangor, Portmadoc, Llanberis, Beddgelert, and other stations in the area.

Mr. Goronwy Williams, a young farmer of Gant Gwynant, who had located the wreck within 40 minutes of hearing the crash, said: "I heard the sound of the plane low over the mountains about 7 o'clock, and, when the engines suddenly cut out, the machine seemed to go into a dive, and this was followed by vivid flashes which lit up the mountains around, and seemed to indicate that the petrol tanks had exploded."

The rescue party, which included members of Portmadoc fire service carrying stretchers, toiling in a hailstorm, reached the spot at 10.30 p.m., after a hard climb in the teeth of bitterly cold rain squalls.

By midnight about 100 helpers had been directed to the desolate mountain top, and they worked by torch light to extricate the bodies from the wreckage and the bog.

SENT FOR SPADES

Mr. G. Moorfield, of the Tyn-y-Coed Hotel, Capel Curig, who went to the spot with a friend, stated: "The first rescue party had to send back for spades and other equipment to dig out the wreckage. Rescue parties worked by the light of hand lanters in appalling conditions."

The plane had nose-dived into a bog, about 1½ miles up the mountainside, almost burying itself.

Mr. Moorfield said wreckage was scattered over a wide area.

Three bodies were discovered close to the wreck, and were taken down the mountainside to waiting ambulances.

TEN AMBULANCES

Ten ambulances and five fire services from Merionetshire and Caernarvonshire went to the scene of the crash, and rescue operations continued under the supervision of Lieut.-Colonel W. Jones Williams, Chief Constable of Caernarvonshire.

A team of mountain climbers, in charge of Mr. C. B. Briggs, Penygwryd Hotel, who had led many rescue teams in Snowdonia, also helped in the search.

A guard remained near the wreckage throughout the night.

The bodies, most of which are unrecognisable, will be brought today to the mortuary at Eryri Hospital, Caernarvon.

SAW A FIRE

It is reported that farmers saw the Dakota coming down and, later, saw a fire.

Villagers at Capel Curig, a few miles away, could see the glow of the burning plane on the mountainside.

One of the first to see the crash was Mr. Owen Williams, of Hafod-y-Rhysgl Farm, close to where the aircraft crashed.

Mrs. Humphreys who lives at a farm near by, said: "I was minding the children for my sister when we heard a loud crash. We ran to the door and saw a huge fire ...

Miss Deirdre Sutton

Statement by Aer Lingus

The following statement was made by Aer Lingus at 1 a.m. to-day:—

"Aer Lingus regrets to announce that D.C.3 aircraft St. Kevin (registration EI-AFL), from Northolt Airport at 17.25 hours on January 10th on a scheduled service, crashed later near Lake Gwynant in the district of Cwn Edno, Caernarvonshire, North Wales.

"The aircraft was carrying 20 passengers, and a crew of three—Captain J. R. Keohane in command; with First-Officer W. A. Newman, and air hostess Miss D. Sutton.

"The number of casualties has not yet been definitely established. The next-of-kin will be notified as soon as possible. A special Aer Lingus aircraft left at 23.00 hours from Dublin Airport, carrying Captain J. Kelly Rogers, assistant general manager (technical), and other senior officers of Aer Lingus."

Planes search

First fatal crash in 15 years

UNTIL last night Aer Lingus had not had a fatal accident in its flying history.

The company was 15 years old last summer, when Mass was said at Dublin Airport during a ceremony to celebrate the accident-free flying record.

In the years of its growth and development Aer Lingus achieved a world-wide reputation for safety and efficiency, and in 1950 it was awarded the Cumberbatch Safety Trophy for its record. This was the first occasion that this award had ever been given to an airline.

MINOR INCIDENTS

Only two other minor incidents have in any way marred this record. The most recent was just before Christmas, 1950, when an Aer Lingus plane overshot the runway at Ringway Airport, Manchester. No one was injured.

Before the war a plane on the Dublin-Shannon route had to make a forced landing but again there were no casualties.

The first route which the company operated was to Bristol, which was inaugurated on May 27th, 1936, when a D.H. 84 took off from Baldonnell Aerodrome. By 1946, the company was flying its first D.C. 3 aircraft, and had extended its network to Shannon, Paris and London, while Amsterdam, Belfast, Glasgow and Rome were later added.

The company's air fleet transports about 2,000 passengers each day, in the peak season.

In 1951 the company had its busiest year, nearly 270,000 passengers used its services, 21% more than in 1950. The Dublin-London route, as usual, carried most of the traffic. More than 123,000 passengers travelled between the two capitals, which represented an increase of 17% over 1950.

Last August, when the company had carried its millionth passenger, the company's aircraft had flown almost 15,000,000 miles without a serious accident.

"THE GRAVEYARD"

The district where the Dakota crashed was known during the Second World War as "the graveyard of the aeroplanes" because many American planes being flown across to Britain crashed in the area.

At one time there were 15 wrecked aircraft within 10 square miles, most of them in places inaccessible except to climbers with full equipment.

So many planes crashed in North Wales that the ceiling for the area was increased by about 2,000 feet, following which the number of crashes decreased, although up to the end of the war such peaks as Tryfan, the Glyders and Siabod continued to take a toll of planes.

Several of the cottages in this area still use equipment salvaged from planes.

TO-DAY'S WEATHER
Bright intervals. Showers. Cold.
(See also Page 5)

No agreement still at Korean truce talks

The United Nations delegates at yesterday's Korean truce talks at Panmunjom, repeated their rejected "after further study" of the Communist supervision proposals because the Communists still want to continue building airfields after the truce is signed. The meeting ended without any agreement being reached.

America's Major General Turner told reporters: "It is now quite clear our differences now concentrate on the airfields issue." The repatriation issue bogged down the prisoners sub-committee. America's Rear Admiral Libby said that the Communists were "scared to death" of the principle of voluntary repatriation, under which prisoners could choose to return or not.

On the fighting fronts the Eighth Army said it had been quiet yesterday apart from two early morning United Nations attacks. The Fifth Air Force has been concentrating on bombing enemy artillery ...

FLYING ENTERPRISE SINKS 35 MILES OFF CORNWALL

Carlsen and Dancy safe

THE 13-DAY SAGA OF THE FLYING ENTERPRISE ENDED AT 4.10 P.M. YESTERDAY, WHEN THE SHIP, AFTER DEFYING THE MIGHT OF THE ATLANTIC GALES AND SEAS FOR A FORTNIGHT, WENT DOWN ONLY 35 MILES OFF CORNWALL, TO A SALUTE FROM THE SIRENS OF A SMALL FLOTILLA OF SHIPS AND TUGS CLUSTERED AROUND HER.

Captain Carlsen and Mate Kenneth Dancy, a few minutes before she sank, climbed up the funnel and dived into the raging Atlantic.

They were in the water only four or five minutes before being picked up by the Turmoil, and Captain Carlsen stood at the rail to bid a last goodbye to his ship as she went down.

When it was certain that the last minutes of the Flying Enterprise had come, Captain Carlsen and Mate Dancy—who had upheld the highest traditions of the sea—climbed up the slanting funnel of the freighter and jumped into the raging sea. They had previously flashed a signal to the surrounding ships to "close."

They were in the water for four or five minutes before being picked up by the Turmoil.

A message from the Turmoil said: "Both men O.K.—now in captain's cabin changing clothes."

A dramatic on-the-spot story of the end of the Flying Enterprise was told by an officer of the U.S. destroyer Willard Keith in the late afternoon in a radio-telephone talk.

Captain Carlsen

"It was an eerie sight in the deepening gloom," he said. "Very slowly, Flying Enterprise rose by the bows and seemed to remain in that position, unwilling to accept her fate.

TELL-TALE SWIRL

"Then, suddenly, she plunged stern first, and only that tell-tale swirl, which many of our men saw in the Pacific war, remained.

"We, of course, had made all necessary arrangements for taking off Carlsen and Dancy had they signalled. I understand that rescue by helicopter was an idea acceptable to both of them, but the aircraft was forced to turn back because of bad weather.

"Towards the end, things were bad. One does not need to be a sailor to know that things are bad when the sea is lapping one's smoke-stack. Turmoil eventually got in very close, and both men jumped."

So ended the six-day vigil of this U.S. destroyer. In the words of one of her crew: "It's been a lesson this week in 'guts and how to take it'."

The first thing Carlsen did was to send a message to the Willard Keith expressing his deep appreciation to officers and men ... the world's Press, broadcasting, television and newsreels.

It is understood that Captain Carlsen and Mate Dancy stayed on board the Turmoil last night.

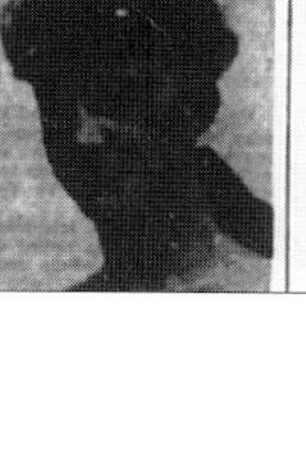

ANOTHER SHIP

The president of the Isbrandtsen Line relayed a message through Reuter's New York office yesterday: "Well done, Carlsen," and promised him command of another vessel—"perhaps another Flying Enterprise."

A ship's bell in the Isbrandtsen office tolled the loss of a ship as the president read to reporters a tribute to Captain Carlsen and a requiem to the vessel.

INQUIRY OPENS

A "terrific crack" at 7 a.m. on December 26th signalled the beginning of the end for the Flying Enterprise, it was stated yesterday at a Coastguard Board of Inquiry in New York into the loss of the Isbrandtsen Company's 6,711-ton freighter. The witness was Mr. John Edward Drake (26), the Enterprise's first assistant engineer. "She had been pitching more than rolling for the last couple of days," he told the Board. "The ship slowed down and hove to while the deck crew came below and got some chain blocks.

"After a few hours I went on deck and saw a three-eighths to one-half inch crack in the deck near the No. 3 hatch on the port side. We managed to keep the engines going until 11 or 12 o'clock (noon), when she took a list. She seemed to roll over and stay over. Between five and ten minutes later she took a second list from 25 to about 40 degrees. Then the lights started growing dim."

LOST POWER

Because of the list, Mr. Drake said, the ship lost its power and turned over to its steam engines.

Captain Carlsen gave the order to abandon ship on Saturday, Mr. Drake said. At first, some of the passengers would not leave the ship—"Some even tied themselves on board."

Mr. Drake said that the seas were running 25 to 30 feet high when he and a passenger jumped from the after port deck into the water. A lifeboat from the Southland rescued seven passengers and eight of the crew.

"What, in your opinion, caused the vessel to crack?" The Chairman of the Board asked Drake. "It was just the pounding of the heavy seas," he replied.

SALVAGE CLAIM

Experts in London last night agreed that ordinarily there is no award for a salvage attempt where the property is not salved.

An official of Lloyd's said that the Lloyd's standard agreement in respect of the salvage of ships was on a "no cure—no pay" basis, but he did not know what contract the owners of the Turmoil had made with the owners of the Flying Enterprise.

Bishops' views on legal adoption

THE view of the Roman Catholic Church on legal adoption was set out in a statement given from the Archbishop's House, Dublin, last night, and dated January 8th, 1952.

It was in the form of a report from an Episcopal Committee established by the Irish Hierarchy to examine the question of legal adoption.

Legislative proposals for legal adoption were submitted on an all-party basis to the Government nearly two months ago, and a Bill sponsored by deputies on both sides of the Dail, has been on the Order Paper for some time. The Bill was not introduced before the Christmas recess because it was not included in the Government's programme of urgent measures.

The following is the statement from the Episcopal Committee:—

1 — Legal adoption, if it be restricted within certain limits and protected by certain safeguards, is consonant with Catholic teaching.

(a) Limits: Parents have a natural right and obligation to provide for their children in regard to religious and moral training, physical well-being and preparation for civic life.

Only for the gravest reasons may parents permanently relinquish this right or consider themselves excused from this obligation.

(b) Safeguards: The safeguards must be such as the Church considers sufficient to protect Faith and morals.

A child's right in respect of Faith and morals must be protected by such safeguards as will ensure its adoption by persons who profess and practise the religion of the child, and who are of good moral character.

An Adoption Bill should contain such reasonable safeguards as will minimise the moral dangers that may arise as a result of adoption.

It is imperative that there should be supervision and control of all institutions holding children for adoption.

2 — The Church regards the natural family as the ideal unit of family life, and, therefore, must oppose any measure in an Adoption Bill that would tend to substitute an artificial for a natural family.

Signed
✠ John C. McQuaid, Chairman, Archbishop of Dublin, Primate of Ireland.
✠ Jeremiah Kinane, Archbishop of Cashel.
✠ Michael Browne, Bishop of Galway.
✠ Neil Farren, Bishop of Derry.
✠ Cornelius Lucey, Bishop of Sila.

Truman asks Senate to ratify pacts

President Truman yesterday asked the Senate to ratify an agreement bringing Greece and Turkey into the North Atlantic Pact.

He also asked the Senate to ratify: the Security Treaty between the U.S. and Japan, the Security Treaty to which Australia, New Zealand and the U.S. are signatories and the Mutual Defence Treaty between the U.S. and the Republic of the Philippines.

Patrick Kavanagh and Anthony Cronin outside Davy Byrne's in Duke Street, Dublin, on 16 June 1954, the fiftieth anniversary of Bloomsday

13 December

The Adoption Act provides for the legal adoption of children, who must be of the same religion as the parents.

1953

5 January

Beckett's Waiting for Godot *is performed for the first time in Paris.*

Dingy and thin as it often was during the war, however, the paper acquired a certain intellectual glamour, described by Anthony Cronin, then a young poet and literary journalist. 'It was a staid journal, with advertisements still on its front page, but it was the intellectual's journal, their parish gazette, more or less by default and because the tone of the other two papers, the *Irish Independent* and the *Irish Press* ... was not to their taste.'[16]

Smyllie placed a heavy emphasis on this literary cachet, devoting generous space to book reviews even in the war years, when the paper itself was cut down to eight pages because of the rationing of newsprint. On 9 June 1945 it published, for the first time in its English-language version, the young Samuel Beckett's poem 'Dieppe'. On 24 June 1946 it published,

1947

Spraying the Potatoes

The barrels of blue potato-spray
Stood on a headland of July
Beside an orchard wall where roses
Were young girls hanging from the sky.

The flocks of green potato-stalks
Were blossom spread for sudden flight,
The Kerr's Pinks in a frivelled blue,
The Arran Banners wearing white.

And over that potato-field
A lazy veil of woven sun.
Dandelions growing on headlands, showing
Their unloved hearts to everyone.

Samuel Beckett's **Waiting for Godot,** *one of the most influential plays of the twentieth century, was first produced in 1953*

And I was there with the knapsack sprayer
On the barrel's edge poised. A wasp was floating
Dead on a sunken briar leaf
Over a copper-poisoned ocean.

The axle-roll of a rut-locked cart
Broke the burnt stick of noon in two.
An old man came through a corn-field
Remembering his youth and some Ruth he knew.

He turned my way. 'God further the work.'
He echoed an ancient farming prayer.
I thanked him. He eyed the potato-drills.
He said: 'You are bound to have good ones there.'

We talked and our talk was a theme of kings,
A theme for strings. He hunkered down
In the shade of the orchard wall. O roses
The old man dies in the young girl's frown.

also for the first time, Beckett's poem 'Saint-Lô', commemorating the period he spent working with the Red Cross in that devastated city in Normandy. Literary events were given prominent coverage. James Joyce's last novel, *Finnegans Wake,* was given a 6,000-word review by Andrew Cass (John Garvin). Evidence of how seriously the paper was taken by writers of the calibre of Joyce and O'Casey came when, in a list of books received for review, it mistakenly referred to 'Finnegans Wake by Seán O'Casey.' Joyce was 'infuriated', and O'Casey wrote to him suggesting that the mistake was deliberate. 'I know many of Dublin's Literary Clique dislike me, and they hate you (why, God only knows), so that "misprint" was a bit of a joke.'

One of Smyllie's most brilliant moves in his efforts to create for the paper this kind of status

5 March

Josef Stalin, ruler of the Soviet Union, dies.

2 June

Queen Elizabeth II is crowned. The British embassy in Dublin is picketed by the Anti-Partition Association.

9 June

Rev. Ian Paisley organises a

Waterford Glass was one of the few industrial success stories in independent Ireland, which otherwise remained overwhelmingly rural through the fifties

And poet lost to potato-fields,
Remembering the lime and copper smell
Of the spraying barrels he is not lost
Or till blossomed stalks cannot weave a spell.

Patrick Kavanagh

from The Irish Times
22 DECEMBER 1948

President Signs Republic Bill

The Republic of Ireland Bill was signed at 11.35 a.m. yesterday by the President, Mr Seán T. O'Kelly, and became an Act of the Oireachtas. The Taoiseach, Mr Costello, and the Minister for External Affairs, Mr MacBride, were present at the ceremony at Árus an Uachtaráin. The signing occupied only a few minutes.

The ceremony was held in the study at Árus an Uachtaráin, in which a copy of the Declaration of the Irish

Mother Mary Martin, founder of the Medical Missionaries of Mary. The extraordinary growth and development of the Irish missionary movement was one of the features of the first half of the twentieth century.

protest at which books are burned in defiance of 'modernism'.

29 October
The Health Act provides free mother and child services to dependants of people insured under the Social Welfare Act (1952).

was giving a regular column to Brian O'Nolan, the civil servant known in his guise as a novelist as Flann O'Brien and in his journalism as Myles na Gopaleen. O'Nolan, an elegant and erudite writer of Irish, offered Smyllie an ingenious solution to an awkward dilemma. How could *The Irish Times* pay homage to the state's policy of reviving Irish without at the same time surrendering to the obscurantism that surrounded it? The paper had always expressed doubts about the policy of seeking to revive Irish as the main vernacular language, and by the early forties polite misgivings had turned into open hostility. In 1942 it seemed that the state was about to close

Brendan Behan

Republic of 1916 hangs. Mr O'Kelly first signed his name to Bills relating to Rates on Agricultural Land Relief and the Expiring Laws Act. Then he was handed a copy of the Republic of Ireland Bill.

He first signed his name to the Irish version of the Bill and then to the English version.

Mr Michel McDunphy, the secretary to the President, filled in the date on the Bill and allotted it the number 22, which indicated that it was the 22nd Act to be passed this year.

The Bill was signed on the office desk, and the President used his own fountain pen.

off the main alternative for those parents (mostly well-to-do Protestants) who did not wish their children to learn Irish—that of sending them to school in Northern Ireland or Britain. The School Attendance Bill contained a provision that the education of a child not attending a recognised school would have to be certified as suitable by the Minister for Education. When the possibility that this law could be used to prevent children from being educated outside the state was raised in the Seanad, the minister did not

1954

6 April

The Flags and Emblems (Display) Act (Northern Ireland) makes it an offence to interfere with a

Union Jack and allows the RUC to remove other emblems if they believe their display will cause a breach of the peace.

18 May
The general election again results in a hung Dáil, with Fianna Fáil the largest party. John A. Costello eventually becomes Taoiseach of a coalition Government.

deny it. *The Irish Times* took up the issue and expressed delight when the Supreme Court declared the provision unconstitutional, showing, the paper said, that minority rights could not be set aside by those 'who would form us all in a standard Gaelic mould.'

By 1948 the paper declared that the 'Irish language experiment', then in progress for twenty-five years, was doomed and that 'all honest citizens must admit it has been a ghastly failure.' Yet it was crucial for the paper to establish that its objection was to compulsion, not to the language itself. And this is where Myles na Gopaleen came in. Myles first appeared in the paper on 4 October 1940, and from then until the end of 1941 his column was almost entirely in Irish. Then, when Myles began to appear every day, Irish alternated with English.

In *Dead as Doornails,* Anthony Cronin recalls that in the early fifties the young Brendan Behan had begun to write a column for the *Irish Press* but that 'since nobody in intellectual Dublin in those days ever saw anything but *The Irish Times,* this was simply not read by most of those

The jacket of the first edition of Máirtín Ó Cadhain's **Cré na Cille.** *First published in 1949, it is perhaps the finest Irish-language novel of the twentieth century.*

The Enterprise express from Dublin to Belfast in the last days of steam

The 1950s was a time of boom in all capitalist countries, with the exception of Ireland. Chronic emigration and unemployment continued throughout the decade, highlighted by this march in 1953.

Thus, in a few minutes, and with a complete absence of pomp, Ireland officially seceded from the British Commonwealth, and became, in fact, a republic. The date on which the Act becomes operative is, however, still undecided.

The Act will now be taken to the Registrar of the Supreme Court, and the Dáil will be informed officially that the Act has been signed by the President.

After the ceremony, Mr Costello told reporters that he was proud to have been present on the occasion of the signing of the Act, which makes clear to the world the country's international position.

Mr MacBride said that the Bill was the final achievement of the national aspirations of the people. It will enable Ireland to be regarded internationally as a republic.

he wanted to impress. I was not even aware of it until after he had been at it for more than a year.' *The Irish Times* summed up Behan's place in Dublin society: 'There are persons of bourgeois respectability in the city of Dublin who nourish a secret unease. It is that one day they may be proceeding on their middle-class way, chatting smoothly with their employer or their bank manager when suddenly across the street will come a loud and ebullient "View-halloo" followed by a colourful and uninhibited commentary on things in general. It will, of course, be Mr. Brendan Behan, who enjoys carrying on conversations with the width of the

19 November
Brendan Behan's Quare Fellow *is performed for the first time in the Pike Theatre in Dublin.*

1955

18 February
John Costello refuses to meet Lord Brookeborough after

Dr Noel Browne, Minister for Health, who sponsored and then resigned over the Mother and Child scheme in 1951

the Acting Prime Minister of Northern Ireland, Bryan Maginess, says that talks could be held only if there is an agreement not to discuss partition.

street between himself and his interlocutor. Mr. Behan has the voice for it but few of his friends have the nerve. Still, it is one of the occupational risks involved in knowing Mr. Behan, and all who know him have decided that it is worth it.'

On the other hand, however, the paper's appeal to the intellectuals was not matched within the ranks of what Myles na Gopaleen called 'the

from The Irish Times 1951
12 APRIL

Contra Mundum

A gallant fight has ended in defeat. Yesterday, after several days of tense struggle behind the scenes, Dr Noel Browne handed his resignation from the post of Minister for Health to the Taoiseach. Although he has been

John Charles McQuaid, Archbishop of Dublin from 1941 to 1972, the rigorist champion of orthodoxy, social conservatism and ecclesiastical authority

28 February
*Huge crowds
attend the new
Seán O'Casey
play in the
Gaiety Theatre,*
The Bishop's
Bonfire, *as
protesters outside
brand it
blasphemous and
cause disturbances.*

26 May
*The British
general election
returns a*

Plain People of Ireland'. The attitude of conservative Catholic Ireland to *The Irish Times* in this period is summed up by Frank McCourt's experiences, recounted in *Angela's Ashes,* of applying for a job with Eason's, the distribution company, in Limerick. The manager gave him a warning: 'Another thing. We distribute *The Irish Times,* a Protestant paper, run by the freemasons of Dublin. We pick it up at the railway station. We count it. We take it to the newsagents. But we don't read it. I don't want to see you reading it. You could lose the Faith and by the look of those eyes you could lose your sight. Do you hear me, McCourt?'[17] When McCourt's delivery bicycle slips on the ice, shops complain that '*The Irish Times* is coming in decorated with bits of ice and dog shit.' The manager, however, 'mutters to

defeated, the honours of the conflict fall to him. We cannot but believe that his stature has been increased even in the eyes of his professional and ecclesiastical opponents. It is certain that the goodwill of the people at large follows him in his fall, and that tens of thousands of families will be sadder for it. His tragedy is that he failed to perceive the extent and power of the forces that were both openly and covertly arrayed against him. It was dangerous enough that his 'Mother and Child' scheme aroused the fierce hostility of a considerable part of the medical profession; it was fatal when his views came into collision with the Roman Catholic Hierarchy. With a united Cabinet on his side, he might have prevailed against the doctors, as his counterpart in Great Britain prevailed against them; but ... he was left to fight a single-handed battle when once the Church entered the arena. Thus—not for the first or second time in Irish history—progress is thwarted.

An Aer Lingus Constellation, the first transatlantic turbo-prop aircraft, which inaugurated the airline's American service in 1947

A Mother and Child scheme, embodying a means test, is in accordance with Christian social principles; a Mother and Child scheme without a means test is opposed to them! So much, if we read them correctly, emerges from the documents which the Hierarchy contributes to the discussion. For ourselves, we cannot pretend to follow the reasoning, and we doubt if it will be followed by the puzzled and disappointed people of this country. Dr Browne proposed to abolish a means test because he is well aware of the humiliations that attend the existence of a means test in too many hospitals—the probings about income which cause annoyance even to the comparatively well-to-do, and acute distress to the poor. There are obvious reasons why the doctors—though certainly not all of them—should object to the absence of a means test, but the plain man, unversed in subtleties, will be at a loss to determine why the Church should take sides in the matter at all. This newspaper has not been uncritical of the ex-Minister's proposals, and holds no brief for his particular scheme. Our sorrow is that he has not been permitted to fight it out on its own merits ...

León Ó Broin, photographed in the eighties. As Secretary of the Department of Posts and Telegraphs in the 1950s, he was one of the moving spirits behind the Broadcasting Authority Act (1960) which established RTE. He was also a distinguished historian.

Siobhán McKenna

us that's the way the paper should be delivered, Protestant rag that it is.' McCourt himself took the paper home 'to see where the danger is.' His mother 'says it's a good thing Dad isn't here. He'd say, Is this what the men of Ireland fought and died for, that my own son is sitting there at the kitchen table reading the freemason paper.' But her son was enthralled. 'There are letters to the paper from people all over Ireland claiming they heard the first cuckoo of the year and you can read between the lines that people are calling each other liars. There are reports about Protestant weddings and pictures and the women always look lovelier than the ones we know in the lanes.

Conservative majority, with the Unionists once again gaining an overall majority in Northern Ireland.

27 May
Sinn Féin reappears prominently on

President Seán T. O'Kelly receives a ticker-tape reception in New York in the late fifties (above) and a more restrained welcome on his return to Dublin (right).

This is a sad day for Ireland. It is not so important that the Mother and Child scheme has been withdrawn, to be replaced by an alternative project embodying a means test. What matters more is that an honest, far-sighted and energetic man has been driven out of active politics. The most serious revelation, however, is that the Roman Catholic Church would seem to be the effective Government of this country. In the circumstances, may we appeal to Mr Costello and his colleagues to admit the futility of their pitiful efforts to 'abolish the border'—their Mansion House Committees, their anti-partition speeches at international assemblies, their pathetic appeals to the majority in the Six Counties to recognise that its advantage lies in a united Ireland? To that majority, the domination of the State by the Church—any

You can see Protestant women have perfect teeth … I keep reading *The Irish Times* and wondering if it's an occasion of sin …'

And in spite of Smyllie's success in making the paper a central part of Irish intellectual life, Frank McCourt's experiences were typical enough. For much of the population the paper was still an exotic occasion of sin. The circulation, in the early forties, continued to hover around the thirty thousand mark. The failure of the business to pay dividends led a group of shareholders to mount a coup against the Arnott family's control of the board, and Frank Lowe, head of Hely's, the Dublin printing

the political landscape as two members in Northern Ireland win seats in the British House of Commons. The ten other seats are taken by Unionists.

21 July
The first regular television service

Ronnie Delaney wins the 1,500 metres at the Melbourne Olympics in 1956 (above) and is welcomed home to Dublin by an ecstatic crowd on his return (right). So far he is Ireland's last gold medal winner on the track.

in Ireland begins with a broadcast from Divis in Co. Antrim.

15 October
Archbishop McQuaid calls for the cancellation of the forthcoming soccer match between Ireland and Yugoslavia because of the imprisonment of Archbishop Stepanić, the Croatian prelate, by the Yugoslav leader Tito.

and stationery company, took over as a director with strong executive powers. By the time Smyllie died, in 1954 (at the age of fifty-nine), he had become an increasingly depressed and marginal figure. It was a mark of his success in recruiting talent that he was succeeded as editor by two men he had brought in to the paper, first Alec Newman and then Alan Montgomery.

By the mid-fifties the paper had moved definitively beyond its Protestant base and had attracted a broader, liberal readership. As Hubert Butler noted in 1955, the paper was 'the only morning paper in Ireland in which independent views are freely expressed every day. If *The Irish Times* had to depend on the five per cent minority of the republic it would have long ago collapsed. So it is obvious that it circulates widely among Roman Catholics who like to think for themselves.'[18]

Thinking for oneself was still, however, a rather difficult art in a country where books were subject to heavy-handed censorship. The paper

Church—is anathema, and from now onwards it can plead some justification for all its fears. It seems that the merits of a theocratic Twenty-six Counties outweigh those of a normally democratic Thirty-two. Has the Government made its choice?

from The Irish Times 1951
12 APRIL

Minister Releases Correspondence

D r Noel Browne last night released the correspondence in connection with his Mother and Child Service Scheme ...

Bishop of Ferns to Taoiseach

10 October 1950

Dear Taoiseach,

The Archbishops and Bishops of Ireland, at their meeting on 10 October, had under consideration the proposals for Mother and Child health service and other kindred medical services. They recognised that these proposals are motivated

by a sincere desire to improve public health, but they feel bound by their office to consider whether the proposals are in accordance with Catholic moral teaching.

In their opinion the powers taken by the State in the proposed Mother and Child Health service are in direct opposition to the rights of the family and of the individual and are liable to very great abuse. Their character is such that no assurance that they would be used in moderation could justify their enactment. If adopted in law they would constitute a ready-made instrument for future totalitarian aggression.

The right to provide for the health of children belongs to parents, not to the State. The State has the right to intervene only in a subsidiary capacity, to supplement, not to supplant.

It may help indigent or neglectful parents; it may not deprive 90 per cent of parents of their rights because of 10 per cent necessitous or negligent parents.

It is not sound social policy to impose a state medical service on the whole community on the pretext of relieving

had, from the start, opposed censorship. In 1930, when the first books were banned, a leader suggested sarcastically that 'the legend "Banned in the Irish Free State" in a publisher's notice will make a fortune for novels which, without this aid, might fall still-born from the press.' In the modern world, 'any form of intellectual censorship is a moral anachronism ... Censorship, indeed, is an admission that the national system of education has been tried and found wanting.'

By the fifties the paper was setting itself more and more strongly against the prevailing atmosphere of church-inspired repression. The Cold War created an atmosphere in which liberals and social democrats were vulnerable to accusations that they were in reality the soft underbelly of communism. In Catholic Ireland, moreover, communism was readily identified

19 October

A capacity crowd of 21,400 turns up to watch Ireland lose to Yugoslavia at Dalymount Park.

14 December

Ireland becomes a member of the United Nations.

Christy Ring (centre), probably the greatest hurler of the century, is foiled by the Waterford goalkeeper, Ned Power, in this dramatic photograph

1956

1 May
The annual
general
meeting of the
Royal
National
Hospital for
Consumption
learns that it

with atheism and immorality. In January 1950, just at the time when Alger Hiss was being sentenced to five years' imprisonment in the United States, a controversy broke out in the letters page of *The Irish Times* in which, for the best part of two months, over fifty writers debated the 'liberal ethic'.

The spark was provided by a prominent report in the paper of a lecture delivered under that title by a Catholic theologian, Professor Féilim Ó Briain. Father Ó Briain suggested that there was a continuity between liberal critics of

the necessitous 10 per cent from the so-called indignity of the means test.

The right to provide for the physical education of children belongs to the family and not to the State. Experience has shown that physical or health education is closely interwoven with important moral questions on which the Catholic Church has definite teaching.

Education in regard to motherhood includes instruction in regard to sex relations, chastity and marriage. The State has no competence to give instruction in such matters. We regard with the greatest apprehension the proposal to give to local medical officers the right to tell Catholic girls and women how they should behave in regard to this sphere of conduct at once so delicate and sacred.

Gynaecological care may be, and in some other countries is, interpreted to include provision for birth limitation and abortion. We have no guarantee that State officials will respect Catholic principles in regard to these matters. Doctors trained in institutions in which we have no confidence may be appointed as medical officers under the proposed services and may give gynaecological care not in accordance with Catholic principles ...

The Bishops desire that your Government should give careful consideration to the dangers inherent in the present proposals before they are adopted by the Government for legislative enactment and, therefore, they feel it their duty to submit their views on this subject to you privately and at the earliest opportunity, since they regard the issues involved as of the gravest moral and religious importance.

I remain, dear Taoiseach, Yours very sincerely,

(Signed) James Staunton, Bishop of Ferns,

Secretary to the Hierarchy,

John A. Costello, TD Taoiseach

Letter to Dr Browne

The letters sent by Mr MacBride to Dr Browne and the Taoiseach were as follows:—

Dear Dr Browne,

Following upon your own declarations and the indications given by me, I had hoped that it would not have been necessary to write this letter. Unfortunately, by reason of the situation which has arisen, and for which I fear you are largely responsible, I have no alternative, as leader of Clann na Poblachta, but to request you to transmit, as soon as possible, your resignation as Minister for Health to the Taoiseach ...

The creation of a situation where it is made to appear that a conflict exists between the spiritual and temporal authorities is always undesirable; in the case of Ireland, it is highly damaging to the cause of national unity, and should have been avoided ...

Letter to Taoiseach

10 April 1951

Dear Taoiseach,

I enclose a copy of a letter which I have sent by hand tonight to Dr Browne, Minister for Health, requesting him to tender his resignation to you ...

the church and communist totalitarianism. 'At its most innocent and futile, it appeared as an occasional letter in *The Irish Times* about "priest-ridden Irish" or "the domination of the clergy." At its most ruthless it found its most vigorous expression in the 34 prelates imprisoned behind the Iron Curtain or exiled from there.' Socialists and liberals, he said, agreed with 'free love' and 'as a necessary consequence, artificial prevention of births ... freedom of abortion, divorce and the State education of the children, who in the new free society were an obstacle to the pleasures and fun of the parents.'

Dr Owen Sheehy-Skeffington replied, accusing the priest of 'fantastically sweeping generalisations' and comparing his denunciations to the notion that 'it is part of the Catholic religion to drink the blood of Protestant babies.' Father Ó Briain defended his views. Brian Inglis attacked them, pointing out that few of the writers whom Ó Briain had cited as representative liberals and socialists would survive in Stalin's Russia. 'In his list are Voltaire, Rousseau, Bentham, Marx and Engels, Zola, Proust, Gide, and Bertrand Russell. "Hell", as the saying goes, "for company." Can it be—dare it be said—that there may be something in an ethic which includes in its ranks so distinguished a gathering?'

Inglis went closer to the bone by hinting that illiberal Ireland was not quite the bastion of morality it might appear to be. 'It would be interesting to find whether the VD [venereal disease] rate in Russia is as bad as the rate here, figures of which are soon to be published that will make our "continence" look pretty silly.' Ó Briain's reply to this claim revealed the depth of personal animosity behind the polite exchanges. Taking up Inglis's suggestion that rates of sexually transmitted disease in Ireland might be surprisingly high, he wrote: 'No doubt some well-to-do practitioners of the liberal ethic do not have to go for treatment to the institutions controlled by our health authorities, but, if and when some clever investigator gives the world these carefully guarded statistics, it will still

has some empty beds for the first time in sixty years.

1 June
The results of the census show the population of the Republic to be 2.9 million. More than forty thousand people have emigrated each year since 1951.

4 November
Soviet forces enter Hungary to crush the uprising there.

2 December
Ronnie Delaney wins a gold medal in the 1,500 metres in the Olympic Games in Melbourne, breaking the existing Olympic record.

12 December
The IRA launches ten

*simultaneous
attacks in
Northern
Ireland,
marking the
initiation of
its border
campaign.*

1957

5 February

*Addressing
the Fine Gael
ardfheis, the
Taoiseach,
John A.
Costello,
suggests a
federal
solution
to the
problem of
partition.*

5 March

*The general
election
produces an
overall
majority for
Fianna
Fáil. De
Valera forms
his last
Government.*

25 March

*The Treaty
of Rome
establishes
the European
Economic
Community.*

remain to be proved that they are a guide to the morality of the Irish people in general.'

Inevitably, this controversy expanded into a debate about censorship. In October 1949 the Censorship of Publications Board had banned the report of the British Royal Commission on Population on the grounds that it advocated 'the unnatural prevention of conception or the procurement of abortion or miscarriage.' This was a clear extension of censorship: no official report had ever been banned before. And in January 1950, while the 'liberal ethic' debate was getting under way, the Censorship Appeals Board overturned the ban. Almost immediately, however, another book dealing with population control, Karl Vogt's *Road to Survival* was banned. The book had been reviewed in *The Irish Times* by an anonymous 'Catholic Sociologist', who wrote to the paper to protest against the ban. He described the book as 'an extremely valuable work on human ecology which has been in circulation for about a year' and protested that 'to ban this book is absurd; for by no stretch of likelihood could it introduce or encourage contraceptive practices among our Christian people. Much rather should the book be widely read, carefully studied, and made the starting-point of consideration of the true Christian solution to the ecological problems of the century.'

In 1950, however, this incipient culture clash between conservative and liberal Ireland was given dramatic form in the conflict over the Mother and Child health scheme introduced by the young Minister for Health in the coalition Government that had ousted de Valera in 1948, Noel Browne. Though the scheme was no more than a modest welfare programme, it was strongly opposed by fervent Catholics within the medical profession and subsequently by the Catholic hierarchy, whose secretary informed the Taoiseach, John A. Costello, that the scheme was 'in direct opposition to the rights of the family.' The controversy rumbled on in the background until April 1951, with Browne attempting to win episcopal support and the bishops, especially the Archbishop of

I take the view that, as the leader of one of the parties in the government, it is part of my responsibility to be in a position to assure the Taoiseach at all times that the members of the party which I have the honour to lead in the Government are trustworthy of the confidence of the Government, the Oireachtas, and the people, and are capable of discharging their duties effectively. As I can no longer give you this assurance in regard to Dr Browne, for the reasons stated in my letter to him, I deemed it to be the proper course to request him to transmit his resignation to you ...

Yours sincerely

(Signed) Seán MacBride,

Minster for External Affairs

from The Irish Times
27 MAY **1957**

Village boycott of school and shops

Irish Times Reporter

Because of a boycott by Roman Catholics in Fethard-on-Sea (population 100) Co. Wexford, the Church of Ireland school and its eleven pupils are without a teacher; Protestant shopkeepers and dealers in the area are doing little business and one man is seeking police protection for his family.

The school closed on 15 May when its Catholic teacher was advised by a number of women in the village that it 'would be better for her if she did not give any more lessons.'

The sexton of St Mogue's Church, one of the three churches of the Church of Ireland Fethard Union—another Catholic—was advised by her neighbours to give up the duties she had been carrying out there for a number of years.

Cause of Trouble

The boycott began on Monday, 13 May, when local people announced their intention of staying away from village shops owned by Protestants. Its cause was the disappearance on 7 April of Mrs Sheila Cloney, the wife of a local farmer, Mr Seán Cloney, and her two children, Eileen and Mary, aged six and three years. Mrs Cloney, who is a member of the Church of Ireland, married Mr Cloney, a Catholic, in London, in 1949.

Some days after Mrs Cloney's disappearance, Mr Cloney was granted a writ of habeas-corpus in the Northern Ireland

School children in Crumlin mid-century

High Court for the production of the two children, said to be held by the mother, whose whereabouts were unknown. In an affidavit Mr Cloney said that he had been approached by a barrister-at-law on his wife's behalf, who told him that the terms of settlement included his agreement that the two children be brought up in the Protestant faith, and that he consider changing his own religion.

The attitude of a number of the villagers is that unless the children are returned to their father the boycott will continue. Some of them believe that Mrs Cloney left with the financial assistance and connivance of local Protestants—these allegations have been strongly denied by the Protestants.

Dublin, John Charles McQuaid, reiterating their objections. It became clear that Browne had not got the support of his Government colleagues, and he was in effect forced to resign.

The Irish Times played an important role in making the controversy a testing-ground for church-state relations. Just before he resigned, Browne sent his secretary to Smyllie with sixteen letters between himself, his party leader (Seán MacBride), the Taoiseach, and members of the hierarchy. He had, he recalled in his autobiography, 'been warned that the Government

13 May

Catholics in Fethard, Co. Wexford, boycott Protestants because of a dispute between a Protestant husband and a Catholic wife.

Walter Cronkite of CBS speaks to camera in front of an almost deserted O'Connell Street in the late fifties. The scene behind him was typical of the time. Ireland was still a quiet, under-developed backwater.

The school-teacher was told on Saturday, 11 May (a week after the High Court action) that the boycott would begin. She approached a local priest and was advised to carry on with her work at the school. She attended the school on Monday and Tuesday, but was again advised by villagers to give up her job. On Tuesday afternoon she informed a number of local Protestants that the school would not be opened the following day. She sent a report to the local education committee and to the Department of Education, giving her reason for the closure as 'a boycott in the area.'

Fall in Trade

Protestant merchants have noticed a fall in business. Few of their Catholic neighbours are dealing with them, although there is some 'backstairs dealing.'

The Protestants are hurt and surprised at the action of their neighbours, and consider that the action of Mrs Cloney is a domestic affair and none of their business. None of them knows the whereabouts of Mrs Cloney or her children.

One Protestant, the father of two children, made a statement to the police at Duncannon, six miles from Fethard, saying that he was apprehensive for the safety of his relatives and asking for police protection.

A Catholic trader said he believed that if the children were not returned to their father the boycott might spread all over the diocese. There would be no peace until they were returned, he said, even though not all of the villagers had their heart in the boycott, or even believed in it at all.

Fethard-on-Sea is part of the Church of Ireland's Fethard Union, an amalgamation of three parishes—Fethard, Tintern and Killesk—which have a combined congregation of about 150. Possibly 40 or 50 of these would attend services at St Mogue's.

The rector, the Rev. A.C.P. Fisher came to the area on 9 May. He has reported the position to his bishop and to the Department of Education. He is seeking a substitute teacher for the school.

might attempt to place an embargo on their publication, but Smyllie, an editor with genuine liberal beliefs, had promised me that should an embargo be attempted, then, at the risk of going to prison, he "would publish and be damned."'[19] The paper, in what was considered a shocking act at the time, did indeed publish the correspondence, marking a significant advance in journalistic willingness to challenge authority in Ireland.

In spite of the church's victory over the Mother and Child scheme, however, that Ireland was in deep decline. Writing in *The Irish Times* in 1952, John Richards Orpen, a member of the Government's Emigration Commission, and Esther Bishop, Vice-President of the Irish Countrywomen's Association, commented: 'Housing conditions in rural Ireland … remain at a low standard … The amenities within most small farms and agricultural workers' houses are, in general, much the same as they were when the land was tilled with a spade and men threshed with a flail … Is it surprising that young girls, who are well aware that we live in a world where labour-saving devices hold pride of place, are unwilling to marry into conditions as they are?'

An upsurge in emigration, combined with an extremely low marriage rate, was having a devastating effect. The preliminary report of the 1956 census disclosed that the population, at 2.9 million, was the lowest since independence (though it was to fall further). In a famous editorial *The Irish Times* commented: 'If the present trend continues Ireland will die, not in the remote, unpredictable future, but quite soon.' Faced with a choice between change and death, Ireland began, very gradually, to accept the necessity for change.

23 May

Alan Simpson is imprisoned under a nineteenth-century law for producing Tennessee Williams's play The Rose Tattoo *in the Pike Theatre, Dublin. While the play is not banned, the appearance of a condom on stage means that the producers have breached the law, 'having produced for gain an indecent or profane performance.'*

7 July

Internment without trial is reintroduced in the Republic.

Bloody Sunday in Derry, 30 January 1972. The Parachute Regiment killed thirteen people at a civil rights rally. In one of the most haunting images of the Troubles, Fr Edward Daly, later bishop of Derry, guides the body of one of the victims, using his bloodied handkerchief as a flag of true...

1958

'Chronic Episcopophagy'

1999

1958–1999

'Chronic Episcopophagy'

In June 1959 Éamon de Valera, now seventy-six, resigned as Taoiseach and offered himself as a candidate for the presidency, an office he would hold until 1973. It was an ambivalent moment. On the one hand de Valera's retirement from active politics marked the end of an era; on the other hand, his determination to remain as the symbolic head of the nation was a reminder that the new era would have to emerge from the deep shadow of the old one. It was as if he wished by his continuing ceremonial presence to remind the nation of the values with which he had helped to imbue it, to keep, from the lofty vantage-point of the presidency, a wary eye on the generation to which he was passing on his achievements.

1958

1 January
The European Economic Community comes into existence.

1959

17 June
De Valera is elected President, but the simultaneous referendum proposal on the abolition of PR is defeated.

23 June
Seán Lemass becomes Taoiseach.

1960

31 March
Dáil Éireann approves a move by University College to Belfield in south Dublin.

12 April
The Broadcasting Authority Act establishes RTE.

9 November
John F. Kennedy is elected President of the United States.

Those achievements, shared with a generation of politicians on both sides of the Civil War divide, had been, even on a global scale, important. Alongside the impact of the First World War, the gradual establishment of an independent, democratic Irish republic had helped, in the words of the historian Eric Hobsbawm, to make 'foreign empires look vulnerable for the first time.' Irish independence did much to prepare the British ruling elite for the inevitability of an end to, or at least a drastic transformation of, its empire. Ironically, in the period between the two world wars Britain controlled more territory than ever before; but, as Hobsbawm puts it, 'never before had the rulers of Britain felt less confident about maintaining their old imperial supremacy.'[1] The Irish experience may be one of the main reasons why, unlike France, which undertook disastrous imperial wars in south-east Asia in the forties and fifties, Britain, for the most part, did not resist the decolonisation of its imperial dependencies after the Second World War.

That war, in which Japan and Germany had overrun much of Asia and north Africa, had shown that the imperial powers were vulnerable and had created successful native resistance movements. By the late fifties it was clear that the imperial system could not be re-established after the immense rupture of the conflict. Syria and Lebanon (in 1945), India and Pakistan (1947), Burma, Ceylon, Israel and Indonesia (1948) broke away in the immediate aftermath of the war. Radical nationalist regimes came to power in Iran, Egypt, Iraq, Syria, Tunisia, and, eventually, Algeria. In British Africa, Ghana became independent in 1957, leading the way for the rest of the imperial possessions (except, until the seventies, those of Portugal) to emerge as separate states. British overseas possessions, which had contained 760 million people in 1944, gradually dwindled until by 1997, when Hong Kong reverted to Chinese rule, they contained just 168,000.

from The Irish Times
EASTER WEEK **1966**

The Embers of Easter
Conor Cruise O'Brien

The Civil War itself is usually blamed for the blight of cynicism and disgust which settled on 'free Ireland.' The real cause is, I believe, the cause of the Civil War itself: the conflict between loyalties and realities, the intolerable knowledge that the Republic proclaimed by Pearse and Connolly was not attainable. Yeats wrote:

Fail, and that history turns into rubbish,
All that great past to a trouble of fools.

My generation grew into the chilling knowledge that we had failed, that our history had turned into rubbish, our past to 'a trouble of fools'. With this feeling it is not surprising that the constant public praise for the ideals of Pearse and Connolly

Conor Cruise O'Brien, Minister for Posts and Telegraphs in the Cosgrave Government. An outspoken opponent of nationalist pieties, especially on Northern Ireland, he is a historian, diplomat, controversialist, journalist and one of Ireland's most internationally distinguished intellectuals.

Éamon de Valera on his 91st birthday, 14 October 1973

should have produced in us bafflement rather than enthusiasm. We were bred to be patriotic, only to find that there was nothing to be patriotic about; we were republicans of a republic that wasn't there. Small wonder that Pearse's vision of an Ireland 'not free merely but Gaelic as well' did not convince us. In Pearse's sense, Ireland was not free; why should it be Gaelic, which was a much more unlikely condition?

Pearse died, not for an island, or part of an island, but for a nation: an entity with a distinct culture, based on its own language. The nation for which he died never came to life. Culturally, Ireland remained a region, or rather two regions, of the English-speaking world. The distinguishing characteristic of the descendants of the Gaels was no longer language but religion, and the territorial division of the island between these people and the children of the Scottish settlers

Yet if the role of precursor to these monumental events gave a certain grandeur to Ireland's rather sleepy independence, the end of the imperial age also brought a realisation of how little the state had done with that independence and of how much it remained, economically if not politically, a British dependency. Other divisions, such as the Cold War between the Soviet Union and the United States—fought, for the most part, with the lives of the poor in Africa, Asia, and Latin America—were complicating the epic conflict between natives and imperialists. And in this new antagonism, Ireland was peripheral. Though anti-communist and pro-western (the Soviet Union kept Ireland out of the United Nations until 1955 because it assumed that Ireland would side with the United States), Ireland did not join the western military alliance, NATO. Only after 1960, when Irish soldiers joined the UN peace-keeping mission in the Congo, did Ireland begin to find a place in the post-war world.

And in a sense de Valera's resignation had happened long before he resigned. He had become resigned to the failure of his policies and believed that there was nothing for his people to do but endure. In 1956, as leader of the opposition, he had responded to the Government's imposition of import levies to try to arrest a growing balance of payments deficit with a warning that 'we have to tighten our belts … The policy of self-reliance is the one policy that will enable our nation to continue to exist. Back in 1917, we had to face the people who were telling us what we would lose by not being incorporated in the British Empire. I remember well that we had to tell people down in Kilkenny: We have a choice. It may be that we have the choice of the humble cottage instead of as lackeys partaking of the sops in the big man's house.'

The irony that, after thirty-four years of independence, he still had to urge the same frugality on his people as in 1917 did not seem to strike him. Nor did he seem to have noticed that huge numbers of his fellow-citizens were

Ten Irish UN soldiers are killed in the Congo.

1961

12 April
Yuri Gagarin of the Soviet Union becomes the first person in space.

1 August
Ireland applies for membership of the EEC.

4 October
The general election results in a hung Dáil, with Fianna Fáil once again the largest party.

31 December
The first television broadcast by RTE takes place.

1962

1 January
Ireland becomes a member of the UN Security Council.

31 May
The Northern Ireland general election results again in an overall majority for the Unionists.

Dr C. S. (Todd) Andrews (left), pictured here with Frank Aiken, the Minister for External Affairs, was a key figure in post-war Ireland. He was successively managing director of Bord na Móna, executive chairman of CIE and part-time chairman of the RTE Authority. In retirement, he wrote two fine volumes of memoirs. He was a notable upholder of the no-nonsense, public service ethic of the revolutionary generation whose time was passing by the nineteen-sixties.

6 July
RTE transmits the first edition of 'The Late Late Show', presented by Gay Byrne.

11 October
The Second Vatican Council meets.

22 October
President Kennedy announces that the Soviet Union has missile bases in Cuba, triggering what becomes the Cuban missile crisis.

choosing to live in the big man's house of England rather than in the humble Irish cottage of his fond imagining. Between 1951 and 1961, 412,000 people emigrated. The reasons were obvious enough. In 1956 and 1957 Ireland was the only country in the western world where the total volume of goods and services consumed actually fell. In 1960 six out of every ten Irish workers earned less than ten pounds a week, compared with just one in ten in Britain. With such an immense gap in living standards and such a short distance to travel, the lure of England was, for most young people, irresistible.

Even while de Valera was still in power, moreover, the main planks of his policy were visibly rotting away. Fianna Fáil had been founded to revive Irish, to keep the maximum number of people on the land, and to secure a united Ireland. The language revival movement had failed so badly that in 1956, when the Gaeltacht area was

in Ulster was the slightly distorted expression of a long-standing spiritual division which men like Tone and Pearse lived and died to close. Such men do not live or die in vain, but the State established by their followers was itself the expression of the failure of their hopes. Pearse's hopes for a bilingual nation, spiritually nourished by the genius of the Irish language and by its ancient literature, were also doomed to disappointment, even so far as concerned the 'three quarters of a nation'. The Irish language survived among a few thousand people in the Western seaboard. Thousands of other people, from the rest of Ireland, did visit these Irish-speaking districts—as a direct result of the Gaelic revival movement—and many of them derived benefit from this. The movement was successful insofar as it enriched a considerable number of lives—and enriched also that perpetual and universal profiteer, the English language. But Irish people generally did not become bilingual, and English remained solidly established as the language both of the home and of business. Most Irish people read English, very often the English of those special editions of the English Sunday newspapers which, in order to placate the Irish censorship, replace their habitual and domestic columns of smut by articles about Lourdes and the Holy Father.

This curious phenomenon reflects the basic situation: that the Irish State is culturally part of Britain, distinguished from the rest of the archipelago so far mainly by its practice of a puritanical form of the Roman Catholic religion and by marked deference to ecclesiastical authority.

Irish became, officially, the first language of the country. It is the language of the Constitution in that, in the event of a conflict between the Irish text and the English, the Irish form shall prevail. This may be the only case in the world in which mistranslation has power to change the original meaning of the text translated, for the Irish form which 'shall be deemed to prevail' is generally believed to be a translation from the English text which shall be deemed to be prevailed over in the event of its having been mistranslated. The greatest tragedy about the creation of a State on the basis of ideals impossible to attain was the release sought through national fantasy. When the answer to Pearse's 'not free merely but Gaelic as well' turned out to be '75 per cent free and 0.6 per cent Gaelic' it proved impossible for Pearse's followers either to accept these figures or to alter the realities they represent. A desperate game of let's pretend followed: Ireland *is* Gaelic—is not Gaelic the first official language?

Ireland *is* free—does not the Constitution declare that the national territory consists of the whole island and its territorial seas? The realistic, as distinct from the fantastic, provisions of the Constitution are in force 'pending the reintegration of the national territory'. Such reintegration, always unlikely, is made much more unlikely by the existence of a Constitution enacted by a small majority of the Catholic three-quarters of a nation, recognising 'the special position' of the Catholic Church, couched in language inspired by Catholic theology and purporting to bind the Protestant majority in Northern Ireland who were never consulted about the matter at all ...

from The Irish Times 1966
27 JUNE

Gunmen Murder Belfast Youth

Political motive suspected

A Belfast youth was murdered by gunmen, and two of his companions wounded, when they were attacked in a side street off the Shankill Road, Belfast, early yesterday morning.

The youth was Peter Ward (18), of 53 Beechmount Parade, off the Falls Road. He had just left a public house in Malvern Street with his two friends and a fourth companion, Richard Leppington (16), of Beechmount Bungalows.

The four were all Catholics. The RUC last night were working on the theory that the shooting had a political or sectarian basis. A police statement yesterday said that a number of men were in Brown Square police station helping the police with their inquiries ...

from The Irish Times 1967
13 DECEMBER

Curtain-up at Last for the Priesthood of Ireland?

By John Horgan

The law preventing Catholic priests in Ireland from attending the theatre is being changed by the Hierarchy, it became clear last night, after several days of unsubstantiated but cheerfully optimistic rumours. The

more realistically defined, it was found to contain just 85,700 people. As for keeping people on the land, rates of emigration in the fifties were higher than they had been at any time since the eighteen-eighties. The steady decrease in the agricultural labour force that had been evident since independence became a stampede from the land in the fifties, with a loss of 200,000 agricultural workers between 1946 and 1961.

And even the ritual condemnation of partition was losing its force. In de Valera's last speech as party leader to a Fianna Fáil ardfheis, in October 1958, he did not mention partition at all. In the previous year's speech he had come

1963

3 June
*Pope John
XXIII dies.*

4 June
*Rev. Ian Paisley
leads a march to
City Hall in
Belfast to protest
against the tributes
paid to the Pope.*

One of Aer Lingus's less successful investments was in the Carvair, a car carrier that it bought in the mid-sixties as a rival to the newly developed roll-on, roll-off car ferries. It was not a success and was abandoned after a couple of years.

Donogh O'Malley, the Minister for Education from July 1966 to his premature death in March 1968. Dynamic, impatient and abrasive, he revolutionised secondary education in the Republic by introducing a universal state-funded free scheme for the first time.

21 June

Giovanni Battista Montini becomes Pope Paul VI.

26–29 June

President Kennedy visits Ireland.

22 November

President Kennedy is assassinated in Dallas, Texas.

close to admitting that a united Ireland was not, in the foreseeable future, a realistic goal. 'I pray to Heaven that I will see this problem solved before I die. I don't want any of you to think that it is more than a prayer to the almighty … We have seen wondrous things happen and in God's mercy we may see the rest. But I cannot promise it to you and nobody else in this country can.' Only a miracle, he seemed to be admitting, could achieve the main aim of his party's policies.

A united Ireland was certainly not going to be achieved by force. The IRA launched an 'offensive' against Northern Ireland in 1956; by

overall significance of the removal of this, one of our most celebrated anachronisms, is roughly similar to the admission of defeat by a group of Japanese soldiers still fighting the Second World War on a Pacific island in the early 'Fifties.

The decision to change the law is believed to have been taken at the last meeting of the Hierarchy in Maynooth …

It puts an end to a fascinating, if archaic, situation, whose roots probably go back to the disputes between prominent prelates and the traditional theatre guilds at the end of the Middle Ages—if not earlier than that. There has been a general Roman law forbidding clerics to attend anything coming under the heading of '*spectaculum*,' and this has been adapted in various ways to local conditions. …

With its implementation, a certain amount of colour will go out of the theatrical life of the country. No longer will theatregoing priests have to skulk in the wings, listening to the language of the actors as they come off-stage, and their fraternal comments on other members of the cast. Dress-rehearsals, too, will be the poorer for their absence, and—perhaps most important of all—they'll now have to pay for their tickets instead of watching performances for free, squashed into the lighting box …

from The Irish Times **1969**
11 DECEMBER

Sorry—No Blacks—2

Last week we disclosed on this page that out of 1,000 landladies offering accommodation approved by the TCD authorities for their students, only 20 would take black students. Today we give the views of some landladies and overseas students on the situation Dublin's coloured students find themselves in …

David Akerele has been in Ireland for five years. He did General Studies in Trinity College and is now doing Honours in History and Political Science there. He was born and educated in England, and his parents are now living in Nigeria.

Mr Akerele and his Belfast wife, Jackie, and baby, Natasha, are in the process of moving flats: it took them six months to find the flat they wanted. Mrs Akerele did most of the inspecting and, although she found a number of places she liked, once she said that her husband was black she was turned down with such excuses as 'I'm sorry, the neighbours wouldn't like it.'

A taste of things to come. A mass protest at Stormont against the decision to establish the New University of Ulster at Coleraine rather than Derry. The decision, made largely on sectarian grounds, united all sides from Derry. The interviewees are Eddie McAteer (Nationalist), Albert Anderson, the Unionist mayor of Derry, and the young John Hume.

Seán Lemass and his wife, Kathleen, in Bonn in 1962 with Chancellor Konrad Adenauer. They discussed the possibility of Ireland joining the Common Market (now the EU), a prospect that faded in the following year when de Gaulle vetoed the British application.

1964

20 March

Brendan Behan dies, aged forty-one.

5 August

The number of Irish soldiers in Cyprus reaches a thousand as more arrive to bolster the UN peace-keeping force.

1961, when it was called off, it had cost eighteen lives (twelve IRA men and six members of the RUC) and a great deal of public money on both sides of the border. The campaign was launched to achieve 'an independent, united, democratic Irish republic,' and the IRA declared that 'for this we shall fight until the invader is driven from our soil and victory is ours.' But its main contribution to unity was that it led to the closure or the cratering of border roads by the British army. The highlights of the campaign were all glorious failures, like the raid on Brookeborough RUC barracks on New Year's Eve, 1956, in which two IRA men, Seán South and Feargal O'Hanlon, were killed. Huge crowds at their funerals and

'But,' said Mr Akerele, 'the flat situation is hopeless really for everyone except working girls. We had a number of things against us. I'm a student, coloured, and we have a baby. It is really a matter of keeping at it until you find the right place.'

When asked if he had come across any blatant racialism in Dublin, other than accommodation, Mr Akerele said that half the time it was impossible to prove. 'You must have political understanding of racialism and what keeps it going or you find yourself becoming a racialist too, in defence. If you have mixed parents—my mother is white—it can turn you against one of them.'

He says that a friend and he had once been refused entry in to a Dublin club. His other friends, who were white, were allowed in. 'But again, you can't prove that it was racialism,' he added.

'If we were here in great numbers there would probably be discrimination in employment as there is in accommodation. The accommodation situation is much the same as London. But most of the coloured people here are students, passing through, so people don't mind too much. If they wanted to settle it would be another thing, but this is unlikely to happen unless some industry develops and a stronger labour force is required,' he said.

'The Church, whether Catholic or Protestant, has great control over the lives of the people in this country. It controls most of the schools. So where do the people get their ideas or fears of coloured people?' he asked. 'Irish people are brought up in such a way that they still think we swing in trees in Africa and that we are savages. For example, if a nun gets raped in the Congo, they think that only the Africans could have done it' ...

Commenting on the proposed Springboks tour in Ireland, he said that it was important to try and get the

the election of four Sinn Féin abstentionist TDs in the general election of February 1957 showed the continuing appeal of diehard republicanism. But the main political effect of the IRA's actions was to provoke de Valera into the introduction, with devastating effect, of internment without trial. With the Northern Ireland government doing the same, the IRA was soon squeezed into ever tighter corners until, in 1961, the campaign was called off. With Catholics in Northern Ireland remaining largely indifferent to the IRA's call to arms, the campaign succeeded merely in proving the resilience of the Northern state.

With so much of the governing ideology in obvious trouble, the appearance of consensus was increasingly maintained by the suppression of alternative views. The censorship of books, which Robert Graves had described in a letter to

18 September
Seán O'Casey dies.

15 October
Labour wins the British general election: Harold Wilson is appointed Prime Minister.

1965

7 January
Following the Beatles' riotous performance at the same venue

The young John B. Keane, pictured in the family pub in Listowel, was one of the most popular and prolific playwrights of the fifties and sixties

THE IRISH TIMES

Price 5d.   No. 33,595   DUBLIN, THURSDAY, JUNE 27, 1963   CITY EDITION

OLD TIME IRISH
COARSE CUT
MARMALADE
A FRUITFIELD PRODUCT

DUBLIN GREETS KENNEDY

President John F. Kennedy waves to the crowds as he passes through College Green, Dublin, on the way to Arus an Uachtarain last night.

WELCOMED LIKE A HOMECOMING HERO

Cheering thousands line route from airport to Arus an Uachtarain

By CATHAL Og O'SHANNON and TONY KELLY

RESIDENT JOHN FITZGERALD KENNEDY, the 35th President of the United States of America and the first U.S. President to visit Ireland, was received tumultuously by 00 people on his arrival for his three-day visit to Ireland.

his tremendous welcome in earlier yesterday, the wel- st Dublin Airport seemed nough: there were fewer than eople allowed into the air- s but it was an enthusiastic ildly excited at seeing the at grandson of an Irish- who is now the most man in the Western world. e President said, he was

glad to accept the Government's invitation to visit Ireland, Ce land from which eight of my grand- parents came to the United States. He was proud too, he said, to visit Ireland because of his father's old and valued friendship with Presi- dent de Valera.

With Mr. Kennedy came his sister, Mrs. Eunice Shriver, wife of the U.S. Peace Corps Director, and

his sister-in-law, the Princess Radziwill. At the airport to greet him with Mr. de Valera and mem- bers of the Government was his younger sister, Mrs. Jean Kennedy- Smith, who had arrived in Dublin earlier in the day.

The President arrived from Ber- lin on board Air Force One, the big Boeing Jet in which he is mak- ing his tour of Europe. It touched down at the airport four minutes before 8 p.m. and taxied to the front of the main terminal build- ing right on schedule.

FIVE HOUR WAIT

By three p.m.—some five hours before the arrival of the 'plane— thousands of people were already at the airport waiting. The main road from Dublin was packed with cars, and the usual 18-minute drive from town took more than an hour. Parking arrangements, however, were excellent. There were large public car parks bear the main entrance into the airport, and hun- dreds of police and stewards were on duty to direct the thousands of vehicles. Everyone who wanted to was able to see the President, although for a great many it was just a fleeting glimpse at a consid- erable distance.

Air Force One made a single circuit of the airfield, then landed

ARNOTTS SALE

Greeted in tongue of ancestors

ON his arrival at Dublin Airport, President Kennedy was welcomed by President de Valera, who opened his address in the Irish language.

Mr. de Valera

The President, Mr. de Valera, said: "Mr. President, I have thought it fitting that my first words of welcome to you should be in our native language, the language of your ancestors, the great Kennedy clan of the Dal gChais who, under the mighty King Brian, nine-and-a-half centuries ago, not far from the spot on which we are standing smashed the invader and broke the Norse power forever.

"Our welcome, Mr. President, is universal and heartfelt. We wel- come you, in the first place, as the head and chief executive, the first citizen, of the great republic of the West upon whose en- lightened, wise, and firm leader- ship hangs the hope of the world.

"We welcome you in the second place as the representative of that great country in which our people sought refuge when driven by the tyrants' laws from their motherland, sought refuge and found themselves and their depen- dents a home in which they pros- pered, won renown and gave distinguished service in return.

"PROUD OF YOU"

"Finally, Mr. President, we wel- come you for yourself as a dis- tinguished scion of our race, who has won first place among his countrymen in a nation of 180 million people. We are proud of you, Mr. President. We admire you for the leadership you are giving. We trust that under God's

Mr. Kennedy

Replying, President Kennedy said: "Mr. President, there are many reasons why I was anxious to accept your generous invitation to come to this country. As you said, eight of my grandparents left these shores in the space of almost months and came to the United States.

"No country in the world, in the history of the world, has endured the haemorrhages which this island endured over a period of a few years for so many of its sons and daughters. These sons and daughters are scattered throughout the world and they gave this small island a family of million upon millions who are scattered all over the globe, who have been among the best and most loyal citizens of the countries that they have gone to, but have also kept a special place in their memory. In many cases their ances- tral memories, of this green and misty island. So in a sense, all of them who visit Ireland come home.

HIS FATHER'S FRIEND

"In addition, Mr. President, I am proud to visit here because of you, an old and valued friend of my father, who has served his country with much distinction, spending over a period of half a century, who has engaged in his own life and in the things that he stood for the very best of Western thought and, equally important, 'Western

PRESIDENT VISITS A DIVIDED BERLIN

Look over the wall a "chilling moment" in heart-warming welcome from the city

By CATHAL Og O'SHANNON

A GRIM-FACED President Kennedy looked over the Berlin Wall, physical symbol of a divided Berlin, yesterday morning at a specially built propaganda hoarding which the East Berliners had built only 20 minutes before he arrived at the Brandenburg Gate. On the other side of the wall a small stand with nine photographers and reporters looked into the west, at the two press stands with more than 300 photographers and reporters.

It was the one, chilling, silent moment of the President's visit to Berlin, which began early in the French zone and ended with his departure for Dublin at 6 o'clock.

The President looked briefly at the hoarding, which asked when he was going to implement the pro- mises of Yalta and Potsdam for ending German militarism," as had been done by the German democratic republic." Just below him, as he stood on his special viewing stand, was the Berlin wall, now nearly 18 months old and 6ft. thick at this point.

Below the wall on the east side and several hundred yards back were a couple of platoons of Vopos, the Volkspolizei who patrol the wall with automatic weapons. On the top of the Brandenburg Tor itself was a single East German soldier, carefully screened behind a perspex screen and with his field glasses trained on Mr. Kennedy, Dr. Adenauer, the West German Chancellor, and Mayor Willy Brandt.

SECURITY PLANES

Over to his left beyond the Soviet war memorial in the western zone, on the roof of the ruins of the Reichstag building, the British military outpost kept a keen eye on the eastern sector. Overhead

been shot by Vopos. At one time, some of the crowd of journalists milling around the stand was so great that some of them were shoved a few yards into East Berlin, but the guards there took very little notice.

A few hundred yards away some East Berliners waved their hand- kerchiefs at the crowd of officials and soldiers at the check point.

Kennedy's Berlin welcome has outdone anything else he has seen in Germany, both in enthusiasm and in sheer numbers. There have been two more or less official estimates of the numbers who turned out to see him, to cheer him, to wave flags and posters at him yesterday. One

(Continued in page 8)

"White Label please"

TAKE ONE TRANSISTOR
from our stock of 22 models. Listen to the pleasure it gives indoors or outdoors. See— and hear your choice at McHUGHS at the Bridge, Talbot Street.

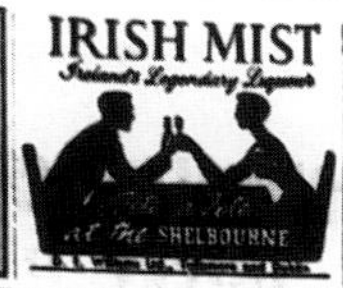
IRISH MIST
Ireland's Legendary Liqueur
at the SHELBOURNE

THE IRISH TIMES

Price 6d. No. 34,081 | DUBLIN, FRIDAY, JANUARY 8, 1965 | CITY EDITION

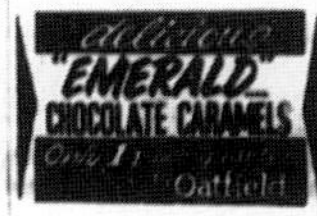
EMERALD
CHOCOLATE CARAMELS
Oatfield

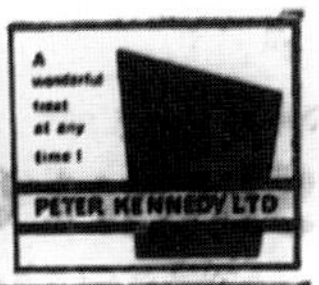
PETER KENNEDY LTD

EXPLOSION SHAKES ABBEYLEIX HOUSE

Occurred after Princess arrived

AN explosion last night shook Abbeyleix House, home of Viscount de Vesci, where Princess Margaret and her husband, Lord Snowdon, are staying. No one was injured.

After intense Garda activity it was discovered that an electricity transformer exploded on the edge of the de Vesci estate, about a mile from Abbeyleix House. The cutting down of an E.S.B. pole on the Abbeyleix-Ballacolla road is believed to have caused the transformer to explode.

Immediately after the explosion, which shook the town of Abbeyleix and shattered windows, gardai cordoned off the de Vesci estate where earlier in the day Princess Margaret and Lord Snowdon arrived from Birr. Viscountess de Vesci is Lord Snowdon's sister.

At first it was thought that a land-mine had caused the explosion. It was then found that an E.S.B. pole in the area had been cut down. For a short time the de Vesci home was without electricity. Power was restored when the house's own power plant was brought into use.

After it had been established that the explosion originated in the transformer, gardai gave chase to a group of about 16 men seen running from the scene. They drove away in three cars.

Two felled trees were also found, one close to the E.S.B. pole and a second at Granston Manor, 16 miles from the estate.

An *Irish Times* reporter, John Horgan, telephoning from Abbeyleix, said late last night that three telegraph poles and three trees had been cut down in the vicinity of the estate.

Police in Abbeyleix were last night keeping in close touch with Garda headquarters in Dublin.

Shortly after midnight a maid at Abbeyleix House said all was quiet. Princess Margaret had apparently taken the explosion calmly. The guests had gone to bed and intended to sleep late this morning.

The explosion occurred shortly before 11 p.m. Soon afterwards, Garda road checks were set up on all roads between Dublin and Abbeyleix. Motorists were stopped and questioned.

Reports that shots had been heard on the estate were traced to back-firing by a Garda's motorcycle.

Residents of Abbeyleix, who rushed into the streets after the explosion, described it as "terrifying." Local Gardai at first refused to comment, saying that they were under instructions to make no statements.

Later Special Branch men said that the explosion was caused when a heavy length of wire was thrown over the high-voltage cable supplying power to Abbeyleix House and parts of the town. The cable short-circuited and blew up the transformer.

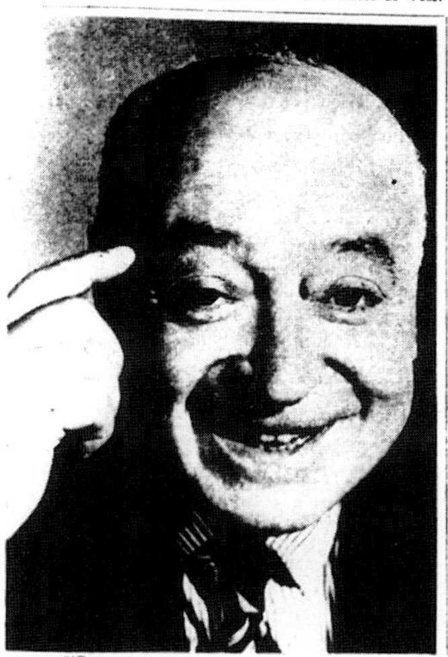

Jimmy O'Dea, acknowledged to be Ireland's greatest comedian, died yesterday in Dr. Steevens's Hospital, Dublin, after an illness of three months. During the last weeks of his illness he surprised his friends by leaving the hospital to attend a function paying tribute to Micheál MacLiammóir and also to complete a television series to which he was committed. His self-imposed duties to the theatre completed, he then returned to the hospital to die. His body will be removed from the hospital to-day at 5.30 p.m. to St. Mary's Church, Haddington road.

THE LAST OF JIMMY

By Myles na Gopaleen

HUMAN sorrow can be an untidy and compartmented thing, as was evident on the death of President Kennedy; it [illegible] varying impact on different people but is uniform in [illegible] personal sadness. That is how Jimmy O'Dea's death [illegible] received, in Ireland and far beyond it.

... by accident or design, the big moments of another player who was on the stage with him.

Outside the theatre, after a rehearsal when things had gone wrong (as they so often do), he was massively unperturbed and always friendly and polite, alike to people he knew and to strangers. And he was ever helpful and covertly generous to those whose fortunes were for the moment at an ebb.

It was a pity that he came so late in his career to TV, for the big face on the little screen showed, as had already been shown in the cinema, the extraordinary mobility, humour and comic charm of those beloved features.

In these lines there may seem to be a satiety of regret and goodwill. But they are only the truth. Farewell, Jimmy!

(A notice of Jimmy O'Dea's career and other tributes are in page 6)

ALIKE TO ALL

NEW SEARCH FOR MISSING PEER

An American air rescue specialist is to launch a new search for Lord Malcolm Douglas-Hamilton, who vanished with his son Niall during a flight over the Cameroun jungle last July.

Dan Brigham, military editor of the New York Journal-American and an air rescue expert, said yesterday that preliminary talks with Congolese airline officials and aviation experts were encouraging. New elements he had uncovered might enable him to find where the 54-year-old Scottish peer's plane went down.

Jewel theft suspect taken to Miami

Allen Kuhn, one of the three suspects in the theft on October 29th from the American Museum of Natural History of the famed Star of India and other jewels valued altogether at $410,000 (about £147,000), who was taken by F.B.I. and New York police to Miami, Florida, on Tuesday night, following a hint that he could lead to the recovery of the jewels, was still there yesterday. He was making mysterious trips around the town, accompanied by his warders and an assistant district attorney from New York.

Kuhn's journey to Miami was arranged in a consultation of the federal district attorney in New York with the Supreme Court Justice there who had committed him to jail for trial when he was unable to furnish bail of $150,000. No explanation was given for the journey unless it was in the intimation of the district attorney that a "break" in the case of the jewel theft appeared imminent.

Sixteen-year-old boy escapes to West Berlin

A 16-year-old boy yesterday fled to West Berlin under the fire of East German frontier guards. He crawled through the barbed wire barriers in the Reinickendorf suburb. None of the 20 or so shots fired hit him.

A total of 3,155 East Germans or east Berliners succeeded in escaping to the west during last year, Herr Lemmer, the Federal Minister for Refugees said in Bonn yesterday. Three quarters of them were under 25.

Speaking about the old age pensioners' visits to West Germany which Herr Ulbricht approved last September, he said that "fortunately" only 220 of the 295,000 East Germans who had come in November and December had stayed in the West. This gave ground for hope, he added, that the "humanitarian" arrangement could continue.

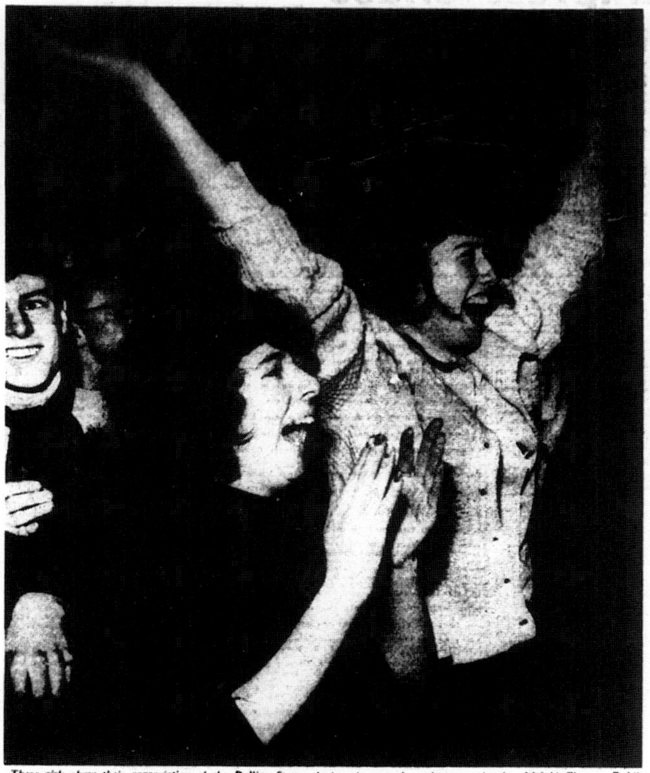

These girls show their appreciation of the Rolling Stones during the group's performance in the Adelphi Cinema, Dublin, last night.

Rolling Stones were "drowned"

Irish Times Reporter

THE Rolling Stones "beat" group, travelling much the same ground as the Beatles nearly two years ago, last night gyrated through two shows in the Adelphi cinema, Dublin, and left thousands of youngsters hoarse, exhausted, and very bruised.

For the uninitiated, the Rolling Stones are second only to the Beatles, making so much money that they have lost count of it, and they don't seem to be particularly worried about the situation.

The audiences who saw them in action last night were mainly very young teenagers; and, unlike when the Beatles were here, had only a small number of adults. But, just like the Beatles "concerts," it was impossible to hear their songs or their announcements and their 20-minute appearance in the two-hour show was principally concentrated on gymnastics and noise. They will appear in Cork to-night.

STOOD IN SEATS

The two shows in Dublin last night were booked out shortly after the booking opened, and the "Stones" arrived in Dublin from Belfast to a very quiet reception in the early afternoon. It was much the same when they gave an extremely disorganised press conference at 4.30 p.m. but full houses greeted them at their two shows.

The reception for them by the teenagers was deafening. At the end of the shows there were the inevitable attempts to rushing the stage; the aisles were jammed and those at the back had to stand on their seats to see the stage.

The only adults who paid any attention to the visit were the Garda Siochana. At one stage there were more police than public in Middle Abbey street. A police spokesman said that they were guarding against a repetition of the scenes which took place when the Beatles were in Dublin when many people were admitted to hospital.

Last night the crowds from the first show had to make their exit ...

INDONESIAN BREAK WITH U.N. BRINGS CRISIS IN S.E. ASIA

Britain determined to stand by Malaysia

PRESIDENT SUKARNO announced last night that Indonesia was no longer a member of the U.N. and that the confrontation with Malaysia would continue. His speech, at a rally in Djakarta, emphasised the growing crisis between his country and the Malaysian Federation.

He told a Djakarta rally held to condemn foreign military bases that Indonesia would continue his "Crush Malaysia" campaign. President Sukarno said his country would not have anything more to do with the United Nations' specialised agencies such as UNICEF, F.A.O. and UNESCO.

The President said that although he had received appeals from several countries to reconsider his decision to withdraw from the United Nations, he stood by it, and this meant completely pulling out. The decision would cause them some difficulties, but it was only by overcoming these difficulties that Indonesia would become a great nation.

Before Sukarno made his announcement, the rally approved a resolution supporting his decision to withdraw Indonesia from the United Nations.

Sukarno said "It was resolved that the Indonesian people have approved my order that Indonesia quit the United Nations."

Only Communist China and its satellites have supported Sukarno's stand in the U.N. withdrawal.

Sukarno also announced Indonesia will not need the help of the United Nations agencies operating in this country.

Sukarno said Indonesia will continue his "Crush Malaysia" campaign.

"I say for Malaysia (you) do not exist," he said.

Sukarno added "Let us face all difficulties. Only through overcoming our difficulties can we become a great nation . . . now march onward, ever onward, never retreat."

The Soviet Union has assured Indonesia that its withdrawal from the U.N. will not affect Soviet policy toward Indonesia. This was reported by Indonesian sources yesterday after President Sukarno in Djakarta had announced a U.N. walk-out.

The walk-out was against the advice of the Soviet Union, whose ambassador in Djakarta was reported to have urged Indonesia to reconsider.

In London, the British Prime

(Continued in page 6)

FORMER U.S. AIRMAN CHARGED WITH SPYING

From a Special Correspondent

NEW YORK, Thursday

A MAN alleged by the Federal Bureau of Investigation to have joined Soviet intelligence seven years ago while serving with the United States Air Force in Berlin was arrested this morning in New York. He is Robert N. Thompson, aged 29, who lives in a New York suburb on Long Island and runs his own fuel oil distribution business.

Mr. J. Edgar Hoover, director of the F.B.I., said that a Russian national, Fedor Kudashkian, was named in the warrant as a joint conspirator with Thompson. Kudashkian used to work for the United Nations Secretariat in New York but now lived in Russia.

Their conspiracy with other persons unnamed was "particularly concerned with furnishing information relating to military equipment and installations, missile sites, code books and intelligence and counter-intelligence activities of the United States Government."

Thompson was born in New York and served six years in the Air Force. His record included a conviction by a summary court-martial on charges of leaving his appointed place of duty, illegally obtaining a revolver, and being unfit for duty because of drink. He was discharged in December, 1958, and then lived in Detroit ...

Bank staffs to get ...

Charlestown Committee will state policy soon

By Michael Foy

THE Committee in the Defence of the West—more widely known as the Charlestown Committee—will become a corporate body on January 31st. On that date its first officers and committee will be elected at a delegate conference in Castlebar. The organisation intends also to launch its own newspaper.

It is expected that the conference will be presided over by the Bishop of Achonry, the Most Rev. Dr. Fergus. Meanwhile, this week, the Minister for Agriculture, Mr. Haughey, has been visiting the west and has called on individuals associated with the Charlestown Committee who, in the past 18 months, have been preparing to launch a programme, based on the ideas and ideals of Glencolumbkille, to save the west from depression and continued depopulation.

The Rev. James McDyer was among the first to be paid an unexpected visit by Mr. Haughey. Last night the Minister was in Westport. Mr. Haughey is due to speak in Castlebar later this month and yesterday agricultural leaders in Mayo interpreted his visit as an indication that he may make a major policy statement about his attitude to agriculture in the congested west.

By the time he speaks, Mr. Haughey will also have available the policy statement of the Committee in Defence of the West. That will be made public at a special meeting in Ballinrobe on January 19th, at which Fr. McDyer will be present.

At this stage, the emphasis is on Mayo, and it is believed that the intention is to organise that county into a bulwark on which can be built the ultimately-envisaged network that will campaign and work for the preservation of the west from Donegal to Kerry; the preservation of its traditional way of life; its pattern of small farming and its closely-knit village and parish community life — geared closely to the economy of the country and requirements of the times.

(Continued in page 4)

THE ENIGMA OF H3

Michael Viney writes in page 10 to-day about H 3, a substance first used by a Rumanian woman doctor, which it is claimed has a rejuvenating effect on old people.

In the same page Leo Bowes writes about the history of the Dublin City Hall.

In to-day's issue

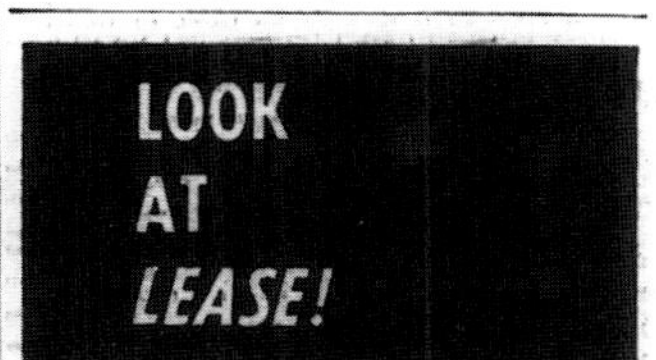
LOOK
AT
LEASE!
AUSTIN MINI

EISENHOWER GOLF TROPHY HELD

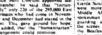

two years earlier, the Rolling Stones play two successful concerts in the Adelphi Cinema in Dublin.

23 February

The remains of Roger Casement are returned to Ireland for burial. He is given a state funeral to Glasnevin Cemetery on 1 March.

1 April

Liam Cosgrave becomes leader of Fine Gael.

16 November

William T. Cosgrave dies.

1966

10 April

President de Valera inaugurates the celebration of the fiftieth anniversary of the 1916 rising at the GPO.

17 April

A census in the Republic shows the population to be 2.88 million.

The Irish Times in June 1950 as 'the fiercest literary censorship this side of the Iron Curtain—and I do not exclude Spain,' was still as brutal as ever. Among the books banned in this period were Kingsley Amis's *Lucky Jim* and Samuel Beckett's *Watt* in 1954, Beckett's *Molloy*, Iris Murdoch's *The Flight from the Enchanter*, Tennessee Williams's *Cat on a Hot Tin Roof* and

match stopped. 'One of the few ties South Africa has with the outside world is sport and this is very important to them. When they send a team abroad, Vorster says that they are ambassadors of South Africa—and, of course, of apartheid.

'The Irish Rugby Football Union say that they do not support apartheid but yet they support the team who come as ambassadors of an apartheid regime. Sport cannot be arrested from the rest of living' …

Symbols of mid-sixties' Dublin. The new Abbey Theatre rises in the shadow of Liberty Hall.

President John F. Kennedy in O'Connell Street, Dublin. His visit in 1963, a few months before his assassination, was the apotheosis of post-Famine Irish Catholicism.

Some Landladies' Views

Mrs Jane Foley has two self-contained flats in her house in Pearse Square, off Pearse Street, Dublin. For the last twelve years they have been let, most of the time, to black students.

'I feel they are just like myself,' she says. 'I never met kinder or nicer people. I would sooner have a black student than a white one. You're sure of your rent and they always keep the room clean. If you go into a black man's room and then a white man's room you can tell the difference. Two white men once took all my blankets and my linen because I didn't get in to check the room.'

Mrs Foley first took in black students when she met a lad from Trinidad with his wife wandering around the square near Christmas time. 'They said they couldn't get lodgings because of their colour. I took them in there and then and moved two of my own children into my room to make space for them.'

Vladimir Nabokov's *Lolita* in 1956, Norman Mailer's *The Deer Park* in 1957, John Braine's *Room at the Top* and Mailer's *The Naked and the Dead* in 1958, and Joseph Heller's *Catch 22* and John Updike's *Rabbit, Run* in 1962.

In this context, the most urgent task was to create at least the basic conditions for open debate by lifting the pall of enforced intellectual conformity. By the late fifties *The Irish Times* had definitively shaken off its old reluctance to challenge the governing consensus of church and state too openly. It stepped up its hostility to the operation of the censorship laws, drawing attention to many of the more extraordinary decisions. In 1955, when Marcel Proust's *Jean Santeuil* was banned, the writer Monk Gibbon

2 June

Éamon de Valera becomes President of Ireland for a second term, at the age of eighty-three.

11 June

A Catholic man, John Scullion, dies fifteen days after being stabbed by loyalists on the Falls Road in Belfast.

President Kennedy at his ancestors' home at Dunganstown, near New Ross, Co. Wexford

8 November

Seán Lemass
announces that
he is to resign as
Taoiseach.

9 November

Jack Lynch is
elected leader of
Fianna Fáil
and the next
day is elected
Taoiseach by
the Dáil.

asked in *The Irish Times,* 'Is it just prurience or stupidity or a kind of unconscious malice?'

In December 1957 the paper published a strong editorial on the subject, prompted by an attack by the former chairman of the Censorship Board, Professor J. J. Piggott, on two current members whom he felt were not diligent enough in rooting out filth. The editorial condemned Piggott and 'the foolish and humiliating Act which is probably without parallel in any democratic country.' It pointed out that since 1946, when the definition of obscenity had been broadened, 'any crank could make a case against a book.' This editorial led to a long

There were objections from the neighbours. 'When I took them in first one of the clergy, I won't say who, came to me and said I would lower the valuation of my house and the houses around me. But I didn't' …

Mrs K—('I'm afraid of being knifed' was the reason she gave for not permitting us to print her name)—has a guest house on the north side of Dublin where she offers accommodation to students—white ones only.

'I had a black student once. He was a friend of someone who was staying with me. He came assuming he was some kind of prince. He went to the extent of opening my telephone coin box. There were women and contraceptives hanging around all over the place. He bought a big record player and only paid the first few instalments on it. I had to advise the shop to take it back. He was living on his wits. Then it turned out he had a wife at home. He was living as if he had a crown on him with all his airs and graces. He never paid his rent. When he returned from his vacation once I only let him back in to collect his things. I don't know what happened to him or if he ever finished. He was a real mystery man.

'I wouldn't let a black inside the door now. I had two fellows from Trinidad before him who were okay until they lost their tempers. A lot of my guests walked out one night when I let them give a party ...

We had a list of eight Dublin landladies who had made it known to the deans of residence of the college concerned that they would take white students only. Of the five that we were able to contact only Mrs K said she would not take black students. The others said they had no objection at all to blacks; that they had them before; that they were very nice and were no trouble at all; they didn't have any at the moment, they 'never seemed to get them nowadays' but if one arrived of course they would take them ...

from The Irish Times **1970**
8 MAY

'In the Dáil'
by John Healy

Survival is the name of the game

The Fianna Fáil Government still stands. As dawn broke over Leinster House this morning the Cabinet of Mr Jack Lynch, reshuffled but with his new Ministers not yet ratified, looked as if it had weathered the worst assault mounted on it in this week of crisis. The debate had not yet finished as we went to press.

That the Government stands this morning is a performance which seems amazing. In the twenty-one-hour long debate shock waves may have swept through the Government Party: at times it seemed inevitable the structure must crumble.

There was the panzer attack by the combined Opposition, there was the astonishing single-handed explosion from within the citadel itself when Kevin Boland launched his speech of explanation: there was a personal statement from the former Minister for Defence denying complicity in any alleged gun-running activities: the counter-statement from a former Army officer from outside Dáil

correspondence in which Owen Sheehy-Skeffington attacked the Censorship Board and Piggott defended himself, insisting that 'pure pornography' included 'books that openly deride chastity and advocate sexual licence as trial marriages and the like ... None but a moral moron would refuse to ban them.' He decried 'Freudian-inspired fiction' and insisted that literary merit had nothing to do with the board's work. 'Hence, books written by whomsoever, must be judged by purely moral standards, unless people are prepared to regard literary merit as of greater importance than moral rectitude.'

Perhaps more serious than the formal censorship of books and films, however, was the informal censorship that operated in the theatre

1967

1 February
The Northern Ireland Civil Rights Association is established to fight against discrimination and repression.

11 April
Charles Haughey's budget grants extra

For fifteen years, following the fire of 1951, the Abbey Theatre had been 'in exile' at the Queen's Theatre in Pearse Street. Here the producer Tomás Mac Anna and members of the company stand at the back of the Queen's on the last day before their return to the rebuilt Abbey.

*money in pensions
and children's
allowances, as
well as allowing
medical expenses
to be written off
against tax.*

11 May
*Ireland and the
United Kingdom
apply for
membership of the
EEC, and for the
second time de
Gaulle blocks
Britain's entry, as a
result of which
Ireland's application
is deferred.*

1 June
*Farmers' represen-
tatives and the
Government meet
and agree to the
release of imprisoned
farmers and the
dropping of fines
against them.*

1968

29 July
*Pope Paul VI issues
an encyclical,
Humanae Vitae,
condemning
'artificial' birth
control.*

5 October
*A rally in Derry
organised by the*

and on radio. The Abbey Theatre, under the former Minister for Finance Ernest Blythe, and Radio Éireann offered the two state-subsidised outlets for the work of Irish dramatists. Yet the list of plays rejected by one or other of them in this period reads like an order of merit: Séamus Byrne's *Little City,* dealing with abortion, rejected by the Abbey in 1952; his *Design for a Headstone,* a searching examination of republicanism, banned from Radio Éireann even while it was in rehearsal; Brendan Behan's *The Quare Fellow,* dealing with capital punishment, rejected by the Abbey in 1954; John B. Keane's *Sive,* dealing with forced marriage in rural Ireland, rejected by both the Abbey and Radio Éireann in 1959; the same author's *Sharon's Grave,* rejected by the Abbey in the same year; Tom Murphy's *A Whistle in the Dark,* showing the violent lives of Mayo emigrants in England, rejected by the Abbey because, as Blythe wrote to the author, no such people as those depicted in the play existed in Ireland.

Jacqueline Kennedy, widow of the assassinated president, and Frank Aiken at the Metropolitan Opera House in New York

At about the same time, these workmen were putting the finishing touches to the foyer of the new Abbey, under the gaze of W. B. Yeats

Éireann so that at ten o'clock last night it was inevitable the House was engulfed in the rumour that the Taoiseach had gone to the Park to dissolve his Cabinet.

The Taoiseach was missing; later this morning it was thought he had gone to see Mr Haughey. At any rate, he was back before midnight and had heard the Kelly statement *apropos* the Minister for Defence read into the record of the House by Mr John Bruton, one of the young Fine Gael members.

Mr Bruton launched his attack just after midnight: a big task for such a junior deputy. And when he came to the pay-off line which was to spear the Taoiseach he fluffed it by losing his place in his notes and very humanly said he'd read that again.

Mr Lynch kept on pulling his thoughts together as if the Bruton speech was just another of the long contributions which the House would hear—but his backbenchers asked Mr Bruton who wrote the speech for him, while others said: 'Give the lad a chance.'

By one o'clock in the morning the rumours of a dissolution had receded, but the assault of words went on: now it was a question of stamina, and Fianna Fáil was sitting it out in the main. It had seventy-four seats, and the deputies hoped Jack Lynch had the answers. It would, they said, be nine o'clock this morning before we would begin to hear those answers.

As I write, it is almost twenty-two hours since the Dáil met to hear the Taoiseach announce his new Ministers. In fact, he shuffled the deck so well only three Ministers held their old portfolios. A new and terribly young Cabinet—a Cabinet of political boys—really should have been the main news of the day: yet last night in Leinster House we had to consult our notes to find out who held what portfolio and just who were the new men: facts which should have branded themselves on our minds had been dislodged in a day of bitter drama.

And who could blame a bunch of deputies for not remembering who had got Defence or Local Government when, within the hour of their nomination by a haggard Jack Lynch, Kevin Boland, his colleague and fellow-Cabinet Minister of the best part of their lifetime in the Dáil, got up and delivered himself of a speech which rocked Fianna Fáil to its foundations and planted a hatchet in the back of his leader, Jack Lynch. It was done openly, fairly and squarely: he came in to defend his resignation from the Cabinet and he let fly and did not worry.

P. J. Hillery had been in for the announcement of the new Cabinet: he left as Mr Boland spoke.

When Mr Boland finished about forty backbenchers clapped him. The Front Bench kept solidly quiet.

It left the party numb and sick and Tom O'Higgins of Fine Gael who followed Mr Boland had a wealth of material with which to belabour the reeling Government party. He used it. So did many of the speakers during the day. The Front Bench personnel changed and the atmosphere bristled: Neil Blaney was going to speak.

To say the Fianna Fáil deputies—the new still-to-be ratified Ministers included—looked grim is an understatement. Mr Colley, Mr Gibbons and Mr Lynch kept their heads buried in their hands or otherwise masked for most of the Boland and Blaney speeches. The smiles of satisfaction which should be on the faces of the promoted did not appear: after the Boland speech there was some doubt among some of the party members if the Cabinet would survive. Opposition deputies, who would go on calling for Mr Lynch's resignation, by lunchtime began to wonder (and indeed fear) that they might well get their request.

The tension built up, rather than diminishing, during the afternoon, and Neil Blaney was busy on his speech. If Blaney,

Three brothers, Pte Willie Boland, Cpl Pascal Boland and Cpl Peter Boland, who served with the Irish UN peace-keeping mission in Cyprus

Another point of conflict came in 1958 with the proposal of An Tóstal to stage two plays, one an adaptation from James Joyce's *Ulysses* and the other the world premiere of Seán O'Casey's *The Drums of Father Ned*. Archbishop John Charles McQuaid of Dublin made it clear that he did not approve of these works; he refused an invitation to open the festival with a votive Mass. The Tóstal committee then asked O'Casey to make changes to his play and asked the director of the theatre festival to withdraw the Joyce piece. *The Irish Times*, which carried two long articles on the controversy by O'Casey, was outraged and suggested sarcastically that in future the festival programme should be submitted to the archbishop in advance for his approval. This drew the fire of the Catholic apologist Alfred O'Rahilly, who described the paper as representing the 'outlook of our Protestant, and also perhaps our agnostic-liberal, fellow-citizens' and diagnosed it as suffering from 'chronic

Northern Ireland Civil Rights Association is banned by the Minister of Home Affairs, William Craig. The RUC baton the marchers off the street.

9 October

Students demonstrate in Belfast for civil rights and form what becomes known as People's Democracy. The Derry Citizens' Action Committee is formed the same day.

22 November

Terence O'Neill announces reforms in local elections, housing, and the Special Powers Act.

11 December

The hard-line William Craig is dismissed as Minister of Home Affairs in Northern Ireland.

1969

1 January

Students and members of People's Democracy begin a civil rights march from Belfast to Derry.

4 January

The civil rights march comes to an end as loyalists violently attack the marchers at Burntollet Bridge, Co. Derry, as the RUC look on.

24 February

An election for the Stormont Parliament results in an overall majority for the Unionists, with pro-O'Neill forces taking twice as many seats as their Unionist opponents.

The onset of the northern Troubles shook the southern establishment. The Arms Trial of 1970 saw Government ministers and others charged with an attempt to import arms for the IRA. All of them, including Charles Haughey—shown here on his way into court—were acquitted.

The Adelphi cinema, Dublin, 1965: fans at the first Rolling Stones concert in Ireland

17 April
*Bernadette Devlin,
aged twenty-two, is
elected as a Unity
candidate in the
Mid-Ulster by-
election for the
British House of
Commons.*

19 April
*Civil rights
supporters are
attacked by loyalists
in Derry. RUC
men and loyalists
swamp the
nationalist Bogside
area of the city and
run riot.*

22 April
*Bernadette Devlin
makes her first
speech in the
British House of
Commons.*

28 April
*Terence O'Neill
resigns as Prime
Minister of
Northern Ireland.*

18 June
*The general
election returns an
overall majority for
Fianna Fáil.*

21 July
*Neil Armstrong
becomes the
first person on
the moon.*

they said, followed Boland and took the Boland line, well then it would be almost impossible to see the Cabinet survive.

My own bet was that Neil Blaney wouldn't.

Mr Blaney's speech was extremely cleverly worded: he has shown himself capable, even in a crisis situation, of tooling words and phrases which are capable of a number of interpretations: it is possible, for instance, to construe the attack on Fine Gael and its peace policy on the North as an indirect attack on Mr Lynch. It was an emotional speech designed to be heard and read by the grassroots: it would have been a great speech at the Árd Fheis or in his father's day thirty or forty years ago. He backed Jack Lynch and his Party and sat down to more applause than Kevin Boland: only one of the Ministers-to-be bothered to clap: the rest, relieved, relaxed and that included Jack Lynch and George

episcopophagy. It has an obsessional disease of bishop-bashing.'

Yet there was, beneath the surface of social control, a palpable desire for escape. In the Limerick Rural Survey of 1962, the most detailed and insightful description of life in the countryside before the radical changes of the sixties took hold, Patrick McNabb noted that even those young people who stayed at home often preferred to seek their entertainment in anonymous surroundings rather than under the eye of the local community. 'Most young people preferred to dance outside their own immediate neighbourhood. Whenever possible they did not support the local halls. Boys in particular, who

11 August

The 'Battle of the Bogside' begins as loyalists, RUC men and B Specials storm into the nationalist area of Derry. Jack Lynch says that the Republic 'will not stand idly by.'

14 August

Six people have died in riots and shooting throughout Northern Ireland by this date. British soldiers enter Derry, and riots break out in Belfast. The next day houses are burned in Belfast.

15 August

British soldiers are deployed in Belfast.

22 August

The B Specials are ordered to hand in their arms.

11 September

The Cameron Commission's report blames much of the violence on the Stormont government and the RUC.

10 October

The Hunt Report recommends the replacement of the

have a car at their disposal, think nothing of travelling long distances to dances, and of visiting three or four different halls in one night … [They] gave the explanation that "you could let your hair down" in outside halls. Since for the most part those people are well behaved at dances, "letting down one's hair" does not mean rowdiness but simply escaping the observation of the home community … Dancing is as anonymous in rural areas as it is in cities. Conversation is pared down to laconic statements about the floor, the band or the weather.'

Behind the vague discontent of the young was an awareness that Ireland was being left behind. Throughout the world, the fifties were the start of an unprecedented economic boom. The United States emerged from the Second World War with its economic dominance enhanced: by 1950 it had 60 per cent of all capital stock held in all advanced capitalist countries and the same proportion of their total output. But the

The remains of Roger Casement were returned to Ireland from London in 1965. Here the cortege passes up O'Connell Street.

Father and son. W. T. Cosgrave and Liam Cosgrave at the races. The elder Cosgrave died in 1965, the year his son succeeded him as leader of Fine Gael.

John Charles McQuaid, archbishop of Dublin from 1941 to 1972, photographed in the last year of his episcopate. A champion of rigorist orthodoxy and conservatism, he was one of the most influential figures in mid-century Ireland.

Colley and Jim Gibbons. P. J. Hillery seemed mildly interested through most of it.

Jim Gibbons made a statement in the afternoon. It was a careful one: he denied involvement as had been charged. He dealt with the man known as Captain Kelly. He gave the House his rating of Captain Kelly. Mr Lynch was beside him. It had its own drama: Mr Gibbons was not comfortable.

There were many good responsible speeches: there were some which did nothing for the institution of Parliament. It was a day in which a man, if he spoke at all, could hardly fail to make a good speech. Jimmy Tully asked a lot of pointed questions: David Thornley showed a sense of awareness of the damage to Parliament. Tom O'Higgins and Paddy Donegan hammered home the enormity of the situation and Paddy Harte, normally a terrier, made a good impromptu and concerned speech.

It is hard perhaps to say it, but as the night wore on and stories came in that Captain Kelly had repudiated the Dáil statement of Mr Gibbons, words began to lose their meaning and the House couldn't be bothered to speculate on who would get promotion to Junior Ministries: there was only one thought, one concern: what new sensations are still to come? But with Fianna Fáil, battered and limp: the name of the new game was: survive.

sense of prosperity was shared by much of Europe. The Soviet Union in the fifties was growing faster than any western economy. Germany and Japan were recovering from their devastating defeat in 1945 with remarkable

Samuel Beckett, winner of the Nobel Prize for Literature in 1969

Ulster Special Constabulary.

23 October
Samuel Beckett is awarded the Nobel Prize for Literature. He refuses to go to Stockholm to receive it.

22 December
Bernadette Devlin is sentenced to six months' imprisonment for her activities during the Battle of the Bogside.

1970

11 January
Sinn Féin splits during its ardfheis in Dublin. 'Official Sinn Féin' (left-wing) and 'Provisional Sinn Féin' (traditional republican) are the result.

16 April
Ian Paisley wins a by-election to the Stormont parliament for the Bannside constituency; his colleague William Beattie wins another in South Antrim.

Walking Derry's walls in 1967 is a group of local politicians and a British Labour Party delegation examining the flagrant discrimination in the city. The four in front are John Hume, Gerry Fitt, Stanley Orme MP (later a junior minister in Northern Ireland under direct rule) and Eddie McAteer, leader of the Nationalist Party.

30 April

The B Specials are disbanded and replaced by the Ulster Defence Regiment.

5 May

Charles Haughey, Minister for Finance, and Neil Blaney, Minister for Agriculture, are sacked by the Taoiseach, Jack Lynch. Kevin Boland, Minister for

rapidity. In Europe, countries that had been as underdeveloped as Ireland—Spain and Finland, for example—were undergoing dramatic industrial revolutions. Agrarian societies such as those of Bulgaria and Romania were developing huge industrial sectors. As yet, the costs of this rapid growth in the form of pollution and environmental degradation were not being counted. The benefits—televisions, fridges, Coca-Cola, cars, and a flood of consumer goods—were immediate objects of desire.

In Ireland a new interest in economics was reflected in 1954 in the decision of the features editor of *The Irish Times*, Jack White, to commission a series of articles on the subject of the national finances from a young Aer Lingus employee, Garret FitzGerald, who wrote under

The last—and vital—word was with the Taoiseach: he had yet to speak and the night was long.

from The Irish Times
9 MAY 1970

Denial by Haughey

A statement was issued yesterday on behalf of the former Minister for Finance, Mr Haughey. It was addressed from Mr Haughey's home at Abbeville, Kinsealy, Malahide, Co. Dublin.

The text of the statement is:

'I regret that, on medical advice, I cannot make a personal statement in Dáil Éireann concerning the termination of my office as a member of the Government.

'Since becoming a Minister, I have endeavoured to the best of my ability to serve my country, Dáil Éireann and the

Government. I have never at any time acted in breach of the trust reposed in me, and I regret that I am now compelled to refer to the circumstances which brought to an end my membership of the Government.

'The Taoiseach informed the Dáil that he requested my resignation on the grounds that he was convinced that not even the slightest suspicion should attach to any member of the Government. I fully subscribe to that view. So far as I have been able to gather, the Taoiseach received information of a nature which in his opinion cast some suspicion on me. I have not had the opportunity to examine or test such information or the quality of its source or sources. In the meantime, however, I now categorically state that at no time have I taken part in any illegal importation or attempted importation of arms into this country.

'At present I do not propose to say anything further, except that I have fully accepted the Taoiseach's decision, as I believe that the unity of the Fianna Fáil Party is of greater importance to the welfare of the nation than my political career.'

from The Irish Times **1972**
2 FEBRUARY

Many march from factories and colleges to embassy

Thousands of workers and students again protested at the British Embassy in Dublin yesterday in a day of almost continuous marches to the building to demonstrate against the killings in Derry on Sunday.

Letters of protest were handed into the embassy by groups ranging from 1,000 workers from the Tallaght industrial estate to a group of schoolgirls. Throughout the day up to 500 people were gathered at the building and their numbers were swelled with the arrival of each contingent of marchers. The building was stoned intermittently and at one stage two petrol bombs were thrown and exploded in the doorway.

Fifty gardaí guarded the steps and entrance and one was injured, though not seriously, when he was struck by a bottle. A Garda spokesman said yesterday that twenty-five gardaí had been injured on Monday night: most of them received stitches for cuts in hospital.

In one of the biggest marches to the embassy the 1,000 workers from the Tallaght industrial estate carried two black

Terence O'Neill, prime minister of Northern Ireland, and Jack Lynch, who succeeded Lemass as Taoiseach in November 1966, meet at Stormont

the pseudonym 'Analyst'. FitzGerald continued to write on economic subjects for the paper for the next twenty years, until he became Minister for Foreign Affairs, and he returned to the paper as a columnist after he retired from active politics. In the late fifties the views he expressed in *The Irish Times* chimed well with those of the Secretary of the Department of Finance, T. K. Whitaker, who in 1958 presented the Government with a report called *Economic Development*. Its argument for a drastic change of policy was based on the conclusion that, in a country with a dwindling population of people with low purchasing power, protectionism could not possibly lead to increased employment. The new Taoiseach, Seán Lemass, accepted this argument, which largely, in any case, mirrored his own views.

Whitaker's programme was by no means left-wing. Indeed his report explicitly stated that it was 'quite unreal to approach the question of development from the aspect of employment.' In the same vein as Garret FitzGerald's analyses in *The Irish Times*, he argued that the 'modernisation' of Irish industry and agriculture should be based on 'active competitive participation in a free-trading world.' This meant not only an end to protection and the opening up of the economy to foreign investment but also a cutting back of

Local Government, resigns in sympathy. Lynch survives a vote of no confidence.

27 May
Captain James Kelly, a former army officer, John Kelly of Belfast and Albert Luykx, a Belgian-born businessman, are arrested and charged with attempting to smuggle arms into the Republic.

28 May
Charles Haughey and Neil Blaney are arrested and charged with attempting to smuggle guns into the Republic.

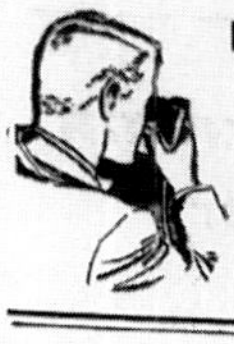
KONICA CAMERAS
Fully guaranteed — and the price is only from £30-5-0. Also full range of other models.
DIXON HEMPENSTALL Open Saturdays until 1 p.m.
Temporary address: 14 Suffolk Street, Dublin 2.

THE IRISH TIMES
DUBLIN, SATURDAY, OCTOBER 24, 1970
PRICE 1s. (5 New Pence) No. 35,692 CITY EDITION

Champagne POMMERY
Pommery & Greno
Prestige de la France

REMY MARTIN

HAUGHEY CHALLENGES TAOISEACH

Demands for resignation follow acquittals in arms conspiracy trial

LYNCH REMAINS CONFIDENT

By Andrew Hamilton

AFTER THE DRAMATIC "not guilty" verdict of the jury in the arms conspiracy trial in Dublin yesterday, Mr. Charles J. Haughey, T.D., the former Minister for Finance, called on the Taoiseach Mr. Lynch, to resign. Mr. Haughey told a news conference: "I think those who are responsible for this debacle have no alternative but to take the honourable course that is open to them."

Mr. Haughey had been questioned about the effects of the trial on relations with Northern Ireland and he replied that there had been "harmful repercussions" as well as damage at home and abroad.

Acquitted with Mr. Haughey were Captain James Kelly, the former Irish Army intelligence officer; Albert Luykx, a Belgian-born businessman, and John Kelly, a Belfast Republican.

The Taoiseach, hearing of the trial verdict in New York, said that if the leadership issue was raised within the Fianna Fail Party, he could look forward to the outcome with confidence. Mr. Lynch is expected back in Dublin tomorrow morning.

The text of Mr. Lynch's statement is: "At the last Ard Fheis I reaffirmed the Fianna Fail policy on partition as enunciated by my two predecessors, Mr. de Valera and Mr. Lemass and endorsed by successive Ard Fheiseanna since. My reaffirmation was approved with acclamation at the Ard Fheis in January of this year.

"I have restated it several times since and again at the United Nations yesterday.

"I believe it to be the only realistic policy for the reunification of our country.

"In taking the decisions I took last May in relation to the attempted importation of arms I felt it was there my duty lay as Head of the Government. I am convinced now as I was then that I made the right decisions.

"As for the leadership of the Fianna Fail Party this can be determined only by a Fianna Fail Ard-Fheis and the Parliamentary Party. If the issue is raised I look forward to the outcome with confidence.

"The Government's proposals to deal with our present economic difficulties were approved unanimously in the Cabinet. Their implementation is essential if we are to overcome the cancer of inflation and maintain the pace of economic progress that we have enjoyed over the past 12 years."

JUBILATION

The trial was one of the most spectacular in the history of the State. The jury's verdict, announced at 5.41 p.m. yesterday just 48 minutes after it had finally retired, was greeted with wild scences of enthusiasm. Amid all the cheering and singing, there were shouts of "Lynch must go" and "We are the real Republicans."

Mr. Haughey's call for the resignation of Mr. Lynch was his first public comment on the leadership question since his dismissal by the Taoiseach six months ago. Last night Mr. Neil Blaney, T.D., and Mr. Kevin Boland, T.D., repeated their demands for a new leader.

The verdict last night brought renewed speculation about the position of Mr. Jim Gibbons, the Minister for Agriculture, within the Government. Mr. Haughey would not comment on Mr. Gibbons's continuance in the Cabinet but Mr. Blaney commented: "I can't see him continuing of his own volition."

The Minister for Agriculture, Mr. Gibbons was said not to be at his home at Dunmore, Ballyfoyle, Kilkenny, early this morning. When telephoned by *The Irish Times* a member of his family said: "He is not available." Asked when the Minister would be home, she said: "I don't know."

Mr. Haughey, speaking to the press after his acquittal, sidestepped questions about his political future. He admitted that the political implications of the trial would be far-reaching. He ruel out the need for a general election. The strongest hint he gave of his interest in the leadership was when ne talked about his candidature in the past and then added: "I am not ruling out anything."

Mr. Haughey also attacked the Taoiseach for his United Nations speech on Northern Ireland on Thursday. It did not, he said, represent Fianna Fail policy. About arms importations he said the whole point of the verdict had been that they had not conspired to bring in arms illegally.

Later Mr. Blaney said: "Mr. Lynch must take the honourable course as indicated by Mr. Haughey. If he did it, it would be good for the unity of the country and the unity of the party."

Mr. Boland commented: "He must see that it is just impossible to stay on."

Mr. Blaney also described the trial as "an international joke, and

"Lynch must go" yells the crowd

JUBILATION AT VERDICT

IN THE main hall outside the courtroom, after the verdict was announced, the large crowd cheered and shouted "We want Charlie" and "Lynch must go."

Captain James Kelly was the first of the four to appear from the court and he was hustled, and congratulated and nearly trampled underfoot by the enthusiastic crowd.

John Kelly appeared next and he was lifted shoulder high and was carried to the main entrance. On the way to the door he waved his arms and shouted, but his words were drowned out by the loud cheering.

Mr. Haughey also received a tumultuous welcome. After leaving the courtroom, accompanied by his counsel, he forced his way through the crowd and stood on the steps in the foyer. Protected by about six Gardai, he addressed the crowd and said: "I am grateful to you all, everyone of you, particularly my own constituents, for the loyalty you have shown me during this difficult time. I will take another occasion to thank you all."

Mr. Haughey was then whisked away by his counsel and the gardai and got out of the Four Courts building by a side door.

Mr. Luykx also had difficulty in getting past the crowd. He waved to the people outside the court and posed for press and television photographers and then went into the Four Courts Hotel.

Rush-hour traffic along the quays outside the court wa held up for a short time because of the overspill of the crowd onto the road.

Inside the Four Courts Hotel, supporters of Mr. Haughey and the other three accused sang "A Nation Once Again" and there were shouts of "We are Republican Fianna Fail" and "Lynch Must Go". One voice shouted "We are only starting."

Senator Bernard McGlinchey, of Donegal, a close friend of Mr. Blaney, when asked if there would be any special celebrations in Donegal, said he did not know but he did not think so. He said there was going to be a Fianna Fail North-East constituency dance in Malahide that night. "Charlie will be going," he added.

Mr. Luykx, when asked by an *Irish Times* reporter to comment on his acquittal, said: "*The Irish Times* has given the best report of the trial. They reported every single word that was spoken and were very fair."

What about his future plans? Mr. Luykx said he would go on living as he always had, rising at 6.45 a.m. and carrying on his job. He considered the trial an "unnecessary interruption of my work." He had been confident that the verdict would be "not guilty."

Asked to comment on the trial, Mr. Luykx said he would have to be very careful about what he said, as he had an appeal against the decision of the judge in the abortive trial who had ruled that he would have to pay the expenses of all parties in that case. He did not know when the appeal would be heard.

In reply to further questions, he said: "I am not a member of any political party and I do not intend joining any . . . yet," he laughed.

You've got grounds for using us.
Grounds for sport and recreation.
Grounds for landscaping.
Grounds for maintenance.
Grounds for Instant Trees.
Grounds for growing. All grounds for Gouldings' professional services.
Fitzwilton House, Dublin 2. Telephone 65891.
Goulding

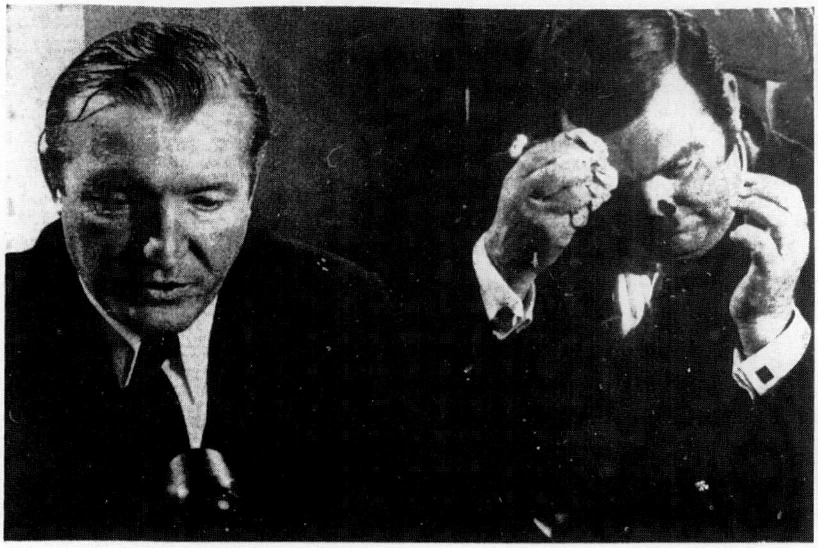

Mr. Charles J. Haughey, T.D., with his solicitor, Mr. Patrick O'Connor, speaking to the press after his acquittal in the arms conspiracy trial yesterday evening. "I was never in any doubt that it was a political trial," he told his questioners.

HAUGHEY TALKS OF POLITICAL FUTURE

"Some dissatisfaction with the Taoiseach"

IN A PRESS conference after the verdict was announced, Mr. Haughey said: "I feel much better than I have felt for some time. I never had any doubt about the outcome. It is a great relief that it is given effect to."

What about the future? — "I intend to continue in my political activities as I have always done."

Would ne care to comment on the leadership of Fianna Fail?— "I would not like to speculate on the leadership, that is a matter for the Fianna Fail Party."

Mr. Haughey, when asked if he would attend the special meeting of the Fianna Fail Party on Wednesday, said that he would certainly attend at the Parliamentary meeting. "There is a meeting fixed for Wednesday. I received notice of it and I will certainly be going. The Dail reopens on Wednesday and this is the usual meeting that takes place."

Asked if he felt there would be political implications arising out of the trial, Mr. Haughey said: "The political implications will be far reaching." He did not want to speculate too much about this, but "I will be dealing with it later."

Mr. Haughey was asked if he felt his reputation had been enhanced as a result of the verdict. He replied that it was not possible to get a better verdict than from 12 good Dublin men.

Mr. Haughey refused to comment on the position of Mr. Lynch as leader of the party, and said that this was a matter that would have to be discussed by the Parliamentary Party. "There is some dissatisfaction with the Taoiseach at the moment (laughter). I will have to confine myself to that remark."

Mr. Haughey said that he did not see any need for an early general election.

Answering questions regarding the prices and incomes freeze recently announced by Mr. Colley, his successor as Minister for Finance, Mr. Haughey said: "The first thing I want to say is that they have not been approved of by the Fianna Fail Parliamentary Party."

Could he describe how the case had come out into the open, what was his version? Mr. Haughey said that the Taoiseach had given his reasons for going into the open and handing the papers to the Attorney-General, but this was not justified. In reply to further questions, Mr. Haughey said that he had been mentioned in the past as a candidate for Taoiseach and "I am not ruling out anything."

What would the country think about him being acquitted? "They cannot come to any other decision except that I have been vindicated."

'A political trial'

Had he considered that it was a political trial?—"I was never in any doubt that it was a political trial."

Asked if he could elaborate on the Government's policy towards the North, Mr. Haughey said that he did not think the Taoiseach had represented Fianna Fail policy as he had explained it at the United Nations. He said that there was a fundamental difference in policy in what he, Mr. Haughey, understood the policy to have been and to be, and it would take a great deal of time to elaborate.

As far as he could assess it, the trial had had serious and harmful repercussions with our relations with the North. It had done a great deal of damage to the country, both at home and abroad. "I think those that were responsible for this debacle have no alternative but to take the honourable course that is open to them," he said.

What was that?—"I think it is pretty evident."

Asked if he would vote with the Government in a Dail divi-

(Continued in page 16)

What Boland expects Lynch to do

THE FORMER Minister for Local Government, Mr. Kevin Boland, who resigned in sympathy when Mr. Haughey and Mr. Blaney were dismissed, said after the trial: "I think the implications for the Taoiseach are clear and I think he will see them.

"The verdict was not just not guilty for these men, but one of guilty against one of his Ministers whom he has officially endorsed in the Dail. He is on the record in the Dail as endorsing this Minister who had now been repudiated by the Courts of Justice. I think the implications will be obvious for the Taoiseach.

"There is no need for me or anybody else to elucidate what he should do in these circumstances. I have that much confidence in him as a man."

He added that he did not think it would be practical to arrange a special Ard Fheis of Fianna Fail following the outcome of the trial.

The former Minister for Agriculture, Mr. Neil Blaney, who was dismissed from the Government with Mr. Haughey and against whom informations were refused in the Dublin District Court, was brief in his remarks after yesterday's verdict. "A stupid trial is over successfully," he said.

Of the political implications of yesterday's verdict, he remarked: "You can wait for those. They will come." Would they come shortly? "Obviously." What would the Government now do? "What the Government decides I haven't a clue."

'Just verdict'

Captain James Kelly, the former Army intelligence officer who was acquitted, said that his first reaction was one of happiness that "we got a verdict that was just." He had not thought of his own future yet but obviously would have to do so. "I have had no job since April 30th," he commented. "I was doing my job as an Army officer and I looked upon the trial in that light.

(Continued in page 16)

LEADERSHIP CRISIS IS NOW IN OPEN

Vital meetings next week

By Our Political Correspondent, Michael McInerney

THE FATE of the Government might be decided by meetings planned for next week following the "not guilty" verdict at the trial at the Four Courts for the past fortnight. The Taoiseach, Mr. Lynch, himself will be on trial both in the Dail and at a three-day Fianna Fail Party meeting.

Calls for the Taoiseach's resignation already have been raised by Mr. Charles Haughey, former Minister for Finance, Mr. Cosgrave, Leader of Fine Gael, and Mr. Corish, Leader of the Labour Party. The Taoiseach himself, in New York last night, however, declared that his policy on the North would continue, that he was convinced the decisions—to call for the resignations of his Ministers—last May were the right decisions and that it was his duty to take them, and that he would fight to retain the leadership of the Fianna Fail Pary "with confidence."

The issue is now set for next week's battles. Mr. Haughey already has denounced the Taoiseach's speech at the U.N. about the North and also the Government's inflation policy. It is clear that Mr. Haughey will fight next Wednesday at the Party meeting on these issues and also on the leadership question. But the battle in the Fianna Fail rooms will be transferred to the Dail, where Mr. Lynch will also be under siege from the Opposition parties.

One of the first shots to be fired by the Opposition will be that the Taoiseach had stated in the Dail

(Continued in page 16)

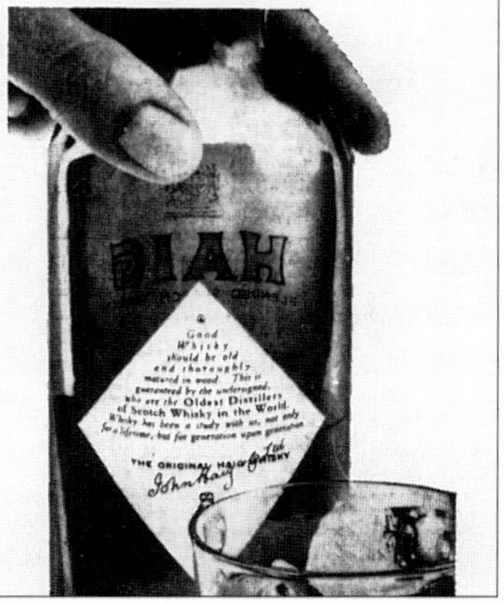

DISPUTE ERUPTS BETWEEN I.B.O.A. AND TAX AUTHORITY

BANK OFFICIALS who returned to work on Wednesday are threatening to place a ban on overtime because of a dispute with the Revenue Commissioners over tax deduction

Increase in

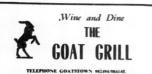

Wine and Dine
THE GOAT GRILL
TELEPHONE GOATSTOWN 982494/984145.

THE IRISH TIMES

PRICE 6p DUBLIN, MONDAY, JANUARY 31, 1972 No. 36,080 CITY

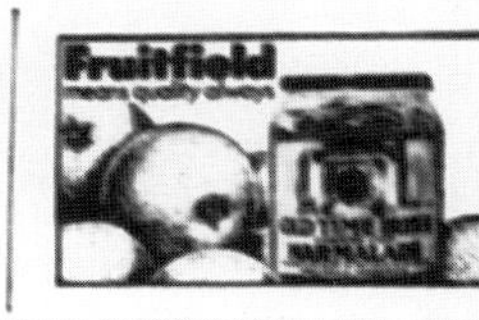

SOLDIERS KILL 13 IN BOGSIDE

Taoiseach to hold Cabinet meeting this morning

KILLINGS WIDELY CONDEMNED

THIRTEEN PEOPLE WERE SHOT DEAD IN DERRY YESTERDAY AFTER A CONFRONTATION BETWEEN A BANNED CIVIL RIGHTS MARCH AND BRITISH PARATROOPERS. THOSE KILLED WERE 12 MEN AND A YOUTH. AT LEAST SIXTEEN OTHERS WERE INJURED BY GUNFIRE AND THE BRITISH ARMY MADE OVER 50 ARRESTS.

The trouble started as the marchers, more than 10,000 strong, came up against a British Army barricade in William street. The march turned down Rossville street and went towards Free Derry Corner where the organisers planned to hold a protest meeting.

Troops followed the marchers into the Bogside to arrest stonethrowers, and then firing began. The British Army claimed that their men opened fire only after they had been fired on by snipers, but eyewitness reports claimed that the paratroopers opened fire first and fired indiscriminately into the large crowd.

Reaction to the shooting was widespread. The Taoiseach, Mr. Lynch, announced that he had been in touch with the British Prime Minister, Mr. Heath, but that " in view of Mr. Heath's response," he had decided to discuss the position with his Cabinet colleagues this morning.

Mr. Lynch, Cardinal Conway, and many Northern political and religious leaders issued statements condemning the shootings, while the Stormont Prime Minister, Mr. Faulkner, said that the blame must rest on the I.R.A. and on those who had organised the illegal march.

Yesterday's events will be raised at Stormont and Westminster today and will almost certainly come up in the Dail tomorrow. Mr. Liam Cosgrave, Mr. Neil Blaney and Mr. Kevin Boland were also among those who condemned the shootings.

HEATH'S RESPONSE UNHELPFUL

Lynch makes approach

By our Political Correspondent

MR. LYNCH, the Taoiseach, announced last night that he had been in touch with the British Prime Minister, Mr. Heath, but that "in view of Mr. Heath's response," the Taoiseach had decided to discuss the position with his Cabinet colleagues this morning.

This means that the whole crisis raised by Derry, implying now a real crisis in Anglo-Irish relations, will be discussed at a specially-called meeting of the Cabinet this morning. A Monday meeting of the Cabinet is most unusual and indicates the gravity of the situation.

The general impression in Government last night was that Mr. Heath adopted the same attitude on this occasion to Mr. Lynch as that of last August 19th, when his telegram told the Taoiseach that he had no business interfering in the internal affairs of the United Kingdom. But, yet only a day later, had invited the Taoiseach to a new meeting in Chequers.

But there is a much more pessimistic atmosphere in Dublin now to that of last August, and the "break" on this occasion could be much deeper and more difficult to resolve. The implications of it all could be of enormous import for both countries, and could, conceivably lead to something near to a breaking off of diplomatic relations.

In a statement last night the Taoiseach said that he had been in direct touch with Mr. John Hume, M.P. to ascertain the facts and then went on: "I am appalled and stunned that British soldiers should shoot indiscriminately into a crowd of civilians who were peacefully demonstrating, resulting in the deaths of ten young men.

"Even if they were in technical breach of the recently-imposed ban on demonstrations this act by British troops was unbelievably and savagely inhuman."

Last night the Taoiseach was so horrified by the disaster that it was considered to be quite possible that he might possibly go to London today.

There, Mr. Lynch could argue that there should be an international inquiry (such as that urged by Dr. Conor Cruise O'Brien last night) conducted by the United Nations so that the full facts could be ascertained, and secondly, if the evidence showed culpability by British troops as—the evidence apparently showed—then U.N. troops should replace British troops in Northern Ireland. Mr. Lynch might press the British to join with the

On the spot report by Dick Grogan	9
British reaction	9
Army statements	9
Lord Brockway	9
Cardinal's call to Heath	8
Dungannon arrests	8
I.R.A. statement	8
Editorial comment	11

members of the official Opposition parties.

Probably the most persistent demand from deputies to Mr. Lynch, and by Mr. Lynch to the British, will be for the withdrawal of the paratroopers from Northern Ireland. Already some other regiments of the British Army in Northern Ireland are said to have protested against the tactics of this regiment and asked that they be taken home.

Last night the Irish Labour Party leader, Mr. Corish, said that he would be asking the Taoiseach in the Dail tomorrow to make a full statement to the House. Dr. Conor Cruise O'Brien is travelling to London today to see Mr. Harold Wilson, British Labour leader, to urge his support for the idea of an impartial international inquiry.

Fine Gael said last night that all through yesterday afternoon and evening Mr. Liam Cosgrave had been in touch with Mr. John Hume, M.P. and with Mr. Paddy Harte who had been in Derry all day yesterday and who kept Mr. Cosgrave fully informed of yesterday's events.

Army commander describes shooting as defence action

Dick Grogan and Martin Cowley

DERRY was a stunned and sickened city last night as its people counted the rising toll of deaths and injuries following yesterday afternoon's carnage in the Bogside when British soldiers opened up with automatic fire on thousands of anti-internment demonstrators.

By late last night 13 people had died and 16 others had been injured in the shooting, which lasted for about 20 minutes.

All the casualties were shot by British soldiers, and yesterday in the city there was widespread condemnation of the army who fired indiscriminately and without warning.

Calls for a general strike and demands that the army, who have been accused by many of "mass murder," should be withdrawn from the streets, have been made by community representatives.

There were 50 to 60 arrests during the afternoon.

Major General Robert Ford, Commander of the British Land Forces in the North, who watched the Army firing yesterday, defended his soldiers' actions by saying that they had been met with nail bombs, petrol bombs, acid bombs and a hail of bullets, but these statements were bitterly repudiated by the marchers.

General Ford told a reporter in Rossville street that his troops fired three shots at three men who had fired 10 to 20 shots from a heap of rubble in front of Rossville flats. Later two of the men were found dead.

Later, in a B.B.C. interview, General Ford said that the task of the Paratroopers had been to seize "as many hooligans as possible." He said that the troops fired only at bombers and snipers. General Ford admitted that he had seen civil rights stewards trying to keep order but alleged that a hooligan element had taken over.

Everyone, including journalists, who accompanied the parade, were agreed that no nail bombs or petrol-bombs had been thrown and there was certainly no hail of gunfire aimed at the troops. The army shot first, hitting an elderly man and a boy in William street, and it was about 20 minutes later that the soldiers let loose at the demonstrators, most of whom had gathered for a meeting at Free Derry Corner.

The protestors there did not hear any firing at the army, and the first firing they heard was directed at them from troops in Rossville street and from an observation post on the city walls overlooking Free Derry Corner.

STONED ROAD-BLOCK

Martin Cowley reports:

The carnage began a short time after youths stoned two Saracen personnel carriers which blocked the marchers' way in William street to Guildhall square where the organisers had intended to hold the rally. By riot standards the stoning was not particularly heavy. The only visible casualty was a girl steward who was hit by a brick and was taken away with blood stream-

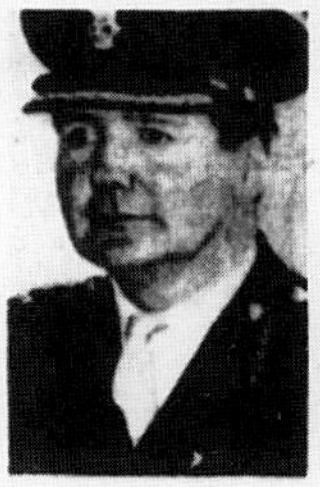

Major-General Robert Ford . . . gunmen fired first . . .

ing from the mouth and nose. With the two vehicles and the big force of troops behind them blocking the road it was impossible for the protestors to carry out their plan to Guildhall square.

After the stoning the situation was deadlocked. Then an army water cannon drove up spraying purple dyes, and then tear gas was thrown. One report said that the gas had been thrown by some of the youths at the troops but no matter who threw it the wind blew the gas into the demonstrators' faces and forced them back. The Army then followed up with more CS gas and the crowd dispersed, some by Chamberlain street to the Rossville flats in Rossville street, and others to the junction of William street and Rossville street.

While most people retreated up Rossville street about 200 youths withstood the effect of the gas and stood throwing a heavy barrage of bricks and stones at troops who were on waste ground on Little James street.

By this time the area was rife

(Continued in page 9.)

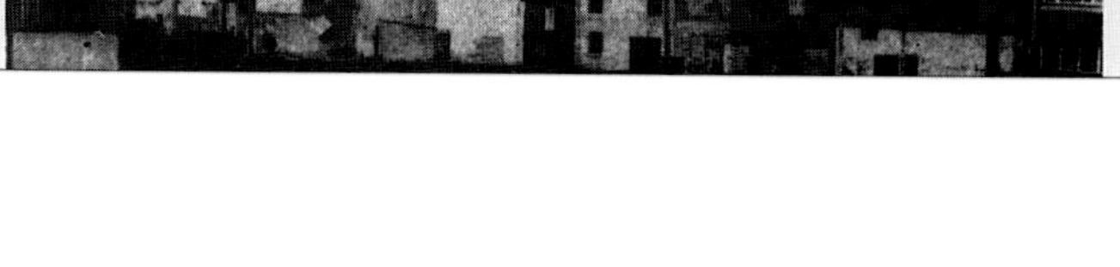

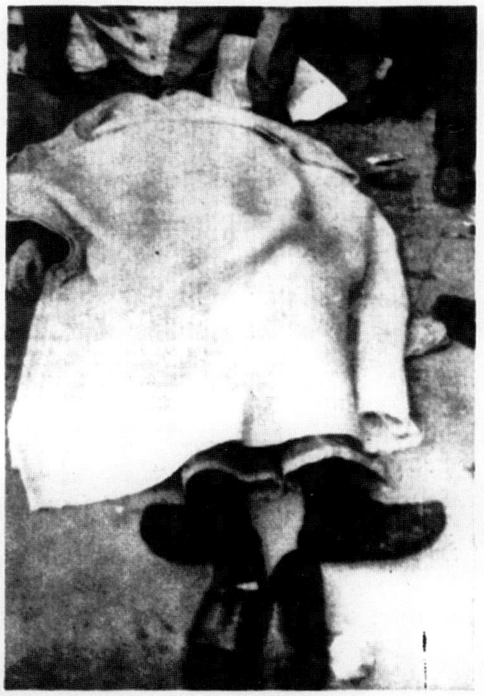

A body in a Bogside street, one of the 13 men shot dead by British troops yesterday.

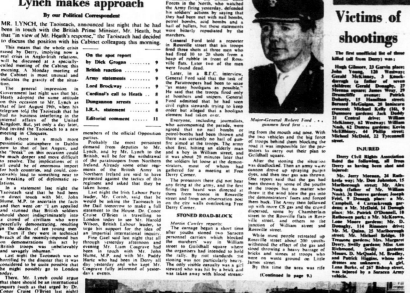

Victims of shootings

The first unofficial list of those killed (all from Derry) was:

Hugh Gilmore, 23 Garvin place; John Young, 120 Westway; Gerald McKinney, 3 Knockdarragh (a father of seven children; Gerald Donaghy, 27 Meenan square; James Wray, 29 Drumcliffe avenue; Patrick Doherty, 15 Hamilton street; Bernard McGuigan, 20 Inniscarn crescent; Michael Kelly (16), 9 Dunmore gardens; Jack Duddy 21 Central drive; William McKinney, 62 Westway; William Nash, 62 Dunree gardens; Kevin McElhiney, 44 Philip street; Michael McDaid, 22 Tyrconnell street.

INJURED

Derry Civil Rights Association listed the following, all from Derry as having been shot and injured:

Mr. Jerry Meenan, 24 Rathkeele way; Mr. Don Johnston, 15 Marlborough street; Mr. Alex Nash (father of Mr. William Nash), 38 Dunree gardens; Joseph Friel, 9 Donagh place; a Mr. Campbell, 4 Carrackreagh gardens; a Mr. McDaid, 14 Donagh place; Mr. Patrick O'Donnell, 10 Rathowen park; a Mr. McKeown, Lone Moore gardens; Mr. D. Donaghy, 114 Rinmore drive; Mr. M. Quinn, 25 Marlborough street; Mr. Michael Bridge, 10 Tremone gardens; Mrs. Margaret Deery, Swilly gardens; Miss Ann Richmond, Swilly gardens; Messrs. D. McQuaid, M. Bradley, and Patrick Higgins, whose addresses are unknown. A girl, Lena Burke, of 267 Bishop street, was injured by a Saracen Army vehicle.

THREE MEN DIE ON BARRICADE

Troops' conduct described

From Nell McCafferty

THREE MEN DIED on a baricade which I vacated below the high flats in Rossville street as four British Army tanks came rushing up the street.

I ran into Colmcille court, a car park behind the maisonettes and burst into a woman's home. As I lay on the floor shots rang out and there was a simultaneous knocking on the door as men cried: "For Jesus sake, missus, let us in, they're shooting."

The woman of the house let them in and I heard more shots ring out. I looked out the window and beyond the picket fence of the back garden a man lay on the ground.

Paratroopers had taken up position at the far end of the courtyard. They rushed forward and surrounded about 30 people whom I had left at the gable wall giving entrance to the courtyard. Among the 30 arrested was a woman whom I watched protesting to the soldiers. A paratrooper struck her across the face with the butt of the his rifle, placed his boot against her stomach, pushed her back against the wall and ordered her to follow the crowd of arrested men.

Later Father Bradley, curate of the Long Tower Church, told me that he had been among the crowd thus arrested. "I said to the soldiers," he told me, "that one of the men had been shot in the shoulder and I pointed him out and said he could not raise his hand above his head like the rest of us. They beat the man then and set upon me, punching, pulling and kicking me. And then for some reason they let me walk away."

About ten minutes later a group of Red Cross officials came into the courtyard. A young female wearing a white coat with Red Cross clearly marked ran into the middle of the courtyard waving her arm at the soldiers. I watched her duck and run for cover as a soldier fired on her. Meanwhile the other Red Cross official dragged a body

26 HAVE DIED THIS MONTH

The death of 13 men shot in Derry yesterday, brought to 232 the death toll since 1969.

Twenty-six people have died this month—18 civilians, three soldiers, one member of the Ulster Defence Regiment and four policemen. Since internment was introduced 169 people have died.—(P.A.)

Faulkner blames I.R.A. and C.R.

By Henry Kelly

THE STORMONT Prime Minister, Mr. Faulkner, last night in a statement laid the entire blame for Derry's carnage on the I.R.A. and the organisers of the civil rights march.

But a quick consultation with some of his own Cabinet Ministers revealed that many of them are seriously disturbed at the first reports they had heard of British Army firing into the Bogside.

It seems at once that a few hours of almost unbelievable shooting in Derry yesterday may turn out to be the most significant and potentially dangerous moment for Mr. Faulkner and his Government to date.

While politicians were generally reluctant to commit themselves too quickly, even Unionists from some sections of the party last night were admitting that wholesale killing like yesterday's is the type of situation which brings the threat of direct rule from Westminster much closer to Northern Ireland. Mr. Faulkner said last night: "Let me say this with great sadness, but with great conviction: Those who organised this march must bear a terrible responsibility for having urged people to lawlessness and for having provided the I.R.A. with the opportunity of once again bringing death to our streets."

Mr. Faulkner described it as "violence and death in a city in which perhaps more than any other the I.R.A. have sought to impose its will."

AFTERMATH

It is certain that tomorrow in the House of Commons at Stormont yesterday's march and its fatal aftermath will be gazed. From Derry come reports that the Catholic population is convinced that British troops from the Parachute Regiment opened fire and killed indiscriminately. From the Army H.Q. at Lisburn come reports that troops only fired when they had been attacked first by snipers and bombers.

Therein lie the ingredients of this week's debate which will be conducted inside and outside Parliament. But the significance for Mr. Faulkner and his Government at this stage cannot be underestimated. And as one Cabinet Minister pointed out last night a further tragedy in the whole situation is that public opinion in the Republic could begin to sway away from Mr. Lynch's moderate political approach to the Northern problem and begin to demand more active participation by the Republic in Northern Ireland's present situation.

BRITISH OFFICER DIES FROM WOUNDS

A British Army officer, wounded in Derry nearly five months ago, died from his injuries in a London hospital yesterday.

Major Robin Nigel Humphrey Aiers-Hankey (35), of the 2nd Battalion, Royal Green Jackets, was shot in the stomach as he guarded firemen fighting a blaze at a timber yard. He was taken to Altnagelvin Hospital for an emergency operation, and six weeks later was moved to the Millbank Hospital, in London.

He came from Winchester, Hampshire, and was married, with two boys, aged five and three.

5½%
tax free

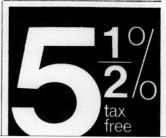

18 June

The British general election returns an overall majority for the Conservative Party. Edward Heath becomes Prime Minister the next day.

26–29 June

Riots break out in Derry and Belfast following the arrest of Bernadette Devlin.

'unproductive' levels of Government expenditure on housing, health, and education. Thus the First Programme for Economic Expansion for the years 1959–64, based on Whitaker's paper, provided little room for capital investment and actual cut-backs in the provision of housing, which Whitaker had claimed in *Economic Development* was perfectly adequate. These cuts in turn led to a housing crisis in Dublin, exemplified in June 1963 by the collapse of condemned houses in Bolton Street and Fenian Street, killing four people.

Yet the opening up of the economy was an immediate and dramatic success. The change in policy coincided with a new era of dominance for multinational corporations. Whereas in 1950 only about 7,500 American companies had international affiliates, by 1966 the number was 23,000 mostly in western Europe. With cheap labour, low corporate taxes and the removal of

coffins with 'Bloody Sunday' and '13' painted in white on them. The coffins were placed one on either side of the doorway and were later burned on the roadway along with placards and a Union Jack. While they were burning, four prayers were recited for the thirteen civilians killed in Derry.

At a brief meeting speakers urged the demonstrators to keep up their protests to get British soldiers out of Ireland and called for the release of political prisoners in the South. Bottles, stones, coins and two petrol bombs were thrown at the building from the crowd …

from The Irish Times
6 MARCH 1972

Patriotism 1972

Two legs gone; one arm sheared off; an eye lost—all in one young female body. That equals someone's idea of patriotism in Ireland in 1972.

Of what are the victims of the Abercorn explosion a symbol? Of Ireland's march to independence, unity and

Bloody Sunday provoked unprecedented outrage in nationalist Ireland, north and south. A mob burned the British embassy in Merrion Square, Dublin.

A no-warning IRA bomb at the Abercorn restaurant in Belfast on 4 March 1972 killed two people and injured 130. Two sisters each lost both legs; one of them had been shopping for a wedding dress.

dignity among the nations? Of Orange insistence that Ulster will remain British? It hardly matters. All are shamed.

Mr John Robb, one of the surgeons who dealt with the broken bodies after the explosion, made an appeal to those responsible. If, he said, the perpetrators are crippled in their outlook, as a result of what had happened in the past, do they honestly believe that by continuing with this form of violence we are going to be able, when it is all over, merely to sweep up the bits and create a new healthy society?

How can this come about, he asked, any more than a surgeon can recreate the human being after he has lost his limbs?

———

We have had a plethora of analyses of violence. Even the most dug-in Unionist can see some point in the cry that the

tariff barriers, Ireland was in a position to attract a decent share of this investment. From mid-1959 to mid-1960 alone the value of the country's exports rose by 35 per cent. Sales of private cars were 40 per cent higher in 1960 than in 1959. Unemployment in October 1960 was 20 per cent below what it had been a year earlier. A headline in *The Irish Times* over an economic forecast by Garret FitzGerald in July 1960 summed up the mood: 'Good times coming.'

The influx of American capital was given a glamorous embodiment by the visit of the American president John F. Kennedy in June 1963. Kennedy provided an astonishing image of Irish Catholic success in the modern world and

27 June

The Provisional IRA is involved in its first action in the nationalist Short Strand area of Belfast.

2 July

Neil Blaney is acquitted in the arms smuggling trial because of lack of evidence.

12 August
Two RUC men are killed in a bomb explosion in Crossmaglen, Co. Armagh. They are the first RUC members to die in a nationalist area in the troubles.

21 August
Gerry Fitt MP and other nationalists form the Social Democratic and Labour Party.

23 October
The remaining defendants in the arms trial are found not guilty.

1971

6 February
The first British soldier to die in the troubles is killed by the Provisional IRA.

20 March
James Chichester-Clark resigns as Prime Minister of Northern Ireland. He is succeeded by Brian Faulkner, who is elected Unionist party leader three days later.

Seán Lemass was Taoiseach from 1959 to 1966. By common consent, he was the most capable person ever to hold the office. He presided over the social, economic and generational changes of the early sixties.

was greeted almost as a god. *The Irish Times* reported the remarkable behaviour of the elite of Irish society at a garden party in the grounds of Áras an Uachtaráin. Tom McCaughren described the scenes as the invited guests 'literally mobbed'

built-in prejudice which will deny to a lad in the Falls Road the chance of a job in some big factory just because he is a Catholic, can be read as violence of a kind.

Then there is the obvious violence. Anti-Unionists point to the shootings by the British Army, to the violence which keeps a man in Long Kesh because he advocates—with pen and voice rather than with gun, maybe—the unity of the country, and to that violence which Lord Gardiner has so emphatically condemned.

Such examples as these have been held to explain or excuse gun and gelignite. What violence offsets the legless and armless women who survived the Abercorn explosion? It is a degree more nauseating than the shooting in his home of a UDR man, whether that man is a Protestant and Unionist or a Catholic who listened to the advice of British politicians and anti-Unionist politicians in the palmy days to go in and take the sectarianism out of the services in the North.

For the Abercorn explosion was not relevant against the British Army; it was not relevant against the British Government or the Stormont Government, except in that it showed the sick society which exists in the North. This attitude presupposes that a better one is in the making. Is it in the competence of anyone who could plant that bomb to bring about a better society? ...

from The Irish Times 1972
12 MAY

Decision joins Republic, NI and Britain in one economic unit

Ends Epoch of Romantic Nationalism

by Michael McInerney, our Political Correspondent

The decision of one million voters to mark yes on their ballots on Wednesday has made Ireland a member of EEC. It has joined together Northern Ireland and the Republic into virtually one economic unit with Great Britain, thus demonstrating the electors' insight in appreciating that Ireland, in isolation from Britain and its market, made no economic or political sense.

In the Irish political sense the million voters have resolved decisively all the problems of the Taoiseach, Mr Lynch, swamping Aontacht Éireann, the Fianna Fáil dissidents, and other 'Republican' parties and groups, and they have also illustrated a nation's utter disapproval of the militant wings of 'Republicanism,' strengthening further the Taoiseach's hand by expressing the discipline of a people. Mr Lynch has won an election without the bother—and the party

The old order. James Dillon, son of the last leader of the Irish Party and himself leader of Fine Gael from 1959 to 1965, with Mrs Thomas Kettle, formerly Mary Sheehy. The Sheehys were one of the great political dynasties of home rule Ireland. In the sixties, their collateral descendants included Senator Owen Sheehy-Skeffington and Dr Conor Cruise O'Brien.

Kennedy and the 'obviously distraught' de Valera. 'Toes were trampled on, high heels sank into lawn, shoes were lost, beautiful hats were crumpled, guests fell over chairs which had remained upturned on the lawn, unused because of the rain. One man determined to get out of the surging, swaying crowd found his shoulder caught under the scarlet cape of a bishop. But too late. The bishop was almost pulled to the ground and his cape was ripped. A pleasant man, however, he was most forgiving. All the while Mr Kennedy shook as many of the grasping hands as possible, including the white-gloved hand of a woman who shouted and waved frantically over the heaving shoulders of the security men, "Jack, Jack, my hand, shake my hand." When he did,

14 April

The Women's Liberation Movement holds its first public meeting in the Mansion House in Dublin.

18 April

The census shows the population of the Republic to be 2.98 million.

11 May

Seán Lemass dies.

22 May

The Irish Women's
Liberation
Movement defies
the law by openly
importing contra-
ceptives through
Connolly Station
in Dublin.

8 July

Two civilians are
killed by the British
army in Derry,
prompting the
SDLP to withdraw
from the Stormont
Parliament.

9 August

Hundreds of
Catholics are arrested
by the RUC and
British army in one
night as internment
is introduced in
Northern Ireland.
Many are not
members of the
republican
movement.
Seventeen people are
killed in the trouble
in the wake of the
arrests, and
thousands of
Catholics flee across
the border, where
they are housed in
army camps.

19 October

Arms are found on
the QE2, docked
in Cork.

Seán Ó Riada and Ceoltóirí Chualainn in the sixties. The group was hugely influential in the rediscovery of Irish music, especially that of the eighteenth-century Irish aristocratic tradition, and anticipated later international successes like the Chieftains.

she turned away and adjusted her hat, and expressed her utter satisfaction to her friends and to the others on whom she had trampled.'

Kennedy also provided a poignant reminder of the legacy of emigration that Ireland was hoping to overcome. The 'success or failure' of the Programme for Economic Expansion, *The Irish Times* had noted in November 1958, 'will be measured by the emigration figures.' And by this criterion, success was immediate and dramatic. Between 1956 and 1961 net emigration was 212,000; in the next five years it was 80,000. During the seventies the historic problem of emigration seemed to disappear altogether, with net immigration during the decade of over 108,000, as many families who had left for Britain in the fifties returned with their children.

The effects of the new policies went far beyond the short-term boost to prosperity. The Republic finally became economically, as

disunity—of declaring a general election; there is now no need for any other mandate.

The million votes, however, were also epochal, and contained a sadness. By recognising the grim economic reality made more grim by the Government's refusal to offer any alternative to full membership, an intelligent electorate decided they could vote only one way: they must go with their British customers.

The sadness consists in the possibility that the vote could mark the end of an epoch of romantic nationalism, an end forced by economic reality, and, in one Labour view, 'marks the undoing of an era which began with 1916 and made vain all the sacrifices of wonderful men.'

There was the sadness too expressed by many 'yes' voters on Wednesday. Some of them clearly had a reluctance in voting 'yes' and one knew they felt they were changing all they had known, and leaving behind patriotism, history, nostalgia, and embracing something new, different, but which yet offered more hope than they had known. It was a form of emigration.

from The Irish Times 1972
5 DECEMBER

In the Eyes of the Law by Nell McCafferty

Housewives' Independence Notions Disappear in the Courtroom

There's no place like a courtroom to dismiss the nonsensical notion entertained by housewives that they are in any degree independent of their husbands. A woman appeared before District Justice Ua Donnchadha in Court 4 at 11.45 a.m. on Wednesday, 29 November, offering herself as bondswoman of her friend, who had been convicted for shoplifting.

'Do you do any work other than housework?' she was asked. No, she did not. 'Are you dependent upon your husband for money?' 'Yes,' she said. 'I cannot accept you then,' said the Justice. It was as short simple and brutal as that, in the world where money matters, women matter not.

Another friend came forward, and was sworn in. Apart from being a housewife, did she work she was asked. 'Yes,' she replied, she was a full-time cleaner in a Dublin hotel for which she was paid £12 a week. 'Might I ask,' said the Justice, 'how you are going to see your friend remains of good behaviour? If you sign this bond, you guarantee she will keep the peace. If she does not, you will forfeit your money.'

'Well,' the woman said, 'my husband is a docker, we would have enough.' 'The only thing that concerns me is your individual solvency,' said the Justice. 'Oh, sure, I'd get the £50 off my husband,' said the woman. 'And supposing your husband said no?' asked the Justice. 'Send your husband along. I'll accept his bond.'

The women left the court in a state of confusion. Outside they asked angrily what was the logic in it. Supposing the husband forfeited the bond, how did the Justice know the wife would not say no? They were unaware, of course, that in this country a husband is not obliged to support his wife above and beyond what he considers she needs. Or that it is he who may decide, arbitrarily, what constitutes 'provision' for those needs.

I asked the woman who had been convicted why her husband did not come along as bondsman. 'Ah well,' she said, 'if he knew about me shoplifting he would kill me. Anyway, he's on the labour, you see, not working, so he's

opposed to politically, independent of Britain. The share of total exports destined for the British market fell from two-thirds in 1956 to one-third in 1981. And whereas even in the sixties British-owned firms accounted for 22 per cent of new industrial investment, by 1980 they accounted for just 4 per cent. Another huge change was that the Republic gradually became an industrial rather than an agricultural society. In 1961 agriculture accounted for over 61 per cent of exports; by 1976 the figure was just 37 per cent, and before the end of the century it would tumble to just 7 per cent.

During the sixties, national output grew by an average of over 4 per cent a year. Tourism boomed. With emigration tailing off, by 1966 the population had risen by 66,000 above the 1961 level of 2.8 million, the lowest ever recorded. With no significant problems of inflation, foreign debt (just £100 million at the end of the decade) or balance of payments, it looked as if the holy grail of full employment might be attainable.

The better economic prospects did not, however, halt the decline of rural Ireland. If

30 November
The Government states that it will bring a case for Northern Ireland internees before the International Court of Human Rights.

4 December
A loyalist bomb kills fifteen Catholics in McGurk's Bar in Belfast.

1972

30 January
Bloody Sunday: thirteen unarmed civil rights marchers are shot dead by British soldiers in

Ian Paisley protesting at Stormont

At Telefís Éireann's Kippure transmitter in 1961, the Minister for Posts and Telegraphs, Michael Hilliard, is flanked by Ed Roth and Éamonn Andrews.

Derry. Another man dies later from his injuries.

2 February
A crowd sets fire to the British Embassy in Dublin in retaliation for the Bloody Sunday deaths in Derry.

14 February
The Widgery inquiry into the Bloody Sunday killings opens.

anything they speeded its collapse. Hugh Brody, in his study of a County Clare village, *Inishkillane*, in the late sixties, noted that 'in many small but significant ways, Irish country people indicate symbolically their involvement with the urban culture to which they are tending to look for social and moral guidance. Young men wear the clothes they think would impress an urban visitor. The housewife places great emphasis on tidiness and cleanliness in the home. The father accepts the son's entitlement to independence. Young girls are preoccupied with the latest Dublin and London fashions. In conversations with tourists, villagers tend to emphasize their awareness of rural limitations and seem to hope that they can establish their superiority to traditional life. In the homes, the stranger is

worth nothing too. Sure, isn't that why I lifted the few things.' They wandered away, wondering how to keep him from knowing of the offence, should the gardaí come to the door looking to see why she had not secured her bond ...

from The Irish Times 1972

The Church goes to the Market

Donal Foley 'Man Bites Dog'

Massive redundancies will take place in the Roman Catholic Church in Ireland when Ireland enters the European Community in January. The redundancies are foreshadowed in a rationalisation plan published today aimed at making the Church a viable religious unit in the Market. The plan was prepared by the Most Rev Dr Mansholt, Bishop of Brussels, at the request of the Irish Management Institute.

Approximately 100,000 Irish Catholic heads are expected to roll as a result of the Mansholt axe. 'There are far too many Catholics in Ireland', the report bluntly states. 'The religious power houses in Ireland could be run with half the number of people operating them at present. What is needed is spiritual automation, with more use of the country's hot line to Heaven.'

Some of the Catholics who will suffer redundancy may find an outlet in the upsurge of vocations which the market will bring, according to the Mansholt plan. 'The deployment of the new vocations is a vital matter for the religious community as a whole. They may have to find work in Germany and other religious community centres.' The report urges the immediate recall of all Irish missionaries abroad, because of the 'dissipation of Irish spiritual assets involved.'

The report calls for greater and clearer lines of communication between religious managers and workers. 'Workers must be given full participation in top Church management. In fact a Time and Motion Study is necessary on Church practices. Many Irish Catholics have gone through the motions for years. This means their religious productivity is well below par. Some are just simply Catholic drones.'

Make It Pay

In order to make the Irish Church a going concern, the Plan recommends a spiritual incentive system which would encourage Irish Catholics to pull their religious weight in the Community. The system would work as a value added merit bonus, payable on death. This would be non-taxable and would be something like the present golden handshake in industry. It is described in the report as a heavenly handshake.

In a special mini report under the heading 'Small Industries' the plan discusses the role of the Church of Ireland. It recommends that the Catholic Church should make a takeover bid for the smaller organisation, offering full membership and an equal share in the special position. Protestants should be guaranteed the same religious dividends and full access to the valuable Bank of Eternal Truth.

The abolition of sin in Ireland was considered in the plan but rejected on the grounds that such a drastic recommendation would have a bad effect on the morals of the country ...

offered white bread and shop ham on the assumption that these are bound to be preferred to rugged home produce, and in the hope of showing the visitor that even if they, the hosts, are Irish country people they still know what is really good. In these anticipations and symbolic gestures—some of them astute, others naïve—the country people seek to demonstrate their esteem for urban life. By the same token they indicate their profound dissatisfaction with local and national tradition.'[2]

Nor should the immediate extent of the boom be exaggerated. By 1967 gross national product per head was still only half the average for north-western Europe and a quarter that of the United States. Rising expectations led, moreover, to bitter industrial unrest and to unsettling changes. From 1964 the amount of property crime, hitherto negligible, began to rise sharply, with burglaries increasing four-fold and robberies eleven-fold by 1975. And the rush of new money destroyed much of the urban landscape of Dublin. Landmarks such as the Royal and Queen's Theatres and the Capitol Cinema were demolished. Ten houses in the magnificent Georgian terrace of Fitzwilliam Street were

Ed Roth, the American who was the first director-general of Telefís Éireann, later RTE television

22 February
An Official IRA bomb at a British army barracks in Aldershot, Hampshire, kills six civilians and a chaplain.

24 March
The British government announces the introduction of direct rule in Northern Ireland.

28 March
The last meeting of the Stormont Parliament takes place.

19 April
The Widgery Report on the events of Bloody Sunday alleges that British soldiers were fired on first; states that no deaths would have occurred had the illegal march not taken place; concludes that the actions of the Parachute Regiment ranged from 'a high degree of responsibility' to firing that bordered 'on the reckless'; and noted that none of the dead were proved to have been handling

a firearm or a bomb. The report is dismissed by nationalists as a whitewash.

10 May

The electorate in the Republic votes in a referendum to accept membership of the EEC.

26 May

The Special Criminal Court is established, removing the right to trial by jury for defendants brought before it.

29 May

The Official IRA calls a cease-fire; it never officially breaks it.

20 June

Republicans end a hunger strike when the Secretary of State for Northern Ireland, William Whitelaw, announces the introduction of special-category status for political prisoners.

22 June

The Provisional IRA announces a cease-fire, to begin at midnight on 26 June.

An anti-Vietnam war protest in Parnell Square, Dublin, in the late sixties

replaced with an ugly office block by the ESB, provoking *The Irish Times* leader-writer to some caustic speculation on the likely fate of Venice in the hands of those who ran Dublin. 'How long would our demolition squads allow her to queen it in the Adriatic? And in Pisa, the Leaning Tower would have come down years ago. The authorities would have taken advice from experts that it was impossible to straighten it.' The fact that many of the developers were generous contributors to Fianna Fáil created enduring suspicions about the ethics of the new generation of political leaders. Chief among them was Lemass's son-in-law,

from The Irish Times 1979

Contraceptive Conversation

Maeve Binchy

Today I had an argument with a stranger, a real live argument with a woman I'd never met before as we stood at a bus stop for what seemed a considerable length of time. 'Very depressing kind of day,' she said. 'Grey,' I agreed. 'But it might cheer up later.' 'Nothing much to be cheerful about, though, is there? Look at the papers,' she said. Obligingly I looked at the front page of *The Irish Times*. Compared to some days, I thought the news was fairly neutral. 'Do you mean Mike Gibson not playing rugby for Ireland any more?' I asked, not quite seeing anything that would cause gloom.

'Never heard of him' she said. It couldn't be the heady excitement of will-we won't-we about the EMS; she was hardly brought down by the fact that the RUC may have been kidnapping Father Hugh Murphy, since he was safe and well; the talks were continuing in an RTE dispute, but that wasn't enough to lay anyone low. No, it had to be Haughey and the Contraceptive Bill. 'Do you mean about having to have doctors' prescriptions?' I asked. 'Indeed I do,' she said. 'Well, I suppose it does make us look very foolish trying to legislate for everyone else's morality and pass the buck to doctors,' I said cheerfully. 'But then I'm a fairly optimistic person, and I'd prefer to regard it as a step in the right direction.'

Charles Haughey, identified in an *Irish Times* editorial of November 1966 as 'the modern man, essentially pragmatic and business minded.'

Adding to the mood of change were the opening of an Irish television station by RTE on New Year's Eve in 1961, and the sweeping liberalisation of Catholicism begun by Pope John XXIII. *The Irish Times* reported de Valera's worries, expressed in his speech at the opening of RTE, that television might lead to 'decadence and dissolution', but the new medium was embraced with considerable enthusiasm by the population as a whole. The Second Vatican Council, held between October 1962 and December 1965, likewise had a huge impact, not just on Irish Catholicism but on the broader culture of the Republic. If, after all, the timeless

9 July

The Provisional IRA cease-fire collapses after nationalists and British soldiers clash in Lenadoon in west Belfast.

17 July

It is reported that seven thousand people have fled across the border to the Republic in the previous week.

*Frank Aiken, Cardinal Cody of Chicago, Mother Mary Martin—the founder of the **Medical Misionaries of Mary**—and Cardinal Conway of Armagh*

Belfast City Hall in the sunshine. The apparent tranquillity of late-sixties Belfast was about to be shattered for a generation.

21 July

*Bloody Friday:
twenty-six
Provisional IRA
bombs in Belfast kill
eleven and injure
130 people, most of
them civilians.*

31 July

*The British army
launches 'Operation
Motorman', which
aims to eradicate
'no-go' areas for
the British army
and RUC in
nationalist areas.*

truths of the church could be renewed and reconsidered, how could orthodox opinion in any other area be taken for granted?

These changes coincided with modest signs that the Unionist monolith in Northern Ireland was also beginning to shift. In May 1962, while Unionists were marking the fiftieth anniversary of the Solemn League and Covenant, the Northern Ireland Labour Party received 26 per cent of the vote, winning in the process an unprecedented level of cross-community support. Internal Unionist criticism of the Prime Minister, Lord Brookeborough, began to mount and he resigned in March 1963, to be replaced by a much younger man, Terence O'Neill. With the pragmatic and mildly reformist O'Neill in power in the North and the similarly inclined Lemass in the South, a new openness was in the air.

There was a stony silence. I wondered had she heard me. After all, she was the one who started the conversation. 'So, even though it's a bit of a joke, it's not all that bad,' I said cheerfully, keeping things going as I thought. 'Is that your view,' she said. 'Well, it's not a very thought-out view,' I backtracked. 'But, it's a kind of instant reaction if you know what I mean.' 'You approve of all that sort of thing,' she said in a kind of hiss. 'Oh yes, I think people have the right to buy contraceptives,' I said, wishing somebody else would come along and stand at the bus stop and shout 'good girl yourself' at me. 'And you'd like to see them in public places,' she said, eyes glinting madly.

'Well, not in parks or concert halls or places like that. But on shelves in chemists, certainly. Then, if people want to buy them, they can, and if they don't, nobody's forcing them to.' I thought I had summed up the case rather well. 'On shelves so that everyone can see them,' she said, horrified. 'Well, they're in packets,' I said, 'with kind of discreet names on them. They don't leap up off counters and affront you.' 'And how might you know all this?' she asked. 'Well, I've seen them in chemists in London,' I said defensively. 'If they're so discreet, how did you know what they were?' she asked, tellingly.

'Well, you'd sort of know. I mean people have to know where they are, for God's sake. I mean they shouldn't have to go playing hide and seek around the chemists with the assistant saying warmer and colder.' The woman wasn't at all amused. 'I'm sure you know where they are because you buy them,' she said. I began to wonder why it is increasingly less likely that I ever have a normal conversation with anyone. 'I once bought a huge amount,' I said reminiscently. 'As a kind of favour to a lot of people. They knew I was going to be in London, and they kept asking me to bring some home.'

She was fixed to me with horror. All her life she knew she would meet someone as wicked as this, and now it had happened. 'I didn't know what kind to get or what the names of them were, so I just went into the Boots chemist beside Marble Arch and asked for four dozen of their best contraceptives and a receipt. They looked at me with great interest.' 'I'm not surprised,' said the woman. 'But really, wasn't I very stupid in those days,' I confided in her. 'I mean, imagine smuggling them all in for people, and not making any profit on them and not even … you know … well, getting any value out of them myself as it were.

She stared ahead, two red spots on her cheeks, and mercifully the bus came. She waited to see if I went upstairs or downstairs so that she could travel on a different deck.

from The Irish Times 1981
16 FEBRUARY

'Thought it was a special lighting effect'
by **Maev Kennedy**

'It was just like a sheet of wallpaper, like the wall itself was burning,' said Geraldine Lynch (18) of her first sight of the fire in the Stardust. She was one of hundreds of teenagers who tried to get into the Mater Hospital yesterday to visit injured friends and relations.

'We thought first it was some special lighting effect, for the disco dancing—the way it was all lit up with just a bit of smoke,' her boyfriend, Ciaran Sheridan (10), said.

The Irish Times renewed its interest in Northern Ireland and in May 1964 was instrumental in bringing a 27-year-old Derry teacher and community activist, John Hume, to public attention. One of the paper's feature-writers, Michael Viney, was in Derry researching a week-long series of articles on the North in which he argued that 'the common people of the North certainly are oppressed and exploited—but not by force of arms or imperialist domination. They are oppressed by armchair, atrophied attitudes to life and politics, which they themselves are tricked into sustaining: on the one hand by a Unionist Party whose public attachment to power and privilege is often mediaeval in its cynicism; on the other by a corps of Nationalists who, with a few exceptions, encourage slogans as a substitute for thought.' Viney saw a short film on the city that Hume had made with a Church of Ireland clergyman, Brian Hannon. The film

24 November
The RTE Authority is dismissed by the Government after a broadcaster interviews the Provisional IRA leader Seán Mac Stiofáin.

25 November
Kevin O'Kelly, news features editor of RTE, is sentenced to three months' imprisonment after he refuses to identify Seán Mac Stiofáin at his trial.

Following the fiasco of the 1956–62 border campaign, the republican movement moved to the left in the sixties. One of its leading personalities was Máirín de Búrca, who was also representative of the gradual advance of women in Irish political life.

7 December

A referendum reduces the voting age from twenty-one to eighteen and removes references to the special position of the Catholic Church in the Constitution.

20 December

The Diplock Report recommends the introduction of courts without juries in Northern Ireland, as well as powers of arrest and detention that allow British soldiers to detain suspects for up to four hours.

1973

1 January

Ireland becomes a member of the EEC, along with Britain and Denmark.

20 January

A car bomb in Sackville Place, Dublin, planted by loyalists or their associates, kills one man and injures thirty.

The fire in the Stardust ballroom in Artane, Dublin, in 1981 claimed the lives forty-eight young people. It was started deliberately.

The funeral of Lt-Gen. Seán Mac Eoin, the 'Blacksmith of Ballinalee', passing along the main street of the village that gave him his nickname. Fifty-two years earlier, in 1921, he had held Ballinalee against superior British forces in one of the most celebrated actions of the War of Independence.

'I heard somebody shout "fire" and I thought he said "fight"—I thought they were shouting about a fight and we'd better get out,' Geraldine said. 'Then we turned round and saw the fire, right up to the ceiling, and we just ran for the main entrance—we were sitting near it, we had been going to sit down at the back and we just changed our minds. There was panic at the door, crowds all shoving and bouncers just sort of shoving people aside to make more room,' she said.

Geraldine escaped with legs badly cut and bruised from being trampled in the rush to the door ...

Christy Ryan was so panic-stricken when the fire broke out that he ran in the opposite direction from the exit he was nearest to. 'I just ran. I was near the balcony, the bit closed off, and then they pulled up the shutters and the fire just shot up. I ran into the middle of the floor, and by the time I got to the middle the lights went off. Then I just followed the crowd. It was panic. I seen a young one running around with her hair and her clothes burning, and you couldn't do a thing.'

'Then I ran round to the front and we were trying to smash in the windows, and the cops turned up and tried to haul us off, and we just turned round and yelled at them—it was mad.'

captured a mood of hope by arguing for 'the independence and seriousness' of the city's Protestants to be allied to 'the discipline and resourcefulness' of its Catholic population. Viney praised the film and urged RTE to show it, which it did. *The Irish Times* then published two articles by Hume under the title 'The Northern Catholic', representing the first significant statement by a man who was to be one of the most important political figures of what was left of the century.

In the articles Hume criticised both unionism and nationalism and argued that 'one of the great contributions ... that the Catholic in Northern Ireland can make to a liberalising of the political atmosphere would be the removal of the equation between nationalist and Catholic.' Representing as he did a new generation of Catholics who had benefited from the post-war reform of higher education in the United Kingdom, Hume broke with the pieties of his tribe and made a passionate case for the

7 February
Loyalists attack Catholic homes during a one-day strike by the Loyalist Association of Workers.

26 February
The Report of the Committee for the Status of Women recommends equal pay, legal mechanisms for combating sexual discrimination, the granting of maternity leave, and day care facilities for children.

constructive involvement of Catholics in Northern Ireland. 'Weak opposition leads to corrupt government. Nationalists in opposition have been in no way constructive. They have—quite rightly—been loud in their demands for rights, but they have remained silent and inactive about their duties. In 40 years of opposition they have not produced one constructive contribution on either the social or economic plane to the development of Northern Ireland ... Leadership has been the comfortable leadership of flags and slogans. Easy no doubt but irresponsible ...' Hume called on Northern Catholics to face 'the realistic fact that a united Ireland, if it is to come, and if violence rightly is to be discounted, must come about by evolution, i.e. the will of the Northern majority.' He also urged them to accept that the Protestant tradition in the North was as strong and as legitimate as their own.

In his second article, Hume turned his attention to unionism, setting out the steps the governing party must take. Unionists would have

Christy appeared in court on Saturday morning charged with using abusive language and behaviour likely to cause a breach of the peace. 'I don't know what's going to happen now. We're supposed to be up in court again on the 20th. Just for trying to get our mates out—it's mad' ...

from The Irish Times
6 MAY 1981

Pleas for calm as Sands's body is brought from jail

By David McKittrick, Northern Editor

Sporadic street disturbances, concentrated in working-class districts of Belfast, continued yesterday following the early-morning death of the Republican hunger-striker, Mr Bobby Sands, on the sixty-sixth day of his fast.

Supporters of Mr Sands have called for a day of mourning in both the North and the Republic when he is buried tomorrow.

The body of Mr Sands, the Provisional IRA man who was elected MP for Fermanagh-South Tyrone last month,

Liam Cosgrave, Taoiseach from 1973 to 1977

The Women's Political Association was influential in advancing the careers of women in Irish public life, one of the most significant social changes of the seventies. Two of the women here, Nora Owen (seated, left) and Gemma Hussey (seated, second from right) later became Government ministers.

was removed yesterday from Long Kesh Prison to his west Belfast home.

Widely differing attitudes were revealed in the reaction of public figures to his death. The Primate of All-Ireland, Dr Ó Fiaich, criticised the British Government's attitude as inflexible, while the Church of Ireland Archbishop of Armagh, Dr Armstrong, described the hunger-strike as 'one of the most calculated pieces of moral blackmail in recent times.'

Mr Sands's supporters have asked for a full day of mourning, with what amounts to a one-day national strike, and have said that people who support the Republican prisoners' demands should wear black armbands or black ribbons and fly black flags from their homes. There are

to accept, he wrote, that nationalism was 'an acceptable political belief,' which people were entitled to express without incurring discrimination or charges of disloyalty. Institutional discrimination against Catholics would have to be dismantled, in the first instance by inviting Catholic representatives to take their place on public bodies. And prejudice would have to be replaced with an acceptance that Catholics were reasonable and responsible people, anxious to secure a better future for their children. If these steps were not taken, he warned, Northern Ireland would be in trouble. 'Unionists must

Commission on Human Rights in Strasbourg of torturing internees in Northern Ireland.

22 November
The Ulster Unionists, SDLP and Alliance parties agree to form a power-sharing Assembly.

6–9 December

Representatives of the Irish and British governments and the new Executive meet at Sunningdale in Berkshire.

19 December

The Supreme Court decides that the ban on contraception is unconstitutional. The Price sisters, imprisoned in England after being found guilty of offences in connection with an IRA bombing campaign, are said to be weak as a result of a hunger strike.

28 December

The German honorary consul in Belfast, Thomas Niedermeyer, is kidnapped near his home in the city.

1974

1 January

Ireland takes over the presidency of the EEC for the first time. The Northern Ireland power-sharing Executive takes office under the Unionist leader Brian Faulkner.

By the early seventies, Séamus Heaney was already established as the best-known Irish poet of his generation

realise that if they turn their backs on the present good will, there can only be a considerable hardening of Catholic opinion …' These warnings were to prove all too prescient.

O'Neill did make efforts to take the opportunities for reform, not least by inviting Lemass to Belfast in January 1965. Lemass's positive reply was delayed for a week because it was addressed to 'Stormont Castle, Dublin.' In spite of mutual nervousness, the meeting provoked little opposition on either side, and *The Irish Times* naturally gave it enthusiastic support. O'Neill's liberal policies did arouse the ire of the Protestant fundamentalist Ian Paisley, and he was reluctant to move too far ahead of his own cautious Unionist constituency. Yet even by March 1968, on the fifth anniversary of his accession as prime minister, *The Irish Times* was still hopeful that in spite of 'the Paisleyite

reports that the National H-Block Committee plans to call a conference, possibly next Saturday, to decide on future plans. It is reported that groups such as the SDLP will be invited.

Meanwhile the committee has said that the period before the funeral 'should not be marred by any action which would detract from the dignity and heroism of Bobby Sands's sacrifice' …

from The Irish Times 1982
23 FEBRUARY

A Step to Watch

Conor Cruise O'Brien

'Doubtless I shall hate it,' wrote W. B. Yeats, 'but not so much as I hate Irish democracy.'

What the poet thought he would hate, but not so much as Irish democracy, was Fascism. Yeats was feeling a bit bruised at the time (1933). His deep love of Ireland was a romantic affair and Irish democracy, whatever else it may be, is not a romantic affair. When Cathleen Ní Houlihan—through the magic of the ballot-box—takes visible, tangible form, she often turns out to be no oil-painting.

Through her elected emanations, the lady had recently trodden all over the poet's dreams with those hard, bony feet of hers.

Censorship she wanted then, plenty of that, but no divorce. It didn't matter what the poet thought about that, or anything else. Poets were *in a minority*, you see, especially Protestant poets.

And he could forget that play he wrote about her, back in 1902, and that girl with the English accent who had the impudence to impersonate her, Cathleen—the real one, who was now telling him, Mr. Yeats, where he got off the bus.

No wonder he hated Irish democracy, and no wonder his mind kept going back to Parnell, and his thoroughly democratic destruction, in the three ghastly by-elections of 1891.

Cathleen has mellowed since then of course. She told Charlie he could exempt writers and artists from tax, and she

infection', O'Neill's 'flair' and 'panache' might yet produce results. 'His five years have brought at the worst some light in the gloomy sky of the North, at best a turning point in recent Irish history. A Tory through and through, an upholder of the perverse and dangerous Orange Order, he has nevertheless contributed something to all the people of this island.'

By then *The Irish Times* was not merely reporting the mood of change but was also participating in it. After Smyllie's death in 1954 the paper had been edited in turn by two of his protégés, Alec Newman and Alan Montgomery, though both, according to Tony Gray, continued to refer to their lost leader as 'the Editor', a habit of mind that expressed their determination to preserve his legacy. In the new era of the nineteen-sixties, however, Montgomery's successor, Douglas Gageby, who took over in 1963, realised that the paper could become much

4 January

The Ulster Unionist Council, governing body of the UUP, rejects the Council of Ireland, by 427 votes to 377.

28 February

Edward Heath loses the British general election to Harold Wilson's Labour Party.

14 May

The Ulster Workers' Council and loyalist paramilitaries begin

Dáithí Ó Conaill, vice-president of Sinn Féin and believed to have been a former chief of staff of the IRA, addresses a republican rally

Abortion was one of the most poisonous issues in Irish life during the unhappy eighties. It was first raised by a coalition of conservative Catholic groups, which sponsored a constitutional referendum to outlaw the practice. It was passed by a 2 to 1 majority.

a strike and intimidation against the power-sharing Executive. The House of Commons removes the ban on Sinn Féin and the UVF.

27 May
Three loyalist bombs explode in Dublin and one in Monaghan, killing thirty-three people.

more than the voice of an embattled minority, holding the fort for liberal values while encircled by the vastly more powerful forces of conservative orthodoxy. There was an opportunity to broaden the paper's base and to give it an ever more central place in Irish life by recognising the increasing importance of women, of the young, and of a more independent-minded strain of Catholicism with little time for blind faith, unquestioning obedience, or direct church interference in political decisions. Gageby responded to these opportunities with detailed coverage of debates within the church, with the more sceptical and irreverent coverage of politics exemplified by John Healy's 'Backbencher' column, and with the increasing prominence of young women journalists, such as Mary Maher, Maeve Binchy,

tells Garret he can go on as much as he likes about not being beastly to Protestants, because she knows there's no harm in him really.

So that's all right.

But stay! There's something else. Cathleen summons her emanations: Charlie, and Garret and Michael hasten to her side. What can it be? She whispers.

Something about *abortion*? But that's prohibited by law. Surely she can't want the prohibition *repealed* …?

The lady's eye flashes: The emanations flicker and quail. The unthinkable is unthought. Then the message comes through: She wants the prohibition of abortion *enshrined in the Constitution*.

Enshrined, that's the idea. In the Constitution, get it? They get it.

Garret, writing: Let's see now. We take divorce *out* of the Constitution, and we put abortion *in*. What a super idea!

'Not secular merely, but Catholic as well.' Who was it said that? Pearse? Davis? Tone?

Michael: It was Connolly. James Connolly. His last words. It's always been Labour Party policy.

Charlie: Not merely will Fianna Fáil put the prohibition of abortion into the Constitution, but we'll put it into the National Anthem as well. *We're* unequivocal about these things. And it wasn't us said anything about divorce, one way or another. That was Garret.

and, later, Nell McCafferty. Even more remarkably, when he appointed Fergus Pyle as Northern Editor, resident in Belfast, *The Irish Times* became the first Dublin paper to have a full-time office there, a mark of how shallow southern anti-partitionism had become. Gageby, though born in Dublin, had grown up in Belfast, and his sense of Ireland as a 32-county entity meshed well with the new mood of cross-border friendship.

28 May

The power-sharing Executive resigns. The Assembly is prorogued the next day, and direct rule from London is reinstated.

The South Leinster Street bomb in Dublin in May 1974. Three bombs exploded within half an hour in different parts of the city. Twenty-five people died and over a hundred were injured. A further six people died in a car bomb explosion in Monaghan.

29 May

The strike by the Ulster Workers' Council ends.

7 June

The Price sisters abandon their hunger strike.

4 July

The British government publishes a white paper announcing a Constitutional Convention to try to formulate a system of government in

There were already signs, however, that change would not be easy on either side of the border. In 1966 the fiftieth anniversaries of both the Easter Rising and the Battle of the Somme provided an opportunity for conservatives on both sides to appeal to the sacrifices of the past. *The Irish Times* marked the anniversary of the rising with a supplement that eschewed piety and stressed the complexity of the event. Along with Nicholas Mansergh, Owen Sheehy-Skeffington, Owen Dudley Edwards and other historians, the contributors included the former diplomat and now academic Conor Cruise O'Brien, who had been associated with *The Irish Times* since his student days, when he was the paper's correspondent in Trinity College, Dublin. He used it as an opportunity for a left-wing critique of the contemporary Republic, comparing its reality with the ideals and example of James Connolly, which he characterised as 'what Ireland

Cathleen: All right, you know the score, the three of you. Get on with it.

As the emanations prepare to leave, Cathleen calls back Garret.

Cathleen (to Garret): I didn't tell you to take divorce out of the Constitution.

Garret (flickering slightly): No?

Cathleen: I told you you could *talk* about *trying* to take divorce out of the Constitution. I don't mind you talking. Shows we're not narrow-minded. If you ever try and do it though, which I doubt, I'll mark your card for you. Oh, and Garret, one other thing. You want to rewrite Articles Two and Three of the Constitution, is that right?

Garret (flickering): Yes, Mother.

Cathleen: Well, I want no messing with my Four Beautiful Green Fields. Remember that.

Garret: You can count on me, Mother.

Cathleen (softening): I know I can, Garret. Sometimes you have me upset with all that modern, liberal stuff. But you're a good boy, at heart. Mind the steps as you go out.

Seán MacBride (right) had one of the most extraordinary careers of the century. Revolutionary, barrister, politician and humanitarian, he was variously chief of staff of the IRA, Minister for External Affairs and Tánaiste, founder of Amnesty International, and holder of both the Lenin and Nobel Peace Prizes.

As I say, the lady has mellowed quite a bit, but you do still have to watch your step.

A reader objects that, in the above, I am joking about abortion, which is not a joking matter. I agree it is not a joking matter, and I am not joking about it. My joke is about collective hypocrisy: a form of joke for which there are respectable precedents, many of them of Irish origin.

The proposed imposition of a Constitutional prohibition, on top of existing Statutory prohibitions, will change nothing whatever in the realities of abortion. Irish women who want an abortion will continue to go where they can get it: to England, just as much beyond the reach of our Constitution as of our Statutes. If the Oireachtas were determined to deal with these realities, it would have to take measures to prevent pregnant women from leaving the jurisdiction. This would require provision for medical examination of all women of child-bearing age at ports, airports and Border posts.

Now, during the recent elections, 'Pro Life' lobbyists in some areas did ask candidates to support exactly those measures. These lobbyists were being perfectly logical and consistent, but that, of course, didn't get them any takers.

Measures of the kind proposed would be inconvenient, unpopular, unpleasant and expensive to administer. No political party will lumber itself with stuff like that. Constitutional amendment, on the other hand, costs little, sounds well, requires no follow-through, keeps you sweet with the lobby in question, and so saves you from being outflanked by the other fellow. Also such an amendment arouses no real opposition, since it is altogether devoid of any real effect, here and now.

In short, an ideal reform, which can be favoured by one and all.

You think I'm cynical? No, I accept that hypocrisy is inseparable from democracy, everywhere and always. As democracy is a good, we should be prepared to put up with some hypocrisy. But not too much, I hope.

And we don't have to put with too much, unless we want to. This is where democracy is different from all other political systems—Fascism, Communism, or whatever.

From them too, hypocrisy is inseparable; but under them hypocrisy is also compulsive. If you don't like the Leader or the Party, you'd better say you do, or lose your job, and perhaps your life.

Under democracy on the other hand, hypocrisy is voluntary. The citizens don't have to practise it, or require it (or

The poet Austin Clarke in old age

requires today.' 'Connolly's Worker's Republic is as far off as ever. The *Irish Independent* which in 1916 continued to call for more executions until it got Connolly, remained the paper of the Catholic bourgeoisie. No significant Labour movement exists North or South. The Labour Party has been dominated by dismal poltroons on the lines of O'Casey's Uncle Payther. The economic progress which has occurred was mainly due to external factors. The same educational system which Pearse condemned survives, controlled by the bishops. There is no cause in this anniversary year for self-congratulation.' By the end of 1968, however, Dr Cruise O'Brien had returned to Ireland and, partly as a result of private mediation by *The Irish Times* political correspondent, Michael McInerney, joined the Labour Party. When, just before Christmas 1968, he addressed a party meeting in Liberty Hall, the paper gave the event front-page coverage and carried the text of his speech.

It was clear that even the Republic was divided about the legacy of the rising. When Éamon de Valera, the living embodiment of that legacy, stood for re-election as President, he was

Northern Ireland that would command the widest possible support.

8 August
President Nixon of the United States resigns after the Watergate scandal.

5 October
IRA bombs explode in two pubs in Guildford, killing four members of the British army.

8 October
Seán MacBride is awarded the Nobel Prize for Peace.

Moccasin **Wallabees**   Kennys

BROWN, CALF,
BLUE, AMBER,
BROWN AND
SAND SUEDE.   PRICE £6.75   Stillorgan Shopping
Centre and
3, Grafton Street.

THE IRISH TIMES

PRICE 6p   DUBLIN, WEDNESDAY, FEBRUARY 2, 1972   No. 36,082   CITY

WINNING RENAULT FEATURES
Performance, comfort, extra features and large luggage
carrying capacity by admiring many and more other
drivers now to the Renault range of cars.

RENAULT

Distributed by Smiths (Distributors) Ltd.,
Deansgrange, Co. Dublin, Telephone 303711.

ANTI-BRITISH PROTEST GROWING

Dail adjourns, planes and newspapers blacked

HEATH WILLING TO MEET LYNCH?

IN ANOTHER DAY of massive anti-British protests and demonstrations, the Dail adjourned yesterday and Mr. Heath announced that Lord Chief Justice Widgery would conduct the inquiry into the Derry killings. B.E.A. and other British passenger aircraft did not land, and airport workers refused to handle British newspapers. There were a number of violent incidents in Dublin and Dun Laoghaire last night.

Before the Dail adjourned, the Taoiseach, Mr. Lynch, said that the madness that had brought death to Derry last Sunday would never be forgotten. In time it would be forgiven out of charity.

Last night, the British Premier was understood to be willing to meet the Taoiseach with the Opposition leaders, Mr. Cosgrave and Mr. Corish, in London.

In Northern Ireland there was continuing violence, and a British soldier was shot dead near Belfast city centre. In Co. Fermanagh a U.D.R. man was shot and wounded while feeding pigs. Belfast witnessed fires, shootings and hijackings on a wide scale.

Today is the national day of mourning, as 11 of last Sunday's victims are buried in Derry. One will be buried in Iskaheen, Co. Donegal today and the 13th will be buried in Derry tomorrow. Cardinal Conway will officiate at the Requiem Mass. In the Republic, there is a shutdown of business and industry and special Masses and religious services are being held. Few buses are expected to run, and other transport services, including Aer Lingus flights, will not operate during the period of the funerals.

In Northern Ireland, Catholic shops and businesses are closed. Yesterday flags on Government offices and public buildings flew at half-mast, as a gesture of sympathy for King Mahendra of Nepal.

In a tough speech at Stormont, the Northern Premier, Mr. Faulkner, said: "Those we represent also have their basic rights and will defend them." Unionist dissidents like Mr. William Craig and Democratic Unionists like the Rev. Wm. Beattie and Mr. John McQuade, joined with liberal Unionists in condemning Mr. Lynch, in a remarkable feeling of unanimity.

Mrs. Anne Dickson, a liberal Unionist, praised the British paratroopers, and Mr. Craig wanted the Bogside and Creggan areas of Derry ceded to the Republic. Mr. Faulkner accused Mr. Lynch of preaching sectarianism when the Taoiseach talked about giving money and support to "our people."

At least four Cabinet Ministers are expected to travel from Dublin to the Derry funerals today. For security reasons their names were not being disclosed last night.

Response to call for day of mourning is overwhelming

By Dermot Mullane

IRELAND TODAY will observe an unprecedented day of national mourning as the funerals of 12 of the 13 victims of Sunday's shooting in Derry take place. In an overwhelming response to the Taoiseach's call on Monday night for such a day, much of the country's commercial and industrial life will be halted while special religious services are held. Flags will be flown at half-mast from all public buildings.

It was clear last night that the country's response had gone far beyond mere compliance with the Government's suggestion that employers should be facilitated, without excessive inconvenience or loss of earnings, to attend religious services. Instead, shops and stores in many areas will remain closed throughout the day. Banks will be closed. Public transport services will be curtailed. Universities and schools will be closed.

Factories and other industrial concerns in many cases also will close for the entire day. Others will close for a period varying from one to three hours and many workers intend to donate half their day's pay to the relatives of those killed in Derry on Sunday. The port of Dublin will be closed throughout the day, and the country's three seaports will close for four hours during the day.

The President, Mr. de Valera, will attend a Solemn Requiem Mass in the Pro-Cathedral in Dublin at 11 a.m. today, which is being offered for the 13 victims.

At least four Cabinet Ministers will attend today's Derry funeral. Deputies will attend the Derry funeral in...

The offices of The Irish Times in Westmoreland street, Dublin, and in Cook street, Cork, will be closed to the public until 2 p.m. today.

Newsagents to open for limited time

THE District Council of the Federation of Retail Newsagents said last night that it had suggested that newsagents' shops should open for limited periods today to facilitate the purchase by readers of the Irish newspapers.

A statement said: "The dissemination of news being an essential service, particularly during this time of crisis, newsagents have a special role to play and have decided to open for a limited number of hours today. They will close for part of their normal business today in sympathy with the bereaved in Derry and to identify themselves with the national day of mourning."

However, a spokesman said last night that it already appeared quite clear that newsagents in some areas would not open at all today. Members of the federation in a number of areas had indicated that there would close all day as surrounding shops were doing so. He cited a number of areas in Dublin and Bray, Co. Wicklow, as places in which newsagents would not open.

...

*The door of the British Embassy, which was shattered by a bomb explosion early today.
—(Photograph: Pat Langan).*

People of Derry in vigil for dead

From Dick Grogan, in Derry

DERRY'S DEAD were carried to Creggan hill last night. All through the night, St. Mary's Church, high over the mourning city, was open, and the people came to pay their respects before the row of 13 coffins that lay on trestles inside the altar rails. In the 24 hours the sad processions from all parts of Derry arrived at Creggan. Each one was followed by hundreds of mourners through the darkened streets.

Today, in the biggest and most tragic multiple funeral the troubled city has yet seen, vast crowds including Church dignitaries and State representatives, are expected to accompany the burial processions.

Cardinal Conway and six Cabinet Ministers from the Republic will attend as two local bishops and 12 priests concelebrate Requiem Mass in St. Mary's for the dead.

Last night, just one priest, the Rev. George McLaughlin, a curate at St. Mary's, met each sad arrival at the church. As men linked arms to keep a path clear for the cortege to the church doors, crowds of people watched, and many women and children wept at each coffin was borne slowly up along the church to take its place, on trestles, beside the previous arrivals.

A litany of the names was whispered through the crowd as each one came—first McElhinney, then McGuigan, Nash and Doherty and Young, and so on ... until the last quiet cortege arrived from the farthest point of all, Waterside.

A simple prayer was recited by Father McLaughlin as men bore the coffins of their neighbours, relatives and friends into the church.

Powerful television lights threw...

TORIES TURN DOWN SECURITY TRANSFER

Wilson N.I. plan rejected

From James Downey, in London

THE BRITISH GOVERNMENT last night rejected the demands of Mr. Harold Wilson and the British Labour Party for the transfer of Northern Ireland security powers from Stormont to Westminster. The Home Secretary, Mr. Maudling, told the House of Commons at Westminster that such an action, quite apart from the serious practical difficulties involved, would be regarded by the Unionists as tantamount to direct rule.

At the end of the Northern Ireland debate, the Opposition divided the House on a motion which spoke of "the need for urgency in Government policy on security decisions and talks leading to a political settlement." The motion was defeated by 304 votes to 266, a Government majority of 38.

Last night marked the formal end of bipartisanship in Irish policy between the parties at Westminster. Mr. Wilson and other speakers on the Opposition side bitterly criticised Ministers for the delay in starting inter-party talks; complained that the British Army was acting, or appearing to act, at the behest of Stormont; and put the Labour front bench, along with back benches, firmly on the side of a united Ireland.

Mr. Wilson expressed his conviction that there could be no political solution without a united Ireland, with proper safeguards for the Protestants, "at the end of the road."

Earlier he had said of the reaction in the Republic to the Derry massacre: "Last week, Mr. Lynch arresting gunmen. Were he to do so today he would be driven from office. It is in a very real sense an all-Ireland problem." Mr. Wilson concluded his speech with the warning that it was the duty and responsibility of the British Parliament to do all in its power to ensure that the future history of Ireland "is not written in blood."

Ministerial speakers in the debate made it plain that the attitude of the British Government, on the...

Unionist Party begins to close ranks

By Henry Kelly

THE Unionist Party in the North, apparently divided in many ways on major issues, has begun to close ranks quickly in the face of what it and the Stormont Government now believe is an all-out effort by Mr. Lynch's Government in the Republic, working in co-operation with Northern Opposition groups, to try to impose unity on Ireland against Protestant and Unionist wishes.

This emerged clearly from a debate in the House of Commons at Stormont yesterday, which was ostensibly about the terrible events in Derry last Sunday, but which turned out in effect to be an expression of Unionist solidarity, whether in the robust terms of Mr. John McQuade, the Democratic Unionist M.P. for Woodvale, or the quieter but no less firm tones of Mrs. Anne Dickson, M.P. for Carrick and Long regarded as a moderate voice.

Even Mr. Phelim O'Neill, who had been described as "not untrue" in a report in this newspaper that he was so disgusted with sectarian politics that he was thinking of leaving the Unionist Party, was fairly definite about where he stood...

7 ATTACKS ON DUBLIN OFFICES OF U.K. FIRMS

Bomb rips out door of British Embassy

Irish Times Reporter

TWO BOMB explosions last night destroyed the Royal Liver Society branch office in Dun Laoghaire and blew a door out of the British Embassy, where thousands have been protesting about the Derry killings since Sunday.

In Grafton street, Dublin, windows in Austin Reed's and Cooks Travel Agency were smashed, while early this morning an attempt was made to set fire to the R.A.F.A. club in Earlsfort terrace. A petrol bomb was thrown at the ground floor window. The premises were not damaged.

At the embassy, four men, masked by stockings, walked out of a crowd of demonstrators outside the building last night and threw about 20 lb. of gelignite through the entrance.

The door was blown in and the façade was scorched, but the building, guarded by bullet-proof windows with reinforced steel shutters, suffered little damage. It stood, blackened and impassive, as the crowd of 7,000 sang "A Nation Once Again".

"We have almost destroyed the symbol of British imperialism in the 26 Counties", a spokesman for the political wing of the Provisionals told the demonstrators. "It will live for another day, another attack".

The crowd sang "The Soldiers' Song" and stood to watch fireworks soar high above the buildings. It was almost like a Guy Fawkes night in Trafalgar square, a little less spectacular, a little more dangerous and exciting.

The crowd, which had cheered on the embassy as speakers from the political wing of the Provisionals talked about the treachery of Mr. Jack Lynch in imprisoning their comrades, moved back when they were warned that a bomb might have been planted.

So did the gardai, who formed two lines along the northern and southern sides of the Embassy building, leaving a no-man's land of about 40 yards between. The crowd began to sing patriotic songs, all, including the gardai, standing to attention for the more "official" airs.

"DUMMY" FIRST

It was sometime before midnight when the masked men moved coolly from the crowd and walked towards the embassy. They hurled a "dummy" first, which kept everyone at a safe distance, then came the real thing and a garda who was not out of the way was the only person injured.

"A Nation Once Again" was struck up by the singers on the Provisional platform; the air was taken up, even by the girls who leaned through the windows of Hollis Street Hospital, and there was a silence of expectancy. Some people said a second bomb had been thrown into the embassy; if it had, it did not go off.

All that happened as foreign reporters marvelled at the military control of the crowd, was the throwing of a couple of petrol bombs, which fell short of their target and succeeded only in annoying a few newspaper reporters sheltering in doorways.

The worst incident was the destruction by fire of the Royal Liver Society district office at 106 Lr. George's street, Dun Laoghaire, last night, when a number of men broke into the building, and placed a bomb in it. A fire followed and spread quickly to furniture and carpets, Dun Laoghaire Fire Bri...

One killed, 5 wounded in North shooting

From Renagh Holohan

VIOLENCE AGAIN broke out in Northern Ireland yesterday and signs of mourning for the Derry victims were evident in all Catholic areas. There were disturbances and shutdowns in Omagh, Strabane, Limavady, Newry, Coalisland, Dungannon, Cookstown, Warrenpoint, Newtownbutler, Carrickmore and Draperstown.

A British soldier was shot dead in Belfast, another was wounded in the hand and a third hit in the leg, a member of the Ulster Defence Regiment was shot and wounded near the Border, a youth was also, and injured by troops in Lenadoon street, Belfast, and a woman was reported to be seriously ill last night after a shooting incident in east Belfast.

More barricades were being erected and there were numerous fires, shootings and hijackings. Army patrols were stoned and bottled, as well as fired at, all over west Belfast.

In Belfast last night, troops were fired on in Derrin pass, Rosnareen avenue, Islandbawn street, Glen road, Tullymore drive, Divis street, Slieve Gallion drive, Kennedy roundabout, and Monagh road. One soldier was hit in the hand and another wounded in the leg in Andersonstown. At the junction of Divis street and Percy street, the military believed that they hit one of their attackers when they returned fire.

Nail bombs were thrown at troops near Divis flats and at the junction of Cupar street and Falls road. Rubber bullets were used to disperse stone-throwing youths in Andersonstown. Two men were arrested in Andersonstown.

Most of West Belfast was littered yesterday with burned-out lorries, discarded barricades, bricks and stones. Men and youths stood round flashpoint corners; the Busy Bee in Andersonstown, the junctions of Falls road and Whiterock road, Whiterock road and Springfield road, and at Grosvenor road, Leeson street and Broadway.

Each time Army vehicles appeared out of the heavy mist, they were stoned.

Troops who stopped were in danger of being shot at, as happened at Leeson street, Andersonstown road, Hastings street and Glen road. Patrols also came under fire in Ballymurphy, Grosvenor road, the corner of Crumlin road and Chief street.

The East Belfast two buses were hijacked by young boys, reported to have been armed, in Mountpottinger road. One was set on fire at Thompson street and the other at Vulcan street in the Short Strand.

£4315

FOR YOU AT AGE 55

Many thousands of men and women in all walks of life are already on the way towards reaping the benefit of wise saving and are looking forward to a capital sum or private income for their later years. If you are aged 45 or younger you will, by setting aside regular monthly, half-yearly or yearly premiums of the required amount, ensure that at age 55 you will receive £4315 or a guaranteed monthly income for as long as you live. Moreover, any accumulated dividends would increase the amount of cash or income at age 55. If you are somewhat older than 45 even the fruits of your saving would come to you at, say, age 60 or 65.

the spy that came out with the gold!

EBS

THE DAY DAIL EIREANN CLOSED RANKS TO FORM A COMMUNITY

IRELAND said the Taoiseach, Mr. Jack Lynch, and he spoke to the nation in conditions of grave national danger, could look to Dail Eireann and have confidence in it...

Public Accounts Committee who are still investigating what happened in...

It was, frankly, unreal and utterly simplistic, but then the usual role of the human political condition that before the clichés of tribute wither on the graves, the battles start to grow again and are not far from grasping any more than last year's...

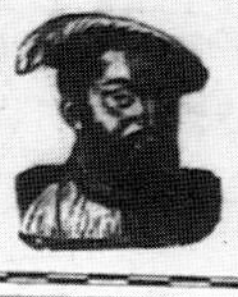

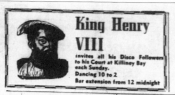

King Henry VIII

invites all his Disco Followers to his Court at Killiney Bay each Sunday.
Dancing 10 to 2
Bar extension from 12 midnight

THE IRISH TIMES

Price 7p — DUBLIN, SATURDAY, MAY 18, 1974 — No. 36,7[illegible] — SPECIAL

BADOIT Saint Galmier
EVIAN Cachat
NATURAL MINERAL WATERS
FROM FRANCE
P. J. NUGENT, 14 DAME STREET, DUBLIN 2

27 KILLED, OVER 100 INJURED IN FOUR CAR-BOMB BLASTS IN DUBLIN, MONAGHAN

Many women, children among victims; nationwide alert on danger of further bombs

THE NATION WAS stunned last night at the toll of 27 lives and over 100 serious injuries in car-bomb explosions which ripped through the centres of Dublin and Monaghan.

The three Dublin blasts, which occurred almost simultaneously at 5.30 p.m., killed 22 people and caused scores of terrible injuries — a toll far greater than any single bombing incident has taken in Northern Ireland since the troubles began there.

At least five people died in the Monaghan Town blast 90 minutes later, just before 7 p.m. Up to 20 were injured, and late last night four people were still unaccounted for.

The Cabinet met in emergency session at Government Buildings within an hour of the explosions. The Minister for Justice, Mr. Cooney, told the meeting that two of the three cars used in the Dublin bombings had been hijacked in Belfast yesterday.

An R.U.C. spokesman confirmed later last night that two of the cars had been hijacked in Belfast yesterday morning, both in Protestant areas. The owner of one was stopped at gun-point by three armed men, two whom held him hostage until 4 p.m. yesterday.

Gardai said that no warning was given before the Dublin explosions, which took place in Parnell Street, Talbot Street and South Leinster Street. Many women and young children were among the victims, as the bombs caused carnage among the crowds of late afternoon shoppers and workers making their way home.

A pre-determined emergency operation, the Dublin Disaster Plan, was activated, with all rescue and hospital services co-operating. Gardai declared a nationwide alert, warning that there was a danger of further bombs in every town and city.

The Taoiseach, Mr. Cosgrave, in a statement which he read on R.T.É. radio and television last night, expressed revulsion and condemnation and said that the Government was as yet unaware of the identity of those responsible.

"What has happened today," he said, "will help to underline the criminal folly and utter futility of violent action as a means for furthering political ends.

"It will also help to bring home to us here, in this part of our island, what the people in Northern Ireland have been suffering for five long years. Today's evil deeds will only serve to strengthen the resolve of those, North and South, who have been working for peace."

A Garda spokesman said just after midnight that the Dublin dead included 15 women: five men, and two children, both boys, aged 2½ years and 1½ years.

The U.D.A. and the U.V.F. denied responsibility. The Provisional I.R.A., in a statement, also denied involvement and condemned the bombings as "vile murder." Official Sinn Fein said in a statement: "We are quite sure that the Protestant workers in Belfast are as horrified at today's events as were their southern co-workers on Bloody Friday in July, 1972."

The Leader of the Opposition, Mr. Lynch, said that every organisation involved in the campaign of bombing in any part of our country over the past four years "has the blood of these innocent victims on their hands."

It was announced later last night that the Fine Gael Ard Fheis, which was due to begin in Dublin this morning, has been postponed.

Monaghan: 5 die and 28 injured

BOMB OUTSIDE PUB

FIVE PEOPLE were killed and 28 injured as a result of a massive car bomb which caused havoc in the centre of Monaghan town yesterday evening.

The bomb went off without warning at 7 p.m. outside Greacen's Bar, Church Square, which is the stopping place for the express bus service. The names of the casualties were not being released last night, but it is believed that Mrs. Peggy White, Belgium Square, Monaghan, who ran the upstairs lounge at Greacen's, much used by bus passengers, was one of those killed. All the fatal casualties appeared to have been in the bar, which was all but demolished, and local firemen, gardai and civilian assistants worked at great risk under the sagging upper storey of the building to extricate the dead and injured.

A pall of black smoke hung over the scene as a wooden cafe nearby and two cars blazed as the rescuers worked. One male victim taken from the bar was decapitated.

A large crater in the concrete street marked the spot where the bomb was planted and the blackened twisted wreckage had been hurled completely over a wrecked bus nearby. Pieces of the car had pierced the bodywork of other motor cars in the vicinity.

The Hibernian Bank building across the street from the pub, had all its windows and doors blown out and the roof wrecked.

EXTENSIVE DAMAGE

Very extensive damage was done to all the buildings in Church Square, including Monaghan courthouse and St. Patrick's parish church. Almost all windows within a radius of 200 yards were damaged, as well as many roofs, and it was dangerous to walk on footpaths. Doctors, priests and nurses worked among the smoke and debris and treated people for minor cuts and shock, apart from those taken to hospital.

While the ambulances raced through the streets, further panic spread as gardai warned of a suspect car in Dublin Street, which was completely evacuated. This car was cleared, however, within half an hour.

At Monaghan County Hospital, the staff worked desperately without attempting to list the casualties. As they worked, further calls came in for aid for elderly people who had collapsed following the explosion. Arrangements were made to clear the medical wards and house the patients fit to be moved in St. Davnet's Mental Hospital as a precaution against any further bombings last night. There were many stories of remarkable escapes, though the explosion occurred at the quietest time of day in the centre of the town. Mr. Jack McMahon said he was in a bar 50 yards from

UDA, UVF deny being responsible

THE UDA and the U.V.F. last night denied responsibility for the explosions but the U.D.A.'s press officer, Mr. Sammy Smyth, said: "I am very happy about the bombings in Dublin. There is a war with the Free State and now we are laughing at them."

Anothe U.D.A. spokesman said that the organisation should not need to be asked whether or not it was responsible. He added: "We completely deny any connection with this." He suggested that the Republic should look "a bit closer to home" for the culprits.

A U.V.F. statement said: "We want to make it quite clear that we are appalled by these explosions. It is indiscriminate and definitely against our policy. At the present time the U.V.F. have made a firm declaration that we will not engage in any physical activities including bombings or shootings.

"We at the moment are engaged in the political field of Northern Ireland and we believe that the political solution to Northern Ireland can only be found democratically by the people of Northern Ireland within Northern Ireland. Therefore we are not concerned with the policy of Eire or indeed the dictates of Westminster politicians."

Provisionals condemn murders

The Irish Republican Publicity Bureau (Provisional), in a statement last night signed by P. O'Neill, said that the I.R.A. utterly condemned "the vile murder and bombings" in Dublin and Monaghan.

It continued: "Needless to say, no branch of the Republican Movement was involved. The events of this afternoon highlight the farcical security situation in this part of the country, which is orientated towards assisting

A man calling himself Captain Craig last night rang the Northern office of *The Irish Times* to warn of two more bombs in Dublin which he said, "were not known about yet."

The man said he was speaking on behalf of the "Red Hand

Synod offers its sympathy

AT the General Synod of the Church of Ireland in Christ Church Cathedral, Dublin, delegates yesterday stood for a minute in silence after the Primate of All Ireland, the Most Rev. Dr. Simms, announced that three bombs had gone off in the city.

Dr. Simms said the Synod expressed its deep concern and sent a message of sympathy and concern to those who have been victims of this outrage.

Later the Synod approved a formal statement which said: "The General Synod of the Church of Ireland, currently meeting in Dublin, having heard of this evening's bomb outrages in this city, expresses to the chairman of the City Commissioners and to the citizens of Dublin its sense of shock and offers its deep sympathy to the bereaved and the injured."

On hearing of the explosions, the Archbishop of Dublin, the Most Rev. Dr. Buchanan, left the Synod Hall to visit victims at Jervis Street Hospital and to inspect the scene of the explosions.

ARMY BLOWS UP SUSPECT CARS

At about 6.50 p.m. yesterday, an Army bomb disposal officer inspected a suspicious package in Dublin's Ambassador Cinema, about 50 yards from the Parnell Street blast. It was found to be harmless.

The Army bomb disposal squad

Picture of death in a Dublin street

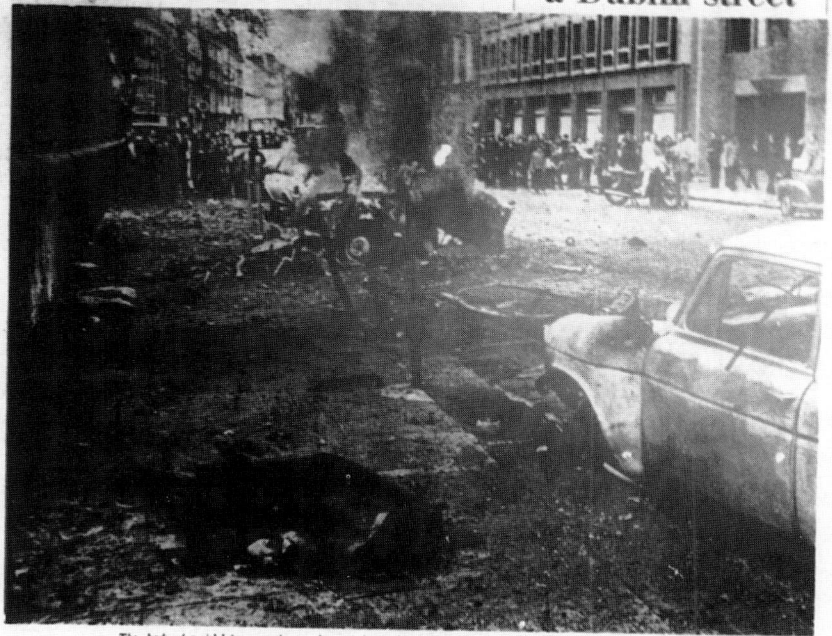

The body of a girl lying near the wreckage of the car-bomb in South Leinster Street, Dublin.—(Photograph: Pat Langan)

WORST MOMENT FOR HEAVY CASUALTIES

Hundreds in Talbot Street

By Nigel Brown and Geraldine Kennedy

IN TALBOT STREET, eye-witnesses said the bomb went off at 5.27. The street was crowded at the time. The car which contained the bomb was parked in Talbot Street, within 20 yards of the junction with Lower Gardiner Street.

The blast hit shoppers and other pedestrians, and cars parked within 50 yards were wrecked. Windows in shops and business premises were shattered all along the two streets. Some 10 cars were completely wrecked.

The dead and injured lay on the pavement, in the roadway and inside shop windows. A fleet of ambulances, private cars and a C.I.E. single-decker bus took the dead and injured, many of whom were badly multilated, to city hospitals.

Crowds stood among the debris in the street before gardai cleared Talbot Street and adjoining areas.

Several bodies were covered by newspapers from a nearby newsboy's stand, at the corner of Gardiner Street.

One girl was decapitated and at least one pedestrian, a girl, had a leg blown off. Two bodies in Guiney's window space were so badly multilated, according to an eye-witness, that they were fused together. A young girl was killed when blown off the pavement, through a door and into the basement of No. 19 Talbot Street. Several other pedestrians were thrown through shop windows by the force of the blast.

THE WRECKAGE

Most shop premises in the area were completely unrecognisable as all nameplates and windows had been blasted away and the contents of showcases were strewn round many streets. The air smelt heavily of burning and fumes filled the streets.

We saw two young men whose faces had been badly injured. Beside the newspaper stand a body lay on the pavement at the junction of Talbot Street and Gardiner Street. Another lay in the gutter on the opposite side of the road. Several more could be seen inside shop windows.

Ten minutes after the blast, the first ambulances had taken away some of the worst injured: they re- find out what had happened to them. People were sobbing and openly crying as gardai tried to clear the adjoining streets of the crowds of onlookers.

CORDONED OFF

It was at least 40 minutes, however, before all the injured had been taken to hospital and gardai then cordoned off the middle section of Talbot Street and began searching through the debris.

A 93-year-old woman was taken, badly shocked, from the top-storey of a house in Talbot Street. An elderly man, who was minding his two-year-old granddaughter, was helped from No. 47 Gardiner

(Continued in page 8)

Faulkner sees unity in suffering

In a message to the Taoiseach, Mr. Cosgrave, last night, the Northern Ireland Chief Minister, Mr. Faulkner, said: "It is with the deepest regret that my colleagues and I have heard of the atrocious outrage in Dublin. We in Northern Ireland, who have had to endure so much suffering and death in recent years, can appreciate fully the tragedy of those who have been struck down and the grief of those who have been bereaved or injured in your own capital.

"For far too long, those of us in Ireland who believe in the democratic process have had to endure the onslaughts of vicious and violent men. Whatever the differences of opinion which may exist in other matters, I believe the responsible people in Northern Ireland and the

Use of troops to man vital North services inevitable

THE USE of British troops to man power-stations and maintain essential services in Northern Ireland seemed inevitable last night, as the Ulster Workers' Council threatened a complete power shutdown from midnight. Extra troops are expected to arrive within the next 24 hours.

In a day of frenzied political activity and uncompromising statements from both sides, the Northern Secretary of State, Mr. Rees, said he would not negotiate with anyone engaged in a political industrial strike and the U.W.C. said that it had no alternative but to withdraw all remaining reserves of power from the grid.

Report: page 5.

Dugdale says she will fast as trial is fixed

The trial of Dr. Rose Bridget Dugdale was fixed for June 24th when she appeared before the Special Criminal Court in Dublin yesterday.

She is charged on 10 counts, which include the robbery of valuable oil paintings belonging to Sir Alfred Beit, on April 26th, and the possession of firearms.

Dr. Dugdale told the court that she proposed to go on hunger-strike if the four Irish people on hunger-strike in Britain were not released. After the hearing she was removed by helicopter to Limerick Prison.

Report: page 16.

Portuguese peace talks to be held in London

The new Portuguese Government has lost no time in making contact with African liberation organisations. It was announced in Dakar, Senegal, yesterday that cease-fire talks would start in London on May 25th between the Government and the P.A.I.G.C., the Guinea-Bissau self-proclaimed provisional government.

In Dar-es-Salaam, Frelimo, the Mozambique liberation organisa-

Bishop says majority backs power-sharing

The Bishop of Connor, the Rt. Rev. Dr. Butler, told the Church of Ireland Synod yesterday that he believed a high proportion of Protestants and Catholics in the North wanted to see power-sharing in Government succeed.

Report: page 13.

France prepares for knife-edge final poll

The final round of voting in the French presidential election takes place tomorrow. Opinion polls indicate that support for the two candidates, M. Giscard d'Estaing and M. François Mitterrand, is evenly balanced.

Report: page 7

Parking summons was dated next November!

Domhnall O Lubhlai, a Dublin teacher who was jailed for a short time last month when he refused to pay a parking fine because he was not issued with a summons in Irish, has received a summons in Irish for a parking offence — dated November 6th next.

Report: page 16

Cork and County Club to move house

The premises of the Cork and County Club have been sold to the Hibernian Insurance Company for demolition and development as an office block. The members of the club will, however, be given accommodation, at a nominal rent, in what their chairman, Mr. U. K. Bowen, described as "a fine modern club".

Report: page 16

Israeli raids on Lebanon continue

The Lebanese Defence Ministry yesterday reported that Israeli planes made a set of raids over southern Lebanon, resulting in at least one death. The raids followed a similar operation on Thursday in which 27 people were killed and over 138 wounded.

Report: page 7

Are all ALFA ROMEOS fabulously expensive? . . . NO!

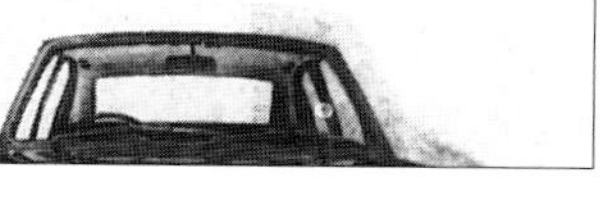

22 October

James Molyneaux is elected leader of the Ulster Unionists in the British House of Commons.

7 November

President Erskine Childers dies.

21 November

Twenty-one people die as IRA bombs explode in two pubs in Birmingham.

3 December

Cearbhall Ó Dálaigh is elected President.

22 December

The IRA declares a cease-fire in the wake of its secret talks with Northern Protestant ministers at Feakle, Co. Clare.

1975

2 April

The Provisional IRA explodes a bomb in Belfast as a warning to the British army because of its truce violations.

British troops on the streets of Belfat on the third anniversary of internment, 9 August 1975

opposed by Fine Gael's Thomas O'Higgins. Fianna Fáil blamed *The Irish Times*, which had insisted that the electorate ought to be given a choice of candidates, for the fact that there was a presidential election at all in 1966. Micheál Ó Móráin, Minister for Lands and the Gaeltacht, revealed the party's thinking in a speech in County Cork: 'For a time it appeared that there would not be any candidate opposing the President. *The Irish Times* spoke, however, demanding that Fine Gael oppose the President ... We all know *The Irish Times* is the mistress of the Fine Gael party and mistresses can be both vicious and demanding. Now it may be necessary for Fine Gael to jump to the crack of *The Irish Times's* whip and gather the relics of the old ascendancy around them. It would, however, be a sad day for our people if the outlook of the President of the Irish people was forged and shaped by the occupants of a back room in Westmoreland Street.' The Fine Gael candidate, Thomas O'Higgins (who had replied that on the subject of mistresses he bowed to the superior knowledge of Mr Ó Móráin), came within ten

even tolerate it) on the part of their representatives. But they often do some or all of these things quite voluntarily. That happens here, perhaps rather more than in other countries.

Yeats was quite wrong. We ought to thank God that we have a lively democracy and a commitment to it. If we let more hypocrisy into it than is probably good for us, it is not for a journalist to complain too much.

The mark is there, to shoot at.

from The Irish Times **1983**
20 JANUARY

Top Garda officers may face dismissal

By Peter Murtagh, Security Correspondent

The Government is considering dismissing a number of very senior officers in the Garda Síochána as a result of the investigation into allegations that the former Minister for Justice, Mr Doherty, authorised telephone tapping against journalists.

Government sources said yesterday that there would be consequences affecting Garda officers following the disclosure that gardaí were involved in bugging a political conversation.

It is believed that some Cabinet members hope resignations will be forthcoming. However, if they are not, the Government is understood to be willing to sack people if necessary.

It was also learned yesterday that a high-ranking officer in the Intelligence and Security Branch was involved in supplying the miniature tape recorder used in the bugging and that the entire operation was done with the knowledge of at least one member of Mr Haughey's Cabinet ...

The tapping was authorised by warrants signed by Mr Doherty. Prior to the warrants being signed, the Garda Commissioner, Mr Patrick McLaughlin, made a recommendation approving them.

It is believed that Mr McLaughlin was asked to do this by another senior Garda officer ...

The secret monitoring of a prominent Fianna Fáil dissident's private conversation, and the official tapping of the telephones of two journalists, Bruce Arnold of the *Sunday Independent* and Geraldine Kennedy, then of the *Sunday Tribune*, who were closely involved in reporting the rebellion against Mr Haughey's leadership of Fianna Fáil, strengthen the view that the surveillance was concerned with internal Fianna Fáil divisions and not at all with matters of national security.

The recording of Dr O'Donoghue's conversation is believed to have been made during a private meeting with Mr O'Malley or another anti-Haughey TD, possibly in a room in Leinster House. The equipment used, a miniature tape recorder, was supplied by Garda sources, according to Mr Noonan's statement.

Editorial

Can of Worms

It may be tempting to regard phone-tapping and bugging as side-shows compared to the economic crisis facing the country. But, arguably, they pose the greater threat.

Economic difficulties are not new, serious though they may be, and there is no great mystery about either their causes or their remedies.

There are, however, some fundamental planks in a democracy, any tampering with which must be seen as extremely grave. One of these is the political independence and reliability of the police force. Any serious questioning of that weakens the citizen's trust in the institutions of the State—a trust that is essential for the proper conduct of parliamentary democracy.

Éamon de Valera's funeral in August 1975

thousand votes out of the 1.1 million cast of beating de Valera.

And if the glamour of 1916 was fading in the Republic, the North was bitterly divided about the meaning of that year. In May 1966 a small group of Belfast loyalists who had revived the name Ulster Volunteer Force in memory of the Ulster Protestants killed on the Somme shot dead a young Catholic labourer, John Scullion, who had the misfortune to be drunk and singing republican songs. A month later four young Catholic barmen who had been drinking after hours in a pub off the Shankill Road were shot at. One, Peter Ward, was killed, and two of the others were seriously wounded. Three men, among them Gusty Spence, were soon charged with his murder. Terence O'Neill flew in from a commemoration on the Somme to announce the banning of the UVF. The past and the present seemed strangely and dangerously intertwined.

The prospects for change received another setback in July 1968 when Pope Paul VI published the encyclical *Humanae Vitae*, reaffirming the church's ban on all means of artificial contraception and setting in the process strict limits to the liberalising forces unleashed by the Second Vatican Council. At this time there were about twelve thousand women taking the contraceptive pill in the Republic.[3] *The Irish*

22 July

Farmers hear that they are to get a £17 million increase in their incomes through the EEC.

31 July

Three members of the Miami Showband and two members of the UVF, dressed as UDR men, are killed by a bomb being carried by the UVF.

15 August

Six Irish men are jailed for the previous year's Birmingham pub bombings.

29 August

Éamon de Valera dies in Co. Dublin, aged ninety-two.

16 September

Three men and a woman appear in court in England charged with bombings in Guildford and Woolwich in 1974.

3 October

A Dutch businessman, Dr Tiede Herrema, is abducted, and his kidnappers threaten to kill him unless three prisoners in the Republic are released.

Times prominently reported the views of Rev. James Good, professor of theology at University College, Cork: 'I have no doubt that the document will be rejected by the majority of Catholic theologians and by Catholic lay people. For my own part, as a teacher of theology, philosophy and medical ethics, I cannot see my way to accepting the teaching on contraception put forward in this document.' His words, as the paper noted in an editorial, were 'unthinkable in the context of a papal decision until now.' It also quoted the prominent Dublin gynaecologist Karl Mullen, who was markedly sanguine: 'Really, there has not been much widespread prescribing of the Pill in this country as a pure contraceptive, but it is used for medical reasons. I feel that very few Irish girls will take contraceptives without medical reasons, and for this reason the Pope's announcement is unlikely to have any effect here.' The paper's own analysis was that 'the document is essentially a reiteration of the

Another related plank is the citizen's right to assume that his privacy is respected, and that it will not be invaded by authority unless he or she gives reasonable cause for that authority to suspect he or she is involved in crime or subversion. In this, as in many other respects, the journalist is the representative citizen, the one who asks questions on behalf of the ordinary man in the street.

———

In this State ... such fundamentals have been taken for granted. To be able to take such things for granted is something to be cherished. The Garda Síochána and the Army have a record of which we can be proud.

Now the Government confirms that these fundamentals have been tampered with ... It is the urgent duty of this Government to make sure nothing of the like happens again, or can happen again ...

The only way, after the Government revelations about listening-in, would seem to be a full sworn inquiry. Then, presumably, the whole of our security and intelligence workings would have to be dragged into the light of day. Could this happen? It is unlikely. The Government will have to fall short of such a procedure. For, if they establish an investigation on a limited basis, the worst will be thought of them, and they dare not, for obvious reasons, expose all our security arrangements. But resignations will be in order ...

from The Irish Times
17 JULY **1985**

The lost potential of Geldof's generation
Conor Brady

Here are another few reasons why I'm cheering for Bob Geldof.

Because I have been watching French television for three weeks and wincing every time Ireland is mentioned. TF2 first runs through the domestic news, then the international stories and finally on to the standard wars and disasters slot. 'Liban' comes up, with shots of mangled bodies and blasted cafes. Then, perhaps, 'Afrique du Sud', with milling crowds and shouting policemen. And then, maybe one evening in three, a shot of green fields or redbricked streets with the voice-over recounting the day's bombing, or the rioting or the shooting in 'l'Irlande du Nord'. There is where we are bracketed ...

The unique Bob Geldof. Outraged by African famines, the former lead singer with the Boomtown Rats organised the huge Band Aid concert at Wembley in London, which raised over £70 million in aid and became a model for further such initiatives.

I'm cheering for Geldof because, for a change, my country and my nationality got themselves a mention before the wider world for something other than violence and killing; because something organised and run by an Irish person did not fall short of expectations; because, although so many things characterise us as a slovenly, careless people, Geldof's marathon concert and Ireland's response to it showed that we can still be inventive, thorough and generous.

I have never met Bob Geldof but I think I know quite a few young Irish people like him. They are different even from people three or four years older in a number of aspects. Some sociologist has said that 1950 is the great attitudinal watershed in Ireland; those born before it see things very differently from those born after. They are, I think, less self-conscious than their immediate elders about their Irishness. They are tougher, for they have a harder time of it than we of the pampered Sixties. But the really significant difference between them and their seniors, I think, is that large numbers of them choose to disengage from this society, rather than get into debate about it and seek to change it.

Their seniors battled it out with their churchmen, arguing over and challenging Church teaching, for example, on Humanae Vitae. They signed on at the university branches of Fine Gael and Labour (some even joined Fianna Fáil). Most of those who mixed it with the bishops seemed to go into journalism or teaching. Quite a few of those who went into politics are now Ministers or members of the Oireachtas.

The post-1950 people generally seem to approach things differently. The gap between their realities and the society about them seems to be so enormous that they will not even attempt to bridge it. They go their own way, make their own rules and get on with their own lives. I remember the night Geldof went on the Late Late Show and, in so many words, told this society to go and copulate with itself. When one considers the claptrap and farce of the so-called Pro-Life amendment, the agony of the amendment of the contraceptives law, the pathetic attempts to find work for the young—all this and much more—one can see why so many of his peers have adopted a similar attitude.

Geldof is an unusual and gifted individual, but not unique. There are hundreds of thousands of young Irish people with a good deal in common with him. Somehow we have failed to tap their potential, to mobilise their capacities and their sense of idealism. What a terrible waste of energy and resources and enthusiasm, while so many small, but

A car bomb in Belfast

Church's claim to be the one true interpreter of the moral law. It seems as if the old fortress mentality of the Vatican has come back, this time as the staunch, beleaguered citadel against modern promiscuity.'

For conservatives, that promiscuity—verbal as well as physical—was embodied in the figure of the long-haired hippy student. Student radicalism began in Trinity College, Dublin, with the formation of a group calling itself the Internationalists, whose activists, however, as the historian Liam de Paor wrote in 1969, were 'readily identifiable as "outsiders" because of their largely English membership and their obsessive interest in English politics.'[4] But, under the influence of the Paris disturbances of 1968, of student involvement in the civil rights movement in Northern Ireland and of the student protests against the Vietnam war in the United States, radical ideas began to affect a significant minority of middle-class youth.

The presence of this new and disturbing minority in Irish life had already been disclosed to an audience far beyond the colleges and bookshops of Dublin. In March 1966 a Trinity student, Brian Trevaskis, was invited on to the immensely popular RTE television programme, the 'Late Late Show', presented by Gay Byrne,

7 November

Kidnappers surrender to gardaí and soldiers, releasing Dr Tiede Herrema unharmed.

29 November

The UDA explodes a bomb at Dublin Airport, killing one person.

5 December

Internment is ended in Northern Ireland.

7 December

Four IRA men hold two people hostage in a flat in Balcombe Street, London. The siege lasts for five days before they surrender.

because he had written a play for the college drama society. He was supposed to discuss drama with Wesley Burrowes, the script-writer for the equally popular RTE serial 'The Riordans'. Instead, a remark he made about the new Catholic cathedral in Galway being a 'ghastly monstrosity' led to a heated debate on the role of the church. Trevaskis went on to praise Noel Browne, to attack the Archbishop of Dublin, Dr John Charles McQuaid, and to decry the treatment of the novelist John McGahern, who had been in effect sacked from his job as a national teacher after one of his books was banned and whom Trevaskis described as a 'martyr'. Even more sensationally, he referred to the Bishop of Galway, Dr Michael Browne, as a 'moron'. The following Tuesday, Dr Browne issued a statement declaring that he was 'not surprised at being called a moron by a student of Trinity College but I am surprised at a means of national communication, paid for by the people, being made available for abuse which is heard over the whole nation.' The controversy intensified when Trevaskis appeared on the 'Late Late Show' again the following week, ostensibly to apologise for his use of the word 'moron'. As soon as he had done so, however, he added that 'the Bishop of Galway knows the meaning of the word "moron", but does he know the meaning of the word "Christianity"?'[5]

The church, politicians and the provincial press were outraged, but *The Irish Times* was notably supportive of Gay Byrne and, if not necessarily of Brian Trevaskis's views, of his right to express them. An editorial after his first appearance suggested that the hysterical reaction to his comments was far more dangerous than the comments themselves: 'more harm is likely to result if the lid is screwed down than if, on occasions, an excess of steam gets blown off in unguarded moments.' The leader-writer took the opportunity too to point out the huge disjunction between private and public speech in Ireland. 'In no country is there more trenchant private discussion than there is here; but the

important, things remain to be done which could make this country a better place to live.

from The Irish Times
14 AUGUST **1985**

'Moving statue' vigil likely to draw 20,000

From Dick Hogan, in Cork

At least 20,000 people are expected to take part tomorrow in a twelve-hour Rosary vigil at the grotto in Ballinspittle, Co Cork, where the 'moving statue' was first reported at the end of last month.

Tomorrow's Rosary, in honour of the Feast of the Assumption, will almost certainly draw visitors from all over Munster and CIE will lay on special buses to the grotto from various destinations. CIE has been providing a regular service from Cork city centre to the shrine and a company spokesman said yesterday this would continue as long as demand existed.

The novelist Kate O'Brien, who died in 1974

Unemployment remained a depressingly intractable problem in the Republlic throughout the seventies and eighties

For the mobile chip vans as well as nearby pubs and shops in Ballinspittle, business has reached record levels since two elderly women taking an evening stroll reported seeing the statue move.

Bord Telecom has installed two new telephone kiosks in the village and Cork County Council has helped with the construction of ladies' and men's toilets near the grotto, which is now being visited by about 10,000 each evening.

The Grotto Committee, using land provided by a local farmer, has also built a car park about five minutes walk from the shrine.

The Committee has reacted to the findings of a team from the Department of Applied Psychology at University College, Cork, which said that a perfectly simple explanation existed for the moving statue.

Led by Mr Jurek Kirakowski, the team conducted experiments at another grotto last week and, using two hitchhikers as 'guinea pigs', succeeded in achieving the same results. Mr Kirakowski said his team had proved that light conditions as well as neck strain could explain the 'movements'.

However, the Grotto Committee suggested that perhaps Mr Kirakowski's team was suffering from neck and eye strain and they noted in a chilly response that a number of the psychologists were wearing glasses. They also wondered

iconoclast at the bar becomes meeker than milk when he is given an opportunity to express himself in public. This discretion, to give it its polite name, arises, not from delicacy of feeling, but from the sheer craven fear that the speaker of home truths in public will suffer for it privately.'

Another editorial after Trevaskis's second appearance marked the fact that his—and Gay Byrne's—refusal to recant under pressure from political and religious quarters was a moment of real significance. 'The entire incident may yet prove to be the best thing that has happened to Irish television. Certainly the manner in which the crisis was met by Gay Byrne and those higher up, whose nerves must have been badly shaken by the pious thunderings of outraged county councillors, proves that there are some people in television not afraid of ideas and not intimidated by sanctimonious outbursts of self-righteous, self-appointed guardians of the public morals.'

These remarks may have been made in relation to RTE but they were clearly also intended as a declaration of intent on the part of *The Irish Times* itself to encourage the new

13 July

The Adoption Act allows for adoptive parents not being of the same religion as the child.

13 August

Thousands turn out for the funeral of three children who were killed when a car driven by an IRA member crashed into them.

14 August

The first in a short-lived series of peace demonstrations is led by Mairéad Corrigan and Betty Williams.

24 August

The Government announces that EEC grants and subsidies reached £121 million in 1975.

2 September

The report of the European Commission on Human Rights is published and finds the United Kingdom guilty of torturing republicans in Northern Ireland.

24 September

The President signs the Criminal Law Bill but refers the Emergency Powers Bill to the Supreme Court to test its constitutionality.

15 October

Following the President's consulting of the Council of State, the Supreme Court finds that the Emergency Powers Bill is constitutional.

18 October

The Minister for Defence, Patrick Donegan, attacks President Ó Dálaigh's treatment of the Emergency Powers bill.

October 1968 in Derry changed everything. On the fifth, the RUC batoned a banned civil rights march off the streets, unleashing the wave of civil unrest that spawned the modern Troubles. Here, a sit-down protest takes place in Guildhall Square on 19 October.

openness of discussion. For it was clear that Brian Trevaskis was not alone, particularly among the young. Liam de Paor reported that 'in late 1968 and early 1969, the observable brisk trade in paperback copies of works by Marcuse, Guevara, Mao, Debray, Lévi-Strauss, Camus and others, showed that the American New Left ideology was being reconstructed in some form in Dublin.'[6]

In February 1969 a vaguely radical group, Students for Democratic Action, led an occupation of the administrative offices of University College, Dublin, demanding reforms in the management of the university and the quality of the education it provided and a delay in the movement of students to the new campus in Belfield until proper library facilities were available there. A mass meeting of about three thousand students then voted to endorse the occupation while at the same time calling for

whether the team believed in God and, finally, they challenged the psychologist to a public debate in Ballinspittle. So far, the challenge has not been taken up ...

from The Irish Times AUGUST **1990**

More and More Noise

John Waters

It is Sunday afternoon. Two young men, neither of them yet twenty, stand talking in the Main Street, Longford. They are part of a larger group of young people, gathered in the middle of town, the way young people will gather everywhere. The two young men are addressing one another in a playful, good-humoured fashion. Then, making a shouted arrangement to meet later on, they move off in opposite directions. Immediately, one of them turns around and shouts after his departing companion: 'Good luck, yebollixye.'

The second man then turns around and rejoins:

Bernadette Devlin speaking in Guildhall Square, Derry, after the arrival of the People's Democracy march from Belfast on 4 January 1969. The march had been assailed by loyalists along the route, most notoriously at Burntollet Bridge, where the attackers included off-duty B Specials.

'Yakuntya.'

The first man again counters with, 'Yebollixye.'

'Yakuntya.'

'Yebollixye.'

This bizarre responsorial psalm continues for what seems like two or three minutes, long after one of the young men has turned the corner onto Ballymahon Street and disappeared.

'Yakuntya.'

'Yabollixya.'

I scan dozens of faces around the street for signs of disapproval or distaste. No one appears to be listening.

Nobody would try to suggest that this form of 'communication' is unique to Longford, or that it is employed by a majority of people there or anywhere else. But neither is it an isolated incident. If pressed to characterise or quantify it, I would say that, in my experience, an increasing number of people, particularly younger people, are 'communicating' with one another in this manner.

it to be suspended in order to facilitate negotiations with the college authorities. Some members of the academic staff came out in support of the students, and others made sympathetic noises.

This Irish version of the worldwide student revolt was not, in spite of the fantasies of some participants, even potentially revolutionary. One well-disposed UCD academic, Liam de Paor, noted: 'The ideological innocence (and indeed the innocence of ideas of almost any kind) of Irish students is an important element in the UCD situation ... Today's student activists do not, by and large, find themselves moved by sympathy for the plight of their fellows at the lower end of the social scale in the same way as many students of the thirties did, nor do they have the same confidence that a model of the good society, in the Soviet Union or elsewhere, exists for emulation. Their

22 October
President Cearbhall Ó Dálaigh resigns.

3 December
Dr Patrick Hillery is inaugurated as President.

1977

16 June
Jack Lynch becomes Taoiseach.

1 July
Garret FitzGerald replaces Liam Cosgrave as leader of Fine Gael.

10 October
Mairéad Corrigan and Betty Williams of the Peace People are awarded the Nobel Peace Prize and $167,000.

1978

17 January
The Well Woman Clinic, offering family planning, opens in Dublin and is picketed by a group calling itself Mná na hÉireann.

18 January
The British
government is
found guilty in
the European
Court at
Strasbourg of
'degrading and
inhuman
treatment' of
fourteen internees
in Northern
Ireland in 1971.

6 August
Pope Paul VI dies.

29 September
Pope John
Paul I dies.

1979

30 March
Ireland joins the
European Monetary
System, cutting links
with sterling.

29 April
The Catholic Guild
of Pharmacists say
they will not sell
contraceptives.

4 May
The leader of the
Conservative
Party, Margaret
Thatcher, is
elected Prime
Minister, the first
woman to hold
the post.

*Neil Blaney, the powerful Minister for Agriculture,
was among those sacked by Jack Lynch over the arms
affair. He was charged along with Haughey and the
others, but the charges against him were dismissed at a
preliminary hearing. Here he is carried from Dublin
District Court by his supporters.*

attitudes are more negative. They oppose capitalist society because, largely, they are dissatisfied with what it has to offer them.'[7]

Although the occupation ended quickly and without violence, the disturbances lasted for over three weeks, and their effects continued to be felt well into the seventies in a persistent strain of student radicalism. Some of this inevitably fed into *The Irish Times*. One of the most radical of the SDA leaders, Kevin Myers, subsequently joined the paper as a journalist and became in time one of its most prominent columnists, though not one who could reasonably be described as left-wing.

If the protest movement in the South was rather tame and innocent, in the North it took on

I do not believe that this is to do with mere ignorance or yobbery. It is, I believe, just one more symptom of the malaise which besets much of modern Irish life, and each one of us to one degree or another. It is part of the way we protect ourselves from the truth.

Economists will, naturally enough, give an economic explanation for everything. A leading Irish economist once tried to persuade me that everything that happens in Ireland should be compared only with phenomena in areas with a comparable population and economic situation. Yorkshire, suggested the particular economist, was quite a suitable model for comparison with this country. But when one sees bookshops closing down all over Ireland, to be replaced by American-style video stores, it is precious little comfort to think that we probably still have a few bookshops more than Yorkshire. Bookshops close down, not because people have no money, but because they have no inclination to buy books. Similarly, people address one another in expletives, not because they know no better, but because they are afraid of knowing too much.

The Get Up the Yard Syndrome has always been a strong feature of life in the country. This was the way a community protected itself against deviance and eccentricity, and attacked conceit and insincerity. To return to a country town after a short absence with the merest hint of an accent, or other airs or graces, was to be slagged unmercifully. The Yabollixya Syndrome is simply an escalation of this. There is a belief at large that, in the new wave of emigration, it is the clever who go and the slow who stay. This is a false impression: quite often the factors which decide who goes and who stays have more to do with personal and family considerations than with academic attainment.

A reasonable proportion of those who remain are clever as well—in fact, given the nature of the society in which they remain, far cleverer than they need to be, and certainly far cleverer than it is wise to admit. Being clever in a small Irish town means having to be aware of too much pain, too much unhope, too much despair. And so you accommodate. Those who remain speak in a common language, a language which allows them to relate to one another without having to betray how they really feel. This is the language of the gibe, the cheerful obscenity and the snort of derision. It is a form of self protection, which allows one to live in a society in which one has little choice and no control.

The tendency of the mass consumer culture to make more and more noise while saying less and less is aped within

The Birmingham Six on their release from prison. They had served sixteen years for a crime they did not commit.

the society which it invades. The name of the game in much of modern Ireland is to pretend to know as little as possible, to hold no opinions other than on matters of no importance and to use no words which are bigger than 'sausages' or 'galvanise'.

Thus, the community, like a frightened hedgehog, rolls itself into a ball. Nothing's changed. Life goes on. Geddup yabollixya. Nothing of any value originates from within the individual or the community. Everything is received: cultural values, notions of style and sophistication, even analyses of your own situation. Clubs called 'Blooms', 'Stringfellows' and 'Paris' pump out music to audiences comprised mostly of teenage boys who just want to jump up and down to the Waterboys. The girls have either left or are too busy studying so as to ensure that they will not be the ones to stay behind. But nobody notices because the Universal City continues to maintain the semblance of sophistication, and the faculties

a far more urgent edge. The Northern Ireland Civil Rights Association, drawing support from Catholic and Protestant liberals, from nationalists and from students, had been inspired by the movement for black liberation in the United States to demand an end to institutionalised discrimination against Catholics in housing and local government. These demands, modest in the context of western European democracy, were, in the one-party Unionist state in which O'Neill's reformist rhetoric had not been translated into real reform, potentially explosive. On 5 October 1968 things moved beyond the point of no return when the RUC attacked a small civil rights demonstration in Derry. The march had been banned by the Minister of Home Affairs at Stormont, William Craig, but went

27 *August*
*Lord Louis
Mountbatten
is blown up
by the IRA
off the coast of
Co. Sligo.*

29 *September*
*Pope John
Paul II visits
Ireland, staying
until 1 October
and celebrating
Mass in the
Phoenix Park,
Dublin.*

*Jack Lynch resigns
as Taoiseach.
Charles Haughey
takes over the
position two
days later.*

1980

3 April

*Three members of
the staff of Kincora
Boys' Home in
Belfast are charged
with acts of gross
indecency against
those in their care.*

27 October

*Republicans in
Long Kesh begin
a hunger strike in
protest at the
loss of special-
category status.*

18 December

*The hunger strike
is called off after
Cardinal Ó
Fiaich suggests
that there will be
movement, and
the republican
prisoners state
that they have
received a
document from
the British
government
conceding their
demands. The
British deny this.*

*Jack Lynch won the greatest landslide in Irish electoral history in 1977 when Fianna Fáil captured 84 seats on a give–away
manifesto that, when implemented, retarded economic development in the Republic for the next fifteen years.*

ahead anyway with three British Labour Party
MPs, the Republican Labour MP for West
Belfast, Gerry Fitt, and the Nationalist politicians
Eddie McAteer, Austin Currie and Ivan Cooper
at its head. Shortly after it set off the RUC
charged the marchers, using what Fergus Pyle in
The Irish Times described as 'a brutal and sickening
display of what can only be called concerted
violence,' punching and batoning them. A call by
County Inspector William Meharg for his men to
'hold their hands, please,' seemed to signal an end
to the batoning, but, as Pyle reported, 'instead of
a pause, this announcement was the prelude to a
methodical and efficient movement forward by
the police, hitting everything in front of them.
Some people in the crowd tackled them back and
poles from placards were flying through the air.'
The police then began spraying the street
indiscriminately with water cannons. Television
images of this violence, captured by the RTE
cameraman Gay O'Brien, shocked public opinion

which would allow society to see what's really happening
have begun to atrophy as a result of the same process. People
stare at 'Neighbours' in smoke-filled bars and imagine
themselves to be at the centre of the universe.

Who says the system doesn't work?

from The Irish Times **1991**
15 MARCH

Birmingham Six free and angry

**By Frank Millar, Carol Coulter, Paul O'Neill
and Donal Conaty, in London**

The Birmingham Six spent their first night of freedom
in over sixteen years in London last night after
earlier expressing their anger at the miscarriage of
justice which had kept them in prison since 1974.

The decision to release the men has thrown the
British legal system into confusion and was followed by
the announcement of a Royal Commission on Criminal

Justice which will examine miscarriages of justice and make recommendations.

The six men were released by the Court of Appeal at about 3.40 p.m. yesterday. The final words spoken to them in court by Lord Justice Lloyd were: 'You are free to go as soon as the formalities are completed.'

At an impromptu press conference on the road outside the Old Bailey, the six men expressed their anger and frustration at their years of imprisonment for crimes they did not commit. As they emerged from the building shortly after 4 p.m., dressed in suits and ties, they were embraced by members of their families and cheered by hundreds of well-wishers.

Also outside to meet them was the British Labour MP, Mr Chris Mullin, who has championed the men's case since 1985, and by Mr Paul Hill, one of the Guildford Four, also released by the Court of Appeal in October 1989.

Within an hour of the appeal court's decision, the British Home Secretary, Mr Kenneth Baker, announced in the House of Commons the establishment of a Royal Commission on Criminal Justice which will report within two years, to be followed, according to Mr Baker, by 'substantial legislation'.

Mr Baker also announced yesterday that the hunt for the real Birmingham bombers is to be resumed by a special West Midlands police squad. A Home Office spokesman added that the squad would now review the findings of the inquiry by the Devon and Cornwall police which led to the successful Birmingham Six appeal, and it would also 'follow up any new lines of investigation that may come to light'.

At a press conference later at Columban Fathers House in north London, one of the six men, Mr Paddy Hill, bitterly denounced what he described as the Irish Government's lack of interest in the case until very recently. 'I have no intention of meeting Mr Haughey,' he told a questioner.

The Government in a statement warmly welcomed the release of the Six and 'the final vindication of their innocence'. The British authorities must now ensure that the level of compensation paid to the men is commensurate with the scale of the injustice, the statement said.

The President, Mrs Robinson, said she was 'delighted at the release of the Birmingham Six and extends to them and their families every good wish for the future'.

The court's decision to allow the men's appeal, their third since 1975, came after attempts by counsel for the Director of Public Prosecutions to argue that the original verdicts were 'safe' but not satisfactory.

Edmund Garvey, commissioner of the Garda Síochána from 1975 to 1978

around the world and created such anger within Northern Ireland that the slide towards chaos became unstoppable.

In January 1969 a march organised by a small student group, People's Democracy, was viciously attacked by Paisley's supporters, some of whom were later identified as members of the auxiliary police force, the B Specials, at Burntollet bridge outside Derry. Remaining Catholic confidence in the RUC completely collapsed. Barricades were erected on several roads leading to the Catholic Bogside area of Derry. When an increasingly isolated O'Neill tried to calm the situation by announcing an official inquiry into the disturbances, two members of his government resigned and twelve of his MPs called for his resignation. O'Neill responded by calling an election, in which he failed to get the overwhelming support he had demanded, and a new generation of Catholic politicians, including John Hume and Paddy O'Hanlon, began to replace the old-style Nationalist Party.

O'Neill tried, belatedly and under pressure from an increasingly alarmed British government,

1981

13 January

Sixty 'blanket men' in 'H blocks' of Long Kesh agree to end their dirty protest as soon as the rights under their former political status are reinstated.

6 February

Hundreds of loyalists wave legally held guns in front of Ian Paisley as the 'Third Force' paramilitary organisation is revealed in public.

14 February

Forty-eight people die in a fire in the Stardust dance-hall in Dublin. It is later found that the fire was started deliberately.

5 May

Bobby Sands MP, an IRA prisoner and hunger-striker, dies in Long Kesh after sixty-six days on hunger strike for the reinstatement of political status.

11 June

The general election produces a hung Dáil, resulting in a coalition

Government of Fine
Gael, Labour, and
independents.

30 June
Garret FitzGerald
of Fine Gael is
elected Taoiseach.

3 October
The hunger strike
ends in Long Kesh
and prisoners are
more or less granted
political status.

to introduce reforms such as a guarantee of 'one man, one vote' in the notoriously corrupt system of local government; but these were both too much for mainstream Unionism—his own cousin, James Chichester-Clark, resigned from the government in protest—and too little for the increasingly militant opposition. The moderate leadership of the Civil Rights Association was replaced by those who favoured confrontation on the streets. Loyalist paramilitaries planted bombs designed—successfully—to give the impression that the IRA was on the war-path. In an atmosphere of rising hysteria O'Neill lost much of his remaining support within unionism and resigned at the end of April 1969, to be replaced by Chichester-Clark.

After the lunch adjournment yesterday, Mr Michael Mansfield, QC, counsel for five of the men, countered by saying that if there were to be a fresh trial there would be no evidence left to put before a jury.

Lord Gifford, QC, for Mr Gerry Hunter, said that all that remained was for the court to quash the convictions as unsafe and unsatisfactory and, perhaps, in doing so 'to express society's deep regret to these men that it has taken sixteen years for this to be recognised'.

Without pausing for an adjournment to consider the court's response, Lord Justice Lloyd said the court would give its reasons later, but its decision was 'because of the fresh evidence which has become available since the last hearing in this court, the appeals will be allowed and you are free to go as soon as the formalities are completed.'

August 1979 at Mullaghmore harbour, Co. Sligo. A Garda gathers pieces of wreckage from the boat on which Lord Mountbatten and three others—the Dowager Lady Brabourne (83), Paul Maxwell (15) and Nicholas Knatchbull (14)—were murdered by an IRA bomb.

The visit of Pope John Paul II to Ireland in September 1979 was the largest public event in the history of the country. He said Mass in the Phoenix Park in Dublin for a congregation of more than a million people.

The three appeal court judges gave no indication when they would deliver their judgment.

There was cheering from the public gallery and from supporters in the body of the court and the six men stood up and held their hands in the air. They shook hands with well-wishers before being ushered out of the dock and taken to the cells where they signed discharge forms and received their discharge grants of £30 each.

Outside the court, relatives had left the public gallery and were gathered in a knot, waiting for the men to come out. Most of them were in tears, unable to speak, and just wordlessly embraced each other, campaigners and journalists they recognised.

Suddenly cheers erupted and horns started to blow as the six men emerged from the front door of the court, embracing relatives who were waiting for them. They shook some of the outstretched hands before walking up the street towards the assembled cameras, microphones and journalists contained in a pen at the top of the street.

In this atmosphere the annual marches of the Apprentice Boys and the Orange Order in July and August took on an extra edge of Protestant triumphalism and were met with a violently enraged Catholic resistance. Riots in Derry prompted the decision of the British Home Secretary, James Callaghan, to send in troops 'to take all necessary steps, acting impartially between citizen and citizen, to restore law and order. Troops will be withdrawn as soon as this is accomplished. This is a limited operation.' But no sooner had the army restored calm in Derry than violence in Belfast reached a fearful climax. Protestant mobs invaded the Catholic Falls Road area behind RUC armoured cars firing machine-guns. Six people were killed, and hundreds of homes were petrol-bombed. By the end of August ten people had been killed in Northern Ireland, 154 wounded by gunshots,

1 November
Garret FitzGerald and Margaret Thatcher meet and agree to establish an Anglo-Irish Council.

1982

27 January
Fine Gael's budget, which attempted to levy VAT on footwear and clothes, is defeated, resulting in the fall of the Government.

745 injured in other ways, property worth £8 million, most of it belonging to Catholics, had been destroyed, and 1,800 families, most of them Catholic, had been forced to flee their homes in Belfast alone.

There was a strong feeling that the fall-out from the Northern troubles might destroy democracy in the Republic. In December 1969 *The Irish Times* gave prominent coverage to a speech by the Minister for Agriculture, Neil Blaney, in which he claimed that Fianna Fáil had never decided 'to rule out the use of force if the situation in the Six Counties demanded it.' The speech—for which *The Irish Times* columnist John Healy dubbed him 'Bang Bang Blaney'—was a direct challenge to the Taoiseach, Jack Lynch, who had in fact ruled out the use of force to 'impose our will on anyone.' Lynch, however, took no action against Blaney until May 1970, when the leader of the opposition, Liam Cosgrave, informed him of a high-level plot to import arms for use in Northern Ireland. On 6

Mr Richard McIlkenny was the first to speak, saying: 'We've waited a long time for this.' Mr Paddy Hill sounded still angry. 'For sixteen and a half years we've been used as political scapegoats for the people in there,' he said, pointing to the Old Bailey, adding that the police had said at the start they were going to frame them. The other four spoke briefly before being swept away with their families in limousines and three vans from the Camden Community Trust to a family celebration.

from The Irish Times
6 FEBRUARY **1992**

'They just kept shooting ...'
from Gerry Moriarty, in Belfast

The punters in Sean Graham's betting office on the Ormeau Road in Belfast were trying to pick the winner of the 2.30 p.m. three-miles hurdle from Ascot when two gunmen walked in and opened up indiscriminately with a rifle and handgun.

A British army foot patrol in Belfast

The H-block hunger strikes of 1981 further deepened the Northern Ireland conflict and gave rise to dramatic public support for the hunger-strikers, as here. Ten men died. Sinn Féin benefited from the upsurge in support for the republican cause among nationalists, becoming a real political force for the first time.

Mr Paul Doran (56) had just walked into the shop to pick up a football coupon for Saturday's matches and was caught in the gunfire, suffering wounds to his buttocks and foot. 'The gunmen just wouldn't stop shooting,' he told his son, Jimmy, from his Belfast City Hospital bed yesterday. 'They just kept shooting and shooting and shooting. Everybody in the place was hit,' he said.

Jimmy Doran was relieved that his father suffered relatively minor injuries but he says he'll never forget the horror of what he saw after he entered the shop to check on his condition. 'It was the worst I have ever seen. These men just had nowhere to go to escape. The floor was totally covered with thick black blood … there wasn't a sound. The police were shaking. The ambulance men were shaking. It was unbelievable.'

The scene was all too typical for Northern Ireland. RUC Land-Rovers and army vehicles were at the scene; police

May the Minister for Justice, Micheál Ó Móráin, who was ill, was forced to resign. Then, on the early morning of 6 May, Lynch sacked Blaney and the Minister for Finance, Charles Haughey. The Minister for Local Government, Kevin Boland, resigned in sympathy with his dismissed colleagues. *The Irish Times* carried an article by Owen Sheehy-Skeffington wishing them good riddance under the headline 'They'll none of them be missed.' In the Dáil the Government received what John Healy described in *The Irish Times* as a battering 'the like of which has not been seen in the House for at least a generation.' But Lynch survived. By the end of the month Blaney, Haughey, an army intelligence officer, Captain James Kelly, and a Belgian businessman, Albert Luykx, had been charged with attempting

refers to the events as grotesque, unprecedented, bizarre, and unique, leading to the coining of the term 'GUBU'.

6 December
An INLA bomb at the Drop Inn Well in Ballykelly, Co. Derry, kills eleven British soldiers and five civilians.

An aerial view of the H-blocks in the Maze prison near Belfast

1983

30 May

*The New
Ireland Forum
convenes but is
attended only by
nationalist
representatives,
who are invited
to give written
submissions as
long as they
oppose violence.*

to import five hundred pistols and 180,000 rounds of ammunition. Charges against Blaney were dropped, however, and the other defendants were subsequently acquitted.

When, in October 1970, the Fianna Fáil dissidents swallowed their pride and voted confidence in Lynch, an *Irish Times* editorial noted that 'they are hanging together—Fianna Fáil is a great organisation. So is the Mafia.' Reporting on the extraordinary scenes at the Fianna Fáil ardfheis in February 1971, when tension between rival factions broke out in fierce anger, John Healy noted the surreal denial of what was happening. 'Well, what do you think of the row?' "What row? I saw no row. There was

officers and soldiers taking positions on the Ormeau Road and neighbouring streets, ambulances ferrying the injured to hospital, the four people then known to be dead being left temporarily in the betting office.

A local priest, the Rev Anthony McHugh, gave the last rites to the dying. 'Four died while I was there with them. Others were brought away in ambulances, some of them very seriously injured. I just pray God that they will survive. There's nothing that I can do but pray for them, and their families, that they can live through this,' he said.

He said that he and everyone else in the area was in a state of shock. Asked what he saw in the betting office, Father McHugh said: 'I saw too much horror, too much blood and death, too much for anyone in any one day. It was horrific' ...

The Lynch landslide of 1977 saw Charles Haughey's return from the wilderness, where he had been since the Arms Trial. He was now Minister for Health. He is pictured here in the company of contestants in the Rose of Tralee competition.

from The Irish Times 1992
12 FEBRUARY

Farewell with feeling and a wintry smile

Mary Holland watches Mr Haughey make a Shakespearean exit

'Cá bhfuil Iago?' The jeering question rang out from the Fine Gael benches and, of course, it drew a laugh. But on C. J. Haughey's last day in the Taoiseach's front-bench seat it turned out to be as inappropriate as it was churlish.

It is difficult to imagine when we will have another Taoiseach (or a speechwriter) who looks to one of

no row. There never will be a row in Fianna Fáil. Never mind the papers …" Of course it never happened. Kevin Boland was never incoherent with rage. Paddy Hillery, his face twisted in a rare display of the real Hillery temper, never told the faithful that they had to choose between Kevin Boland and Fianna Fáil. The Taoiseach, Mr Jack Lynch, was never booed, and no-one chorused "Union Jack, Union Jack" as he plodded manfully through his policy for Northern peace and integration.'

Lynch's decisive, if belated, action prevented civil war. But by the time he intervened, money from the Southern exchequer had played, according to the historian Jonathan

10 June

Gerry Adams of Sinn Féin defeats Gerry Fitt of the SDLP and becomes MP for West Belfast.

7 September

A referendum is carried 2-1 to prevent the possibility of abortion being legalised without a referendum.

269

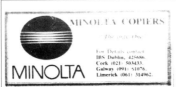

MINOLTA COPIERS
"The only One"
For Details contact
IBS Dublin, 425686.
Cork (021) 503433.
Galway (091) 51076.
Limerick (061) 314962.
MINOLTA

THE IRISH TIMES

Price 47p incl. VAT
44p sterling area

MONDAY, JULY 15, 1985

No. 40,197 CITY

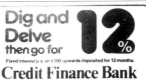

Dig and Delve then go for 12%
Fixed interest p.a. on £100 upwards deposited for 12 months.
Credit Finance Bank
12/13 South William Street, Dublin 2. Tel. 777046 and Branches.

Bob Geldof backed for Nobel prize

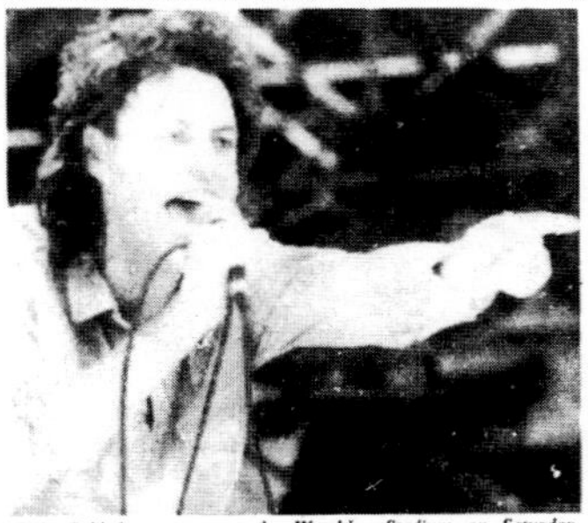

Bob Geldof on stage at the Wembley Stadium on Saturday night. — (PA wirepicture)

By Willy Clingan

THE TAOISEACH, Dr FitzGerald, yesterday gave his full support to the growing calls for a Nobel Peace Prize for Bob Geldof, the organiser of the Live Aid event which raised an estimated £45 million throughout the world, including a remarkable £3 million in Ireland, for African famine relief.

Ireland contributed more per head of population than any other country in the world, far exceeding the original target of £500,000.

Last night, RTE's co-ordinator of the Irish fund-raising effort, Mr Tony Boland said £2.8 million had been pledged or donated during the 16-hour concert. He said another £110,000 had been raised through auctions held over the air.

Much more still remains to be auctioned, he added. "We had queues of people coming in to RTE to hand in things — ladies brought wedding and engagement rings, we got oil paintings, mink coats, television sets, computer games . . . the list is endless."

On top of this, it is likely that some of the donations made at Allied Irish Banks branches came from people who did not get through to RTE to have their contribution included in the main total. Staff at 82 AIB branches worked voluntarily to receive donations.

The Irish response overshadowed the British contribution. Britain pledged £3.5 million sterling, including £205,000 sterling from Northern Ireland. The extraordinary success of the Irish effort was being put down yesterday — at least in part — to the persistent and patently sincere urgings of the RTE presenters on radio and television.

Most of the money raised was pledged over the telephone, and will be paid into the banks as soon as possible. Telecom Eireann put through over 100,000 calls on its free telephone service.

Late on Saturday night, the Taoiseach said on television that the Government was contributing £250,000 in recognition of the overwhelming response of the nation.

Yesterday, Dr FitzGerald said on RTE radio that he would support calls for Bob Geldof to be awarded this year's Nobel Peace Prize. "I think that all parties here would be willing to support that, and that it would get support in other parliaments too."

He said he would be moving as soon as possible to get all-party support for a formal proposal. Earlier, the Fianna Fail leader, Mr Haughey, said Geldof deserved the prize.

A member of the Norwegian parliament, Mr Sissel Ronbeck, yesterday nominated Geldof for the Prize for "his unique effort to save suffering Africans".

In the aftermath of the concert yesterday, attention started to focus on how the money raised will actually be spent. Live Aid organisers said it was hoped to get the first benefits through to the people in need within six weeks. It was also hoped to spend a good deal of the money on long-term aid measures, including irrigation projects.

Sixties legends come to life again; 70,000 revel in Wembley spectacle; How RTE organised the chaos: page 9; 500,000 moved in Ethiopia: page 7.

Mr Kevin Jenden, the chief co-ordinator for operations undertaken by Band Aid — the relief agency established by Geldof — will visit Africa on a fact-finding mission later this month. He said yesterday that he would like to see a consortium set up which would link his organisation with Oxfam and the Save the Children Fund. It would be immoral, he said, if separate agencies duplicated their efforts in one region and allowed people in untouched areas to starve to death.

Last night, Band Aid's accountant, Mr Philip Rusted, said he would work out a total budget from the money available to help Ethiopia, Sudan and the sub-Saharan regions.

Candidates for the Nobel prize, which is awarded annually in six different categories for contributions to "the good of humanity", may not nominate themselves. Instead, they have to be nominated by qualified persons. In the case of the peace prize, parliamentarians are qualified persons. A committee of five, elected by the Norwegian parliament, awards the peace prize and the winners receive the awards on December 10th.

Baby talk, Money talk

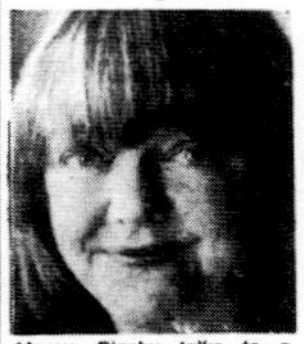

Maeve Binchy talks to a surrogate mother, whose book on her experiences is published today: page 13.

My Own Place

Senator Michael D. Higgins writes about Galway: page 13.

Tomorrow

The Arts in Ireland series continues with a look at a half a dozen young artists to watch.

AIB fund helpers may be punished

By Michael Foley

BANK employees who worked on Saturday as part of the Live Aid fund-raising effort may be disciplined by their union, the Irish Bank Officials Association.

The general secretary of the IBOA, Mr Job Stott, said yesterday that only a small number of staff with Allied Irish Banks had disobeyed a union directive, issued last Friday, which instructed staff not to work on the special fund-raising effort. The decision about what to do with those who worked would be up to the IBOA's executive council.

Mr Stott said only about 20 per cent of staff decided to work and he believed the number of branches reported by the AIB to have opened, over 86, was an exaggeration. However, even if the figure was correct it was still small, considering there are around 280 branches, he said.

Mr Stott conceeded that it was a difficult problem, given that people ignored the union's advice for good motives and had been influenced by publicity about Live Aid. There had been a degree of emotional blackmail and the IBOA did not believe AIB was involved for purely altruistic reasons. Mr Stott pointed to the publicity the bank received. The union directive was in the interests of AIB staff and it was they who would suffer in the long run in their relationship with their employer.

Meanwhile, a spokesman for AIB said that all money in the fund, including any interest earned, would be presented to the Band Aid Trust. He said it was impossible to estimate yet how much money was in the bank, as many people had simply pushed cheques through the letterboxes of branches which were closed.

More than 2,000 staff had given their time free, he said. "There was no pressure from AIB. People wanted to come in and be party of it all." He knew of 86 branches which had opened, but believed that many more opened for short periods in the afternoon.

By all accounts those who did go to work enjoyed themselves. Most branches had the concert playing loudly and the staff wore casual clothes.

Reagan back in control after major operation

From Sean Cronin, in Washington

PRESIDENT REAGAN is doing "very nicely", the White House said yesterday, following his operation on Saturday when surgeons removed a tumour about two inches in diameter from his colon and almost two feet of his lower intestine.

The tumour shows no evidence of cancer, a preliminary examination indicates, but a detailed microscope analysis is being made and the result will be known today.

Mr Larry Speakes, the President's press secretary, said Mr Reagan is reading briefing papers in his room at the Bethesda Naval Hospital. Doctors said he will remain hospitalised for seven to 10 days. "I'm amazed at how good I feel," he was quoted as saying after the operation.

Before the operation, Mr Reagan transferred his presidential powers temporarily to Vice-President George Bush, who returned to Washington from his summer home in Maine. Mr Reagan's action, in a letter to Mr Strom Thurmond, President pro-tempore of the Senate, and to the speaker of the House, Mr Tip O'Neill, made Mr Bush the first acting-President in this country's history.

Mr Reagan rescinded his unprecedented decision when the operation was over almost eight hours later. The 25th Amendment to the Constitution which deals with incapacitated Presidents and was ratified on February 10th, 1967, was the instrument of transfer although Mr Reagan said he did not think it applied in his situation. Former Senator Birch Bayh, the liberal Democrat who drafted the amendment, said that in his view it did apply.

Mr Reagan spent Saturday night in the recovery room and was ready to walk back to his bedroom yesterday morning, Mr Speakes told White House correspondents. However, doctors at the naval hospital overruled him and he was put in a wheelchair for the short journey along a hallway to his room.

Doctors criticise delay in tests on Reagan. Page 7.

The President asked for the Sunday newspapers, Mr Speakes went on, to read the comics, he added not the news sections. Mr Reagan told his chief of staff, Mr Donald Regan, that he wants action by Congress this week on the 1986 Budget.

Surgeons said Mr Reagan is free from pain and has been given a localised injection of morphine. He can work on state papers and

(Continued on page 8)

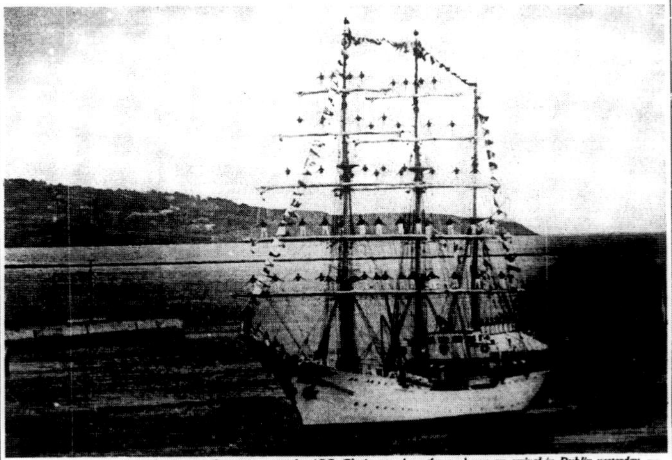

Crew members of the Colombian sail training vessel, ARC Gloria, stand on the yardarms on arrival in Dublin yesterday. — (Photograph: Matt Kavanagh. Report: page 8)

Taoiseach rules out further Budget

THE Taoiseach, Dr FitzGerald, yesterday rules out a mini-Budget later this year and defended the Government's handling of the ICI affair: page 10.

UN soldier killed

A Finnish member of the UNIFIL force has been killed by a landmine in southern Lebanon: page 7.

Home work plan

Journalists at the *Daily Mirror* are taking legal advice over a plan by management to "invite" about 20 staff members to work from home: page 7.

Mayor shot dead

A mayor and his bodyguard were killed in the Philippines yesterday by suspected New People's Army guerrillas and military agents were blamed for the abduction of a Filipino priest: page 7.

Durham gala

Conor O'Clery found bowler hats, sashes, tough men and bands and banners at the Durham miners' gala: page 7.

Tourism policy

The Government is to publish a policy document on tourism shortly: page 8.

Belgian vote

The Belgian coalition Government has survived a vote of confidence arising from a report on the Heysel soccer stadium disaster: page 6.

TV TONIGHT

Lee Marvin stars in "Point Blank," John Boorman's classic thriller, at 10.05 p.m. on BBC 1 tonight. RTE 2 features Stravinsky's "Firebird" in "Festival" at 8.10 p.m. Full radio and TV guide: page 17.

Shopkeepers count the cost in Portadown

From Niall Kiely in Belfast

AFTER days of disturbances between Loyalist rioters and the RUC, the Co Armagh town of Portadown quietened yesterday as shopkeepers cleared-up after Saturday night's riot, the police nursed their injuries, and the arrested protesters awaited Court appearances this morning.

Several dozen premises were damaged and some looted by rampaging youths on Saturday as stones, bottles and shards of plateglass were thrown at the RUC. Twenty-four policemen and 19 rioters were injured, with 19 arrests. Of the 19 people arrested on Friday, two were later found to be members of the Ulster Defence Regiment.

There was outraged reaction by some Loyalist politicians to the re-routing of Orange marches which preceded the disturbances. One spokesman for the Rev Ian Paisley's DUP, denounced "foul-mouthed drunken rioters," although he then went on to call for the resurrection of Carson's army. "Surely with three weeks' notice, we can organise something better than a riot," said the Rev Ivan Foster.

A spokesman for the Ulster Defence Association condemned police action and said the amount of force used by the RUC was excessive. "They were absolutely wild and I am amazed that no one was killed or hit in the head by a plastic bullet," said Mr John McMichael.

"They were bouncing off walls and off shopwindows just above the heads of people in the crowd.

Mr Billy Bleakes, of the Official Unionist Party, described the re-routings as "a blunder of the utmost magnitude."

A DUP councillor from Portadown, Mrs Ethel Smith, said security policy was now in ribbons and she predicted that Orange marchers would soon march through the Catholic Tunnel area of the town despite police actions.

A Derry DUP Assembly member, Mr Gregory Campbell, who participated in Saturday night's Portadown protest, said yesterday that the Taoiseach's praise for the RUC was proof of Dublin involvement in the re-routing decision.

Mr Will Glendinning of the Alliance Party, said responsibility for attacks on police would have to be laid with march organisers.

Senator Brid Rodgers of the SDLP, said yesterday that it would require more than a few re-routings for Nationalists to give their wholehearted support to the RUC and an SDLP district councillor in Co Down, Mr Jim Magee, criticised police failure to provide adequate protection for Catholics in Ballynahinch over the Twelfth weekend.

The Rev Foster said the lesson of Portadown was that such protests were futile. He suggested that all Twelfth demonstrations should have been cancelled last week and the entire membership of the Orange Order should have converged on the Co Armagh town.

"The British Government is not impressed by threats nor is it troubled by drunken rioters. If

SA tour dropped by New Zealand

THE New Zealand Rugby Union has abandoned a proposed tour of South Africa by the All Blacks team, saying that a court ruling had made it impossible to go ahead with the tour as planned.

A statement read to the New Zealand High Court by the union's lawyers said no practical purpose would be achieved by appealing against Saturday's ban on the team's departure until the end of a full hearing. "Consequently, the All Black tour of South Africa, which was due to start on July 24th is cancelled," the statement said.

Judge's ruling: page 7.

The chairman of the rugby union, Mr Ces Blazey, said the group's ruling council would meet tomorrow "to consider all the options which are available to us." He would not comment on suggestions that the union may try to arrange another tour of South Africa later in the year.

The Prime Minister, Mr David Lange, who had called on the union to scrap the tour, made no immediate comment.

The tour was strongly opposed by the Government and Mr Lange has said it would make New Zealand "part of the armoury of apartheid."

The legal action was brought by the two rugby-playing lawyers, Mr Patrick Finnigan and Mr Phillip Recorden.

Rugby sources in Wellington said alternative tours could take place to Ireland and England or Argentina. —(Reuter)

Petrol price

Mayo sweep to victory in Connacht final

From Michael Finlan, in Roscommon

AS OFTEN before, the Mayo football team demonstrated again yesterday that they are a green and red puzzle enclosed in an enigma wrapped in a mystery.

The whole world, its aunt and uncle, had forecast that Roscommon would swallow Mayo whole and spit out the bones in the Connacht final, but it was Roscommon that was eaten alive on their very own football field.

The Mayo supporters in the crowd of about 18,000 almost had to pinch themselves to make sure they weren't dreaming as their team, from which they never know what to expect, was transformed into a smooth-running instrument of destruction that carried out its lethal mission with despatch and efficiency.

At the end of the 70 minutes the score was two goals 11 points for Mayo and eight points for Roscommon, and Mayo will now play the winners of the Leinster final.

There was a sad appropriateness in the fact that the final point in yesterday's game was scored by Dermot Earley, one of the greatest of all footballers, for whom it was his last game after 20 years during which he was the supreme star of Roscommon.

A triumphant chant of "Mayo, Mayo" went up from the followers of the green and red at the end of the game and one of them observed: "I was beginning to forget how to cheer, its been so long since we've had a really worthwhile victory."

Yesterday's final was to have

commentary. The same thing happened at a Munster hurling final a few years ago when a GAA official told me he never heard of Radio na Gaeltachta."

Saturday was Oaks day at the Curragh and it belonged to England as the Dick Hern-trained filly, Helen Street, ridden by Willie Carson, beat Ireland's Alydar's Best to the winning post, but it was Ireland's day yesterday at Crystal Palace where Marcus O'Sullivan beat Ray Flynn into second place in the 1,500 metres AAA championships final for an Irish one-two.

Sport is on pages 2, 3, 4, 5, 6.

WHO SAID UNIT TRUSTS WERE DEAD?

Not Taylor and Associates

However, on the back of a poor 1984 some "informed" commentators suggested that

MONTHLY INCOME SHARES

An extra boost every month

Save now for retirement and you could be sure of a regular income with the Irish Permanent.

Investing in Monthly Income Shares means you receive an interest cheque on the first of each month. (Minimum capital £3,000).

At Irish Permanent we've got it all for you.

Assets exceed

THE IRISH TIMES

PRICE 65p (incl. VAT) 55₊ sterling area   DUBLIN, MONDAY, JULY 2, 1990   No. 41,718 CITY

Heroes' welcome for team

Streets lined by at least 500,000 joyful fans

Jack Charlton waves to supporters on arrival at Dublin Airport. — (Photograph: Joe St Leger.)

Irish Times reporters

AT LEAST half a million people are estimated to have taken to the streets of Dublin to welcome the returning World Cup team last night.

The Garda, normally reliable at estimating crowd numbers, declined on this occasion, saying that numbers were so enormous they were impossible to calculate.

Most observers agreed, however that the team was greeted by the biggest and most joyous public reception the city has ever seen.

Perhaps half of the city's population, joined by tens of thousands from other parts of the country, took to the streets to greet their football heroes on a grand scale.

A sea of Tricolours saluted the team from Dublin Airport to the city centre. The city ground to a halt, with traffic jams miles long on roads near the route from the airport to the civic ceremonies which awaited them at the Bank of Ireland in College Green.

The motorcade, with the team on an open-topped bus, took more than three hours to travel the seven miles from Dublin airport to College Green, after a huge welcome at the airport, led by the Taoiseach, Mr Haughey.

"I want to thank you all for being wonderful, wonderful supporters and also a credit to Ireland," Mr Jack Charlton, the team manager, told the thousands who filled College Green, where the official reception was given by the Lord Mayor, Alderman Sean Haughey.

Charlton urged people to "please go away quietly" at the end of the formal ceremonies. During the long wait for the team, with some people standing for up to six hours in the city centre, there was a steady stream of casualties, mostly women, suffering from the effects of hypothermia and exhaustion.

At Dublin airport, and again at every vantage point from Whitehall church to the Bank of Ireland, where the civic reception was held, countless thousands gathered at every vantage-point to see their heroes. Despite the long wait the crowds remained remarkably good-humoured. Music by Paddy Cole and the Gerry O'Connor Allstars at Clery's in O'Connell Street and platform at College Green helped sustain good spirits and keep masses of younger supporters entertained.

The team arrived later than expected from Rome, where Saturday night's 1-0 quarter-final defeat against Italy. The Aer Lingus 737, the "St Jack", specially dedicated for the day, landed shortly after six o'clock. It was then that players and officials got their first sight of the massive turnout.

Wives, girlfriends and family members were joined by Mr Haughey and several government ministers in welcoming the team. Jack Charlton, hands in pockets, attempted to look relaxed, but was clearly moved by the

Inside

Five pages of photographs and reports on the celebrations in Rome and Dublin: pages 3, 4, 5, 6, 7

feel very proud of the job they've done," he added. "I hope we'll do better in the future, when maybe instead of coming back with nothing, again, we'll bring something home to you."

Hundreds of extra gardai were on duty to guide the motorcade through the packed streets of the city, but there were no problems other than those caused by traffic choking the main Belfast-Dublin road. The occasion passed off with unparalleled good humour. When the team finally reached College Green the crowd chanted "We want Jack" repeatedly as political speeches were read from the platform.

Eventually they had their wish, with Charlton introducing each of the 22 players who had travelled to Italy for the World Cup tournament. "I would like, because we took 22 and only 16 played, to introduce each one individually, because we are a squad and a group."

He told the crowd they were "wonderful, wonderful supporters and a credit to Ireland." He also described the journey into the city as "the most terrifying experience of my life" because of how close people had been to the wheels of the vehicle in the motorcade.

After the team took their final curtain call at College Green, they led the crowd in singing "Molly Malone". Jack Charlton told the tired, but elated thousands: "Be careful going home, and goodnight. Thank you."

Mandela to address Dail after rapturous reception

By Colm Boland

THE deputy president of the African National Congress, Mr Nelson Mandela, will address a special session of the Dail today and have talks with the Taoiseach, Mr Haughey, following his rapturous public reception in Dublin when he accepted the Freedom of the City.

Mr Mandela thanked the people of Ireland for their solidarity in the struggle against apartheid during his address to the crowd outside the Mansion House yesterday. "Thank you for being there when we needed you most," Mr Mandela said to loud applause. "In prison and behind big walls we would hear your message of solidarity loud and clear."

He warned that, although they had entered a period of momentous change in South Africa, "the road ahead is still fraught with danger." International sanctions must be

Visit, report and photographs: page 2; Black movements split over strike in Natal: page 9.

this last mile in our long and difficult struggle."

Mr Mandela had particular words of thanks for the Taoiseach and the Minister for Foreign Affairs, Mr Collins, for resisting pressure for the relaxation of EC sanctions at last week's summit in Dublin Castle.

Earlier, during a lunch hosted by the Irish Congress of Trade Unions and the Irish Anti-Apartheid Movement, Mr Mandela said that the ANC had taken particular inspiration from the Irish struggle for independence. The boycott weapon had been one important lesson from the Irish experience.

At the Freedom of the City ceremony at the Mansion House, the Lord Mayor, Alderman Sean Haughey, presented Mr Mandela with a Cavan Crystal model of the globe and said he had achieved the status of the world statesman. "In effect, you have the whole world in your hands," Mr

Pollsmoor Prison in Cape Town."

Mr Haughey said that Mr Mandela's friend and comrade, Mrs Adelaide Tambo, came to City Hall to accept the Scroll of Freedom on his behalf. "On that occasion she pledged that one day, Nelson Mandela, a free man, would come to Dublin to accept formally the Freedom of the City. Today is that day. Today, the people of Dublin walk taller because you are amongst us."

During his speech inside the Mansion House and outside on the public platform, Mr Mandela graciously acknowledged that he was sharing the limelight with the returning international soccer team, and, paying tribute to their fighting spirit, said he would like to believe that their magnificent performance was partly because he was amongst them, in spirit at least.

Mrs Winnie Mandela signed the visitors' book with her husband. "Ireland has been a tremendous source of strength to the people of South Africa in the struggle against apartheid. Compliments and Best Wishes."

Mr Mandela, on doctor's orders, missed last night's special concert in the Gaiety Theatre, "Tribute to Mandela," featuring

Security call after killing of RUC men

From Marie O'Halloran, in Belfast

AS DETECTIVES investigate the IRA killing of two RUC officers in one of the busiest shopping areas of Belfast on Saturday, politicians have called for more protection for policemen on street patrols.

Yesterday, Belfast city councillors laid a wreath at the security gates at Castle Street near where Constable Harold John Beckett (47), and Constable Gary Carl Meyer (35), were shot from behind, one dying almost instantly and the second three hours later in hospital.

Unionist and Alliance party councillors had been commemorating the 74th anniversary of the Battle of the Somme outside the city hall and went to the site of the shooting for a brief religious service. The two RUC men were community police officers in the

Bureau de Change

16 December
The kidnapped businessman Don Tidey is released.

1984

12 August
The RUC kill an unarmed civilian, Seán Downes, with a plastic bullet. They were trying to arrest the American Martin Galvin of Northern Aid, who was barred from entering Northern Ireland, at a Sinn Féin rally.

12 October
The IRA comes close to killing Margaret Thatcher and many members of her Cabinet as it explodes a bomb at the Conservative Party conference in the Grand Hotel, Brighton. Five people die in the explosion.

1985

4 May
It is revealed that a man is being tested for AIDS at Galway Regional Hospital, the first known potential case in the area.

Christy Moore, one of the most popular Irish singers from the nineteen-seventies on.

Bardon, a 'crucial role' in the formation of the Provisional IRA. The IRA split in December 1969 over the issue of whether Sinn Féin should end its policy of abstaining from the Dáil, with the traditionalist minority forming a Provisional Army Council. This split was repeated the following month at the Sinn Féin ardfheis. Although both wings of the IRA began to rearm and to prepare for violent conflict, it was the Provisionals' determination to replace political protest with armed revolution that would be most significant.

Gradually at first and then quite dramatically, Northern Ireland slipped into anarchy. The Provisionals gained support as defenders of the Catholic community when, on 27 June 1970, they fired on Protestants attacking the enclave of Short Strand in Belfast, killing four men. A few days later the British army imposed a disastrous curfew on the Falls Road area, sealing it off for

Shakespeare's most sublime tragedies to sum up more than three decades in public life. Mr Haughey had quoted from the last scene of Othello:

'I have done the state some service; they know't
No more of that.'

Earlier, followed by his Cabinet walking in single file, he had come into the Dáil and taken his accustomed seat, just below the Ceann Comhairle. There was a short prayer and then Mr Haughey rose to speak, slowly and with great feeling. He talked of his affection for the Dáil over 35 years, his vivid memories of great figures 'who have passed through its portals and who are no longer with us' and of important parliamentary occasions he had witnessed in this 'democratic forum of the nation'.

He thanked the people of Ireland for their support and affection and wished them every happiness. It was not a time to speak of his own achievements. If he sought any accolade it would be simply, 'He served the people, all the people, to the best of his ability.'

It says a lot about the heightened mood of a crowded Dáil chamber that nobody seemed to think this demand was excessive nor the language of the speech just a shade overblown.

True, Dick Spring, uneasy at Mr Haughey's recent inclination to reach for an English playwright in times of crisis, said he had decided to bypass 'Julius Caesar' in favour of Flann O'Brien's comment on Finn McCool: 'I am an Ulsterman, a Connachtman, a Greek.' The quote was a bit too clever for the occasion and people looked nonplussed ...

By five o'clock there were fewer than a dozen people left in the Dáil and Austin Deasy was making jokes about Pedigree Chum. Mr Haughey listened impassively from his seat in the back row. A few hours on and we were already a long way from Shakespeare and much, much closer to Patsy Kline. It seemed a pity that he hadn't had a chance to finish Othello's final plea for a fair press:

'I pray you, in your letters
When you shall these unlucky deeds relate,
Speak of me as I am; nothing extenuate,
Nor set down aught with malice.'

thirty hours while they searched for arms. This time the Official and Provisional IRA both fired on the army, who retaliated by killing four people, including a press photographer. The Provisionals then launched a bombing campaign, setting off a hundred small explosions by mid-September.

In August 1970 John Hume inspired a story in *The Irish Times* to the effect that a new political party was to be formed and that only the choice of leader was holding up the public announcement. His aim, essentially, was to push the Belfast MP Gerry Fitt into accepting the leadership of a new democratic nationalist movement. The story worked: the Social Democratic and Labour Party was launched later that month, with Fitt at its head. But the new party was powerless to stop the violence. The Provisional IRA, having killed its first British soldier in February 1971, was set on sweeping aside the political campaign to reform Northern Ireland and replacing it with an armed campaign to abolish it. And in August 1971, when the

*The wreck of the **Betelgeuse**, which exploded while discharging oil at the **Whiddy Island** terminal in Bantry Bay, Co. Cork, in 1979. Fifty people died.*

13 July
Bob Geldof's Live Aid concerts in London and America raise approximately $70 million for famine relief in Ethiopia.

15 November
Garret FitzGerald and Margaret Thatcher sign the Anglo-Irish Agreement.

1986

2 January
The Progressive Democrats are formed by Des O'Malley and Mary Harney.

15 January
The first 'test-tube baby' (fertilised in vitro) is born in Dublin.

3 March
Loyalists hold a one-day strike to protest against the Anglo-Irish Agreement, resulting in widespread disruption and violence.

6 June
John Stalker is suspended from the investigation into

RUC 'shoot-to-kill' policies in the early eighties, amid allegations of corruption; many people believe this to be a smear campaign because of his work in Northern Ireland.

26 June

A referendum on making divorce available in the Republic is defeated: 61% vote against.

1987

10 March

Charles Haughey becomes Taoiseach of a minority Fianna Fáil Government after the casting vote of the Ceann Comhairle.

12 March

Dr Garret FitzGerald resigns after ten years as leader of Fine Gael.

8 May

Eight IRA men and a civilian are killed in an ambush by the SAS in Loughgall, Co. Armagh.

26 July

Stephen Roche wins the Tour de France.

British government responded by introducing internment in a disastrously one-sided and ill-prepared manner, it was given the perfect opportunity. Violence intensified, and during that month alone thirty-five people were killed. A cycle of atrocity and counter-atrocity had been set in motion. Sectarian attacks led to the biggest enforced movements of population in Europe since 1945 as Protestants and Catholics were forced to seek refuge in exclusive ghettos.

And the continuing capacity of Northern violence to destabilise the South was demonstrated again in January and February 1972 when the British army's Parachute Regiment gunned down thirteen unarmed civil rights marchers in Derry. A protest march in Dublin culminated in the burning down of the British embassy while gardaí looked on. Yet public opinion in the Republic was quickly sobered by IRA atrocities, such as an Official IRA bombing of the Parachute Regiment's headquarters in Aldershot, Hampshire, in February, killing five women who worked in the canteen, and the Provisional IRA's bombing of the Abercorn restaurant in Belfast, killing two women and injuring 136 people.

The Irish Times reported vividly on all these events. At first it was inclined to see them as a short-term horror that would quickly lead to a new Anglo-Irish settlement. Even in the midst of the arms crisis in May 1970 *The Irish Times* seemed confident that Irish unity would come about within the foreseeable future and by peaceful means. 'Forces in Britain and the weight of our EEC membership must render the Border anachronistic in a relatively short time. Britain needs a peaceful neighbour to trade with and to be a reasonable security on her flank. This may suit us as long as we are able to run our own affairs. The change must come; it may be rapid; it will be peaceful. Harold Wilson is not so foolish as to think that the 1920–21 arrangement has been other than a failure.'

In 1971, as Apprentice Boys were preparing to march in Derry, the paper was anxious that

from The Irish Times **1994**
18 NOVEMBER

Emotional Albert has his finest hour

Dáil Sketch by Joe Carroll

'It's amazing. You cross the big hurdles and when you get to the small ones you get tripped.'

Even Albert's most savage critics had to hand it to him for the way he handled the most difficult decision of his long political career. There was no messing.

As soon as the Dáil session opened at 10.30 a.m., Albert was on his feet and in the first sentence he had announced that he was going to resign as Taoiseach. It would be for 'the good of the country'.

The packed Chamber sat up. The motion of confidence was supposed to go on until 5 p.m. but suddenly Albert had pulled the plug and was on his way to the Park.

As he told the Dáil later, 'I'm straight up. I tell it as it is. That's me. That's what I've been and always will be.' It was a stream of pure Albertese …

His parting words as Taoiseach summed up his philosophy better than any biographer could. 'Above all in

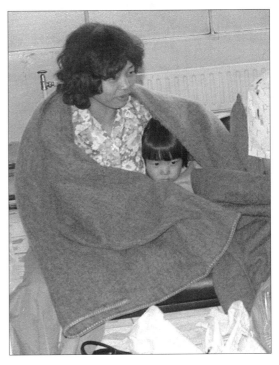

Vietnemese refugees in Ireland

Albert Reynolds, Taoiseach from 1992 to 1994. Although his tenure as Taoiseach was short, he made a vital personal contribution to the Northern Ireland peace process.

14 August
The British government orders an inquiry into the conviction and imprisonment of four people for involvement in the Woolwich and Guildford pub bombings in 1974.

19 October
Stock market crashes occur throughout the world, the worst since 1929.

8 November
An IRA bomb at a memorial service in Enniskillen, Co. Fermanagh, kills eleven people.

1988

6 March
Three members of the IRA are shot dead by the SAS in Gibraltar as they carry out a trial run for a bomb attack. They were unarmed and had offered to surrender before being shot.

16 March
Two civilians and a member of the IRA are killed by a loyalist gunman,

The aftermath of the IRA attack in which Christopher Ewart-Biggs, the British ambassador to Ireland, and Judith Cooke, a civil servant, were murdered in July 1976

Michael Stone, who hurls grenades and fires on those attending the funeral of the IRA members killed in Gibraltar.

19 March
Two British soldiers are killed during the funeral of an IRA man, Kevin Brady, killed by Michael Stone three days earlier.

Republicans would show restraint and understand that 'strong action now will be seen only as an attack on Orangemen—and Protestants in general. No matter how misguided, no matter how they have misused their fifty years of power, they are still Irishmen, and an attack on them will be interpreted by many Protestants, even those outside the Order, or out of sympathy with the order, as purely sectarian.' Yet even when such restraint was not forthcoming and sectarian warfare broke out during the internment crisis, the paper was still inclined to see the chaos as the prelude to a British withdrawal. An editorial shortly after the introduction of internment explained that 'we are

politics and in business I was delighted to have been a risk-taker because I believe that if you are not a risk-taker you'll achieve nothing … I'm quite happy that having taken the risks the successes far outweighed the failures.'

Brave words for a man who had taken a risk on Harry Whelehan and lost the highest prize in Irish politics as a result. But you felt he was really thinking of his finest achievement—the silencing of the guns …

Before he left the Chamber, Albert looked up at the Press Gallery. He paused and said: 'I'm no use to you now. I never kept a diary.'

Then with a break in his voice he added: 'It's amazing. You cross the big hurdles and when you get to the small ones you get tripped.'

And those were his last words in the Dáil as Taoiseach.

Liam Cosgrave, the British Prime Minister, Edward Heath, and the Ulster Unionist leader, Brian Faulkner, signing the Sunningdale Agreement in 1973

from The Irish Times
1 JULY 1996

Funeral gathering hears of grieving husband's 'best pal' taken brutally from a small, close family

By Frank McNally

The murdered journalist, Veronica Guerin, was laid to rest in Dardistown Cemetery near Dublin airport on Saturday afternoon, after leaders of church, State and the media joined her family and friends for one final tribute.

Earlier, in the most poignant moments of the funeral service, Ms Guerin's seven-year-old son, Cathal, helped other young relatives in presenting gifts of his mother's prized possessions. These included her wedding album, a photograph of her with her footballing hero, Eric Cantona, and the International Press Freedom award which her husband, Mr Graham Turley, said was a testimony to her dedication to journalism.

Mr Turley paid a moving tribute to his wife, speaking of her love of 'Sunday papers, football and her family'. In a sometimes faltering voice, he told mourners that when he and Veronica married in 1985, 'we promised each other we'd have great fun, and we really did. Believe you me, we had great fun'.

watching … all the tactical errors, that are made on the routine road to a withdrawal. It has been seen before in more distant parts of the world.' The assumption of the leader-writer was that a united Ireland of some form was now a certainty and that the essential problem was the narrowing of the sectarian divide. 'Our Political Correspondent put it well recently: when the Border goes, who will end partition?'

The massacre in Derry on Bloody Sunday strengthened the paper's view that the violence was part of the end game of empire. An editorial on the day after the massacre commented that 'it is as if Britain, shorn of her empire, has been able to concentrate in the small area of the six north-eastern counties of Ireland all that talent for arrogance, blindness and malevolence that an imperial Power in decline manifests when faced with a small but determined people.' On the day of what the paper hoped would be peaceful protests in Dublin it wished that the public might 'keep the pressure on their leaders for an insistent drive towards a settlement of Irish-British relations.' *The Irish Times* still believed that a transformed Ireland was in the offing. 'We need to know ourselves what this new Ireland is

20 August
Eight British soldiers die in an IRA bomb attack at Ballygawley, Co. Tyrone.

30 September
An inquest into the shooting of the three IRA members in Gibraltar finds that they were lawfully killed.

1989

13 February
A solicitor, Pat Finucane, is shot dead in his Belfast home by the UFF. Some weeks earlier the Conservative MP Douglas Hogg had stated in the House of Commons that some defence lawyers are unduly sympathetic to the IRA.

24 February
The Dáil approves Fine Gael's Legal Separation Bill, which allows legal separation by the courts once it is proved that a marriage has broken down for a year.

4 June
The Chinese army massacres

President Mary Robinson and Queen Elizabeth in London

pro-democracy demonstrators in Tian'anmen Square, Beijing.

12 July
A snap general election fails to produce a Fianna Fáil overall majority. Charles Haughey resumes as Taoiseach as a coalition Government of Fianna Fáil and the Progressive Democrats is approved by the Dáil.

going to be like and we need to tell others— especially the one million in the North. We need to be clear in our minds when we use the term "our people".'

The sense of living through an end game was heightened in March 1972 when the British government suspended the Stormont parliament and introduced direct rule from London, ostensibly for a year but in fact indefinitely. Henry Kelly in *The Irish Times* noted the melancholy air at the last sitting of the Parliament. 'Stormont ended quietly, almost in anti-climax. In the restaurant a Unionist Senator looked towards a table of MPs and Ministers. "Captains and Kings," he muttered. Then he added, "My foot."' But neither direct rule nor large-scale protests by working-class women in Catholic Belfast persuaded the Provisional IRA

With their son, he said, they had formed a small happy group that nobody would ever get between. In losing Veronica, he was saying goodbye 'not just to my wife and the mother of Cathal, but to my best pal, because that's what she was. She was my best pal'.

The President, Mrs Robinson, and the Taoiseach, Mr Bruton, led the mourners who filled the small airport church to overflowing. Among those who also attended was the former mayor of New York, David Dinkins. 'I was in Ireland for a meeting and when I heard of this assassination, I felt I had to come,' he said afterwards.

The airport chaplain, Father Declan Doyle, told the congregation that on Sunday of last week priests throughout the diocese had preached sermons on the theme of violence against women. Veronica had heard this sermon 'and three days later she was dead, shot down in cold blood'.

Her shooting was wider than the issue of violence against women, he conceded, but it was an example of the 'violence of the strong against the weak; violence by those with power against the vulnerable; violence by the unscrupulous against those who obey and uphold the rule of law in our society; violence by those who ask few questions and tolerate few questions being asked of them against those who dare to question and enquire'.

Questioning was part of the human spirit, a necessary part of the search for truth and freedom, he said. But 'the search for truth leads us through winding ways and into strange company. It has few markers to guide the way. It can be lonely and isolating'.

'Veronica knew more than most the pitfalls of the search for truth … Coming here to mass on Sundays, her belief in God, her faith—all that formed part of the Veronica Guerin who was able to risk mistakes, to investigate fearlessly, to humbly appraise a situation. Her faith and her life made sense if you see them this way.

'St Augustine said, "You have made us for yourself O Lord and our hearts are restless until they find their rest in Thee". Veronica had a restless heart. She searched long and hard and deep and wide. Now she is at rest. May she rest in peace for all eternity' …

to call off its campaign, even when, at the end of May 1972, the Official IRA declared a cease-fire.

There was a moment of hope after November 1973 when the Unionists, the SDLP and the Alliance Party formed a power-sharing Executive, and their achievement was followed a month later by the Sunningdale agreement between the British and Irish governments and the Northern Ireland parties. This underlying optimism drained away, however, as the violence continued and Protestant opposition to the provision for a Council of Ireland mounted. As early as February 1973, when the Loyalist Association of Workers staged a one-day strike to demand the release of the first Protestant internees, Henry Kelly, the Northern Editor of *The Irish Times*, had noted that 'if Protestants ever want to bring Northern Ireland to its knees, all they need to do is strike.' This the Ulster Workers' Council commenced to do in May 1974 when it staged a strike aimed at bringing down the power-sharing Executive. Harold

15 September
John Stevens and his inquiry team arrive in Belfast to investigate collusion between loyalist paramilitaries and members of the RUC and UDR after files on nation-alists fall into the hands of loyalist terrorists.

18 October
The Guildford Four are released after spending fifteen years in jail.

10 November
The Berlin Wall is torn down.

The Fine Gael and Labour coalition Government of 1983–87 under the leadership of Garret FitzGerald

THE IRISH TIMES

PRICE 65p (incl. VAT) 55p sterling ar\ | DUBLIN, SATURDAY, AUGUST 25, 1990 | No. 41,765 CITY

INSIDE

CAO 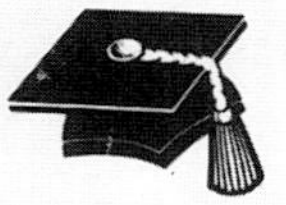 An eight-page pull-out guide

Guide to college places

The CAO offers — Full list of all first round university place offers

The Points — Details of cut-off points at which 1990 course offers have been made

Guide to offers — How to read the offers list and find your place

DIT and RTC — Details of offers and points

Options — Courses and options with no college for those offers

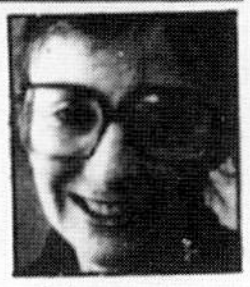

● Compiled by Christina Murphy

Freephone College Advice Service

A free telephone advisory service on college entry and points will be provided by *The Irish Times* today from 10 am to 6 pm. By dialling the number 1 800 231 231 direct from anywhere in the State, callers will be connected free of charge to the advisory service staffed by Christina Murphy and John Walshe with a team of 12 experts from The Institute of Guidance Counsellors.

Keenan due in Dublin today

By Renagh Holohan and Christine Newman

MR Brian Keenan, the Belfast schoolteacher who has been held captive by Islamic fundamentalists in Beirut for over four years is due in Dublin today. The Government jet with the Minister for Foreign Affairs, Mr Collins, on board was due to leave early this morning to pick up Mr Keenan in Damascus, where he was handed over to the Irish Ambassador to Syria, Mr Declan Connolly.

Mr Keenan (39), who holds an Irish passport, was released in Beirut at 7 p.m. Irish time and driven to Damascus by Syrian officials. His freedom was achieved following a prolonged diplomatic campaign by the Government and intense lobbying by his family and friends. He was kidnapped in West Beirut on April 11th, 1986, while walking to the American University where he worked as an English teacher.

His release last night came after two days of mounting speculation and anxiety that initial reports would prove unfounded, as they had on several previous occasions. Also aboard the Government jet going to pick up Mr Keenan were his two sisters, Mrs Brenda Gillham and Mrs Elaine Spence, a medical team, and officials from the Department of Foreign Affairs.

In a statement last night, the Government said it was overjoyed at the release and expressed the hope that it would be followed everywhere in the Middle East by the freeing of all hostages, no matter where they were being held, or by whom. The Government expressed its deep appreciation to the governments of Iran and Syria for their assistance in securing Mr Keenan's freedom.

Government can claim a victory; Political, church leaders welcome release; Gulf crisis may have hastened release: page 5. Diplomatic efforts focused on Keenan's Irish passport; Kidnappings are backlash of the most oppressed: page 4. Editorial comment: page 9.

At a press conference in Iveagh House last night, Mr Collins said: "I believe this could very well be the start of the release of all the hostages in the Lebanon."

Crying with joy, the two sisters received the news of their brother's release at 8.40 p.m. last night in a Dublin hotel.

Mrs Gillham and Mrs Spence said it was their "happiest wee hour" when they appeared in the foyer of the hotel on either side of Mr Collins, who escorted them out with his arms around them.

A Foreign Affairs spokesman said early this morning that he had no reports on Mr Keenan's health after his long confinement but he had obviously been well enough to travel by car from Beirut to Damascus, a journey of over two hours. The earliest he will be in Dublin is 7 pm tonight, but the length of time that the jet will spend on the ground in Syria is unclear.

The Islamic Dawn organisation, in a brief communique to a Beirut newspaper, said it had freed Mr Keenan. A statement from the same group was issued earlier this year after the release of American hostage Mr Robert Polhill.

News that Mr Keenan was still alive did not come until the end of April this year, more than four years after his kidnapping, when a released American hostage, Mr Frank Reed, said he had shared a cell with Mr Keenan and an English journalist, Mr John McCarthy. Mr Reed said: "Brian and John had been held together for a long time, they were good friends and both were in good shape, as they had exercised together doing press-ups."

Last night Mr Reed, speaking from Washington, said he had been told two days in advance that he was about to be released and he assumed the same had been the case with Mr Keenan. The news of Mr Keenan's release was the best and most important he had had since his own release, he said.

The Northern Ireland Secretary, Mr Peter Brooke, said he and his ministerial colleagues in Northern Ireland were delighted and relieved to hear of Mr Keenan's release. "I reiterate the Government's total condemnation of terrorism and hostage taking" he said.

The Government jet was due to leave about 6 a.m. this morning for the five-hour flight to Damascus. It will refuel in Rome, where it will pick up Mr Padraig Murphy, the political director of the Department of Foreign Affairs, one of the diplomats who played an important role in the negotiations leading to Mr Keenan's release.

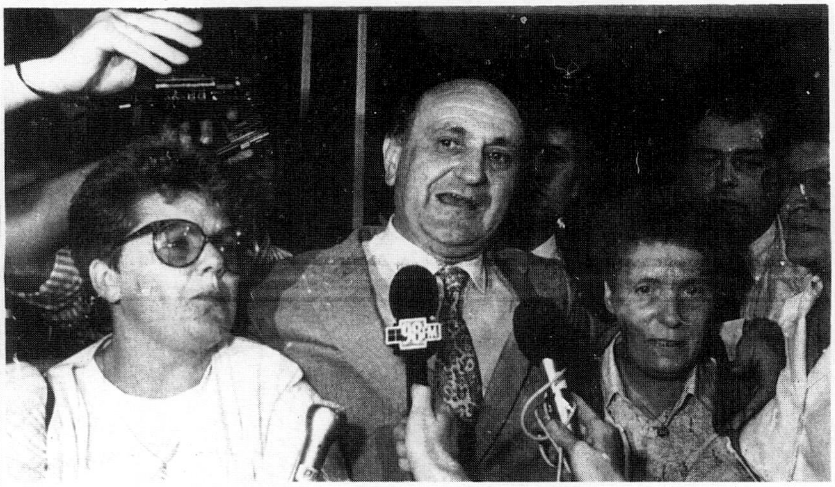

Mr Brian Keenan's sisters, Mrs Elaine Spence (left) and Mrs Brenda Gillham, with the Minister for Foreign Affairs, Mr Collins, in Dublin last night after news of their brother's release came through. — (Photograph: Paddy Whelan)

NEXT WEEK

GOING TO COLLEGE '90

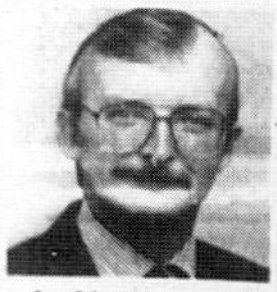

A 24-page colour tabloid supplement on Monday with advice and information by Christina Murphy and John Walshe on:

- The cost of college
- Student accommodation
- Repeating the Leaving Cert
- Vacancies in British colleges
- Private colleges

BED AND BREAKFAST

Behind an Irish tradition

MONDAY

YEAR OF THE TOURIST

Three-part series
On a boom season

TUESDAY — THURSDAY

Taoiseach denies Dail recall centres on Goodman

By Renagh Holohan

THE Dail is being recalled for an emergency session on Tuesday to pass a section of the Companies Bill which will allow a corporation facing financial difficulties to get court protection to prevent its creditors from forcing it into receivership.

The Taoiseach, Mr Haughey, last night denied that the legislation was being enacted specifically to aid Goodman International and said it would be available to all companies with temporary problems as a result of the crisis in the Middle East and the consequent unstable financial markets.

The new measure, which will enable the courts to appoint an examiner who could freeze a company's assets for up to 12 months, is expected to be passed in one day by the Dail and the Seanad. Mr Haughey said that opposition leaders were agreeable to the recall. He expected that events in the Middle East would also be discussed.

Mr Haughey said the Bill, which has been some five years before the Oireachtas and its committee, was due to be passed in October in any event. The Government, he said, did not intend giving specific financial aid to any corporation; the mechanism of seeking the protection of the courts would be generally available to all companies encountering financial difficulties and had the prospect of restructuring themselves.

Asked how Goodman could survive, the Taoiseach said: "I do not know; it is not a function of government to look after companies in the private sector, but I know that the Goodman organisation has been in very close discussion with its bankers, so it is a matter for them. But this legislation would be available to companies which would be in the sort of difficulties which appear to beset Goodman at the moment."

Section nine, the Taoiseach said, was equivalent to legislation in the United States called Chapter 11 and the Bill to enact it

Bill to protect companies from creditors: page 2. Editorial comment: page 9.

would be published on Monday, when the Minister for Industry and Commerce, Mr O'Malley, would elaborate on its details. There was no question of the State guaranteeing credit to any corporation, or of Departments issuing letters of comfort. Although he was aware of the difficulties some companies were facing, representations had not been made to him.

The Fine Gael spokesman on industry and commerce, Mr John Bruton TD, said last night that Section nine was a completely untried system of company rescue and did not seem to adequately cover day-to-day finance for continued operations.

The Labour Party leader, Mr Dick Spring, said it would be "incongruous to the point of being obscene" if the Dail were recalled solely to discuss the commercial problems of one individual when up to 400 Irish citizens were trapped in the Gulf.

Brendan McGrath writes:

Before the Government statement at 5.00 pm, the stock market in Dublin was swept by rumours that an administrator might be sent in to manage Goodman International, with the former PMPA administrator, Mr Kevin Kelly, being mentioned.

Mr Kelly is on holiday and could not be contacted but some industry sources felt that such a move would be unlikely, while the Goodman spokesman would only say that the group's meat plants are being managed by the existing management, that all the plants are working flat out and that all cattle being bought are being paid for on the same day.

The spokesman added that Goodman International is continuing discussions with its bankers and he denied a report that Mr Goodman has been given until the end of next week to take measures that would lead to the reduction of the group's debts.

Gorbachev warns Iraq of UN action

AS PRESIDENT Saddam Hussein sent his occupation troops to surround beleaguered embassies in Kuwait, President Gorbachev stepped deeper into the Gulf crisis with a warning of tougher UN action.

The Soviet leader sent a message to Mr Hussein telling him bluntly that if he did not abide by UN Security Council orders to get out of Kuwait and free foreign captives, the UN would be obliged to approve "additional measures".

"Sidestepping these demands will inevitably prompt the Security Council to adopt appropriate additional measures," he said, according to Tass.

In his message, Mr Gorbachev said Moscow was standing by its denunciation of the annexation of Kuwait and urged Mr Hussein to abide by the UN resolutions.

The urgency for new powers to police the sanctions became clear yesterday with evidence that Iraq has succeeded in importing military and chemical warfare equipment by air in breach of the United Nations embargo.

Disclosing the details in Washington, Mr Marlin Fitzwater, President Bush's spokesman, said that Mr Thomas Pickering, the United States ambassador to the UN, had presented evidence of the sanctions-breaking imports to the other four permanent members of the Security Council during continued talks on means of enforcing the embargo.

Iraqi troops were still surrounding the embassies in Kuwait of Britain, the United States and more than 20 others early today as diplomats remained defiant in the face of President Hussein's order that they close midnight and move out.

As the deadline approached, there were mounting fears that Iraq was preparing to fulfil its threat to evacuate the embassies by force — but diplomats from the resisting countries were intending to stay put until the last possible moment. Telephone lines were severed yesterday and troops were stopping people moving in and out of the buildings.

In Amman, the Spanish ambassador, Mr Ramon Armengoa, said the deadline had been extended to 8.30 a.m. today.

Mr Armengod, said Iraq had threatened to use force against diplomats who defied orders to evacuate their missions by this morning.

The threat, which appeared to extend Baghdad's original Friday deadline, was delivered in a message to the West German embassy in Baghdad, signed "Iraqi authorities," he said.

Iraqi troops and tanks surrounded the British Embassy and staff were still inside after the deadline passed.

A British Foreign Office spokesman said power supplies to the embassy had been cut. "Diplomats in the embassy are sitting by candlelight. The embassy is surrounded by Iraqi soldiers and tanks," he said.

The United States has declared that any attempt to close its embassy — manned by a skeleton of 10 — will be viewed as an act of war.

The European Community will ask for an emergency meeting of the UN security council if the diplomatic status of European ambassadors in Kuwait is violated when the Iraqi deadline expires, an Italian Foreign Ministry spokesman said in Rome.

The spokesman said the EC political co-operation committee was studying the possibility of grouping all the European Community ambassadors in Kuwait City in one place for when the deadline expires to dramatise the violation of diplomatic norms. But, he indicated no final decision had yet been made on that idea. — (Reuter, AP, London Independent Service, AFP, UPI)

University points drop slightly

By John Walshe, Education Correspondent

ENTRY requirements for many ...

those who are made offers will not accept them. Eventually some 12,000 places will be filled, compared with 10,500 last year ...

Parc denies INO claims of low morale, fear among Baghdad staff

STAFF at the Parc hospital in Baghdad are having their movements restricted, have been deprived of meat in their rations and based on a rice diet at this time.

"Despite assurances (which we understand were given by yourselves) that they would be in a ...

"totally untrue." "The INO made no attempt to check their statement with Parc before going public," the company said.

reporting for duty as normal. All 19 specialist units in the hospital were functioning properly, but a continued embargo on movement ...

More storms are expected today

By Padraig Yeates

ALARM systems all over Dublin were set off by last night's electrical storms but the heavy ... simply due to the localised nature of the cloudbursts, which were not occurring at their weather stations.

The atmosphere had been con...

THE IRISH TIMES

PRICE 65p (incl. VAT) 55p sterling area | DUBLIN, FRIDAY, NOVEMBER 9, 1990 | No. 41,829 CITY

INSIDE TODAY

WORKING & LIVING

Digital's high-tech warehouse

New EC rules on jobs

10-PAGE COLOUR SUPPLEMENT

PRAGUE POLICY

Czechs look to the EC

FERGUS PYLE PAGE 13

HITTING FIFTY

Wiser and happier

PAGE 15

Judgment on Ellis reserved

The Supreme Court has reserved judgment on the appeal by Mr Desmond Ellis against his extradition to Britain ■ page 11

Force in Gulf not ruled out

The use of force in the Gulf was not ruled out, the Soviet Foreign Minister, Mr Shevardnadze, told the US Secretary of State, Mr Baker, in Moscow yesterday ■ page 13

Xtra-vision worth £5½m

Cambridge's takeover of Xtra-vision values the video chain at £5½m, down from its £40m high ■ page 18

GPA group profits up

GPA Group, the aircraft leasing concern has improved first half profits 22% to $140.3 millions. ■ page 18

INDEX

Home News ... 2, 4, 5, 6, 7, 8, 9, 11, 16
Sport ... 20, 21, 22
World News ... 12, 13
Business & Finance ... 18, 19, 20
Arts, Reviews ... 14
News Features ... 15
Letters to the Editor ... 17
Weather ... 16
Entertainments ... 26
TV and Radio ... 27

Historic victory for Robinson

By Denis Coghlan, Political Correspondent

MS MARY ROBINSON will be confirmed as the first woman President of the State when the final election counts take place in Dublin today and the second preference votes of Fine Gael's Mr Austin Currie are distributed.

Although Fianna Fail had not formally conceded defeat last night, the first count results which gave Ms Robinson 39 per cent of the national vote, as against 44 per cent for Mr Brian Lehihan and 17 per cent for Mr Currie, sealed the fate of the Fianna Fail candidate.

Transfers from Mr Currie to Ms Robinson were estimated to be running at a ratio of 7:1, which would give her a final percentage of about 52 per cent, against 48 per cent for Mr Lenihan.

Ms Robinson, who was nominated by the Labour Party and supported by the Workers' Party and the Green Party, spoke of the result as "a great, great day for the women of Ireland" and thanked all who had voted for her.

The Presidential campaign was the most controversial and hard-fought on record, with marked volatility in the electorate as it responded, first to disclosures concerning Mr Lenihan's telephone call to Aras an Uachtaráin in January, 1982, and then in sympathy to his sacking from Cabinet.

The former Tanaiste said yesterday that he had been "witch-hunted" and that history would vindicate him. The most unethical aspect of Irish politics they had seen during the campaign, he said, had been the involvement of Fine Gael, Dr Garret FitzGerald and an Irish national newspaper in the matter of a telephone call.

Mr Lenihan said he was proud to have been "the first choice of the highest number of voters in the country", and he felt that the turnout, from the party's point of view, was a good result. They had been beaten by "a rainbow coalition of interests" and he was the only one to have fought an absolutely clean campaign". He intended to continue his career in politics, he said.

Even as Mr Lenihan and Fianna Fail Ministers were projecting the imminent loss of the Presidency as a minor setback, rather than as a political failure of immense proportions, Fine Gael was also counting the political cost of the defection of half of the party's vote to Ms Robinson.

INSIDE

A reluctant runner who went the distance: page 2; Ahern lays blame on tapes issue; O'Rourke says FG campaign was shameful: page 4; The undoing of an 'unbeatable' candidate; Airwaves: page 5; Dublin vote was key to victory; Map and charts: page 6; How the State voted; Powers of the President: page 7; How the result will affect the main parties: page 8; Robinson profile: page 9.

Editorial comment: page 17

Mr Austin Currie blamed his poor showing on his late entry to the race and upon the fact that Fine Gael activists had already committed themselves to Ms Robinson. They had not changed their allegiance, he said, and other Fine Gael voters had joined them in an "anti-Lenihan vote".

Mr Currie felt that his conduct during the campaign, his television performance and his judgment would "not be lost on people" in terms of his future political career. Significantly, however, he declined to comment on whether he would continue to support Mr Dukes as leader of the party. He said that all political campaigns had "implications for political parties and the leaders of political parties".

The outcome of the election will be decided today through the transfers of Mr Currie's second preference vote and, in that regard, the political controversy over the telephone call affair had a major effect.

In early October, Mr Lenihan was in a strong position and stood to gain one-in-three of those votes, according to opinion polls. After the sharpening of political divisions between Fianna Fail and Fine Gael, however, the ratio of transfers between the parties worsened to one-in-seven. That ratio is now expected to put Ms Robinson into Aras an Uachtaráin.

The leader of the Progressive Democrats, and Minister for Industry and Commerce, Mr Desmond O'Malley, said he was "very pleased" by the result. He felt Ms Robinson would make "an excellent President", and he congratulated her on her "considerable victory".

As to possible repercussions within the coalition Government, Mr O'Malley said that the outcome of the election would "not affect the Progressive Democrats' coalition arrangement with Fianna Fail".

Ms Robinson represented the result as a victory for women and announced that it was a great, great day for them. The women, she said, had gone out and voted because they had a sense of purpose, and it was "a great day for us, for our children and our grandchildren, and I thank you all for having been involved in it".

The leader of the Labour Party, Mr Dick Spring, felt that the election of Ms Robinson was something that his party would capitalise on. There were many areas of the country where Labour was now in a position to organise itself because of the campaign, he said.

The president of the Workers' Party, Mr Proinsias De Rossa, regarded the outcome as "a death knell for civil war politics". Ms Robinson's vote represented the triumph of tolerance over prejudice, he said, of principle over pragmatism and of idealism over opportunism.

The Green Party welcomed the outcome and anticipated that the new President would represent "a more environmentally friendly and modern pluralist face of Ireland".

HOW THE STATE VOTED

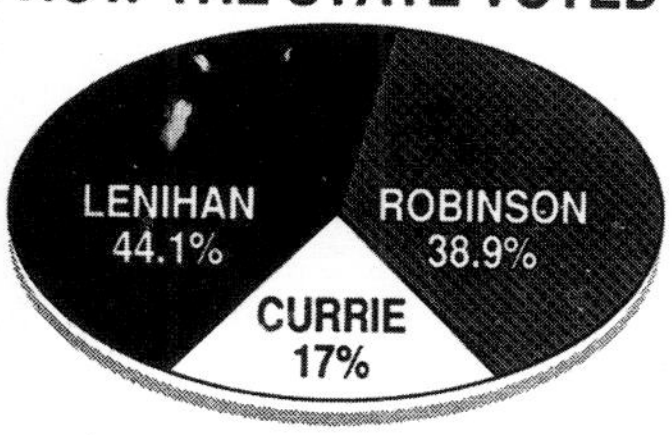

PROJECTED OUTCOME AFTER DISTRIBUTION OF SECOND PREFERENCES

LENIHAN	47.4%
ROBINSON	52.6%

Dukes denies crisis in FG as FF turns blame on PDs

By Denis Coghlan, Political Correspondent

THE Fine Gael leader, Mr Alan Dukes, has rejected any notion of bowing to internal party pressure and resigning his position, following the collapse of the Fine Gael vote and the poor showing of Mr Austin Currie in the Presidential election.

As the result of the election began to fulfil the worst fears of Fine Gael deputies, who have become increasingly restive in recent months under his leadership, Mr Dukes told *The Irish Times*: "There is no question of my stepping down. With the party gaining in the opinion polls, the last thing it requires is a leadership contest which I would, in any case, win. The real leadership issue is in Fianna Fail."

Even as he spoke, a Fine Gael councillor, Mr Michael Connor-Scarteen of Kerry said he would support a move by the Parliamentary Party to remove Mr Dukes and he expressed a preference for Mr John Bruton.

The defiant attitude of Mr Dukes, and his threat to fight any attempt to oust him as leader, may cause his opponents to hesitate in challenging him openly. In recent months, reports of a conspiracy against him sent some deputies running for cover, while others felt that he would 'go quietly' if the pressure became intense.

The looming failure of Fianna Fail to retain the prize of the Presidency will also have repercussions within that party, even though they may not immediately call into question Mr Haughey's leadership.

As the outcome became evident, representatives of the party tended to blame the Progressive Democrats for what happened, while the sister of the sacked Tanaiste, the Minister for Education, Ms Mary O'Rourke, insisted that there was "no leadership crisis in Fianna Fail".

Ms O'Rourke felt that Fianna Fail should have opted for a general election, rather than dismiss her brother, and she admitted to feeling "very troubled about it." At the same time, she said: "We have a very strong leader and it's back to business as usual."

Anti-Coalition sentiment due to the role played by the Progressive Democrats in the sacking of Mr Lenihan surfaced in Cork last night with a call from Mr Ned O'Keeffe, for the party to withdraw from Coalition.

The East Cork Fianna Fail deputy said that the Progressive Democrats had forced Mr Haughey's hand in the sacking of Mr Lenihan and it was now clear that the party had "suffered greviously because of its involvement with the Progressive Democrats."

There was "very serious unrest" throughout the organisation because of what had happened, he went on, and that feeling had deepened because the Progressive Democrats had actively campaigned for Ms Robinson and had spoken for her. In spite of his attack on the Coalition arrangement, Mr O'Keeffe said he had no problem with Mr Haughey's leadership and he felt that he would not be challenged.

Mr Haughey and his colleagues have sacrificed so much already to preserve the Government that they will be determined to make it last. The Progressive Democrats have already indicated their willingness in that regard.

The election has also provided clear and positive benefits for the parties of the left who supported Ms Robinson, and particularly for the Labour Party, which masterminded her campaign. But the fruits of that victory may be slow to come, judging by the standing of the political parties in

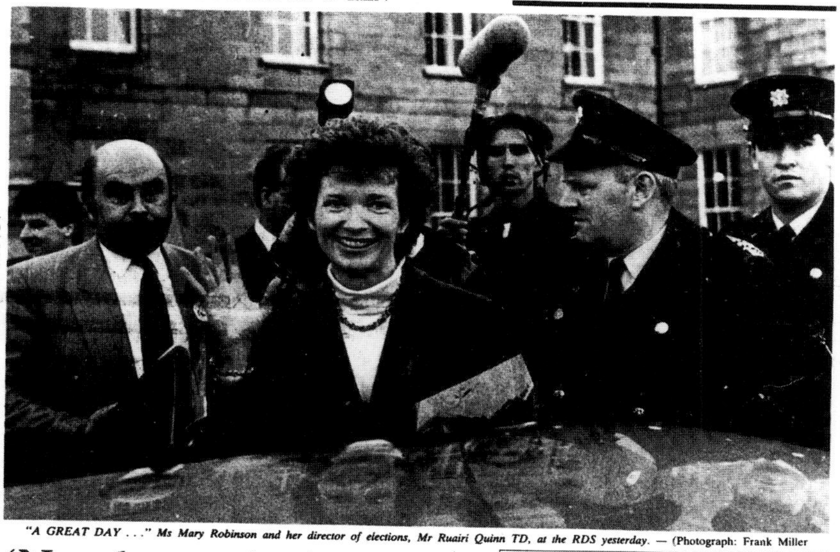

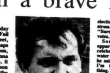

"A GREAT DAY . . ." Ms Mary Robinson and her director of elections, Mr Ruairi Quinn TD, at the RDS yesterday. — (Photograph: Frank Miller

'Nearly made it' group puts on a brave face

By John Waters

AT TWO o'clock yesterday afternoon in the Fianna Fail headquarters in Mount Street, Dublin, we waited, for perhaps the last time in this election, for the arrival of the Fianna Fail candidate. By this time, it appeared that Mary Robinson had won, that she would be the next President of Ireland; our job was to discover whether, in fact, Mr Lenihan had lost.

The building was strangely quiet. The election might not yet have been either won or lost, but there was little difficulty in deducing the party's view of the likely outcome. There were no ministers in the building, no TDs, no senators, only a handful of party workers. The signs were bad: if they were good, a party worker said "the lads would have been dropping in over lunch". There were no lads. But the candidate himself was due at any minute. First, however, came director of elections Bertie Ahern. Bertie, looking more relaxed than for the last three weeks, informed journalists that it was still too early to say what the outcome might be

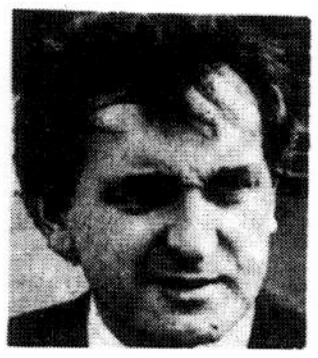

Mr Ahern

accept full blame for themselves and talk about voting trends as though they were in the nature of strange political weather patterns, totally beyond the control or understanding of politicians.

But for Bertie this hour had not yet come. Not quite, at any rate. Yes, he said, it would be correct to say that they were worried. But it was early days yet. Bertie, however, was getting closer to the bottom line. "We nearly made it," he said. "But nearly never won a race." What could this mean, we

election. He had, he wanted to stress, obtained the most votes. "Sure I won on first-preference votes," he pointed out.

Someone asked, without apparent irony, how he would be celebrating. "I'm confined to water for celebration purposes," he said, adding quickly: "Not that I'm feeling penitential or anything."

And what about his future if he failed to win the election?

"My future career is well set in Irish politics. It has been for a number of years and it's going to continue in a very active way. I had no intention of taking on the Presidency at any stage in a retirement capacity. I was interested in doing a good job and, well . . . the people decide otherwise . . . or have done . . . may, *may* decide otherwise on what's appearing. That's democracy. But I'd like to pursue an active life in parliamentary politics."

Would he like to be reinstated in the Government?

"I'd like to pursue an active life in parliamentary politics."

Meanwhile, he said, getting up to go to the count centre at the RDS, things were in a state of

SUZUKI
No. 1 in small vehicles in Japan
INTRODUCE
for their Swift and Alto ranges
A 3 YEAR UNLIMITED MILEAGE WARRANTY

HIGHER INTEREST RATES
UP TO **11%**
with the **SUPERGRO** INVESTMENT SCHEME
Interest

16 November

Legislation makes it illegal to incite hatred against homosexuals.

22 December

Samuel Beckett dies in Paris.

1990

11 February

Nelson Mandela is released from prison in South Africa.

30 June

The Republic of Ireland is knocked out of the World Cup after losing 1–0 to Italy.

1 July

Nelson Mandela visits Dublin and is reported as saying that the British government should engage in talks with the IRA. At least half a million people welcome the Republic of Ireland's soccer team home to Dublin.

24 August

The Belfast man Brian Keenan is released from captivity by the Islamic Jihad in Beirut.

The McAliskey house in Co. Tyrone where a loyalist gang attacked and attempted to murder Bernadette McAliskey (née Devlin) in January 1981

Wilson, the British Prime Minister, made a notorious broadcast in which he described the people of Northern Ireland as 'people who spend their lives sponging on Westminster and British democracy.' The effect on middle-class Protestant opinion was disastrous, pushing many previously apathetic people into support for the strikers. Many Catholics were equally offended. In *The Irish Times* Nell McCafferty described her mother in Derry listening to the broadcast. '"What?" my mother sat up. "Spongers? Is he calling us spongers? In the name of God … is he telling us we're spongers?" She made for the radio.' When the strikers won and the Executive collapsed, *The Irish Times* furiously noted that 'in all the shame that Britain has suffered at the hands of her departing colonials this lying down to the bigots of Belfast ranks high in infamy.'

The Irish Times tried to keep optimism alive, however, and an editorial at the end of May reflected that 'the new idea of power-sharing is not dead … something has been rescued, an idea, and it will, and must, go marching on.' Yet gradually, as the violence of the IRA, of the

from The Irish Times 1996

The Gay B&B

Nuala O'Faolain

There's a small guesthouse in central Dublin, in a pleasant, prettily decorated, nineteenth-century house. They're all the rage now, these town-house places. Just inside the door, in an illuminated frame, there's a large photograph of the President. That's common enough. Only—not so common—beside Mrs Robinson there's a portrait of Danny La Rue. He performed the opening ceremony of the place a couple of months ago.

The guesthouse is attached to a gay sauna club. You get free admittance to the club (worth £7.50) when you stay a night in the guesthouse (B&B, £25 single). It's Ireland's first gay-run accommodation, and it's mainly meant for gay men, although anyone, of course, can stay there. And it's as stunning a sign of social change in Ireland as you're likely to come across.

It asks more of the rest of us, in the line of abandoning old attitudes, than gays have hitherto done. Last week, for example, we had World AIDS day. Everyone knows what gay men have suffered through AIDS, and more or less everyone on such a day, if they think about it at all, feels sympathetic. It's easy to be sympathetic towards somewhat distant people, especially when they are comfortably defined as victims. The guesthouse, however, is a detail in the life of a perfectly self-confident, if sexually specialist, part of the community, which has its own entrepreneurs and its own business life. Sympathy is quite irrelevant. Then again, next Friday 170 gay men and lesbian women will attend a gala dinner in a hotel in Dún Laoghaire, where they will present the Minister for Justice, Mrs Geoghegan-Quinn, with the Hirschfeld Award.

This award is to mark the forthright way in which the Minister presented the arguments for Ireland's progressive sexual equality legislation. It is fully expected that a wonderful night will be had by all. And the conferring of the award will be another moment in social change. A great many people in Ireland still have the knee-jerk reaction that the only thing the Department of Justice could possibly want with homosexuals would be to keep an eye on them. But there are no threatening laws now, no in-built criminality, nothing which a homosexual person can get into trouble for that anyone else wouldn't get into trouble for too. Obviously, all the implications of this have yet to work their way into every corner of the social fabric. For example, the army appears to have an unresolved problem. But the Gay and Lesbian Federation is now as likely as the Irish Farmers' Association or

Bono, the biggest pop star Ireland has produced. His band U2 has been one of the best—some say the very best—in the world through the eighties and nineties. This photograph dates from the band's early days.

Shane McGowan, lead singer with the Pogues

security forces and of the loyalist paramilitaries continued, the paper was forced to retreat from its belief in the early years of the conflict that the violence was just an end-of-empire phenomenon. Indeed it was forced to demand a dismantling of all epic ideologies and to demand, first and foremost, an end to bloodshed and a commitment to compromise. After 17 May 1974, when loyalist bombs caused carnage in Monaghan and Dublin, an editorial spelt out the cost of romantic rhetoric. 'It was easy to place the present bloody strife of Irishman versus Irishman in a falsely romantic setting of the past ... We recognise the frightfulness of the bodies and the blood on our streets. We do not always recognise the implications of the phrases which so often are bandied about—phrases about the inalienable rights of this or that section of the people, phrases

24 October

It is revealed that the Fianna Fáil presidential candidate, Brian Lenihan, phoned President Patrick Hillery in 1982 to ask him not to dissolve the Dáil after the defeat of the coalition Government's budget that year.

22 November

Margaret Thatcher is defeated as British

Stephen Roche on the Champs Élysée en route to victory in the 1987 Tour de France, the only Irishman to win the world's most gruelling sporting event

Charles Haughey, once again Taoiseach, was there to greet Roche on his victory. A few weeks later, an American bald eagle landed in the west of Ireland, having been blown across the Atlantic by storm winds. Martyn Turner conjoined the two events in this classic cartoon.

the Pre-School Playgroup Association or the Soroptomists or any other body to invite a Minister to dine with them and receive an award. They're not just normal—they bid fair to be boringly normal.

Yet it is not possible to recover in just a few months from the millennium or two during which homosexuals were formally reviled and ostracised. Gay people themselves probably adjust more quickly than outsiders can—they always knew that in everything except sexual orientation they were much like everyone else …

Twenty years ago, Liam and Tony opened Studio One, the country's first gay club, and they got a certain amount of harassment from members of the Legion of Mary, who reported them to the Garda. Just for existing, really. But that was the very least you would expect, given the times. De

about the freedom to do this or that. When any man fails to reckon his neighbour's freedoms as important as his own, the result can be released in explosions like those in Dublin yesterday.'

If the bombs of 1974 turned public opinion in the Republic definitively against violence, there was already strong evidence that the IRA's claims to act on behalf of the Irish nation had no basis. The relatively limited hold of militant nationalism over public opinion was clearly demonstrated in May 1972 in a referendum on whether or not Ireland should join the EEC. Both wings of Sinn Féin campaigned strongly for a 'no' vote, and the authority of the internees was invoked. 'The boys in Long Kesh say vote no.'

Prime Minister and leader of the Conservative Party.

9 November
Mary Robinson becomes the first woman President of Ireland.

1991

14 March
The Birmingham Six are released in London after wrongly spending more than sixteen years in jail for the Birmingham pub bombings.

21 April
A census is carried out in the Republic; it will show the population to be 3.53 million.

17 July
Ian Paisley and other unionists visit Dublin to picket the Department of Foreign Affairs because of the resumption of the Anglo-Irish Conference, which was suspended for the eleven-week duration of the inter-party talks in Northern Ireland.

The Boss. Charles Haughey was the most controversial political leader in Ireland since independence. Not fully in control of Fianna Fáil until the second half of the eighties, he failed to win an overall majority for the party in five general elections.

The eighties were a time of economic gloom in the Republic, with public finances seemingly out of control. It led to protests such as this one by construction workers.

Valera was only dead a few months when Studio One opened. On the whole, everyone had a great time. And the club did well: visitors to Ireland—the late Johnny 'Crybaby' Ray, for example—would dance there, and Irish gays took their place among the nations of the earth, so to speak …

The club was there for years, behind the house that has now been made into a hotel. It used to be a grocery shop. But the old man died, and the upper storeys were empty, and Dunne's Stores took away the custom. Most of the street was derelict. Now three blocks of new apartments are going up. The private education colleges which are taking over inner Dublin have moved into the vicinity, bringing in hundreds of young people. Some of the pubs have become international-type bars. Life is pouring back into an area which has done nothing but decay for years.

A few years hence the plain, grey street will be altogether modernised, and the way it was for so long will be forgotten. It will seem quite unremarkable that the local hotel is a gay one. Our citizens will be like Amsterdamers are now, or Berliners—not amazed by anything. Nobody then will see anything unusual in little things such as that the hotel's

But the contest between nationalist orthodoxy on the one side and the prospect for economic advancement (especially, in rural Ireland, the benefits of the Common Agricultural Policy, with its high prices and generous subsidies for farmers) proved to be no contest at all. 83 per cent, including a huge majority in every constituency, voted in favour of the EEC. It was, in more ways than one, a turning-point. Membership of the EEC (later called the European Union) would have huge economic, social and cultural consequences. But, less obviously, the vote was the moment at which the Republic declared itself against civil war. It had decided that its dream was modern prosperity, not atavistic revenge.

While Northern Ireland remained inextricably linked with Britain, membership of the EEC helped the Republic to move out of the economic and political shadow of its larger neighbour. And it also helped to tip the balance

1992

22 January

The trial of a UDA man and British military intelligence agent, Brian Nelson, hears that four shootings were carried out by the UDA in 1988, resulting in two deaths, despite Nelson's handlers being forewarned of them.

30 January

Charles Haughey resigns as Taoiseach and

The key members of the Sinn Féin executive in the early eighties, following the effective take-over of the republican movement by its northern wing. From the left: Joe Cahill, Martin McGuinness, Gerry Adams, and Danny Morrison.

leader of Fianna Fáil over the allegation that he knew of the tapping of journalists' phones in 1982.

5 February

Five Catholics are shot dead by the UFF in a bookmaker's shop in the Lower Ormeau Road, Belfast, in what it says is retaliation for the Teebane bombing.

11 February

Albert Reynolds is elected leader of Fianna Fáil.

of the conflict between tradition and modernity decisively in favour of modernity. After 1973 it was simply impossible to imagine an alternative project for the Irish future that could even begin to compete with the European one. Before the EEC, a case could still just about be made for an isolated, protected, conservative Ireland. It could still be proposed that the main goal of Irish people was to preserve intact a set of religious, cultural and social values they had inherited from their ancestors. At least in the way the Irish talked about themselves, this ideal still had immense prestige. Even though it was contradicted in daily life all the time, it still had the authority of religion, of the education system, and of political rhetoric.

The EU destroyed those illusions and bought off the conservative heartlands of rural Ireland. It offered modernity in a form that seemed at first to be purely material. It was modernity not as sex and secularism and confusion but as subsidy cheques, mechanised milking-parlours, beef mountains, and headage payments. It seemed to be about money, not

brochure says 'Good morning. We do hope you had a good night's sleep and indeed an enjoyable night on the town.' Or that you get a complimentary glass of champagne with your full Irish breakfast on a Sunday.

Evidently, many Irish men suffer greatly because they are gay. Every day you see the viciousness with which straight men punish them for what their existence says—that the peace and quiet of the heterosexual marriage bed isn't everything. There must be many, many men in Ireland who will never in their lives be held in a passionate embrace, because heterosexual bigotry has forced them into darkness. But that is only part of the story, and the story so far. Liam and Tony represent another possibility. They've never been victimised. They've been happy and amused, most of the time. They apologise to nobody. Moreover, a few weeks ago, the elegant facade of the guesthouse won a prize in the Business Face of Dublin Awards, sponsored by Jury's Hotel Group. They accepted their certificate from the Lord Mayor. That's where they're at. They're businessmen.

When maternity leave for mothers first came in—only twelve years ago—some employers looked on fondly as their women employees went off to have a baby. Once. Then when women took time off to have second babies, or even third ones, they got furious. 'They're taking advantage of the legislation,' I remember one boss saying to me.

They thought there could be progressive legislation, but that things would stay the same—that nothing would really threaten the status quo. But legislation changes everything. The decriminalisation of homosexuality will have effects more far-reaching than most people have bothered to imagine. The guesthouse is just a little thing but it is a portent of the Ireland to come.

from The Irish Times 1997
JULY

Scenes from the Death of the National Movement

Fintan O'Toole

In July 1997 Charles Haughey, former leader of Fianna Fáil, admitted that he had received £1.3 million from a businessman between 1987 and 1992.

A decade ago, shortly before he returned to power for his third stint as Taoiseach, Charles Haughey presented a programme called 'My Ireland' for Channel 4. Full as it was of sentimental clichés dressed up in about politics, society, or culture. It probably helped too that in the initial period of EU membership rural Ireland gained while urban Ireland lost out. In the countryside, new bungalows were springing up like mushrooms moistened by the sweet mist of prosperity that seemed to descend on the fields. In the towns and cities, mass unemployment was laying down deep roots as traditional, uncompetitive and labour-intensive industries shut up shop.

Before it quite knew it, the conservative heartland had bought into a modernising project much more radical in its implications than anything it could ever have imagined. The road paved with European currency units was leading inexorably to a transnational, federal superstate. Yet the economic benefits of continuing to follow it, and the economic costs of trying to go back, were so great that there was no real choice except continuing to put one foot in front of another. Things came to a crunch in 1992 with the referendum on the Maastricht Treaty on

18 February

In what becomes known as the 'X' Case, the Attorney-General obtains an injunction preventing a fourteen-year-old rape victim from travelling to Britain to have an abortion. A psychiatrist states that the girl is in a state that could lead her to take her own life.

18 June

69% of voters in the referendum accept the Maastricht Treaty.

Tony Gregory, the independent inner-city Dublin TD whose casting vote gave Charles Haughey power following the inconclusive February 1982 general election in return for a package of measures to assist his constituency. The arrangement was known ever after as the Gregory Deal.

THE IRISH TIMES

PRICE 75p (incl. VAT) 65p sterling area | DUBLIN, TUESDAY, FEBRUARY 18, 1992 | No. 43,218 CITY

Pregnant girl threatened suicide

'It is better to end it now than in nine months' time', she told psychologist

By Jim Cusack

THE 14-year-old girl who has been restrained by the Attorney-General, Mr Harry Whelehan, from terminating a pregnancy allegedly caused by rape is capable of committing suicide, according to a clinical psychologist who has examined her.

The girl has told her parents that she wanted to kill herself and "coldly expressed a desire to solve matters by ending her life". Mr Justice Costello stated in his judgment granting an application for an injunction restraining the girl from travelling to England for an abortion.

The girl has received clinical treatment since returning from England 13 days ago after her parents were made aware that an injunction was being sought to restrain their daughter and themselves from terminating the pregnancy.

She remains under supervision while in the care of her parents, who live in the greater Dublin area. The family is middle class and the girl has been receiving a convent education.

The family, described by gardai as "highly respectable", was said to have been co-operative throughout the present proceedings. The girl's parents voluntarily agreed to return from London to Dublin when informed by a Garda officer of the injunction.

In his judgment yesterday, Mr Justice Costello confirmed that the girl had been subjected to sexual abuse by the father of one of her school friends since she was 12 years of age. The judge described the man, who has been questioned by gardai, as "depraved and evil".

Mr Justice Costello said that the girl had been subjected to serious sexual abuse by the man since the early part of 1991. Last December, he had had "full sexual intercourse with her, to which she did not consent". She did not tell anyone about the abuse until January 27th last. Her parents, who were known to have become increasingly concerned at her withdrawn behaviour, discovered from the family doctor that she was pregnant.

She was referred to hospital three days later and the gardai were alerted. A statement was made to gardai on February 3rd. A day later, after the hospital had confirmed the pregnancy, she and her parents decided to have it terminated.

INSIDE

Text of judgment: page 6
Garda file on alleged rape incomplete; Women's group warn fewer will report rape; Opposition TDs to seek debate on judgment: page 7
Dr Anthony Clare's view: page 8

The parents let this be known to gardai and raised the possibility of making arrangements for DNA testing of foetal tissue samples for possible use in evidence against the alleged rapist. It was when gardai raised this question with the office of the Director of Public Prosecutions that the matter was made known to the Attorney-General, who then set in train the legal action to prevent the abortion.

Delivering his judgment yesterday, Mr Justice Costello revealed that the girl had said that she "wanted to kill herself by throwing herself downstairs" and that, while in London, she had said that she wanted to throw herself under a train.

According to the report from the psychologist who examined the girl, the "psychological damage to her of carrying a child would be considerable and the damage to her mental health would be devastating." The girl told the doctor: "It is hard at 14 to go through the nine months. It is better to end it now than in nine months' time."

The judge found that, although "complicated and difficult", the facts of the case did "not inhibit" the court from applying the "clear rule of law" laid down in the Eighth Amendment to the Constitution. He also found that the amendment amounted to a derogation by Ireland from the principles in EC law abolishing restrictions on the movement of nationals wishing to travel to another State, where abortion is legal, in order to have a pregnancy terminated.

He found that the threat to the life of the girl in this case came not from surgical intervention, but from herself.

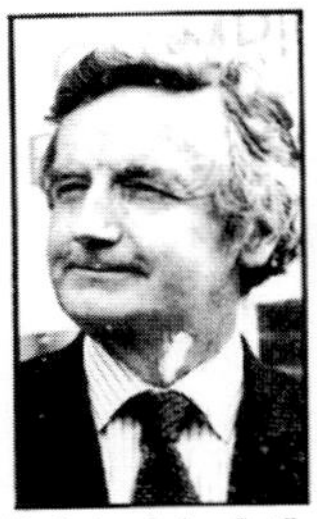

Mr Justice Declan Costello . . . applying "clear rule of law".

INSIDE

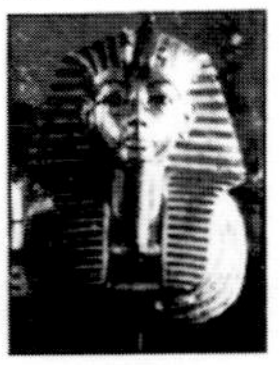

EGYPT

A special 12-page colour supplement on tourism in the land of the Pharaohs

TOO MANY DEGREES

Is TCD giving too many degrees to outsiders: Some of the college's academics think so
PAGE 11

THE FINAL CURTAIN?

Mary Leland on the crisis facing Cork Opera House
PAGE 10

Israeli army on alert

The Israeli army has been put on alert in preparation for retaliatory attacks for the killing of Sheikh Moussawi ☐ page 9

Irish to join UN peace force

At his first EC ministers meeting as Foreign Minister, Mr Andrews confirmed that Ireland would be sending a small contingent of gardai and Army personnel to join the 13,000-strong UN peacekeeping force in Yugoslavia ☐ page 9.

INDEX

Whelehan to advise against change in law

High Court judgment depends on family's goodwill

By Geraldine Kennedy and Maol Muire Tynan

THE Attorney General, Mr Harry Whelehan, will advise the Government today that no changes in the law or the Constitution on abortion are required following yesterday's High Court decision to prevent a 14-year-old alleged rape victim from travelling to England for an abortion.

It was thought unlikely that the girl or her family would appeal the case to the Supreme Court last night, although this could not be confirmed.

Legal sources also indicated that the implementation of the High Court judgment would depend on the family's goodwill, and that they would not be subjected to garda surveillance to ensure that they did not leave the jurisdiction over the next nine months.

It is understood that provision was made for the girl and her family to return to the court at any time if circumstances changed.

Mr Whelehan has been asked to brief the Cabinet this morning on the circumstances surrounding the case which he took to the court last week independently of the Government.

All of the Opposition parties will be seeking information from the Taoiseach, Mr Reynolds, in the Dail today on the implications of the case.

Mr Justice Declan Costello, in his judgment yesterday, restrained the 14-year-old girl and her parents from procuring or arranging a termination of the pregnancy either within the State or abroad. He also restrained her or her parents or agents from leaving the jurisdiction for a period of nine months.

The judge found that the risk that the girl may take her own life if an order was made "is much less and is of a different order of magnitude than the certainty that the life of the unborn will be terminated if the order is not made".

The leader of the Labour Party, Mr Dick Spring, has already written to the Ceann Comhairle calling for a suspension of today's Dail business to allow "a matter of public importance requiring urgent attention" to be debated.

He will call on the Taoiseach, Mr Reynolds, in the light of the judgment, to outline the steps that will now be taken to provide relief for the distress and trauma suffered by the family involved and what further steps the State proposed to take in the matter.

The Fine Gael spokesman on justice, Mr Alan Shatter, has tabled a special notice question to the Taoiseach asking him to state the circumstances which gave arise to the Attorney General making the court application; and what future policy will be applied by the Government in such circumstances.

The leader of the Workers' Party, Mr Proinsias De Rossa, said that in the short-term the party would be raising the matter in the Dail today and tabling a private members' motion calling for the resignation of the Attorney General. "In the longer-term those who have been shocked and appalled by this case must now begin preparing the ground for a further referendum to remove this hideous provision from our Constitution", he said.

Government sources indicated last night that the case was proving an extremely traumatic start for the new administration under Mr Reynolds, and that the Government took the view that it must be dealt with "sensitively".

Ministers were told from the outset by the Attorney General that he was exercising a non-Governmental role given to him by the courts. However, the sources added that the Cabinet was looking forward to today's briefing from the Attorney General in the knowledge that the Government still had a major problem that required urgent political consideration.

A Government spokesman refused to comment either before the judgment or afterwards, but a spokesman for the Progressive Democrats admitted: "We are very concerned about the present situation".

In a statement issued last night, the chairman of the Progressive Democrats, Mr Michael McDowell, said the decision was "as unnecessary as it is difficult to understand". Its implicit social values are not shared by the majority of "right-minded people", he said.

"The facts revealed in the judgment could clearly have led to a different result. The result is not what people voted for in 1983; they were assured then that this would never happen," Mr McDowell said.

He believed the decision to bring the matter to the courts was demonstrated to be wrong and had "potentially devastating consequences not just for the girl, for her family, but for all girls and women, for men, our values and self-respect and for our standing among civilised people".

He urged the State to take whatever steps are necessary to ensure these circumstances are never repeated — whatever the outcome of the present case.

Editorial comment: page 13.

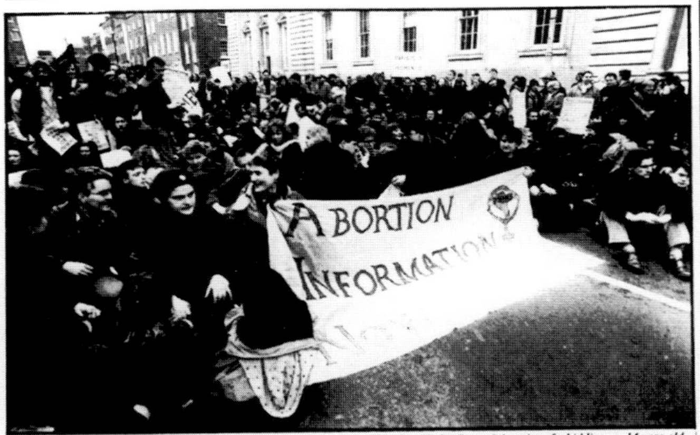

A demonstration yesterday outside Government Buildings against the High Court injunction forbidding a 14-year-old alleged rape victim from obtaining an abortion in Britain. The banner includes a telephone number which has been deleted by The Irish Times, *in compliance with the High Court ruling of December 1986, which found that the provision of assistance, including information, to a pregnant woman seeking an abortion was in breach of Article 40 of the Constitution. This judgment was upheld by the Supreme Court in February 1988.* — (Photograph: Eric Luke)

The Citroën XM. Automatically, it costs the same as a Manual!

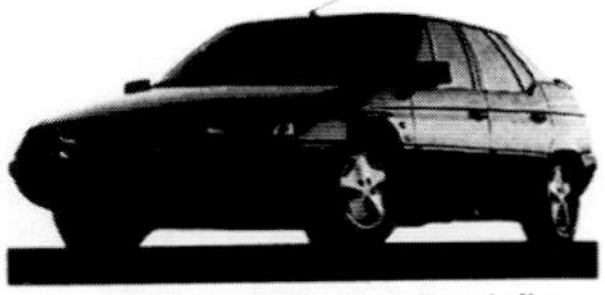

Announcing a remarkable and very limited offer from Citroen.

A superb Citroen XM Automatic, for the price of a Citroen XM with manual transmission. All XM's will also feature a free tilt and slide electric sun-roof.

Normally, these added luxuries would cost almost £3,000, but right now they're yours at no added cost at all.

NIO silent on alleged involvement of SAS

From Gerry Moriarty, in Clonoe, Co Tyrone

THE security forces and the Northern Ireland Office have refused to confirm or deny claims by Sinn Fein and some local people that the gun battle in Clonoe, Co Tyrone, on Sunday night, in which four IRA members were killed, involved SAS undercover soldiers.

Earlier, eight or more IRA men had attacked the nearby Coalisland RUC barracks. The men fled the scene and as they were transferring to getaway cars in the car park of St Patrick's Catholic church in Clonoe, they were caught up in a fierce exchange of fire with British soldiers.

Four IRA members were killed and two other men were injured as well as a British soldier. It is believed two or more men may have escaped.

Sinn Fein said the Clonoe incident bore all the hallmarks of an SAS undercover operation, while some local people complained of a "shoot-to-kill" policy by the security forces ... known to the police as IRA members, according to the RUC. One of the men was Mr Kevin Barry O'Donnell (21), from Coalisland, who was acquitted by an Old Bailey jury last March of possessing two Kalashnikov rifles with intent.

He was convicted of having the weapons under suspicious circumstances and sentenced to nine months youth custody. He was arrested following a car chase through London. Mr O'Donnell was released as he had served the nine months while on remand in custody.

Residents tell of fierce battle at church: page 5

The IRA last night admitted that members of its east Tyrone brigade had been killed and claimed that at least one of the four men killed had his hands in the air (in the act of surrender) when he was shot.

The four men were named last night as Mr O'Donnell, of Stewartstown Road, Coalisland; ... O'Farrell (22), also from Lisnakil Court, and Mr Patrick Daniel Vincent (20), Kingarve Road, Dungannon.

Local people said there was a heavy security presence in the Clonoe area on Sunday. An RUC spokesman said he had heard reports of the SAS being involved in a stake-out at Clonoe.

The Northern Security Minister, Dr Brian Mawhinney, said the men who died were clearly on a murder mission. "Their grieving families are going to have to ask those who sent them: 'Why'? What good could ever come out of the barrel of a heavy duty gun?"

The DUP leader, the Rev Ian Paisley, said that the "pro-active initiative" by the security forces at Clonoe was welcomed. He suggested that the shooting of the four men was related to the recent meetings on security between the four main political party leaders and British Prime Minister, Mr John Major.

The operation by the security forces against the IRA has also raised suggestions that the para-...

NI youth killed in video shop

From Mark Brennock, in Belfast

A 17-year-old shop assistant has been killed in an apparent sectarian shooting at a video club on the Upper Crumlin Road in North Belfast, the 32nd person to die in Northern violence so far this year.

A masked gunman burst into the club shortly after 8 pm yesterday evening, opening fire on the youth, named locally as Andrew Johnson, a Protestant from Silverstream, Ballysillan. He was working behind the counter in the shop when the man entered and fired four shots, killing the teenager almost instantly. A second member of staff, a young girl, was not harmed in the attack. The Irish People's Liberation Army later claimed responsibility for the shooting in a telephone call to a local radio station.

The gunman escaped in a car which had been stolen earlier in Flax Street in the Ardoyne area of Belfast. The car was later found burnt out in the Ligoniel area about a mile from the scene ...

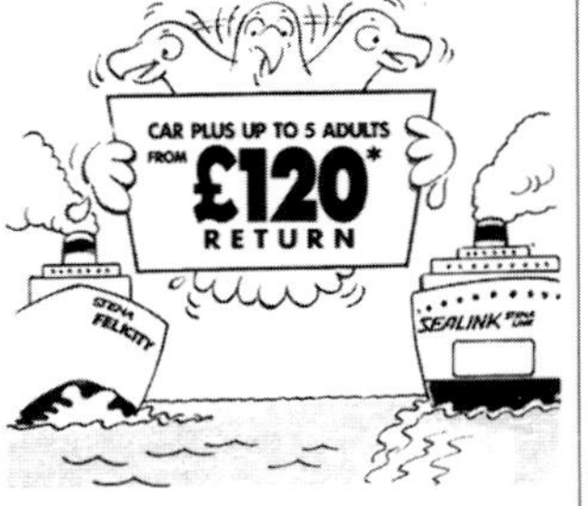

THE GREAT IRISH SEA DOUBLE TAKE.

Buy a return car ticket from Rosslare to Fishguard for £120, using midweek (Monday -Thursday) daylight sailings in each direction and you get a similar return

THE IRISH TIMES

PRICE 75p (incl. VAT) 65p sterling area | DUBLIN, THURSDAY, MAY 7, 1992 | No. 43,285 CITY

Dr Casey resigns as Bishop of Galway

By Andy Pollak, Religious Affairs Correspondent and Conor O'Clery, in Washington

DR EAMONN CASEY has resigned "for personal reasons" as Bishop of Galway, according to a statement issued on his behalf by the Catholic Press Office late last night. The Pope has accepted the resignation.

Dr Casey travelled to Rome last weekend and tendered his resignation to the Vatican's Congregation of Bishops on Monday. In last night's statement Dr Casey said he intended to "devote the remainder of my active life to work on the missions".

He was expected to return to Ireland on Tuesday but was delayed in Rome because of the Vatican's reluctance to accept his resignation immediately.

Dr Casey arrived back in Galway from Rome yesterday and is understood to have had discussions with a solicitor from Arthur O'Hagan and Son, the Dublin law firm which advises the bishops.

It is understood that before travelling to Rome, Dr Casey had spent several days in Malta considering his position. The Papal Nuncio, Archbishop Emanuele Gerada, who would have been informed of his intention to resign, comes from Malta.

The bishop, normally one of the most outspoken and visible members of the Hierarchy, has been keeping a noticeably low profile recently. Earlier this week *The Irish Times* made unsuccessful efforts to set up an interview with him, having heard reports of his possible resignation, in order to discuss matters which might have a bearing on the reasons for his decision.

One of these included payments amounting to $115,000 to a woman in Connecticut and a lawyer in New York on July 25th, 1990, and other regular payments to the woman over a period of 15 years since the mid-1970s.

The woman involved instructed a solicitor with the Dublin firm of Kenny, Stephenson and Chapman, to take legal proceedings against Bishop Casey last summer. Counsel was also instructed but the woman withdrew her instructions to pursue the case earlier this year.

It is also understood that a lawyer representing Dr Casey in the United States was involved in recent negotiations for a possible further payment of up to $150,000 to a relative of the woman in Connecticut, but that these also came to nothing.

Earlier this week Dr Casey was also forced to cancel a meeting with the executive of Trocaire, the Catholic Third World aid and development agency which he has headed since its foundation 19 years ago.

It is understood that the events which precipitated Dr Casey's resignation go back to the period in the early 1970s when he was Bishop of Kerry. He became Bishop of Galway in 1976.

Dr Casey, who was 65 last month, has been a popular figure among the bishops for many years for his commitment to campaigns for the poor and underprivileged. He started campaigning for the homeless in Britain in the 1960s and was a co-founder of the housing lobby, Shelter.

The following is the full text of a statement issued last night on behalf of Dr Casey by the Catholic Press and Information Office.

"Dr Eamonn Casey, the Bishop of Galway, has offered his resignation to Pope John Paul II. His Holiness has accepted it. Bishop Casey is retiring for personal reasons.

"The diocesan chapter has elected Monsignor James McLoughlin as diocesan administrator. Monsignor McLoughlin is the Vicar-General of the diocese and parish priest of the cathederal parish. He has served as secretary to Bishop Casey and his predecessor, Bishop Michael Browne. He will oversee the administration of the diocese until a successor to Bishop Casey is appointed.

"In a statement last night, Bishop Casey said: 'I have been extremely happy as Bishop of Galway for the last 16 years. In the first place I thank the priests and religious for their wholehearted acceptance of me as their bishop and for their generous co-operation at all times.

'I ask them to continue to support me in their friendship and prayers. I shall always remember them in mine.

'It has been an immense privilege to have served the people of Galway diocese. The kindness and affirmation I have received will always remain with me.

'My faith has been immeasurably strengthened by their faith. I pray they will continue to build the local Christian community. I thank in particular those who have helped me in so many ways in responding to the many needs of our community.

'My greatest joy in my ministry has been the celebration of the Sacrament of Confirmation. I would add here a special word of acknowledgement to all the teachers of the diocese.

'As a member of the episcopal conference for almost 23 years I shall remember with special warmth the friendship and solidarity I have always experienced among my brother bishops and in particular the bishops in the West.

'I wish also to express my appreciation of the fellowship which I have shared with the Bishop and the members of the Church of Ireland and the members of the Methodist and Presbyterian traditions.

'As chairman of the executive of Trocaire since it was launched in 1973, I thank all the people of Ireland for their immense generosity to the Third World and the staff of Trocaire for their consistent dedication and commitment.

'I intend to devote the remainder of my active life to work on the missions. In this way and with the help of God I will continue my lifelong commitment to the Church and His people.' "

The embodiment of Catholicism's human face: page 10

Editorial Comment: page 11

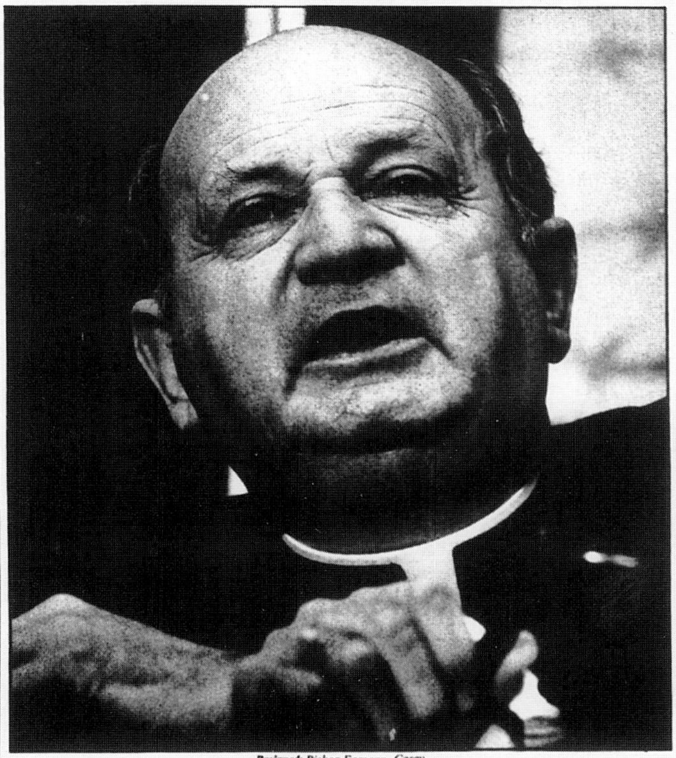

Resigned: *Bishop Eamonn Casey.*

New talks likely in postal dispute

By Ed O'Loughlin and Patrick Nolan

WHILE BOTH SIDES in the postal dispute have said that they are willing to negotiate without preconditions it is thought unlikely that any direct talks can begin before next Monday.

The director of letters and services at An Post, Mr John O'Callaghan, and the general secretary of the Communications Workers' Union, Mr David Begg, both declared yesterday that they were prepared to negotiate without preconditions to end the dispute.

However, it is believed that both sides may have differing beliefs on what the agenda of such a meeting should be and that this is likely to take at least until the weekend to clarify. Direct negotiations before then are ruled out by the timing of the CWU's annual conference in Tralee, Co Kerry, which ends tomorrow.

The chairman of the Labour Relations Commission, Mr Kieran Mulvey, said last night that it was too early for direct intervention but the commission's conciliation service would be maintaining contacts with both sides over the next few days.

The Communication Managers' Union said yesterday that it has contacted the Minister for Communications, Mrs Geoghegan-Quinn, to express its concern at An Post's announcement that 2,600 staff in the Dublin area will not be paid this week.

An Post made the announcement on Tuesday following the suspension of all staff in the Dublin payments office for refusing to process payments to the temporary workers at the centre of the dispute.

The CMU's general secretary, Mr Patrick Nolan, said that An Post's action was a calculated attempt to escalate the dispute beyond the Central Sorting Office in Dublin but that the CMU would resist all such pressure.

The dispute began on April 27th when about 100 temporary employees began work at the Central Sorting Office in Sheriff Street. About 600 permanent employees have been suspended for refusing to co-operate with them.

International mail has been paralysed, while mail volumes in Dublin and rural areas are down to three and 33 per cent respectively.

Addressing the CMU conference yesterday the union's general secretary, Mr Begg, alleged that An Post wanted to reintroduce a radical "viability plan" which the former Minister for Communications, Mr Brennan, dropped last year. He claimed that the company wanted to "develop a new angle" by taking on the industrial strength of the union. The management also wanted to reduce the workforce by 1,500 and to replace them by casual workers. He said it appeared that the company wished to implement its controversial proposal to erect roadside letter-boxes in rural areas.

Mr Begg told delegates representing almost 20,000 workers that the dispute was about the CWU's right to negotiate and that An Post had breached the Labour Relations Commission's procedures. He maintained that the dispute had to be viewed in the context of events which occurred in the past six months, including the bank dispute and a prolonged dispute in RTE.

Telecom 'being prepared for privatisation': page 8

INSIDE

THE BLUE ANGEL

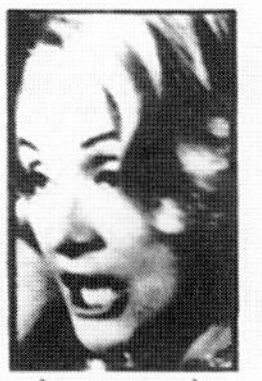

A t· ·bute to the extraordinary career of Marlene Dietrich, who died in Paris yesterday, aged 90

PAGE 9

PROPERTY MARKET

Dublin housing scheme sold within days

Palladian villa on the market

Ringsend flats from £39,500

12-PAGE COLOUR SUPPLEMENT

Ceasefire shattered

Fighting in Sarajevo and outlying cities ruptured the latest EC-backed ceasefire, less than 24 hours after it was signed □ page 6

Manslaughter investigation

A manslaughter investigation has begun as the death toll in the Corsican soccer stadium disaster rose yesterday □ page 6

Smurfit shares drop sharply

Shares in the Jefferson Smurfit group fell sharply yesterday following worse than expected results from its US operations □ page 12

INDEX

Home News.......... 2, 4, 5, 7, 8
World News 6
Sport.......... 14, 15
Weather 2
Arts 9
News Features 10
Letters to the Editor 11
Business & Finance 12, 13
Entertainments.......... 18
TV and Radio.......... 19

Well Done

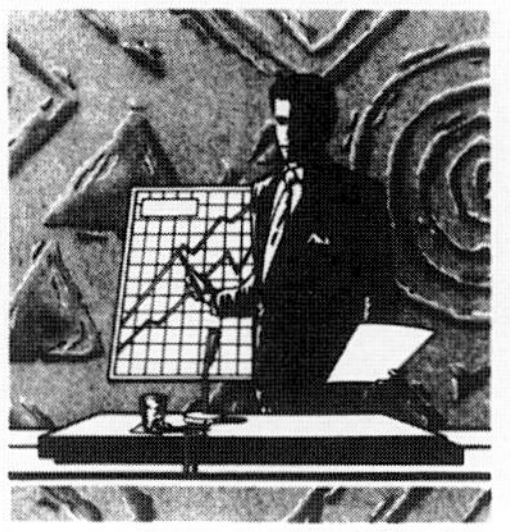

Enjoy

Dail expected to approve referendum legislation today

By Maol Muire Tynan, Political Reporter

LEGISLATION allowing for a referendum to be held on the Maastricht Treaty will comfortably pass all stages in the Dail today despite Opposition criticism that insufficient time has been allowed to discuss their amendments.

Meanwhile, a Government spokesman has confirmed that the Taoiseach, Mr Reynolds, is likely to travel to Rio de Janeiro for the UN Conference on Environment and Development a week before the Maastricht poll takes place. Mr Reynolds is expected to leave for the conference on June 10th, returning to Dublin four days before the referendum on June 18th.

His decision to proceed with the trip was last night seen in political circles as a sign of the Government's confidence that the treaty will be ratified.

As the Dail debate on the Maastricht legislation continues today, the leader of Democratic Left, Mr Proinsias De Rossa, has strongly criticised the Government decision to allocate just 75 minutes for the committee and remaining stages of the Bill this evening. Accusing the Government of rushing the legislation through "with indecent haste", Mr De Rossa said it made an utter joke of the Taoiseach's recent comments on Dail reform.

Democratic Left intends to table a series of amendments at the second stage, demanding that the protocol to the treaty be deleted and that the referendum be postponed until November.

Fine Gael this afternoon plans to table a motion appealing to the Government to hold a constitutional referendum on the right to travel and abortion information prior to the Maastricht vote. But, even if the amendment is rejected, the party is expected to support the legislation enabling the referendum to take place.

A Labour Party spokesman said they will continue to explore ways of reaching an all-party consensus on travel and information. A vote on the issue is due to take place next Wednesday night in the Dail on Labour's Private Members Bill which the party whips have agreed can be dealt with in just three hours of debate, the spokesman added.

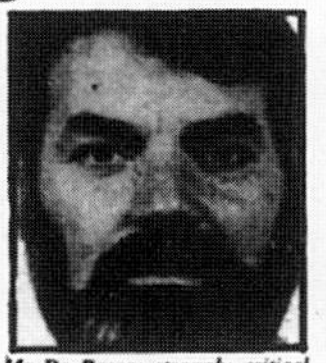

Mr De Rossa: *strongly critical.*

The thrust of that Bill is to hold a referendum on travel and information rights for all citizens. Labour has said that if agreed at second stage, it will enable the Maastricht referendum to go ahead "without misgivings".

The spokesman said the Taoiseach had not indicated "outright opposition" to the move in a letter to the Labour chief whip, Mr Brendan Howlin.

Geraldine Kennedy adds:

Speculation that a full Garda investigation has commenced in an effort to establish whether the latest abortion case was a hoax could not be confirmed by political nor Garda sources in Dublin last night.

This follows the attempt by a Derry man, in his mid-20s, to seek State assistance to stop his ex-girlfriend, a Dublin woman in her 30s, from procuring an abortion in England. The Chief State Solicitor's office wouldn't comment yesterday on whether it had yet referred the case to the Attorney General's office.

Dail Report: page 5. Group fears wide scope of EC union; Women travel to Holyhead for data: page 8

O'HAGAN DESIGN

7EVEN DAY SAVER

MUST END SATURDAY

3 Piece Leather Suite, Brown	£1,795
'Figaro' 2/3 Seater Sofas, various colours	£595
'Betty' Compact Sofabed	£99
'Fabian' 2 Seater Sofas 'Aztec' only	£199
Pine Desk with 2 Drawers & Adjustable Top	£99
6' x 3' Pine Bookshelf. Reduced to	£69
2 Door Pine Wardrobe with Shelves	£199
Small Students Pine Desk only	£47
Black Leather Highback Fireside Chair. Reduced to	£159
2 Seater Leather Couches, Black or Brown	£475
'Tivoli' Pine Frame Mirror only	£15
Cane Bedroom Chair	£79

5 November
*The coalition
Government falls.*

25 November
*The general
election results in
the Labour Party
more than
doubling its seats,
to thirty-three. A
referendum is held
on constitutional
amendments on
the right to travel,
the right to
information, and
the right to have
an abortion;
voters pass the
first two and reject
the third.*

economic and political union, when anti-abortion activists appealed for a 'no' vote. Faced with a choice between taking a stand on the most visceral moral issue and the possibility of rocking the EU boat, conservative Ireland put its mouth where the money was and voted in favour of the treaty.

At the time Ireland joined the EEC, however, its social conservatism was still manifest in the exclusion of women from the political sphere and from basic legal equality. During the general election campaign of February 1973 *The Irish Times* made a concerted effort to put discrimination against women on the agenda. It drew up a list of issues on which voters should question candidates and canvassers: equal pay and opportunities, the right of women to serve on juries, free legal aid, support for single parents, and access to contraception. To draw attention to the fact that no woman had served in the Government in the history of the state, the paper's Women First page picked a putative all-female Government. As Minister for External

high-sounding abstractions, it nevertheless offered the odd glimpse of a deeper truth. One came in a sequence of the Great Helmsman at the wheel of his yacht, the *Celtic Mist*, metaphorically steering the ship of state through rough winds and high swells. In the voice-over, he spoke as if he were God: 'When the storm sweeps in from the Atlantic and the sea rages with awesome power, one feels very close to the centre of creation' …

For a moment, the extraordinary fact that a career politician owned an island and a yacht, that he had become inexplicably wealthy, was obscured in a fog of folksy nostalgia and statesmanlike poses. And then his son Ciarán put his hand on the wheel of the boat. 'Don't touch my wheel,' barked the statesman. 'Don't you dare touch my wheel.' The remark was meant, presumably, as self-mockery. But it came across as much less ironic and much more honest than everything that had gone before. For the two concerns expressed in those few words—power and possession—seemed much closer to the essence of Charles Haughey than all the posturing that had gone before.

And a second sequence was, in retrospect, even more bizarrely eloquent. Again, Charles Haughey was flaunting

The Chieftains, quite simply the finest exponents of traditional Irish music in the second half of the century. This brilliant ensemble has had widespread international success and acclaim.

President Ronald Reagan in Ballyporeen, Co. Tipperary, in 1983

his possessions. At a rececourse, he talked about his ownership of horses and of the fun of seeing them run in his very own colours. Then a figure in a ten-gallon hat, the actor Larry Hagman, famous around the world for his portrayal of the flamboyantly corrupt businessman J. R. Ewing in 'Dallas', approached the Fianna Fáil leader and shook his hand. After some banter, Hagman put his hand in his inside pocket and took out a piece of paper which he presented with a flourish and a leer to the once and future Taoiseach. As the camera zoomed in, we could see what the piece of paper was—a dud thousand-dollar bill with the face of J. R. Ewing on it.

It was like a scene from some bad over-the-top satire, expressing in crude caricature a common perception of Charles Haughey as the kind of shady politician who would take money from an archetypal dodgy businessman. Yet here

Affairs, for example, it chose the poet Máire Mhac an tSaoi, with the distinguished public official Thekla Beere as Minister for Industry. As Taoiseach, however, the paper chose the young Senator Mary Bourke (subsequently known as Mary Robinson), who, it noted, might have settled for a pleasant time after her surprise election in 1969. 'But Ireland's youngest senator has instead stirred up a steady whirlwind ... In a little over three years she has made more impact on Irish life than virtually anyone in Dáil Éireann, male or female, and she would no doubt prove as formidable and daring in the position of critical leadership.' The point, however, was not taken: the new coalition Government of Fine Gael and the Labour Party still had no women members.

1993

13 January
Albert Reynolds is re-elected Taoiseach.

20 March
An IRA bomb in Warrington, Cheshire, kills a child and claims the life of another some days later.

The reforming energies of that Government were dissipated too by the continuing threat from the IRA. After the murder of the British ambassador, Christopher Ewart-Biggs, in July 1976 the Government gave new powers to the Gardaí, including the right to hold suspects for up to seven days. *The Irish Times*, now edited by Fergus Pyle (who held the chair from 1974 to 1977 when Douglas Gageby returned for a second time as editor), published an investigative series on brutality perpetrated in the interrogation of suspects by a 'Heavy Gang' within the Garda Síochána. These reports 'distressed' a senior member of the Government, Garret FitzGerald, to the extent that he raised the issue in the Cabinet and decided 'if necessary to force the issue to a conclusion by threatening resignation.'[8] His concerns, however, were not shared by many of his colleagues, and the matter was more or less allowed to lapse.

Tensions over the point at which measures to defend democracy began to threaten democracy itself persisted, however. In September 1976 President Cearbhall Ó Dálaigh referred the coalition's Emergency Powers Bill to the Supreme Court to test its constitutionality. In October the court ruled in favour of the bill, though, as an *Irish Times* editorial pointed out, it also underlined the importance of a detainee's right to communicate and to receive legal and medical advice. Three days after the ruling the Minister for Defence, Patrick Donegan, addressing soldiers at Columb Barracks, Mullingar, described the President as a 'thundering bollocks.' *The Irish Times* insisted that Donegan would have to resign and asked, 'Are his views shared by other members of the Government—above all, are they shared by the Taoiseach?' Donegan, however, neither resigned nor was sacked. Instead it was Ó Dálaigh, 'to protect the dignity and independence of the Presidency,' who resigned. The paper blamed the Government for failing to distance itself properly from Donegan's 'boorish reaction' and 'grossly bad manners.'

Sonia O'Sullivan, the first Irishwoman to win a medal in a major track event

it was, not an invention but a piece of fly-on-the-wall documentary realism. And it was being presented, not by some scurrilous subversive, but by Haughey himself.

Watching Haughey exhibit his wealth so openly on the programme, you realised that the display itself was a critical aspect of his survival. For he had mastered over many years the difficult art of hiding in plain sight. Instead of seeking to conceal the scandalous truth that he had accumulated great wealth from what was supposedly a life of public service, he had made it so obvious that it became simply an accepted aspect of Irish reality …

So his wealth became at the same time entirely open and utterly mysterious. It could be seen but not spoken about, observed but not explained. Like the weather or the internal combustion engine, we took it for granted without ever knowing how it really worked.

It is a trick that can only be pulled off when it is not consciously a trick at all, when it arises from deep personal conviction. And this is what is now most obvious about Charles Haughey's naked display of unexplained wealth.

The University of Limerick has been the most innovative and original development in Irish higher education since the sixties.
Its founder president, Dr Ed Walsh (left), was controversial, argumentative, iconoclastic and supremely efficient, but never dull.

Tony O'Reilly, the richest man in Ireland

As well as divisions over the North, and the cleavage between liberals and conservatives, there was also a feeling that Ireland was becoming increasingly split between rich and poor. It was, too, feeling the sense of dislocation that comes with massive and rapid transformation. In 1971 the urban population of the Republic was 52 per cent, the first time in history that town and city-dwellers had been a majority. During the seventies and early eighties the Republic became definitively an urban society. Dublin, for instance, grew faster in the seventies than any other western European capital city.

The Republic also became a much better-educated society. In 1971 only a half of fourteen to nineteen-year-olds in the Republic were in full-time education. By 1990 the figure was three-quarters and rising. And it became a less religious society. The number of new entrants to religious life in 1990 was much less than half of what it was in 1970. While Mass attendance

30 October

After a week of loyalist murders in retaliation for the Shankill bomb, members of the UFF enter the Rising Sun bar in Gresteel, Co. Derry, and open fire, killing eight civilians.

18 November

It is revealed that the British government and republicans have been involved in secret talks.

24 November

British customs officials seize two tons of explosives, three hundred rifles and a dozen other weapons in the largest known arms shipment intended for the UVF.

15 December

Albert Reynolds and John Major issue the Downing Street Declaration in London. While it guarantees the position of Northern Ireland in the United Kingdom, it allows for the creation of a united Ireland if a majority of people within

Jack Charlton, manager of the Irish soccer team from 1986 to 1996. In the first half of the nineties, he was probably the most popular person in the country.

Packie Bonner saves Timofte's penalty to help Ireland beat Romania in Turin during the 1990 World Cup. Ireland got to the quarter-finals of Italia '90, its best performance in a World Cup.

The homecoming from Italia '90. As Charlton asked, what would people have done if Ireland had won it?

Northern Ireland
and the Republic
vote to unify
the country.

1994

26 April
The first multiracial
elections are held in
South Africa and
result in the African
National Congress
receiving 63%
of the vote.

18 June
Six Catholic civilians
are shot dead in
O'Toole's bar in
Loughinisland,
Co. Down, as they
watch the Ireland v.
Italy World Cup
match; among them
is the oldest victim of
the troubles, who is
eighty-nine.

31 August
An IRA cease-fire
comes into effect at
midnight and is
welcomed by
republican and
nationalist cavalcades
and rallies in
Northern Ireland.

10 October
The Combined
Loyalist Military
Command calls a
cease-fire, to be

The New Ireland Forum in session in Dublin Castle in 1984

*enforced by the
UDA (including
UFF), UVF, and
Red Hand
Commando.*

17 November

*Albert Reynolds
resigns as Taoiseach
over the controversy
surrounding the
appointment of the
President of the
High Court and the
way in which the
latter dealt with the
extradition of the
paedophile priest
Brendan Smyth.
The President of the
High Court,
Harry Whelehan,
also resigns.*

remained very high by international standards, other indicators of religious practice fell sharply. Nearly half of all Catholics went to confession at least once a month in 1974; fifteen years later that figure was down to less than a fifth.

The status of women changed fundamentally. In 1971 only 8 per cent of married women were in the work force in the Republic. By 1988 this had increased to 23 per cent, still low by international standards but a huge change in the social order nonetheless. And, even more profoundly, one of the most distinctive things about Catholic Ireland over recent centuries—its high fertility level—changed. In 1991, for the first time, fertility in the Republic fell to a level where births were just replacing deaths. This in itself is evidence of a massive change in the relationship between men and women, and in the relationship of ordinary people to their church. It meant that Irish people were now using artificial contraception as a standard practice, even though the Catholic Church continued to regard it as a sin. The Irish abortion rate rose as high as the Dutch,

He flaunted it because, in his own eyes, he had a right to it. So deeply did he believe in his own greatness that it seemed simple justice that he should have whatever he wanted. He could act so shamelessly because in the world that he had constructed, he had nothing to be ashamed of …

Now that he has been snared, the gulf between his rhetoric and his reality is breathtaking. A man whose love of abstract grandiloquence did not preclude petty, self-serving and bare-faced lies. A man who almost wept when talking of his devotion to the institutions of the State and then thought little of treating a tribunal of inquiry established by both houses of the Oireachtas with contempt. A man of infinite pride without sufficient self-respect to keep him from common beggary. A self-proclaimed patriot whose spiritual home was in the Cayman Islands. A lover of his country who could treat it as a banana republic. A man who called for sacrifices from his people but was not prepared to sacrifice one tittle of the trimmings of wealth and luxury to the cause of preserving the dignity of the State he professed to love. A man who in his Channel 4 film could declare himself 'perhaps a little sentimental, even romantic, in my loyalties to people'; and then privately sneer at an 'unstable' friend who had just given him a gift of £1.3 million …

Paedophile priest grins as crowds abuse him

By George Jackson in Derry

The paedophile priest, Brendan Smyth, grinned yesterday as he was extradited from Northern Ireland to face 74 sex abuse charges in the Republic.

The priest of the Norbertine Order was extradited to the Republic hours after he was released from Magilligan Prison in Co. Derry where he had served a four-year term for sexually abusing children over 20 years in west Belfast.

On his release, Smyth (71) was taken to Limavady, Co. Derry, where he appeared for an extradition hearing in the town's magistrates' court.

even though abortion remained illegal and almost all Irish abortions were performed in England.

In 1974 *The Irish Times* underwent a transformation in its own status. The Arnott family had sold its shareholding in the newspaper during the nineteen-fifties and nineteen-sixties and the controlling or voting stock had passed into the hands of a number of investors. By 1974, under the commercial direction of Major T. B. McDowell as chairman and under the editorial direction of Douglas Gageby, the company's fortunes had improved to the point where a take-over from outside Ireland seemed a real possibility.

The shareholders decided to sell their shares to a newly created *Irish Times* trust which secured the newspaper against take-over while guaranteeing its editorial independence. The broad

1995

22 February
John Bruton and John Major launch the Framework Document, a blueprint for discussion by the Northern Ireland parties.

29 March
The British government announces that it

Brendan Smyth, the convicted paedophile priest. The Smyth affair brought down the Albert Reynolds government and shook the Irish Catholic church to its foundations.

will hold an exploratory dialogue with Sinn Féin.

11 July
The Drumcree confrontation at Portadown results in loyalist violence and a compromise whereby the nationalist community consent to the Orange parade through their area. In the aftermath of the gesture from the nationalists, David Trimble and Ian Paisley dance hand in hand down the road in celebration. A 'Siege of Drumcree' medal is struck in another sign of loyalist triumphalism.

outlines of editorial policy were set out in the Articles and Memorandum of the Trust and these continue to govern the newspaper's operations to this day. Major McDowell became chairman and chief executive of the Trust and of The Irish Times Ltd, the operating company. In 1996 he was succeeded as chief executive of The Irish Times Ltd by Louis O'Neill and in 1999 as chairman of The Irish times Ltd by Don Reid.

Reviewing the state of the nation at the end of 1978, the assistant editor of *The Irish Times*, Jim Downey, noted that while Irish society was now 'alive, vivid and thrusting,' it was also deeply divided. Those who had engineered the change of policy in the nineteen-sixties, he wrote, 'could not foresee that our transition to affluence would be so speedy and disruptive, that a new class system would be developed—and stratified—so soon, that our old easy-going, tolerant, egalitarian ways would be discarded with our poverty, that the "haves" of our society—professional people included—would fight for an even better position by a ruthless use of the methods practised so successfully by the skilled working class, or that the voice of social conscience would be fainter in the seventies.' As affluence increased, especially

The revelation that Bishop Éamonn Casey of Galway, one of the most charismatic of the Irish hierarchy, was the father of a child following an affair many years previously was the story that began the final erosion of public confidence in the Catholic Church, a feature of the nineties.

When the hearing ended, verbal abuse was shouted at Smyth by a crowd of 200 outside the courthouse. One man shouted: 'Rot in hell, you bastard'. But the convicted paedophile looked towards the crowd and laughed at them …

The extradition hearing lasted nine minutes. The warrants attached to each of the 74 charges related to sex-abuse offences allegedly committed by Smyth in the Republic between 1 January 1967 and 30 June 1993.

Smyth faces 47 charges of indecent assaults on females, 12 sex-assault charges on females under the 1990 Rape Amendment Act and 15 charges of sexually assaulting males.

During the hearing, Smyth stood in the dock beside an RUC sergeant. He remained silent except to reply 'yes' when he was asked if he understood five specimen charges …

After the hearing, Smyth was driven to City of Derry airport where he boarded an aircraft at 1.28 p.m. which took off at 1.35 p.m. for Dublin.

from The Irish Times **1997**
23 APRIL

Sympathy for 'broken man' prompted personal present

Mr Ben Dunne handed Mr Charles Haughey bank drafts worth £210,000 when he dropped in on him in Kinsealy for a cup of tea, the tribunal was told. As he left he took the drafts from his pocket and said: 'Look, that's something for yourself,' and Mr Haughey said: 'Thank you, big fella.'

Mr Dunne was giving evidence of the fifth and final payment made by him to the former Taoiseach. The other four were made via intermediaries, including his friend Mr Noel Fox and Mr Haughey's close associate, Mr Des Traynor. But this was a direct transaction.

Mr Dunne explained how he came to have the bank drafts. For reasons totally unconnected to Mr Haughey or any other politician, he had acquired three bank drafts, each worth £70,000, payable to a Mr Cox, a Mr Montgomery and a Mr Blair. He told the tribunal these were totally fictitious names, and bore no relation to any person who might exist of that name.

He got the drafts from his solicitor, Mr Noel Smyth, and put them in his pocket 'for the particular personal use I was

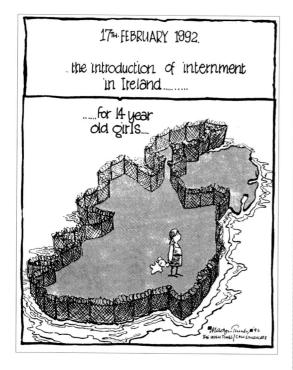

These two Martyn Turner cartoons sum up the absurd and tragic 'X' case. A fourteen year-old-girl, pregnant as the result of a rape, was first denied the right to travel to England for an abortion. The law was changed.

going to use them for'. He had them in his pocket when he went to play golf in Baltray, north Dublin, with friends. 'I was very conscious of them in my pocket every time I was taking a tee or checking a score card,' he said.

He rang Mr Haughey and said he was in Baltray and would call for a cup of tea. 'I dropped in. I felt he was not himself. We chatted. My son had just been diagnosed with kidney problems which would require a transplant and we were talking about that. On the way out I took the drafts from my pocket and said, "Look, that's something for yourself", and he said, "Thank you, big fella".'

'Under no circumstances did he make any reference to financial difficulties or say "Times are tough" or anything like that. I just felt he was down. I've gone through situations in my own life when I knew I was down.

'I felt sorry for the man. For no particular reason, he looked like a broken man. I could not put my finger on it.' Mr Dunne told Mr McCullough that during the litigation with his siblings he had thought that this money had been given to other members of his family, but when he examined the bank books he realised it had gone to Mr Haughey.

He agreed with Mr McCullough that the drafts had been sent by Mr Traynor's secretary to the Irish Intercontinental Bank to the same Cayman Islands bank as the previous money he had paid for Mr Haughey's benefit.

in the economic miracle of the nineties, these concerns with the ambiguities of progress would become a constant undertone to the paper's reflections on change.

One reaction to the uneven and confusing nature of progress was an attempt to put the clock back and return to the moral certainties of an era of Catholic dominance that was already being wrapped in a mist of nostalgia. Conservatives chose the issue of abortion—even though it was illegal in the Republic—as the ground on which to make their stand, demanding that the Constitution be amended to outlaw abortion for all time. With Fianna Fáil, now led by a rehabilitated Charles Haughey, and Fine Gael, resurgent under Garret FitzGerald, engaged in a tight struggle for dominance, both parties agreed to put an amendment to a referendum.

The Irish Times was especially hostile to the abortion amendment. During July 1982 alone it carried three editorials attacking it as sectarian and divisive. The first was accurately summed up by the headline: 'Drop it.' The second, on the Protestant festival of 12 July, reminded readers of the role Protestants had played in the state and of the view from the North: 'they on the other side of the Black Pig's Dyke are watching us as we are watching them.' The third asked: 'Have we enough conviction of our republican traditions to wish to make of the Twenty-six counties a

12 August

The RUC baton residents off the Lower Ormeau Road, Belfast, to allow a loyalist parade to pass through the area. Riots erupt in Derry over a loyalist parade in the city.

8 September

David Trimble is elected leader of the Ulster Unionist Party, taking over from James Molyneaux, who held the position since 1979. The Irish Press (together with the Evening Press and Sunday Press) is wound up after sixty-four years of existence.

Ben Dunne, former supermarket magnate, with his son Mark. Dunne's revelations about payments made by him to finance Charles Haughey's lavish life style started a landslide of disclosures about Haughey in the late nineties.

5 October

Séamus Heaney wins the Nobel Prize for Literature.

24 November

A divorce referendum in the Republic results in a narrow majority in favour of the introduction of divorce on stringent terms.

28 November

The British and Irish governments issue a joint

pluralist state?' A later editorial described the amendment campaign as 'the second partitioning of Ireland.' And although the amendment passed with a comfortable majority, it left not only division but a legacy of legal complications.

The conservative reaction in Ireland was part of a wider turn to the right in the western democracies, symbolised by the election in 1979 of Margaret Thatcher in Britain and of Ronald Reagan in the United States. The oil crisis of 1979, the West's loss of competitiveness in heavy industry, the increasing globalisation of the economy and the immense impact of new electronic technologies all contributed to the undermining of the broadly social-democratic consensus that had emerged after 1945. Large-scale job losses, dizzying technological changes and a renewal of the Cold War, with a

He said he had no dealings with Mr Traynor, nor had Dunne's Stores, and there was no reason why the bank drafts should have ended up in Mr Traynor's hands. Nor did he have any dealings with the Ansbacher bank in the Cayman Islands.

Since that episode he had met Mr Haughey twice, once at a dinner party and again when he met him for lunch.

from The Irish Times
EASTER 1998

Goodbye to the bloody days

Raw emotion, joy, wonder and disbelief swirled around Castle Buildings yesterday. And when the light of dawn came it chased away the political darkness of Northern Ireland to reveal a promise that things could be different. Frank Millar was there.

John Hume canvassing during the nineteen-eighties

They really did make history here yesterday. In joy and wonderment and something approaching disbelief, friends and allies—and even some old adversaries—allowed themselves the luxurious embrace of fresh hope and the sense of new beginnings …

All morning the assembled press corps had waited patiently, grateful for snippets of information about the timetable, moaning but gently about the endless delays. No matter that the vending machine had run dry. The sun was shining, the snow gone, and it felt good just to be here. When it came, it would be worth waiting for.

But as the one o'clock deadline became three, then four, and the rollercoaster rose and crashed, word filtered through that David Trimble was having problems with his party. Two MPs and some officers had apparently told him they could not accept a deal putting Sinn Féin in a government 'without the IRA having decommissioned a single bullet.'

consequent risk of nuclear annihilation, all contributed to a widespread feeling of insecurity.

In Ireland, all these factors, coming on top of continuing and apparently endless violence in the North, contributed to a sudden sense of instability. Unemployment rose to hitherto unimaginable levels (close to 300,000 by the early nineties) as a booming young population poured onto a shrinking labour market. The national debt, traditionally kept under close control, began to spiral. Mass emigration, thought to be a thing of the past, returned to the highest levels since the fifties, with many of the new young emigrants ending up with the never-never status of 'undocumented aliens' in the United States. And at the head of the natural party of power, Fianna Fáil, the comforting figure of Jack Lynch had been replaced by the dark Machiavellianism of Charles Haughey.

statement announcing the appointment of an arms decommissioning body under the guidance of the former American Senator George Mitchell.

30 November
President Clinton visits Belfast and Derry. He receives a tumultuous reception in the two cities and in Dublin the following day.

1996

24 January
The Mitchell Report is published by George Mitchell. It states that there is no possibility of decommissioning from the IRA before all-party talks begin. It also sets out a set of principles committing participants in any talks to peaceful means.

9 February
The IRA ends its cease-fire with a huge bomb at Canary Wharf, London.

George Mitchell, who chaired the long series of talks that culminated in the 1998 Belfast Agreement, the best chance Northern Ireland has had for peace in a generation

28 February

Allegations of child abuse in the nineteen-fifties are made against the Goldenbridge Orphanage, Dublin.

9 May

The Madonna House Report deals with fifteen cases of child abuse at the former Sisters of Charity orphanage in Dublin.

The *Irish Times* security correspondent, Peter Murtagh, discovered in October 1982 that Haughey's Minister for Justice, Seán Doherty, had attempted to transfer a Garda sergeant in his County Roscommon constituency and that, in the so-called Dowra affair, a witness in an assault case against Doherty's brother-in-law had been detained by the RUC, preventing him from giving evidence. After the general election that followed in December, in which Haughey lost office and a coalition Government of Fine Gael and the Labour Party took over, Murtagh discovered that the phones of two prominent political correspondents, Geraldine Kennedy and Bruce Arnold, had been tapped by the outgoing Government. He also published damning new

The 'D' word was back. But it couldn't be. Could it? Most emphatically came the signal from the young briefers presumably tasked to tell us that the document Mr Blair and Mr Ahern were waiting to present to the world wasn't the one they'd agreed. Yes they had done a deal with the SDLP. But Sinn Féin's participation was meant to be conditional on the actual decommissioning of IRA weapons.

Had they defined that in the agreement? No, it was a verbal understanding, came the reply.

They could hardly be serious. Did they appreciate the pariah status that would be theirs if they did this to Tony Blair? But Mr Trimble was indeed facing serious problems. Jeffrey Donaldson was allegedly in revolt. Mr Taylor, too, was reportedly doubtful. A grim faced Roy Beggs MP came to read the document and apparently judged it untouchable. Could they really have it in mind to overturn the leader?

Would he be forced to resign before the day was out?

Irish officials suddenly found themselves in need of exercise, bumping into the journalists they had so carefully avoided through the week, presumably gathering as much information as they dispensed.

No, the UUP claims were not true. The document had not been changed.

No, the Strand One deal with the SDLP had not stipulated decommissioning as a condition of Sinn Féin's involvement in the Assembly executive. No, the two leaders would not be hanging around while the UUP had a trauma. And yes, the deal would be done 'because it has to be'.

That presumably was President Clinton's message as he responded to the crisis, using his influence to help effect the vital last words which would enable Mr Trimble—for the moment at least—to face down his doubters.

Mr Blair gave Mr Trimble the assurance he sought that, if the existing provisions to deal with office holders who did not remain committed to exclusively peaceful means proved ineffective he would support changes to make them so. And he confirmed he shared the UUP view that decommissioning measures should come into effect immediately.

The importance of words was never more plainly revealed. And on reflection, the last-gasp fright may have served a vital purpose in impressing on the paramilitaries that the procession into the world of democratic government really is incompatible with the world of private armies and the dispensation of summary justice.

Nelson Mandela, freeman of the city of Dublin

30 May
Sinn Féin wins 16% of votes in the Forum elections.

7 June
Detective-Garda Jerry McCabe is shot dead during an IRA robbery in Adare, Co. Limerick.

10 June
Multi-party talks start in Northern Ireland without Sinn Féin.

15 June
An IRA bomb destroys a large section of the city centre of Manchester.

26 June
The journalist Veronica Guerin is shot dead near Dublin by a member of a criminal gang.

8 July
A Catholic taxi-driver, Michael McGoldrick, is found shot dead in Portadown at the end of the first day of this year's Drumcree confrontation.

11 July
The RUC beat residents off the road

to allow the Orange Order down the Garvaghy Road, Portadown.

20 July
Michelle Smith wins the first of three gold medals in swimming at the Atlanta Olympics.

2 October
Brigid McCole dies of hepatitis C. Six days later the Blood Transfusion Service Board admits liability.

29 November
It is revealed that the businessman Ben Dunne paid £208,000 for an extension to the home of the Fine Gael TD Michael Lowry.

*Brian Keenan following his release from captivity. He had been held hostage in Beiruit for over four-and-a-half years. His book, **An Evil Cradling**, was an award-winning best-seller.*

details of the Dowra affair, revealing that the arrest of the witness had been initiated from Doherty's office. The revelations led to an internal Fianna Fáil challenge to Haughey, which narrowly failed.

For the rest of the century *The Irish Times* continued to probe Haughey's use of power. In

The depth and passionate nature of republican support is illustrated in this photograph of Patrick McIntyre being cheered off from the Four Courts in Dublin following the refusal of the Irish courts to extradite him to Britain.

At the time though it seemed to add a sour note, to take some of the gloss off the occasion. And in highlighting the issue at the last lap, the UUP seemed to have notched-up still further Mr Trimble's task in selling the deal to the wider unionist electorate.

They had made history. But it was probably too much to have expected them to do it with great grace. And, again on reflection, it was maybe as well they didn't.

For in a moment of great personal triumph, Mr John Hume reminded everyone of the barriers and obstacles ahead. This was not the end, or even the beginning of the end, more the end of the beginning. But for all that, one hell of a beginning—and greater in scope, ambition and opportunity than most would ever dared have imagined.

from The Irish Times
EASTER 1998

Unheard melodies

The peace players at Stormont have done something evolutionary and there is a fitting Easter energy about it, a sense of arrival rather than wreckage.

Séamus Heaney

'Heard melodies are sweet, but those unheard are sweeter.' It may seem flippant to greet history with a play upon John Keats' lines, but language itself seems to have gained a new friskiness through the signing of the inter-party agreement yesterday. Even the term 'party tunes' loses a bit of sectarian weight and begins to suggest something more innocent and celebratory. By devising a set of structures and a form of words which have the potential to release all sides from their political and historical entrapment, Senator Mitchell, the Taoiseach, Prime Minister Blair and all the talks participants have done something evolutionary.

If revolution is the kicking down of a rotten door, evolution is more like pushing the stone from the mouth of the tomb. There is an Easter energy about it, a sense of arrival rather than wreckage, and what is nonpareil about the new conditions is the promise they offer of a new covenant between people living in this country. For once, and at long last, the language of the Bible can be appropriated by those with a vision of the future rather than those who sing the battle hymns of the past.

Irish troops serving with the United Nations on patrol in South Lebanon. The Irish army has maintained a distinguished record of service with UN peace-keeping missions.

Herd melodies are what the opponents of the process have offered all along and will continue to offer. The Rev Ian Paisley and the Rev William McCrea of the DUP have tried to turn constituencies into congregations, and have had more appetite all along for apocalypse rather than for the process of negotiation. They promise to do their best between now and the referendum on 22 May to have the agreement rejected by those whom they call the people of Ulster—by which they mean loyalists and unionists.

What the agreement does, however, is to offer the possibility of a northern Irish world where that hitherto coded phrase would actually mean what it says: from now on, 'the people of Ulster' is going to have to include the nationalist and republican minority as well. If a North-South Council and an assembly at Stormont acceptable to all can be established, the minority will finally escape from a state where their 'Ulsterness' was a 'Britishness' forced upon them and become instead a shared attribute. Ulster will remain a site of contention, politically and culturally, but at least the contenders will have assented to play on the same pitch and by agreed rules.

It was good to watch David Trimble rise to the occasion with some style and force in his brief statement to the press after the plenary session, and to hear him take the long view

1990, when Haughey's lieutenant, Brian Lenihan, was running for President, questions arose about the pressure that Haughey and Lenihan had put on a previous President, Patrick Hillery, in 1982, when they had urged him not to dissolve the Dáil after the collapse of FitzGerald's Government. Lenihan denied on television that he had made calls to the President. *The Irish Times* obtained a tape from a research student on which Lenihan said that he had in fact made the calls. At the insistence of Haughey's minority coalition partner, the Progressive Democrats, Lenihan was dismissed from the Government. The incident may not have contributed greatly to Lenihan's subsequent defeat in the Presidential election by Mary Robinson—there was a wave of public sympathy for him after his dismissal— but it considerably deepened Fianna Fáil's animosity to the paper. So did its coverage of the scandals, including the extraordinarily generous treatment of a beef company, Goodman International, that continued to surround Haughey. Only in 1996, however, when the

15 January
The first application for divorce in the Republic is made to the High Court.

2 February
At least forty thousand people attend the Bloody Sunday march in Derry to mark the twenty-fifth anniversary of the shooting dead of fourteen civilians in 1972 and demand a neutral inquiry into the murders.

11 March
The Hepatitis C Tribunal blames officials of the Blood Transfusion Service Board for the contaminated blood scandal.

17 April
The Blood Transfusion Service Board admits liability in the hepatitis C cases caused by contaminated blood.

21 April
Charles Haughey denies that he received £1.3

THE IRISH TIMES

PRICE 85p (incl. VAT) 75p sterling area | DUBLIN, THURSDAY, JULY 10, 1997 | No. 44,878 CITY

PROPERTY

Wexford mansion to make over £750,000

POLITICS

Goodbye to all that: P J Mara on his roots, on radio shows — and on Charles J Haughey

DRUMCREE

Errors were made but this time things are better

GOLF MASTERS

Leaderboard for Week 19 in £20,000 fantasy contest

● PROPERTY SUPPLEMENT ● INTERVIEW: 15 ● MARY HOLLAND: 16 ● SPORT: 20-24

Hume to discuss North crisis with Taoiseach today

THE "posture" of the Taoiseach could have a "significant influence" on events in the North this weekend, unionist sources said last night. In another development, the SDLP leader, Mr Hume will lead a delegation to discuss the crisis with Mr Ahern in Dublin this afternoon. Hundreds of extra troops have been drafted into the North ahead of two major marches in Belfast and Derry: **page 11**

Pressure on pound eases as sterling loses strength

SPECULATION on the outcome of the Bank of England monetary meeting today on interest rates dominated trading on Irish currency markets yesterday, with an acceptance that a rise of at least a quarter of a percentage point in British rates is now inevitable. Pressure eased on the pound as sterling lost some strength: **page 18**

Sellafield wins award: The Sellafield plant has won an international award for its environmental practices. Winning the ISO 14001, according to British Nuclear Fuels, is a recognition that the plant conforms to "the highest international standards": **page 5**

NATO, Ukraine sign charter: NATO leaders meeting in Madrid took a giant step forward yesterday in the restructuring of European security when they signed a charter with the Ukraine: **page 13**

EU structural spending to rise: EU structural spending is set to rise to £206 billion: **page 2**

Tyson's boxing licence revoked: Mike Tyson has had his boxing licence revoked and fined $3 million, after a decision by the five-man Nevada State Athletic Commission yesterday. While the decision will be reviewed every year, it means the boxer is out of the sport for at least a year. It is the stiffest penalty ever handed out in the sport but the reality is that Tyson will probably get his licence back when first allowed to apply for it, 12 months from now: **page 21**

Mother throws baby to safety: A mother had to throw her three-and-a-half month old baby out a window, when a fire broke out at a house in Mulhuddart, Co Dublin: **page 2**

Post-mortem on Limerick woman: A post-mortem will be carried out today by the State Pathologist into the death of a 60-year-old Limerick woman: **page 4**

Live cattle trade with Egypt unlikely: The live cattle trade with Egypt is unlikely to resume until BSE is completely eradicated: **page 2**

BA stoppage causes havoc: A 72-hour stoppage by British Airways cabin crew caused havoc with the airline's flights yesterday: **page 13**

Man on murder charge breaks down: A man charged with murder broke down yesterday as he told the Central Criminal Court, "I didn't mean to kill anyone": **page 4**

Woman awarded damages: A woman who had to have a second sterilisation at the Rotunda Hospital after haemorrhaging following the first operation was awarded damages yesterday: **page 4**

Cambodia's royal family flees: Cambodia's royal family have fled the country: **page 13**

Most school bullies 'unhappy': Most school bullies are unhappy, a conference has been told: **page 5**

Burke's view analysed: In Edmund Burke's view, the British national subject was "solid, faithful and industrious while the French was capricious and faithless", Prof Seamus Deane told a symposium yesterday. Burke viewed the fate of Queen Marie Antoinette as a classic working out of standard tragic theory. "In her sexual attraction and monarchial attraction she epitomises the attractiveness of *ancien règime* politics": **page 5**

Press competition 'essential': The Tánaiste has said that competition in the newspaper industry is essential if there is to be diversity: **page 10**

Independent denies claim: Independent Newspapers has denied being approached to sell its share in the London *Independent*: **page 18**

Merger backed: Leinster milk producers have backed the Avonmore and Waterford Co-ops merger: **page 19**

Lotto jackpot not won: There was no winner of last night's lottery jackpot. The numbers were 10, 14, 15, 22, 35, 38 and bonus 37. Five people shared a jackpot of £13.2 million in the British lottery with the winning numbers 3, 5, 13, 22, 24, 43 and 23.

Haughey may face £1m tax bill for accepting Dunne payments

...RAISE MONEY BY WRITING YOUR UNMIS-TAKEN MEMOIRS— CALL THEM 'BEGGAR'S BELIEF'....
BILL
LEGAL FEES
TAX

As no such monies have been paid, no repayment arises
Mr Haughey in 1994 when the Dunne family asked for their money back

A careful perusal of the documents on their own do not corroborate the allegations made against me
Mr Haughey, April 3 1997, in a letter to the Tribunal

I now accept that I received the £1.3 million from Mr Ben Dunne and . . . that he handed me £210,000 in Abbeville in November 1991
Mr Haughey, July 9 in a statement to the Tribunal

By Mark Brennock and Colm Keena

THE former Taoiseach, Mr Charles Haughey, faces a possible tax bill of about £1 million following his dramatic admission yesterday that — despite his earlier insistent denials — he did receive more than £1.3 million from Mr Ben Dunne.

Mr Haughey, who is due to give evidence under oath to the Dunnes payments tribunal next week, saw his reputation shredded in public yesterday after politicians and commentators condemned him in the wake of his statement to the tribunal admitting that he had misled it, his own lawyers and Dunnes Stores by insisting that he had received no money from Mr Dunne.

But the opprobrium heaped on the former Fianna Fáil leader yesterday may only be the start of his difficulties. Apart from the likely interest of the Revenue Commissioners, Dunnes Stores has indicated that it will seek repayment of the £1.3 million it says was "improperly diverted" from the company.

Mr Haughey's dramatic *volte-face* sent shock waves through the political system. Fine Gael has tabled a Dáil motion seeking a new tribunal of inquiry into payments by businesses other than Dunnes Stores to Mr Haughey. The Labour Party leader, Mr Spring, said that the Dáil should sit to consider "this extraordinary day in Irish politics".

The Taoiseach, Mr Ahern, said that the Government would decide what was necessary after it has seen the tribunal report. He had an open mind on an inquiry into Mr Haughey, he said. "I will cover nobody. We will deal with this report comprehensively."

THE STATEMENT OF MR CHARLES HAUGHEY TO THE DUNNES PAYMENTS TRIBUNAL

THE following is the text of the statement of Mr Charles J. Haughey, read to the tribunal by his counsel, Mr Eoin McGonigal SC:

"I wish to thank the chairman for yesterday's adjournment. As a result of reviewing the excellent work of the tribunal and considering the very helpful documentation recently received from Mr Ben Dunne's solicitor, I now accept that I received the £1.3 million from Mr Ben Dunne and that I became aware that he was the donor to the late Mr Traynor in 1993, and furthermore, I now accept Mr Dunne's evidence that he handed me £210,000 in Abbeville in November 1991.

"In making this statement, I wish to make it clear that until yesterday, I had mistakenly instructed my legal team. They have however agreed to continue acting for me for the duration of the tribunal. I wish to thank them in this regard. I will give evidence to the tribunal when required to do so."

IMPACT, the trade union representing tax officials and inspectors, has called for Mr Haughey's assets to be frozen along with the so-called Ansbacher deposits, which have contained up to £40 million in the names of Irish residents.

Mr Haughey changed his story for the second time yesterday after his legal team was shown telephone logs detailing contacts between him and Mr Ben Dunne's solicitor, Mr Noel Smyth. Last week, after repeated denials, Mr Haughey acknowledged that, as a matter of "probability", he indeed received money from Mr Dunne while not knowing Mr Dunne was the "donor". This was his first change of story.

It is understood Mr Haughey's statement to the tribunal on Monday contained no reference at all to the controversial meetings with Mr Smyth. On Tuesday, however, the tribunal produced copies of documents from Mr Smyth's office showing that Mr Haughey had made numerous phone calls to Mr Smyth's office around the times Mr Smyth had said he had had meetings and conversations with Mr Haughey.

Having received what he yesterday called this "very helpful documentation", Mr Haughey changed his story for the second time to admit:

- that he had received the £1.3 million after all;
- that he had known since 1993 that it came from Mr Dunne;
- that he had personally been handed £210,000 by Mr Ben Dunne, as Mr Dunne described;
- and that he had "mistakenly instructed" his legal team on the matter.

His admissions mean that he did not tell the truth when he told the tribunal, in a letter earlier this year, that he had not received this money. He also gave the same untruthful denial in the past to solicitors for Dunnes Stores and similarly to Mrs Margaret Heffernan. Neither did he disclose the payments to the Buchanan inquiry.

The admission that he personally received the £210,000 is crucial, as that money went into the Ansbacher deposits, the same place the other payments ended up. This therefore provides additional evidence that the entire £1.3 million followed a trail from Mr Dunne to Mr Haughey.

In a day of sensational revelations at the tribunal it also emerged that Mr Ben Dunne offered Mr Haughey a further £1 million earlier this year to help him meet the potential tax liability on the money previously given to him. Mr Haughey declined.

The offer was made on Mr Dunne's behalf by his solicitor, Mr Noel Smyth, who told the tribunal that he estimated Mr Haughey would face a tax bill of at least £1 million on the £1.3 million given to him by Mr Dunne. The figure could be considerably higher if interest and penalties were included.

Yesterday's dramatic developments mean that the tribunal's work will now be shortened by up to a week.

The trail followed by the money given to Mr Haughey will still have to be proven in evidence, but the process will be speeded up greatly by Mr Haughey's admission that he received the entire £1.3 million.

Evidence will be given today by individuals from Guinness & Mahon and Irish Intercontinental Bank, the two Dublin banks into which the £1.3 million was paid. Evidence will also be heard from ACC Bank. The tribunal has already been told that a loan Mr Haughey had with this bank was paid off with money which came from Mr Dunne.

Mr Haughey is scheduled to begin giving evidence on Monday.

Classic
QUARTERLY ACCOUNT
A HIGH RETURN OF UP TO
6.6% GROSS
WITH ACCESS TO YOUR FUNDS

That secret love's no secret as the straight man finally sings

WE left Dublin Castle humming an old Dr Hook song: the one that

Ben Dunne's million-

an Irish Intercontinental Bank account was a "nexus" linking him

THE IRISH TIMES

PRICE 85p (incl. VAT) 75p sterling area

DUBLIN, MONDAY, JULY 6, 1998

No. 45,184 CITY

IRISH OPEN
Carter defeats Montgomerie in play-off at Druids Glen
● SPORT SUPPLEMENT

GAELIC GAMES
All-Ireland champions Kerry finish strongly to oust Cork

SICK SYSTEM
Alison O'Connor examines patients' anger at their doctors
● WELL & GOOD: 8

CYCLE SCIENCE
Using aerodynamics and advanced materials to win the Tour de France
● SCIENCE: 11

Cardiac pacemaker company to take over Clonmel plant

A US medicare company, the Minnesota-based Guidant Corporation, is to take over the vacant Seagate plant in Clonmel and provide more than 500 jobs in the manufacture of cardiac pacemakers, the Tánaiste will announce today. The computer company closed last December with a loss of 1,400 jobs: **page 3**

Frustrating day for peace envoys in Kosovo

THE US special envoy, Mr Richard Holbrooke, and the Russian Deputy Foreign Minister, Mr Nikolai Afanassyevsky, have returned to Belgrade after a frustrating day urging ethnic Albanian political leaders in Kosovo to put aside their differences in the search for peace: **page 12**

Bord Fáilte could go: Bord Fáilte could be replaced by an all-island tourist body, provided such a move wins the support of both the Northern Ireland Assembly and the Oireachtas: **page 16**

Heat deaths in Europe: More deaths have been reported in a heat wave sweeping southern Europe while 1,000 firefighters and soldiers yesterday fought to prevent fires from engulfing a mountain north of Athens: **page 12**

TEAM result today: The result of the ballot by TEAM Aer Lingus workers over the FLS buy-out of the company will be known today: **page 3**

National day of commemoration: The President, Mrs McAleese, the Taoiseach, Mr Ahern, the Tánaiste, Ms Harney, the Labour leader, Mr Ruairí Quinn, and the Fine Gael deputy leader, Mrs Nora Owen, were among those who attended the annual national day of commemoration, which started with an ecumenical prayer service, at the Royal Hospital, Kilmainham, to honour those Irish men and women who died in past wars or on service with the UN: **page 5**

Arts director resigns: The Galway Arts Centre has just lost its executive director, the second in 18 months: **page 2**

Mandatory reporting opposed: Eleven Rape Crisis centres are opposed to mandatory reporting of sex abuse because it poses a threat to client confidentiality: **page 4**

Building boom goes on: Ireland will have the fastest-growing construction industry in Europe until 2000, analysts say: **page 16**

Mandela angry with communists: An attempt by the once-powerful South African Communist Party to challenge the "capitalist" policies of its allies in the ANC has attracted President Mandela's wrath: **page 13**

Law on Arabic language: The Algerian government has enacted a law which bans the use of any language other than Arabic in the administration, public meetings, radio, television and business: **page 12**

EMU states face budget warning: Finance ministers from the 11 EU countries due to enter monetary union in January are expected to get a warning on budgets from the European Central Bank president today: **page 16**

Sudan famine concerns: Fresh concerns are being expressed about the extent of the famine threatening southern Sudan and the effectiveness of the relief operation: **page 13**

Farmer, TD dispute claims: A major conflict now exists between a retired Co Meath farmer and Fianna Fáil TD Ms Beverley Cooper-Flynn over his claim that she sold him a Clerical Medical Insurance product when she was working for the National Irish Bank. Mr James Howard is standing by his allegation that Ms Cooper-Flynn introduced him to the controversial investment scheme run by NIB: **page 5**

Coroner's court figures: Suicides and traffic accidents were the main causes of death in cases before Dublin City Coroner's Court in the first six months of 1998: **page 5**

EHB payments review: The Eastern Health Board expects to complete a review of the welfare payments it makes to asylum-seekers by October: **page 4**

Envoy to be awarded citizenship: The Taoiseach has said the departing US ambassador, Mrs Jean Kennedy Smith, is to be made an honorary Irish citizen: **page 3**

£2.1m jackpot not won: There were no jackpot winners in the weekend £2.1 million lottery. The numbers drawn were 6, 23, 27, 31, 32, 41 and (18). Two tickets shared £13 million in the UK lottery. The numbers were 9, 15, 25, 29, 32 and 49 and (14).

Fears grow of serious disorder if Drumcree standoff continues

Orangemen massed behind the wire fence erected by security forces face a phalanx of RUC officers in riot gear, as they take two loyalists into custody in one of the few incidents at Drumcree yesterday.
Photograph: Eric Luke

By Deaglán de Bréadún,
Northern Editor, in Drumcree
and Andy Pollak in Belfast

TENSION was high throughout Northern Ireland last night as fears grew that the coming week could see widespread demonstrations in support of the Orange Order protest at Drumcree and that these protests could lead to serious civil disorder.

There were road blockages and some violent incidents in loyalist areas in Belfast and and other areas of Northern Ireland last night. In the city, about 50 youths threw bottles and stones at the RUC near the loyalist Sandy Row area. They erected barricades of wooden pallets and blocked the road for a time. The RUC fired a number of plastic bullets.

Petrol bombs were thrown at the RUC on the Lower Ormeau Road. The police returned fire with plastic bullets. At Lansdowne Road in north Belfast, burning cars blocked the road, while burning cars also blocked roads in Carrickfergus, Co Antrim.

In Drumcree itself, tension mounted as the standoff between police and Orangemen stretched into the night. Some 1,500 members of the Order settled down for the night in the vicinity of Drumcree parish church at Portadown, Co Armagh, preparing to sleep in

INSIDE

PAGE 6
● *Deaglán de Bréadún on a town effectively under martial law*
● *Sporadic street violence by loyalists*

PAGE 7
● *Return the way you came, Ingram tells Orangemen*
● *Troops' role to support RUC in case of clash with crowds*
● *Nuala O'Faolain: page 14* ● *Editorial Comment: page 15*

tents and cars and vowing to remain there until they were allowed to march down the Garvaghy Road, despite nationalist objections and the prohibition announced by the Parades Commission. A marquee was being erected for those with no accommodation.

The security forces beamed arc lights onto the crowd in the field in front of the barrier, but RUC officers said other parts of the North were of greater concern. "Portadown is quiet because it is under control and it is the centre of focus," one officer said.

The Rev Ian Paisley left the scene at Drumcree church this morning after spending two hours in meetings with local Orange officials in a room attached to the church of Ireland parochial hall there. He visited Orangemen at

the barrier and told them, to applause, that the Parades Commission should resign.

Given the security presence in Portadown and the scale and strength of the barrier at Drumcree, it is not considered physically possible for any group to break through to the Garvaghy Road. Yesterday two loyalists managed to breach the first line of the blockade before they were taken away by RUC officers.

Late last night, senior Ulster Unionist Party sources were unable to confirm a report in this morning's *Daily Telegraph* that the party leader, Mr David Trimble, has warned the British government that his position as First Minister will become untenable if the march is not allowed down the Garvaghy Road.

Mr Trimble told the Assembly on Wednesday that the march should proceed and the Parades Commission ban on it progressing down the Garvaghy Road was a "massive assault on the civil rights of an important sector of the community in Northern Ireland".

The Parades Commission is to announce fresh decisions today on a range of Orange parades. Its chairman, Mr Alistair Graham, warned last night that nationalists might be disappointed with some of the decisions, which gave rise to speculation that the controversial march through the nationalist Lower Ormeau Road in Belfast would be permitted.

Contact was maintained between the Taoiseach, Mr Ahern, and the British Prime Minister, Mr Tony Blair, throughout yesterday. A Government spokesman would make no comment on developments last night, though it was clear they were being viewed with some apprehension.

Meanwhile, the RUC Chief Constable, Mr Ronnie Flanagan, has stressed he will not overturn the decision of the Parades Commission. "The march will not be forced down. It is our responsibility to uphold the law and it is our responsibility to enforce the lawfully binding decision of the Parades Commission."

Email
& Internet access
for everyone
in your office

£1,699 +VAT

Orangemen sleep under the

Charles Haughey with his mother and Monsignor James Horan, the energetic promoter of Knock Airport in Co. Mayo. The Dublin establishment was generally sceptical about the airport—to put it mildly—but it was built nonetheless and opened in 1986.

million from the businessman Ben Dunne.

22 April
The paedophile priest Brendan Smith pleads guilty in Dublin to seventy-four charges of indecent and sexual assault.

1 May
The Labour Party wins the British general election, bringing

paper helped to reveal that Haughey had received huge payments from a businessman, Ben Dunne, did the full extent of his venality begin to emerge, shattering for ever the screen of patriotic idealism that had covered Haughey's career.

By then the other great institution of twentieth-century Ireland, the Catholic Church, had also been tainted with scandal. The church's victory in the abortion referendum of 1983 and in a referendum to repeal the constitutional ban on divorce in 1986 had seemed to shore up its authority. But those bitter controversies had torn apart the Catholic consensus in the Republic and lost the church its sacred supra-political status. Though it was slow to realise it, the church hierarchy no longer occupied an ethereal plane above criticism or questioning. This became stunningly clear in May 1992 when *The Irish*

of the past in talking about historical and political relations which have developed between the British and the Irish islands in the course of a millennium. The proposed 'strand three' British-Irish Council suddenly took on ampler meaning.

Here was a Unionist leader conceiving of a pre-Plantation Ireland, promising a shift in consciousness rather like the one that occurred when white Americans began to conceive of the pre-*Mayflower* history of their country and those who inhabited it before their arrival.

Another phrase that extended its reach was 'totality of relations'. In the course of the negotiations, this was applied to the overall configurations and arrangements operative between London, Dublin and Belfast, with a glance towards a future when Edinburgh and Cardiff might come into the picture as the sites of newly devolved assemblies within the United Kingdom.

On Friday, however, it was impossible not to acknowledge the reality of the American dimension and the crucial role played by the Senator from Maine, whose experience and patience and undentable dignity have been of inestimable value. When the crunch came, however, the direct phone link to the White House was essential to tilt the balance towards success.

And yet, direct access would not have had the same resolving effect had President Clinton not previously established his credentials as a personally committed player in the settlement game. His availability and intervention set the crown upon efforts of his own and others that have been indispensable. Ever since Senator Kennedy and the friends of Ireland in Washington made peace in Northern Ireland a part of their agenda, 'the totality of relations' has worked on a new and hugely enabling scale.

One reassuring thing about the whole process is the feeling that an action—in the tragic, dramatic sense—has been completed. In fact, what came to mind as I watched John Hume outside Stormont Buildings was the poet Louis MacNeice's notion that Ireland is a place where a person might live to see the consequences of one particular action. Hume was already a figure of some charisma when I knew him as a student two years ahead of me at St Columb's College, but on Friday he was beyond charisma and into history.

Charles Haughey's occasional republicanism made him a consistent critic of the RUC. Martyn Turner noted the irony of the police protection he received—and needed—on a visit to Northern Ireland.

Ireland had the presidency of the European Union in 1990. This press conference in Dublin Castle featured the president of the EU Commission, Jacques Delors, and the Minister for Foreign Affairs, Gerry Collins.

Times's Washington correspondent, Conor O'Clery, broke the story that the popular and colourful Bishop of Galway, Éamonn Casey, had used diocesan funds to help pay for the upkeep of the son he had fathered with an Irish-American woman. That story would have had an immense impact at any time, but its significance was heightened by the fact that it came just at a moment when the church's great triumph on the abortion amendment of 1983 was beginning to unravel. A brief front-page story in *The Irish Times* on 12 February 1992 gave the first limited details of what became known as the X case. The paper broke the news that the Attorney-General, Harry Whelehan, had taken legal action to prevent a fourteen-year-old girl, pregnant as a result of rape, from seeking an abortion. In a cartoon for the paper, Martyn Turner depicted Ireland surrounded by a barbed-wire fence, with a little girl holding a teddy bear standing behind it. The caption read: *The introduction of internment in Ireland … for 14-year-old girls*. Turner's cartoon was instrumental in the family's decision to fight the case. The girl and her mother visited him and asked for the original, which was subsequently used to raise funds for the Rape Crisis Centre. Eventually the Supreme

eighteen years of Conservative Party rule to an end.

21 May
Noel Browne, doctor, politician and socialist, dies.

6 June
A general election returns a coalition of Fianna Fáil and Progressive Democrats: Bertie Ahern succeeds John Bruton as Taoiseach.

12 June
President Robinson is appointed UN High Commissioner for Human Rights.

9 July

Charles Haughey's counsel admits that he received £1.3 million from Ben Dunne.

19 July

The IRA reinstates its cease-fire, to come into effect at midday the following day.

25 August

The McCracken Report is published and brands Charles Haughey a liar and Michael Lowry a tax cheat.

7 October

Ray Burke resigns as Minister for Foreign Affairs on

Court ruled that the abortion amendment in fact permitted the termination of pregnancy in circumstances where the life of the mother was in danger, and the girl, who had threatened suicide, was allowed to travel to England.

The Casey affair, moreover, turned out to be a rather innocent prelude to a series of much more damning revelations of the sexual abuse of children by members of the clergy. The most extraordinary was the case of the Belfast priest Brendan Smyth, who had abused children in Ireland, Britain and the United States at least since the early fifties and whose crimes were covered up by a church that simply moved him on to a new parish whenever the outrage of parents became too embarrassing. A UTV documentary by Chris Moore revealed that the Catholic primate, Cardinal Cahal Daly, was among those who had known of Smyth's crimes and had failed to report them to the police. It also revealed that a request from the RUC for Smyth's extradition from the Republic to face charges in Belfast had not been acted on for seven months in the office of the Attorney-General, Harry Whelehan. Since the Fianna Fáil

Dónal Lunny, a hugely influential figure in the Irish music revival of the past generation

He has seen things through in a moving and courageous way. In the course of the last thirty years, he suffered abuse from republicans in Derry, from Unionists and Loyalists and from elements in the Dublin media, but even

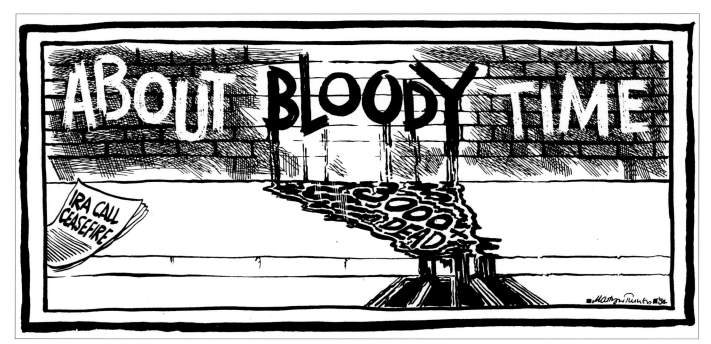

Martyn Turner reacts to the first IRA ceasefire in August 1994

when he sounded exhausted, he stood his ground in principle and conviction. He has kept going and now will have the satisfaction of getting started in a new gear.

Still, even the best disposed unionist cannot be expected to have any such satisfaction at the turn events have taken. Unionist opposition to the document will equally derive from principle and conviction, and what will make acceptance of the new situation so cruelly testing for them is Sinn Féin's inclusion in the democratic fold, since in the unionist mind Sinn Féin is to blame for the devastation which the IRA wrought on the economic and social life of the province—'their' province—over the past years. Terrible things done in the name of Ireland (and yes, of Ulster too) have put a darkness over the lives of individuals, families and communities. For too many people alive in the North, on both sides, it is never going to be a case of 'calm of mind, all passion spent'.

Everybody has to contend with what Thomas Davis called 'felt history'. Revisionists have created new perspectives (and contentions) and generations of gifted Northern poets have let the linguistic cat out of the sectarian bag, setting it free in the great street carnival of 'protholics and catestants,'

Fans at a U2 concert

Tony Ryan (right) founded Guinness Peat Aviation in 1975. It was a huge success during the eighties but almost collapsed following a failed market flotation in 1992. It was rescued by General Electric and in effect absorbed by it. His family also controls Ryanair.

Taoiseach, Albert Reynolds, was determined to appoint Whelehan President of the High Court over the objections of his coalition partner, Dick Spring, this suddenly became a crucial political issue. Reynolds was forced to resign. A new coalition between the Labour Party and Reynolds's successor was derailed by a story written by *The Irish Times*'s political correspondent, Geraldine Kennedy, detailing the information that other Fianna Fáil ministers had about the case.

In this period, as the end of the century approached, the gap between history and current affairs seemed at times to narrow almost to nothing. Only now was it becoming possible to understand the nature of the state that had emerged from the nationalist struggle. In March 1996 the headline over an *Irish Times* editorial was 'Stark days of revelation'. It was prompted by the release of files from the National Archives showing that over 2,100 'illegitimate' babies had been secretly exported from Ireland to America between 1949 and 1970, in a trade organised by nuns, sanctioned by the Archbishop of Dublin, John Charles McQuaid, administered by civil servants, and endorsed by Government ministers. That the story itself was covered in such detail in 1996 was itself a profound mark of change, for in fact that policy of exporting babies had not been

the day negotiations begin at Stormont. He had allegedly received an illegal payment of £30,000 from a property developer.

31 October
Mary McAleese wins the presidential election and becomes the first person from Northern Ireland to hold the position.

5 November
Dick Spring resigns as leader of the Labour Party.

16 November
In what becomes known as the 'C' Case, it emerges that a girl who was raped is seeking to go to Britain to have an abortion.

A protest in Dublin at the closure of a pirate radio station

but in Drumcree and on the Lower Ormeau Road, neither the victories of creative spirit nor the dodges of post-modernism are going to have much immediate effect. And yet it is at the level of creative spirit, in the realm of glimpsed potential rather than intransigent solidarity, that the future takes shape.

Indeed, what happened yesterday gives reassuring substance to that rather elevated sentiment. In the solemn mood at the end of the plenary session, Gerry Adams's invocation of the spirit of the United Irishmen even sounded as if it might not be a turn-off for their deradicalised descendants.

'Our island is full of comfortless noises,' I wrote in the mid-1970s, in a poem that began in shock at the killing of the British Ambassador, Christopher Ewart-Biggs, and ended with a recollection of British army helicopters hovering over the protest march at Newry a few years earlier, on the Sunday following Bloody Sunday. The line was a bitter echo of one spoken by Caliban in *The Tempest*, Shakespeare's late play of reconciliation and transcendence, and was intended to imply a deadly contrast between the sounds of violent destruction on the island of Ireland and the melodies of fulfilment that coursed through the air on Prospero's island.

In the play the malformed and maltreated Caliban reveals his susceptibility to the sweetness of music, but in those days the visionary mood of his famous speech felt like a mockery of what people in the North were experiencing in their daily lives. 'The isle,' Caliban says, 'is full of noises, sounds and sweet airs/That give delight and hurt not.' What

21 November

The Children's Court rules that the girl in the 'C' Case, who is in the care of the Eastern Health Board, is free to travel to Britain to have an abortion.

27 December

Billy Wright, leader of the Loyalist Volunteer Force, is shot dead in Long Kesh prison by the INLA.

entirely secret. As early as October 1951 *The Irish Times* had revealed that 'almost 500 babies were flown from Shannon for adoption last year' and added that the figure for the first nine months of 1951 was already higher than that. The report referred to eighteen parties of children leaving Shannon in the first week of October alone. But the story had no impact at the time. The files released in 1996 showed that at the time the only comment within the Department of External Affairs had been that 'it would be interesting to know how *The Irish Times* obtained the figure.'[9] What could be the source of national outrage in 1996 had not been, in the early fifties, a fit subject for discussion.

The editorial of March 1996 was prompted too by continuing revelations of the physical and

Sinéad O'Connor

Van Morrison, Ireland's most enduring rock star

is eopch-making about the document agreed at Castle Buildings on the Good Friday of 1998 is the fact that it just might be instrumental in turning this delightful, unhurting music into the as yet unheard music of the future.

from The Irish Times **1999**
12 MAY

Child sex abuse inquiry to start in September

By Maol Muire Tynan, Political Reporter

The first victims of childhood sexual abuse will have an opportunity to have their experiences officially heard next September under a new commission established to inquire into the scandal.

The possibility now exists that hundreds, if not thousands, of victims may avail of the opportunity to explain, 'in a healing forum', the abuses they suffered under the care of religious orders or State institutions, including primary and secondary schools, from at least 1940 to the present day.

Meanwhile, legislation to remove the current restrictions under the Statute of Limitation laws to victims of childhood sexual abuse is to be introduced during this Dáil session.

sexual abuse of children in the care of the church or by paedophile priests: by the end of the decade about fifty priests or brothers were either convicted or awaiting trial on charges of child abuse. 'When the social history of our times is written,' said the editorial, 'the early months of 1996 will figure as a period of stark revelation, a final drawing away of the veils from a darker, hidden Ireland. These days and weeks have marked a convergence of suppressed grief, of buried secrets and of enduring pain.'

Yet there was some reason to hope that Ireland could escape from the painful past that seemed to have doomed the North to the slow, familiar obscenity of sectarian violence. Throughout the eighties the conflict settled down into a pattern of regular, small-scale killings punctuated by large-scale atrocities horrible enough to provoke revulsion and despair but not momentous enough to provoke a sustainable mass movement for peace. From June 1993 onwards, however, it was becoming clear that a tentative peace process was under way. The world in which the conflict had begun was transformed. The Cold War, with its premium on anti-imperialist rhetoric and messianic calls to world revolution, had ended with the collapse of the Berlin Wall in 1989 and of the Soviet Union shortly afterwards. The strategic imperatives that had made the United States unwilling to risk any upset to its ally Great Britain had weakened. The Republic had ceased to be the rural, obediently Catholic society so alien to Northern Protestants and had emerged, especially from the early nineties onwards, as a thrusting high-technology economy with astonishingly rapid rates of growth. Britain had lost its pretensions to imperial greatness, and the symbols to which unionists attached their loyalty—the monarchy, the empire, the Protestant faith—had either disappeared or fundamentally altered their meaning.

The Irish Times, through its correspondents in Belfast and Washington, managed to give its readers a reasonably accurate picture of what was going on behind the scenes as Sinn Féin and the

1998

10 January
The Secretary of State for Northern Ireland, Mo Mowlam, holds talks with UDA prisoners in Long Kesh prison in an effort to keep their cease-fire secure.

30 January
A former Olympic swimming coach, Derry O'Rourke, is sentenced to twelve years' imprisonment for the sexual abuse of young girls.

20 February
A dissident republican bomb tears through Moira, Co. Down.

23 February
Republican dissidents strike again, this time bombing Portadown, Co. Armagh.

3 March
A Catholic man and a Protestant man are shot dead by the Loyalist Volunteer Force in a pub in Poyntzpass, Co. Armagh.

THE IRISH TIMES

PRICE 85p (incl. VAT) 75p sterling area | DUBLIN, FRIDAY, DECEMBER 11, 1998 | No. 45,319 CITY

BUSINESS THIS WEEK

The Little Helpers?

Taking stock of Tesco's Irish operation

Donegal's bitter harvest

13 pages of jobs

SOUND & VISION

Why Steve Earle went into the West

THE NORTH WEST

Helping those in the grip of marital abuse

The Irish Times on the Web
www.irish-times.com

Clinton's testimony video used to bolster impeachment views

REPUBLICANS and Democrats used clips from the video of President Clinton's testimony denying sexual relations with Monica Lewinsky to bolster their respective views on impeachment. It was the first time the public was allowed to see parts of this video of Mr Clinton's testimony under oath: **page 12**

Inflation falls to its lowest level since March 1998

INFLATION fell to just 2.1 per cent at the end of November as mortgage interest cuts kicked into the figures. The fall to 2.1 per cent brings inflation to its lowest level since March 1998: **Business This Week**

Funeral of murder victim: The body of Siobhán Hynes, the 17-year-old schoolgirl found dead on near Carraroe last weekend, was laid to rest yesterday: **page 6**

Pinochet in court today: The former Chilean dictator Gen Augusto Pinochet is to make his first court appearance in London today as a legal challenge to his deportation is made: **page 13**

Ahern, Blair may delay decision on visit: The Taoiseach and the British Prime Minister may postpone until after the weekend a decision on whether to travel to Belfast next week in an attempt to conclude agreement on the Northern Ireland executive: **page 7**

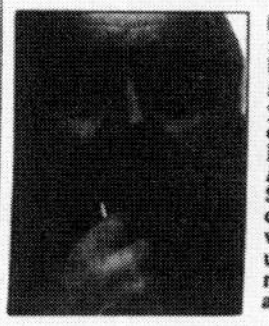

National debt £28.3bn: The national debt is standing at £28.3 billion — significantly below the £30.69 recorded at the end of last year, according to the chief executive of the National Treasury Management Agency. But in an *Irish Times* interview, Dr Michael Somers criticised the Department of Finance and the Central Bank, whom he partly blamed for holding up progress in developing the bond market and being reluctant to accept change: **Business This Week**

Arafat confirms failing health rumours: Confirming rumours of his failing health, the PLO President, Mr Yasser Arafat, said this week: "I don't know if I'll live one year or two years": **page 12**

Taoiseach attacked for bringing partner abroad: The Church of Ireland *Gazette* has described as "astonishing" that Ms Celia Larkin should accompany the Taoiseach as he goes about state business: **page 6**

Widow wins action against building society: A widow won her nine-year battle against a building society's claim that she had to repay a £100,000 loan made to her and her husband: **page 4**

Manager of Year award for Kerr: Brian Kerr was named Sports Manager of the Year: **page 19**

Truth about battered husbands 'suppressed': Ms Erin Pizzey accused the feminist movement of suppressing the reality of violence against men by women: **page 4**

Slain hostage admitted spying: A Chechen official showed a videotape in which one of four murdered Western hostages said they had been spying for British intelligence: **page 12**

Short cut home 'lead to victim's death': A murder victim's short cut home led to his death, a jury heard: **page 4**

Commonwealth 'no longer relic of British empire': Ireland would receive a very warm welcome back into the Commonwealth, with whose members it already has many close links, the secretary-general of the organisation said. The modern Commonwealth is no longer a relic of the British Empire but a co-operative association of free and sovereign nations, Chief Emeka Anyaoku told the Irish association in Dublin last night: **page 9**

Ex-soldier jailed for 15 years: A former soldier was jailed for 15 years for having a car bomb which was twice the size of the Omagh bomb: **page 4**

Jury returns verdict of misadventure: A jury returned a verdict of misadventure at an inquest into the death of a prisoner who died after a fire in his cell: **page 6**

Rise in crimes against women: Rape, sexual assault and other violent crimes against women are increasing, the Minister of State for Equality said: **page 2**

Optimism on duty-free sales: Confidence is growing that duty-free sales will continue after June 1999, the Dáil was told: **page 9**

WEATHER

It will be dry over the northern half of the ...

Gardai to investigate leaks from planning tribunal

Media warned against publishing material

By Paul Cullen

THE planning tribunal chaired by Mr Justice Flood has called in the Garda to investigate newspaper leaks of confidential documents relating to its work.

Mr Justice Flood is also seeking written undertakings from the main daily and Sunday newspapers that they will not publish any confidential material provided to or circulated by the tribunal.

Mr Justice Flood has set the newspapers a deadline of 12 noon today to comply with his request. If they fail to do so, he has indicated he may seek a High Court order restraining them from publishing confidential material relating to the tribunal.

The penalty for a journalist or any other person who is judged to have obstructed or hindered the tribunal in its work is a fine of up to £10,000 or two years in jail, or both. A letter written on behalf of the tribunal chairman to the newspapers makes specific reference to these punishments.

The Garda investigation into the leaks started in the past few days, and follows complaints by the former minister for foreign affairs, Mr Ray Burke, and a number of builders who are the subject of allegations relating to planning corruption.

They argued that the flow of newspaper leaks was interfering with their ability to work with the tribunal. Lawyers claimed their clients were afraid to provide any further confidential material to the tribunal, for fear it will be leaked.

Lawyers for Mr Burke indicated their future participation in the tribunal could depend on how it dealt with the issue of leaks.

A Garda spokesman said last night it was investigating allegations of offences under Section 3 of the Tribunal of Inquiry (Evidence) (Amendment) Act, 1979. This is the section which provides for fines and terms of imprisonment for anyone who obstructs or hinders the work of the tribunal.

The decision to call in the Garda follows an attempt by the tribunal to deal with the matter directly. A number of journalists were requested to meet tribunal lawyers after stories appeared under their name.

They include Mr Jody Corcoran of the *Sunday Independent*, which last month published extensive extracts from the affidavit filed by Mr James Gogarty, the retired building firm executive who is the tribunal's main witness.

The publication of this document prompted the Government to express concern that such leaks could undermine the tribunal. Mr Gogarty's former employer, Joseph Murphy Structural Engineering, and another builder against whom he has made allegations, Mr Michael Bailey, both called for an immediate Garda investigation into the matter.

It is understood Mr Corcoran was unable to help the tribunal with its investigations, and cited the journalists' right to protect their sources. The tribunal wrote subsequently seeking a copy of the affidavit which was in the possession of the newspaper, but this request was not complied with.

The tribunal could sit in Dublin Castle today if any of the newspapers indicate a wish to make oral submissions to the chairman.

Mr Gogarty, who is 81, is due to become the first witness to take the stand at a public sitting of the tribunal scheduled for January 12th.

The tribunal was set up to investigate allegations of corruption relating to planning matters in north county Dublin. Its investigations have since been widened to include allegations about payments to politicians.

It was established over a year ago following revelations that Mr Burke received £30,000 in cash from JMSE in 1989. Last June, the terms of reference were changed after it was discovered that Mr Burke had received a second payment of £30,000 from Rennicks Ltd, a subsidiary of the Fitzwilton Group.

Cork's 'goldy angel' left trumpetless atop St Fin Barre's

By Dick Hogan, in Cork

WHO stole the trumpets? And who fears vertigo so little that he (for it is presumed it is a he), scaled the daunting spires of St Fin Barre's Cathedral in Cork to remove them? These questions are occupying the Garda authorities in the city.

The great Victorian architect, William Burges, designed the ca-...

... parcel of Cork's history for 130 years. No one could put a price on Burges's creation. It was a sad escapade, the spokesman said, adding: "It is something we just do not understand. Why would anyone do such a thing?"

And to what avail? The trumpets are known far and wide as an essential part of the cathedral. Who could sell them? Who would buy them? In any event, after all her years on guard duty over the ...

After many days of misery and tears, a grand occasion

The winners of the Nobel Peace Prize, Mr David Trimble and Mr John Hume, display their Nobel medals at the Grand Hotel yesterday following the awards ceremony in Oslo City Hall. Photograph: Matt Kavanagh

North gets a small taste of fairytale as heroes of peace process honoured

From Deaglán de Bréadún, in Oslo

GREAT hatred, little room. Much sadness, sparse joy. Many days of misery and tears, very few grand occasions. That's been the history of the Northern Ireland Troubles for the last 30 years.

But yesterday, at last, it was time for a celebration. There were fanfares by cockaded soldiers in fairytale uniforms who blew silver trumpets. There was a king and a queen and they looked the part, too. There was snow on the streets, with Christmas just around the corner, and children in bright clothes cheering as they sang about peace and lit eternal flames.

There were glamorous people, camera crews that focused on smiling faces and not twisted wreckage, politicians who wore broad grins and dropped tantalising hints about a compromise on the "D-word". There was champagne on ice, there was a banquet, there was even a little hope if you dropped your guard long enough.

It's a tradition after every year's Nobel ceremony that the winners appear on the balcony of the Grand Hotel in downtown Oslo to wave to a torchlight procession below.

David Trimble and John Hume appeared in their evening suits, the odd couple, awkward but amiable. They didn't know what to do with their hands, whether to wave or give a thumbs-up sign. Some onlookers nicknamed the pair *"Urbi et Orbi"*.

There was a surge of cheering and general goodwill from the crowd, although some seemed weak on the specifics of the prizewinners and their role. "It's very good that they fight for the IRA," one young person commented.

Earlier in Oslo City Hall, under massive and intriguing Nordic murals, the two leaders received their gold medals and their Nobel diplomas. The £344,000 cheque comes separately, it was said, but both men say they haven't had a chance ...

... missioning.

He said he had not insisted on "precise dates, quantities and manner of decommissioning". He had sought only a "credible beginning". All he had asked for was a declaration that the so-called war was over — and this could be proved by such a beginning.

After the ceremony, the prizewinners, their families and guests adjourned to the Grand Hotel, with, among other famous faces, Mrs Jean Kennedy Smith and Bishop Edward Daly — grey now, but he will always be the young priest waving the white handkerchief on Bloody Sunday.

Compassion of the people recognised: page 10

Contrasting words of the romantic and the realist: page 11

Editorial comment: page 17

Take a Clear Stance

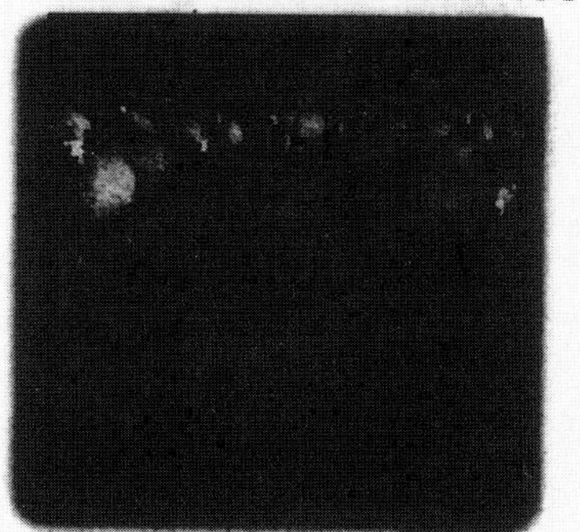

Why pay more on your Home phone bill when you could choose Esat Clear, the Home Phone and Internet company?

• Phone anywhere in Ireland for the price

THE IRISH TIMES

PRICE 85p (incl. VAT) €1.08 75p sterling area | DUBLIN, WEDNESDAY, FEBRUARY 17, 1999 | No. 45,374 CITY

Retail Investment
Developers pay £14m for Dundrum shopping centre
❑ COMMERCIAL PROPERTY

Mercantile Success
Robert O'Byrne on Waterford's regeneration
❑ FROM THE SOUTH-EAST: 2

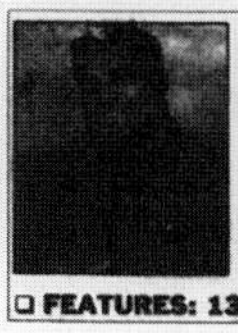

Eye in the Sky
Up in the air with AA Roadwatch
❑ FEATURES: 13

Poet and Naturalist
Seán Lysaght talks to Eileen Battersby
❑ ARTS: 12

9 771393 350034 07
The Irish Times on the Web
www.irish-times.com

Ahern asks senior Finance officials to brief journalists

THE Taoiseach asked two senior officials in the Department of Finance to brief journalists last night on his role in the G-Tech and tax concession controversies. He had earlier refused to take Special Notice Questions on these matters in the Dáil. Two assistant secretaries in Finance, who had dealt with the Lottery contract and the benefit-in-kind concession in the 1994 Finance Act, said there was no departure from normal procedures in either case by the then minister for finance, Mr Ahern: **page 5**

Gardai examine apparent abduction of young woman

GARDAÍ are trying to ascertain if the apparent abduction of a young woman in Naas, Co Kildare, early yesterday is linked to the disappearance of women in the area. A senior Garda source said they had contacted the special unit set up to investigate possible links between the previous disappearances of six women in the area: **page 4**

Hospital service plan: The board of Tallaght Hospital has submitted a service plan for this year to the Department of Health and Children, as required under the deadline in its Letter of Determination: **page 5**

Farmer demonstrations: Farmers are to hold demonstrations today in 28 towns throughout the State in protest at proposed changes in the EU's Common Agricultural Policy: **page 3**

Singer dies: Singer and actress Agnes Bernelle has died. She was born in Berlin in the 1920s but her family fled Germany to escape Nazism and went to live in London. She got married and moved to Dublin. She appeared in plays, wrote her memoirs, made records and was the subject of an RTÉ documentary, *The Berlin of Agnes Bernelle*. She worked with many people, including Orson Welles to Peter Cook: **page 3**

Euro falls: The euro has fallen to new lows against the US dollar and sterling, making an interest rate cut less likely despite mounting political pressure: **page 16**

Three horses die: Animal welfare groups last night called for an inquiry after three horses died in a pile-up at a race meeting in Co Durham: **page 22**

Gogarty cross-examination: The main witness at the planning tribunal, Mr James Gogarty, faces the prospect of the long-promised "big ambush" by lawyers today: **page 5**

Internet service charge: A new "flat rate" Internet service from Telecom Éireann could more than halve the company's current lowest-priced net connection charges within two weeks: **page 16**

House bulldozed: A couple who bought a semi-detached house in Howth came home one day to find their neighbour's house had been effectively bulldozed away, leaving "a battleground" next door: **page 4**

Lung cancers: An Irish person dies every six hours from lung cancers, 90 per cent of which are due to tobacco smoking: **page 2**

Ward recalled for Welsh match: Andy Ward is recalled to the Ireland rugby team for Saturday's Five Nations' Championship game against Wales in Wembley, the only change to the side which lost to France: **page 20**

GM concerns: British ministers last night insisted consumer safety remained their number one priority amid mounting public controversy over genetically modified (GM) foods. The Prime Minister, Mr Tony Blair, insisted his Science Minister, Lord Sainsbury, would not be "hounded" from office following newspaper allegations about his links with a company controlling the patent rights to a key gene used in the genetic modification process: **page 9**

Clondalkin growth: Clondalkin, the print and packaging group, is looking for strong growth following a 22 per cent rise in pre-tax profit: **page 16**

Ultrasound scan services: The National Maternity Hospital did not have full ultrasound scan services available at weekends in 1992: **page 4**

War slave labourers: Some of Germany's leading companies have agreed to establish a fund to compensate second World War slave labourers: **page 10**

Kickboxer broke jaw: A champion kickboxer who broke a student's jaw because he wrote down the registration number of a car has been given a one-year suspended sentence: **page 18**

WEATHER

CHART FOR NOON TODAY

IT WILL become milder

Drive to break weapons deadlock planned

By Deaglán de Bréadún, Northern Editor

A MAJOR drive to break the decommissioning impasse is to take place over the coming fortnight, following yesterday's cross-community vote in the Northern Ireland Assembly to accept new government departments and North-South bodies.

The British and Irish governments and the main pro-agreement parties will be in constant consultation to break the deadlock.

The White House is renewing its involvement and there is a major focus on the expected report from the head of the decommissioning body, Gen John de Chastelain.

As an indication of the gathering pace of political contacts, the first-ever party-to-party meeting between the Ulster Unionists and Sinn Féin is scheduled to take place this morning at Stormont.

Previously, Mr Trimble met the Sinn Féin leader, Mr Gerry Adams, in his capacity as First Minister but this will be the first time for delegations representing both parties to meet.

There had been widespread predictions from the anti-agreement camp and the media that Mr Roy Beggs jnr would oppose the party leadership in yesterday's vote, which would have placed Mr Trimble in a minority position among unionist members.

The East Antrim Assembly member said last week he would be unable to support the leadership stance. But a determined effort was made by senior unionists to persuade him to change his mind. In the end, the only UUP Assembly member to vote No was Mr Peter Weir, who had lost the whip after a previous defection.

The balance of forces between Yes and No unionists remains 29-29. With the support of other parties the proposal from Mr Trimble and Mr Séamus Mallon on new structures was passed by 77 votes to 29.

In a statement issued immediately after the vote, Mr Beggs indicated he had been strongly influenced by a meeting of the UUP executive on Saturday which unanimously voted to block the appointment of Sinn Féin ministers until the IRA had decommissioned.

The result in the Assembly was welcomed by the Sinn Féin president, who missed the vote to attend a meeting with Mr Tony Blair at Downing Street. Mr Adams said he hoped Mr Trimble would "take strength" from the fact that the political landscape had changed since the days of monolithic unionism and that he had the support of a range of parties yesterday, reflecting the referendum results North and South.

"I put it to Tony Blair that the next steps were over to the British government," Mr Adams said. This meant the activation of the procedures for setting up the executive and transferring powers by the March 10th deadline.

Meanwhile, White House sources were saying the Clinton administration was stepping up its activity in the peace process, now that the President's impeachment difficulties had been overcome. "This president's legacy will include his work on Ireland."

Turning of Beggs is triumph for Trimble, reports and analysis: ***page 8***

Haughey left AIB officials chasing £1m debt

By Colm Keena

DETAILS of Mr Charles Haughey's extraordinary financial relationship with AIB in the 1970s, during which he ran up a debt of over £1 million, were disclosed at the Moriarty tribunal yesterday.

Dozens of bank letters and memos concerning Mr Haughey's affairs were read into the record by a lawyer for the tribunal, so that the settlement of Mr Haughey's £1.143 million debt, for £750,000 in January 1980, could be put in context.

The documents showed that Mr Haughey told his AIB bank manager in 1976 that he intended to be in politics for another 10 years and could direct a lot of business towards the bank. At the time Mr Haughey had debts with AIB of £246,871.

Although Mr Haughey repeatedly failed to live up to promises he made to the bank, AIB continued to issue him with cheque books and to honour his cheques. Mr Haughey's debt with the bank rose from more than £100,000 in the early 1970s to £1.143 million by the end of the decade. During the period he also had debts with the Northern Bank Finance Corporation of more than £200,000.

Yesterday's evidence conflicts with Mr Haughey's evidence to the McCracken (Dunnes Payments) tribunal. Mr Haughey is detailed in the AIB documentation as repeatedly meeting with bank officials, negotiating his overdraft facility and discussing aspects of his business affairs.

However, Mr Haughey told the McCracken tribunal that the late Mr Des Traynor "took over control of my financial affairs from about 1960 onwards. He saw it as his personal responsibility to ensure that I would not be distracted from my political work by financial concerns." Mr Haughey said he "never had to concern myself about my personal finances".

The Moriarty tribunal heard yesterday that Mr Haughey told AIB in March 1975 that he bought his home and estate, Abbeville, Co Dublin, for £140,000 in 1968/1969. He also owned a stud farm in Meath and other properties, and he put a value of £1.252 million on his assets. He said he paid out £32,600 per annum in wages and other costs. His income as a TD was £7,000 per annum.

In September 1975 Mr Haughey's bank manager at AIB in Dame Street, Dublin, Mr Michael Phelan, wrote to his superiors saying that despite the unattractiveness of a proposition being put by Mr Haughey, he recommended it be sanctioned "bearing in mind . . . the likelihood of Mr Haughey being a man of influence in the future".

In May 1970, Mr Haughey was dismissed from government as a result of the arms crisis. In 1977 he was appointed Minister for Health and Social Welfare. In September 1979, when his debt exceeded £1 million and just months before the resignation of Mr Jack Lynch as leader of Fianna Fáil, Mr Haughey telephoned his bank manager and said he wanted to deal with "this dangerous situation once and for all".

By December 1979, when settlement terms for his debt were being negotiated with AIB, he had been elected Taoiseach. If he had been declared bankrupt, he would have lost his seat in the Dáil.

Mr Haughey's debt of £1.143 million was cleared with £750,000 from Guinness & Mahon bank in January 1980. The money came from an account in the name of the late Mr Traynor, though it is not known who the funds belonged to.

In October 1976, when a bank official formally asked Mr Haughey to hand over his cheque books, Mr Haughey "became quite vicious", according to a bank memo.

In September 1979, when Mr Phelan went to Mr Haughey in the Department of Social Welfare, the bank manager said there had been cheques for £31,776 written on Mr Haughey's accounts between July 16th and September 5th. "He [Mr Haughey] seemed very surprised by the high figure on the drawings and implied Abbeville had gone mad buying unnecessarily," Mr Phelan noted.

INSIDE

How Haughey diced with soaring debt; Gross breach of privacy alleged; Land sold to meet demands: **page 6**

Day the bank ran out of patience: **page 7**

Vincent Browne on the questions for Ahern; Political analysis by Denis Coghlan: **page 14**

Guerrilla leader's arrest sparks embassy protests

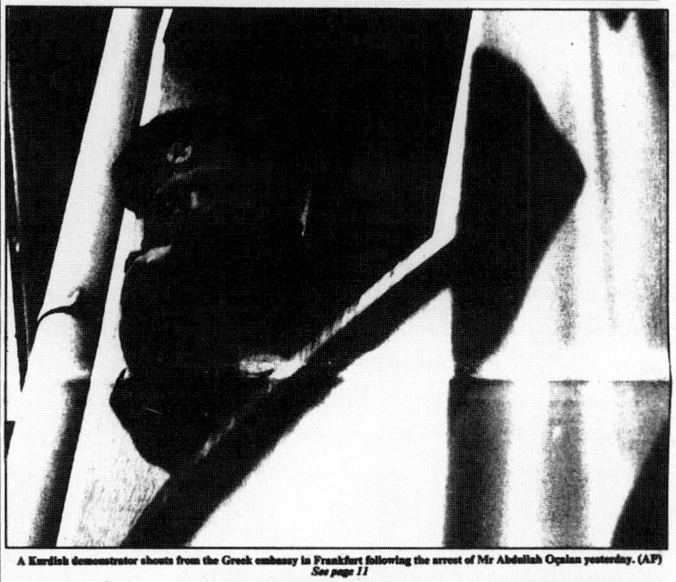

A Kurdish demonstrator shouts from the Greek embassy in Frankfurt following the arrest of Mr Abdullah Oçalan yesterday. (AP)
See page 11

Kurdish anger over capture

TURKEY yesterday captured the Kurdish guerrilla leader, Mr Abdullah Oçalan, and brought him home to stand trial, spiriting him out of Kenya.

Kurdish protests across Europe, originally called to protest at Greece's refusal to grant Mr Oçalan refuge, intensified.

The demonstrations were directed largely against Greece, which secretly sheltered Mr Oçalan in its Nairobi mission before he fell into Turkey's hands.

Washington denied any "direct involvement" in Mr Oçalan's arrest.

The Greek Prime Minister, Mr Costas Simitis, came under attack from critics for allowing the rebel leader to be delivered to Turkey.

Greece recalled its ambassador from Kenya over the incident.

The Turkish Prime Minister, Mr Bulent Eçevit, his voice shaking with emotion, announced: "The head of the separatist organisation has been in Turkey since three o'clock this morning. He will account for his actions in front of the Turkish justice system."

Goodman link to bank from which

Big on performance, Even bigger on value.

If you're looking for quality, high performance systems at great prices, take a look at these specs. So for bigger, better value call the world's largest direct PC manufacturer* now. *source: IDC

PROFESSIONAL DESKTOP
Dell® Dimension™ V400c
- Intel® Celeron™ Processor 400MHz
- 64MB 100MHz SDRAM
- 128KB Full Speed Cache
- 8.4GB ATA-33 Hard Drive
- Integrated ATI Rage Pro AGP 8MB Video Card
- 17" Colour TCO95 SVGA monitor (0.28 Dot Pitch, 15.9" Viewable Area)
- Integrated Yamaha XG 64 Voice Sound (Speakers optional) or 10/100 Ethernet Controller (UTP)
- 17/40 x CD-ROM Drive
- 2 PCI, 1 ISA and 1 PCI/ISA shared expansion slots
- Mid-Sized Desktop Chassis
- Microsoft® Windows 98

MULTIMEDIA DESKTOP
Dell® Dimension™ V400c
- Intel® Celeron™ Processor 400MHz
- Intel® 440 AGPset
- 64MB 100MHz SDRAM
- 128KB Full Speed Cache
- 8.4GB ATA-33 Hard Drive
- 17" Colour TCO95 SVGA monitor (0.28 Dot Pitch, 15.9" Viewable Area)
- ATI Xpert 98D 8MB 3D AGP Video Card
- 14/32 x CD-ROM Drive
- Integrated Yamaha XG 64 Voice Sound and Harmon Kardon 195 Speakers
- US Robotics 56 KB/s Modem
- 2 PCI, 1 ISA and 1 PCI/ISA shared expansion slots
- Mini-Tower Chassis

MOBILE COMPUTING
Dell® Inspiron™ 3500 c300 XT
- Mobile Intel® Celeron™ Processor 300MHz
- Intel® 440BX Chipset
- 13.3" XGA (1024x768) TFT Screen
- 32MB SDRAM (upgradeable to 256MB)
- 128KB High Performance Cache
- 3.2GB ATA-33 Hard Drive (upgradeable to 6.4GB)
- Modular 24x CD-ROM Drive and 3.5" floppy disk drive (DVD Optional)
- 256bit Neomagic (NM65) video with 2.5MB VRAM
- 2 Cardbus PCMCIA type II slots
- Lithium Ion battery
- Touchpad with 2 buttons
- Zoomed video support
- Infrared communications port (IrDA 1.1 compatible)

Dick Spring, the most successful leader in the history of the Labour Party and Minister for Foreign Affairs, 1992–7, canvassing in Ballymun, Dublin, with the local TD, Róisín Shortall

10 April

All the parties participating in the multi-party talks at Stormont reach an agreement that they believe will bring about political structures to which nation-alists and unionists can give allegiance. People throughout Ireland greet the news with joy.

IRA sought a way out of the dead end of violent attrition and the British and Irish governments tested the possibilities for a settlement that, instead of seeking to isolate both republican and loyalist paramilitaries, would attempt to incorporate them in a democratic compromise. In July 1993 it reported the suspicion, relayed through senior unionists, that the IRA and the British were having secret talks. In September it reported that discussions between John Hume and the Sinn Féin leader Gerry Adams had identified the possibility that the IRA would call a cease-fire in return for a formal British recognition of the right of the Irish people as a whole to 'national self-determination', a possibility that became real when the Downing Street Declaration of December 1993 was

Under the present system, a plaintiff can only take a legal action within three yeas of reaching the age of eighteen. Such is the nature of sexual abuse [that] a victim may be incapable of initiating such an action until long after their eighteenth birthday. However, the changes would mean that adults, even in middle age, will not be debarred from instituting a damages suit.

The Government has also decided to refer the issue of limitation periods to the Law Reform Commission for its recommendation.

In the first apology from Government for the wrongs inflicted on children who suffered such violation, the Taoiseach yesterday said the starting point to dealing with the matter was 'simple'.

'We must start by apologising. On behalf of the State and of all citizens of the State, the Government wishes to make a sincere and long-overdue apology to the victims of childhood abuse for our collective failure to intervene, to detect their pain, to come to their rescue,' Mr Ahern said.

Following Cabinet approval of a range of measures relating to childhood abuse, the Taoiseach, the Tánaiste, Ms Harney, and the Minster for Education, Mr Martin, called a press conference to announce several proposals, including a 'dedicated professional counselling service' which would also be introduced in all the regions ...

from The Irish Times
12 MAY 1999

Perpetrators of bombings still evade justice

Opinion/Vincent Browne

Malachy, my younger brother, was a medical student at Trinity in May 1974. We had met in Trinity earlier in that magnificent summer's afternoon of Friday, 17 May, and afterwards I had gone down to the offices of Independent Newspapers in Middle Abbey Street, where I then worked. I was coming down the stairs when I heard the first dull thunder-like sound at about

Dawson Stelfox, the first Irish person to stand on the summit of Mount Everest

followed by an IRA cease-fire in August 1994. In August 1994 it reported the general shape of the framework documents that would set out the basis for a negotiated settlement.

One of the positive factors was the determination of the Clinton administration in the United States to give as much weight to the views of the Irish Government as to the British. As Clinton told *The Irish Times* in an interview a week after the declaration, 'US policy on Northern Ireland is made in the context of the deep ties of friendship and history the American people enjoy with the peoples of both Ireland and Britain.'

When the IRA declared 'a complete cessation of military operations' on 31 August 1994, *The Irish Times* summed up the mood of cautious optimism. 'There must be a welcome. And there must be caution. It may not yet be the day to hang out the flags and colours to mark a full and final peace. But with the IRA cease-fire since midnight, it becomes possible to hope that such a happy condition is now within measurable reach.' The absence of the word 'permanent' from the statement induced scepticism from the British government and from Unionists, but Gerry Adams assured *The Irish Times* that in interpreting the cease-fire as permanent the Irish and US governments had responded 'positively and correctly.' The prospects for peace were enhanced in October when the Combined Loyalist Military Command responded with a cease-fire of its own.

On 9 February 1996 the IRA, unhappy with the lack of progress towards political negotiations, exploded a bomb at Canary Wharf in London, killing two innocent men. *The Irish Times* reflected the shock felt in both countries. 'Words are hardly adequate to condemn the bombing at Canary Wharf which has once more caused the world's television screens to fill with images of innocent people injured and mutilated in the name of Irish nationalism ... At one blow, the normality of peace has been undone and replaced once again by the fear of random

Bertie Ahern at the count following the general election of 1997. He is about to become Taoiseach.

any other party despite a relatively bad turn-out for them.

5 July

'Drumcree mark 4' looms as the RUC and British army block the route of the Orange Order to prevent them from marching down the Garvaghy Road in Portadown. A week of loyalist violence sweeps Northern Ireland.

violence.' Yet the paper stressed the need to avoid panic reactions and to try to rebuild the peace process. Eventually, that sober optimism was justified when, on 10 April 1998, a comprehensive peace agreement was signed in Belfast.

The agreement, providing for shared power in Northern Ireland, for North-South bodies with executive powers and for new institutional links between both parts of Ireland and both Westminster and the devolved parliaments of Scotland and Wales, was extraordinarily radical and innovative, placing Ireland, as it had been in the early years of the century, near the forefront of global political developments. Recognising the right of the citizens of Northern Ireland to be 'Irish or British or both', it marked a new recognition of the complexity of political and ethnic allegiances at the end of the twentieth century. And by creating in Northern Ireland a political space over which no government

5.30 p.m. and at the door of Independent House when I heard the second. Having worked in Northern Ireland from 1970, I was sure these were bomb explosions.

Unexpectedly, Malachy had followed me down to Middle Abbey Street and we both ran out to O'Connell Street to see from where the bomb blasts had come. We saw people running down from North Earl Street and went up there and then on to Talbot Street.

We walked through the initial debris and I was making a mental note of the windows that were shattered, the initial signs of damage to shop fronts and the cars which were brunt out. At first there seemed nothing very different from countless such scenes I had witnessed in Belfast over the previous several years. Then we saw a body and then another and then another.

There was stillness about Talbot Street. Almost a complete stillness. Just occasional groans coming from the debris.

Almost at our feet there was a man lying on the pavement, with a large piece of a car fender jabbed into his side. He was a big man, probably in his mid to late thirties,

The Cranberries, one of the most successful of the many Irish bands of the nineties

dark curly hair, wearing a dark suit and white open-necked shirt. We tried to lift him but he was too heavy. A stranger came to help us and we carried him awkwardly up towards Moran's Hotel and into the foyer.

He was just about conscious and bleeding profusely. The staff at Moran's would not allow us leave him in the foyer or carry him into the dining room. They insisted we take him downstairs. We did as we were told and we let the man fall on the stairs on the way down.

We went back outside and by then people were screaming. Along with several others, we started to go back down Talbot Street where we had seen other injured people but a garda was shouting that there was another bomb about to go off and we all ran back towards Amiens Street station. Within a minute or two we realised we were no safer there than in Talbot Street and along with several other helpers we returned.

A woman was lying on the footpath outside a shoe shop. She was just about breathing. We lifted her up and she disintegrated in our arms. Her body simply fell apart inside her clothes. We laid her back down.

exercised a territorial claim, it pushed out the boundaries of the very notion of sovereignty that had shaped so much of Irish history over the previous hundred years.

The Irish Times continued to change and develop. In 1986 a new, full-colour printing press was installed in the d'Olier Street premises and in 1991 the Atex computer-based composition system was added. New sections meant that the newspaper began to grow in size.

In 1986 also, Douglas Gageby stepped down as editor and was succeeded by Conor Brady. The newspaper continued its steady growth in circulation and in 1993 passed the 100,000 mark for the first time. By the end of the year 1999 the daily average circulation was projected at a figure comfortably in excess of 112,000.

The range of editorial services grew too. In 1987 the newspaper opened Ireland's first bureau in the then Soviet Union, headed by Conor O'Clery. Other permanent bureaux opened in

12 July

Three children die in a sectarian arson attack on their home in Ballymoney. Massive pressure is put on members of the Orange Order to abandon the Drumcree confrontation; most do, but a hard core remain, vowing to stay for as long as it takes.

6 August

The international swimming body, FINA, bans

Washington, Paris and Beijing, as well as the long-established bureaux in London and Brussels.

In the late nineteen-nineties a significant expansion of the newspaper's regional network within Ireland took place. By the end of 1999 *Irish Times* staff were operating regional bureaux in Belfast, Cork, Waterford, Sligo, Limerick and Athlone. In 1996 the newspaper launched its website editions, making *The Irish Times* available electronically and instantly to readers all around the world.

When the Irish state was still young and fragile, one of its most important ideologues, the writer Daniel Corkery, tried to define what made Ireland Irish. He came up with three things that were so obvious and solid that no-one could dispute their overwhelming presence: '(1) The Religious Consciousness of the People; (2) Irish Nationalism; and (3) The Land.'

There were several other people groaning on the roadway. Malachy saw a young woman and thought she could be saved if got to hospital quickly. No ambulances had come: it was now certainly twenty minutes after the bomb had exploded. I saw a man getting into a car further down Talbot Street, towards O'Connell Street. I ran to him and explained that a woman could be saved if she could be brought to hospital immediately and asked if he would take her. He hesitated and said he would. I returned to where Malachy was with the woman and we started to carry her towards O'Connell Street. It took us about three or four minutes and when we got there the man and his car were gone.

A Garda inspector had taken charge and was directing those involved in the attempted rescue to line up the bodies at the junction of Talbot Street and Gardiner Street. It was as though he could not cope with the terrible agony of those still alive.

It seemed to take a lifetime for an ambulance to arrive: certainly none arrived for at least forty-five minutes. Then the

When Michelle Smith de Bruin won three gold medals and a bronze at the Atlanta Olympic games of 1996, Ireland celebrated. Three years later, de Bruin's career ended in disgrace when she was held to have tampered with a drug test and was banned from swimming for four years.

first one that came had no stretchers, only the frame for stretchers, which meant that just a single person could be placed in the ambulance and then only on the floor between the two frames.

We stayed on the scene for another hour or so and then went back to the offices of Independent Newspapers where I wrote what we had seen for the following day's *Irish Independent*. The only thing I remember about the newsroom that evening was another stillness.

We then went across O'Connell Street to Daly's pub on the quays, and there was more stillness there. I had been unaffected by it all up to then, partly distanced, trying to remember what was happening for the piece I was going to write. We had a few brandies—one of the few occasions in my life I drank brandy. We both stood there silently at the bar staring straight ahead, crying …

from The Irish Times 1999
22 MAY

We are sleeping now without dreams

By Elaine Lafferty

'It's nice to see another lady. Welcome to hell.'

That was the greeting I received from a Turkish woman journalist who has been living in a hotel in the heart of Kosovo for well over a month. Hell is at this moment an apt description for this shredded and scarred land that Serbs are willing to die for. It is a place of bombed buildings, cratered streets and charred Albanian homes.

There are two routes into Kosovo that several journalists have taken over the last fifty-eight days of the war here. One, via Albania or Macedonia, has been taken by a handful of reporters travelling with the Kosovo Liberation Army (KLA) through the legendary 'accursed mountains' into the heavily forested hills just over the border.

The other method has been tightly organised bus and van trips lasting several hours, closely supervised by the Yugoslav military. Extremely sensitive about photography and video, the authorities have allowed limited access even to the approved destinations.

The BBC, for example, was permitted just under half-an-hour last week to film the village of Korisa, where a NATO bomb struck a farmland site, killing 87 Albanians and

No-one could have disputed the inescapable power of these great forces. The political partition of Ireland in the early twenties had left, in effect, a Protestant British province in the North and in the South a Catholic state. In the South, religion, in the shape of the Catholic Church, was so pervasive that Ireland supplied not just its own church but much of American, African, Australian and British Catholicism with priests and nuns.

The importance of nationalism was equally self-evident. The state itself had emerged from a violent struggle for independence from Britain, fuelled by a deep belief that Ireland was a place apart, with its own history, language, culture, and destiny. Nationalism was so powerful that the major political disputes were not between nationalists and others but between fervent nationalists and even more fervent nationalists.

And the land itself was an object of both religious devotion and national pride. The Catholic peasantry had wrenched it from the grasp of the old Protestant landlords, creating in the process a society of smallholders fiercely protective of their few acres. Ireland was essentially a rural society, and its towns and cities were regarded with contempt and suspicion. The economy was utterly dependent on agriculture.

Roughly until the early nineteen-seventies, Corkery's three pillars of Irish identity were still standing. Ireland was still so Catholic, so saturated

7 September
The 'Real IRA' declares a cease-fire after coming under immense pressure to do so following the Omagh bombing.

27 November
Paul Ward is given life imprisonment for the murder of the journalist Veronica Guerin two years previously.

10 December
John Hume and David Trimble receive their joint Nobel Prize for Peace in Oslo.

1999

2 January
Launch of the Euro means end of Irish punt as independent

The staff at Raidió na Life, Dublin's independent Irish-language radio station

Gay Byrne, the best-known face and voice in Ireland since the early sixties, finally retired from broadcasting in 1999. His 'Late Late Show' had been the longest-running chat show in the world.

wounding 100 more. (NATO said the village was a Serb military encampment.)

A sprinkling of journalists, including those from the *New York Times*, the *Los Angeles Times* and the *Washington Post*, as well as some Greek and Turkish reporters, have been permitted to leave Belgrade without a military escort. This week *The Irish Times* was also allowed to travel through the region without restrictions …

On the way into Pristina, the devastated capital of Kosovo, we passed through the area of Vucitrn, a village that has been troublesome to Serbs for centuries. (A Catholic church document dated 1644 shows that the town's 2,000 families only spoke Albanian or Turkish.) Now the village is off limits, explained our Serb driver, because it is mostly Albanian and filled with Ushtkas, the Serb name for KLA members.

'It is too dangerous,' he says, picking up speed. Still, we see rows and rows extending for miles of burnt-out Albanian homes. They are redbrick with red tiled roofs. They have obviously not been hit by aerial bombs, as many of their roofs and walls are intact. Instead, the windows are gone or the exterior walls are blackened from fire that has roared from the interior …

We finally arrive in Pristina, a city that unfolds in a valley from the hills above. There is electricity and water here, but little else is normal.

There are a handful of working telephone lines. Military and police are everywhere, literally every few yards throughout the city. Building after building has been levelled, nearly too numerous to mention. Office buildings, schools, banks, the post office, government buildings, apartment houses and single-family homes. It is clear from the size of craters here that NATO missiles have done the damage.

In an adjacent area of town, rows of shops owned by Albanians have also been destroyed. There is no evidence of bombs or missiles, just broken windows and fire. Beauty shops, cafés, accountants' offices are all in shambles and looted. Desks and office chairs are overturned, drawers with papers are strewn about. This area was destroyed by human hands.

Dragona Milic (25), a Serb whose home has been bombed, spends her nights with her family and friends in a makeshift cellar beneath a building. It is illuminated only by candles. There is no ventilation, the low ceiling is made of waterlogged wood planks, and the place is damp. Live electrical wires dangle from one brick wall. Foam-beds and blankets line the concrete floor.

Proinsias de Rossa, seen here with the popular comedian Brendan O'Carroll, joined his Democratic Left party with the Labour Party in 1999

with religion, that it seemed closer to Africa or Asia than to Europe. With the outbreak of civil conflict in Northern Ireland, nationalism was, if anything, resurgent. And the Republic was still a largely rural society.

Yet by the end of the century that Ireland was almost completely gone. Irish Catholics were, as Bishop William Walsh put it in *The Irish Times*, 'hurt, sad, angered, frustrated, fearful and insecure.' In 1998, for the first time, the main Catholic seminary in Dublin got no new recruits at all. Nationalism of the traditional variety was practically dead. In the Republic in 1998, 94 per cent of voters in a referendum on the Northern Ireland peace agreement approved of that deal. In the process they dropped the main demand of Irish nationalism: that Northern Ireland be recognised as an integral part of the Irish state. And the land has lost its grip. Ireland was primarily an urban society, with just 10 per cent of the work force employed in agriculture. Those who remained were not romantic peasants but business people who spent much of their time filling out forms for EU subsidies.

Yet, for all the trauma of those upheavals and the legacy of thirty years of sectarian conflict, Ireland could count itself among the twentieth century's winners. The Republic had definitively joined the rich elite of nations whose citizens enjoyed opportunities unimaginable to the

currency. Euro loses over 10 per cent of its value in first six months of trading.

15 March
Rosemary Nelson, a prominent solicitor, is murdered by a bomb placed under her car in Lurgan, Co. Armagh.

25 March
NATO begins air war against Serbia over crisis in Kosovo. War continues until June, when Serbs capitulate.

6 April
Record Exchequer surplus of over £1 billion in the Republic due to buoyant tax receipts.

20 April
Mr Justice O'Flaherty of the Supreme Court and Mr Justice Kelly of the High Court resign following criticism by the Chief Justice of their handling of

As the century moved towards its end, the future of the Northern Ireland peace process was in the balance. The IRA refused to decommission its arms, on the grounds that it was not specifically required to do so under the Belfast Agreement. The Unionists refused to implement the agreement fully without decommissioning.

majority of the population of a world in which desperate deprivation was still the common lot of humanity. Economic and cultural transformations amounting to a social revolution had been managed without the violence that normally accompanies a revolution.

The bitter familiarity of emigration had turned to the unexpected experience of immigration. The possibility of complete economic collapse which had seemed so real in the nineteen-eighties had given way to the problems of maintaining any kind of communal values in the face of sudden and extraordinary national wealth. Excuses for the failure to live up to the egalitarian promise of the nationalist revolution—poverty, British domination, the priority of completing the 'unfinished' project of uniting Ireland—had been lost and the power to actually change the country for the better had been gained. In a sense, even though the idea of sovereignty for which the revolution had been launched was, by the end of the century, so deeply qualified as to be redundant, Ireland had more sovereign power than ever before.

About 15 children and 10 adults spend their nights here now because their homes are either gone or devoid of electricity. Their ages range from five years to 68.

'Bombs cannot make peace between Serbs and Albanians,' says Ms Milic. 'Everybody is dying here. We have given everything to the Albanians. They have books in their

Seamus Heaney, winner of the 1995 Nobel Prize for Literature

July 1999, Mr Gareth Cooney, counsel for the Murphy Group, takes a break from the Flood Tribunal, set up to inquire into aspects of the planning process

own language, they have nice homes. They have more rights than anybody. This war didn't start with Serbs. I am tired of hearing about Albanian refugees. What about us? Can you sleep at night when there is bombing every night? We are sleeping now without dreams.'

At a bus station in the centre of town, about 100 Albanians, mostly old women, are waiting to board for Skopje in Macedonia. This is the third bus that has left today.

A whispering Albanian woman tells us that it costs DM 20 and the trip takes about four hours. A crowd is gathered, and people are hugging those about to board. Tears are plentiful. We ask one of the women why she is leaving, but again we are in the presence of Serbs, who are urging us to leave because it is 'too dangerous'.

The Albanian woman shrugs. A Serb says to her: 'You are leaving because of NATO bombs, right?'

The Albanian woman glares.

'No! The police!' she hisses and hurries away.

And in the last years of the century even the terrible human cost of the Northern Ireland conflict was placed in a sobering perspective. With the series of appalling wars that followed the break-up of Yugoslavia in the early nineteen-nineties, the terrifying potential of ethnic strife was fully revealed. Words that were supposed to have fallen out of the European vocabulary—concentration camp, genocide, refugee camp, massacre—became again the common language of news reporters. From a global perspective, those words were a rueful reminder that the bloodiest century in human history would not easily relax its grip on horror. From an Irish perspective, they created a dark image of what the island's fate might have been and a wary hope that, somehow or other, it had finally escaped those awful possibilities.

Notes

1900–1923

1. Quoted by R. B. McDowell in *Crisis and Decline: The Fate of the Southern Unionists*, Dublin 1997, p. 3.
2. Lionel Fleming, *Head or Harp*, London 1965, p. 160.
3. Worldwatch Institute, *State of the World, 1999*, New York 1999, p. 135.
4. D. G. Boyce in *The Revolution in Ireland, 1879–1923*, London 1988, p. 123.
5. David Pierce, *James Joyce's Ireland*, New Haven and London 1992, p. 107.
6. C. S. Andrews, *Dublin Made Me*, Dublin 1979, p. 45.
7. Joseph V. O'Brien, *'Dear Dirty Dublin': A City in Distress, 1899–1916*, Berkeley 1982, p. 63.
8. Quoted by R. F. Foster in *Paddy and Mr Punch*, London 1993, p. 225.
9. W. B. Yeats, *The Secret Rose and Other Stories*, London 1982, p. 41.
10. R. F. Foster, *W. B. Yeats: A Life, vol. 1*, Oxford 1997, p. 336.
11. R. B. McDowell, *Crisis and Decline: The Fate of the Southern Unionists*, Dublin 1997, p. 29.
12. Alvin Jackson, *The Ulster Party*, Oxford 1989, p. 320.
13. Anthony Read and David Fisher, *The Proudest Day: India's Long Road to Independence*, London 1997, p. 127.
14. *Lenin on Ireland*, Dublin 1974, p. 8.
15. Mary E. Daly, *Dublin: The Deposed Capital, 1860–1914*, Cork 1984, p. 240 ff.
16. Mary E. Daly, *Dublin: The Deposed Capital, 1860–1914*, Cork 1984, p. 265.
17. Mary E. Daly, *Dublin: The Deposed Capital, 1860–1914*, Cork 1984, p. 269.
18. Adrian Pimley in D. G. Boyce (ed.), *The Revolution in Ireland, 1879–1923*, London 1988, p. 199.

19. Vincent J. Esposito (ed.), *A Concise History of World War I*, London 1965, p. 30.

20. Eric Hobsbawm, *Age of Extremes: The Short Twentieth Century, 1914–1991*, London 1994, p. 29.

21. Worldwatch Institute, *State of the World, 1999*, New York 1999, p. 152–3.

22. James Stephens, *The Insurrection in Dublin* (third edition), Dublin 1965, p. 33.

23. *1916 Rebellion Handbook*, republished Dublin 1998.

24. James Stephens, *The Insurrection in Dublin* (third edition), Dublin 1965, p. 38–9.

25. P. S. O'Hegarty, *The Victory of Sinn Féin*, republished Dublin 1998, p. 3, 5, 42.

26. Conor Kostick, *Revolution in Ireland: Popular Militancy, 1917 to 1923*, London 1996, p. 36.

27. Jonathan Bardon, *A History of Ulster*, Belfast 1992, p. 462.

28. Aodh de Blácam, *What Sinn Féin Stands For*, Dublin 1921, p. 150–1.

1924–1957

1. P. S. O'Hegarty, *The Victory of Sinn Féin*, Dublin 1998, p. 91, 125.

2. See Dermot Keogh, *Twentieth-Century Ireland*, Dublin 1994, p. 40, 399.

3. Dan Bradley, *Farm Labourers: Irish Struggle, 1900–1976*, Belfast 1988, p. 15.

4. Pat Feeley, 'Servant boys and girls in County Limerick', *Old Limerick Journal*, December 1979, p. 34.

5. Pat Feeley, 'Servant boys and girls in County Limerick', *Old Limerick Journal*, December 1979, p. 129.

6. R. B. McDowell, *Crisis and Decline: The Fate of the Southern Unionists*, Dublin 1997, p. 175.

7. Brian Inglis, *Downstart*, London 1990, p. 80.

8. Lionel Fleming, *Head or Harp*, London 1965, p. 127.

9. Lionel Fleming, *Head or Harp*, London 1965, p. 161.

10. Brian Inglis, *Downstart*, London 1990, p. 87.

11. Niall Sheridan in Timothy O'Keeffe (ed.), *Myles: Portraits of Brian O'Nolan*, London 1973, p. 44.

12. Lionel Fleming, *Head or Harp*, London 1965, p. 121–2.

13. C. S. Andrews, *Man of No Property*, Dublin and Cork 1982, p. 136–7.

14. Lionel Fleming, *Head or Harp*, London 1965, p. 169.

15. Robert Fisk, *In Time of War*, London 1985, p. 162–3.

16. Anthony Cronin, *No Laughing Matter*, New York 1998, p. 112.

17. Frank McCourt, *Angela's Ashes*, London 1997, p. 394.

18. Hubert Butler, 'The Minority Voice' in *In the Land of Nod*, Dublin 1996, p. 28.

19. Noel Browne, *Against the Tide*, Dublin 1986, p. 186.

1957–1999

1. Eric Hobsbawm, *Age of Extremes*, London 1994, p. 211.

2. Hugh Brody, *Inishkillane: Change and Decline in the West of Ireland*, London 1974, p. 40–1.

3. Dermot Keogh, *Twentieth Century Ireland*, Dublin 1994, p. 267.

4. In Philip Pettit (ed.), *The Gentle Revolution*, Dublin 1969, p. 64.

5. Gay Byrne, *To Whom it Concerns*, Dublin 1972, p. 86 ff.

6. Philip Pettit (ed.), *The Gentle Revolution*, Dublin 1969, p. 63.

7. Philip Pettit (ed.), *The Gentle Revolution*, Dublin 1969, p. 62–3.

8. Garret FitzGerald, *All in a Life: An Autobiography*, Dublin 1991, p. 315.

9. See Mike Milotte, *Banished Babies*, Dublin 1997, p. 17.

Index

Note: Page references in **bold** denote illustrations

Acknowledgments

The publishers are grateful to the following for permission to reproduce photographs and cartoons listed on the pages below:

Aer Lingus 166 (top), 172 (top), 173, 177, 188, 207; Camera Press Ltd 2; Culver Pictures 171; Dalton, J. Brendan 182 (top); Department of Enterprise, Trade and Employment 160; Duncan, G. A. 10, 139, 170, 185, 197; Electricity Supply Board 175; Fennell, Frank 243; Fógra Failte 180 (top); Fr Browne SJ Collection—Irish Picture Library 126 (top), 127, 136 (Fr Browne Collection), 150 (Fr Browne Collection), 155 (Fr Browne Collection, 156 (Fr Browne Collection), 164 (Fr Browne Collection), 165 (Fr Browne Collection), 167 (top and bottom) (Fr Browne Collection), 172 (Fr Browne Collection), 176 (Fr Browne Collection); Hugh Lane Municipal Gallery of Modern Art, Dublin (courtesy of the Lavery Estate) 49; Hulton Getty Ltd 146; Illustrated London News Picture Library 98; Independent Newspapers 68, 159, 192; Inpho Sports Photography 294, 296 (top and bottom), 322; Irish Air Corps 132; Irish Labour History Museum 51; Irish Picture Library 17, 32, 92, 126 (bottom); Irish Press 147, 162, 169, 295 (top); Irish Times Photo Library x, 4, 5, 9 (bottom), 16, 23 (top), 26, 34, 35, 38, 40, 41, 43, 46, 48 (bottom), 55, 64, 69, 79, 88, 89, 100, 109, 110, 114, 116, 117, 125, 135, 148, 152, 153, 154, 166 (bottom), 178, 179, 180, 183, 186, 187, 189 (left), 191, 198, 204, 205, 206, 208, 210, 212, 213, 214, 215, 217, 218 (left and right), 219, 220, 221, 222 (top and bottom), 223 (top and bottom), 225, 226, 227, 228, 230, 231, 233, 234, 235, 236, 238, 239, 240, 241, 245, 246, 247, 249, 250, 251, 253, 255, 256, 260, 261, 263, 264, 265, 269, 270, 271, 273, 274, 275, 278, 280, 281, 282, 284, 286, 287, 289, 290, 291, 293, 295 (bottom), 297, 299, 302, 304, 305, 306 (top), 308, 309, 310, 314 (left), 316, 317, 319, 324, 326, 327; Lafayette Photography 161; Lensman 133, 182 (bottom), 189 (right), 193, 232, 237, 279, 311 (right), 313 (left); National Gallery of Ireland 9 (top), 25 (with the permission of Miss Julien O'Sullivan), 52 (bottom), 58 (top), 158 (with the permission of James Le Jeune); National Library of Ireland 3, 8, 11, 14, 18, 20, 21, 22, 24, 27, 28, 29, 31, 36, 37, 39, 42, 44, 45, 47, 48 (top), 52 (top), 53, 57, 58 (bottom), 59, 60, 62, 63, 65, 66, 67, 73, 74, 75, 76, 77, 78, 80, 81, 82, 83, 84, 85, 91, 94, 97, 102, 104, 107, 115, 118, 119, 120, 124, 140 (left), 168; O'Malley, Tony 134; Pacemaker 200, 252, 268, 303; Premier Photographers 56; Public Records Office, Northern Ireland 33, 144; Report/Derek Speirs 306 (bottom); Rodwell, Crispin 267, 288; RTÉ Illustrations Library 15, 143, 151, 216, 242, 254, 272, 276, 292, 298, 307, 314, 321; RTÉ Illustrations Library Cashman Collection 71, 72, 86, 121, 123, 130, 131, 137, 142, 145 (top), 174; Silver Image Photography 323; Sotheby's Picture Library 6; Thorp, Terry 283 (bottom), 312 (top); Tuach, Rod 262; Turner, Martyn 285, 300, 301 (left and right), 311 (right), 312 (bottom), 326; Ulster Folk and Transport Museum 19; Ulster Museum 12, 30, 99, 122, 129 (courtesy of the Lavery Estate); United Press International 190.

The publishers are also grateful to the following for permission to reproduce the material listed below, most of which first appeared in The Irish Times:

A.P. Watt Ltd on behalf of Michael B. Yeats for 'September 1913' by W.B. Yeats; Binchy, Maeve, for 'Contraceptive Conversation'; Brandt and Brandt for 'The Brother' from *The Best of Myles* by Myles na Gopaleen (Flann O'Brien); Browne, Vincent, for 'Perpetrators of Bombings Still Evade Justice'; Calder Publications and The Samuel Beckett Estate for 'Saint Lô' and 'Dieppe' from Samuel Beckett's *Collected Poems*; David Higham Associates for 'No More Sea' from Louis MacNeice *Collected Poems* (publisher Faber); McCafferty, Nell, now a journalist with the *Sunday Tribune*, for 'Housewifes' Independence Notions Disappear in the Courtroom'; O'Brien, Conor Cruise, for 'The Embers of Easter' and 'A Step to Watch'; O'Faolain, Nuala, for 'The Gay B&B'; Penguin Books Ltd for 'Spraying the Potatoes' from *Selected Poems* by Patrick Kavanagh; Waters, John, for 'More and More Noise'.

Despite their best efforts the publishers were unable to trace all copyright holders prior to publication of this book. However, they will make the usual and appropriate arrangements with any who contact them after publication.